I0821540

Ancient Christian Texts

Commentaries on Job, Hosea, Joel, and Amos

Julian of Eclanum

TRANSLATED AND EDITED BY

Thomas P. Scheck

SERIES EDITORS

Gerald L. Bray, Michael Glerup, and Thomas C. Oden

An imprint of InterVarsity Press
Downers Grove, Illinois

InterVarsity Press
P.O. Box 1400, Downers Grove, IL 60515-1426
ivpress.com
email@ivpress.com

InterVarsity Press® is the book-publishing division of InterVarsity Christian Fellowship/USA®, a movement of students and faculty active on campus at hundreds of universities, colleges, and schools of nursing in the United States of America, and a member movement of the International Fellowship of Evangelical Students. For information about local and regional activities, visit intervarsity.org.

Unless otherwise indicated, all Scripture quotations are the author's translation.

While any stories in this book are true, some names and identifying information may have been changed to protect the privacy of individuals.

Design: Cindy Kiple
Images: Saints Peter and Paul by Crivelli, Carlo at Accademia, Venice/Art Resource, NY
Monogrammatic cross: Early Christian Monogrammatic cross from Monastero, at Kunsthistorisches Museum, Vienna, Austria. Erich Lessing /Art Resource, NY

ISBN 978-0-8308-2547-9 (print)
ISBN 978-0-8308-2548-6 (digital)

Printed in the United States of America ♾

InterVarsity Press is committed to ecological stewardship and to the conservation of natural resources in all our operations. This book was printed using sustainably sourced paper.

Library of Congress Cataloging-in-Publication Data
A catalog record for this book is available from the Library of Congress.

P 25 24 23 22 21 20 19 18 17 16 15 14 13 12 11 10 9 8 7 6 5 4 3 2 1
Y 44 43 42 41 40 39 38 37 36 35 34 33 32 31 30 29 28 27 26 25 24 23 22 21

To my friend and colleague Barry David,
professor of philosophy at Ave Maria University,

and to my nineteen-year-old son John,
missionary to Mexico.

CONTENTS

GENERAL INTRODUCTION

Ancient Christian Texts (hereafter ACT) presents the full text of ancient Christian commentaries on Scripture that have remained so unnoticed that they have not yet been translated into English.

The patristic period (AD 95–750) is the time of the fathers of the church, when the exegesis of Scripture texts was in its primitive formation. This period spans from Clement of Rome to John of Damascus, embracing seven centuries of biblical interpretation, from the end of the New Testament to the mid-eighth century, including the Venerable Bede.

This series extends but does not reduplicate texts of the Ancient Christian Commentary on Scripture (ACCS). It presents full-length translations of texts that appear only as brief extracts in the ACCS. The ACCS began years ago authorizing full-length translations of key patristic texts on Scripture in order to provide fresh sources of valuable commentary that previously were not available in English. It is from these translations that the ACT series has emerged.

A multiyear project such as this requires a well-defined objective. The task is straightforward: *to introduce full-length translations of key texts of early Christian teaching, homilies and commentaries on a particular book of Scripture.* These are seminal documents that have decisively shaped the entire subsequent history of biblical exegesis, but in our time have been largely ignored.

To carry out this mission each volume of the Ancient Christian Texts series has four aspirations:

1. To show the approach of one of the early Christian writers in dealing with the problems of understanding, reading and conveying the meaning of a particular book of Scripture.

2. To make more fully available the whole argument of the ancient Christian interpreter of Scripture to all who wish to think with the early church about a particular canonical text.

3. To broaden the base of the biblical studies, Christian teaching and preaching to include classical Christian exegesis.

4. To stimulate Christian historical, biblical, theological and pastoral scholarship toward deeper inquiry into early classic practitioners of scriptural interpretation.

For Whom Is This Series Designed?

We have selected and translated these texts primarily for general and nonprofessional use by an audience of persons who study the Bible regularly.

In varied cultural settings around the world, contemporary readers are asking how they might grasp the meaning of sacred texts under the instruction of the great minds of the ancient church. They often study books of the Bible verse by verse, book by book, in groups and workshops, sometimes with a modern commentary in hand. But many who study the Bible intensively hunger to have available as well the thoughts of a reliable classic Christian commentator on this same text. This series will give the modern commentators a classical text for comparison and amplification. Readers will judge for themselves as to how valuable or complementary are their insights and guidance.

The classic texts we are translating were originally written for anyone (lay or clergy, believers or seekers) who wished to reflect and meditate with the great minds of the early church. They sought to illuminate the plain sense, theological wisdom, and moral and spiritual meaning of an individual book of Scripture. They were not written for an academic audience, but for a community of faith shaped by the sacred text.

Yet in serving this general audience, the editors remain determined not to neglect the rigorous requirements and needs of academic readers who until recently have had few full translations available to them in the history of exegesis. So this series is designed also to serve public libraries, universities, academic classes, homiletic preparation and historical interests worldwide in Christian scholarship and interpretation.

Hence our expected audience is not limited to the highly technical and specialized scholarly field of patristic studies, with its strong bent toward detailed word studies and explorations of cultural contexts. Though all of our editors and translators are patristic and linguistic scholars, they also are scholars who search for the meanings and implications of the texts. The audience is not primarily the university scholar concentrating on the study of the history of the transmission of the text or those with highly focused interests in textual morphology or historical-critical issues. If we succeed in serving our wider readers practically and well, we hope to serve as well college and seminary courses in Bible, church history, historical theology, hermeneutics and homiletics. These texts have not until now been available to these classes.

Readiness for Classic Spiritual Formation

Today global Christians are being steadily drawn toward these biblical and patristic sources for daily meditation and spiritual formation. They are on the outlook for primary classic sources of spiritual formation and biblical interpretation, presented in accessible form and grounded in reliable scholarship.

These crucial texts have had an extended epoch of sustained influence on Scripture interpretation, but virtually no influence in the modern period. They also deserve a hearing among modern readers and scholars. There is a growing awareness of the speculative excesses and spiritual and homiletic limitations of much post-Enlightenment criticism. Meanwhile the motifs, methods and approaches of ancient exegetes have remained unfamiliar not only to historians but to otherwise highly literate biblical scholars, trained exhaustively in the methods of historical and scientific criticism.

It is ironic that our times, which claim to be so fully furnished with historical insight and research methods, have neglected these texts more than scholars in previous centuries who could read them in their original languages.

This series provides indisputable evidence of the modern neglect of classic Christian exegesis: it remains a fact that extensive and once authoritative classic commentaries on Scripture still remain untranslated into any modern language. Even in China such a high level of neglect has not befallen classic Buddhist, Taoist and Confucian commentaries.

Ecumenical Scholarship

This series, like its two companion series, the ACCS and Ancient Christian Doctrine (ACD), is an expression of unceasing ecumenical efforts that have enjoyed the wide cooperation of distinguished scholars of many differing academic communities. Under this classic textual umbrella, it has brought together in common spirit Christians who have long distanced themselves from each other by competing church memories. But all of these traditions have an equal right to appeal to the early history of Christian exegesis. All of these traditions can, without a sacrifice of principle or intellect, come together to study texts common to them all. This is its ecumenical significance.

This series of translations is respectful of a distinctively theological reading of Scripture that cannot be reduced to historical, philosophical, scientific or sociological insights or methods alone. It takes seriously the venerable tradition of ecumenical reflection concerning the premises of revelation, providence, apostolicity, canon and consensuality. A high respect is here granted, despite modern assumptions, to uniquely Christian theological forms of reasoning, such as classical consensual christological and triune reasoning, as distinguishing premises of classic Christian textual interpretation. These cannot be acquired by empirical methods alone. This approach does not pit theology against critical theory; instead, it incorporates critical historical methods and brings them into coordinate accountability within its larger purpose of listening to Scripture.

The internationally diverse character of our editors and translators corresponds with the global range of our audience, which bridges many major communions of Christianity. We have sought to bring together a distinguished international network of Protestant, Catholic and Orthodox scholars, editors and translators of the highest quality and reputation to accomplish this design.

But why just now at this historical moment is this need for patristic wisdom felt particularly by so many readers of Scripture? Part of the reason is that these readers have been longer deprived of significant contact with many of these vital sources of classic Christian exegesis.

The Ancient Commentary Tradition

This series focuses on texts that comment on Scripture and teach its meaning. We define a commentary in its plain-sense definition as a series of illustrative or explanatory notes on any work of enduring significance. The word *commentary* is an Anglicized form of the Latin *commentarius* (or "annotation" or "memoranda" on a subject, text or series of events). In its theological meaning it is a work that explains, analyzes or expounds a biblical book or portion of Scripture. Tertullian, Origen, John Chrysostom, Jerome, Augustine and Clement of Alexandria all revealed their familiarity with both the secular and religious commentators available to them as they unpacked the meanings of the sacred text at hand.

The commentary in ancient times typically began with a general introduction covering such questions as authorship, date, purpose and audience. It commented as needed on grammatical or lexical problems in the text and provided explanations of difficulties in the text. It typically moved verse by verse through a Scripture text, seeking to make its meaning clear and its import understood.

The general Western literary genre of commentary has been definitively shaped by the history of early Christian commentaries on Scripture. It is from Origen, Hilary, the *Opus imperfectum in Matthaeum*, John Chrysostom and Cyril of Alexandria that we learn what a commentary is—far more so than in the case of classic medical, philosophical or poetic commentaries. It leaves too much unsaid simply to assume that the Christian biblical commentary took a previously extant literary genre and reshaped it for Christian texts. Rather it is more accurate to say that *the Western literary genre of the commentary (and especially the biblical commentary) has patristic commentaries as its decisive pattern and prototype.*

It is only in the last two centuries, since the development of modern historicist methods of criticism, that modern writers have sought more strictly to delimit the definition of a commentary so as to include only certain limited interests focusing largely on historical-critical method, philological and grammatical observations, literary analysis, and socio-political or economic circumstances impinging on the text. While respecting all these approaches, the ACT editors do not hesitate to use the classic word *commentary* to define more broadly the genre of this series. These are commentaries in their classic sense.

The ACT editors freely take the assumption that the Christian canon is to be respected as the church's sacred text. The reading and preaching of Scripture are vital to religious life. The central hope of this endeavor is that it might contribute in some small way to the revitalization of religious faith and community through a renewed discovery of the earliest readings of the church's Scriptures.

An Appeal to Allow the Text to Speak for Itself

This prompts two appeals:

1. For those who begin by assuming as normative for a commentary only the norms considered typical for modern expressions of what a commentary is, we ask: please allow the ancient commentators to define *commentarius* according to their own lights. Those who assume the preemptive authority and truthfulness of modern critical methods alone will always tend to view the classic Christian exegetes as dated, quaint, premodern, hence inadequate, and in some instances comic or even mean-spirited, prejudiced, unjust and oppressive. So in the interest of hermeneutical fairness, it is recommended that the modern reader not impose upon ancient Christian exegetes modern assumptions about valid readings of Scripture. The ancient Christian writers constantly challenge these unspoken, hidden and indeed often camouflaged assumptions that have become commonplace in our time.

We leave it to others to discuss the merits of ancient versus modern methods of exegesis. But even this cannot be done honestly without a serious examination of the texts of ancient exegesis. Ancient commentaries may be disqualified as commentaries by modern standards. But they remain commentaries by the standards of those who anteceded and formed the basis of the modern commentary.

The attempt to read a Scripture text while ruling out all theological and moral assumptions—as well as ecclesial, sacramental and dogmatic assumptions that have prevailed generally in the community of faith out of which it emerged—is a very thin enterprise indeed. Those who tendentiously may read a single page of patristic exegesis, gasp and toss it away because it does not conform adequately to the canons of modern exegesis and historicist commentary are surely not exhibiting a valid model for critical inquiry today.

2. In ancient Christian exegesis, chains of biblical references were often very important in thinking about the text in relation to the whole testimony of sacred Scripture, by the analogy of faith, comparing text with text, on the premise that *scripturam ex scriptura explicandam esse*. When ancient exegesis weaves many Scripture texts together, it does not limit its focus to a single text as much modern exegesis prefers, but constantly relates them to other texts, by analogy, intensively using typological reasoning, as did the rabbinic tradition.

Since the principle prevails in ancient Christian exegesis that each text is illumined by other texts and by the whole narrative of the history of revelation, we find in patristic comments on a given text many other subtexts interwoven in order to illumine that text. In these ways the models of exegesis often do not correspond with modern commentary assumptions, which tend to resist or rule out chains of scriptural reference. We implore the reader not to force the assumptions of twentieth-century hermeneutics upon the ancient Christian writers, who themselves knew nothing of what we now call hermeneutics.

The Complementarity of Research Methods in This Series

The Ancient Christian Texts series will employ several interrelated methods of research, which the editors and translators seek to bring together in a working integration. Principal among these methods are the following:

1. The editors, translators and annotators will bring to bear the best resources of *textual criticism* in preparation for their volumes. This series is not intended to produce a new critical edition of the original-language text. The best urtext in the original language will be used. Significant variants in the earliest manuscript sources of the text may be commented upon as needed in the annotations. But it will be assumed that the editors and translators will be familiar with the textual ambiguities of a particular text and be able to state their conclusions about significant differences among scholars. Since we are working with ancient texts that have, in some cases, problematic or ambiguous passages, we are obliged to employ all methods of historical, philological and textual inquiry appropriate to the study of ancient texts. To that end, we will appeal to the most reliable text-critical scholarship of both biblical and patristic studies. We will assume that our editors and translators have reviewed the international literature of textual critics regarding their text so as to provide the reader with a translation of the most authoritative and reliable form of the ancient text. We will leave it to the volume editors and translators, under the supervision of the general editors, to make these assessments. This will include the challenge of considering which variants within the biblical text itself might impinge upon the patristic text, and which forms or stemma of the biblical text the patristic writer was employing. The annotator will supply explanatory footnotes where these textual challenges may raise potential confusions for the reader.

2. Our editors and translators will seek to understand the *historical context* (including socioeconomic, political and psychological aspects as needed) of the text. These understandings are often vital to right discernment of the writer's intention. Yet we do not see our primary mission as that of discussing in detail these contexts. They are to be factored into the translation and commented on as needed in the annotations, but are not to become the primary focus of this series. Our central interest is less in the social location of the text or the philological history of particular words than in authorial intent and accurate translation. Assuming a proper social-historical contextualization of the text, the main focus of this series will be upon a dispassionate and fair translation and analysis of the text itself.

3. The main task is to set forth the meaning of the biblical text itself as understood by the patristic writer. The intention of our volume editors and translators is to help the reader see clearly into the meanings that patristic commentators have discovered in the biblical text. *Exegesis* in its classic sense implies an effort to explain, interpret and comment on a text, its meaning, its sources and its connections with other texts. It implies

a close reading of the text, using whatever linguistic, historical, literary or theological resources are available to explain the text. It is contrasted with *eisegesis,* which implies that interpreters have imposed their own personal opinions or assumptions on the text. The patristic writers actively practiced intratextual exegesis, which seeks to define and identify the exact wording of the text, its grammatical structure and the interconnectedness of its parts. They also practiced extratextual exegesis, seeking to discern the geographical, historical or cultural context in which the text was written. Our editors and annotators will also be attentive as needed to the ways in which the ancient Christian writer described his own interpreting process or hermeneutic assumptions.

4. The underlying philosophy of translation that we employ in this series is, like the Ancient Christian Commentary on Scripture, termed *dynamic equivalency.* We wish to avoid the pitfalls of either too loose a paraphrase or too rigid a literal translation. We seek language that is literary but not purely literal. Whenever possible we have opted for the metaphors and terms that are normally in use in everyday English-speaking culture. Our purpose is to allow the ancient Christian writers to speak for themselves to ordinary readers in the present generation. We want to make it easier for the Bible reader to gain ready access to the deepest reflection of the ancient Christian community of faith on a particular book of Scripture. We seek a thought-for-thought translation rather than a formal equivalence or word-for-word style. This requires the words to be first translated accurately and then rendered in understandable idiom. We seek to present the same thoughts, feelings, connotations and effects of the original text in everyday English language. We have used vocabulary and language structures commonly used by the average person. We do not leave the quality of translation only to the primary translator, but pass it through several levels of editorial review before confirming it.

The Function of the ACT Introductions, Annotations and Translations

In writing the introduction for a particular volume of the ACT series, the translator or volume editor will discuss, where possible, the opinion of the writer regarding authorship of the text, the importance of the biblical book for other patristic interpreters, the availability or paucity of patristic comment, any salient points of debate between the Fathers, and any special challenges involved in translating and editing the particular volume. The introduction affords the opportunity to frame the entire commentary in a manner that will help the general reader understand the nature and significance of patristic comment on the biblical text under consideration and to help readers find their critical bearings so as to read and use the commentary in an informed way.

The footnotes will assist the reader with obscurities and potential confusions. In the annotations the volume editors have identified Scripture allusions and historical references embedded within the texts. Their purpose is to help the reader move easily from passage to passage without losing a sense of the whole.

The ACT general editors seek to be circumspect and meticulous in commissioning volume editors and translators. We strive for a high level of consistency and literary quality throughout the course of this series. We have sought out as volume editors and translators those patristic and biblical scholars who are thoroughly familiar with their original language sources, who are informed historically, and who are sympathetic to the needs of ordinary nonprofessional readers who may not have professional language skills.

Thomas C. Oden, Gerald L. Bray, and Michael Glerup, Series Editors

VOLUME EDITOR'S INTRODUCTION

A Brief History of the Pelagian Controversy

This volume contains the first English translation of four commentaries on Scripture by Julian (380–ca. 445), the "Pelagian" bishop of Eclanum, Italy. I use quotation marks here because the term *Pelagian* is problematic. Julian never used this word to describe himself. His adversaries, especially Augustine, Jerome, the Roman bishops, and the imperial power, labeled him so. Yet modern scholarship does not necessarily concur that the doctrines defined as Pelagian were actually held by the persons accused. The author of a recent monograph argues that Pelagianism was in fact the heresiological construction of a heresy and that what the members of this movement preached was something different.[1] At the very least, most modern scholars concede that it is impossible to speak of Pelagianism as a monolithic movement as if there were no differences among its exponents. It was Augustine and Jerome who tried to present the movement as unified.

To understand Julian and situate him in his historical context, it is first necessary to become acquainted with the heresy with which he is associated. Pelagianism is named after the British monk Pelagius (ca. 360–ca. 420), a zealous and learned Christian leader and Pauline exegete in the ancient church who conflicted theologically with St. Augustine (354–430) and St. Jerome (ca. 347–ca. 419) in the second decade of the fifth century.[2] After being acquitted by two Eastern synods and exonerated by at least one Roman pope, Pelagius was eventually branded as a heretic in the West. In his Christology and trinitarian doctrine, Pelagius was orthodox.[3] Traditionally the principal error of the Pelagian heresy is its doctrine of sin. Pelagius and another contemporary figure named Caelestius claimed that the sin of Adam affected only himself; it did not implicate or cause the downfall of the entire human race. According to Caelestius, Pelagius, and Julian, while Adam's transgression set a bad example for his posterity, his sin and guilt could not have been transmitted to his descendants, especially newborn infants, to make them guilty and culpable for what he had done and therefore worthy of eternal damnation. In

---

[1]Cf. Ali Bonner, *The Myth of Pelagianism* (Oxford: Oxford University Press, 2018).

[2]See Stuart Squires, *The Pelagian Controversy: An Introduction to the Enemies of Grace and the Conspiracy of Lost Souls* (Eugene, OR: Wipf and Stock, 2019).

[3]Cf. A. Dupont, "The Christology of Pre-Controversial Pelagius," *Augustiniana* 58 (2008): 235-57. See also A. Dupont, "Die Christusfigur des Pelagius. Rekonstruction der Christologie im Kommentar von Pelagius zum Römerbrief des Paulus," *Augustiniana* 56, nos. 3–4 (2006): 321-72.

his interpretation of Romans 5:12, for example, Pelagius bypasses the idea that Adam transmitted to the human race an inheritance of guilt, physical death, ignorance, and concupiscence. It is interesting to note, however, that in this passage, Pelagius simply lists the arguments of those who are against the transmission of original sin. He does not explicitly say that he supports their teaching, though this is the impression one has. The tone of Pelagius's writings strikes me as churchman-like. In any case, Catholics and Protestants, following the main lines of Augustine's teaching (though not necessarily all his inferences and particular interpretations of biblical texts), have generally agreed that all human beings enter this world subject to fallen conditions, mysteriously implicated in Adam's sin, and in need of grace and redemption. This predicament is the result of our entailment in Adam's sin and condemnation and is not merely the result of our own actual sins carried out in imitation of Adam. J. N. D. Kelly formulates Pelagius's teaching as follows:

> He rejected as Manichaean, as well as stultifying to endeavor, the notion that human nature has been corrupted by original sin transmitted from Adam, and can raise itself only by God's help. Although a habit of sinning has set in, a man is always free to shake it off, and by the exercise of his will to choose either right or wrong. Indeed, so far as from there being any necessity of sinning, a man is in principle able to live without sin. Regarding sin as a voluntary act, he denied that new-born babies, who have no choice, can be guilty of it, yet he upheld the traditional practice of having them baptized. Assuredly men always need God's grace; but Pelagius defined grace, not as an inner power transforming them, but as their original endowment with rational will, the divine forgiveness they obtain through baptism, and the illumination provided by the law of Moses and the teaching and example of Christ.[4]

Beatrice explains that for Caelestius (and Pelagius), "babies are born without original sin, that is, they are in the same condition as Adam was in the Garden of Eden before he sinned. This is because sin is not something that can be transmitted or passed on."[5] Julian of Eclanum concurred with this Pelagian doctrine, and this particular Pelagian teaching (that is, the reduction of Adam's fault to that of a bad influence) has been repudiated in the magisterial teaching of the church.[6]

The difficulty in discerning the extent to which Pelagius and Julian's writings were infused with the other errors of which they were accused by their orthodox opponents is illustrated by the striking fact that many of their written works were transmitted in the West anonymously or under false attributions to saints. And so long as their ascription to Pelagius (or Julian) was unknown, the writings were treasured. For instance, Ali Bonner

[4]J. N. D. Kelly, *Jerome: His Life, Writings, and Controversies* (New York: Harper & Row, 1975), 309-10.

[5]Pier Franco Beatrice, *The Transmission of Sin: Augustine and the Pre-Augustinian Sources*, trans. Adam Kamesar (Oxford: Oxford University Press, 2013), 19.

[6]See *Catechism of the Catholic Church*, second edition, revised in accordance with the official Latin text promulgated by Pope John Paul II (Citta del Vaticano: Libreria Editrice Vaticana, 1997), 396-412.

has studied the manuscript tradition of Pelagius's *Letter to Demetrias* and pointed out how influential it was throughout the medieval period. When authorship of these writings by Pelagius (or Julian) was discovered in modern times, suddenly these same works began to be accused. Lamberigts comments with respect to Pelagius:

> It would appear, however, that the tradition was not always so ill at ease with Pelagian perspectives as was the case with Augustine of Hippo, certainly if one takes into account the fact that several so-called Pelagian documents have survived to the present day because the said tradition had ascribed them to other, "orthodox," Christian authors. Perhaps the most striking example thereof is Pelagius' *Epistula ad Demetriadem*, authorship of which was ascribed for a significant period of time either to Jerome or to Augustine himself on account of the quality of the ascetic content of the work. When scholars came to be convinced that the work could be ascribed with certainty to Pelagius, it suddenly acquired the epithets "un-evangelical" and "non-Pauline," a somewhat surprising change of perspective given the fact that Pelagius's writings tended to afford a significant amount of space to commentary on the letters of Paul.[7]

It appears that scholars in the Greek Orthodox tradition likewise take a more moderate stance to interpreting the polemics between Augustine and Pelagius and Augustine and Julian. John McGuckin, for instance, argues that

> Eastern Christianity to this day senses that Augustine's clash with Pelagius was unnecessarily limiting, and that while all the initiative for grace and redemption, at every level and stage, lies with God, the same God expects each believer to do his or her part in responding to the divine assistance. For the East, grace was not simply an assistance of God in the soul, but more so the transfigurative indwelling of God.[8]

McGuckin adds further that in the later theological tradition the heresy of "Pelagianism" has generally been drawn up in reference to Augustine's theology of grace and "what Augustine said were Pelagian implications, not to what Pelagius was actually saying. Pelagius believed that God gave grace to human beings, certainly, but his primary grace was the freedom to choose and respond."[9] When interpreting the works of Pelagius and Julian I have taken an irenic and ecumenical approach that takes into account the positions of the Eastern fathers of the church, and thus the received tradition of Eastern Orthodoxy, rather than limiting myself to an Augustinian interpretation that is progressively narrowed by medieval Scholasticism and Magisterial Reformation Protestantism.

[7]Mathjis Lamberigts, "Recent Research into Pelagianism with Particular Emphasis on the Role of Julian of Aeclanum," *Augustiniana* 52 (2002): 176. I am presently working on a new, complete translation of all of Pelagius's commentaries on the epistles of St. Paul.

[8]John A. McGuckin, *The Path of Christianity: The First Thousand Years* (Downers Grove, IL: IVP Academic, 2017), 453.

[9]McGuckin, *Path of Christianity*, 455. Lamberigts concurs: "With respect to peripheral accusations such as the distinction between the Kingdom of God and eternal life mentioned above, it has been satisfactorily proven that this distinction stems in its formulation from Augustine and is nowhere to be found in Pelagius." "Recent Research into Pelagianism," 182.

The Life and Career of Julian of Eclanum (ca. 380–ca. 445)

We now turn to Julian of Eclanum's involvement in the Pelagian controversy.[10] Julian is first encountered in ancient Christian literature as the son of an Italian bishop named Memor, or Memorius, and the recipient of an epithalium, or wedding poem, composed by his father's friend St. Paulinus of Nola (ca. 355–431) between 401 and 404.[11] Julian had been a lector in the church over which his father presided. In addition to Paulinus of Nola, Augustine of Hippo was familiar with his family and wrote of them respectfully and affectionately prior to the outbreak of the Pelagian controversy. After the sack of Rome in 410, Pelagius and Caelestius fled to Africa.[12] At the time, Pelagius was regarded in the West as an outstanding spiritual director. He, along with Augustine and Jerome, was solicited to offer spiritual counsel to the noble woman Demetrias, who had taken a vow of virginity.[13] Pelagius went to Carthage and thence to Palestine. Caelestius stayed in Carthage, where he was accused of heresy by Paulinus, the former deacon of Ambrose in Milan. He was found guilty of six charges by Aurelius, bishop of Carthage, in 412.[14] In June 415, Pelagius was acquitted of heresy charges in a synod in Jerusalem presided over by John of Jerusalem.[15] In December of the same year, Pelagius was again acquitted of heresy charges by fourteen Eastern bishops at the Synod of Diospolis

[10]Gennadius of Marseilles (ca. 495) composed a summary of the career of Julian in ch. 45 of his continuation of St. Jerome's work, *On Famous Men*. Cf. NPNF2, 3:394. Gennadius's reference to Julian's charity famously led to the "canonization" of Julian by Pietro de Natali in his "Catalogue of Saints," composed between 1369 and 1372. The author ignored Gennadius's added remark that disparages Julian's motives. Cited by J. Lössl, "Julian of Aeclanum's Tractatus in Osee, Iohel, Amos: Some Notes on the Current State of Research," *Augustiniana* 51 (2001): 23.

[11]Paulinus of Nola, *Carm.* 25 (CSEL 30:238-45). See P. G. Walsh, trans., *The Poems of St. Paulinus of Nola*, ACW 40 (New York: Newman Press, 1975), 245-53.

[12]For the historical details and dates in this section, I have used primarily J. P. Burns, "Augustine's Role in the Imperial Action Against Pelagius," *JTS* 30, no. 1 (1979): 67-82; M. Lamberigts, "Augustine and Julian of Aeclanum on Zosimus," *Augustiniana* 42 (1992): 311-30; Beatrice, *Transmission of Sin*; M. Rackett, "What's Wrong with Pelagianism? Augustine and Jerome on the Dangers of Pelagius and His Followers," *Augustinian Studies* 33, no. 2 (2002): 223-37; and E. TeSelle, "The Background: Augustine and the Pelagian Controversy," in *Grace for Grace: The Debates After Augustine and Pelagius*, ed. Alexander Y. Hwang, Brian J. Matz, and Augustine Casiday (Washington, DC: Catholic University of America Press, 2014), 1-13.

[13]Cf. P. Brown, "The Patrons of Pelagius: The Roman Aristocracy Between East and West," *Journal of Theological Studies*, N.S., 21, no. 1 (1970): 56-72; and Robert F. Evans, *Four Letters of Pelagius* (New York: Seabury Press, 1968).

[14]The charges (preserved by Marius Mercator, *Commonitorium super nomine Caelestii* 36) are listed by Burns, "Augustine in the Action Against Pelagius," 69n3: "1 Adam was made mortal and would have died whether he had sinned or not. 2 Adam's sin harmed himself alone and not the entire human race. 3 Children are now born in the same state in which Adam was originally created. 4 The sin and death of Adam do not affect all humans, nor does the resurrection of Christ extend to all. 5 The law, like the gospel, leads to the kingdom of heaven. 6 Even before the coming of Christ some human persons lived without any sin."

[15]Bishop John's character was highly praised by the Roman pope Anastasius (399–401). Cf. NPNF2, 3:432. See Giulio Malavasi, "John of Jerusalem's Profession of Faith (CPG 3621) and the Pelagian Controversy," in *Studia Patristica, Vol. XCVIII. Papers Presented at the Seventeenth International Conference on Patristic Studies Held in Oxford 2015. Vol. 24: Augustine and His Opponents*, ed. Markus Vincent (Louvain: Peeters, 2017), 399-408. Malavasi (407) concludes the following: "This profession of faith proves that John was well informed about the theological debate: his rejection of original sin, his clear position in favor of the co-operation between grace and free will to attain virtue and, finally, his middle position on sinlessness, clearly show that he was completely aware of what the Latins were debating in Palestine. He decided to take a position, which, though not completely Pelagian, was certainly closer to Pelagius than Jerome. This can help explain why the Palestinian bishops who gathered in Diospolis decided to proclaim Pelagius as orthodox, and that Augustine, Jerome and Orosius were right when they charged John of being a friend or a protector of Pelagius."

(Lydda) in Palestine.[16] This synod was possibly attended by St. Chromatius of Aquileia and Jovinus.[17] The eleventh accusation was based on words taken from Caelestius's book, where it was objected against Pelagius that he had said that "everyone can have all virtues and graces and that they destroy the diversity of graces which the apostle [Paul] teaches." Pelagius replied that this was a "malignant and blundering charge." "We do not . . . destroy the diversity of graces; rather we say that God gives all the graces to one who is worthy to receive them, as He gave them to the apostle Paul."[18] To this response the synod replied, "Your views on the gift of the graces found in the holy apostle are reasonable and in accord with the mind of the Church."[19] The modern Greek Orthodox scholar, John A. McGuckin, assesses this vindication as follows:

> And when Pelagius came to Jerusalem and was forced to answer ecclesiastical charges that the way he taught underestimated God's grace and placed too high a premium on human effort (saving ourselves by good works) the learned bishop John exonerated him there, finding nothing wrong with his ascetical teachings at all.[20]

Pelagius's troubles, however, did not end with these acquittals. Through Augustine's initiative, the cases of Pelagius and Caelestius were reopened and they were condemned in provincial synods in Africa. The Africans reported their actions to Pope Innocent of Rome, who in late January 417 excommunicated Caelestius, Pelagius, and their followers.[21] Pope Innocent died in March 417 and was succeeded by Pope Zosimus. Caelestius appeared in Rome and requested a hearing. Letters and a profession of faith, which Pelagius addressed to Innocent, also arrived. Zosimus looked into the matter and acquitted Pelagius and Caelestius in September 417. Burns writes, "Pelagius' profession of faith astonished the Roman clergy and attendant bishops who could not understand how such a man could be accused of heresy."[22] Lamberigts writes in summary of Pope Zosimus's rehabilitation of Caelestius,

[16]B. R. Rees, *Pelagius: A Reluctant Heretic* (Wolfeboro, NH: Boydell Press, 1988), 135-39, very helpfully provides an appendix (2) in which he translated into English an outline of the charges against Pelagius and his replies at the Synod of Diospolis in 415.

[17]Cf. P. F. Beatrice, who is the first to argue that the Chromatius in attendance was indeed the famed bishop of Aquileia, friend of John Chrysostom. "Chromatius and Jovinus at the Synod of Diospolis: A Prosopographical Inquiry," *JECS* 22, no. 3 (Fall 2014): 437-64.

[18]*The Deeds of Pelagius* 16, 39; John E. Rotelle, OSA, ed., *The Works of Saint Augustine: A Translation for the 21st Century, Answer to the Pelagians*, vol. 1.23, trans. Roland J. Teske, SJ (New York: New City Press, 1997); *The Deeds of Pelagius* 32, 357. Also cited in Rees, *Pelagius*, 137.

[19]*The Deeds of Pelagius* 32, 357.

[20]McGuckin, *Path of Christianity*, 453.

[21]According to Beatrice, *Transmission of Sin*, 243, Innocent's excommunication of Pelagius and Caelestius was based on theological assumptions and doctrines that were fairly different from those on which the African bishops, and above all Augustine, generally relied. Innocent's pronouncements say nothing about original sin or hereditary guilt, but simply confirm the necessity of grace for progress in the Christian life and of baptism for newborns. Beatrice claims that Augustine drew unwarranted theological inferences from Innocent's action in his *C. duas ep. Pel* 2.4.7. See *Transmission of Sin*, 245.

[22]Burns, "Augustine and the Action Against Pelagius," 71.

> A sharper critique of the anti-Pelagian movement is inconceivable. Therefore one may believe that Caelestius did not try to mislead Zosimus in order to be set free [as Augustine misleadingly claimed] but that he was set free while stating that the doctrine of original sin as understood by Augustine, was against the catholic doctrine.[23]

Beatrice states the matter this way: "Zosimus completely rehabilitated Caelestius and Pelagius, declaring them in full communion with orthodoxy. Moreover . . . he accepted essentially without reservation their rejection of the Augustinian notion of *peccatum ex traduce* [sin by transmission]."[24] The African bishops did not obey the instructions found in the papal letters that arrived in Carthage on November 2, 417. Instead they dispatched countering letters to Rome to which Zosimus responded on March 23, 417. The Roman pope persisted in his conviction that the case had not been proven. He refused to comply with the request to take further action against Caelestius. A dramatic contest between Rome and Carthage had arisen. The next event occurred on April 30, 418 when an imperial rescript was published. It condemned Caelestius and Pelagius as heretics and denounced them for disturbing the peace of the church and of the city of Rome. The cooperation between imperial authority and the African episcopacy isolated Zosimus, who then submitted to this outside pressure and issued his *Epistula tractoria* to all the bishops of the East and West for subscription. The theological content of the surviving fragments of the *Tractoria* is analyzed linguistically by Beatrice.[25] He claims that it does not amount to being a full recognition by Rome of the Augustinian theology of original sin, but an attempt at compromise, "more in word than in substance, between the theological tradition of Rome, which was influenced in a markedly profound way by orthodox Greek theology."[26] Julian was among the eighteen Italian bishops who refused to subscribe to the *Tractoria*. These bishops were deposed and afterward exiled under the edicts issued by Emperor Honorius in 418. Eugene TeSelle wonders whether the papal action may have been a "premature decision":

> Eighteen bishops in Italy and Illyria, led by Julian of Eclanum, asked that the issues be examined in a general council. They had a credible argument. The controversy had been decided after only a few years of formal debate (415–18); the condemnation had come from the imperial court and only then, under duress, from the pope; and many regions were unacquainted with the doctrine of original sin and had scarcely heard of Augustine's approach to grace and free will.[27]

[23]Lamberigts, "Augustine and Julian of Aeclanum on Zosimus," 319. Beatrice, *Transmission of Sin*, 249, concurs with this and writes, "With these weighty decisions, pope Zosimus seemed to completely contradict the work of his predecessor, who had excommunicated Pelagius and Caelestius. In reality, however, all he did was to stay true to the doctrinal tradition of the Roman church, which was much closer to orthodox Greek views than to the pessimistic anthropology of the Africans."

[24]Beatrice, *Transmission of Sin*, 249.

[25]DS 231. Beatrice, *Transmission of Sin*, 252-56.

[26]Beatrice, *Transmission of Sin*, 256

[27]TeSelle, "Background," 6.

Julian now addressed two letters to Zosimus in the fall of 418, using very harsh language. About the same time, Julian addressed a letter to Rufus, bishop of Thessalonica (410–431), on his own behalf and that of eighteen fellow recusants. For Julian it was very clear that the Roman clergy had changed sides because of fear of the imperial edict. They contradicted their earlier attitude and were now declaring human nature to be evil. Pope Zosimus died on December, 26, 418, and was succeeded by Boniface I on April 10, 419. Augustine responded to Julian's letter to Rufus and to another epistle of Julian to the clergy of Rome in his *Contra Duas Epistulas Pelagianorum*. According to Augustine's account, Julian had tried to persuade the Eastern bishops that Augustine's doctrine was Manichean, and Julian had denounced Pope Zosimus for vacillation. Moreover, Julian had accused the Roman clergy of unjustly condemning the Pelagians and had argued that the Roman church had embraced heresy and that the Western bishops had been victims of imperial extortion.

After composing two letters to Pope Zosimus, Julian replied to the first book of Augustine's *De nuptiis et concupiscentia*. His work was dedicated to a fellow recusant named Turbantius. Julian again accused the church of having embraced Manicheism. Julian sent portions of this four-book work to Valerius, friend of Augustine. The title of Julian's book accused Augustine of condemning marriage and assigning its fruits to the devil. Augustine answered the accusations in the second book of *De nuptiis et concupiscentia*. When Augustine received Julian's complete work, he published a more detailed answer in his *Contra Julianum Pelagianum*. In this work Augustine quoted his opponent at length.

Julian and other deposed Italian bishops took refuge with Theodore of Mopsuestia in Cilicia. Julian occupied himself with a translation of Theodore's *Commentary on the Psalms* from Greek into Latin, thus demonstrating his competency in the Greek language.[28] Julian answered Augustine's reply to him in a lengthy work dedicated to Florus, a fellow recusant. Augustine cites extensively from Julian's attack in his *Opus Imperfectum*.[29] Julian returned to Italy when Pope Celestine I succeeded Boniface I in September 422. He may have hoped for rehabilitation, but the endeavor was not successful and he was exiled a second time. Julian apparently died in Sicily between 443 and 445.[30]

Julian's Surviving Exegetical Writings

Commentary on the Song of Songs. Until the beginning of the twentieth century, only fragments and excerpts from Julian's writings had been preserved under his name in the West, most of these in the form of quotations and allusions recorded in Augustine's works against him. Fragments of a *Commentary on the Song of Songs* by Julian are attested by

[28]See Theodore of Mopsuestia: *Commentary on Psalms 1–81*, trans. Robert C. Hill (Atlanta: Society of Biblical Literature, 2006).

[29]P. Brown, *Augustine of Hippo: A Biography* (Berkeley: University of California Press, 1967), 389, writes of Augustine's polemics against Julian, "There is an element of tragedy in this encounter. Seldom in the history of ideas has a man as great as Augustine or as very human, ended his life so much at the mercy of his own blind-spots."

[30]Rees, *Pelagius*, 142, places Julian's death in 443–445. Other sources place his death as late as 454.

Bede the Venerable. This is probably the work Julian refers to in the preface to Hosea as a commentary on the books of Solomon. Holder writes of it,

> [Bede's] commentary begins with a polemical preface in which Bede refutes the teachings of Julian of Eclanum, a fifth-century Italian bishop who had opposed Augustine by defending Pelagian notions affirming free will and denying original sin. Perhaps inspired by his time in exile under the tutelage of the Antiochene exegete Theodore of Mopsuestia, Julian had written a treatise *De amore* in which he advanced a literalistic interpretation of the Song of Songs as a celebration of human sexuality. . . . Bede calls Julian a "snake in the grass" because he presented heretical doctrine under the guise of seductive eloquence. Further on, however, Bede quotes Julian's completely innocuous interpretation of the hair of the bridegroom in Song 5,11, with apparent approbation.[31]

It is noteworthy that despite his view that the main theme of the Song of Songs is a literal defense of the goodness of human sexuality after the fall of Adam and Eve, Julian also uses allegorical exegesis in this commentary, including Marian interpretations.[32] Bede rejected Julian's Mariological interpretation of Song 8:1-2, which identified the Blessed Virgin as the mother referred to. In these texts, Julian had argued that there was nothing sinful about human birth, since the Lord was completely encircled in flesh yet was free from sin.[33] It seems most unfortunate that Julian's commentary does not survive.

Exposition of the book of Job. A date in the early to mid-420s for Julian's *Exposition of the Book of Job* is reasonable. The unique manuscript attributes the *Expositio* to Philip the Presbyter (a disciple of St. Jerome). Unfortunately, it is damaged at the end and terminates with commentary on Job 42:7. Thus, it does not contain an interpretation of the Lord's restoration of Job's fortunes (Job 42:10-17). The manuscript was first printed by Abbot Amelli, archivist of Monte Cassino.[34] Schanz confused this commentary on Job with the *Expositio interlinearis libri Job*, printed among the *spuria* of Jerome.[35] His mistake was slavishly copied by the writer of the article on Julian in the *Dictionnaire de théologie catholique*. In an important monograph, A. Vaccari proved that Julian of Eclanum was the author.[36] His arguments were based on the doctrine, vocabulary, style, exegesis, sources, and the biblical text used (namely, Jerome's new version).[37] Vaccari showed that the incorrect attribution arose from a banal confusion between the authentic work of

[31]See A. G. Holder, "The Patristic Sources of Bede's Commentary on the Song of Songs," in *Studia Patristica* 34 (Louvain: Peeters, 2001), 371.

[32]See A. Holder, "The Anti-Pelagian Character of Bede's Commentary on the Song of Songs," in *Biblical Studies in the Early Middle Ages*, ed. Claudio Leonardi and Giovanni Orlandi (Florence: SISMEL, Edizioni de Galluzzo, 2005), 98.

[33]Holder, "Anti-Pelagian Character," 100.

[34]*Spicilegium Casinense* 3, no. 1 (1897): 333-417, from Cod. Casin. 371; cited by J. H. Baxter, "Notes on the Latin of Julian of Eclanum," *ALMA* 21 (1951): 8.

[35]See PL 23, 1407-1470. Schanz, *Geschichte der röm. Litteratur*, 4, no. 2 (1920): 510; cited by Baxter, "Notes," 8.

[36]A. Vaccari, *Un Commento a Giobbe di Giuliano di Eclana* (Rome, 1915).

[37]Cf. M. Annecchino, "I Temi Dottrinali-Esegetici nell'Expositio in Iob di Giuliano D'Eclano," in *Munera parva: studi in onore di Boris Ulianich*, ed. Gennaro Luongo (Naples: Fridericiana Editrice Universitaria, 1999), 288; and CCSL 88, xii, n. 43. It is noteworthy that Baxter declares Julian to be "the greatest master of the Latin language since Tertullian" "Notes," 5.

Philip and that of Julian, and also the fact that Julian knew the work of the disciple of Jerome. Vaccari also used the material collected by the French scholar G. Morin, who successfully attributed to Julian the *Tractatus prophetarum Osee Iohel et Amos*, a work that had previously been published among the works of Rufinus.[38] Morin's work enabled Vaccari to demonstrate that even the *Expositio in Iob* was to be attributed to the author of the *ad Florum*, which was considered a certain work of Julian. J. Stiglmayr persistently contested the result, yet Vaccari has prevailed.[39]

Vaccari showed that Julian's *Exposition* was inspired by the Antiochene John Chrysostom and the Greek writer Polychronius (d. ca. 430),[40] who is obscurely referenced in passages that are not well preserved in the manuscript.[41] There is also a connection to Olympiodorus, but since the latter lived a century and a half after Julian, it must be assumed that both of them drew from a common source.[42] Julian was also familiar with views of Philip the Presbyter (d. ca. 455), disciple of Jerome.[43] Philip, whose commentary dates around 393–397, appears to have been the first to adopt Jerome's new Vulgate translation as his reference text.[44] Philip's *Commentary on Job* survives only in fragments but provides important evidence of the Vulgate. It exists in a long and a short recension.[45] Julian imitates Philip by adopting Jerome's version. Julian's *Exposition of the Book of Job* is the oldest surviving patristic commentary on Job that covers (virtually) the entire book.[46] St. Gregory the Great's famous exposition of Job dates to 579, thus 150 years after Julian. My own estimation is that Julian is unsurpassed as a Christian exegete of the books he took under his consideration.

Annecchino observes that Julian's *Expositio in Iob* contrasts strongly with his anti-Augustine manifestoes, *ad Turbantium* and *ad Florum*, because it is free from doctrinal controversy. The great motifs of Pelagian preaching are absent from it.[47] The *Expositio* is more of a "hymn to reason, not in the sense that rationalism itself is exalted, but in the sense that it highlights a great confidence in man's rational abilities that make him free

[38]See PL 21, 959-1104.

[39]J. Stiglmayr, "Der Jobkommentar von Monte Cassino," *ZKT* 43 (1919): 269-88; and J. Stiglmayr, "Zum Jobkommentar von Monte Cassino," *ZKT* 45 (1921): 495-96.

[40]He was the brother of Theodore of Mopsuestia and bishop of Apamea on the Orontes in Syria Secunda. Only fragments of his commentary survive in the catenae.

[41]See under Job 3:8; 6:19; 16:7.

[42]Cf. Annecchino, "I Temi," 289.

[43]See under Job 18:15; Vaccari, *Un Commento a Giobbe di Giuliano di Eclana*, 92-93; cited in CCSL 88, xvi n. 77. Cf. Gennadius, *De vir. Ill.* 63.

[44]Cf. ACCS Job, xxiii.

[45]CPL 643 and 757; PL 26, 619-802 and 23, 1407-70.

[46]There is a survey of patristic commentaries on Job in ACCS and in Kenneth B. Steinhauser, "Job in Patristic Commentaries and Theological Works," in *A Companion to Job in the Middle Ages*, ed. Franklin T. Harkins and Aaron Canty (Leiden: Brill, 2016), 34-70. *Anonymi in Iob Commentarius* predates Julian, but it covers only the first three chapters of the book. Philip's commentary survives in fragmentary form. K. B. Steinhauser, ed., *Anonymi in Iob Commentarius*, CSEL XCVI (Vienna: Verlag der Oesterreichischen Akademie der Wissenschaften, 2006).

[47]For these paragraphs I was greatly aided by the work of Marialuisa Annecchino, "I Temi," 288.

from a frustrating fatalism."[48] The preface to the *Exposition* can be divided into two distinct parts.[49] The first half lays the foundations of Julian's doctrine: (1) the importance of the teachings of a virtuous life for achieving virtue and (2) the recognition of an inborn natural human goodness, which allows a person to live virtuously. At the basis of these doctrines lies the awareness of a free will, which can be inspired by positive examples and which allows us to live a life free from sin. In the second half of the preface, the theme of human suffering and divine justice is announced through Job's dialogue with his "friends." The preface ends with the recognition of divine providence, which is realized, among other things, through the works of creation.

Julian opens his exposition of the speech by quoting the words of St. Paul: "All things whatsoever that have been written were written for our instruction" (Rom 15:4). Julian argues that if it is important that the things that have been written not disappear in silence, it is more important that the actions of the holy people, which have been set forth for our imitation or to teach us, not vanish into thin air. For Julian, the importance of the exemplary model for the achievement of virtue is one of the main purposes of Christ's coming among people (cf. Job 10:9-11).[50] Christ became human in order that humans, by looking at the model of perfection, could strive for perfection (cf. Job 17:8-9). We are justified in speaking about holy Job, so that in him we can recognize the goodness of human nature. In Julian's theology, humanity is responsible for its own condemnation and salvation. These themes are significantly placed among the first lines of the preface to Job and thus occupy an emblematic role in Julian's thought.

Julian says that when their merits are made public, just people will shine like a splendid lamp (cf. Job 12:4-5). They will be recognized for their merits because they acted in full freedom. This freedom is granted from creation to enable people to live according to the divine laws. It exists even among those outside of Christian revelation. It is a force activated by the law of God and the example of Christ. Julian justifies the choice of the life of the holy Job, not to honor him through the exaltation of his good works but to show posterity that the way of virtue is accessible to everyone. Praising Job, in short, does not increase the esteem that God has of him but rather strengthens the hopes of those who want to become virtuous, so that through Job's example we become aware of the fact that virtue is not inaccessible (Prol).

It is interesting to note the resemblance between Julian and Pelagius's interpretation of Job. In Pelagius's famous letter to Demetrias, *Ad Dem* 6.1-3 (which was attributed to various saints for most of its reception history), Pelagius describes Job as a man who fought against the devil to the very end. The Lord himself testified on his behalf

[48]Annecchino, "I Temi," 288.

[49]Annecchino, "I Temi," 295.

[50]References to Job, Hosea, Joel, Amos in this section of the introduction refer both to the texts cited and to Julian's comments underneath.

(Job 1:8; 2:3), and this testimony was not undeserved, for "he always feared the Lord," and "at no time did he dare to scorn one whom he believed to be ever present with him but said: I am safe, for my heart does not reproach me for any of my days" (Job 27:6). Pelagius cites Job 31:29, 32, 13 and 24 as evidence that Job anticipated the behavior commanded by Christ and exemplified by Paul. Pelagius writes,

> What a man Job was! A man of the gospel before the gospel was known, a man of the apostles before their commands were uttered! A disciple of the apostles who, by opening up the hidden wealth of nature and bringing it out into the open, revealed by his own behavior what all of us are capable of and has taught us how great is that treasure in the soul which we possess but fail to use and, because we refuse to display it, believe that we do not possess it either.[51]

Returning to Julian, in the second half the preface, Julian summarizes and anticipates the debate between Job and the "friends" who came to visit him. Job's "friends" maintained that physical miseries are linked to moral decadence. The dispute reaches a crescendo after the accusations and defenses unfold in a series of very significant statements. Julian begins by noticing that the debate is divided into three parts. In the first round, Job defends himself from the accusations of his "friends," who say that he has been complaining without moderation. Job affirms that this must not be ascribed to his guilt, since his sufferings have been utterly unspeakable. In the second round, Julian emphasizes the questionable attitude of friends, who came with the intention of consoling him but ended up afflicting Job's dispirited mind by attributing to him the responsibility for the calamities that struck him. The third part highlights how the "friends" attempt to show that Job is guilty precisely because he was struck by misfortune. But this is invalidated by the fact that many people of a corrupt life lead a prosperous existence.

Julian notes that Job justifies his defense also by addressing those who have been silent, because they could not refute his words. Job enumerates actions he performed on various occasions that were in accord with justice and done with a spirit of deference to the divine will. Annecchino shows that the tendency of Julian's discourse, through the lengthy dialogue between Job and his friends, wherein each one is the spokesperson for a well-constructed religious position, responds to the typical characteristics of an *apologia*, in which the accusations and defenses are intertwined.

> The whole discourse, by exposing the earthly condition of man through the misfortunes of Job, tends, in the restoration of the latter, to the exaltation of divine justice. Sometimes one has the impression of being in the presence of a text that is following the typical canons of a legal defense.[52]

The preface concludes by exalting divine providence. Overall, Julian wants to show how even those who have been tested the most severely cannot be conquered by the devil

[51]B. R. Rees, *The Letters of Pelagius and His Followers* (New York: Cambridge University Press, 1991) 42-43.
[52]Annecchino, "I Temi," 301.

if they will to live their humble human condition according to the virtue and freedom with which humanity has been endowed. Job has become an example for achieving virtue. Julian recognizes in the first words of the biblical story the moral qualities of this man: Job was *simple* in that he was far removed from any contamination of vices (Job 1:1). This means he was not a hypocrite (8:20). Job was *upright* because he feared the Lord (1:1). True wisdom lies in respecting the divine prohibitions and obeying God (28:28), and this is how Job had lived. However, the greatness of Job's soul was best praised in his endurance of hardships (1:2-3). Job recognized the inconstancy of ephemeral goods and never surrendered morally to the circumstances that afflicted him.

K. Steinhauser commends Julian's insight in understanding the main theme of the book of Job: "He is one of the few ancient commentators on Job who comes close to the actual theme of the book, when he states that God permits the good to suffer in order to demonstrate their devotion and increase their merit."[53] In fact, the word *meritum* appears sixty-four times in Julian's text, which makes clear that for Julian human beings can earn merit before God. Steinhauser speculates reasonably that Julian's motives for expounding Job were determined by his dispute with St. Augustine over grace and hereditary sin. Julian chose to write a commentary on Job rather than on Romans "because the book of Job provides a more benign environment for the development of Pelagian thought and a more effective vehicle for its expression."[54] We should recall, however, that Pelagius himself wrote substantial commentaries on the Pauline epistles. Steinhauser thinks that Romans was Augustine's preferred battlefield with the Pelagians, whereas Job was theirs. Allegedly, Romans gave Augustine the tactical advantage whereas Job gave his opponents the high ground. Romans allegedly affirms the existence of hereditary sin whereas Job speaks of a sinless person.[55] Dealing with Job left Augustine with the embarrassing task of proving that this Old Testament saint was a sinner:

> One is reminded of a similar development in the Donatist controversy. The Donatists continuously extolled Cyprian, the martyred bishop of Carthage, as their ideal teacher and model of courage, thus leaving Augustine in the embarrassing position of having to condemn Cyprian in order to condemn them. Julian of Eclanum, the Pelagian genius, perceived a golden opportunity and decided to capitalize on this opportunity by writing a commentary on Job.[56]

Citing Pelagius's use of Job in his *Epistle to Demetrias*, Steinhauser reasonably claims that the Pelagians found in Job a corroboration of the good Gentile who was living in accord with natural law that Paul testified to in Romans 2:15-16. Julian agrees

[53]Steinhauser, "Job in Patristic Commentaries and Theological Works," 57.

[54]Kenneth B. Steinhauser, "Job Exegesis: The Pelagian Controversy," in *Augustine: Biblical Exegete*, ed. Frederick Van Fleteren and Joseph C. Schnaubelt (New York: Peter Lang, 2001), 300.

[55]Steinhauser, "Job Exegesis," 305.

[56]Steinhauser, "Job Exegesis," 305-6.

(cf. Job 23:12). Pelagius affirms from the Old Testament examples of Abel, Melchizedek, Abraham, Joseph, and Job that human beings have "the ability to reform themselves without any additional intervention on the part of God. Human beings, who do not exercise this freedom, insult God. The concept of natural sanctity without hereditary sin could only be scandalous to Augustine."[57] I would comment here that the words "without any additional intervention on the part of God" are Steinhauser's, not Julian's or Pelagius's. They are really an inference drawn by Augustine and applied to those who did not identify his doctrine of grace with the teaching of the church. In my view, A. Dupont summarizes Pelagius's views more accurately and in a manner that I believe could be applied to Julian as well:

> He rejects every thesis that alleges that God commends to man something impossible and that God's commandments cannot be fulfilled by individuals separately but only by all in community. Notice that Pelagius states that it is possible for the individual to observe God's commandments. This opens the possibility of a righteous, sinless life. Pelagius condemns those who with Mani reject marriage or those who like the Cataphrygi are against remarriage. Pelagius finally emphasizes human freedom (*liberum arbitrium*), *without denying the human need for God's help*.[58]

The italicized words are of great importance since critics of Pelagius and Julian often rely on an argument from silence. With respect to Julian, Ogliari says that for him, "although man remains responsible for his moral activity, God's helping grace is also at work co-operating with him whenever something good is achieved."[59] We know that according to the report of Melania the Younger, Pelagius actually wrote,

> I declare anathema anyone who thinks or says that the grace of God by which "Christ came into this world to save sinners" (1 Tim 1:15) is not necessary, not only at every hour and at every moment, but also for every act of ours. And those who attempt to do away with this doctrine deserve eternal punishment.[60]

I cannot imagine Julian disagreeing with Pelagius's declaration. Yet it is commonly assumed that the "Pelagians" did not mean it when they anathematized those who denied the need for divine grace. In a carefully written study, Dupont and Malavasi conclude that the fact that Augustine and Jerome found fault with Pelagius's interpretation of grace does not imply they shared the same theology of grace between themselves.

> Our study of their respective exegesis of Rom. 9,16 and Phil. 2,13 clearly illustrated that they upheld a different vision on the relation between good human volition and divine

[57]Steinhauser, "Job Exegesis," 304.

[58]Dupont, "Christology of Pre-controversial Pelagius," 248, italics added.

[59]Donato Ogliari, *Gratia et Certamen: The Relationship Between Grace and Free Will in the Discussion of Augustine with the So-Called Semipelagians*, Bibliotheca Ephemeridum Theologicarum Lovaniensium 169 (Louvain: Peeters, 2003), 242, citing *Ad Florum* 5,48.

[60]Cited by Augustine, *Grat. Chr.* 1.2.2.

grace. Thus, we also find diversity within the anti-Pelagian camp. Whether Augustine was fully aware of Jerome's doctrine of grace is not completely clear, but if he was, he likely deemed Jerome's doctrine as incomprehensive and insufficient.[61]

What follows is a more detailed synopsis of Julian's interpretation of the book of Job.[62] To begin with, he regards the book as composed by the Holy Spirit (1:8). This is noteworthy because Julian's teacher, Theodore of Mopsuestia, whose *Commentary on the Psalms* he had translated into Latin and whose "Antiochene" approach to exegesis had greatly influenced him, apparently rejected the divine inspiration of the book of Job. Angela Kim Harkins reports that for Theodore, Job's angry outbursts (cf. Job 3) were irreconcilable with the portrait of him being a moral exemplar and "raised serious questions about the book's inspired status."[63] She further notes that the Acts of the Council of Constantinople in 553 preserve fragments of Theodore's critical comments on Job in which he rejected the book in its present form.

Second, the text that Julian interprets is Jerome's new Latin version of Job translated from the Hebrew, not the Old Latin translation of the Septuagint (LXX) version. The Hebrew version is about 20 percent longer than the LXX. In his preface to the Vulgate version of Job (AD 393), Jerome reports to his readers that the LXX version is significantly reduced:

> Wherefore, let my barking critics listen as I tell them that my motive in toiling at this book was not to censure the ancient translation [the Old Latin rendering of the LXX], but that those passages in it which are obscure, or those which have been omitted, or at all events, through the fault of copyists have been corrupted, might have light thrown upon them by our translation; for we have some slight knowledge of Hebrew.[64]

Julian adopts Jerome's text while making some seventy references to Greek readings. According to Annecchino's analysis, Julian used the version of the LXX handed down by the Codex Alexandrinus (mid-fifth century).[65] Julian often offers several readings of a single passage introduced by *uel uel* and *aut aut*, and about fifty introduced by *aliter*. Annecchino notes that the use of the latter adverb, which is absent in the *Tractatus*, is really interesting because, in addition to the cases in which it is used between one interpretation and another, it sometimes makes a transition between the translation of the LXX

[61]A. Dupont and G. Malavasi, "The Question of the Impact of Divine Grace in the Pelagian Controversy," *Revue d'Histoire Ecclesiastique* 112 (2017): 566-67. I believe my own recent articles confirm this as well: Thomas P. Scheck, "Jerome's Use of Origen's Exegesis of Romans 9 in His Epistle 120.10 to Hedibia," *St. Vladimir's Theological Quarterly* 62, no. 4 (2018): 349-371; Thomas P. Scheck, "Election as Foreknowledge from Justin Martyr to St. Jerome," in *The T&T Clark Companion to Election*, ed. Edwin Chr. Van Driel (forthcoming).

[62]Annecchino, "I Temi," 287, says that this exegetical work is closer to the literary genre of the *scholia* than to that of the commentaries.

[63]Angela Kim Harkins, "Job in the Ancient Versions and Pseudepigrapha," in *A Companion to Job in the Middle Ages*, ed. Franklin T. Harkins and Aaron Canty (Leiden: Brill, 2016), 16.

[64]NPNF2 6.491.

[65]Annecchino, "I Temi," 295.

and the comment linked to Jerome's biblical text. In two cases it is placed between the text and explanation (14:5; 41:24); at other times it is placed between the biblical quotation, presented both in Jerome's and the Greek versions, and explanation; in some cases it is not connected to the biblical text or to the commentary that comes before; in two cases it lies between the text of the LXX and the commentary based on the LXX.[66] Noteworthy is that Julian's interpretive technique does not seem altered by the text forms. He puts the literal interpretation first, conforming to the context of the passage and in respect of the contextual coherence, which is considered decisive in establishing the real meaning of the text, beyond any subjective or symbolic interpretation.

In basing his commentary on the new Vulgate translation, Julian has followed the path taken by Philip, disciple of Jerome, as mentioned above. It is noteworthy, however, that Julian does not copy Philip's heavily allegorical approach to interpreting Job. Simonetti and Conti describe Philip's exegesis of Job in these terms:

> The interpretation proposed by Philip is on two different levels. The first is the historical level which deals with the misfortunes of Job and explains them in a literal way. The second level is characterized by an extremely allegorical interpretation that considers Job as a figure of Christ and his three supposed friends as symbols of the heretics. These two kinds of interpretations run in parallel lines throughout the work. For instance, the seven sons of Job prefigure the sevenfold grace of the Holy Spirit, and his three daughters the law, the prophets and the gospel. Job, who curses the day of his birth, signifies Christ, who has taken upon himself the entire mortality of the human race and deprecates the transgression of Adam.[67]

In contrast with such a strongly allegorical reading, Julian focuses on the historical level without denying the prophetic and messianic aspect of some of Job's oracles.

Thematically, and resuming the issues mentioned above in our discussion of the preface, Julian says that Job's life is praised in Scripture because in him the goodness of human nature can be recognized, even without his having been taught by the law of Moses. Job shows that human nature was sufficient unto itself to know the one true God, to reject sins and pursue all virtues (Preface; 16:19; 23:13; 33:15-16). Job's prudence and perfect circumspection concerning sin are shown by his response to his trials (Job 1:22). He did not sin with his lips or do anything wrong before God (23:15). The theme of the book, then, is that God takes pride in those who are innocent, who practice sincere and unfeigned virtue, and who live according to his law. Julian, commenting on Job 17:8-9, writes,

> For the Lord wanted to conceal his own justice in order to broadcast the merits of his servant [Job], in order that by his example every innocent person will not only stand up confidently against the hypocrite, but, moreover, while proceeding down the continuous way of virtue, will always increase his own former pursuits for the sake of those who are following.

[66]Annecchino, "I Temi," 289-90.
[67]ACC Job, xxiii, citing PL 26, 658-61.

Job's friends, who measure merits on the basis of prosperity and misfortune (Job 12:6), argue that Job is suffering these things because of his previous sins (4:2). They say that God's justice does not permit him to show vengeance to those who have done nothing worthy of censure (4:7), that Job had only affected a reputation of justice, and that he did not have any solid virtue (8:11-12; 34:5). Indeed, they say that Job had committed grave sins against charity (22:6-7). In fact, in their estimation, Job has received less chastisement than his merits deserve (20:1-2, 18). Yet according to Julian, it is Job's friends (excluding Elihu) who are the hypocrites, not Job himself (27:8; 38:1-2). Innocent and just persons, like Job, are to be contrasted with those who displease God by feigning virtue. The "friends" accuse Job of sin, based on his sufferings, but his conscience is upright (10:3-4; 11:1-2; 23:15). Job is like Christ, who for the sake of saving the human race, endured the humiliation of the cross, so that by his example the innocent person could stand up strongly against the accusations of hypocrites (17:8-9). In addition to possessing the virtues of justice, chastity, and moderation (31:12-13), Job had served the poor and was merciful to them (31:16). He had invited the vulnerable to his table (31:17), since the virtue of humanity was ingrained in him (31:18). He also had done good in chance encounters with the poor, clothing the naked, and showing compassion and hospitality to strangers (31:19, 32). He had never cheated his laborers (31:38-40) and had even loved his enemies (31:29). Such behavior sprang from his fear of God (31:23, 35). Job did not worship idols, which shows that he not only strove after good morals but also held fast to right religious thoughts (31:26-27).

It seems important to add, however, that according to Julian, Job does not claim to have lived an entirely sinless life (Job 6:3; 13:14, 23; 31:33). Granted what the book itself tells us, that Job was an innocent, upright, and God-fearing man, who did not sin in his response to his losses (1:1, 22; 2:10). Granted that in 17:2 (Vulgate) Job himself says in the lemma, "I have not sinned." Julian acknowledges the truth of these affirmations and says that the latter passage could refer to the continuous time of his life, or else that he has avoided vices since lapses in his adolescence (13:26; 20:11; 33:8-10). Granted that Job judges as false Bildad's effort to expose him as a sinner on the basis of his calamities (9:1). Steinhauser raises the question, "What better way could there be to refute Augustine's insistence upon universal hereditary sin than by putting forth the concrete example of a holy man who did not sin?"[68] In Julian's defense, it seems only fair to indicate that, whatever Julian may have thought about Augustine's doctrine of hereditary sin, Julian states that Job does not claim sinlessness (13:14; 31:33). Rather, Job denies that he had been a hypocrite in his prior life (13:16), and he thinks that the measure of the punishment and torture inflicted on him has been excessive and incongruent with the life he had lived previously (6:1-2; 8:1-2; 10:19-21; 13:14, 23; 15:11; 19:6; 20:1-2, 3, 18). Job does not deny

[68]Steinhauser, "Job Exegesis," 306.

that he deserved chastisement from God, but he thinks the reproof he received has been excessive. Moreover, Julian points out repeatedly that Job does not boast about his own virtues (6:1-2; 23:11; 30:27; 31:35); rather, he was forced to defend himself against the vicious charges of his hypocritical friends who accused him of insolence and bitterness and of having committed criminal acts (22:6-7). But Job recalls his virtues reluctantly and with a sense of embarrassment. These passages seem sufficient to refute the claim that Julian views Job as a model of utterly sinless perfection that is attainable apart from the constant assistance of the grace of God.

By revelation Job recognizes that mysteries are coming later on that will bring him remuneration and consolation for his virtue (19:27). Yes, he will be vindicated, and his fidelity to God will be revealed and the accusations of his friends exposed (19:28). For Julian, the overall lesson of the book is that although Job is unable to know the justice of God's judgments (39:5), the Creator had never ceased to care for him and Job had never been robbed of God's providence (38:4, 5-6; 39:33-34 LXX & Vulg = RSV 40:3-4; 40:1-3; 42:3). It is noteworthy that according to Julian, Job prophesies the coming of Christ and predicts the Lord's passion (9:24; 17:8-9), his incarnation and resurrection, and the resurrection hope for his followers (14:12, 14, 18-19; 15:12; 19:25, 27; 26:5-6; 38:13, 14, 16-18). Contrary to a seeming majority opinion of modern exegetes of the book of Job, Julian claims that Job does not deny the future resurrection hope (7:9; 14:7, 12, 14).

Ultimately, as Job stands before the greatness of God, with the help of reason, he discovers the divine mysteries and understands that he is a part of it. He humbly accepts his human condition and lays bare his conscience before God. From the examination of past life (Job 29) and present (Job 30), he shows how, both in prosperity and in misery, he never moved away from justice, mercy, chastity, and temperance (31:7-13). He rightly states that by his constant pursuit of kindness, the virtue of his humanity was engrained in him (31:18). The endeavor to practice virtue, which is born of the fear of God (31:23), frees humanity from pain because although the just and the sinner are subjected to the laws of death, not all will suffer death. In fact, after (physical) death, life will be restored (30:23-24). In the image of Behemoth and Leviathan, symbols of negative power that can be overwhelmed and defeated by humans through virtue, all the force that can spring from it and from the positive example is expressed (41:16).

Additionally, it is interesting to note that Julian thinks the language used in Job 1:6 and 2:1-3 is figurative, since angels do not literally stand before God in the manner of attendants. God is invisible and boundless (cf. Job 11:8-9), and Scripture frequently presents things that were *said* as things that actually *took place* (22:17). Julian here follows Jerome's line of interpretation of a number of texts of Scripture, which describe things that took place in spirit as things that were actually carried out.[69] Finally, Julian does not deny spiritual and allegorical applications of the book. He thinks the Leviathan creature represents the power of spiritual wickedness (41:25).

In her study of the themes of Julian's *Exposition of Job*, Annecchino summarizes Julian's theology as follows:

> Julian, in this writing, summarizes all his doctrine. The human being, as gifted with free will, finds his salvation not in a fatalistic saving grace, which transcends him by crushing him irreparably, but in his dignity as a free man. Although the theme of grace does not constitute a central point of Julian's discourse, since he is intent on claiming the native goodness of human nature, it is clear that he does not deny divine help in the life of man, indeed he recognizes its multiformity. This grace of God, however, can only help and not create good will; if it were not so, the freedom of will would be annulled which is the greatest manifestation of God's benevolence towards men. Free from *tradux peccati* [transmission of sin] man—and this is the central core of Pelagian morality—who is born full of innocence; he can tend to virtue and live far from sin by virtue of his innate strength, freedom and the will, aided by the divine law and the example of Christ, supported by reason which, even within the limits of its creaturely condition, makes it fear God, making it go beyond the limits of human abilities.[70]

To this I would only add that it appears to me that neither Pelagius not Julian intended these emphases as directed against the idea that humanity constantly stands in need of the divine grace and assistance for the achievement of virtue. Rather, their theology is directed against Manichaeism and fatalism, which is apparently how they interpreted Augustine's doctrine of irresistible grace.

Julian's tractates on Hosea, Joel, and Amos. In 1580, R. L. de la Barre published this work for the first time among the works of Rufinus of Aquileia.[71] This association presumably suggests that the theological content was assessed favorably. De la Barre was succeeded by D. Vallarsi, who in 1745 reissued the work as an appendix to his edition of Rufinus. In 1849 Vallarsi's text was re-edited by J. P. Migne.[72] Carl Paucker proposed on linguistic grounds that Julian was the author of these commentaries that had previously been ascribed to "Pseudo-Rufinus," but death prevented the fulfillment of his hope of a later and fuller study.[73] Then, in 1913, Germain Morin developed Paucker's suggestion

[69]For instance, Jerome sees Hosea's union with a prostitute (cf. Hos 1) as a figurative story, not a marriage consummated literally. The story of Jeremiah burying a loincloth in the land of the Parthians (cf. Jer 13:1-7) was something done in spirit, not in reality. The story of Ezekiel's translation into the inner shrine of the temple (cf. Ezek 8:3-4) was something done without Ezekiel's physical presence in that location. Cf. Jerome, *Commentary on Hosea*, bk 1 preface (ACT 2:150).

[70]Annecchino, "I Temi," 309.

[71]Cf. Gisbert Bouwman, *Des Julian von Aeclanum Kommentar zu den Propheten Osee, Joel und Amos. Ein Beitrag zur Geschichte der Exegese* (Rome: Pontificio Istituto Biblico, 1958), 24-37; and Lössl, "Julian of Aeclanum's Tractatus," 11-37.

[72]PL 21, 959-1104.

[73]C. Paucker, *Vorarbeiten zur lat. Sprachgeschichte*, ed. H. Rönsch (Berlin, 1884), III, 3, ii, p. 53. Cited by Baxter, "Notes," 6.

and successfully attributed to Julian of Eclanum the tractates on Hosea, Joel, and Amos.[74] His principal evidence (drawn from Paucker) was the striking similarity in language and style between Julian's *Libri VIII ad Florum* and the *Tractates*. Bouwman describes Morin's achievement as "one of the finest accomplishments in modern patristic studies."[75] The text in the Migne edition had been extremely defective, but thanks to new manuscript discoveries, aided by the research of Morin, Baxter, and Bouwman, Julian has now been edited in a modern critical edition by Lucas De Coninck and M. J. D'Hont, the basis of the present translation.[76] Bouwman describes Julian's *Commentaries on Hosea, Joel, and Amos* as a long forgotten pearl of ancient Christian literature, which is completely free from any taint of the Pelagian heresy (although he thinks Pelagian expressions are found frequently in the commentaries on Job and Song of Songs).[77]

Despite the initial attribution, it is hardly conceivable that Rufinus of Aquileia (345–410) was the author of these commentaries. There is no ancient evidence (from Jerome or Gennadius) that Rufinus composed such works. The author is rather critical of Origen's allegories, whereas Rufinus admired them and had defended and translated Origen's highly allegorical homilies on the Hexateuch. The author praises Jerome's scholarship in the preface and actually adopts Jerome's new Vulgate translation of the Hebrew as his base text. (He had also adopted the Vulgate for the Job exposition.) Yet Rufinus is known to have been a severe critic of both Jerome's person and of his new translation of the Old Testament.[78] In fact, both Rufinus and Augustine argued in opposition to Jerome that the Greek Septuagint was the divinely inspired and ecclesiastical version of Scripture. This is all decisive evidence against Rufinian authorship of these commentaries.

When assessed against the backdrop of his own times, Julian's adoption of Jerome's new translation of the Old Testament as his base text of Scripture is strikingly bold and innovative. He had been preceded only by his predecessor Philip, disciple of Jerome. Julian's extensive use of Jerome's commentaries in his own work confirms the respect he held for Jerome's overall scholarly achievement. Julian explicitly ascribes theological importance to Jerome's new translation in these words:

> Let the reader of our work recognize which version I followed and what was the main consideration I had in mind when I took up this very difficult task of writing a commentary. Especially if he belongs to those who train attention on the reading [in the liturgy],[79] let him know that it was not for no reason that I deliberately chose this most recent version

[74]Germain Morin, "Un ouvrage restitué à Julien d'Eclanum: Le commentaire du Pseudo-Rufin sur les prophètes Osée, Joel et Amos," *Revue Bénédictine* 30 (1913): 1-24.

[75]Bouwman, *Des Julian von Aeclanum Kommentar*, 8.

[76]CCSL 88.

[77]Bouwman, *Des Julian von Aeclanum Kommentar*, 137, 79.

[78]Cf. Rufinus's *Apology Against Jerome*, 2.33-35.

[79]I have followed J. Lössl, "A Shift in Patristic Exegesis: Hebrew Clarity and Historical Verity in Augustine, Jerome, and Julian of Aeclanum and Theodore of Mopsuestia," *Augustinian Studies* 32, no. 2 (2001): 167n37 in adding the bracketed words for clarification.

> known as "according to the Hebrew." For in the earlier versions faults of expression frequently corrupt the meaning, of the doctrinal teaching or of the narrative, so that divination rather than work seems to be required. But this latest translation, although it has not added much rhetorical brilliance to the coherence of the original text itself, nevertheless by its integral soundness of expression it frequently avoids those previously mentioned losses of suppressed meanings.[80]

Julian's attitude toward Jerome's new translation and his effort to assimilate Jerome's learning into his own stands out in contrast to the theory and practice of Augustine, who at least in his early period did not think Jerome was qualified to translate the Bible from Hebrew, and he tried to dissuade him from that task. Augustine wrote the following to Jerome in the inaugural letter of their famous dispute over the proper meaning of Paul's conflict with Peter recorded in Galatians 2: "I would be very surprised if anything could still be found in the Hebrew texts which had escaped the notice of all those [Hexapla][81] translators who were such experts in that language."[82] He fashions the following syllogistic argument to dissuade Jerome in his effort: The passages that the Seventy translated were either obscure or plain.[83] If they were obscure, one must believe that Jerome's new version is just as likely to be mistaken. If the passages were plain, it is not believed that the Seventy could have been mistaken. So how could Jerome's translation be anything but erroneous or redundant?[84]

Jerome eventually replied to this logic (not without sarcasm) as follows: a whole series of Greek and Latin writers have composed commentaries on the Psalms; Augustine too has published a work on the Psalms, which is at variance with the other writers. Jerome asks, Why, after all the labors of so many competent interpreters, does Augustine differ from them in his exposition of some passages? If the Psalms are obscure, it must be believed that he is as likely to be mistaken as the others; if they are plain, it is incredible that these others could have fallen into mistakes. In either case, Augustine's exposition of the Psalms has been an unnecessary labor, and on his principles, no one would ever dare to speak on any subject after others have pronounced their opinion. Jerome reproaches the incivility of Augustine's attack: Why does Augustine grant himself the liberty to contribute to the church's exegetical tradition of the Psalms yet is intolerant of Jerome's effort to make a new Christian Latin translation of Scripture directly from the Hebrew? Jerome

[80]*Commentary on Hosea*, preface.

[81]The Hexapla refers to a six-column edition of the Old Testament edited by Origen of Alexandria. In addition to the Septuagint version, it provided three additional Greek translations (Aquila, Symmachus, Theodotion).

[82]Augustine, Ep. 28, in C. White, *The Correspondence (394-419) Between Jerome and Augustine of Hippo* (Lewiston, NY: Edwin Mellen, 1990), 66. J. Lössl writes, "Already in ep. 28 dating from the year 394/395 he declared Jerome's translation of Job from the Hebrew as superfluous and went as far as to question Jerome's competence as a translator." "Shift in Patristic Exegesis," 157-58.

[83]The "Seventy" refers to the legend that King Ptolemy of Egypt employed seventy Jewish scholars to translate the Hebrew Bible into Greek.

[84]Augustine, Ep. 28.

writes, "No, it should rather be your duty, as a civilized human being, to show the same indulgence to others as to yourself."[85] Jerome goes on to say that he has not attempted to do away with the works of his predecessors by his fresh work on the Hebrew text. Therefore, Jerome adds, if Augustine is averse to reading his version, no one is compelling him to read it against his will. Let him drink with satisfaction the old wine; but Augustine should not despise Jerome's new wine.

In a later letter, Ep. 82.34, Augustine claims to have become convinced of the benefits of Jerome's translation of the Scriptures from the original Hebrew. Yet at least one modern scholar has noticed that Augustine seems to deliberately neglect Jerome's scholarship in exegetical works that could have directly benefited from Jerome's learning. E. Plumer, the modern translator of Augustine's *Commentary on Galatians,* finds it surprising that Augustine did not draw on Jerome's erudite exegesis of Galatians in his own commentary on Paul's text, though he had access to Jerome's work and had criticized it in published letters.

> At the very least, one would have expected him to borrow some linguistic point or other from Jerome, particularly as we find Augustine very soon afterwards emphasizing the importance of linguistic expertise for the interpreter of the Bible, painfully conscious of his own lack in this regard, and (no doubt thinking primarily of Jerome) commending the work of the Hebraists to biblical interpreters [*De Doctrina Christiana* 2.11.16; 2.16.23]. Yet where is the evidence of Augustine's having taken his own advice?[86]

In contrast to Augustine's deafness to the value of Jerome's scriptural exegesis and translation work, it appears to me that no reader of Julian's *Commentaries on Job, Hosea, Joel, and Amos* could come away wondering about the evidence that Julian learned from Jerome's Hebrew scholarship; it is found on every page. Julian has adopted Jerome's text as his own. Where pertinent to the prophetic context, he has assimilated Jerome's expositions. I have endeavored to aid the reader in detecting this by recording parallel passages in the footnotes. One can also learn a great deal by observing the way Julian differs from Jerome as an interpreter of these books.

Date and sources of Julian's tractates on Hosea, Joel, and Amos. Scholars do not agree on when these commentaries were composed. Morin dates them early, between 421 and 423, before the translation of Theodore's *Commentary on the Psalms.*[87] Bouwman places them in the late 430s (439) after Julian's return to the West. He describes them as Julian's last and most mature works.[88] De Plinval dates them 432–436.[89] He was followed by Duval.[90]

[85]Jerome, Ep. 112, in White, *Correspondence,* 135.

[86]E. Plumer, trans., *Augustine's Commentary on Galatians* (Oxford: OUP, 2003), 53.

[87]Morin, "Un ouvrage," 19n36.

[88]Bouwman, *Des Julian von Aeclanum Kommentar,* 60.

[89]G. de Plinval, "Julian d'Éclane devant la Bible," *RSR* 47 (1959): 354n31.

[90]Yves-M. Duval, "Iulianus Aeclanensis restitutus. La première edition—incomplète—de l'oeuvre de Julien d'Éclane," *Revue des Études Augustiniennes* 25 (1979): 168.

I tentatively follow the suggestions of J. Lössl in placing them in the mid- to late 420s.[91] In his preface to Hosea, Julian observes that among the Latins particularly there has been a long silence in commenting on the prophets, yet among the Greeks and Syrians some exegetes have arisen who have endeavored to discuss these writings. He says he has read a few things written by St. John Chrysostom, who adapted nearly his whole work to homiletical exhortation rather than commentary.[92] Julian goes on to report that on Hosea, Origen of Alexandria (ca. 185–ca. 254) composed "charming allegories rather than solid and tenable historical explanations."[93] Apparently, Julian read Origen's Greek works on the Prophets.[94] Jerome had indicated that Origen also wrote a work in Greek titled "Why Is the Name of Ephraim Used in Hosea?" Jerome says that this work aimed to show that whatever was spoken against Ephraim in Hosea should be referred allegorically to the persona of the heretics.[95] Jerome himself adopted this antiheretical application extensively in his own commentary on Hosea, which in allegorical digressions contains an enormous amount of polemic against heretics. This feature is completely absent from Julian's commentary. I have counted 246 occurrences of the term *heretic* or *heresy* in Jerome's commentaries on Hosea (160), Joel (7), and Amos (79), whereas in Julian's three commentaries these terms hardly occur at all.[96] Julian evidently felt that such allegorical excurses, which apparently originated in Origen's Greek exegesis, were inappropriate and far removed from the commentator's task of expounding the contextual coherence of the prophetic texts. As mentioned above, Julian also shied away from such diversions in his Job commentary. It does not seem just, however, to conclude from Julian's criticism of Origen on this particular point that it means that Julian was generally hostile to Origen's exegesis. My estimation is that Julian would have been quite sympathetic to Origen's strongly anti-Gnostic (= anti-Manichean) exegesis of Romans, for instance, as was Pelagius for certain.[97] Such a stress found in Origen resembles Julian's and Pelagius's anti-Manicheism and stress on free will.

After mentioning John Chrysostom and Origen, Julian goes on to give us his opinion of Jerome himself:

> Jerome, a man of enormous intellectual capacity and persistent zeal for scholarship, wrote commentaries on the books of the prophets to be sure, but he was content to navigate

[91]Lössl, "Julian of Aeclanum's Tractatus," 17-18.

[92]St. John Chrysostom (ca. 345–407) was patriarch of Constantinople. The sample of Chrysostom's exegesis of Hosea referred to here has not survived. See Bouwman, *Des Julian von Aeclanum Kommentar*, 129.

[93]Origen's commentary on Hosea is no longer extant. It is noteworthy that Julian read it but seems to frown on it for its excessive use of allegory. Jerome further says that Origen wrote a separate commentary on Hosea, the manuscript of which was damaged at the beginning and the end. Jerome's reception of Origen was far more positive than Julian's.

[94]We know that Jerome possessed Origen's twenty-five-book *Commentary on the Twelve [Minor] Prophets*, transcribed by the hand of the martyr St. Pamphilus himself, and said, "which I hug and guard with such joy, that I deem myself to have the wealth of Croesus." *On Famous Men* 75.

[95]Jerome, *Commentary on Hosea*, bk 1 preface (ACT 2:150).

[96]I have found one instance of *heresy* under the lemma to Hosea 1:2-5.

[97]See my work, *Origen and the History of Justification: The Legacy of Origen's Commentary on Romans* (Notre Dame, IN: University of Notre Dame Press, 2008), ch. 2.

> between the two traditions [Greek Christian and Jewish], and he was either unwilling or unable to exhibit any concern to seek contextual coherence.[98] Thus his entire speech flowed either through the allegories of Origen or through the fabulous traditions of the Jews. Therefore, since it seems to me that he [Jerome] passed over many useful things, I have decided that the work would be a religious one before God and useful to men, if in obedience to you, I should undertake to write a commentary on the prophets, as our capacity has allowed by the help of divine grace. (*Hos Prol*)

Noteworthy here is that Julian recognizes Jerome's scholarly contribution to the church and admits that he has been inspired to write his own commentaries on the prophets by his great predecessor, whom he regards as a man of great intellect and persistent scholarly zeal. Yet he simultaneously criticizes Jerome's exegetical works for excessive attachment to Origen's allegorical exegesis and for unfounded esteem for Jewish traditions. Julian thinks that Jerome should have paid more attention to expounding the historical context of the prophetic texts. Slightly later in the preface, Julian says that he himself is not interested in the investigations into "novelties." I believe he means that Origen provided many novelties by his allegorical interpretations that related the details of prophetic texts to the heretics who were afflicting the church. Jerome incorporated many of these into his works and added more "novelties" from the Jewish exegetical tradition—that is, etymologies, stories, and explanations that had not previously been familiar in the Latin West. According to Julian, not all of these new things contribute to the coherent explanation of the prophetic texts. Even previously unknown Jewish traditions need to be sifted and compared to the context. In other words, in Julian's view Origen's and Jerome's scholarly work on the prophets has left room for successors to achieve other tasks. J. Lössl comments on the lengthy passage cited above:

> Julian's notion of what is the meaning of his text is also far more restricted than Jerome's. Having Jerome's commentary on the Minor Prophets in front of him and indicating, without mentioning Jerome's name, that he draws from it, Julian makes clear that he wants to discuss neither historical and philological *quisquiliae* [odds and ends] like the Jewish Rabbis nor indulge in allegorical and typological exegesis in the tradition of Origen. This criticism is directed against Jerome. Julian cannot but acknowledge the quality of Jerome's translation, and his commentary reveals in every single paragraph its indebtedness to Jerome's commentaries on Hosea, Joel, and Amos, but that does not prevent Julian from mercilessly pointing out that in Jerome's commentaries the simple narrative, historical, and prophetic fabric of the text, its most basic, simple, meaning, is buried under an avalanche of marginal details.[99]

[98]Bouwman, *Des Julian von Aeclanum Kommentar*, 81, notes the importance of the concept of "contextual coherence" (*consequentia*) to Julian. It is shown statistically by the fact that *consequentia* occurs fourteen times, and *consequenter* forty times, in his three commentaries on the prophets. Julian thinks Jerome (and Origen) often ignored this aspect.

[99]Lössl, "Shift in Patristic Exegesis," 169-70.

This seems to be a very accurate assessment. Yet it hardly seems fair to take Julian's words cited above as an affront to Jerome, as Bouwman does.[100] Jerome himself tells us that he conceives the chief work of a commentator to be that of compilation.[101] He admits that he does not necessarily endorse all the views he records, nor does he provide definitive interpretation of all texts, but rather leaves many interpretive choices open to the reader. Jerome says that his overall goal was to acquaint his Latin readership with the Greek Christian and Hebrew interpretive tradition.[102] These are very noble ambitions to which he dedicated his life, and it is a credit to Jerome that he supplied the Latin church with an enormous reservoir of exegetical and homiletical material. Yet Jerome's aims do not determine how Julian understands the task of a commentator. Baxter summarizes Julian's method under a discussion of his favorite words, *consequentia* and *consequenter*:

> These words are among the most characteristic and the most frequent in Julian's vocabulary. As a sober commentator of the Antiochene school, despising the allegorical method of exegesis and intent on bringing out the literal and historical meaning of Scripture by the close study of the context and the natural development of narrative or argument, he keeps continually insisting on the sequence of ideas, the logical unfolding of the story, and he well defines his position in the words of Hos 10:10: "the rule of explanation is best which is taken from the context of the reading." Hence his incessant use of *consequenter, consequentia*, and of *contextus*, in all the treatises which flowed from his pen.[103]

From Jerome, Julian learned that all three books of Hosea, Joel, and Amos reflect the historical circumstances of the reigns of the kings mentioned in Hosea 1:1.[104] This view, Jerome tells us in the preface to Joel, is derived from Jewish tradition. Whatever modern exegetes may say about the tenability of this claim with respect to Joel, Julian accepts this theory and makes the corresponding historical background of these particular reigns, as testified in Kings and Chronicles, the fundamental context in which the prophecies were delivered. Moreover, Julian adopts from Jerome nearly all that he reports

---

[100]Bouwman, *Des Julian von Aeclanum Kommentar*, 82, says that Julian has hardly a good word to say of Jerome's commentaries on the prophets. But can dissent from particular interpretations be equated with disparagement?

[101]When Jerome was accused of Origenism by Rufinus of Aquileia, based on the way he compiled Origen's exegesis of Ephesians into his own commentary on Ephesians, Jerome responded in his *Apology Against Rufinus* 1.16 (NPNF2, 3:491): "What is the function of a Commentary? It is to interpret another man's words, to put into plain language what he has expressed obscurely. Consequently, it enumerates the opinions of many persons, and says, Some interpret the passage in this sense, some in that; the one try to support their opinion and understanding of it by such and such evidence or reasons: so that the wise reader, after reading these different explanations, and having many brought before his mind for acceptance or rejection, may judge which is the truest, and, like a good banker, may reject the money of spurious mintage. Is the commentator to be held responsible for all these different interpretations, and all these mutually contradicting opinions because he puts down the expositions given by many in the single work on which he is commenting?" See R. Heine, *The Commentaries of Origen and Jerome on St Paul's Epistle to the Ephesians* (Oxford: Oxford University Press, 2002). For another striking example of Jerome's tendency to compile Greek exegesis into his Latin commentaries, see his extensive use of Didymus the Blind in his *Commentary on Zechariah* (Jerome, *Commentary on the Twelve Prophets*, ACT 2:1-115).

[102]Jerome, *In Ieremiam* 3, *Praef; In Zachariam* 6:9-15.

[103]Baxter, "Notes," 25.

[104]See Julian, preface to Joel.

about history, topography, biblical realities, Jewish exegesis, and alternate interpretations. Thus, from start to finish he is sitting at Jerome's feet and learning from him as a teacher. According to Julian, the message of Hosea, which is also closely related to that of Joel and Amos, is that "our God declares that he has received the synagogue as his wife, as it were, but that she violated the terms of the union in the fashion of adulteresses, and, what is more, she subjected herself to the worship of different gods [in the form of Jeroboam's calf-bulls]" (Joel 1:8-9). Therefore, God has threatened to bring disasters on the people of Israel, while also holding forth his offer of mercy to the penitent. In Joel the threat takes the form of a forthcoming locust plague that hopefully will inspire terror and remorse in the hearts of the listeners. It will be removed once God has been placated. In Amos, whose focus is on the ten tribes, God's providential care for the surrounding nations is also revealed. He examines them in judgment as well as the Jewish nation (Amos 1:3-5), for he is the God of the Gentiles as well as the Jews. No human being's pursuits are deprived of consolation or punishment in the divine recompense. Julian offers a beautiful summary of God's singling out Israel from all nations under Amos 3:1-2. Elsewhere he says that many prophetic promises point to greater blessings under the Messiah (Joel 2:26-27), yet not every detail of these prophecies can be applied to the spiritual interpretation under the gospel times (Joel 3:4-8). Rather, digressions occur in the course of the words of the prophets that point to messianic times, but then the prophet reverts to his own times once again.

Julian agrees exegetically with Jerome (over against Theodore of Mopsuestia) that Hosea 5:10 refers to Judah's rejoicing at the extent of the lands annexed to themselves when their brother Israel was driven out by the Assyrian captivity. He follows Jerome's interpretation of Hosea 6:7 that Israel fell by imitating Adam, an interpretation that some modern theologians have reproached as a "Pelagian" interpretation. Scores of other examples of Julian's discipleship to Jerome could be documented. Yet despite his tremendous debt to Jerome, both for his text of Scripture and for the exegetical and historical content, Julian does not simply copy Jerome's interpretations in the manner of a plagiarist. On the contrary, he critically engages it and is capable of reproaching Jerome's exegesis, sometimes impertinently, yet almost always anonymously (in the sense that he does not name Jerome as his target). Yet his criticism of Jerome is not personal but historical-critical.[105] At times Julian disagrees with Jerome's exegesis as unbecoming to the historical context and coherence of the prophetic books. Julian frequently offers a range of possible interpretations of the text, introducing them with the *vel, aut* ("or") or *aliter* ("Here is another way"). To me this indicates humility and a spirit that does not aim to impose a dogmatic straitjacket on every text he interprets.

[105]J. Lössl points this out in *Julian von Aeclanum*, 165n86. He calls attention to and discusses the following passages: *Tr. Proph.* Praef; Hos 1:2-5; 2:14-17; 9:7-8, 15-17; 12:9, 11; 13:11; Joel 1:13-14; Amos 3:13-14; 8:3; 9:1, 5.

Here are samples of passages where Julian seems to regard Jerome as having faltered in his interpretations.

- Under Hosea 1:2-5, commenting on the words, "I will visit the blood of Jezrahel on the house of Jehu," Julian thinks that historical background in 2 Kings 9-10 might be adequate to explain Hosea's reference to Jehu (this is Jerome's interpretation), but the closer context in Hosea favors the view that here Jehu stands in place of the nation of Israel.
- Under Hosea 2:14-17, Julian mentions a meaning of "Baal" Jerome had reported as stemming from the Jewish tradition, but Julian finds the context of Hosea alone sufficient for ascertaining the sense.
- Regarding Hosea 9:8, Julian mentions that "some" (Jerome) think that the watchman of Ephraim refers to Jeroboam. Julian presents Jerome's interpretation in full but then dissents from it based on the immediate context.
- Under Hosea 9:15-17, Julian again reports that "some" (Jerome) have taken the passage to refer to Saul, but Julian finds this an overly subtle interpretation and presents one that he finds "clearer and more applicable."
- In his commentary on Hosea 11:8-9, Julian reproaches Jerome by name for his claim that in a certain sense God will never enter a city, which would put the verses in opposition to Psalm 87:2 and 46:5.
- Under Hosea 12:11, Julian once more finds the immediate context sufficient to explain the meaning rather than far-fetched references presented in Jerome's commentary.
- In his preface to Joel and under Joel 1:1, Jerome had discussed the etymologies of names of the Twelve Prophets and their sires and interpreted these terms allegorically. Julian finds this childish and criticizes the practice (Joel 1:1).
- In distinction from Jerome, Julian interprets Joel as describing a real locust plague that fulfilled predictions made in Deuteronomy 28. The basic description is literal, not symbolic of nations harassing Israel, as Jerome had claimed based on Jewish tradition (cf. Julian on Joel 1:4; 2:19-20).
- Under Amos 7:4-6, Julian adds that Jerome's interpretation of the locust plague as symbolic of Israel's enemies is inconsistent with history, since the prophet says that these plagues were warded off by his prayers whereas the Assyrian and Babylonian enemies were victorious. Thus, contextual coherence is the leading principle of Julian's exegesis and the basis for his dissent from Jerome (when he exhibits such dissent).
- Under Amos 2:13-16, Julian dismisses a Jewish interpretation Jerome had provided. At Amos 5:25-27 he strongly reproaches Jerome by name.
- Under Amos 9:1a-c, Julian reports anonymously what Jerome and Theodore had thought, that the altar referred to was that of the temple in Jerusalem. Julian objects: "But the context of the passage refutes such an understanding. For no mention of Judah had preceded, but he was expressly threatening the ten tribes." Contextual coherence and historical consistency is the main principle once again. Yet it is clear that Julian does not repudiate allegorical or symbolic interpretation in principle, since he offers an allegorical application of the locusts to human souls (Joel 2:4-11). Julian's symbolic exegesis in this section has clearly been informed by Jerome's commentary on Joel 1:4 and his commentary on Zechariah 1:18-21, which no doubt had been based

> in Origen. This particular example shows the inadequacy of the scholarly attempt to make rigid dichotomies between Alexandrian and Antiochene approaches to exegesis.[106]

In general, Julian's interaction with Jerome strikes me as that of the respectful engagement of a very intelligent pupil with the learned but not infallible views of a revered and pioneering scholar.

Many modern scholars claim that the logical and thematic tensions that exist in the writings of the prophets are to be attributed to the fact that different editors from different centuries were permitted to interpolate their ideas into the prophetic books.[107] Julian's comment under Amos 5:3 deals with this question of whether there are inconsistencies in the prophets. He handles the problem as follows:

> The history of Kings makes clear that the misfortunes of captivity did not rush in all at once, but the people were chastised at many times, while their amendment was awaited.[108] And for that reason our God addresses them through the prophets by a voice that changes its tone. At one time he says that their ruin is definite, since ruin had to be declared. At another time, he promises them prosperity, if they amend. Therefore, do not surmise that there is any discrepancy in the statements, as though he were restricting them to one time; rather he distributes the judgments that have been set forth over long periods of time and they are appropriate for the circumstances. Then you will find that coherence is maintained in everything, and truly, the reign of the profane people was diminished bit by bit by increasing adversities, until it reached the destruction of the final captivity. Accordingly, we should understand that the decimation of the nation was carried out in those cities and regions, which were laid waste while the capital city of Samaria was still standing.

For Julian the discrepancies and seeming inconsistencies in the tone and message of the prophecies found in Hosea, Joel, and Amos can be attributed to their lengthy periods of ministry and to the varying historical circumstances they were addressing. Obscurity arises from the way the prophets intermingle judgments that pertain to various times into single oracles (Amos 3:13-14; 5:25-27). In my view, Julian's rigorous historical and contextual approach to interpreting these books deserves consideration at the table of modern exegesis of Hosea, Joel, and Amos.

Use of Theodore of Mopsuestia? Scholars disagree on the question of whether Julian had Theodore of Mopsuestia's *Commentaries on the Prophets* directly at his disposal while writing his own. He does not mention Theodore among his sources in the preface to Hosea, although he does mention Origen, Jerome, and John Chrysostom. Morin found evidence for Julian's use of Theodore in Julian's reference to the "Syrian" interpretation of

106 See J. Behr's comment about this, *Formation of Christian Theology*, vol. 2, *The Nicene Faith*, part 1 (Crestwood, NY: St. Vladimir's Seminary Press, 2004), 12.

107 See for example the approach taken by Bernhard Duhm, *The Twelve Prophets: A Version in the Various Poetical Measures of the Original Writings*, trans. Archibald Duff (London: Adam and Charles Black, 1912).

108 Cf. 2 Kings 15:29; 17:3-6.

Hosea's real marriage to a prostitute, which agrees exactly with what Theodore says. Bouwman concedes that Julian knew of Theodore's interpretation of Hosea's marriage as factual but thinks that some of the corresponding interpretations between Julian and Theodore may have been derived from Theodore's *Commentary on the Psalms* and not directly from the published form of Theodore's exegesis of the prophets.[109] Julian's comments about Hebrew idiom correspond with what Theodore says (Hos 1:2-5). Julian does not follow Theodore's example in ignoring the Lord's reference to Hosea 10:7-8 in Luke 23:30 and Paul's citation of Hosea 13:14 in 1 Corinthians 15:55. Theodore agrees with Julian that Joel lived in the time of Hosea. Julian disagrees with Theodore that the locusts are figurative of Israel's enemies.

Julian's conception of prophecy. Julian recognizes the messianic dimension of particular prophecies. He thinks that Hezekiah foreshadows Christ (Joel 2:26-27) and that events fulfilled under Hezekiah are fulfilled more abundantly under Christ (2:32). Yet not everything the prophet weaves into his speech is connected to a spiritual understanding (3:4-8). Several passages from Julian's *Commentaries on Hosea, Joel, and Amos* deserve special attention, since he seems to make use of his definition of prophetic vision (*theoria*) to interpret Old Testament prophecies in the light of their New Testament fulfillment.[110] Hosea 1:10 is cited by St. Paul in Romans 9:25-26 as being fulfilled in the reception of the Gentiles into the church. Julian believes that in his original context the prophet Hosea is describing the return of the Israelites from the Babylonian captivity, but he does so with language that in no way corresponds to the historical facts, but transcends them by far—for example, when he says, "And the number of the sons of Israel will be like the sand of the sea which is without measure, and shall not be numbered" (Hos 1:10). With wording like this, the prophet wants to call attention to the fact that Israel's return from Babylon is an image of a much more wonderful liberation, which alone corresponds to the description that is given. It is not that Israel's return from Babylon is the text's literal meaning whereas the Christian ecclesiastical application is the allegorical meaning. No, rather, the prophet has predicted both, so that the imperfection of the historical partial fulfillment points to the future messianic events. Hosea 1:10 provides the occasion for Julian's definition of prophetic vision. He says that when Paul indicates that Hosea's promise was fulfilled in the time of the gospel, his aim is not to deny what the whole context of the prophecy of Hosea drives home—namely, that a release from the Babylonian captivity had also been promised:

> He [Paul] merely wanted to show what principle we ought to observe in the interpretation of the prophetic writings, that is, when anything was revealed in a narration of Jewish matters that was vaster than the insignificance of one nation had room to contain, we need to

[109] Bouwman, *Des Julian von Aeclanum Kommentar,* 129.

[110] In this section I have closely followed Bouwman, *Des Julian von Aeclanum Kommentar,* 108-10.

> know that it has been fulfilled partially in that people, and by [prophetic] vision (*per theoriam*) it is applicable to others also, that is, to all the nations. But as the learned have agreed, [prophetic] vision (*theoria*) is the perception of those realities which are of greater importance, considered generally in brief images or cases. Therefore, this summoning back of the Jews from Babylon was not properly spoken of according to history, but that liberation signified allegorically what has been acquired through faith in Christ.

Julian grants that the prophetic speech has promised both without qualification. Thus, the thing of moderate size that preceded made known the peaks that were to follow. "For what had first been expressed in exaggerated terms hardly equaled the magnitude of the things that were to come later" (Hos 1:10-11). What Hosea had said of the Babylonian times, Paul transferred to the facts of the Savior. Annecchino summarizes Julian's exegetical principle this way:

> That is, the prophet has two objects of his prophecy in his mind and uses the first to announce the second. The prediction is one and occurs twice: first partially in Jewish history, then fully in the history of the Messiah. This happens when the anticipation of an episode in the life of Jesus is caught in Jewish history. The two events, as historically real, have a literal meaning in which there is no first and second but rather a sense virtually double literal.[111]

No New Testament passage cites Hosea 2:16-24 as being fulfilled in the New Testament period. However, Julian provides an interpretation of it within the framework of a general typological correspondence between Israel and the church. He says it is fulfilled more clearly if we apply it to the calling of the gospel. Yet Hosea 11:1 *is* cited in Matthew 2:15 as a type in the technical sense. From what Julian says, it appears that in this instance the prophet himself is not aware of the higher fulfillment. Julian says that since the context of the prophecy shows that this was said concerning the Jewish people, apostolic authority pointed out that this can also be transferred to the person of the Lord Jesus Christ—namely, the one through whom those things that had been given to the Jews as insignia of the divine religion were conferred even more abundantly and more graciously on us. Bouwman comments that this is not a mere accommodation of the Hosea passage by Matthew but rather a unique allegorical interpretation within the framework of a general typology whereby Israel equals Christ.

The words of Hosea 13:14 are cited in 1 Corinthians 15:55. The miraculous liberation from the siege of Sennacherib is an image of the freedom that Christ has given to us. Julian says that he has already explained this in accordance with the history predicted by the prophet. Yet it is also capable of signifying even greater things: "Therefore, that liberation which was accomplished under Hezekiah is unfolded more abundantly and graciously by the freedom that Christ bestowed" (Hos 14:10). One observes that the New Testament citation provides the occasion to Julian for a broader typological interpretation that once again is based on the typology of Israel's equivalence with the church.

[111]Annecchino, "I Temi," 293.

Although New Testament prooftexts are not found for Joel 2:23, the foundation of the typology is the correspondence between Hezekiah and Christ. Julian says that we should apply the things that were done by Hezekiah to the affairs of our Redeemer: "Thus though they were indeed fulfilled somewhat in [Hezekiah's] time, yet under the gospel they seem to have acquired vast surpluses of meaning. For he [Christ] is the true 'teacher of justice' (cf. Joel 2:23 Vulgate) 'in whom all the treasures of wisdom and knowledge are hidden' (Col 2:3)." Joel 2:28-32 is quoted in Acts 2:17-21. Julian observes that Peter recalled this passage when the Holy Spirit came down into the apostles (cf. Acts 2:17-21). But the only point he wished to make initially is that the apostles' miraculous gift of tongues fulfilled Joel's prophecy about the outpouring of the Spirit. Yet Peter added to say that when the day of the Lord comes, it will be with the power and uproar described in Joel's prophecy, when the stars are struck down and the world collapses (cf. Mt 24:29; 2 Pet 3:10-12). Faith alone will suffice for salvation at that time.

> Therefore, just as it does not interfere with the prophet's meaning to apply what the whole book describes as Jewish history to the situation of the gospel, so also—or rather, far more, at least with the well-educated reader—it is never allowed to deny the credibility that is suitable to the context if some prophecy can be applied to the situation of believers from the nations too.

Julian thinks the audacity of those must be renounced who recklessly and ignorantly contend that the prophet had indicated solely that time about which the apostle Peter preached. For the entire context of Joel is shown to embrace first the times of the Jewish people but, secondly, ours, "as a finishing touch as it were." Julian goes on to say that the prophecy of Joel was fulfilled in its first stage at the time of Hezekiah. However, the events of that time had not merely a historical but also a prophetic significance. This prophecy has even a third level of meaning: the eschatological. As Christ linked the downfall of Jerusalem with the end of the world, so shall the shaking of nature that occurred at the death of the Redeemer take place more fully at the world's end.

The foundation of Julian's interpretation of Joel 3:17-21 is the typological correspondence between Jerusalem and the church. Julian says that the blessedness of Jerusalem foretold in Joel embraces the mysteries of the church, which endured the assault of hostile power, of the Jews, and of the pagans:

> Just as we read that this was done in part under Hezekiah, so also we proclaim it was fulfilled more abundantly under the "mediator of God and men" (1 Tim 2:5). He indeed . . . promised that he would dwell in the midst of the city of Zion when he said: "Behold I am with you all the days, even to the consummation of the world" (Matt 28:20).

Julian claims that the punishments Amos threatened against the Jews in Amos 8:7-12 were indeed fulfilled when they went into exile but also when they later rejected the Lord. He says that the context of the reading demands the continuance of historical application to the Jews, but the same things are also valid for signifying future things—namely, those times in which the Jews sinned most criminally and fell most gravely. Amos 9:11-12 is cited in Acts 15:16-17. Julian explains,

> Therefore, by following the teaching of the apostles, we have come to know that the books of the prophets must be understood in such a way that the events of their own times are embraced according to the context. And through the sudden digressions or accumulations of senses, they also have indicated future events, and have taught that their greatness is seen in the narration of epitomes. For thus has the form of the present passage established, that, as far as the history is concerned, both the rule of the Babylonians has been dissolved, and the captivity which the Jews suffered has been abolished, and the long-awaited freedom that was often promised has shone forth upon the troubled. Nevertheless, if you examine this freedom against the measuring rod of virtue, you will say indeed that an excessively small amount happened to mortals and to those who endured the bitter things of this life. But this liberation, which the mysteries of Christ have brought to the faithful, when it has finally come, is limitlessly longer, incomparably higher.

Here Julian makes clear that the historical sense of the passage is the liberation from the Babylonian exile. However, Christ has delivered us in a much fuller sense. The remainder of the interpretation is strongly allegorical. The term *digression* (*excursus*) is understood by Baxter as a literary digression.[112] For Vaccari it is "something subjective in the poet's mind, a digression of thought, a kind of transient *ecstasis* which is then reflected in the extrinsic expression."[113] Bouwman adds that in Julian's time, digressions frequently mean *ecstasis*; however, he thinks that *excursus* concerns more the grammatical sense, while *ecstasis* the prophetic-mystical one. They allow the prophet to rise for a moment on the historical plane to look at the distant future, then return to the contemporary situation without ever abandoning the object that he penetrates more deeply.[114]

Conclusion

De Plinval concludes his study of Julian's *Tractates on the Prophets* by criticizing the secondary and derivative character of his work. He finds that Julian has rewritten Jerome's commentaries in a spiritually mediocre and secularizing fashion. Julian allegedly stands far below the works of Jerome and Theodore as a second-tier personality.[115] This assessment strikes me as unfair when one considers the degree to which Jerome's own works are indebted to his Greek predecessors, whether Origen or Didymus the Blind, his commentaries on Ephesians and Zechariah, respectively, being cases in point.

De Plinval correctly recognizes that for exegetes like Origen, Ambrose, Augustine, and Jerome, virtually every verse in the Bible could be interpreted spiritually as applying

[112]Baxter, "Notes," 30.
[113]A. Vaccari, "La θεωρία nella scuola esegetic di Antiochia," *Biblica* 1 (1920): 118.
[114]Bouwman, *Des Julian von Aeclanum Kommentar,* 90.
[115]De Plinval, "Julien d'Éclane devant la Bible," 362-66.

to Christ and the church, whereas Julian allowed for this kind of interpretation for only a few privileged passages, primarily those cited by New Testament authors. Yet De Plinval thinks this has resulted in an impoverishment of Julian's exegesis and ultimately in a wrongheaded theology. While I acknowledge that these significant differences exist in the extent of the use of allegory, I do not detect a resulting impoverishment on the side of Julian's exegesis. In any case, at the very end of his *Commentary on Hosea*, Julian admits that greater depths of spiritual interpretation are possible for the material he has treated primarily historically. But is Julian's reduction or elimination of allegorical digressions that attack heretics, for example, an impoverishment or an improvement of Christian exegesis of the Old Testament? I see little harm in what Julian has done and think the church has room for both approaches and others as well. In general, I agree with J. Lössl, who has found some of De Plinval's assessments unjustified:

> De Plinval was certainly right in calling the *Tractatus* a "re-writing" of Jerome's commentaries on Hosea, Joel and Amos. He could have called it by an equally fashionable expression a "relecteur" (re-reading). It was a "re-writing" influenced in spirit, if not letter, by Theodore's commentaries on Hosea, Joel and Amos. But De Plinval was wrong to consider the *Tractatus* an inferior work for that. He might have come to a different conclusion, if he had compared the three authors in detail. Bouwman had compared the texts, but had failed to appreciate Julian's originality as a writer and thinker. His verdict that Julian has merely "copied" Jerome is contradicted by his own findings concerning Julian's language, style, compositional technique, exegetical method and theological content. For these are not only similar, but also dissimilar to Jerome's and Theodore's. Both, similarities and dissimilarities alike need to be studied in more detail.[116]

I hope the present translation will facilitate the study of these ancient Christian commentaries.

Conventions Used in This Translation

My translation is based on the Latin text found in L. De Coninck and M. J. D'Hont, eds., *Iuliani Aeclanensis expositio libri Iob, tractatus prophetarum Osee, Iohel et Amos, accedunt operum deperditorum fragmenta post Albertum Bruckner denuo collecta aucta ordinate*, CCL 88 (Turnhout: Brepols, 1977). Since Julian adopted Jerome's Vulgate version as his base Scripture text, I have tried to conform his lemmata (the cue headings that contain the Bible text to be commented on) for Hosea, Joel, and Amos as closely as possible to those of Jerome in the latter's commentaries on these books (ACT, vol. 2). As the starting point for rendering Julian's other Scripture citations, I have used the online Douay-Rheims English translation of the Vulgate (www.drbo.org/), always updating the archaic English. For his references to the "Greek," I have used the online Septuagint in Brenton's version (www.ellopos.net/elpenor/greek-texts/septuagint/default.asp). Although Brenton's English rendering is of the LXX in Codex Vaticanus, whereas Julian's Greek text corresponds most closely with Codex Alexandrinus, in the vast majority of cases the two texts agree.

[116]Lössl, "Julian of Aeclanum's Tractatus," 36-37.

In the commentaries, echoes of the lemma are indicated with italics. The critical edition does not contain an abundance of Scripture references and allusions. I have supplied as many as I could (using the Revised Standard Version Catholic Edition), often conjecturing as to which passages Julian may have had in mind. For the Scripture citations in the footnotes I have used English locations according to the RSV. These are not always identical to the LXX and Vulgate locations.

I wish to acknowledge the collaboration of the following students from Ave Maria University: C. M. C. Wood, Elise Larres, Rachel Corcho, and Andrew Kuenstle. In addition to these diligent students, the patristic scholars Stuart Squires and Giulio Malavasi, as well as the editors of InterVarsity Press's Ancient Christian Texts series, gave me valuable feedback on the introduction.

EXPOSITION OF THE BOOK OF JOB

[Preface]

The apostle testifies, "All things whatsoever that have been *written* were written for our instruction."[1] If this is true, how much more have those things that are reported as the *deeds* of holy people been handed down in tradition for us to imitate, to keep them from perishing due to the silence of the pen. They have been provided in advance for authoritative instruction. And so the life of saint Job is praised because in him the goodness of human nature can be recognized.[2] Even without the teaching authority of written law, he shows that human nature was sufficient unto itself both to reject sins and pursue all virtues.[3] For it was indeed created that way by God. But Job is praised not because it advances his merits that such a man becomes known to all. For even if he had not been praised, in the sight of God he would not have lost anything in the estimation of his honor. But the reason was so that in him those who come after may realize that virtue is attainable for those who are willing to approach it. Due to his intimacy with virtue, the holy man was not distracted (*deductus*[4]) either by his losses or by his bereavements. Secondly, it is pointed out how great God's goodness is toward us. Whatever good things we do are so pleasing to him that he seems to point out our goodness, as it were, and brag about it, almost as if he were boasting.[5] We learn the following also from this book, that every saint of God often experiences temptations and tribulations. This is not due to his having offended [God], but in order to test the person's devotion and to increase his merit.[6]

It is asked, of course, whether we believe holy Job lived before the law [of Moses] or after the law.[7] But it seems more likely that he came before the time of the law, because that fits both with reverence for the lawgiver and with the justice of the man himself.

[1]Rom 15:4.

[2]Job is mentioned in Ezek 14:14-20 alongside Noah and Daniel, each of whom has a well-known reputation for justice. Angela Kim Harkins says, "It appears that Job's power of intercession merited his inclusion here [in Ezekiel], as the prophet notes that these skills would fail all three holy men on the day that is to come." "Job in the Ancient Versions and Pseudepigrapha," in *A Companion to Job in the Middle Ages*, ed. Franklin T. Harkins and Aaron Canty (Leiden: Brill, 2016), 14-15. Job is also mentioned in Sir 49:9 as a part of the praise of the prophet Ezekiel, and he is recorded as a paragon of virtue in Jas 5:11.

[3]Kenneth B. Steinhauser, "Job Exegesis: The Pelagian Controversy," in *Augustine: Biblical Exegete*, ed. Frederick Van Fleteren and Joseph C. Schnaubelt (New York: Peter Lang, 2001), 306, comments on these words: "Here the fundamental self-sufficiency of human nature is affirmed." Gisbert Bouwman seems to concur with such an assessment when he says that "Pelagian expressions" occur frequently in the Job and Song of Songs commentaries, whereas they are entirely absent from the three prophets commentaries. *Des Julian von Aeclanum Kommentar zu den Propheten Osee, Joel und Amos. Ein Beitrag zur Geschichte der Exegese* (Rome: Pontificio Istituto Biblico, 1958), 79. Yet compare John Chrysostom's comment on the same text in Job: "Notice the words 'from any [evil; cf. LXX],' and not simply from one evil and not from another. Where are those who assert that human nature is inclined toward evil?" ACCS 6:1-2.

[4]Cf. Job 19:18. The Latin word can also mean "brought down."

[5]Cf. Job 1:8.

[6]K. Steinhauser comments on this passage: "[Julian] is one of the few ancient commentators on Job who comes close to the actual theme of the book, when he states that God permits the good to suffer in order to demonstrate their devotion and increase their merit." "Job in Patristic Commentaries and Theological Works," in Harkins and Canty, *A Companion to Job in the Middle Ages*, 57. *Meritum* appears sixty-four times in Julian's text, which makes clear that for Julian human beings can earn merit before God.

[7]See under Job 16:19; 33:15-16.

Otherwise, this one who had pleased God[8] would be believed to have shown contempt for the law of him whose authoritative instruction in any case he did not think it fitting to approach, being, as it were, sufficient in himself.

One should know, moreover, that saint Job's whole speech against his friends is divided into three parts.[9] For immediately in the beginning, when they blamed him for complaining excessively, he shows that even if he were roused to all bitterness by those things that had befallen him, this should not be attributed to him as a fault. And in order to convict them, he adds to this in various ways by relating his sufferings; and then he makes a transition. And, what is more, he shows that they are friends only in outward appearance, but in reality they are enemies. For though they came to console him, they heap up causes for grief by scoffing at his sufferings. For high and low they try to pin the blame of sin on him for his hardships. Finally, he shows that it is in vain that they want to prove him to be responsible for his misfortunes, since it is an established fact that many persons of a defiled life are not without prosperity in the present. However, when his friends are reduced to silence, since they were unable to refute the things that he said, as a greater apology for himself, he recounts as well those things that he had done justly and piously.[10] After this, Elihu undertakes a discussion of the providence of God, and he uses many arguments to prove it.[11] This speech is clearly helpful, and its theme corresponds to his purpose. For even God enters into the conversation and mixes it up in words of disputation with saint Job.[12] He, so to speak, adjudicates everything that had been said above and discourses on the providence of affairs. He cites as evidence those things that were done at the beginning of the world: that is, the visible creation, four-footed creatures, flying creatures, and the things native to the earth and things that take delight in the waters.[13] Whoever stands out as a diligent reader [of this book] will be able to find these things in the reading itself.

[Chapter 1]

1:1 In the land of Uz (*Hus*) there was a man by the name of Job.

There is a simple narration of events, and it seems far removed from showing favoritism to persons. For his parents and ancestors are not praised, as is customary for eulogists, but the one whose good blessings are to be set forth is placed in the center of the discourse. *In the land of Uz (Hus)*. People think that this refers to the land of King Sihon near the Promised Land, which was captured by saint Moses.[14] [The Septuagint] said, "In the land of Ausis." "And he was simple and upright and fearing God." The method of the narration is maintained, so that, since he had told who he was [and] where he was from, he added what kind of man he was. *He was simple*, in that he was separated from any mingling with vices. He added *upright*, lest his simplicity be believed to be in him not from his pursuit of virtue but from the kind of nature he had.[15] This is why

[8]Cf. Job 1:22; Heb 11:5; Jas 5:11.

[9]Cf. Job 6–11; 12–20; 21–30.

[10]Cf. Job 31.

[11]Cf. Job 32–37. The word *providentia*, which derives from Stoicism, is used thirty times in his Job commentary.

[12]Cf. Job 38–41.

[13]Cf. Job 41.

[14]Cf. Num 21:21-32; Deut 2:24-37. A. Vaccari, *Un Commento a Giobbe di Giuliano di Eclano*, Scripta Pontificii Instituti Biblici 27 (Rome, 1915), 157, found a parallel in the Scholia of Olympiodorus, deacon of Alexandria, here and throughout Julian's commentary.

[15]Both second-century Gnosticism and fourth-century Manichaeism held that salvation was determined by the nature one receives at birth, not by one's works or merits. A good nature would always be saved and never perish, and a bad nature would always perish and never be saved, irrespective of deeds. Valentinus, an Egyptian who taught in Rome from 135 to 160 and probably the most influential of the Gnostics, held to a sort of natural

he clarified the two preceding words with the addition of a third, *and fearing God*. The reason, then, that he was *simple and upright* was because he *feared God*. "And avoiding evil." He shows briefly what precisely it means to fear God—namely, to avoid being incited by any evil.

1:2-3 And there were born to him seven sons and three daughters. And his possession was seven thousand sheep, three thousand camels, five hundred yoke of oxen, five hundred she asses, and a family exceeding great.

The fruitfulness of children and the extent of his wealth is shown in order to proclaim more fully the greatness of his soul, which patiently endured bereavement and losses. "And this man was great among all the people of the east." He had everything that human beings believe make them happy: the adornment of good character, the comfort of affection, extensive property, and no scanty amount of inheritance.

1:4 And his sons went and made a feast in their houses, everyone in his day. And they sent for and invited their three sisters to eat and drink with them.

This has in view the good of the father's instruction. For his children live among themselves in such great harmony that at no time are they separated from a single banqueting table.

predestination that divided humanity into three categories. The redeemer, Jesus, saves people from the world by giving them saving knowledge, or gnosis. The gnosis is available only to the spiritual (*pneumatikoi*). The second kind of nature is the "soulish" (*psychikoi*) and refers to ordinary members of the Catholic Church, who can achieve some kind of salvation by faith and good works. The third group is the rest of humanity, or the "natural" (*hylikoi*), who have no chance at redemption. Clearly, according to such a system, human freedom in salvation is unreal, at least for most people, and merit is inconsequential. Julian strongly opposes such an approach.

1:5 Job sent to them and sanctified them.

Sanctified, that is, he would cleanse them with water, just as it is commanded in Exodus, that the people should *sanctify* themselves.[16] And she is called Bathsheba (*Bersabee*) because she *sanctified* herself after her adultery.[17] "And rising up early he offered holocausts for every one of them: Lest perhaps my sons have sinned." A serious reproach is not precluded here, that he seems to be overlooking the sins of his children without correction, which certainly does not fit his being a just man. But, since there was nothing for him to reprimand, being solicitous and very devout, he does not neglect to pray for them and make amends for what could have happened. "Lest perhaps my sons have sinned, and have blessed[18] God in their hearts." In the Greek it does not say, *Lest perhaps my sons have sinned, and have blessed God in their hearts*, but rather, "He offered holocausts for each of them and one calf for sin for their souls."[19]

1:6 Now on a certain day when the sons of God came to stand before the Lord, Satan also was present among them.

Angels are called *sons of God* as a sign of their immortality. In order for there to be a fitting

[16]Cf. Ex 19:10.

[17]Cf. 2 Sam 11:4.

[18]The Douay-Rheims note here reads, "For greater horror of the very thought of blasphemy, the scripture both here and ver. 11, and in the following chapter, ver. 5 and 9, uses the word bless to signify its contrary." www.drbo.org/chapter/20001.htm.

[19]Job 1:5 LXX. Julian will frequently reference the Greek version (about seventy times). According to Marialuisa Annecchino's analysis, Julian used the version of the LXX handed down by the Codex Alexandrinus (mid-fifth century). "I Temi Dottrinali-Esegetici nell'Expositio in Iob di Giuliano D'Eclano," in *Munera parva: studi in onore di Boris Ulianich*, ed. Gennaro Luongo (Naples: Fridericiana Editrice Universitaria, 1999), 295. The reader should be aware that the Septuagint version of Job is considerably shorter than the one known from the Masoretic Text (and thus Jerome's Latin version). As many as 390 lines or about 20 percent of the material found in the Hebrew text of Job does not appear in the LXX. For a discussion, see Harkins, "Job in the Ancient Versions."

occasion for the devil to request permission for himself to tempt Job, the angels are well said to *stand before* God, being observers of various human beings and actions. Thus, the devil seems to have been incited by the praiseworthy acts of Job. It makes no difference, then, whether we say that God truly appeared to the angels in the form that he desired, not in the truth of his nature, so that an occasion would be offered for the devil to attack Job; or the malignant power became visible; or whether we believe that he has rendered into words what was in the will and zealous desire of the devil and in the knowledge of God. For it is customary in Holy Scripture to record things that are *said* as things that have been *done*, and conversely, to narrate those things that dwell only in our perceptions and thought in such a way as if they are carried out in reality and in works, so that invisible realities may more easily become known through visible actions.[20]

1:7 And the Lord said to him, Where do you come from? And he answered and said: I have gone round about the earth, and walked through it.

By his answer, the devil wanted the following to be understood, that he had circuited the earth and had found no one who was not obedient to his rule. For that reason, the Lord presents Job to the one who was boasting, as it were—Job who was estranged completely from the devil's interests and will.

[20]See further under Job 2:1-3. Along similar lines Julian (following St. Jerome's interpretation) claims that Hosea's union with a prostitute was a figurative story, not a physically consummated marriage (cf. Hos 1:2-5); the story of Jeremiah burying his loincloth in the land of the Parthians was done in spirit, not reality (cf. Jer 13:1-7); and Ezekiel's translation into the inner shrine of the temple of Jerusalem (cf. Ezek 8:3-4) was something done without his physical presence in that location. Also noteworthy is the correspondence of Julian's views here and under Job 2:1-3 with Isho'dad of Merv, who says, "There was never a special meeting where Satan dared to speak, to formulate questions and receive answers—nothing of the sort—but these facts are reported in a narrative style for the edification of the listeners. . . . They never took place in reality." Cf. ACCS 6:4.

1:8 Have you noticed my servant Job, that there is no one on earth like him, a simple and upright man?

The testimony that was recorded at the beginning of the book is granted by God to Job.[21] This proves that this book was composed by the Holy Spirit.

1:9-10 Satan answered and said to him, Is it for nothing that Job fears God? Have you not made a fence for him, and his house, and all his substance round about?

The favorable moment for the accusation arises from his material prosperity, when he says that Job fears God not from a religious frame of mind but due to the pile of his goods.

1:11 But stretch forth your hand a little, and touch all that he possesses, and see if he does not bless[22] you to your face.

You will find the proof of his devotion when his prosperity has been taken away and adversities have been introduced.

1:12 Behold, all that he has is in your hand.

The devil had said to God, "Stretch forth your hand, and touch all that he possesses."[23] Lest the favorable moment for the accusation should be left to God, and the devil should say that the Lord had dealt too gently with his servant, power is given to the devil to vent his anger on Job. Thus, to the extent that he is the fiercer attacker, so much the more does the virtue appear of him who is to be attacked.

1:13-15 Now on a certain day when his sons and daughters were eating and drinking

[21]Cf. Job 1:1.
[22]See note on Job 1:5.
[23]Job 1:11.

wine in the house of their firstborn brother, there came a messenger to Job, who said, The oxen were ploughing, and the asses feeding beside them, and the Sabeans rushed in, and took all away, and struck down the servants, and I alone have escaped to tell you.

In the house of their firstborn brother: the devil chooses the day of temptation so that he may then assail holy Job with a variety of losses and sorrows. It is while the feasts of his children were being carried out on the earth, while sacrifices were being offered. Job at that time would have been secure regarding God's propitiousness. Not without reason on that day on which the report came concerning the stolen bulls and asses, mention is made also of his children's feasting. But this shows that all the bitter things by which the spirit of the just man was to be struck happened simultaneously.

1:16 And while he was yet speaking, another came and said, The fire of God fell from heaven, and it struck the sheep and consumed the servants.

Now it should not seem surprising that the devil is said to have brought down *fire from heaven*, since it is possible even for humans to discover the nature of fire, either by rubbing sticks together, or with the insertion of water, or sometimes by means of glass vessels.[24] *The fire of God fell from heaven.* The reason the devil brings fire down from heaven is to throw Job's mind into a state of greater confusion, so that he may not suppose that he is suffering evils by chance, but surmise that they are coming from God himself, whom he used to serve very devoutly.

[24]The last presumably refers to the use of a magnifying glass in direct sunlight. Rubbing sticks together is a well-known method of starting fires. The use of water to generate fire may refer to the practice of refracting sunlight through a water-filled glass vessel.

1:17 And while he was yet speaking, another came and said, The Chaldeans formed three companies, and fell upon the camels and took them; moreover they have struck down the servants.

In Greek it says, "Horsemen formed three companies."[25] In all this, the messengers are announcing two evils: the stealing of the livestock and the killing of the shepherds. Thus, if the losses do not shake him up, at least feelings of compassion over the death of human beings may move him.

1:18-19 He was speaking, and behold, another came in and said, Your sons and daughters were feasting in the house of their firstborn brother. A violent wind came and shook the four corners of the house, and it fell upon your children (*liberos*) and they are dead.

The spirit of saint Job is tested by the devil's great artifice. Thus, having started with the lighter temptations, he brought it about that the one that was more serious was the last to be reported. Thus, if he bore the loss of his inheritance patiently, and did not deem it worthy to shed tears over it, he would be shaken from the loss of his own children (*pignorum*). And, if he was insufficiently pious to refrain from groans, if he showed himself too lacking in moderation, he would be convicted of having forgotten God.

1:20 Then Job arose and tore his tunic.

From this it is evident that all these things came to pass within a single day. For no sad news altered the joy of the children feasting together. Surely they would not have devoted themselves to feasting amid all the great losses of their father. *He tore his tunic*, since he was about to reveal feelings of grief over the loss of

[25]Job 1:17 LXX.

his children. Thus, what he was silent about in respect to the loss of his inheritance is shown to have come not from having his spirit stunned but from virtue. "He worshiped and said." *He worshiped*; that is, he did not let go of his reverence for God, even when set amid so many adversities.

1:21 Naked I came forth from my mother's womb, naked shall I return thither.

The man's great steadfastness is being shown. His many lost properties do not bother him, and the death of his children does not compel him to say anything unbecoming against God, as is customary for those who are grieving. Instead, he merely puts on the attire of one who is mourning. "The Lord gave, the Lord has taken away." In these words in particular is the virtue of saint Job recognized. For although he was uncertain of [the identity of] his enemy, and he thought that the evils were being carried out against himself by the God whom he worshiped, he did not draw back from his pious pursuit of God. "Blessed be the name of the Lord." I follow the decision of my Lord in all things. I do not refuse riches, when he *gives*, nor do I become exasperated over the injustice of poverty, when he *takes away*.

1:22 In all this Job did not sin by his lips, nor did he say any foolish thing against God.

Here is shown both the man's prudence and his perfect circumspection concerning sin. For he abstains not only from those words by which God could have taken offense but also from those that in grief are normally attributed not to one's reason but to sorrow.

[Chapter 2]

2:1 And it came to pass.

When the just man had given clear proof of his virtue in the midst of the initial commencement of the struggle, the angels were in awe, but the devil, who was vexed by the man's resolution and steadfastness, attempts to challenge him to combat in some other way.

2:1-3 And it came to pass, when on a certain day the sons of God came to stand before the Lord, Satan also stood among them, so that the Lord said, Where do you come from? He said, I have gone round about the earth. And the Lord said, Have you considered my servant Job, for there is none like him on earth? And does he still keep his innocence? But you have incited me to afflict him without cause.

It is asked whether this took place in this way, as it says in the simple narration of the words. Or, as is customary in the Scriptures, is what the devil wished for and what God allowed being conveyed in the form of deeds that were carried out, so that it may stick more tenaciously in the memory of future generations?[26] For things *done* transmit a stronger remembrance of it than things *said*. In fact, neither reason nor the faith allows that angels *stand before* God in the manner of attendants. For God is invisible and his nature is boundless, as is frequently asserted in testimonies from the Old and New Scripture.[27] And if the holy angels are not able to be present locally with God, how much more the devil? What, therefore, does this mean when it says that *the angels stood before God, and Satan with them*? That just as the holy angels were rejoicing over Job's manner of life, for there is equal joy with them and God over the salvation of human beings,[28] so the devil was vexed by his virtues, and he eagerly endeavored to shake him out of a tranquil state of mind by harming him by means of new misfortunes. And since he thought that the reason Job was devoted to God

[26] See the explanatory note at Job 1:6.
[27] Cf. Ex 33:20; Jer 23:24; Jn 1:18.
[28] Cf. Lk 15:7, 10, 32.

was because he was rich in property and a father blessed with a throng of children, he meditated in his will that, if it were permissible to rob him of the goods in which that one rejoiced, he could then be exposed as one who was not truly religious. And so God, knowing both the wishes of the devil and the steadfastness of his servant, allows him to be robbed of possessions, deprived of children, filled with sores, in order to prove that Job had been devoted to God out of his zeal for virtue, not prosperity. Therefore, these things that were present in the will of the devil and permitted by God are spoken of as things that were done, so that the appearance of a contest that was hidden could meet the eyes, after the things in the future unfolded. *Keep his innocence*: which the severity of misfortunes and the weight of grief customarily shakes. *That I should afflict him without cause*: it should be noted that God says that what he allows to happen by some kind of dispensation is his own doing.[29] *Without cause*: so that I, as if ignorant, may make Job's justice, which was known to me, come into scrutiny.

2:4 Satan answered and said to him, Skin for skin, and a man will give everything for his life (*anima*).

The devil saw that he had not overthrown the steadfastness of the saintly man by the onslaught of the first temptation. Therefore, he came once again before the face of God and alleged that those things by which Job had been tempted were, so to speak, not great things. He says that Job should be tested not by things placed outside of him but by things that strike his very self. For he adds that Job, following the custom of the rest of men, had endured the loss of his things as a pretense, lest he should endanger his salvation[30] by speaking insultingly of God. For it is common to human beings to ward off greater costs by smaller losses, and often by extending the hand in opposition, to ward off danger to the safety[31] of one's head.

2:6 Therefore the Lord said, Behold, he is in your hand.

Behold he is in your hand. The devil's allegation seems worth putting to the test, and the Lord does not refuse to do this. For if the request had been unjust, it never would have been allowed by the just One who has knowledge. Therefore, the test proposed by the devil comes from God. But just as that one who tries to attack by means of these things is convicted of being evil, so is he patient who knows that his servant is made and rendered more illustrious by means of these things. "But spare his life." Because the devil's whole contest was to oppose Job, the state of the holy man's person needed to be kept intact, so that, just as he had resisted with his whole man in the first encounter, he could approach the second combat even with part of himself intact. For if the mind's (*animae*) reasoning capacity or the health of his life had been extinguished by the incursion of some disturbance or frenzy, all the terms of the contest would have been dissolved.[32]

2:7 Satan went forth from the presence of the Lord and struck Job with a very grievous boil.

Some say that it was elephantiasis.[33]

[29]Cf. Job 12:24. In a manner that echoes the teaching of John Chrysostom, Pelagius, Theodore of Mopsuestia, and Diodore of Tarsus, Julian interprets the scriptural passages that apparently describe God's direct act in terms of his allowing it to happen. Cf. M. F. Wiles, *The Divine Apostle: The Interpretation of St. Paul's Epistles in the Early Church* (London: Cambridge University Press, 1967), 97n1.

[30]Or "health."

[31]Or "salvation."

[32]Annecchino notes this passage and comments, "Job is virtuous because he faces the struggle with pain in full consciousness. A struggle carried out in a state of mental illness would have thwarted the essence of the prophet's effort." "I Temi," 304.

[33]According to L & S, this refers to "a very virulent kind of leprosy." Isho'dad of Merv also claims that Job's disease was elephantiasis. *Commentary on Job* 2:7; ACCS 6:1-2, 12.

2:8 Sitting on a dunghill.

In the Greek it says, "He sat on a dunghill outside the city," and among the Greeks there is much more at this point.[34]

2:9 But his wife said to him, Do you still continue in simplicity? Bless[35] God and die.

By his wife's words it is shown that Job continually gave thanks to God, while his limbs were being wrenched apart, and, what is more, amid all this extreme pain he said that he was being kept alive by mercy. This is why his wife says to him as if it followed logically, If he bestows life on you at the special pleading of your prayers, it is better for him to take it away, when he becomes angry at the sound of your complaint.

2:10 He said to her, You have spoken like one of the foolish women. If we receive good things from the hand of the Lord, why should we not receive evils?

He is calling wealth and poverty *goods* and *evils*. The reason poverty must be borne very patiently is because it has many companions and comrades in it, though on the other hand one who has wealth is nearly alone. *You have spoken like one of the foolish women*. The rebuke of the mind is not broken by a disability of the body; for he checked the harmful suggestion of his wife with a raised voice, not a soft one, and with a stern countenance. He says, *You have spoken like one of the foolish women*: that is, you surpass them all in foolishness, you do not know what things pertain to the devotion of servants, [that we are] to embrace, not argue about, the will of the Lord, and to receive with a grateful heart both those things that seem bitter and those that are favorable.

2:11 Therefore, when three of Job's friends heard all the evil that had come to him, each one of them came from his own place, Eliphaz the Temanite, Bildad the Shuhite, and Sophar the Naamathite, to visit him.

Since the calamity of so great a man had been broadcast so far away, it makes sense in the context that many came together from different countries, either to have a look at this new development or to console him in his miseries. But only these three are named, whom either greater inquisitiveness had aroused or who were superior to the rest in honor. *Eliphaz the Themanite*: In Greek it says, "Eliphaz the king of the Themans." Now Theman is a city of the Idumeans, as the prophet Amos testifies when he says, "I will send a fire into Theman."[36] *And Bildad the Shuhite*: In Greek it says, "Bildad the sovereign (*tyrannos*) of the Aucheans (*Aucheon*)," which they say is a city of the Moabites. *Sophar the Naamathite*: [In Greek it says,] "Sophar king of the Minaeans," that is, of the Ammonites. *To visit him*—that is, to alleviate the condition of his suffering by sharing his sorrow. What is shown to be understood from this is that for many days they sat by his side in silence.

2:12 And when at a distance they had lifted up their eyes, they did not recognize him.

The honor of his body was turned to horror,[37] so that the recognition of him by his familiar friends was eclipsed, though not completely

[34]The LXX (in Brenton's translation of Codex Vaticanus) adds to the beginning of v. 9, "And when much time had passed, his wife said to him, How long will you hold out, saying, Behold, I wait yet a little while, expecting the hope of my deliverance? for, behold, your memorial is abolished from the earth, [even your] sons and daughters, the pangs and pains of my womb which I bore in vain with sorrows; and you yourself sit down to spend the nights in the open air among the corruption of worms, and I am a wanderer and a servant from place to place and house to house, waiting for the setting of the sun, that I may rest from my labors and my pangs which now beset me; but say some word against the Lord, and die."

[35]See the note at Job 1:5.

[36]Amos 1:12.

[37]As in English to some extent, these words make a play in Latin.

taken away. "And they wept aloud, and tearing their garments they sprinkled dust on their heads towards heaven." In Greek it says, "And sprinkling earth on their heads they looked up towards heaven." The dust is thrown up toward heaven not as an affront to the worship of the divine but to lay bare the feeling of compassion by making one's head filthy by such a sprinkling.

2:13 And they sat with him on the ground seven days and seven nights, and no one spoke to him.

Their feelings of compassion had not given his friends opportunity to mingle in speech. Therefore, Job is the first to break out into words that give a clear indication of his great sorrow. They are not words that formulated a philosophic tenet. And amid his torments and reverence for the Creator, between these two indeed he does not dare to attribute his sufferings to anyone, yet he wishes that he had not been born.[38] And he detests the very commencement of his existence and utters curses against that time that lacked sensation and substantial existence. This is something that is customary for people who are filled with offense or bitterness. *No one spoke.* Why are they silent, these men who had come together for the very purpose of alleviating by their speech the harshness of the evil that had occurred? Doubtless it is because the evils that they were beholding had exceeded the measure of their expectations.

[Chapter 3]

3:1-3 After this Job opened his mouth, and cursed his day, and he said, Let the day perish on which I was born, and the night in which it was said, A man [child] is conceived.

He shatters the obstinate silence, when some had departed, but these men remained, who had come in friendship and who had been emotionally affected by sharing in his sorrow and pain. He sees that temporal delay was becoming burdensome, because the silence was dragging on. He utters words not to reproach God but to express the misery of his condition.[39] He says that it would be better not to exist (*esse*) at all than to exist like this. *Let the day perish on which I was born.* So great was the onset of pain from the disease, which had spread through the body of holy Job, that no opportunity could be found for a speech that asks particular questions.

3:4-6 Let that day be turned into darkness, let a darksome whirlwind seize on that night.

With diverse imprecations he reproaches the time of day and night, and he heaps these things up into a pile of cursing. He mentions things that are accustomed to ruin the pleasure of rest and light. But in all this it is not reason or logic that is being expressed, but solely the bitterness of one who is suffering severely.

3:7 May that night be solitary.

May that night be solitary, which due to its bitterness and horror cannot come into communion with the remaining [nights] that tranquility commends.

3:8 Let them curse it who curse the day, who are ready to rouse the Leviathan.

May this night and the day of detestation attack, for the terror and devastation of the dragon that is brought up from the deep onto the land deserves it. For the tradition of the Hebrews and Syrians understands the Leviathan to be that thing of which David says,

[38]Cf. Job 3:3.

[39]Annecchino comments on this passage, "Julian does not see in these words any offense to God, but rather the bitterness of those who have become aware of their own miserable creaturely condition." "I Temi," 304.

"This is the dragon which you formed to play therein."[40] Although it seems to hold forth the figure of spiritual wickedness, yet when he emerges and is cast onto the land, he is shown to be one who will cause such great slaughter of men and livestock that everyone's curses would rightly be heaped up against it. In Greek [it says], "But let him who will curse that day curse it, [even] he that will capture the great whale."[41] Just as the one who imprecates the day has referred this to God, in order that the outcome of his prayer may be fulfilled, and says, "Let not God above call for it,"[42] so also he begs that God fulfill the accumulated curses against the night. "Let him curse it," therefore; that is, may he cause the prayers of my cursing to be fulfilled. For with him alone is it possible to wrest the times of day and night from their order and course, to whose power it belongs also to kill that "whale," whose strength is invincible.

3:13 For now I should have been asleep and still.

If I had nothing to do with this life, which is full of work and distress, long periods of leisure would welcome me. There would have been no distinction between the condition of those who, after the cares of the world and the names of honor, pass into the place in which there is no distinguishing of conditions, ranks, or offices. "And I would have rested in my sleep." That is, I would be free and safe from the evils I suffer.

3:14 With kings and consuls of the earth.

In Greek it says, "With kings and councilors." He has called them *consuls*, therefore, not based on their office but their duty. "Who built solitudes for themselves." Their riches are spent on superfluous uses, while from numerous buildings they strive to make solitary places into frequented places. They establish some of these buildings in order to perpetuate the memory of their own name. In passing he has touched on the vanity of mortal pursuits of those for whom speedily approaching death puts an end to their great endeavors.

3:15 Or with princes who possess gold.

He shows the just reasons for his request. For if those also, who lived in honor and pleasure, return no profit from their past life when they are overtaken by death, how would it not have been advantageous to me, who am beset with bitter hardship, not to have come to the very commencement of life?

3:16 Or as a hidden untimely birth.

He has recorded *hidden* for "unformed," whose completion, because it is not present to our sight, is rightly called *hidden* and remote.

3:17 There the wicked have ceased from tumult.

Though the state of the one who is suffering is one thing, that of the one inflicting the injury something else, yet one end will remove both, so that both the former rests from his pain and the latter from his deeds.

3:18 They have not heard the voice of the taskmaster.

After death, he says, there is no difference between king and private person, between the one who drives another on and that one who is driven, but one condition renders all equals.

3:20 Why is light given to him that is in misery, and life to them that are in bitterness?

[40]Ps 104:26.
[41]Job 3:8 LXX.
[42]Job 3:4.

He who is enveloped by the darkness of grief does not feel the pleasure of this *light*. He for whom it is necessary constantly to groan and grieve lacks the gift of *life*.

3:23 To the man whose life[43] is hidden, and God has surrounded him with darkness.

He does not seem to partake of *life*, and somehow lives without it, who is estranged from the sensation of pleasure, sensation that various causes produce.

3:25-26 For the fear that I feared has come on me, and that which I was afraid of has happened.

For the fear that I feared: those things that I am suffering did not befall me, as it were, without premeditation; for when I saw in others both the evils of poverty and the various disabilities of the body, our common bodily nature admonished me to be afraid that such a thing might also fall to my lot. And this is also why I am compelled to dread an increase of the evils that I am enduring. This expectation makes death seem better than life. Now as for what he added, "Was I not quiet?" the Greek has "I was not quiet." That is, I have not continued in the enjoyment and prosperity of my possessions. He is saying that he *feared* that the evil of this crisis might strike, with the result that he would utter a voice of complaint contrary to the resolution of his seriousness, if he should suffer any torment. And therefore he says, *Was I not quiet?* That is, when the sharpness of the pain had struck me, I wanted silently to hide what I was suffering; but so great was the violence of the evil raging in me that I am compelled to reveal my torments with a voice of lamentation.

[43]The CCSL text reads *vita* (life) here, which seems to be Julian's reading. Other Vulgate manuscripts read *via* (way).

[Chapter 4]

4:1 Then Eliphaz the Themanite answered, and said.

Amid the justice of God's judgments and the bitterness of the wound and the pain, his friends grew weary of his countless questions and his perplexity. They arrange the commencement of their address in such a way that they could agree both on the things proclaimed simply for consolation and on the things considered more deeply as a rebuke. And, as is usually done in uncertain cases, they prefer to impute what he is suffering not to the unjust judgments of God, as it were, but to Job's deserts. Now to be sure, they commence the discussion with a milder speech, but as it progresses, it becomes clear that they are unleashing their own very harsh verdict.

4:2 If we begin to speak to you, perhaps you will take it ill.

Here *speak* does not simply mean to engage in conversation but to oppose your statements and thoughts. The Greek has, "Have you often spoken in distress?" After Job cursed the time and moment of his birth, as a way of consoling himself in his hardships, Eliphaz does not bear to turn a deaf ear to his complaints, [treating them] as if they had been intended to offend God. Instead, he girds himself with zeal to defend the divine, and he thinks that he can convict saint Job concerning the harshness of his present words—namely, that he is suffering these things because of previous sins.

4:3 Behold, you have taught many, and you have strengthened the weary hands.

Behold you have taught many: the present facts are at odds with your former view. For you are the one who often illumined others who had fallen into sorrow, and you gave the aid of your hand to the lowly, that they might rise up. How is it that you yourself do not hold to the firm tracks with constancy and are not strong enough to raise yourself from ruin? Those things that you frequently taught others ought to have sufficed to console you. These things are being said either in the usual manner of consolation, based on the pursuit of a higher life, or else with irony.[44] It is not that Job had done these things, but thusly had Job previously thought concerning himself.

4:5 But now the scourge [has come] on you.

By these words he wants to show that before the experience of these things, Job had a certain virtuous opinion of himself, virtue that is indeed proven not to have existed, since the case makes this certain.

4:6 Your fear, your fortitude, and the perfection of your ways.

Those things in which you were boasting are also exposed as not having previously existed in you, when you could give them up so quickly, that amid your complaints of lamentation no vestige and sign of them remained in you. You had said that you were silent, quiet, and still at the onslaught of torments and sufferings.[45] Why then are you bursting forth in words that indicate a weak mind?

4:7 Remember, I pray you, who has ever perished being innocent?

With an argument that is general in nature, he even attempts to drag him into agreement with his words, since the justice of the divine examination does not permit that he show his vengeance against those who have done nothing worthy of censure. Thus, it circles back on those who have been pernicious in whom it could lay claim to vengeance.

4:8-9 On the contrary, I have seen those who work iniquity perishing by the blast of God.

He is considering the proper duty of justice: just as it inflicts no evil on the innocent, so it does not allow the crimes of the guilty to go unpunished. *Perishing by the blast of God*, "and consumed by the spirit of his wrath." God requires no work, no effort to punish sinners, but he pursues the apportioning of his rebuke by his command alone.

4:10 The roaring of the lion and the voice of the lioness and the teeth of the whelps of lions are broken.

By the names he has invoked, he wanted to indicate that riches by their own power cannot protect any human being against the judgment of God, not one. By the names *lion*, *lioness*, and *whelp of lions* is shown the ferocity of powerful men and of their despoilments, which they carry out on their subjects, the savage fury against those on whom the severity of divine punishment is deservedly thrust. However, the speech subtly looks back to Job, so that he may recognize by the testimony of the correction received that he was one such person.

4:11 The tiger has perished for want of prey.

In Greek it says, "The ant-lion."[46]

4:12 Further, a concealed word was spoken to me.

To provoke him all the more by his authoritative words, he says that while he was, so to

[44]On Julian's use of irony, see Annecchino, "I Temi," 291.
[45]Cf. Job 3:26.

[46]*Myrmicoleon*. This is the LSJ definition found at http://logeion.uchicago.edu/myrmicoleon and also Sir Lancelot Brenton's rendering, *The Septuagint with Apocrypha: Greek and English* (Peabody, MA: Hendrickson Reprint 1987), 668, note.

speak, submerged in deep thought, he has discovered these things that he is about to declare, and thus they are definitive and carefully weighed. Thus, he appears to have perceived these things with the magisterial authority of a revelation, and they have not been composed so much by the reflection of his own thought as by the voice of someone else who is issuing a warning. In Greek it says, "But if there had been any truth in your words, surely none of these evils would have befallen you."[47] *Concealed* refers to one who denies rather than to the one who affirms.

4:13-16 In the horror of a vision by night, fear seized upon me; there stood one whose countenance I knew not.

At night time, when our senses are free from meeting corporeal things, we are accustomed to occupy ourselves entirely with thoughts and to examine every doubtful and uncertain thing with a deeper reflection of the mind. That is when a thought appears that occurs as more agreeable to the mind of the one who is deliberating. It bears the form and outward appearance of things, and we believe and it seems to be standing there. In order to express this, therefore, Eliphaz claims that he saw an image and heard a voice speaking. *There stood one whose countenance I knew not,* "an image before my eyes, and I heard the voice, as it were, of a gentle wind." In order to accuse saint Job of temerity in his words, he begins to discuss the dignity and nature of God. He says that no human being, however much he focuses his mind, is able to arrive at a perfect knowledge of him. And he tries to express under his own persona that which is proper to the nature of mortals—namely, what he experiences when he wants to think more deeply about God, what men who are overwhelmed by a deep sleep are accustomed to experience in the middle of the night, when various forms of things trick the senses and phantoms of diverse images without shape are discerned, or when the blowing of a light breeze is felt and nothing happens that can be seen by the eyes. In this way, therefore, also the human mind itself, as it thinks about God, is exhausted by the greatness and majesty of things, so that it understands that it has accomplished nothing.

[47] Job 4:12 LXX.

4:17 Shall man be justified in comparison with God?

The things that were said earlier were of general application, although Job could prove that they nevertheless are not fittingly said with respect to his own character. Therefore, Eliphaz adds something else that seems to properly touch Job, so that he would not be able to complain further about the things that he suffers. For if no one's life is completed in such a way that he can be allowed to be compared with divine perfection, then no one ought to boast over the small measure of his justice. And if he cannot boast, because he is far inferior, he should not complain that what he is suffering is shown to be unjust, through the fact that he does not fall short of perfection in any way. *Shall he be justified in comparison with God?* His whole aim has this in mind, that no one can say that he is enduring [anything] undeservedly who understands that he falls well short of that measure that corresponds with the Deity alone.

4:18 Behold, those who serve him are not stable.

He wants to show that it is impossible for human nature to live in such a way that it incurs no offense. For if those who were dedicated to virtue with great zeal, whom he calls his servants, were not able to escape blameworthy lapses, such as Moses, who so offended [God] that he was denied entrance into the Promised Land,[48] what should we believe of those whose more remiss life pays regard to the basics of his body? "And in his angels he found wickedness." He has said *angels* for priests, according to the following: "The lips of the priest shall keep the law, and they seek truth, because he is the angel of the Lord."[49]

4:19 How much more those who dwell in houses of clay?

The state of weakness and the awareness of guilt takes away the liberty to complain; nor is he able to show that he is enduring the things he suffers undeservedly, who is not able to lay claim to the perfection of his virtues.

4:20 And because no one understands, he will perish forever.

No one understands that he should not place his hope in the merit of his own virtues, but in the mercy of God. And the reason he is far removed from pardon is because he does not approach to make amends.

4:21 They will die, and not in wisdom.

The reason *they will die* is because the wisdom that taught them about the forgiveness of God was not present in them, that they should not have been secure concerning their own justice.

[Chapter 5]

5:1 Call, therefore, if there be any that will answer you, and turn to one of the saints.

Consult others about what you ought to feel in respect to your person, and learn from their response. You will find that no one guarantees security for himself on the basis of his own merit. Here is another interpretation: if when you bring forward evidence of some uprightness in yourself, you judge that the harsh words that you had uttered were just, ask anyone you please from among men or any of those who are placed in positions of intimacy with God, and see whether any one comes forward to approve your words.

5:2 Anger truly kills the foolish one, and envy slays the little one.

To complain about one's misfortunes is evidence of foolishness, which indeed is kindled with greater bitterness at that time when one sees the prosperity of another when you yourself have been afflicted.

5:3 I have seen a fool with a strong root, and I cursed his beauty immediately.

Favorable circumstances do not expose excellent men. For even if those who are bad suffer no inconveniences, yet they are nevertheless worthy of repudiation, so that misfortunes may be called down on them justly.

5:5 His harvest the hungry man shall eat, and the armed man shall take him by violence, and the thirsty shall drink up his riches.

He is recounting different kinds of disasters, which usually happen to those who sink into misfortunes on account of the perversity of their character.

5:6 Nothing on earth is done without a cause, and sorrow will not spring out of the ground.

If all things correspond to preceding *causes* and nothing comes about by chance, then merit has preceded as the source from which

[48]Cf. Num 20:10-13.
[49]Mal 2:7.

the bitterness of this *sorrow* arose. For indeed this is the condition appointed to man, so that, since he is left to his own effort, he may be filled with rewards for the quality of his zeal. Here is another interpretation. He is saying, Since you overlooked those things that have been said, you should not have been completely shaken by those things that happened to you; nor should you have gone to court with the miseries of the earth, or of the waters, or of any inanimate thing, which have been formed for our use and service by the Craftsman. They are not to be attributed to common chance; things that have been brought on by *causes*, they speak of an examination of judgment.

5:7 Man is born to labor and the bird to fly.

To feel one's misfortunes is only human; each thing keeps the law of nature imposed on it.

5:8 Wherefore I will pray to the Lord.

He is saying that he himself will do that which he wants to persuade Job to do, to give up seeking the why of the misfortunes that have come on him but rather turn his prayers and supplications to God, who is the Lord of all and whose laws all things obey. *I will pray to the Lord* since I can lay claim to no security for myself on the basis of my works.

5:9 Who has done great and inscrutable things.

[Eliphaz] recounts the riches of divine providence, which are suitably bestowed on each and all commonly throughout all generations.

5:10 Who gives rain on the face of the earth.

From the greatness of his power and the outpouring of his kindness, he infers what is safer for human beings. By acknowledging that one is guilty, one places one's hope of salvation not in one's own merit but in God's forgiveness.

5:12 Who scatters the designs of the malignant.

Since he had pointed out the generosity of the divine goodness, which poured out benefits to humans through a large channel, now he points out the power from which hidden plans cannot escape, nor can those things come into effect that are ordained even by the wise[50] contrary to his will.

5:13 Who catches the wise in their craftiness.

That which they had thought they had provided, he makes so ineffective that it is as if they have been driven back in a narrow space and are unable to move themselves forward. At the end of the verse, he divulges what was veiled earlier, when he says, "And scatters the counsel of the wicked."

5:14-15 They shall meet with darkness in the day, but he shall save the poor from the sword of their mouth and from the hand of the violent.

The gift of divine power looks to one and the same thing, to nullify the attempts of the wicked, not to allow those things that are done contrary to justice to come into effect, and to bring help to those who are weary and who are deprived of solace.[51]

5:17 Blessed is the man whom God reproves.

Since saint Job was very discouraged that such things had happened to him against his hopes, [Eliphaz] says also that after the plague he should not despair about God becoming propitious to him again; for it is a kind of testimony to divine love that he bridles the freedom to sin by means of

[50]Cf. Job 5:13.
[51]Cf. Mt 11:28.

scourges. *Blessed is the man whom God reproves.* He had recounted various kinds of miseries that have come on sinners for this reason, because they did not want to appear guilty themselves in some respect, or to approach satisfaction by the confession of their iniquity. Therefore, he says that when one is compelled to correction or knowledge by his scourging and severity, he should not be reputed to be amid miseries.

5:19 Out of six troubles he shall deliver you.

To be sure, the sum total of the number that is recorded seems to agree with these things that he has added.[52] But generally what he wanted to demonstrate is this: if Job trusted in God and believed that God had reproved him not by anger but by his providence, Job would plead from then on that due to God's protection he was free and safe from many dangers.

5:21 You will be hidden from the scourge of the tongue.

Not from the curses of detractors but from the arrogant commands of enemies who abuse their captives.

5:22 You will not be afraid of the beast of the earth.

Because of the savageness of their manners, he calls his enemies *the beast of the earth.*

5:23 But [you will be] in league with the stones of the field.

You will grow old within the boundaries of your inheritance that were established long ago, and a hostile attack will not drive you from your place of habitation.

5:24 And visiting beauty (*speciem*).

In Greek it says, "And the visitation of your beauty (*pulchritudinis*) will not sin." "And visiting your beauty you will not sin." That is, when he looks at the prosperity of your home, he will keep it for you continually, and he will not allow that you be prevented from retaining these things by any change. The following words in the psalm are also like this: "And none of them that hope in him shall offend."[53]

5:25-26 You will know also that your seed shall be multiplied; you will enter into the grave with an abundance.

The number of multiplied offspring will attend you with greatest honor in the last rites.

5:26 You will enter into the grave with an abundance, as a heap [of wheat] is brought in its season.

Not in the manner of chaff will you be worthlessly cast away, but you will be eagerly stored up like a ripened crop.

5:27 Behold, this is even so, as we have searched out.

He shows in this brief verse that what he spoke about earlier was not a vision, but the thought of an attentive mind. "When it has been heard, consider it carefully in your mind." That is, the vengeance of God is not lacking to the bad, nor his mercy to the good.

[Chapter 6]

6:1-2 But Job answered and said, O that my sins and the calamity that I suffer were weighed in a balance.

[52]Cf. Job 5:20-22.

[53]Ps 34:22.

The argument both of holy Job and of his friends begins with less weighty things and grows hotter as it advances. For Eliphaz the Themanite applied goads of remorse, just as if Job were a guilty man. He did this not from the outspokenness of his words but from the subtlety of their meaning, while he reduces Job to the company of those who are unable to promise themselves any perfection of justice.[54] And holy Job responds not as one who is loudly defending himself by asserting his own justice, but he simply complains about the excessiveness of the reproof.

6:3 As the sand of the sea, this appears heavier.

Just as I recognize that I am not perfectly just, so I know that what I am suffering is unjust. "Whence also my words are full of sorrow," because the reproof, by exceeding moderation, compels me to break out into the words of my complaint and to say that I am not experiencing my Lord as judge but withstanding an enemy and an assailer.

6:4 For the arrows of the Lord are in me.

He is saying, You all indeed whom no feeling of pain affects discuss philosophers in respect to foreign evils, and you discourse on suffering; but I, who am experiencing the bitterness of plagues in my body, am forced to indicate what I suffer by wailing. "The indignation of which drinks up my spirit." He has continued with the metaphor taken up and says, as if struck by an arrow, I am experiencing the "poison" of infixed iron. "And terrors." He persists in the words with which he had begun, wanting to explain the magnitude of his torments and compare his wounds to arrows shot into his guts. In Greek it says, "When I begin to speak, they pierce me."

[54]Cf. Job 4:7; 17.

6:5 Will the wild ass bray when he has grass?

This is a subtle rebuke that would have struck back at the insults of his friends against him. He is saying, If nature has given these senses to wild and domesticated animals, so that they are not forced to make noise except when they need food, could I have wailed about my sufferings, unless the bitterness of pain compelled me, unless a cause exists that compels me?

6:6 Or can an unsavory thing be eaten?

No one consumes *unsavory things* as food or things full of bitterness. "To the thirsty soul even bitter things seem to be sweet."[55] Necessity, therefore, extorts what the will did not admit or suffer.

6:7 The things that before my soul was unwilling to touch, now, through anguish, are my food.

In Greek it says, "My spirit (*anima*)[56] cannot cease; for I perceive my food as loathsome, as the smell of a lion."

6:8 Who will grant that my request may come?

I am compelled to this due to the excess of pain. Thus, I go around in order to display this through my prayers, which is wont to be a terror to other men.

6:9 And that he who has begun may himself crush me.

He who has begun to lead me away from the pleasantness of life by the tortures that have been applied, may that very one hasten the end of my life through the accumulation of suffering.

[55]Prov 27:7 LXX.

[56]The LXX has ὀργή, "wrath."

"That he would release his hand, and cut me off." May he not allow me to be beaten and vexed slowly with a suspended hand, but one that has been applied more firmly, so that it may accomplish that through which I can be extinguished. And from the necessity of the plea may I pass on to be delivered to the place of favor, if by the intervention of death the voice of lamentation will be snatched from me.

6:10 And this would be my comfort.

While the violence of the disease fatally assails me, may I who am certain about my exit not complain about the extent of my pains.

6:11 For what strength do I have to hold out?

What constancy of spirit, or what perfection of purpose and virtue will be so great, that I could disguise what I am suffering?

6:12 My strength is not the strength of stones.

That I should bear what I suffer without feeling pain.

6:13 Behold, there is no help for me in myself, and my familiar friends also have departed from me.

In the absence of endurance and of reason, which could heal me, I am also destitute of the solace of friends.

6:14 He who takes away mercy from his friend, forsakes the fear of the Lord.

Deeply and justly shaken by his desolation, he brings to light the full meaning of truth and the weighty consequence, which he does as one who does not feel the affection of compassion of his friends in his adversities, one who has forgotten the fear of the divine.

6:15 My brethren have passed me by as the torrent.

During the period of delay of conversation,[57] they did not take in any of the horror or pain; or else, by their passing contact, they did not perceive any of my misfortune.

6:16 The snow shall fall on those who fear the hoary frost.

In Greek it says, "Like snow or congealed ice melts at the approach of heat, and it is not known that they existed, so I also have been deserted by everyone; I am ruined, and have become an outcast from the home."[58] *The snow fell*[59] *upon them.* He had said that his brothers passed by with quick passage due to their horror of contamination.[60] Therefore, he announces what punishment awaits merciless souls and those who form cowardly counsels for themselves. He says, "They that flee light evils will be driven into far greater and heavier ones."

6:19 Consider the paths of Theman, the ways of Saba.

That is, [consider] the people who came from these countries. "Theman, the ways of the Sabaean." Such is the exposition in Greek. He adds that he found Thema, not Theman, and Seba, not Saba, whose path is through impassible land or desert.[61] Thus, the sense would be the following: like those who make a journey through the desert in the hope of finding water, and they do not find either springs or running water, and they easily perish from

[57]Cf. Job 2:13.
[58]Job 6:16-18 LXX.
[59]The lemma had the future tense.
[60]Cf. Job 6:15.
[61]According to Vaccari, *Un Commento a Giobbe di Giuliano di Eclano*, 169-70, Julian is referring here to the Greek author Polychronius, brother of Theodore of Mopsuestia. Cf. CCSL 88, xvi n. 73.

thirst, so also I have been deprived of the hope I had placed in my relatives and ancestors.

6:20 They were confounded, because I had hope; they came to me and were covered with shame.

They that had been glad of my familiarity when I was in my regular condition now blush at my friendship and loathe and despise me as one who lacks his wealth.

6:22-23 Did I say, Bring to me, and give me some of your wealth, or deliver me from the hand of the enemy?

That is, bring some solace for my miseries.

6:24 Teach me, and I will be silent.

He is saying, You have blamed me, as one who had behaved bitterly and immoderately. But if I was burdensome to you and because of this you took the opportunity of shaming me, say so. Or, if those things that fell on me are not grave, prove it. But if both my suffering is grave and I was not burdensome to you, you were obligated to interpret my words charitably. "And if perchance I have been ignorant in anything, instruct me." Since I do not seek any of your wealth, I ask this alone, that you convict me of the error, if I argued something wrongly about the arrangement of this troubled life amid my miseries.

6:26 You concoct speeches only to rebuke.

Though you are able to bear witness when questioned by me—that is, whether I am in a grave condition in your eyes, whether I am weighed down by a light suffering, and you must admit to both—yet you are willful transgressors of the truth in respect to my injustice.

6:27 You rush in on the orphan.

Upon the orphan, as it were—that is, on one who is destitute of all help, I who do not deserve your afflictions but who am convenient to injure.

6:29 Answer, I beg, without contention.

By convicting them of not acting amicably and of speaking against conscience, Job tries to show that just judges cannot rightly blame him for his harsh words or for his longing for death. "And by speaking that which is just, judge ye." Be the very judges of common sayings, but only in such a way that the reckoning of your verdict complies with justice, not contention.

[Chapter 7]

7:1 The life of man on earth is a military service.

When I discuss the condition of mortal nature and am roused to be filled with bitterness over the day of my birth,[62] I do not say what folly and error would seem to dictate, but I bring out what acquaintance with common life acknowledges. *The life of man upon earth is a military service;* that is, it is brief, unrecoverable, full of anguishes. For just as *military service* is not undertaken for the entire lifespan of a man, but it terminates with a pension, so also the life of mortals ends after a short number of days. "And like the days of a hireling": because no man knows leisure, no matter what the rank of the state in which he is placed, but employs care and labor to the present life.

7:2 As a servant longs for the shade, as the hireling looks for the end of his work.

Nothing separates all of us human beings from the condition of slaves; for there is no human

[62]Cf. Job 3:3.

being who leads life without fear. For the poor man fears the power of the rich; the rich man the envy of another, whether his equal or a superior; the superior fears the proscription of kings; kings fear lawless rebellion and the plots of conspiring subjects. What *shade* (that is, nighttime) offers to slaves, then—namely, that they are relieved from the burden of labor and from the presence of the master, this is what the final end of life gives universally to mortals, whom various cares vex. Again, here is another way [to interpret this]. The burdens of diverse forms of anguish also draw near to the condition of a short life, so that what is lived briefly is also lived with the greatest affliction.

7:3 So I also have had empty months.

He says, Nearly all of us human beings exert ourselves in divine worship in the hope of receiving a reward, and the expectation of repayment makes us devout; but for me, as I see it, the wages for my devotion have been taken away. Not only have [my months] received no good things, but they have received grave evils. However, he referred the whole thing to a cause by saying this: if the rest of men desire death, since they cannot endure the miseries of the life they share in common, how is it that you believe that I am to be faulted if, when beset by such grave evils, I judge it better not to exist at all than to exist like this? *Empty* means empty of rest or of the feeling of pleasure.

7:4 If I sleep, I say, When shall I arise?

The time of rest contributes to the increase of my suffering, for when the senses are distracted from thinking about other things, then I am driven to think about and feel my sufferings all the more.

7:5 My flesh is clothed with rottenness and filth.

In Greek it says, "I waste away, scraping off the bloody gore with clods of earth."

7:6 My days have passed more swiftly than the web is cut by the weaver, and are consumed without any hope.

Not only do I hold on to nothing good, but neither can I hope any longer, as the end of life approaches.

7:7 Remember that my life is [like] the wind.

Why do I infer from the sight of sufferings that my end is fast approaching, when I should turn my eyes to the very nature of mortals, which vanishes as easily as a breeze?

7:8 Your eyes [are] on me, and I shall subsist (*subsistam*) no more.

In Greek it says, "My eyes [are] on me, and I am (*sum*) no more." By this he has expressed the suddenness of death.

7:9 So he that shall go down to the lower world does not come up.

He is not denying the resurrection here, but he is saying that there is no return and going back to the condition of the present life.[63]

7:11 Wherefore I will not spare my mouth.

So many bitter things converge into the state of my life, so that it is of short duration and full of hardship, and it is not allowed to call back my foot to it from the *lower world*. Rightly, therefore, do I complain about my birth, and I accuse the day of my conception.[64]

[63]Many modern scholars disagree with Julian's claim here. For example, Roland E. Murphy, O.Carm., comments on Job 7:9, "It is quite clear from this and other passages (e.g., 10:21; 14:10-12; 16:22; 17:13-16) that Job has no hope in a future life with God; Sheol is really darkness, nonlife, even if it can serve as a respite from his suffering (3:11-22)." *The Book of Job: A Short Reading* (Mahwah, NJ: Paulist Press, 1999), 26. I believe that Julian's views are solidly based and will be clarified in other passages.

[64]Cf. Job 3:1-3.

7:12 Am I a sea, or a whale, that you have enclosed me in a prison?

Every great thing, not feeble things, should perceive the greatness of your power. *In a prison*: he said *prison* for calamity.

7:13-14 If I say, My bed shall comfort me, you will frighten me with a dream.

I am so worn out by continuous evils, and at no time do the adversities that I suffer become inactive, so that the duration of night in which the cares of minds are relieved brings me no reprieve or rest.

7:16 I have done with hope, I shall now live no longer.

This is what he said earlier: "Behold, there is no help for me in myself."[65] With the strength of my endurance shattered, I cannot promise myself anything concerning the end of evils and a change to good things.

7:17-18 What is a man that you esteem him? You visit him early in the morning, and you prove him suddenly.

As far as pertains to the logical coherence of the statements, here is the meaning that arises. Though you employ so much proof of your goodness toward man, so that you testify from your bounty that he matters to you, when you gift him with honor and prosperity, suddenly, as if you do not know him, you test him and want to prove him by means of conflagrations. If therefore you inquire into my life by means of scourges, no torments are necessary. Accept the confession and bring out the death sentence against the guilty one. Another subtle meaning occurs concerning the same passage. Why do you hide your knowledge? Is it to make the merits of your servants appear? For you assume the outward appearance of one who is ignorant, so that you may manifest who they are, not to yourself but to others. Whence, if this is the cause of my vexation, "I have sinned,"[66] because I uttered a voice of complaint and lamentation. Here is another way. Since you fashioned us with an infirm and contemptible nature, why do you stand forth as a diligent examiner of our daily actions?

[65]Job 6:13.

7:20 I have sinned: what shall I do to you?

In Greek it says, "If I have sinned, what can I do to you?"[67] That is, how have my wrongly done deeds injured you? "O keeper of men?" He means, watcher and observer of every work. In the Greek another verse begins here: "O keeper of men," and then it has, "O you who understand the mind of men. Why have you set me opposite to you?"[68] In the Greek it says, "And [why] am I a burden to you?" while I respond outspokenly and I, a slave, bring the Lord into a contest. *Why have you set me opposite to you?* He is saying, Since you knew that I would be a sinner, why did you allow me even to come into life? Or was it for me to add to the accumulation of offenses, when I am compelled to expostulate against you concerning my misery? "And I have become burdensome to myself." Life has become burdensome to me because it is destitute of evidence of your propitiousness.

7:21 Why will you not remove my sin?

Will you take away the voice of my complaint either by the intervention of death or by the cessation of torment? "Behold, now I shall sleep in the dust." The continuation of my torment will quickly cause me to be buried and will

[66]Job 7:20.

[67]The Rahlfs LXX has "to you," but the Brenton edition (Vaticanus) does not.

[68]Job 7:20c.

remove me from the number of those on whom the providence of your kindness is expended. "And if you seek me in the morning, I shall not exist (*subsistam*)." The affection of pity is introduced due to the swiftness of the passage.

[Chapter 8]

8:1-2 But Bildad the Shuhite answered and said, How long will you say such things?

This one who contradicts Job's long-winded errors strives to accuse the entire content of the debate, in which saint Job had complained about the excessiveness of punishments, just as he had failed to defend his own justice. After he satisfied himself about his birth, Job showed from the greatness of suffering that the complaint and causes of his indignation were not unjust. And disputing with God as if with a just plea, he said that such severe vengeance of sins should not be demanded from a man of such a corruptible and short life. Bildad accuses him of insolence and bitterness and says, Give a rest to the bitterness of your words, and do not think that if you talk a lot you can improve your case. Here is another way. Without a doubt, the friends believe that the plagues have been inflicted by God, and holy Job continues in the same opinion complaining.

8:3 Does God pervert (*supplantat*) judgment?

So that it remains to be understood that such a sentence against Job has been given because his offenses (*meritis*) demanded it.

8:4 Even if your children have sinned against him.

Even if your person is purged from fault by your words, do not the sins of your house reflect the fault of your instruction? Therefore, it does not suit you to spend your time complaining, but it is to your advantage to be purged by a confession and by offering prayers.

8:5 Yet if you will arise early to God.

All things can be read by changing the times, which is indeed customary in the Holy Scriptures, so that the sense is this: although the perverse instruction of your children involves you in a guilty charge, yet the punishment by their death would never have been apportioned to you if you had continuously and meritoriously pursued your devotion.

8:6 If you will walk clean and upright, he will presently awake onto you.

Your prayer will be efficacious if you take care not to have merely the appearance of justice, but the reality (*veritatem*). You will easily appease God, and he will quickly bring you back into your former state.

8:8 For inquire of the former generation.

In order to give authority to his words, [Bildad] summons the testimony of the previous generation. His aim is to show Job that what he has said or is about to say is clearly known by long experience. Here is another way. From the examples of those who came before him, he wants him to learn what he had said, that God is easily won over by the prayers of the just, and that not only are adversities removed by his appeasement but also prosperous and favorable things are restored. So, for example, consider the way Abraham and his descendants were protected amid adversities by calling on God.[69] Here is another way. The reason I want you to look back to the examples of the ancients is to keep you from despising our counsels in view of our youthful age.

[69]Cf. Gen 13:4; 21:33; 26:25.

8:9 For we are but of yesterday, and are ignorant.

The reason testimony must be sought from elders is because our brief span of years could not confer to us perfect knowledge of things. "For our days are but a shadow." Since we began to exist only a short time ago, after a short time we will not exist.

8:10 And they will teach you. They will speak to you.

After the insertion of the line in the middle, he added what he ought to listen to from the thoughts of the fathers.

8:11-12 Can the rush be green? When it is yet in flower it withers before all plants.

By seeking a comparison from things that have no firmness in themselves, he wants it to be understood that saint Job only affected a reputation of justice, and he did not take care to have any solid virtue. And for that reason he was deceived by a tenuous hope. For those things that grow not from their own roots but thanks to liquid perish when that same liquid ceases to exist.

8:13 Even so are the ways of all that forget God, and the hope of the hypocrite shall perish.

He has revealed what he wanted to be understood by the metaphor that was cited.

8:14 His folly shall not please him.

When he sees that he possesses no fruit from the shadow of virtue, which he has followed, [Job] will understand that he has been deceived in his own opinion of himself.

8:16 It seems full of moisture before the sun comes up.

Before the time of testing, he flatters himself about his abundant virtue.

8:17 His roots are on a heap of stones.

These verses are similar to that parable that is introduced in the Gospel, where the seed that is described as having fallen on rocky soil is said to be unable to grow deep roots and subsequently withers in the heat of the sun.[70]

8:18 If one swallows him up from his place, he will deny it.

He continues with the metaphor. He says, Why do I say that a hypocrite is like a field of reed grass or a rush that lacks water?[71] Nay, rather, he is no different from those things, which enjoy moisture, which, when they arise on a heap of stones, perish as quickly as if they had never existed. And if one could inquire about the *place* in which they had arisen,[72] he would *deny* those things and say that he does not know.

8:19 For this is the joy of his way, that others may spring again out of the earth.

This is the law of nature, that others are substituted in the place of those who perish.

8:20 God will not cast away the simple.

He has set the name *simple* over against the hypocrite.

[70]Cf. Mt 13:5-6; Mk 4:5; Lk 8:6. The Vulgate reads, "Can the rush be green without moisture?" Julian's lemma is abbreviated. A rush or bulrush (*scirpus*) is a grass-like herb with a hollow stem that grows in marshy places.

[71]Cf. Job 8:11-13.

[72]Cf. Job 8:8.

8:21 Until your mouth is filled with laughter.

The Septuagint has "But he will fill with laughter the mouth of the true, and their lips with thanksgiving."

[Chapter 9]

9:1 But Job answered and said, Indeed, I know it is so, and that man is not justified when compared with God.

He is not saying that he agrees entirely with Bildad's view, but only with part of it. For Bildad had maintained that God, endowed with both justice and power, opposes the impious just as he cherishes the good.[73] Saint Job says that this is true. But when Bildad wanted to expose him as a sinner on the basis of the things that had happened to him, this Job pronounces to be false.[74] Here is another way. Job did not support the judgment of the one who was railing against him by assenting to his words; but he pronounces to be true what Bildad had said earlier—that is, "Inquire of the former generation, and search diligently into the memory of the fathers."[75] For no man is found who does not choose and make distinctions in matters, yielding in his respect for a superior to come down hard on the person of the inferior.

9:3-4 If he [man] wants to contend with him [God], he [God] is wise in heart and mighty in strength.

Each thing is listed that pertains both to the divine wisdom and power. Surely, by considering these things no one would dare to testify that Job is enduring adversities undeservedly.

9:5 He who removed mountains and they did not know it.

By consideration of all these things, the men choose to say that Job lacked the merit of innocence rather than that God was lacking justice.

9:6 Who shakes the earth out of its place, and the pillars thereof tremble.

He speaks of *pillars* in view of the stability of their unshakable mass and for their firmness.

9:7 Who commands the sun and it rises not.

He is saying, Not only do the things on earth but also the things in the sky feel his power; for he stops even the course of the sun when he wants, and changes the arrangement of the stars, as was done under Joshua, son of Nun.[76] Here is another way. All things are mentioned as an indication of the divine power, through

[73]Cf. Job 8:4-6.

[74]Job's "friends" have claimed that Job's trials are simply the just repayment to him for his previous sins, whereas Job proclaims his own justice and approval before God (cf. 13:18). In 4:17, Eliphaz had accused Job of comparing himself with God's justice by his proclaiming his own innocence. Here in response to Bildad's similar charge (cf. also 15:14), Job admits that no human being is justified in comparison with God, but that does not entail any admission on his part of his having lived a hypocritical and unjust life prior to his trials. Even to bring in the comparison to God's virtues is a matter of great praise of Job (25:1-2). It is interesting to note that during the Pelagian controversy, Jerome accused the Pelagians (to my mind unjustly) of placing themselves at the same level as God by their claim that man can be just and without sin if he wills it. In an ironic way, Jerome's accusations seem to echo the charges of Eliphaz and Bildad against Job. In *Dial Pel* 1.12, based on citations from Job 9:20; 16:22; 19:24; 31:35 (many of which do not match his Vulgate translation), Jerome claims that Job is convicted of having spoken many things against the ruling of God, and to have summoned him to the bar. Therefore, Job is not just in Jerome's assessment. Jerome claims this in spite of Job 42:7-8; Ezek 14:12-20. J. N. D. Kelly, *Jerome* 319 concurs on this point, that Jerome treats the Pelagians unjustly in his *Dialogue*: "Although Critobolus protests that the perfection the Pelagians envisage is a relative one adapted to the human condition, Atticus brushes this aside and credits them, quite unfairly, with postulating an absolute perfection which would make man the equal of God." See also Michael R. Rackett, "What's Wrong with Pelagianism? Augustine and Jerome on the Dangers of Pelagius and His Followers," *Augustinian Studies* 33, no. 2 (2002): 223-37.

[75]Job 8:8.

[76]Cf. Josh 10:12-14; Sir 46:4.

which the scales of human testing are thrown into confusion.

9:8 Who alone spreads out the heavens.

He is saying, It is no wonder if he uses the elements for the sake of his own will, through which he has willed a thing, since he is the one who created these things when they did not exist.

9:9 Who makes Arcturus and Orion.[77]

The cause of his power is revisited, whereby either the rising of the sun can be prevented by his command or the quick motion of the stars be made invisible. For all things obey the will of him by whose command they came into existence. "And the inner parts of the south." The *inner parts of the south* are said to be that part of the world that is inaccessible to mortals on account of the excessive heat of the sun.

9:10 Who does things great and incomprehensible.

Those things that are being done constantly confess the greatness of his works, the changes of the atmosphere, the change of times, the succession of seasons, the interchange of nights and days. Therefore, by the heavenly signs he wished to indicate atmospheric changes that help and bring benefits to human beings.

9:11 If he come to me, I shall not see [him].

Something else is added to the things earlier through which terror can be increased. He says, Not only is he wise and powerful, but also invisible, so that by coming unforeseen, he can be justly feared.

9:12 If he examine on a sudden, who shall answer him?

Reason yields to power, and it does not dare ask into the causes of his works when reverence for the maker is thought of.

9:13 God, whose wrath no man can resist, and under whom they stoop that bear up the world.

For the same reason no one dares seek from him a rational accounting of his works. Here is another way. Above he had said, "The pillars thereof tremble,"[78] and here, *under whom they stoop that bear up the world.* He wanted nothing else to be understood by each, except that the stability and firmness of the earth bow to his will.

9:15 Even if I should have something just, I will not answer him.

Overwhelmed with wonder at his power, I can set forth nothing concerning the purity of my conscience, but it is necessary that I hasten to the helps of my supplications.

9:16 And though he should hearken to me when I call, I do not believe that he hears me.

This is the limit of his appraisement; that is, while I think how great he is, he does not allow me to believe that my words could easily be admitted to his hearing. He listed everything that was relevant to pointing out the divine strength and power, in order to show that he knows all the more that God is almighty. And he summons this very thing as evidence in defense of his case. For that reason he cannot protect himself against those things by which he is beset, because his strength is no match for him that strikes him, and that power is

[77] Arcturus refers to the principal star in the nearly stationary constellation Boötes (the Bear Keeper). The rising and setting of the constellation Orion were believed to be attended by storms; according to the myth, Orion was a hunter transported to heaven.

[78] Job 9:6.

removed that he uses while taking a stand on the opposite side.

9:17 For he shall crush me in a whirlwind without a cause.

All that he recounted as proof pertained to his power, not justice. That is why here he adds *without a cause*, in order to show his good reasons, if justice were to preside over his examination.

9:19 If [it be a question of] equity of judgment, no man dare bear witness for me.

As the sides are summoned into court, no one will dare absolve me from blame in the divine judgment.

9:20 If I should want to justify myself, my own mouth shall condemn me.

That is, if I apply my defense speech to my justification (*purgationem*), I will accomplish nothing more than offending your ears, since you do not want me to be innocent. I will incur the bad repute of being a blasphemer. Here is another way. He will change my words. "If [I wanted] to show myself innocent, he shall prove me in the wrong." He takes this from the comparison to judges who affix a criminal charge in whatever cases they have submitted. According to your opinion, my justification (*purgatio*) will not be an acquittal but the onset of a guilty charge.

9:21 Although I should be simple.

I am so thrown into disorder amid those things of which I am conscious and those that I suffer in confusion, that I seem to myself to have lost the knowledge of good and evil.

9:22 One thing there is that I have spoken, he destroys the just and the wicked.

It is as if when discernment [between the two] is removed, which looks to the duty of justice (*iustitiae*), the justice (*ius*) of power alone is set in motion.

9:23 If he scourge, let him kill at once, and not laugh at the pains of the innocent ones.

This is a familiar cry [for] those who are beset by excessive pain. Here is another way. *Let him not laugh* at those who are tried by bitter and hard things, but at those who want to assign blame on the basis of sufferings.

9:24 The earth is given into the hand of the wicked one; he covers the face of its judges.[79]

In Greek it says, "But the just are laughed at from the earth." *The earth is given into the hand of the wicked one.* As far as concerns the context of the passage, he seems to be saying this: the part of him that is earthly (namely, his body) has been surrendered to torments and distresses, and the power to afflict it has been given to the wicked one. Surely, through this it has come to pass that those who look on cannot bear a sound judgment concerning the merits of the afflicted one. But as far as concerns the prophecy that is laid claim to by the merits of the person, Job leaps from the context of the argument and has opened his mouth about future mysteries. He predicts the Lord's passion, saying that due to the paltriness of the outer, which they had crucified, they were unable to recognize the worth of the inner.[80]

9:25 My days have been swifter than a runner.

In Greek the order of the words is not the same, nor do the lines begin at the same point. For instead of this it is recorded as follows: "The just are laughed at from the earth." The explanation is this: he despises the distresses

[79]The final part of this verse reads like a messianic prophecy in the Vulgate: "And if it be not he, who is it then?" Thus Julian's interpretation, that "the earth" refers to Christ.
[80]Cf. 1 Cor 2:8.

received by the just for the sake of virtue and cares little if they suffer any adversity. But as for what he added, "from the earth," it is as if he were to say, Such is this life, and mortal affairs are filled with much unfairness. But he refers everything to his own persona, as if he were to say, I endure such things when placed in the pursuit of piety, and he does not free me from the onrushing evils. For just as his friends make a general speech that could apply to the just and the wicked, so even holy Job makes use of a discourse with general application. They speak so as not to be openly cruel to him, but he speaks so as to flee from the vice of bragging. Another verse says the same thing: "They are handed over to the hands of the wicked ones."[81] Explanation: it is a frequent occurrence to see the just handed over as plunder to the wicked, as if he were to say, I have been allowed to endure such things from wicked men. Another line says, "He covers the faces of its judges."[82] Explanation: he makes them worthy of honor and contemptible of authority. "But if it be not he, who ***[83] is it?"[84] But if these things do not happen in such a manner, prove it. In everything, he produces proof by making proper distinctions.

9:26 They have passed by as ships carrying fruits.

By the addition of words he has amplified what he had said at first. For he added *as ships carrying fruits* as though he had not explained the flight of the passing time by the comparison to the steps of a runner; and as if this were still not sufficient, he added, "As an eagle flying to the prey." Here is another way to read this in a different manner. In its speed, my life competes with ships, whereby he indeed indicates the swiftness of the human passage.

[81]Job 9:24a LXX.
[82]Job 9:24b LXX.
[83]There is an erasure or illegible letters in the manuscript.
[84]Job 9:24c LXX.

Here is another way: [Ships] that indeed are driven along by very strong winds at the end of autumn, or that cannot suffer delay in view of the zeal of the merchants.

9:27 When I say, I will not speak so, I change my appearance.

When the resolution for patient endurance draws me back from complaining, yet the violence of the pain impels me again to the same things.

9:28 I feared all my works, knowing that you did not spare the offender.

In Greek it says, "I quake in all my limbs, for I know that you will not forsake me in my innocence." Here is another way: this is why I wanted to moderate my tearful cries.

9:29 But if I too am so wicked, why have I labored in vain?

In Greek it says, "Since I am wicked, why have I not died?" Here is another way: If my rather strict life and my solicitous intentions, which is the examiner of works, was not able to defend me from guilt, why have I lost that sense of enjoyment that arises from a more negligent life?

9:30-31 If I be washed, as it were, with snow waters, yet you shall plunge me in filth, and my garments shall abhor me.

The horror of his sores fights against the purity of his life, so that his skin is believed to have been corrupted from the filth of his mind.

9:32[85] For I shall not answer a man that is like myself.

So that I could freely inquire of him about the rationale and justice of my affliction.

[85]CCSL mistakenly reads "31" here.

9:34 Let him take his rod away from me, and let not his fear terrify me.

Let the whole face of terror be removed, so that the equity of judgment can stand firm under the protection of freedom.

9:35 I will speak and will not fear him.

And may I live free from besetting evils. In the future may I fear nothing in respect to outspokenness of speech. In Greek it says, "For I am not conscious of iniquity in myself."

[Chapter 10]

10:1 My soul is weary of my life.

[My soul] that is settled in the denial of those things which I ask about. "I will let go my speech against myself." Although he will say nothing of importance about his great reverence, he comes to fear that his speech may commit some offense. Another way: I will turn my complaints against myself, since I can lay claim to my justice before no one. "I will speak in the bitterness of my soul." He adds what he will speak *in the bitterness of his soul*; namely, I will neglect complaining about my sufferings, and inquire into the reasons for my condemnation.

10:2 I will say to God, Do not condemn me.

In Greek it says, "Do not teach me to be impious."

10:3-4 Does it seem good to you?

In Greek it says, "Does it seem good to you if I be impious?" Here is another way: it is a peculiar feature of calumny, when the reliability of the truth is neglected, to say what is not real. Job experienced something like this, so that though he was not guilty, yet he endured the blame of a guilty man. "Do you have eyes of flesh? Does it seem good to you if you falsely accuse [me] and help the counsel of the wicked?" They are the ones who think they can rightly conjecture about the nature of the blame of my torments, and they declare what sort of thing the pain of my body shows. "Or will you see as man sees?" So that you inquire into my life based on the torments, not knowing about the uprightness of my conscience.

10:5 Are your days as the days of man, and your years as human times?

So that something done in the past or in earlier time could be hidden.

10:6-7 That you should inquire after my iniquity, and search after my sin, and should know that I have done no wicked thing, whereas there is no one who can deliver out of your hand.

This is a matter of human ignorance, that when blame is at issue, he wants to bring into the light that which is unknown by the torments. An appeal of this very serious verdict often acquits, and the judicial examination is transferred to another. But though you are carrying out a lawsuit involving a severe judgment, no one's intervention can correct what you have decreed.

10:8 Your hands have made me and fashioned me.

Nothing in my condition is foreign to you, nothing estranged from the rights of your dominion, [nothing] which you think little of, and which you would meanly abuse as an irrelevant thing.

10:9-11 Remember, I ask, that you made me as the clay. Have you not milked me as milk, and curdled me like cheese, and clothed me with skin and flesh?

Why do you forget your goodness in respect to me, which was my sole reason for existence? Since you have caused us to have the beginning of our nature from such worthless material, he says, yet you did not cause us to perish quickly, as those who were responding to the substance from which we had taken our origin. For we who were mortals in view of the paltriness of our constitution, you granted us to imitate immortality by the substitution of offspring. You brought about, by much application of your providence in the very coming into being of individuals, first that the liquid substance of our seed did not perish in the insides of our mothers, but what was fluid *was put together with skin, flesh, bones and sinews*. Some of these things you provided for strength, others for feeling, others were supplements of perfection.

10:12 And your visitation.

He says, Not only did I take form by the working of your hand in the secret place of my mother's uterus, but even when I came forth into the light, I shared in the life that you were responsible for.

10:13 Although you conceal these things in your heart, yet I know that you remember all things.

Although my ill treatment attests that you are neglecting your possession, yet reason does not allow you to be affected by feelings for the things you have created.

10:14 If I have sinned, and you have spared me for an hour, why do you not suffer me to be clean from iniquity?

If the sins of my past life have earned pardon from you, why do you summon them back to the present day, and establish me as so guilty that you believe I was not forgiven?

10:15 And if I be wicked, woe unto me; and if just, I shall not lift up my head, being filled with affliction.

With two opposites set forth, he added the new and the same end. For he applied punishment to the wickedness, but he linked to justice the humility that affliction customarily brings about. "And if I should be just, I cannot breathe out, for I am filled with dishonor and I am captured like a lion for slaughter."[86]

10:16 And for pride you will take me as a lioness.

Though I consist of such paltry and abject material, he says, when I consider what is the inspiration of your goodness, the life that I enjoy, why do I experience the violence of your severity, again as a force of great strength, as a force of great power?

10:17 You renew your witnesses against me.

By the added words in which he says, "And pains war against me," he has made known who these witnesses are of whom he complains that they have been brought forth against him.

10:19-21 I should have been as if I had not been. Dismiss me, therefore, that I may lament my sorrow a little, before I go to a land that is dark and covered with the mist of death.

In the first part of the book, where he complains about the excessiveness of his torments, he offers the underworld as a comparison to his tearful life, and he recounts the advantages of death.[87] Here, where he is discussing the whole condition of mortal life, he describes the state of sad places, in order to increase the

[86]Job 10:15 LXX.
[87]Cf. Job 3:1-22.

heap of miseries, because after the present afflictions it is necessary for human beings to reach such an end. *Dismiss me, therefore, that I may lament.* "Allow me to rest a little."[88]

[Chapter 11]

11:1-2 Then Zophar the Naamathite answered, and said, Shall not he that speaks much, hear also? Or shall a man full of talk be justified?

Do you think that by talking a lot you will improve your case and reduce us to silence, as if we revered your lengthy oration? By making use of just arguments, saint Job not only showed that he was estranged from criminal charges, but he also called God forth to his trial to reveal his uprightness. Zophar tries, therefore, to convict him first of verbosity, then of a lack of uprightness. And with his prejudiced opinion about God's power and wisdom, he tries to show that Job had erupted in the outspokenness of his words without proper consideration. For it would have been fitting instead for Job to remember the weakness of his nature. Here is another interpretation. They accuse both the sense, which arises from the context of the argument, and the prolixity of his speech, and they endeavor to lead him into a confession of guilt, which he himself refuses to do.

11:3 And when you have mocked others, shall no man confute you?

You have mocked; that is, you have convicted [us] of being in error.

11:4 For you said, My speech is pure.

The public expression of his *speech* did not make this claim, but the context of the argument shows it.

11:5 And I wish that God would speak with you.

In order that you would be overwhelmed by the profundity and reasoning of his statements, and cease to weary him in your defense. It amounts to a serious accusation to equate your own works with the works of God and to claim for yourself the testimony of justice.

11:6 And he would show you the secrets of wisdom.

That is, the rational manner in which he created everything. He is saying, If he would now make manifest those things that long ago he removed from our sight, you would understand how great his power is and the magnitude of his wisdom. "And that his law is manifold." If *his law is manifold,* and the lineage of his commandments is diffused far and wide, you are forced to admit that you do not comprehend his precepts or that you were unable to carry them out.

11:7 Perhaps you will comprehend the tracks of God, and will find out the Almighty perfectly?

Lest you be able to confine within the comprehension of your own thought him who knows no limits to time and who rejoices in his own eternity. By the forms of the proofs that have been summoned, he is unable to demonstrate what he said. Therefore, he takes refuge in a general declaration about the divine power, and he compensates for his own failure by praising the measureless God above.

11:8-9 He is higher than heaven.

The Greek says, "Heaven [is] high, but the earth is deep. And what will you do?"[89] He is

[88]Job 10:21 LXX.

[89]Brenton's version of the LXX (Codex Vaticanus) lacks "but the earth is deep."

saying, If we are unable to comprehend the visible things that have been made by God who measured them, how is it not a matter of ultimate insanity that our impudent tongue takes up arms against God? "He is deeper than the underworld, and how do you know? The measure of him is longer than the earth, and broader than the sea." By the measures of all the elements that are spread out far and wide, he seems to have set forth the measure of the divine wisdom. For higher up he mentioned it. Here is another way. Just as he is immeasurable in his nature, so is he incomprehensible in the rational reckoning of his works. *The measure of him is longer than the earth.* He is saying, Why do I question you about the lower parts of the earth—that is, about the underworld? By what measures is the earth itself extended, which meets your eyes, and why has it been compacted into such a size, so that it was made neither larger nor smaller? And by what limits is the sea enclosed, what is its measure in length and breadth? What gulfs does it have and what curves? You will not be able to answer these questions when asked. Surely by this you are admonished about human weakness.

11:11 For he knows the vanity of men.

He also is not ignorant of the actions of men, just the rational account of his works is not known by men. For he is so much aware that he does not permit what is done perversely to be unavenged.

11:12 A vain man is lifted up into pride.

As if he manufactured something great by his subtle disputation, he employs this conclusion, which stings Job and accuses him openly of having vain convictions. "And he thinks himself born free like a wild ass's colt." Since the reason of nature and of God's works is profound, foolish human beings think that nothing that comes from the contemplation of him applies to themselves. Instead, they live in the fashion of beasts in whom the force of reason is a foreign thing.

11:13 But you have hardened (*firmasti*) your heart and have spread your hands to him.

You have hardened (*obdurasti*) it in obstinacy, and with a stretched forth hand you have complained that you are experiencing injustice. *Your hands*: as if he is challenging God to a fight.

11:14-16 If you will put away from you the iniquity that is in your hand, then you could lift up your face without spot and also forget misery.

As if he convicts him using reason, so he recommends beneficial counsel.

11:18 And being buried you shall sleep secure.

Here *buried* does not refer to the grave but to the protection of a more remote location.

[Chapter 12]

12:1 But Job answered and said.

He himself asserts for himself and vehemently extols that argument by which his friends want to depress and come down hard on saint Job. For they endeavor to prejudge him concerning the omnipotence of God, whereas he says that they have corrupt judgments out of fear of the divine omnipotence.

12:2 Are you then men alone?

Do you think that there has been no one before you, nor will there be any wise man like you after you?

12:3 For who is ignorant of these things that you know?

"Are you alone?"[90] Since Zophar was convinced that he himself had made use of subtle arguments and had prepared things by his discussion that were unanswerable, saint Job says, the things that Zophar had brought up were not matters of great intelligence. Since indeed not only are human beings able to perceive the things about which he had lectured concerning the power of God, but also speechless animals and those elements too that are inanimate. "I also have a heart as well as you." Since you and I have one nature, I too can know what you know.

12:4-5 He that is mocked by his friend, as I, shall call on[91] the Lord, and he will hear him.

The very fact that you are all trying to humiliate me and wish to make a laughingstock of me can itself commend me to God. "For the simplicity of the just man is laughed to scorn, the lamp despised in the thoughts of the rich is ready for the time appointed." *The simplicity of the just man*, which provokes unjust scorn among you and is scoffed at in your *thoughts*, will shine like a bright *lamp* at a time when it should have been necessary to publicize his merits. *The thoughts of the rich*, that is, yours.

12:6 The tents of robbers abound, and they provoke God boldly, though it is he who put everything into their hands.

The subtlety of your entire conjecture tends toward this, that you measure merits on the basis of prosperity and misfortune. Thus, you want to show that I am guilty, and that you men are just, because no opposing breeze blows against you. This is openly to accuse the justice of God, or a way to find fault with his patience. *The tents abound*. Those whom previously he had called "rich"[92] he now accuses by the name of *robbers* with respect to the bad portions.

12:7 Doubtless, ask the beasts, and they shall teach you.

From that line where he said, "For who is ignorant of these things that you know,"[93] up to this passage, things have been inserted in between. For contextual coherence demands the following arrangement: "For who is ignorant of these things which you know? Doubtless, ask the beasts, and they shall teach you," that, if God is the maker of all things,[94] he is singularly endowed with ineffable wisdom and power.

12:11 Does not the ear discern words, and will not your jaws eat up the taste?

The Greek has "[The ear] discerns words of understanding." Here is another way. Just as the teaching of nature holds that one senses a diversity of sensations by the different functions of the members, and human effort did not bring it about that the ears would register sound, the palate [registers] the diversity of tastes, so by the instruction of nature one attains to the knowledge of the divine immensity and power.[95]

12:12-13 Is there wisdom in the ancients and prudence in length of time? With him is wisdom and strength; he has counsel and understanding.

One should read this as irony, so that it can be linked to what follows. Here is another way. Lest they think that they are saying something

[90]Job 12:2.
[91]Another reading is "call on" in the imperative mood.

[92]Job 12:5.
[93]Job 12:3.
[94]Cf. Job 6:9.
[95]Cf. Rom 1:20.

great or that they have introduced something profound, in his speech holy Job likewise describes these same things in detail that they recounted with great effort in order to reproach him. Here is another way: this is what he has grasped, that nothing can be compared with the divine power.

12:14 If he pulls down, there is no one who can build up, and if he shuts up a person, there is none that can open.

This is proof of the divine power, he says: if he dissolves the fabric of a human being, when his soul departs, and he drives him into the bars of his tomb, no one can call him back to life.

12:15 If he withhold the waters, all things shall be dried up, and if he send them out, they shall overturn the earth.

The proof of lesser things is being cited from greater things. He says, Why do I speak of individual human beings? He can destroy everything, either by great rainstorms or by extreme drought.

12:17 He brings counsellors to a foolish end and judges to insensibility.

When they are robbed of success in the things they have foreseen.

12:18 He looses the belt of kings and girds their loins with a cord.

When supreme power is transferred to others, he lays them low from their heights and strips them of power.

12:19 He leads away inglorious priests.

His purpose is to render human wisdom null and void by comparing it with divine wisdom. Hence he very finely said that *inglorious priests* are led, surely meaning those persons who are likewise teachers to others. It is as if he had said, Compared with the divine wisdom, even those who profess the duty of being teachers are not wise.

12:20 He changes the speech of those who speak truly.

He is not referring here to those who speak truly, but to those who were thought to speak truly. He convicts them of falsehood when he makes what they had predicted turn out in a different way. Here is another way. He has called them *those who speak truly* whose plans he could let falter into nothingness. Here is another way. "He takes away the doctrine of the elders." Job shows them that the frustration of their deliberations occurs without any following of their authority.

12:21 He pours contempt on princes.

Both those who are concerned with teaching and the leaders of the people who are in charge of running common affairs. When God opposes them, they lose the whole summit of dignity by which they had been eminent. "And he lifts up those who were oppressed." After showing what God can do to those persons who are considered to be illustrious, he adds what help and protection he imparts to the lowly, so that the divine power may be known by both [these classes of people].

12:22 He reveals deep things out of darkness and brings forth into the light the shadow of death.

When he causes those who had been oppressed to breathe again, once the iniquitous rule has been expelled, then he will bring forth into the light those things that had previously been pressed together and overwhelmed by the night—that is, the merits of both the upright and the wicked.

12:23 He multiplies nations and will destroy them, and he will restore them to wholeness after they have been overthrown.

He says, By means of prosperity and adversity he frequently brings about increases and decreases among the peoples.

12:24 He changes the heart of the princes.

He himself is said to do what he permits to be done by the intervention of someone's merit.[96] *He changes the heart of the princes* "and deceives them that they walk in vain where there is no way." So that they either choose or follow harmful things instead of beneficial. Here is another way: they often promise great things from their awareness of their strength; after they are invaded they turn their backs to their enemies out of fear and in their confusion look for wastelands and seek hiding places.

[Chapter 13]

13:1 Behold, my eye has seen all these things.

Things that they believed provided proof of their singular prudence. By lowering these things to the level of common knowledge,[97] he does not allow them to sense great things about themselves.

13:3 But yet I will speak to the Almighty.

Since the speech of my argument showed that I perceived the same things that you had spoken of as things that were unknown to others, yet it is something else that your accusation of my case and questioning calls for: that I recognize that what I am suffering is just.

13:4 Having first shown that you are forgers of lies.

The Greek has "For you are all unjust physicians and bad healers"; that is, you make the wounds worse and do not cure them. Here is another way. Whoever applies the truth of grace, even though he considers it an honor of him to whom he thinks this truth can help, he does not escape blame for falsity, since the outward appearance of virtue never excuses vice.

13:5 And I wish you would hold your peace, that you might be thought to be wise men.

It is a foolish thing to wound the person who needs to be cured. You came to console,[98] and you are increasing the causes of grief. The speech brought forth badly must not have convinced you of your folly.

13:7 Has God any need of your lie?

As if what God does could not be excused in any other way, thus do you vindicate his whole work under the name of power. Here is another way. You who want to bring a legal defense, look into those cases of yours. For you cite words contrary to conscience; for you know some things about me, and you do not fear to falsify other things.

13:9 Or shall it please him, from whom nothing can be concealed?

The form of your public speech will not prevail with him to the extent that a lie could be proof in the injury to the truth.

13:10 He shall reprove you.

It does not concern his honor but is a false charge, because you defend him not by means of justice but flattery.

[96]See the note under Job 2:1-3.
[97]Cf. Job 13:2-3.
[98]Cf. Job 2:11.

13:11-12 As soon as he shall move himself, he shall trouble you. Your remembrance shall be compared to ashes.

It will not be acceptable in such a great duty of your praise that it be necessary for you as well to incur an offense against him; and when you vindicate the movements he displays against you, you will so perish that the calamity brought in does not allow anything to remain as a sign of you.

13:13 Hold your peace a little while, that I may speak.

So much so has your discussion not frightened me, that I myself am even confident in searching for the causes of my afflictions, and I declare to you the evils of applying correction.

13:14 Why do I tear my flesh with my teeth and carry my soul in my hands?

Though he does not dare to excuse himself from sin entirely, yet he complains about the excessiveness of the tortures. Why, he asks, am I tortured by such great tearing of my internal organs that my soul, placed in my hand, as it were, is in danger of being poured out?

13:15 Even if he should kill me, I will hope in him. But yet I will reprove my ways in his sight.

In order to render null and void the judgment of his friends who were endeavoring to prove that he had acted against God by the bitterness of his complaints, he says both that he will seek the reason for his troubles and he promises that he will hold fast to the steadfastness of hope during the graver misfortunes. *I will reprove*: that is, the examination and the judge.

13:16 For no hypocrite shall come before his presence.

I want the rational account of my life set forth because I am not in doubt that I am being tested by his knowledge. Surely I would not do this if I were concealing one thing in my conscience, alleging something else in my speech. Here is another way. In accordance with his own statements higher up, he says that they will not have confidence in the judgment of God in which assuredly there will be no place for feigned justice.

13:17 Hear my speech and perceive with your ears hidden truths (*aenigmata*).[99]

By the term *hidden truths*, through the inspiration of the Holy Spirit, he seems to be promising grander and even concealed things, that is, future mysteries. He said *hidden truths* because by the brevity of the statements he had left more to be understood than he had articulated to be heard.

13:18 If I shall be judged, I know that I shall be found just.

The reason he confidently wants his ways to be brought before the public is because he is not in doubt not only about his acquittal but even about his being approved.

13:19 Why am I consumed holding my peace?

He says that he is *consumed holding his peace*, not that he did not say anything but that his claims and defense do not seem to have been acknowledged.

13:20-21 Two things only may you not do to me: withdraw your hand far from me and let not your dread terrify me.

He scoffs at his audience as if they are inexperienced and unequally matched, and he turns his words to God and asks him to remove from him both the bitterness of the threat and the

[99]For a brief discussion of this term, see Annecchino, "I Temi," 291.

violence of the blows, and then he promises that he will be confident in his own assertion.

13:22 And call me, and I will answer you; or else I will speak, and do thou answer me.

Then an equal format to the disputation will be preserved, and I will be able to answer boldly, or if it has seemed so, to occupy the first step of the questioner, when no terror overwhelms one's confidence.

13:23 How many iniquities and sins do I have? Show me my crimes and offenses.

In his customary manner he does not claim that he has not sinned, but he says that he has not done things deserving of such great blows. Thus, he asks not that the class or species of sin be pointed out to him, but its measure.

13:24 Why do you hide your face?

He has held to the scheme that is preserved in a trial before judges, that when a guilty enemy is convicted before the laws and justice, the verdict is declared against him after a veil has been spread before the face of the judge.[100] For he applies it to fulfill the comparison that he had invoked. "Do you write bitter things against me?"[101] "And do you think me your enemy?" My worthlessness does not permit me to come into that suspicion, that I am believed by you, as it were, equally as an enemy, though I do not differ from a dry leaf.[102]

13:25 Against a leaf, that is carried away with the wind, you show your power.

By the worthlessness of the comparison he has expressed that he was speaking not from the impudence of his mind but from the purity of his innocence.

13:26 For you write bitter things against me.

Bitter things—that is, judgments that are bitter to me. "And you want to consume me for the sins of my youth." It is an established fact that the life of the present time cannot be called to court when the suspicions are directed against lapses during childhood.

13:27 You have put my foot in a fettering band and have observed all my paths.

You have applied such a great watch over all my actions and you have looked on whatever I have done with such focused vision that you did not allow my foot to move forward beyond the course of what is right, and to be free to wander by turning aside.

13:28 I who am to be consumed as rottenness.

The fragile propensity of my nature to fall does not allow such an attentive guardian and such a strict severity of the examiner.

[Chapter 14]

14:1 Man born of a woman, living for a short time, is filled with many miseries.

Our nature, in order to proclaim the end from the beginning, attests to its destruction by its birth; necessarily, one born from a mortal is mortal.

14:2 He comes forth like a flower, and is destroyed, and flees as a shadow.

Many things come together that yield to your reproach and strictness: the brevity of life, the continuance of miseries, and the constant race toward death.

[100]Cf. Job 9:24. I am not certain what ancient legal custom is being described here.
[101]Job 13:26.
[102]Cf. Job 13:25.

14:3 And do you think it fitting to open your eyes upon such a one?

In the legal defense of his own action, he invokes the general situation of all living things, that when communion with the human race was commended to him, he adds the pursuit of his own virtue to the heap of words out of which his speech is composed.

14:4 Who can make clean him who is conceived of unclean seed? Is it not you who are alone?[103]

This comparison of yours, which seems to burden humanity, acquits. For it is a matter of great praise that what has been composed displeases you.[104] *Who can make clean?* An accusation of nature amounts to saint Job's purification from guilt.[105] For if that [accusation] cannot be referred to its author in view of the condition of frailty that is inborn to itself, how is it blameworthy that a holy man could be charged with being inferior to God? *Who can make clean?* According to the Septuagint, "For who will be clean from filth? Not even one, even if his life on earth is one day long."[106]

14:5 The days of man are short, the number of his months is with you, you have appointed his bounds which cannot be passed.

"But you have appointed his months to be numbered, you have established his time, which shall not be exceeded."[107] Here is another way: one person will indeed die, though he lived but one day, but another has months of life that have been predetermined, and perhaps to someone else there may be a longer amount of time; yet it is necessary for him to die and to fulfill the debt of his condition. Here is another way. The same meanings are often repeated for one and the same case.

14:6 Depart a little from him, that he may rest.

He does not want God's providence to be removed from man, as it were, from an irreligious mind, but he asks that his inquisition and censuring be suspended. Here is another way. The Greek says, "Depart a little from me, that I may rest."[108]

14:7 A tree has hope; if it be cut, it grows green again.

This is why I most justifiably ask for a remission of my griefs in the present, since that hope is not mine after death, which there is for a cut tree, that I could sprout again from my roots and be restored. *A tree has hope.* In the things said previously he had described the brevity of mortal life, the lengthening of the afflictions, the fact that time does not stand still, the hastening of man's race toward death.[109] Now in the comparison with a *tree* he endeavors to prove his worthlessness, that a thing cut down could quickly rise again from the roots, but a

[103]The RSV reads, "Who can bring a clean thing out of an unclean? There is not one." Pier Franco Beatrice, *The Transmission of Sin: Augustine and the Pre-Augustinian Sources*, trans. Adam Kamesar (Oxford: Oxford University Press, 2013), 96-97, discusses this verse and observes that the Hebrew version simply "laments the miserable and ephemeral condition of human beings, and the utter fragility of their existential condition" (96). However, the Vulgate translation accentuates the idea that the human being comes into the world already tainted by impurity. "This formulation leads to an even more pessimistic assessment (if that were possible!) of the process of generation" (97). Beatrice concludes, "It is clear that the Greek translator, and later the Latin one, wanted to impose on the biblical text a nuance that it did not possess in its original form" (97).

[104]Cf. Job 25:1-2.

[105]Cf. Job 15:3.

[106]Job 14:4 LXX. The Greek version of this verse played an important role in the arguments used in support of the doctrine of original sin. It was even noted repeatedly by Origen; see S. Bagby, *Sin in Origen's Commentary on Romans* (New York: Fortress Academic, 2018), 62.

[107]Job 14:5 LXX.

[108]This is neither how the Brenton text (Vaticanus) reads nor the Rahlfs edition, though in the apparatus the latter edition does list Julian's reading as a variant.

[109]Cf. Job 14:2.

dead man cannot return to life. *A tree has hope*. Here is another way. He is describing the case of the human condition, and he utters words not suited so much to his faith as to the matter at hand, words that can indeed suffice in response to those who did not have knowledge of such a great hope, or else that could most rightly fit the present state of man.

14:12 When a man has fallen asleep he shall not rise again; till the heavens be broken, he shall not awake.

It is not possible for him to appear to be casting doubt on the resurrection by the things he said higher up,[110] since he predicts and signals the very time of the resurrection, and he confesses that those whom he claims will awake from their slumber do not perish but live.

14:14 Do you think that a man that is dead may live again?

This doubt comes from the greatness of the thing, not from the feeling of hopelessness, which surely he already excluded by his words higher up. "All the days in which I am now in warfare (*milito*), I expect until my change come." Since it is necessary for a soldier (*militem*) to be involved in constant dangers, he nicely calls the time of the present life *military service* (*militiam*). *My change* is close to the apostle's statement: "It is necessary that this corruptible be clothed with incorruption and this mortal be clothed with immortality."[111]

14:16 You indeed have numbered my steps.

The severity of a parent is evidence of love. The parent who does not allow his son to wander off from his own chastisement wants to have a proven son.

[110]Cf. Job 7:9; 14:7.
[111]1 Cor 15:53.

14:17 You have cured my iniquity.

The Greek says, "And you have marked if I have sinned unwillingly."

14:18-19 A mountain falling passes away, waters wear away the stones, so in like manner do you destroy man?

When he was filled with a prophetic spirit, he had shown that the hope of resurrection undergirds the human being.[112] Therefore, he wants to prove it even by the application of reason, while he vindicates it by a comparison with worthless things.

14:20 Have you strengthened him for a little while, that he may pass away forever?

This whole thing needs to be read as irony all the way to the end of the speech (*eclogae*).[113] *Have you strengthened him for a little while?* Similar to this is the following passage from the psalm: "Have you made all the children of men in vain?"[114] "Will you change his face, and send him away?" Will you convert favorable circumstances into adversities? Will you repay a needy man from one who abounds, and a dejected man from one who is honored?

14:21 Does he not understand whether his children come to honor or dishonor?

When death takes away all feeling for one's own posterity by which the living are influenced.

14:22 But yet his flesh, while he lives, shall have pain.

From a speech with general application, at the end he has turned to his own role in the

[112]Cf. Job 14:14.
[113]J. H. Baxter, "Notes on the Latin of Julian of Eclanum," *ALMA* 21 (1951): 29, indicates that *ecloga* means a speech or chapter (in the Bible), a discourse in general. Cf. Job 24:1; 28:1.
[114]Ps 89:47.

discussion, that by God's chastisement he was leading a life filled with pain.

[Chapter 15]

15:1 And Eliphaz the Themanite, answered, and said.

Saint Job had not only shown that Zophar's words deserved ridicule, but he also had reproved all the men in common, because they thought that wisdom had to be judged according to the ends of a lifetime. And since he had also discussed many things not only concerning human nature but likewise concerning the divine power, Eliphaz takes offense. He tries to accuse [Job] openly of multiple iniquities. And since he is lacking proof, he takes refuge in making a comparison with the people of antiquity. And in this he does not bear a humble mind with respect to himself, but he thinks that he is wiser than everyone else.

15:2 Will a wise man answer as if he were speaking in the wind, and fill his stomach with burning heat?

[Eliphaz] wants the proof of Job's foolishness to appear in the length of his speech, and he thinks that Job's words were dictated by anger; they were not brought forth by reason. "Will a wise man answer as if he were speaking in the wind?" Since saint Job, after the beginning of his speech, had left his fellow disputants behind and had turned his words to God, Eliphaz says that it does not befit a wise man to neglect the person of his fellow disputant and to speak, as it were, to the air, and to orate to the end on whatever pleases him without the fear of being contradicted.

15:3 You reprove him by words, who is not your equal, and you speak what is not profitable to you.

Your purification from guilt is an accusation against God;[115] for if you are afflicted undeservedly, he who is afflicting you is most justly branded with iniquity.

15:4 As much as is in you, you have made void fear and have taken away prayers from before the Lord.

By your complaints, you put aside reverence for God and subject him to scorn as you attack his justice. For no one will care about appeasing by prayers the one whom your speech fearlessly made light of.

15:5 For your iniquity has taught your mouth.

Language is formed based on the nature of your heart, and speech expresses what the perversely afflicted mind dictates.[116]

15:6 Your own mouth shall condemn you, and not I.

More correctly, you will attribute the bitterness of our response not to us but to your own statements, which required this. *Your own mouth shall condemn you.* Compare your words and subject matter, and you will mark yourself down for error, when you see that you have transgressed the measure of your nature by the insolence of your speech.

15:7 Are you the first man that was born?

So that you refuse to be judged according to that rule by which all are checked, but all are checked by that form of assessment that you yourself have established. *Are you the first man* so that you claim for yourself greater knowledge of all things based on the experience of a longer life?[117]

[115] Cf. Job 14:4.
[116] Cf. Mt 15:18-19.
[117] According to Gen 5:5, Adam died at the age of 930.

15:8 Have you heard God's counsel, and shall his wisdom be inferior to you?

Was it at your discretion that he granted his own statutes and decrees, so that you should constantly chastise his mistakes as one who is superior?

15:10 There are with us also aged and ancient men, much older than your fathers.

By whose teaching and authority we learned those things that we did not know.

15:11 Is it a great matter that your God should comfort you?

Even if the measure of chastisement had surpassed the measure of your transgressions, the justice of the censor could have revoked that which exceeded your deserts, had not the obstinacy of your speech stood in the way.

15:12 Why does your heart elevate you, and why do you stare with your eyes, as if you were thinking great things?

Amid his feelings of pain, Job was pointing out the inspiration of the Holy Spirit by the appearance of his body. And, as if forgetful of the present, he was rendered more attentive to the viewing of deep realities. Thus, without any ambiguity he perceived and spoke of the mystery of the Mediator, of his faith in and of the time of the resurrection. For this reason, Eliphaz believed that from the elation of his mind that appearance of his body was formed.

15:14 What is man that he should be without spot?

Eliphaz is convicted by the rebuke that saint Job had perceived well about the nature of man. He would not have blamed holy Job by accusing the nature of man if he had said the same and not different things. For this reason Eliphaz means that the nature of human beings is subject to suffering. It is likewise prone and inclined to sin. *What is man that he should be without spot, and that one born of a woman should appear just?* From the words of saint Job he reckons that an occasion has been given him to argue against Job. And he reckons that he can bind him on the basis of what he has conceded. Saint Job had said, "Man born of a woman, living for a short time, is filled with many miseries."[118] Eliphaz infers from this and says, "If this is the nature of mortals, as you yourself testify, so that in view of the frailty of mortality and the constant change of his state, it would not be able to be compared with God, you too are forced to confess that you are a sinner."[119] But the defect that Job applied to [human] bodies, Eliphaz attributed this to their moral character.

15:15 Behold, among his saints no one is unchangeable.

No one is so devoted to virtue that he is incapable of the opposite. Now by *saints* here he means Abraham and his descendants. "And the heavens are not pure." He is not saying that the *heavens* are blackened by the filth of anyone's sin but that the only nature subject to no change is God's. For often the calm appearance of the *heavens* is obscured by an overlay of clouds.

15:16 How much more is man abominable?

To whom the pursuit of evil customs creates an eagerness and longing to sin.

[118]Job 14:1.

[119]Cf. Job 14:4. Annecchino, "I Temi," 307n89, notes that the accusation against the Pelagians of wanting to compare themselves to God is a recurring theme in Jerome's anti-Pelagian works. See for example Jerome's Epistle 133.8 *Ad Ctesiphontem*,; *Dial Pel* 1.12; and my note under Job 9:1.

15:17 I will show you, hear me.

By saying, *I will show you, hear me,* he wants him to learn from him what he says he received from the elders. This is a sign of a wise man, to know that man is incapable of complete justice and perfection.

15:18 Wise men confess and hide not their fathers.

That is, they do not conceal by whose authoritative instruction they were educated.

15:19 To whom alone the earth was given.

To the wise whose thought this is, that they set their salvation in supplications for themselves more than in the pursuit of virtue, since they are incapable of it. *The earth was given*—that is, as an inheritance that is long and secure, with no fear of a robber.

15:20-21 The wicked man is proud all his days. The sound of dread is always in his ears.

The alarm that comes from conscience lacks security even in times of quiet.

15:22 He does not believe that one could return from darkness.

When adversity occurs, the good of his conscience is unable to guarantee better things for him.

15:23 When he moves himself to seek bread, he knows that the day of darkness is ready at his hand.

Even if he is not involved in great labor and behaves as one who is remiss in activity, the horror of death always stands over him.

15:25 For he has stretched out his hand against God.

He adds the reason and renders an account for why an arrogant man would encounter those things that he recounted. And he explains the vices of the mind under the form of the body.

15:26 He has run against him with his neck raised up.

Since he had put on the role of one fighting against God, he describes by whose aid the rash man is accustomed to stir up ventures.

15:28 He will dwell in desolate cities, and in desert houses.

To the previously stated calamities that he says are owed to the impious, he adds other adversities as well: that the exile hunts from his desert house and does not enjoy his wealth inexhaustibly.

15:29 Neither shall his substance continue, neither shall he push his root in the earth.

Not only will his *substance* and wealth be diminished, but he will not even have hope of propagating offspring.

15:30 He does not depart out of darkness.

He will not alter the sad situation by any change to joyful things. "The flame shall dry up his branches." He has preserved the metaphor in order to say that *his branches* are to be dried out by the burning wind. He has indicated posterity in the comparison to trees.

15:31 He would not believe, being vainly deceived by error, that he may be redeemed with any price.

A handful of money will not redeem someone whom vice and guilt dooms to a death sentence.

15:32 Before his days be full, he shall perish.

He will not be allowed to reach old age but will be snatched away by a premature death.

15:33 He shall be struck as a vine when its grapes are in the first flower and as an olive tree that casts its flower.

By means of a simile he says that he is to be deprived of all succession of goods, the way a vine or olive tree loses its fruit when cold strikes the former in its first flower, when summer heat strikes the latter.

15:34 For the congregation of the hypocrite is barren.

He strikes at the character of saint Job by this generalization of speech. "And fire shall devour their tabernacles." This applies either to the corruption of judges or to the avarice of robbers.

15:35 He has conceived sorrow and has brought forth iniquity.

When he steals things that belong to others and does not allow the use of things that have been seized, the only fruit of his work is the labor alone.

[Chapter 16]

16:1-2 Then Job answered and said, I have often heard such things.

With one line he accuses them of two errors. They are recalling as novelties things that were overused in the speech earlier, and they are forgetful of the duties of friendship when they heap up the causes of his pain. Just as Eliphaz and his friends want saint Job's suffering to be a testimony to his sins, so on the other side saint Job endeavors to summon the things that had happened to him as his own justification from guilt. For under the outward form of a rhetorical training exercise, as an affront to Job, Eliphaz had recounted things that customarily happen to the impious.

16:3 Shall they have no end?

The reason no limit is applied to their inane words is because your speeches are not balanced with prudence and well-considered, nor is what you all speak full of importance, whatever effort is applied.

16:4 I also could speak like you.

If I behaved idly as you all do, and the sensation of my pain did not restrict me to words of importance, I could easily pour forth whatever words came to my tongue.

16:5 I would comfort you also with words.

This kind was easy, [a speech] that announces a reproach rather than applies the compassion of consolation to you.

16:7 But what shall I do? If I speak, my pain does not rest.

From this inanity of your speeches, I am led off, as it were, with a kind of bridle of my vexation, which is so great that the intention neither to speak nor be silent diminishes it. *Does not rest:* [Theodore has][120] instead "Does it not rest?" "And if I hold my peace, it will not depart from me" instead of "Does it not depart?"

16:9 My wrinkles bear witness against me.

All the vigor of a man in the very bloom of life has been consumed. The whole form of my body has changed into that of an old man whose appearance is summoned as testimony

[120]The manuscript is corrupt here.

of my accusation, while my sufferings are attributed to my offenses. "And a false speaker is raised up against my face." My accuser is armed with private testimony against me.

16:10 He has gathered together his fury against me, and threatening me he has gnashed with his teeth.

Using a comparison to human custom, he has expressed the bitter attacks of pain within himself and the violence of the raging evil. *He gathers together his fury.* As far as is revealed in the speeches of saint Job, it appears that his fellow disputants are incensed by the progression of his speech and have gone beyond the moderation of a disputation. They have reached the point of bitterness in the quarrel and the wrath of those who are wrangling.

16:11 They have opened their mouths upon me.

In the Greek all these things are recorded in the singular.[121] "They have struck me on the cheek." The strivings of the undisciplined customarily reaches the point of this outcome, that they abandon moderation in disputation and arm themselves with reproaches and wrangling, with the result that they are scarcely able to contain themselves even by hands. Either this is indicated in the present lines or else all these things are spoken with rhetorical stress.

16:12 God has shut me up with the unjust man and has delivered me into the hands of the wicked.

He refers to God as the cause of the insult that he endures from the speech of his friends. And he says that he would not have been able to endure anyone's injury except that he had been stripped of so many helps. This is why he added:

16:13-15 I who was formerly wealthy have been suddenly broken to pieces. He has set [me] up to be his sign.

He did not train on me alone the gestures of an angry man, as it were, but for the display of his power and proof of his skill, he cheaply reckoned [me] against whom he directed his javelins. *I who was wealthy have been suddenly broken to pieces.* So that he deprived me both of bodily health and the consolation of wealth. "He has held my neck. He has compassed me round about with his lances; he has wounded my loins. He has torn me with wound upon wound, he has rushed in on me like a giant." Since he had said that he was laid prostrate by God his assailer, he pursues in his speech the comparison to an enemy and to a powerful adversary. And he endeavors to explain things situated in the intellect by means of physical indications, and he announces what he feels by means of what customarily has met the eyes.

16:16 I have sowed sackcloth on my skin.

This is what he said: "He has torn me with wound upon wound."[122] Thus, he showed that two serious things happened to him, that he lacks that with which the body is covered and healed.

16:17 My face is swollen from weeping.

He shows that he expended tears not as a penance but out of pain. "These things have I suffered without the iniquity of my hand."[123] Surely he means that if he were guilty he would have paid for what he had done by weeping, not for what he was suffering.

[121]That is, "He has" rather than "They have."

[122]Job 16:15.

[123]Job 16:18.

16:18 These things have I suffered without the iniquity.

You are grieved for good reason, for there were no grounds for such great torment. *I have suffered these things.* He feels pain, well aware that it goes contrary to his merits; therefore, he does not want the fact that he has been surrendered to torments to be concealed, but he wants his suffering to come into the light. He does not want the memory of his suffering to be buried in oblivion, but he wants his suffering to reach everyone's ears because he is confident[124] about the uprightness of his life.[125] And this is why he added:

16:19 O earth, do not cover my blood.

It is fitting for one who has been beset by such pain as surpasses human nature to endure to authoritatively address the *earth,* so that it does not seem undeserved for him by the inspiration of the Holy Spirit to lay claim to such great confidence for himself. For while situated outside the law, the man says that which is found in the writings of the sacred law. For the voice of God says to Cain, "The voice of your brother's blood cries out to me from the earth."[126] Therefore, it pertains uniquely to the just that their sufferings, deaths, and battles are not hidden.

[124]Reading *securus* for CCSL's *sucurus.*

[125]Annecchino comments, "The author of the *Expositio* is of another opinion [than Eliphaz] according to which suffering is in no way generated by iniquities (16:18). If it were not so, the same old age, showing a consumed body, would bear witness to some fault (16:9). Correlating guilt with pain suffered means questioning the Providence and justice of the Creator; Providence, if the things of mortals are uncertain and without guidance, justice if the diversity of merits is not weighed by any balance (20:5-6). The fact that the wicked live unpunished and the innocent are exposed to every form of adversity is the proof that there is no correspondence between guilt and punishment (21:22)." "I Temi," 307.

[126]Gen 4:10.

16:20 For behold, my witness is in heaven.

The words by which he had professed the virtue of his innocence and the purity of his prayers seemed to be asserted in opposition to realities that pointed in a different direction. Therefore, the confident one takes refuge in the worthiness of an incorrupt witness who is able to judge not based on things that meet the eyes but on his very conscience.

16:21 If my friends are full of words, my eye pours out tears to God.

It is understood here that his friends revealed his offense by their murmuring, while he spoke things greater than suited human measure. And this is the reason he turns and accuses them of garrulousness and testifies that his case is with God.

16:22 And O that a man might so be judged with God as the son of man is judged with his companion!

Because you show yourselves offended by my outspoken speech, O friends, greater confidence has arisen in me to assert myself, if the assailer's persona would stand by me as an equal. But now, as my conscience raises me up, so the weight of divine reverence drives me back.

16:23 For behold, short years pass away.

It is consistent that he comes into doubt, as it were, concerning the benefit of his justice and he complains about the shortness of life.

[Chapter 17]

17:1 My spirit shall be wasted.

In view of the greatness of the afflictions, he believes that he is to die before joyful times succeed in place of the sad times. "My days shall be shortened, and only the grave remains for me." [The Greek has] "I pray for burial, and it does not happen to me."

17:2 I have not sinned, and my eye abides in bitterness.

Either this is to be referred to the continuous time of his life or else he is saying that after lapses during his adolescence, which he corrected by better pursuits, he has solicitously avoided vices.

17:3 Deliver me and set me beside you, and let any man's hand fight against me.

Since these adversities that I suffer bear witness that you hate me, release me from such a prejudice, so that constituted under the fairness of your examination, I may confidently welcome the incriminations of any accuser.

17:4 You have set their heart far from instruction.

He repeats in his own speech the words that his friends cited in respect to his suffering, that the reason his children perished was because they mishandled their education and their claim that Job himself had stood forth as such a violent man during the time of his prosperity that he won the loyalty of his own servants by sharing the plunder with them.[127] This is why he coherently added, "He has made me, as it were, a byword of the people."[128]

17:5 He promises plunder to his companions, and the eyes of his children shall fail.

The Greek has "For they have turned away their heart from wisdom."[129] Willingly and knowingly, he says, they transgress justice and behave as those who have forgotten the truth. Another line [in the Greek says], "Therefore you shall not exalt them."[130] "You shall not exalt"; that is, I am not able to exalt: I am not able, he says, to prefer their words to my statements, nor to reckon their thoughts better than mine. And he gives the reasons why he could not do this: "You have stood by on the side of iniquity."[131] It is not surprising, he says, if you prepare contradictions to my statements contrary to my conscience, you who have striven to place perverseness before what is right. Whence, he says, is this true? "My eyes have failed over my children."[132] You cannot confess ignorance of my evils, since the plundering of my property and the loss of my children, which impaired my eyesight, reached the ears even of those situated far off.

17:6 He has made me, as it were, a byword.

The horror and cursing over my suffering is constantly on everyone's lips.

17:7 My eye has grown dim from indignation.

He is aroused at the bitterness of the wounds, likewise by the curses of those who speak reproaches.

17:8-9 The just shall be astonished at this.

The Greek has "Wonder will hold true men upon this." Not those, he says, who will be of the right judgment, as you are affected by a similar rumor, but they will collapse into ultimate grief since they see that what I suffer has happened beyond the limits of human power. "For the unjust has risen up against the just." Consequently, he says, they will be of such

[127]Cf. Job 17:5.

[128]Job 17:6.

[129]Job 17:4 LXX, although the Brenton text (Vaticanus) reads, "you have hidden their heart."

[130]Job 17:4 LXX.

[131]Job 17:5 LXX, although the Brenton text (Vaticanus) reads, "He shall announce evil to their side."

[132]Job 17:5 LXX.

a will and thought that they even render testimony to my justice, and those who rob me will accuse me of impiety. *The just shall be astonished at this*, "and the innocent shall be raised up against the hypocrite, and the just man shall hold on his way." From the context of the disputation, he advances to greater things while being filled with illumination into higher matters. Thus, he utters what he feels about the end of his suffering, or else about the Lord's dispensation. Both these things can be understood in one way; namely, *the just shall be astonished* at the depth of the divine counsel and will. For the Lord wanted to conceal his own justice in order to broadcast the merits of his servant, in order that by his example every innocent person will not only stand up confidently against the hypocrite but, moreover, while proceeding down the continuous way of virtue, will always increase his own former pursuits for the sake of those who are following. *The just shall be astonished at this.* Either saint Job understands as much as he declared or he spoke things greater than were capable of occurring to his understanding. When these things are fulfilled, they convince us that what he said was a prophecy. For who is not *astonished* either that holy Job, for the sake of testing his virtue, was surrendered to tribulations or that the Son of God, for the sake of the salvation of the human race, arrived at the humiliation of the cross, so that by his example the innocent person could stand up strongly[133] against the one who hypocritically feigns virtue and not be terrified by any kind of punishments?

17:10 Wherefore be ye all converted.

You are furnished with eyes only for the images of things of the present, and you are unable to view with the eyes of the mind those that are concealed in the depths of the [divine] superintendence.

17:11 My days have passed away; my thoughts are dissipated.

After touching on the great matters, he returns again to the course of his own insignificance, and he says that in the agitation of his mind he could not track down what he should hold on to for certain.

17:12 They have turned night into day, and after darkness I hope for light again.

This is a familiar experience, that sleepless nights pass that are occupied either by stirred up emotions or pains.

17:13 If I endure, the underworld (*infernus*) is my house.

The constant horror of death shuts out the moderate endurance of sufferings. For when can I promise a change to prosperity, since I already see the time of my life spent in miseries?

17:14 I have said to rottenness, You are my father, my mother.

I have been so corrupted by the long and continuous decay of my body, that to me it does not seem to have occurred at any particular time, but I believe I was either born from this rottenness or with it.

17:15 Where is now then my patience?

Here he is not calling the virtue of endurance *patience*, but the very cause of his suffering.

17:16 All that I have shall go down into the deepest hell (*infernum*).

The whole time of my life has been consumed, when I might have hoped for better things.

[133]Job 17:9b says, "and he that has clean hands shall be stronger and stronger."

[Chapter 18]

18:1-2 Then Bildad the Shuhite answered and said, How long[134] will you throw out words?

There is one intention both for saint Job in all his statements and for his three friends, that he show himself estranged from their recriminations, and that they, as if in defense of God, endeavor to show him to be guilty, based on those things that have happened to him. *How long?* By the occasion of his response, it is understood that it was not written down in the same order and manner in which the disputation was conducted. For neither the words full of saint Job's bitterness nor the heated and incited speech of his friends would have preserved their ordered measure, nor would a book of controversies and speeches have been contained by that brevity that it does contain. Whence Bildad too complains about those making a racket about his speech and those claiming that it lacks discipline, to express that which occurred to each one in the conflict. And he demands that an opportunity be given to himself as to one who is not inferior.

18:3 Why are we reputed as beasts?

You claim for yourselves alone the opportunity to speak, as those who are wiser, while excluding it from us.

18:4 You who destroy your soul in your fury.

Having, as it were, procured silence from his friends, he hurls the javelins of his words against saint Job, against whom he was particularly seeking an opportunity for himself to speak. "Shall the earth be forsaken for you, and are rocks being removed out of their place?" He is saying, Just as the elements have received a definite status by the arrangements of their Creator, so the merits of things are checked off as paid, in view of their characteristics, as is decreed by the same Creator. Therefore, although you are complaining about the fairness of God's judgments and do not want to undergo what sinners deserve, doubtless you wish that the entire ordering of God's works be changed.

18:5 Shall not the light of the wicked be extinguished?

For the standard of fairness established by God and presiding at the judgment demands this.

18:7 The steps of his strength (*virtutis*) shall be constricted.

By the different forms of afflictions, he explains what fruits follow wickedness. "His own counsel shall cast him down headlong." It is a common thing in the Holy Scriptures to speak as follows. They are said to have undertaken by their own desire and pursuit that condition into which people fall headlong when the verdict of judgment is passed.
It is not that someone desired the adversities but that he behaved in such a way that it was necessary that he reach the outcome of the adversities. Therefore, the end of the business is appraised from the nature of its commencement.[135]

18:8 For he thrust his feet into a net.

No effectual achievement will follow the aim of his works; rather, on the contrary, he will be chained inextricably to the adversities.[136] This customarily comes to pass to the one seething amid anguishes.

[134] Or "unto what end."

[135] For similar scriptural interpretations, see under Hos 1:2-5; 8:4; Amos 2:6(-7).

[136] Cf. Job 18:9.

18:12 Let his strength be wasted with famine.

Ever since he said that adversities advance unto sinners as a consequence of God's judgments, he was delighted, as it were, by the justice that assesses[137] merits, and he adopts the outward display of one wishing for something.

18:13 Let it devour the beauty of his skin and consume his arms.

The Greek has "While he is still alive, death shall devour his firstborn (*primogenitum*)."[138] Firstborn (*primogenita*) death. He said *firstborn death*, wanting to indicate the one and only, as it were, in respect to eminence, and the one that could not be compared with others, in view of his own bitterness. For every firstborn is preferred to those born later. Or one should understand *firstborn arms*—that is, sons whose death customarily afflicts parents very grieviously.

18:14 Let his confidence be rooted out of his tabernacle.

With all resources consumed that can provide solace or bring aid to one who is lying at the point of death, let no hope be left in which one who is about to fall could lean. "And let destruction tread on him like a king." The Greek has "And let distress (*necessitas* = ἀνάγκη) and a charge from the king seize him." He says indeed that he found this more clearly in another passage where it says, "Let actions on the necks be exhibited to the king."[139] And the sense is, He says, not only does the wicked one suffer evils from inferiors, but he is even reduced to miseries from those who preside and hold command.

[137]Cf. Baxter, "Notes," 31.

[138]The Brenton reading (Vaticanus) is "And death shall consume his beauty."

[139]This is apparently an alternative Greek version that differs from the LXX. Julian may be referring to Philip the Presbyter. Cf. Vaccari, *Un Commento a Giobbe di Giuliano di Eclana*, 153.

18:15-16 Let the companions dwell in his tabernacle.

Elsewhere it says more clearly, "Let him dwell in tabernacles not his own."[140] This indeed has been recorded very coherently in accordance with the Greek version. For the one who incurs an offense meriting royal confiscation becomes an exile even from his own house as well as in other affairs. *Let the companions of him who is not dwell in his tabernacle.* "Let his roots be dried up beneath, and his harvest destroyed above." The explanation that reckons *him who is not* as said of the devil is far removed from the contextual coherence of the reading.[141] Thus, it befits God to say that he always is, in accordance with the following: "I am who I am."[142] The devil, on the other hand, is not said "to be." But here the intention of the statements pleads for complete desolation and abandonment by saying *the companions of him who is not. He who is not* surely has no companions. It is as if he were to say, Let no one dwell in his tabernacles. He has made this meaning obvious in the verse that follows.

18:17 Let the memory of him perish from the earth.

In order that Bildad may not appear to have spoken inconsistently, so that, when he said, "Let his roots be dried up beneath," he added, "and his harvest destroyed above,"[143] he added what he wanted to be understood through such a series of statements, by saying, "Let the memory of him perish from the earth." For it could happen that the maturation of the crops

[140]This is apparently an alternative Greek version that differs from the LXX. Cf. Vaccari, *Un Commento a Giobbe di Giuliano di Eclana*, 154.

[141]According to Vaccari, *Un Commento a Giobbe di Giuliano di Eclana*, 91-93, Julian is referring to Jerome's disciple, Philip the Presbyter.

[142]Ex 3:14.

[143]Job 18:16.

would occur before the drying up of the roots, which takes place over a long period of time. *Let the memory of him perish from the earth.* All the things indeed that customarily happen to the unjust are spoken of in general, but these words refer obliquely to saint Job, because he suffers such things in view of his own merits, as God marks him down as paid.

18:20 The last (*novissimi*) shall be astonished at his day.

One should refer *first* and *last* either to the genealogical family of the race or to distinguish the sequence.

18:21 These then are the tabernacles of the wicked man, and this the place of him who does not know God.

It is as if he were to say, Here is the fruit and these are the wages of sins.

[Chapter 19]

19:1-2 Then Job answered and said, How long do you afflict my soul?

Saint Job understood that he in particular was being bitten by the teeth of his friends, although they were making assertions in general terms, or rather, obliquely, about what wickedness deserves. And therefore, when they are not receptive to clearing him from guilt in his statements, he complains about his compulsion to respond that has been imposed on him.

19:3 Behold, these ten times you confound me and are not ashamed.

It is a matter of shame and disgrace to oppress one who is lying on the ground and to step on someone who has fallen.

19:4 For if I have been ignorant, my ignorance shall be with me.

This charge by which you pursue me comes to you not from necessity but from perversity of mind. For my sins will not injure you, who rise up in such bitter speeches against me. In fact, it will tell against me if I have committed anything either in deed or in speech that truth would not approve of.

19:5 But you have set yourselves up against me and reprove me with my reproaches.

You summon testimony against me not from my deeds but from the vexation of my body.

19:6 At least now understand that God has not afflicted me with an equal judgment.

If your determination to contradict seduces you, at least the facts themselves, which you perceive, ought to procure certainty for you. For what is concealed in the kind [of affliction] is revealed in the measure [of it].[144] For the tortures are greater than the guilt; surely the appearance of punishments is manifest, though suspicion rummages about looking for sins.

19:7 Behold, I shall cry suffering violence, and no one will hear me.

The silence of the judge proceeds from the form of the deed. Therefore, the voice of the objector is not allowed, since it more cruelly excelled the one who was established. My outcry ought either to be curbed by reason or soothed out of pity.

19:8-9 He has hedged in my path round about, and in my footpath he has set

[144]For this theme, see 6:1-2; 8:1-2; 10:19-21; 13:14, 23; 15:11; 17:8-9; 20:18.

darkness. He has taken the crown from my head.

By this metaphor, he says that his hope of escaping from his miseries has been taken away from him; for he says that even *darkness,* which removes the ability to look ahead, has been employed to hinder escape.

19:10 He has destroyed me on every side and has taken away my hope, as from a tree that is plucked up.

In order to increase the evil of hopelessness, he was not content to say *a tree* that is "cut down" but *plucked up.* When its roots perish with itself, it is not able to rise into another sprout by germinating.

19:11 His wrath is kindled against me, and he has counted me as his enemy.

He has excluded judicial moderation by the terms *wrath* and *enemy.*

19:12 His robbers have come together and have made themselves a way by me.

Either Job is complying with the simile that he had adopted in order to say that he is exposed to the attack of the enemies and that they more often go back and forth without any obstacle on their open road, or else he is referring to the fact that messenger followed messenger, who announced to him those evils that had befallen him. For it is reported as follows: "While he was still speaking, behold, another messenger came."[145] *His robbers have come together.* He has developed the metaphor that he had introduced with the term *enemy.* In fact, since Job said that God came to attack him, as a kind of hostile king, he now added, *His robbers have come together.* It is as if he said, his soldiers. For scriptural usage calls the spies of enemies *robbers.*[146] Therefore, even by the things he added he has adorned the form of the desired comparison:

19:16 I called my servant, and he gave me no answer; I entreated him with my own mouth.

He looks toward greater mistreatment. A situation that is not far off, but present, can be despised.

19:17 And I entreated the children of my womb.

The Greek has "children of my concubines." *Children of my womb,* on whom I had expended no less affection than if they had come forth from my flesh.

19:18 Even fools despised me.

As it were by certain stages he says that he has been brought down (*deductum*)[147] from the highest heights to the deepest depths. For first of all, he says he was robbed of his kingdom when he says, "He has taken the crown from my head."[148] But since it did not immediately follow that, since he had been stripped of honor, he likewise seemed exposed to attack, he added, "Thus, he has counted me as his enemy."[149] Still, the solaces of parents, or dependents, had remained. He says that he lost even these when they were all taken away.

19:19 My counselors, and he whom I love most is turned against me.

This is what he said previously: "And I entreated the children of my womb."[150]

[145]Job 1:17.

[146]Cf. Gen 42:9-34.

[147]Cf. preface, n. 4.

[148]Job 19:9.

[149]Job 19:11.

[150]Job 19:17.

19:20 The flesh being consumed, my bone has cleaved to my skin.

The violence of the raging disease has attacked not merely on the surface, but down deep. "And nothing but lips are left about my teeth." He recorded lips for thin skin.

19:21 Have pity on me, have pity on me, at least you my friends.

When such a dire appearance of my calamities meets your eyes, it did not become you to insult my miseries, but it would have been befitting to be struck with the affection of pity and with compassion.

19:23-24 Who will grant me that my words may be written? Who will grant me that they may be marked down in a book with an iron pen, and in a plate of lead, or else be graven in flint stone?

When our souls are troubled, we often express things that are disordered, and we desire that afterward these things be consigned to oblivion, as things to be ashamed of. But, on the other hand, we want those things that are said seriously and in a considered fashion to be fixed in the memory and to remain in the mouth of many people. Therefore, saint Job too wants to show that it was not with a deeply troubled mind that he had poured out what he had said, but that his words were well arranged and filled with truth and reason. Thus, he desires that they be written not merely on paper but also engraved on *lead* and *flint stone*, so that they may be preserved unto a great age and for a long time.

19:25 For I know that my Redeemer lives, and in the last day I shall rise out of the earth.

[The Greek has] "For I know that he is eternal who is about to deliver me on the earth; my skin that endures these things will rise again."[151] *For I know that my Redeemer lives.* The Greek has "For my body that draws such things will rise again."[152] *For I know that my Redeemer lives.* Just as he wanted there to be testimony to his sound statements, if he defended them from oblivion by having the writings carved into metals, so he gave the reason why he wanted them consigned to a longer remembrance—namely, in order that they would receive testimony of approval by a judge's verdict when brought into examination. Therefore, being filled with a prophetic spirit, he foretells our Savior and his incarnation and resurrection, as he says, *I know that my Redeemer lives, and in the last day I shall rise out of the earth.*

19:27 Whom I myself shall see.

Since he was afflicted by his present troubles, by the revelation of the Holy Spirit he recognizes that mysteries are coming later on, clearly to bring remuneration and consolation for his virtue. Thus, he says that he will see God clothed with the nature of his own flesh.[153] This very clearly concerns the mystery of the Lord's incarnation.[154] And this does not have in view a testimony to a lesser grace, because he so fully and openly declares his hope in the resurrection already at that time! *Whom I will see.* In this passage the Greek is far different.[155]

[151]Job 19:25-26 LXX.

[152]This presumably is another Greek version that does not match the Brenton version (Codex Vaticanus). Cf. John 2:19-22; 11:25-26; 12:32.

[153]The Vulgate of Job 19:26 reads, "And from my flesh I shall see God."

[154]Cf. John 1:14.

[155]The Brenton version of Job 19:25-27 (Codex Vaticanus) reads, "For I know that he is eternal who is about to deliver me, [and] to raise up upon the earth my skin that endures these [sufferings]: For these things have been accomplished to me of the Lord; which I am conscious of in myself, which mine eye has seen, and not another, but all have been fulfilled to me in [my] bosom."

19:28 Why then do you say now, Let us persecute him?

Since, therefore, in that judgment that I now already behold with the eyes of my mind, the faithfulness of one's works and statements is to be revealed, why do you want to claim obstinately by your statements that I am guilty? Why do you endeavor to affix guilt on me, which my conscience does not acknowledge?

19:29 Flee then from the face of the sword.

That is, by repentance and amendment prevent the wrath of the coming avenger's sentence of judgment.

[Chapter 20]

20:1-2 Then Zophar the Naamathite answered and said, Therefore various thoughts succeed one another in me.

Since saint Job said that he was justly complaining, if not of the kind of punishment but of the amount, Zophar tries to snatch even this from him in the speech of the respondent. Thus, he says that Job was enduring things less than his merits deserved. For indeed he says that he has reached this conclusion not from any prejudice or dislike but from a due weighing of both sides.[156] For among the excuses of Job, by which he said that he did not deserve such a great calamity, Zophar says that the umpire, as it were, established even the appearance of the things that Job suffered. And it seemed more correct to fasten sins on Job himself, not a charge of injustice on God.

20:3 The doctrine with which you reprove me, I will hear, and the spirit of my understanding shall answer for me.

Although the things that you allege move me in some measure—namely, when you say that the reckoning of punishments exceeds the measure of sin—nevertheless, by carefully considering that what the spirit's intention suggests is true, the defect is to be found in your merits rather than in God's justice.

20:4-5 This I know from the beginning, since man was placed on the earth, that the praise of the wicked is short, and the joy of the hypocrite but for a moment.

Not without reason he adds what is lighter to what is heavier—that is, when he recorded *hypocrite* after *wicked*—but [he said this] to touch him properly whom he thought always had the outward appearance of a holy man but with an awareness of guilt. *Praise of the wicked.* He has recorded *praise* for glory and honor. *And the joy of the hypocrite but for a moment.* If the censure of equity demanded this, that the prosperity of the wicked be short, it follows that adversities and griefs should be longer. You see, therefore, that your voice of complaint is not able to suit you, due to the very status of the judgments.

20:6-7 If his pride mount up even to heaven, and his head touch the clouds, in the end he shall be destroyed.

By a variety of comparisons he proceeds to show the fleeting glory of the wicked. "And those who had seen him shall say, Where is he?" A sudden change in conditions customarily causes a sense of wonder.

20:8 As a dream that flees away, he shall not be found.

This is similar to what the psalm says: "They have suddenly ceased to be, they have perished by reason of their iniquities, as the dream of them that awake."[157]

[156]Cf. Baxter, "Notes," 18.

[157]Ps 73:19-20.

20:9 The eye that had seen him shall not see.

It is not that the same person does not meet the eyes of those who see, but that the whole sphere of action has been changed by the introduction of the calamity. "Neither shall his place any more behold him." *Place* is recorded here not for a piece of ground or a building but for social standing and honor.

20:10 His children shall be oppressed with want, and his hands shall render him his sorrow.

Appropriate fruit will follow his works, and the wages will reveal the merit of the preceding action.

20:11 His bones shall be filled with the vices of his youth.

He did not say that the sins of youth are to be imputed to the old man, but he says that he so continuously practiced the vices to which a youth was accustomed that he dragged these things out all the way to old age. And as though he was not content with having indicated the final period of life, he adds, "And they shall sleep with him in the dust." It is as if he were saying, He reached the final end of life with intimate knowledge of disgraceful acts.

20:12 For when evil shall be sweet in his mouth, he will hide it under his tongue.

Since he had said *sweet,* he recorded *mouth* and *tongue,* which have the proper function of judging tastes. *For when evil shall be sweet in his mouth.* He was brought by the long practice of sinning to the point that no horror over the vices arose in him but delight. And zeal came along to keep him from losing out on any evil habit. *He will hide it.* That is, he carefully guards it.

20:13 He will spare it and not leave it.

He has referred to the affection of a lover. For we are accustomed to treat more mildly those things that we embrace with passionate love (*amore*). For he expressed this in the things he added:

20:14 His bread shall be turned in his belly, the gall of asps within.

As long as he was speaking about tastes, he linked the services of mouth and tongue. When he now comes, as it were, to dissolved food, he has fittingly found a place for the belly, where all food ordinarily is sent through the mouth and tongue. Now what he wanted to say is this: That which he had believed to be sweet, he will not only experience it as bitter but will find it even to be lethal.

20:15 The riches that he swallowed, he shall vomit up.

He has preserved the form of the comparison undertaken. Thus, what he had said was first taken in by the mouth, and was later sent to the belly, he added that it is to be vomited up.

20:16 He shall suck the head of asps, and the viper's tongue shall kill him.

The nature of its own works will be harmful to it, so that the venom derived from it becomes the cause of its death.

20:17 Let him not see the streams of the river, of the brook of honey and of butter.

After the invocation of so many evils, it does not seem for the sake of any increase that he added that he will not have an abundance of favorable conditions. Whence, lest that which the conclusion of the speech asked for seem forgotten, he has denied in an exchange of good things he will have an end of grievous things. *Let him not see the streams of the river.* The Greek has "May he not see his herds coming to the milk-pail."[158]

20:18 He shall be punished for all that he did and yet shall not be consumed.

He is not oblivious to the charge of his response. For since saint Job had pleaded about the excessiveness of his own sufferings, Zophar himself says that if he is enduring all these adversities that he has recounted, yet he suffers less than he deserves; that is, the punishment cannot be equated to or exhaust the merits of his faults.

20:19 Because he broke in and stripped the poor.

Lest the general nature of his statements not graze him whom no evidence of sins had convicted, Zophar tries to prove him already guilty and pernicious by specific cases. "He has violently taken away a house which he did not build." That is, he did not correct what he had done wrongly by a subsequent repentance.

20:20 And though he has the things he had coveted, he shall not be able to possess them.

When the vengeance that is owed takes away the enjoyment of sin.

20:21 There was nothing left of his meat, and therefore nothing shall continue of his goods.

Zophar wants to brand Job with the vice of avarice and say that his inhumanity was the reason for his poverty.

20:22 When he shall be filled, he shall be brought into straits.

He wanted what he said to provide proof of Job's great inhumanity, that the abundance of possessions, which often made him inebriated, brought to him the disposition of generosity and sharing. *When he shall be filled.* This is said with a change of the tense—that is, when he had been filled and by the ingestion of food had reached the point of a distended stomach and a bellyache.

20:23 May his belly be filled, that [God] may send forth the wrath of his indignation on him.

Here too, just as higher up, the disputant was moved, as it were, by the credibility of things and breaks out with the feelings of one wishing for something, with the orderly sequence plainly overturned. For when the examination of judgment has been removed, we approve of those things that we want to happen, whereas here he pursues them by his wishes, as if the consideration had already been weighed in the balance. "And rain down his war on him." The constant persistence of his scourging seems to imitate the concourse of raindrops. By the continuance of the evils, [God] never allows him peace, that is, rest.

20:24 He flees from weapons of iron and shall fall on a bow of brass.

The preceding evils are followed by others that are more severe.

20:25 [The sword] is drawn out, and comes forth from its scabbard, and glitters in its bitterness; they shall go and come upon him.

To increase the attack, he does not want the hostile persons to encounter him, but that the very weapons be taken up against him, and the

[158]Job 20:17 LXX.

grim things themselves and the hostile elements to rise up against him.

20:26 All darkness is hid in his sight.[159]

The darkness grows dim by its own spreading out in view of the space of atmosphere. It becomes heavier by the denseness and gathering. "Has devoured him." The Greek has "A fire that burns will devour."[160] "A fire that is not kindled." That is, continuous. It does not require the service of human beings for its maintenance.

20:27 The heavens shall reveal [betray or expose] his iniquity, and the earth shall rise up against him.

Each of these elements will experience rage in view of his offenses (*meritis*).

20:28 The offspring of his house shall be exposed.

Stripped for eradication.[161]

[Chapter 21]

21:1-2 Then Job answered and said, Hear, I beseech you, my words, and do penance.

Their arguments attempted to cause the possibility of Job being convicted as a guilty man. With two propositions they said, If you are innocent, he who afflicted you is unjust; but if he is just, you are proven completely guilty. He promises that he will expose these arguments with such ease that he would not merely compel them to silence but even to repent of their statements and opinions. *Hear, I beseech you, my words.* He is confident about the uprightness of his response, and demands patient ears from them, so that his speech received in silence may not merely shut out their contradicting voices but even compel the impeachment of their previously spoken statements. *And do penance.* He says not to Zophar alone but to all of them that they should receive his statements with attentive ears, since their verdict against him was equivalent and similar.

21:4 Is my debate against man, that I should not have just reason to be troubled?

Neither scorn for the injustice nor vengeance consoles the sensation of my pain. For if he who harasses me were inferior, I would not grieve but summon the magnanimity of soul. But the equivalent thought of storing up the injustice would have averted the sting of the pain. But now the just cause of my grievance presses down on me, since I am beset by him whom I admit stands forth prominently in the distance on a singular height.

21:5-6 Hearken to me and be astonished, and when I remember, I am very afraid.

Hard and excessive questioning was set forth at that time. He says not only that they must be filled with astonishment but even that they themselves endure a lot of fear and trepidation by reflecting on deep things. For even the present proofs testify to how much the Creator's providence or justice over human affairs is assailed: providence, when the affairs of mortals are reported to be uncertain and without governance; justice, when no diversity of merits is weighed in the movement of the scales. You said that all that happens has in view the judgment of God; how then are the opposing examples contested? And he added, "Why then do the wicked live?"[162]

[159]CCSL has *oculis* (lit. "eyes") whereas the standard Vulgate reading is *occultis*, "secret places." It is not clear if the CCSL is in error here. No textual variants are mentioned.

[160]Job 20:26 LXX.

[161]*Evulsio* occurs in Jer 12:17 Vulgate.

[162]Job 21:7.

21:7-8 Why then do the wicked live, and why are they advanced and strengthened with riches? Their seed will continue before them, a multitude of kinsmen, and of children's children in their sight.

Contrary to the thought of Zophar, who had said, "I know that the praise of the wicked is short, and the joy of the hypocrite but for a moment,"[163] he describes not only the many favorable circumstances in which the wicked abound but also that these conditions last for a long time.

21:9 Their houses are secure.

One should take note with what additions of successive things he is careful to augment the first things.

21:10-12 Their cattle have conceived and do not abort; their cow has calved and is not deprived of her offspring. Their children dance and play. They take the timbrel, and the harp, and rejoice at the sound of the organ.

He summarizes everything that characterizes their life that is not merely abundant but even joy-filled. It is full of affection and has much solace, heaps of gold and silver, fertile herds and flocks. And lest these things seem to have been reserved for rural custom, he added those things that the arts invented to soothe the ears or that urbane lewdness devised.

21:13 They spend their days in wealth, and in a moment they go down to the underworld.

A respondent could object, But those things that have been recounted will be altered by the succession of sad things. To answer this he has added that [the wicked] so enjoy constant delights that the swiftness of death banishes even the sad feelings that ordinarily arise from the imminent end of life.

[163]Job 20:5.

21:14-15 Who have said to God, Depart from us, Who is the Almighty, that we should serve him?

To convict the judgment of his fellow disputant he had set forth two things to himself to show that some are wicked and yet happy. Therefore, he fully described the portion of happiness through its outward forms; it remains to show the wickedness of the same men by open proofs.

21:16 Yet because their good things are not in their hand, may their counsel be far from me.

Since he had interpreted the prosperity of the wicked by a lengthier speech, lest he seem to approve it likewise by a judgment, he has revealed his own thought by the insertion of this statement: *Yet because their good things are not in their hand, may their counsel be far from me*. That is, since they boast over those things that chance can both give and take away,[164] I do not want to be associated with their wealth under such a judgment.

21:17-18 How often is the lamp of the wicked put out? They shall be as chaff before the face of the wind, and as ashes that the whirlwind shall scatter.

He sets forth as things that are harmful to his own case statements that agree with the sense of those men. For if we wish to understand this as said under the persona of saint Job, he will be found not to be refuting but agreeing with their judgment. Therefore, in order to continue in the course of the quarrel, he inserts things that he will make void.

[164]Cf. Job 1:21.

21:19 God has preserved the sorrow of a father for his children.

He himself proposes for himself what they could have said, as if he were to say, You will perhaps say this, even if the wicked man himself does not suffer any adversity per se, yet a vengeful reproach will rage against his posterity; therefore he added, "For what is it to him?"[165] That is, when by the intervention of death he is deprived of all sensation, he will not be struck by grief over the affliction of his children.

21:21 For what is it to him?

Up to this passage he has been interpreting the objections of his friends.

21:22 Shall anyone teach God knowledge, who judges those that are on high?

By the insertion of this single line, he has solved the question that had countered his own statements. For he seemed to have flung the charge of ignorance at God, if he who had sinned did not lay claim to it for himself but in someone else. Therefore, saint Job says that he knows indeed that knowledge of all things and complete knowledge are with God. Yet they who have said that all things are done by the judgment of justice are not able to prove rationally how these things are done. For indeed, even I confess that often there is vengeance against the wicked; yet it does not follow that wherever affliction exists, fault is also found. But by what rationale does God punish some of the wicked, but he allows others to go away unpunished? And why does he permit others to experience adversities though they have not sinned? It is not ours to know this. For he is the one who by the depth of his own wisdom can both refute the clever and who alone can have true judgment. When this line that he had inserted is removed, a contextually coherent meaning links the things below with the things above. *Who judges those that are on high.* Here one should understand *those that are on high* as the angels.

21:23-25 One man dies strong, healthy, rich and happy; but another dies in bitterness of soul without any riches.

In order to refute the thought of those men, who wanted to refer everything to the equity of the divine judgment, two cases are set forth, unequal both in respect to merits and outcomes, so that it may clearly appear that in the state of things in the present the justice that they were affirming is lame.

21:26 And yet they shall sleep together in the dust.

Though there may be a great divergence between the lives of the rich and the poor, yet a similar and equal end will overtake them both.

21:27 Surely I know your thoughts.

What you have said is exposed as false by the evidence of things that occur. But he has nicely recorded *I know,* in order to show that the reason he easily tore down what they had said is because he had understood it.

21:28-29 For you all say, Where are the tabernacles of the wicked? Ask any one of them that go by the way, and you shall perceive that he understands these same things.

He shows that it is a matter of no great wisdom, and one that could fall into the mouth of the common crowd, to bring a speech to a close by using a general accusation against vices and to accuse one whom he regards as guilty without naming any specific instances of sins.[166]

---

[165]Job 21:21.

[166]Cf. Job 21:30.

21:31 Who shall reprove his way to his face, and who has repaid him what he has done?

It is obvious and ready at hand to say that punishment awaits all the wicked and no sins can go unpunished. But the following is a matter that pertains to the repository of reason, to convict the one whom you are accusing by bringing facts out into the open without any verbal jeering.

21:32 He will be led to the tombs, and will watch in the heap of the dead.

[*He will watch*] for "he will be," since the one thing depends on the other, for no one *watches* unless he first *is*. For the sake of doing justice to the coherence of the context, he recorded *he shall watch* for "he will be." Here is another way: But since he is dead, would you perchance say that punishment has been exacted against him? From the same fact that is common to the good and the evil, all guilty persons cannot be convicted; for where that one went, many went before, and all will follow on the same journey.

21:33 He has been sweet to the gravel of Cocytus.

The Greek has "He has been sweet to the stones of the torrent." *He has been sweet to the gravel of Cocytus*. As if already long ago the lower world seems to have selected him as desired. Now he recorded the name *Cocytus* from the usage of common speech,[167] just as he followed the usage of those who call the names of the stars Arcturus, Orion, and Hyades.[168]

[167]Cocytus is a mythic river in the Lower World.

[168]Cf. Job 9:9; 38:31. Hyades refers to the seven stars in the head of Taurus, whose rising, which occurs in the month of May, was thought to betoken rain.

21:34 How then do you comfort me in vain, whereas your answer is shown to be repugnant to truth?

He accuses them by the witness of facts that they cannot prove him guilty concerning his sufferings. He says, Though many regard my life based on the judgment of the wicked, merits are not to be appraised based on outcomes. Therefore, it is clear that you profess yourselves to be my friends in appearance, but by your words you fill out the role of enemies. For you came to alleviate my miseries. Instead you make them far worse by your speeches.

[Chapter 22]

22:1 Then Eliphaz the Themanite answered and said.

Eliphaz saw that both his own verdict and that of his friends was taken apart by the response of saint Job. He discerns that he is unequal to the task of finding solutions to the things that had been set forth. So he takes refuge in the defense of prejudice and sets the greatness of the Creator in opposition to the question. It is as if he were to say, You have summoned the examples of facts and attempted to show that in marking down the merits of men as paid, justice did not hold fast to its own rights, and that the prosperity of the wicked was repugnant to the equity of judgments, as you have inferred by your great knowledge. To solve this objection, even if we could not produce any rational explanation, yet it is easy for God to show why he acted in such a way.

22:2 Can man be compared with God?

The cleverness of your argument has shown that the wicked prosper contrary to the dignity of the scale of justice, so that, as logical consistency would suggest, it would be understood that the morally upright are exposed to afflictions, and thus you are proven innocent when you are afflicted. If therefore you are not guilty at all, then the one who afflicted you is proven to be a doer of wrong. But by no argument could you tear this from me, for I do not believe that there is injustice in God's judgments. And he can render a rational account for his own works, by the greatness of his knowledge, something that I am incapable of doing.

22:3-4 What does it profit God if you be just? Will he reprove you out of fear?

We indeed are moved to every action by a twofold affection—namely, by hope or fear—while we either want something to profit us or we take precautions lest it do us harm. But God is estranged from each of these necessities. For he neither needs our goods nor is he helped by them. Nor is he ever frightened by evils; that is, he gains nothing from our devotion. Nor does an obstinate mind steal anything from him. What cause then has aroused him to destroy you, if not the excess of your iniquity?

22:6-7 For you have taken away the pledge of your brethren without cause.

Higher up saint Job had said that what could be sung by those that go by the way pertains to common speech, to wind up a case against the vices by a general oration, and fail to reveal the person's guilt by specific cases.[169] Therefore, Eliphaz now attempts to fasten these specific instances of sins on him, but he does so more by way of calumny than conviction. "Without cause you have stripped the naked of their clothing, [failed] to give water to the weary, and withdrawn bread from the hungry." He heaps up and augments these things that he has proposed in opposition, so that Job's character, which was not content with sinning moderately, might appear all the more abhorrent. For it seemed tolerable that *you have taken away the pledge of your brethren*, especially if the terms of some contract compelled this; but he adds *without cause*, so as to increase the wicked crime with which he was accusing him. Likewise, those other things he adds proceed to weigh him down with an abundance of accusations.

22:10 Therefore, you are surrounded with snares, and sudden fear troubles you.

He had said that [Job] had sinned not triflingly and as if from a lack of strength, but grandiosely and with great force. Therefore, he boldly asserts against him that he has been punished, so that the transgression and punishment appear to be paid out in the same moment. *And sudden fear* (formido) *troubles you*. Elsewhere it says, "fortitude (*fortitudo*)."

22:11 And did you think that you should not see darkness?

You also added this to the charge of your evil deeds, that you did not believe that revenge would follow. At any rate, if you had ever thought about it, it would have called you back from the dangerous path of your works or frightened you less by being already foreseen.

22:12-14 Do you not think that God is higher than heaven? And you say, What indeed does God know? And he judges, as it were, through a mist. The clouds are his covert, and he walks about the poles of heaven.

It is an indication of a sacrilegious mind to sin with such carefreeness that it does not believe that the witnessing eyes of the judge are moved by the things it is doing, and that the

[169]Cf. Job 21:29.

sharp-sightedness of the Knower is excluded from the knowledge of the facts through this inane means, and that it thinks that God cannot approach nearer, in view of the immensity of locations, and be present to all things as the arbiter of the facts. *And he walks about the poles of heaven.* The Greek has "And he walks about the circle of heaven."[170]

22:15 Do you desire to keep the path of ages, which wicked men have trodden?

That is, to enter down those same roads by which they walked who revealed the arrogance of their spirit at the beginning of the world by building the tower.[171] Here is another way. By such perversity of thought you are proven clearly to be willing to take up arms against God, and to imitate the giants who tried to climb into heaven by the stubbornness of their mind.[172]

22:16 Who were taken away before their time.

Their wicked ventures merited that the length of their life be cut short by the incited severity. "And a flood has overthrown their foundation." Since they were utterly wiped out by a deluge, he rightly says, *A flood has overthrown their foundation.*

22:17 Who said to God, Depart from us.

Not that he uttered these words of sacrilege with his tongue but that their works and wicked actions expressed this. For they were doing the sorts of things that seemed to be casting God out from themselves, and they thought that he could do nothing.[173]

22:18 Whereas he had filled their houses with good things.

The outpouring of his generosity nourished prosperity, prosperity fed their arrogance, arrogance led ultimately to sacrilege. Thus do blessings become the tinder of sinning for those who use them badly.

22:19 The just shall see, and shall rejoice, and the innocent shall laugh them to scorn.

When criminal actions are checked by punishment, the pursuit of virtues grows stronger and a joyful innocence pleads for its fruits.

22:20 Is not their exaltation cut down, and has not fire devoured the remnants of them?

He provides proof, as it were, of those things that he had said before. Thus, he says that those men of arrogance, of whom Job was an imitator, are not merely *cut down*, but they have even become extinct to posterity, since fire went after their roots.

22:21 Submit yourself then to him, and be at peace.

Leave off the brash voice of your complaints, he says, and hold in check the turmoil of your stomach and heart, so that when the waves of your thoughts subside, you can attain to the hope of salvation with repentance as your guide.

22:22 Receive the law from his mouth.

Be a hearer, be a disciple of that which has been divinely promulgated, whose judgment

170 Job 22:14 LXX.

171 Cf. Gen 11.4, 6.

172 Cf. Gen 6:4. The mythological reference (cf. L & S, *gigas*) would be to the fabled sons of Earth and Tartarus, giants with snakes for legs, who stormed the heavens but were smitten by Jupiter with lightning and buried under Mount Aetna. Cf. Ovid, *Met.* 1.152; 5.319; Horace, *Carm.* 2.19.22; Cicero, *De natura deorum* 2.28.70; Martial, 9.51.6; Vulgate: Sir 47:4; Num 13:34.

173 Cf. Job 22:17b.

this is, which seems clearly imprinted in these things, so that it crushes the proud and raises up and fosters the lowly.

22:23-24 If you will return to the Almighty, you shall be built up, and he shall give flint for earth, and torrents of gold for flint.

Since he had said previously, *you shall be built up*, fittingly he has promised that *flint* is to be given him *for earth*. On flint are made the foundations of a house that will not fall.[174] But in light of the abundance of all things, the flint, which is not advantageous for growing crops, is to be turned into *torrents of gold*.

22:25 And the Almighty shall be against your enemies, and silver shall be heaped together for you.

Not only will you be covered with divine protection, but you will even be given an abundance of all things.

22:26 Then you shall abound in delights in the Almighty.

The Almighty will provide you with such a reason for joyful delight, that whatever tastes sweet, smells pleasant, feels soft would seem to flow into your senses from him. "And you shall lift up your face to God." It is a testimony of confidence if no guilt turns one's face toward the ground.

22:28 You decree a thing, and it shall come to pass to you.

Things worthy of approval and just are vowed,[175] and they are allotted an easy, effectual achievement.

[174]Cf. Mt 7:24.
[175]Cf. Job 22:27.

22:30 The innocent shall be saved, but he shall be saved by the cleanness of his own hands.

Supported by penitence, you will be freed from guilt in such a way that you would appear never to have been in the wrong.

[Chapter 23]

23:1-2 Then Job answered, and said, Now also my words are in bitterness.

He had not been so battered by the speeches and arguments given earlier that he should be turned to bitterness over the curses of his friends, above and beyond the harshness of the pain. For a general indictment of vices had not dislodged anything from the dignity of his conscience. Therefore, he replies with less mental turmoil. But when he began to be indicted with specific criminal charges, he feels the goads of greater anger. And he says, Now plainly there is a just cause of sadness for me, not only in light of the bitterness of my wounds but also for the reproach of your insults. *Now also my words are in bitterness.* Now plainly I experience worse feelings of my pain; a deeper wound is pressed into me. Having laid aside all reverence, you open wide your mouths in open recriminations.

23:3 Who will grant me that I might know and find him, and come even to his throne?

Since they have thus conspired in falsehoods as testimony against me, equity alone can vindicate me from the attorney's reproaches. Therefore, that very tribunal of the judge is what I must seek by my prayers, so that when my complete case is brought into the open, I may shout out freely before him concerning my afflictions, inquire after a rational accounting for my miseries, and at least find out the reason when he responds.

23:5 That I might know the words that he would answer me.

Whether the witness of your false charge were to approach, or that of my conscience.

23:6-7 I do not want him to contend with me with much strength; let him propose equity against me.

As far as I know by the witness of my conscience, I see that these things that I suffer have to do with his power alone, not his justice. Therefore, I desire that the judge's knowledge be granted to me, since equity alone can cast a favorable vote for me.

23:8-9 If I go to the east, he does not appear; if to the west, I shall not understand him. If to the left, what would he do? I shall not take hold of him; if I turn myself to the right, I shall not see [him].

He had said, "Let him propose equity";[176] that is, let him make the moments of those debating equal. Let him not be inferior in advantages and overwhelmed. Let him first reckon that he is powerful against the one to whom the affair belongs, then that he is invisible, thirdly that he fills and contains every part of the world by his immensity. For by the names *east* and *west*, *right* and *left*, he wanted to indicate the four zones of the world.

23:10 But he knows my way and has tried me as gold that is tested through the fire.

He adds this to increase the disparity, that though I may not be able to see how great he is, he in truth knows me in such a way that nothing can be hidden from him, even of my works. For he has often cast me for examination like a lump of shining metal into the furnace.

[176]Job 23:7.

23:11 My foot has followed his steps.

The reproach of criminal acts wrenched from him a confession to his own praise, with a somewhat concealed sense of shame. He discloses his virtue in order to drive out the heap of vices [of which he had been accused].

23:12 I have not departed from the commandments of his lips.

He says that the *commandments of God's lips* is the power of reason stamped on his nature. It was able to teach human beings justice after the manner of the law, as the apostle also says: "For when the Gentiles who do not have the law do by nature the things which are of the law, though not having the law, they are the law to themselves."[177] "And the words of his mouth I have hid in my bosom." I have applied diligence of watchfulness to keep from slipping through negligence.

23:13 For he is alone, and whatsoever his soul desires, that he does.

He reveals the reason that makes him stick to the narrow paths of God without deflection from the tracks. This compels him carefully to keep his commandments. He says, I conceived with my mind this esteem for God, because he is the only one for whom this name [of God] is truly fitting. As for those who are called gods, he does not admit any of them into the company of his power. For everything is easy for God to do, and nobody can resist his power and will.

[177]Rom 2:14. Steinhauser, "Job Exegesis," 307, thinks that Julian's aim here is to "develop a theory of natural law based on reason whereby reason makes human nature totally self-sufficient in avoiding sin and doing good." If "self-sufficiency" is defined as personally and meritoriously culpable before God for good and evil works, I agree.

23:14 And when he shall have fulfilled his will in me, many other like things are also at hand with him.

He wants to show that his sufferings are proof of the divine power, and therefore he added that he could work *like things* with equal power.

23:15 And therefore I am troubled at his presence.

When I have recourse to my conscience and find nothing in it that is averse to the light, and I consider the proofs of his power, I am upset by the great ambivalence of the counsel, whether it discusses the whole matter to the best of their ability or feigns its own justice by some provision to suit the occasion.

23:16 God has softened my heart.

Whatever strength he had fostered in me by virtue of his patience has wasted away the whole of the scourge that I suffer and by the ignorance of counsel.

23:17 For I have not perished because of the darkness that hangs over [me], neither has the mist covered my face.

He has recourse to the testimony of his conscience, and confidently declares that the reasons for his outcome come not from the defilement of his works, which rejoiced in the light, once the thick darkness of night had flown away.

[Chapter 24]

24:1-2 Times are not hidden from the Almighty.

[Job] raises the same question he had discussed previously, but now with a profession of his faith. And moreover he says that he certainly knows that by marking down as paid the merits of human beings, justice will pursue the portions of his reproach; but, in the present, many things happen that seem to negate judgment. And by this continuous course of meaning all the way till the end of his speech (*eclogae*), he describes the crimes of the wicked. He says, *Times are not hidden from the Almighty*; that is, in his knowledge there dwells a full awareness of all our moments. It is as if he were to say, God does not disregard any time of our works, even as we change them constantly; yet we, who touch him with the devotion of our mind, do not know what days he weighs out for our examination by patient endurance, which days he weighs out for postponement.

24:2 Others removed the landmarks.

It must be noticed, in this reproof of vices, that they are reckoned either lighter or heavier according to how they are handled with respect to the virtue of the soul. Thus, saint Job and his friends are influenced differently; the friends only accuse the acts of inhumanity, whereas Job describes the crimes of iniquity, violence, robbery, lewdness, pride, and impiety. "They have taken away flocks by force, and fed them." He professes boldly that he sins who is bold enough to hide the bad things he does. The Greek has "They have carried off the flock with the shepherd."[178]

24:3 They have driven away the ass of the fatherless; they have taken away the widow's ox for a pledge.

His condition of being exposed to public commiseration, which in itself provoked a feeling of humanity in view of his abandonment (that is, the fatherless and the widow), this was unable to bridle the ferocity of their greed.

[178]Job 24:2 LXX.

24:4 They have overturned the way of the poor.

While nothing satisfies avarice, they increased their own wealth even by the meager income of the poor, which they sought by continuous effort from daily work for their own survival. Here is another way. When the cause of the poor had come into their judgment, the false charges that were raised drove out the appeals for justice.

24:5 Others like wild asses in the desert go forth to their work.

Two accusations are being made simultaneously (namely, of arrogance and robbery) because they are carried without bridles with a neck free from the yoke of common fairness through roads exposed to plundering. "And by watching for a prey they get bread for their children." He is careful to express the freedom of rapine by an example.

24:6 They reap the field that is not their own.

He runs through each form of evildoing that wickedness was accustomed to carry out.

24:7 They send people away naked.

He is more moderate than his friends, who through the anger of their mind were oblivious to a sensible reproach, and said, "You have despoiled the naked."[179]

24:8 Who are wet with the showers of the mountains, and having no covering embrace the stones.

He says, They are so in need of a hovel, due to the distress of their extreme poverty, and they are exposed to rainstorms, as the mountains, not roofs protect them from the rain. And on this account they are forced to take refuge either in caves or in rocks exposed to the winds. *Who are wet with the showers of the mountains.* This whole passage seems to have in view the example of the wild ass that was used in another exposition.[180] Thus, the acts of rapine of violent men are better understood using a description of a stupid wild beast. Thus, his words, *Who are wet with the showers of the mountains,* seems to be more fitting for wild asses.

24:10 From the naked and them that go without clothing and from the hungry they have taken away the ears of corn.

He diligently adds something that could increase the charge of wickedness.

24:11 They have taken their rest at noon among the stores of them.

One sins with the brow exposed when due to ingrained habit extending over a long time one does not fear the testimony of the evil work that is in those things. "Who after having trodden the winepresses suffer thirst." With these words he expresses avarice that does not know how to be satisfied and that always seeks other people's things.

24:12 Out of the cities they have made men to groan, and God does not suffer it to pass unavenged.

This is what we took note of higher up, that saint Job indeed admits that everything is to be brought before the divine examination, yet the form of judgment is not proven in the present. *Out of the cities they have made men to groan.* It pertains to a tyrannical rule to show no respect for locations and for wrong to exist instead of law.

[179]Job 22:6.

[180]Cf. Job 6:5; 11:12; 24:5.

24:13 They have been rebellious to the light, they have not known his ways.

Since it is a proper function of light to keep the tracks of travelers from going astray, he expressly calls those who continue going down perverse roads in this life *rebellious to the light*.

24:14 The murderer rises at the very break of day, he kills the needy and the poor man; but in the night he will be as a thief.

He has indicated two things: that he is not lazy when it comes to doing evil, and he allows no time to pass by without sinning.

24:15 The eye of the adulterer observes darkness, saying, No eye shall see me.

He has expressed what is quite common for the depraved, that they do not want to entrust to a witness the base things they do; or else, when they dash headfirst into wicked deeds, they are animated more by the hope of concealment.

24:16 He digs through houses in the dark, as in the day they had appointed for themselves.

He was not content with having hit on the custom of adulterers in words only, but he puts their deeds as well on display to increase the abhorrence, and he says that they are not afraid to break through the fortifications of houses in order to perpetrate crimes. "And they have not known the light." With eyes of shame dug out, they drive strangers from the light of moral integrity. *And they have not known the light*. Elsewhere it says, "By day they have sealed themselves";[181] that is, they have concealed themselves so that they were unknown, as are those who display the outward form of being honest but live as men of crime and as thieves.

24:17 If the dawn suddenly appear, they regard it as the shadow of death.

They hate that by which they know they are exposed, and they love that by which they think they can be veiled.

24:18 He is light on the face of the water; cursed be his portion.

The Greek has "He is light from the face of the water"; that is, like water he will easily slip by, so that he is unknown to all. *He is light upon the face of the water, cursed be his portion*. Out of horror for the crimes, he erupts into the words of a man cursing. He says, *He is light upon the face of the water*; that is, he is snatched away to destruction with such great ease that with the swiftness of one perishing he overcomes the waters that are borne straight downward. "Let him not walk by the way of the vineyards." By the term *vineyard*, he wants him to be driven out from the habitation of all land that is cultivated.

24:19 Let him pass from the snow waters to excessive heat, and his sin even to the underworld.

The expression is twisted around: as snow disappears and is melted into water by the heat, so he desires the vigor of the man to be dissolved whose evil deeds he described earlier in his speech.

24:20 Let mercy forget him.

Since he had said previously, "and his sin even to the underworld"[182]—that is, he is absolved by no intervention of pardon—he has well added, *Let mercy forget him*, so that it concerns not pardon but anger from the horror over his works. "May worms be his sweetness." Since the

[181]Job 24:16 LXX.

[182]Job 24:19.

fruit of works customarily influences the spirit of the one who exerts himself in his labor, may a delightfulness of flavor arise in this one too, in view of those things that he has carried out, of such a kind that would soothe his senses!

24:21 For he has fed the barren.

He is describing the vice of luxury and fornication, while he says that intercourse with a wife is sought after not for the sake of having more children. "And she who does not give birth, and to the widow he has done no good." The virtue of humanity could not touch the spirit of the libidinous man, since there is no fellowship between vices and virtues.

24:22 He has pulled down the strong by his might.

The following passage in the psalm is similar to this: "He will crouch and fall when he shall have power over the poor."[183] *The strong by his might.* The Greek has "the helpless." When he has effectually achieved what he wanted, he will tremble over the condition of mortal life. "And when he stands up, he does not believe in his life." When he will have prospered in his ventures, he does not believe that his life could fall into adversities by a turn of events.

24:23 God has given him room for repentance, and he abuses it in pride.

Since the punishment does not catch up to the sinner immediately, he is offered space and time for correction. When this time is spent increasing the criminal acts, the measure of just vengeance is compiled.

24:24 They are lifted up for a little while.

The brief prosperity of the wicked cannot bring them long-term security in their state. "And they shall be humbled as all things, and shall be taken away." That is, [as all things] which are like this: "And as the tops of the ears of corn they shall be broken." It is as if he were to say, The frailty inherent in the ear of grain is great in view of its slenderness.

24:25 But if it be not so, who can convince me that I have lied?

The pronouncement seems to be incomplete.[184] For after the hesitation the affirmation is not brought in so as to justly agree with what he had introduced. Therefore, it is recorded in the fashion of those who say, *But if it be not so*, or rather, since it is so, it is established that I have not lied. *But if it be not so, who can convince me?* He infers at the end what he had pleaded through the whole course of the speech, that those abandoning the testimony of works were not able to prove that he was guilty with respect to those miserable circumstances that had befallen him, inasmuch as it was an established fact that often in the present the wicked are not punished. "And set my words before God." The Greek has "And set my words as nothing."[185]

[Chapter 25]

25:1-2 Then Bildad the Shuhite answered and said, Power and terror are with him.

Bildad sees that Eliphaz's argument, whereby he wanted to prove that saint Job was guilty with respect to his sufferings, had been plainly refuted by holy Job's response, that there were many impious persons who did not suffer any adversity. Therefore, he departs from this style of argumentation, that he should say that the one whom he sees has fallen into harsh

[183] Ps 10:10.

[184] Baxter, "Notes," 48, says that *semiplenus* means "only half-finished, half-completed."

[185] Job 24:25 LXX.

circumstances of life is guilty, and he insists on the following aspect, in order to accuse Job. He preaches the divine *power*, and he says that Job sinned because he had dared call God to judgment. *Power and terror are with him.* Since Bildad is pressed by the force of reason, he is obliged to agree with saint Job's words. Thus, he leaves out the equity of judgment for the present and preaches the *power* of God. And since he cannot prove that Job is guilty, he tries to discount him by a comparison. But by this tactic he does not notice what this adjustment brings about, that he is actually apportioning Job great praise.[186] For it is a matter of supreme merit when a man is unable to be equated to the virtues of God! "Who makes peace in his high places." Who has wonderfully mingled the natures of the elements, which are not only various but even contrary, as they come together among themselves. Thus, hot things and cold, wet things and dry unite in one body of the world. *Who makes peace.* He wants to consider the proof of his *power*, which by an equal judgment of agreement is applied in his service from so many countless thousands of angels.

25:3 Is there any numbering of his soldiers? And on whom does his light not arise?

The throngs of his attendants attest to the greatness of the king and the benefits so diffused throughout the whole world that no one could be excluded from them.

25:4-5 Can man be justified when compared with God? Behold, even the moon does not shine.

On the verge of speaking about the changeable nature of the elements, he summoned the testimony of the moon, so that he could more easily prove what he wanted. For it is a unique quality of the moon that, when it waxes and wanes, it cannot hold to one state. "And the stars are not pure in his sight." Since a moonless night often obscures their twinkling.[187]

[Chapter 26]

26:1-2 Then Job answered and said, Whose helper are you?

Since Bildad had been overwhelmed by the reasoning of the argument and completely neglected the cast of his opponent, he betook himself to a summary of the divine praise, and thought that the estimation of God could be brought into danger, if saint Job proved himself innocent—for he who had inflicted the calamity appeared unjust, if the one who had received it were believed to be just. What is more, the reason he defended the justice of God by the legal defense of his own favor, holy Job says, was not the duty of a religious mind, to believe that God needs the aid of a human defense. *Whose helper are you,* "is it not of him that is weak?" The case seemed to have been conducted in divisions, as it were, so that they laid claim to the justice of God against saint Job, who had removed the suspicion of guilt from himself. Therefore, holy Job reproaches this. He says that this pertains not to the praise of God, but is an affront, if someone believes that God is aided by a person's own strength.

26:3 And you have shown your very great prudence.

So that you firmed up one who was wavering by the subtlety of your argumentation, and removed the part that was being pressed.

26:4 Whom did you desire to teach? Was it not him that made the things that breathe?

He divides the rational account of the rebuke into two parts, so that of the things he is about

[186]Cf. Job 14:4.

[187]Cf. Job 15:15.

to say, one seems to apply to his power, the other to his wisdom; that is, he who is powerful through himself does not need help from someone else, and he who is wise in himself is not helped by another's counsel. *Who made your breath.*[188] In order that there be no doubt about the secondary things, the primary things convince; for living is prior to being wise; but no one is wise unless he first lives; therefore, you owe your wisdom to him who bestowed life on you.

26:5-6 Behold, the giants groan under the waters. The underworld is naked before him.

After stating first the division that he made between power and wisdom, Job puts forward his evidence. Thus he says, Both the things that live in the depths of the sea, even if they are of tremendous bodily size (and for that reason he calls them *giants*, which we should understand as monstrous beasts) and even *the underworld* itself, which shuts out the sight of viewers by its dense gloom—[both these realms] either perceive his power or are ever exposed to his eyes. *Behold, giants groan under the waters.* The Greek has "Will the giants be delivered by a midwife under the waters, and in their neighbor?"[189] This bears the following meaning: Will the dead rise who are under the waters on earth? "They will be delivered by a midwife" means "rise," from the metaphor of women giving birth. The meaning is this: Just as the skill of midwives brings the child forth from the womb, so is it possible to call back the dead even from the underworld? Surely only God is capable of this. *The underworld is naked before him.* It is impossible, he says, to hold back those who have been brought to an end by death when God wants to raise them. For at his command alone it is forced to vomit up those whom it had swallowed. "There is no covering for destruction." Even though [the underworld] is covered by the thickness of darkness, nevertheless it appears transparently before the eyes of its Lord.

26:7 He stretched out the north (*aquilonem*).

He made the huge northern (*borealem*) region, which is uninhabitable and deserted on account of the excessive cold, just as on the other hand the southern region is inhospitable due to its excessive heat. "And hangs the earth upon nothing." The earth that has been commanded to uphold itself balanced in the middle clearly testifies to the power of its own Creator.

26:8 He binds up the waters in his clouds, so that they do not break out and fall down together.

Since the whole thing that he had said seemed to expect proof of his power, he now adds the means by which the power of wisdom could be known. For that which was to be for destruction, if it were to fall together on the earth, he subdued into discipline by certain chains, as it were, so that it was divided out and dispersed beneficially into soft raindrops.

26:9 He withholds the face of his throne, and spreads his cloud over it.

It was consistent that the things that he had created by his power, he held together by the duty of judge, and he imposed rudders on affairs, as it were, from the height of the tribunal. But the one who presides in carrying things out is removed from the sight and viewing of men by a great mystery.

[188]The LXX has "breath" (πνοή) here.
[189]Job 25:5 LXX.

[Chapter 27]

This commendation of his virtue that arose from his fear of God clearly is conducive to the removal of the suspicion of boasting and levity.

27:7 Let my enemy be as (*ut*) the ungodly, and my adversary as (*quasi*) the wicked one.

If I cannot be suddenly led away from the previously mentioned course of my training, so that I feel and declare contrary to the reliability of the facts, it is necessary that I call you unjust and *ungodly*, in whom I have denied that justice inheres. But the words he recorded, as (*ut*) and as (*quasi*), are those of one not wishing for this but pronouncing it.

27:8 For what is the hope of the hypocrite if through covetousness he take by violence?

The reproach of hypocrisy is branded into his friends with a general censure, because earlier they feigned both honesty and friendship, and later on they greedily seized on the opportunity to detract.

27:9-10 Will God hear his cry? Or can he delight himself in the Almighty?

He is describing in order the evils that await those who choose to feign rather than to do honest things. "And call on God at all times." He has nicely recorded *at all times*, for it pertains to a good conscience alone to stay composed amid the evils of tribulation concerning the protection of God.

27:11 I will teach you by the hand of God.

He says that he will hand down to them by his authoritative teaching the evils that are inflicted on hypocrites through the hand of God. And in order to show his certain knowledge of the things that he will hand down, he adds a heap of them on the side. He claims that they are not unaware of what he is going to relate. The Greek has "I will announce to you the things that are in the hand of God, the things that are with the Almighty, and I will not lie."

27:12 Behold, you all know it.

Since they themselves had said that they knew that "the praise of the wicked is short, and the joy of the hypocrite but for a moment."[190]

27:13 This is the portion of a wicked man.

This is said (not without stinging those who hear) as an invective with general application.

27:14 If his sons be multiplied, they shall be for the sword.

Although he touches on feigned friendships with a speech like this, nevertheless he defends the case of his own appraisal. Thus, he says he would not have been able to feign virtue, since he recognized such fruits of hypocrites.

27:15 They that shall remain of him, shall be buried in death, and his widows shall not weep.

The Greek has "And no one shall pity their widows." Here is another way. They will be so overwhelmed by the weight of evils, he says, that they would not even have power to shed tears.

27:16 If he shall heap together silver as earth, and prepare garments as clay?

The Greek has "gold" [in place of *garments*].

[190]Job 20:5.

27:17 He has prepared indeed, but the just man shall be clothed.

[In v. 16] he is posing a question, if what is said never comes to pass; but if it is ever established as having been fulfilled, then he is bringing a solution.

27:18 He has built his house as a moth, and as a keeper he has made a booth for the shade.

So that when all usefulness of things has been used up, traces remain as a sign of the calamity received. *He has built his house as a moth, and as a keeper he has made a booth for the shade.* When he showed the vain efforts of those who have pursued the shadows of the virtues without any solidity, doubtless he showed that he was estranged from such a pursuit.

27:19 The rich man when he shall sleep takes nothing with him.

The things that are one's own (namely, external wealth) are betrayed in the final end; for just as the goods of character go with us, so whatever was acquired as comforts and tools of the flesh remains behind.

27:20 Poverty like water takes hold of him.

In the manner of onrushing water, he will be overwhelmed beyond hope by the evils coming on him.

27:21 A wind shall carry him away.

Using a comparison to those things by which crops and sprouts are ruined, adversities are recounted by which the wicked are scourged. "And as a whirlwind shall snatch him from his place." Variously the evils are recounted that he will encounter who has cared only to pursue his reputation and not conscience.

27:22 And he shall cast on him, and shall not spare; out of his hand the one fleeing will flee.

Since he had shown that the one whom no virtue had armed is exposed to being wounded by the onrushing calamities, now he puts on the character of his attacker, as it were, from whose hand a javelin is borne and hurled so swiftly that it does not differ from the speed of the one fleeing.

27:23 He shall clasp his hands on him.

He has completed the comparison of one pursuing with a hostile spirit a man in flight.

[Chapter 28]

28:1 Silver has beginnings of its veins.

In order to link the things lower down with the things higher up, the meaning is as follows. Often, he says, God subjects the wicked to punishment and robs them of their goods and drives them out of their possession of property. However, he does not do this because he begrudges the wealth of the bad, for he is the one who at the beginning of creation mixed the substance of gold and silver into the veins of the earth for the future benefit and use of human beings. Hence, what he generously bestowed, he judiciously snatches from the wicked. *Silver has beginnings of its veins.* Since at the end of this speech he will speak of the goods of true wisdom,[191] now he recounts the services that seem to imitate it, and he says that what nature removed from sight is brought forth into public view by the hands of prudence. *Silver has beginnings of its veins.* This is all that saint Job pleads in the present speech (*ecloga*), in order to show that

[191]Cf. Job 28:28.

concerning the power of God he perceives things greater by far than his friends [had perceived]. For by the pursuit of divine knowledge he has been led to a concern for a better life, by which surely he is not able to be forced to mislead. And on account of this he says the things he feels concerning his friends. Second, he has learned to locate the good of man not in bodily happiness, nor in those things that pertain to the body, but in the mind and wisdom. Not in that wisdom which pays attention to providing for earthly things, which often brings forth into the light that which nature has concealed, but in that wisdom that instills the fear of God[192] and drives out the practice of vices.

28:2 Iron is taken out of the earth.

He provided some metals for beauty, others for cultivation or labor, that it might be adorned on the top and strengthened down below. "And stone melted with heat is turned into brass."

28:3 He has set a time for darkness.

He gave gifts of wisdom to mortals and reduced the alternation of day and night within limits. *He has set a time for darkness.* In order to promote the praise of the divine gifts, he marvels at how, when one substance meets human eyes, the force of reason still seeks another in it; that is, they think as necessary things not the earth that they dig up, or the mountains that they cut into, but that which the Creator mixed into them. And for greater wonder he adds, *He has set a time for darkness.* That is, he has distinguished day and night, so that during the day, with the light as a witness, the eyes could judge concerning the diversity of things, but with the onset of night one color drenches everything. To the gift of sight and light he joined that wise reason could penetrate hidden substances even lying in secret. "And he considers the end of all things." The Greek has "He considers the ends of times." Human work is divided out in view of the variations in the times. Thus, one concern stirs mortals during the winter, another during the spring, another in the summer, and something else in the fall. "The stone also that is in the dark and the shadow of death." He is saying, Even things that are devoid of reason know to some extent what we know by the instruction of nature—namely, to work during the day, to rest at night, to sow in winter, to harvest in summer. For they know what food to seek, what dangers to flee from. With no slip of memory, they seek a safe place to sleep in too. But only to the human being instructed by reason is it proper to know those things that are hidden or remote. Therefore, he recorded *stone in the dark* and *the shadow of death*, as if he were saying, Only the wisdom of man has tracked down and brought forth into the light those kinds of metals that are so hidden away and removed from sight that they are thought to have been thrust into hell. *Stone in the dark*. He recorded *stone* for the boundary by which the spaces and rights of property are customarily marked. The expression is obscure enough, but it suggests the following interpretation: since he had discussed the discovery of bronze and iron, he describes with what difficulty both were discovered, in order to increase in admiration. It is as if he were to say, From those things wisdom brought some usefulness into the open, things that seemed estranged from any suspicion of advantage. For bronze melted out of completely inert stone, but from wasteland and wilderness, and that which was tilled only by water and that which promised no nourishment for the use of the poor, the hand of reason dug out iron that was necessary for agriculture.

[192] Cf. Job 28:28.

28:4 The flood divides from the people that are on their journey, those whom the foot of the needy man has forgotten.

What wonder is it, he says, if he appointed certain times for day and night, when he marked off with a limit life itself and death, so that this light would not maintain complete control, nor greedy death steal everything? For indeed, the violently onrushing condition of mortality separates *from the people that are on their journey*—namely, from him who is still a sojourner of this earth—him who cannot help the hand of the needy from the law of death.

28:5-6 The land out of which bread grew in its place has been overturned with fire. The stones of it are the place of sapphires, and the clods of it are gold.

That which is called wisdom by the majority through sharing the name has exerted its talent in this direction, that it has even fathomed things placed underground, and eager for greater profits, it neglected the crops as it dug out gemstones and rich *clods* for *gold*.

28:7 The bird has not known the path.

Although they sail through the air by their flight and touch roads that are near heaven, yet they are unable to approach those by which wisdom travels. *The bird has not known the path*. The context of the exposition seems to demand that he is describing the effects and duties of wisdom, which he set out to describe, and he assigns to its duties that under its lead men approach those places in the hope of profit, which were previously remote from the access of mortals. And in his own way by using hyperbole he says that such desolate wastelands are approached by men that the places where the foot of man has entered are remote from birds and wild beasts themselves.

28:8 The children of the merchants have not trodden it.

Since he discusses this in order to show that men penetrate deserted places, why, on the other hand, does he deny that the desolate places are worn down by the feet of merchants? Hence, he seems to have shown the rarity of travelers and to have denied the frequent traffic of merchants. "Neither has the lioness passed by it." Neither birds nor creeping things nor four-footed creatures have known those things that reason has discovered by its rigorous investigation of secret things and by its keen sense of inquiry.

28:9 He has stretched forth his hand to the flint.

He searches carefully for unknown metals of marble and looks into the veins of the mountains diffused with various colors. "Neither has the lioness passed by it."[193] Of all the species of animals, none are gifted with reason except the human being. Though he bestowed greater bodily goods on others, so that one rejoices in his strength, another in his speed, another rises up with wings and flight, he honored man alone with the activity of reason.

28:10 And his eye has seen every precious thing.

[*Seen* means] caused to appear. Here is another way: *his eye has seen every precious thing*—that is, not only those things that were useful but also those that were fitting for adornment, such as clothes from wool, fabrics for the rich from the threads of the Persian worms,[194] wine from certain kinds of plants, ointments and other remedies from herbs.

[193]Job 28:8.
[194]This refers to silkworms.

28:11 The depths also of rivers he has searched.

His curious hand explores the unknown stones submerged in water. "And hidden things he has brought forth into the light." His reason spread knowledge about the previously unknown usefulness of things. In fact, since before humankind the elements subsisted alone, after he was created, the human being with the guidance of his reason came to understand what usefulness could be gained from each of them. He learned what kind of land was suitable for sowing seed, which kind was fit for transplanting, what benefit could be obtained from particular plants, which woods were useful to build ships, which were more suitable for buildings, and what kinds were made only for the fireplace to stoke fires. And in this manner by the vast diversities of things the prudence of man guided his genius so that they would be useful.

28:12 But where is wisdom to be found?

His talent exerted itself to make the usefulness of these things known. But the activity of reason alone by itself was unable fully to search out what our proper thoughts should be concerning the valuation of God. Here is another way. Let the name of wisdom make a mockery of the listeners. It had led the talents of men through the many arts and brought to light things previously unknown. Now by the preference for precious things he is commending that wisdom that is true and in which the good of man is located. Here is another way. After showing that man excelled the rest of the animals by far through his reason, he prefers the worship and knowledge of God to reason itself, to convince his own detractors that those animals have far better perceptions about God than those men do. *Where is wisdom to be found?* The Greek has "whence."

28:13 Man knows not the price thereof.

He goes back over each of the things by which he had described that with which wisdom is thought to have occupied itself, and he says that the functions of true wisdom could not be involved in the preparation or provision of such things, nor should its worth be associated with wealth or else with delights.

28:15 The finest gold shall not be given for it.

This passage is similar to the Proverbs of Solomon in which the worth of wisdom is preferred to everything that is reckoned great by human beings.[195]

28:16 It shall not be compared with the dyed colors of India.

If anything glows red with gold, sparkles with gemstones, blooms with colors, it is sought for the use and adornment of human beings. But in human beings, living precedes adornment. It is an established fact that wisdom by which life is *compared* is better by far than all the precious and beautiful things. *It shall not be compared.* He had described that the diligence of human beings, which seems to imitate wisdom, went through all those things. Thus, it sought for veins of silver in hidden away places, it condensed the sands of rivers into gold, it collected gemstones from watery depths. Therefore, he says that true wisdom, of which God is the teacher, is not found in these locations or pursuits.

28:18 High and eminent things shall not be mentioned in comparison of it.

He shows that not only amassed riches but also the heights of honors and the highest

[195]Cf. Prov 3:15; 8:11; 16:16; 17:24; 20:15; 21:20; 31:10.

peaks of official dignity become worthless in comparison with it. "Wisdom is drawn from what is hidden." Since in order to honor wisdom, he had depreciated all the things that entice the eyes, flatter the other senses, or make a mockery of our imaginations, he also vindicates [wisdom] from that injustice, in order that it may not appear to lie open to everybody; that is, it may not be reckoned to dwell in the pursuits and the functions of the common crowd.

28:19 The topaz of Ethiopia shall not be equal to it.

The Hebrews call *topaz* "smaragdon."

28:20 Whence, then, shall come wisdom, and where is the place of understanding?

By the form of a question, he extols its merit, lest as if set out in public view it become worthless by the very ease of those approaching it.

28:21 It is hidden from the eyes of all.

He advances to the peak of honor because it is not touched by human knowledge, nor is it found in hidden away places, but it is located only in the knowledge of God.

28:22 Destruction and death have said, With our ears we have heard the fame thereof.

For the wisdom by which one approaches the worship of divinity not only takes precedence over all the things that human diligence has sought for; it is even clear from this, that we find just ones devoted even to this wisdom that taught them to fear God, that he not only vindicated them from destruction or death but others as well. Thus, justly, as if it has no rights over them, it says that the fame of them has reached only to their ears. *Destruction and death have said.* Wisdom presides over this, through which we are instructed in the worship of the true religion, so that *destruction and death say* that we who are placed far from its jurisdiction are without knowledge.

28:23 God understands the way of it, and he knows the place.

He had said higher up through what means or where it could not be found. Therefore, so as to increase its worth, he has said by whom it has been found and by whose teaching it could be known.

28:24 For he beholds the ends of the world and all things.

Lest the difficulty of discovery that he had shown higher up by the grand ostentation of speech would be thought to hinder even God, he describes the immensity of his power, because it easily meets the eyes of one who considers all the exposed spaces of the earth in every place where the heaven extends.

28:25 Who made a weight for the winds.

Even another testimony is employed, so that the possibility of comprehending wisdom from God may be indicated. He is saying, He *who made a weight for the winds* found by his own subtlety that which had escaped the grasp of men. He weighs by a definite examination those things that among us are thought to be the lightest, as things weighed on scales, and he knows with such certainty the immensity of the waters, which exceed the reckoning of our calculation, so that he seems to have measured them. Here is another way. As proof of his providence that he wanted decreed for mortals, he joined together elements that were at odds with each other by established measures, in such a way that one would not be the destruction of another by its own larger part.

He made a weight for winds, lest everything collapse either from winds greater than was fitting or else they not bring help by weaker ones. "And he weighed the waters by measure." Either he brought into order those (waters) that were under the firmament,[196] so that they did not equally run down into the lower regions, or he gave them equal space by limiting their positions to those that are on the earth.

28:26 When he gave a law for the rain.

Since at the beginning of creation he formed by his own disposition a way to govern the world by means of changes in seasons and moderating air temperatures.

28:28 And he said to man, Behold, the fear of the Lord, that is wisdom.

His authority of his first command extends to the communion of the human race. For when he issued the injunction to abstain from the tree,[197] he was not begrudging the taste of fruit but seeking humanity's obedience.

[Chapter 29]

29:1 Job also added, taking up his parable.

One properly speaks of a *parable* when more is contained in the meaning than is declared in the words. Either the coherence of things means more than is on the surface or the understanding is completed by reason. For either the lengthy description of divine power or the commendation of wisdom that was briefly summarized discussed all this, so that by means of these things a testimony to saint Job's virtues could be offered.

29:2 Who will grant me, that I might be according to the months past, according to the days in which God kept me?

It is not that he does not know who could summon him back to the *past* prosperity, since he is certain that it could be granted even in the present by him who first bestowed it. Rather, he has introduced the speech of one who is wavering for the sake of affect and in the manner of one expressing his wishes. *Who will grant me, that I might be according to the months past?* He first says those things that have in view the divine generosity, and he lingers in unfolding God's acts of kindness toward himself and skillfully postpones saying anything about his own virtues so that, when he has published his own goods, you would understand that he has not lapsed into vain boasting but was forced [to say these things] by necessity. By this he shows that the reason he had developed such character in himself is that he had never thought meanly of God, as, for instance, his friends were assuming.

29:3-4 When his lamp shined over me. My head.

When I enjoyed such great prosperity that the gifts of heavenly grace were clearly reflected in me. "And I walked by his light in darkness. When God was secretly in my tabernacle." As far as the literal meaning[198] of the words is concerned, it seems to be contradictory. For how could he *walk in darkness* who was rejoicing in the splendor of light? But since he had actually said *lamp,* the use of which is necessary at night time, he responded to the occasion first mentioned, which had arisen from the term; or else he wanted that to be understood that he made evident in the subsequent verse, that he recorded *darkness* for *secretly.*

[196]Cf. Gen 1:7.
[197]Cf. Gen 2:16-17.

[198]For this sense of *superficies,* see Baxter, "Notes," 51.

29:5-6 When I washed my feet with butter. And my servants round about me.

He recounts everything that has in view commending his benefits. For to be crowded with the duties of servants and to overflow with wealth is not an indication of virtue proper but of the munificence of the generous donor.

29:7 When I went out to the gate of the city, and in the street they prepared me a chair?

He is proclaiming either past dignity or abundance of property, so that the change of state which followed may instill more pity.

29:8 The young men saw me, and hid themselves, and the old men rose up and stood.

This is both a testimony of reverence and of authority, that either the old men rise up or the young men leave (for whom customarily solemn maturity is something foreign).

29:9 The princes ceased to speak and laid the finger on their mouth.

Appointed silence and restricted speech, attentive ears and awestruck faces of those standing about attested to the merits of his very influential tongue.

29:11 The ear that heard [me] blessed me, and the eye that saw [me] gave witness to me.

The hearer was so influenced by the light of my thoughts and the grandness of my statements that he did not conceal his own judgment. For on the basis of their own experience even those to whom the reputation of my works had reached claimed that they had heard the truth.

29:12 Because I had delivered the poor man that cried out.

Lest he should seem to have proclaimed the gifts of his own genius while he charmingly winds up his speech, he added the reason why the throng of those standing about him imagined that you knew that what was praised pertained not to eloquence but to justice.

29:13 The blessing of him that was about to perish came upon me.

He said *him that was about to perish,* not him whom perdition awaited based on his merits, but one who was beset by danger unless protection came to his aid. "I comforted the heart of the widow." He either promised her the comforts that she would have reaped from the provision of a husband or he prevented her from being treated unjustly since she seemed especially exposed to this by her condition.

29:14 I was clad with justice, and it clothed me like a robe.

In order to show that he has been greatly concerned for justice, he nicely sought for an example from the robes in which we go around. He says, As the body needs constant covering and is impatient of its own nakedness, so an intimate sense of justice was ingrained with deep affection in my actions. "And my justice was a diadem." Not only have I put justice around myself like clothing but I have even taken such delight in its charm that I thought of wearing an ornament and a sign of royal authority on my head.

29:15 I was an eye to the blind.

On account of the linking of subjects, this seems to apply both to the aspect of mercy and justice, because in the discussion of doubtful things and in the ferreting out of hidden things, he often discovered those things that those whose business it was did not see. For he adds:

29:16 And the cause that I knew not, I searched out most diligently.

Lest I be deceived by the first look at the unexamined business.

29:17 I broke the jaws of the wicked man.

A concern for justice was preeminent so that I did not listen negligently to those things that were called to my examination; my authority allowed me to punish with very great severity what I had ascertained was true.

29:18 And I said, I shall die in my nest, and as a palm tree I shall multiply my days.

I thought that the fruits of justice were such that it bestowed on those who cultivated it not only prosperity but even long life.

29:19 My root is opened beside the waters.

By various comparisons he shows that he believed that he had to be given favorable circumstances.

29:20 My glory shall always be renewed.

The condition and state of my life will allow no impairing of the help[199] of justice.

29:21-23 They that heard me waited for my sentence. They waited for me as for rain.

They hung on my words, not trusting in their own sentiments and judgment, and what I sanctioned was wondrously approved by the consent of all; and so great was the uprightness of my statements that it roused not merely the pursuits of the listeners but also affectionate feelings of goodwill toward me. Whence this is not a repetition of the things above, but something new, so that the former seems to have in view his authority, the latter his prestige.

29:24 If at any time I laughed on them, they did not believe.

His solemnness was so mingled with good cheer that he met not with dread over his excessive gloominess, nor scorn concerning his paltry permissiveness.

29:25 And though I sat as a king with an army standing about, yet I was a comforter of them that mourned.

The honor conferred on me and the ardent obedience about me did not strip me of my feelings of humanity, but I remembered that I too was human, whenever a cause for tears occurred.

[Chapter 30]

30:1 But now the younger in time scorn me.

These words testify to the authority, prestige, and power of his former life, as he has proclaimed. For to the extent that the state of his former happiness had been more pleasant, so much the more bitter now it makes his feelings of pain after things turned into the opposite. "Whose fathers I would not have deigned to set with the dogs of my flock." This provides evidence of extreme poverty, through which also the vileness of his condition is shown, not only the fact that he lives on charity but also that he is appointed to offer shepherd's care of the food of dogs.

30:2 The strength of whose hands was to me as nothing.

By these words he takes care to show the outstanding nature of his previous life and the

[199]For *suffragium* in the sense of *auxilium*, see Baxter, "Notes," 50.

degree to which there was no vice of pride in the midst of his own state and theirs. "And they were thought unworthy of life itself." He did not come to this by the vice of arrogance or by the elation and haughtiness of pride, but for the sake of the extreme condition of persons and abject worthlessness.

30:3 Who brayed in the wilderness.

By the sound of a confused voice they were indicating the abundance of their distresses.

30:4 And they ate grass and the bark of trees.

The impoverished life of lowly persons is being described all the more keenly so that he may make headway in reaching the peak of griefs in disrespect of such persons.

30:5 Who snatched up these things out of the valleys, when they ran with a cry.

He is emphatically describing poverty as well as burning and violent hunger, in which nothing was left.

30:6 They dwelt in the desert places.

That is, they were stripped of the comforts of both food and shelter.

30:7 They pleased themselves among these kinds of things.

It is as if he were to say, By withdrawing from the society of human beings, they lived like wild beasts.

30:8 The children of fools, and not appearing on the earth.

By this addition he has revealed how he wanted the things stated earlier to be understood.

30:9 Now I am turned into their song.

It is common among men to sing with a melodious voice the collapse of a certain state and the change of things for the worse. The following is like this: "They that sat in the gate carried on against me, and they that drank wine made me their song."[200] *Now I am turned into their song.* Up to this point a lengthy description both of his prosperity and of an external disaster was advancing in order to increase the causes of his grief by the comparison of the portions.

30:10 They abhor me and are not afraid to spit in my face.

Just as fearing contact is a sign of great horror, so daring to spit is a sign of great scorn.

30:11 For he has opened his quiver and has afflicted me.

That which is despised, which is mocked, which is spit at, he says that he endures, because he is shaken by the attack of a higher hand. It is as if he were to say, The reason such great things are allowed against me even as most contemptible things is because I have been brought into these miseries with God standing in opposition. The following words of the Lord are like this: "You would have no power over me except it were given to you from above."[201] "And he put a bridle into my mouth." Lest as one gravely doomed I should invite a milder sentence.

30:12 My calamities [are] at the right hand of my rising.

The Greek has "of my offspring." Since by the term *quiver* he had said that God was armed

[200]Ps 69:12.
[201]Jn 19:11.

for his own destruction, he completes the comparison taken up and indicates what sort of arrows he shoots with his upraised right hand, saying, "My calamities forthwith arose." He maintains the figure of an attacker even in the rest and says that his companions have been soldiers in the assault and fight against him.

30:15 I am brought to nothing; as a wind you have taken away my desire.

When those things have dispersed, which either used to or were capable of inciting my feelings in themselves—that is, when I have been deprived of both comforts and services—I came to realize that there was no hope left to me by which I could be supported. "And my welfare (*salus*) passed away like a cloud." He said that his *welfare passed away*—not his life—which was placed in the comforts of home and bodily health.

30:16 And now my soul fades within myself, and the days of affliction possess me.

Not without reason did he say *possess*, but this was to show that nothing within him was free from the sensation of pain.

30:17 In the night my bone is pierced with sorrows, and they that feed on me do not sleep.

My tormenters do not allow a respite either in the change of time or by exhibiting satisfaction.

30:18 With the multitude of them my garment is consumed.

When there is not sufficient flesh to eat, eager vermin consume clothing as well.

30:19 I am compared to dirt, and am likened to embers and ashes.

Since he had said that he was wrapped with a multitude of vermin, as with a tunic, fittingly from the source from which so many bubble forth, he compared himself to dirt, which is customarily found in sewers and on buried corpses.

30:20 I shall cry to you, and you have not heard me; I stand up, and you do not regard me.

You refuse to show me any feelings of mercy, so long as you do not hear my appeal and do not turn your eye toward my sufferings.

30:21-22 You are changed to be cruel toward me. You have lifted me up and set me, as it were, on the wind, and you have mightily dashed me.

I see not only that you have shared no help with me, but I sense that you are in reality a violent attacker as well; for I have been raised up higher in order that I should fall more heavily. Now he said this using the metaphor of wrestlers.

30:23-24 I know that you will deliver me to death, where a house is appointed for every one that lives. But yet you do not stretch forth your hand to their consumption; and if they shall fall down, you will save.

He seemed to have removed all differences in merits when he said, *Where a house is appointed for every one that lives*. Therefore, he gives attention to this: although the just and the sinner equally are liable to the laws of death, yet he who has pleased you will not be led into everlasting destruction. For after the collapse of his body, he will be restored unto life.

30:25 I wept once for him that was afflicted.

Previously he discussed the pursuit of justice.[202] Now he brings into view the affection of great mercy that was in him. *I wept once*. The grand

[202]Cf. Job 29:17-20.

pursuit of piety is revealed in him; for if, as he himself says, he "broke the jaws of the wicked man, and out of his teeth I took away the prey,"[203] what reason for tears did he have when he saw that someone was afflicted? But the former passage had in view the function of authority, the latter that of mercy. Justice was carried out in the former passage; the bowels of compassion were struck by the latter.

30:26 I expected good things, and evils came upon me.

I thought that equal, not opposite fruit would answer to the things above.

30:27 My inner parts have boiled without any rest.

By repeated interruptions he reveals how sparing he is and embarrassed to proclaim his own virtues. For when his praises have been briefly touched on, he tarries in narrating his griefs.

30:28 Without indignation I rose up and cried out in the crowd.

The greatness of pain compelled me to burst out in public wailing, and I cried out as if out of my mind; with a sound state of mind I discussed the matter of indignation. He cried out:

30:29 I was the brother of dragons.

The Greek has "I was the brother of sirens and a companion of sparrows." "And companion of ostriches." It is normal for those suffering from poor health to believe that an alleviation of pain comes to them by frequent changes of environment. Therefore, he says this using the metaphor of *dragons* and *ostriches*, because when the evils stirred themselves up, he pursued wastelands and deserts.

30:30 My skin has become black on me, and my bones are dried up with heat.

It was consistent that one who lived in the desert and was defended by no protection of a roof would burn in the blazing rays of the sun.

30:31 My harp is turned to mourning.

All delight, which was usually applied to soothe the senses, has been driven out by the onset of grief.

[Chapter 31]

31:1 I made a covenant with my eyes, that I would not so much as think on a virgin.

The understanding is well linked with the previous verse.[204] Not even at the time, he says, when the sweetness of the harp soothed my ears did I allow any lustful feeling to dwell in my heart, even though the sound of lute-playing artfully affected my senses. *I have made a covenant with my eyes.* After the pursuit of justice and the feeling of mercy, the virtue of chastity is made public. And since it was beneficial to his posterity to imitate that which the confession of the saintly man announced about himself, he points out that he carefully avoided, as a great evil, the vice of sexual impurity, and he tarries at length in extirpating the evil that is familiar to human beings.

31:2-3 Is not destruction to the wicked?

He was not satisfied with saying that by sexual impurity he would be rendered unworthy of being indwelt by God, but he added that *destruction* would await him, who had polluted himself by unlawful sexual intercourse. "For what part should God from above have in me?"

[203]Job 29:17.

[204]Cf. Job 30:31.

Therefore, "I made a covenant with my eyes,"[205] since I believed that God was always present as a witness to my actions.

31:5 If I have walked in vanity.

This also is said about the same pursuit of virtue.

31:6 Let him weigh me in a just balance.

He proceeds to speak about his great awareness of virtue, that if he is summoned to judgment, he will possess it in reality, no less than his profession shows.

31:7 If my step has turned out of the way.

He says not merely that he did not fall into the precipice of sexual impurity but that he walked along the prescribed footpaths of moral integrity without stumbling and that he held firm to the right tracks. "And if my heart followed my eyes." Watchful concern for chastity so held me in my post that if the influence of some beautiful form passing by caught my eyes for a look, I was not led astray into base desire by any willful act.

31:8 Let me sow and let another eat.

Odious luxury attests how it will be respecting the pursuit of the affection of chastity; for he would never have pleaded this for himself so earnestly if he considered this vice trivial and esteemed it lightly.

31:9 If my heart has been deceived over a woman.

He quite often tarries by repeating the same things since he wants to create a remedy for this disease, which is familiar to human beings.

31:10 Let my wife be the harlot of another.

He is armed against sin by the bitter thought of adultery, so that the dread of the accursed thing may lead to caution.

31:11 For this is a heinous crime.

He proceeds to weigh down heavily on what he wants to be carefully on guard against, and from the fruits of the works he discourages the works themselves. He shows the merit of the thing to those whom he wants to avoid punishment.

31:12-13 It is a fire that devours even to destruction. If I have despised abiding judgment with my manservant.

After first mentioning his virtues of justice, mercy, and chastity, he adds another—namely, the virtue of moderation. For he would not have defended himself against the expostulations of petty servants with the master's authority but by satisfying reason.

31:14 For what shall I do when God shall rise to judge?

Before the sentence of the Judge, the guilt of my own conscience would have overwhelmed me, if in the appraisal of things I had followed the differences of conditions, not the merits of the cases, and if fairness rather than persons had not moved me.

31:15 Did not he that made me in the womb make him also?

Why would diverse merits create a prejudice over a name if one creator's hand made both?

31:16 If I have denied to the poor what they desired.

In order that it might not appear that by treating his servants humanely he did not

[205]Job 31:1.

practice a real liberality but was only taking care of his property, he says that he extended the hand of mercy and kindness to strangers as well. Here is another way. One who does not wait to satisfy the desires of the needy gives without delay. "And I have made the eyes of the widow wait." The caring affection of one who is merciful offers of his own accord what he thinks must be asked of him.

31:17 If I have eaten my morsel alone.

Not only does he say that he worked outside with a bountiful hand, but, what pertains to greater kindness, he says that he invited to share his table those whose condition exposed them to injury by the powerful and to robbery.

31:18 For from my infancy mercy grew up with me.

In order to show his constant and sufficiently personal pursuit of kindness, he said that the virtue of humanity was ingrained in him.

31:19 If I have despised him that was passing by for want of clothing, and the poor man that had no covering.

He says that he always focused his sight on doing good even in chance encounters with poor people, and his heart was impacted by the afflictions of strangers.

31:20 If his sides have not blessed me.

Even with their tongue being silent, those bodily members that his acts of blessing reached are said to have burst into speech.

31:21 If I have lifted up my hand against the fatherless.

Since previously he confessed that which is more, when he said, "If I have eaten my morsel alone, and the fatherless has not eaten thereof,"[206] how is it that he seems to add to the pile of virtue that which is less? Clearly such praise of this virtue is increased from its continuation, because he always practiced it in such a way that no intermission ever occurred. *If I have lifted it up against the fatherless.* Lest he seem to have done his works of mercy not from his own property but from things he had pillaged from others, which even his friends indeed raise as an objection to him,[207] he nicely adds, *If I have lifted up my hand against the fatherless.* That is, I have not brought to another what someone else received from me.

31:22 Let my shoulder fall from its joint.

Since he first mentioned his virtues, just as so grave an imprecation records the truth, so it removes from them the suspicion of fickleness.

31:23 For I have always feared God as waves swelling over me.

He gives the reasons why such a fertile crop of virtues sprang up within him—namely, because a very great fear of God, and one of the sort that the comparison indicates, cultivated the soil of his heart.

31:24 If I have thought gold my strength.

He could not place any support or delight in external and perishable goods, however grand they may have been, he who possessed his own private wealth of soul that was vast. The lord of great treasure[208] thought little of lesser things.

31:26-27 If I beheld the sun when it shined, and the moon advancing in brightness, and I have kissed my hand with my mouth.

206 Job 31:17.
207 Cf. Job 22:6-7.
208 Cf. Job 31:25.

I was not so moved by the beauty and splendor of the stars that I believed them to be gods and devoted any worship and veneration to them. In this it should be noted that he not only strove after good morals but also held fast to right thoughts concerning religion.

31:28 Which is a very great iniquity?

To believe that created things are gods is an injustice to the Creator, and to want to place that which has been made ahead of the Maker, this is not pardonable ignorance but punishable wickedness.[209] A person plainly denies God who does not confess the one who is true and alone.

31:29 If I have been glad at the downfall of him that hated me.

How far removed he is from the pursuit of doing harm. He even experiences some grief at the evils that afflict his own enemy! A person is incapable of wounding who necessarily feels pain over the one who has been wounded.

31:30 For I have not given my mouth to sin by wishing a curse to his soul.

From the same virtue he came to restrain his tongue from cursing, from which [tongue] the seriousness of his character and the proper training of his senses had proceeded.

31:31 If the men of my tabernacle have not said, Who will give us of his flesh that we may be filled?

The extent of his love and the ardor of his passion is more often indicated in these words. But he wants to say that he presented himself as common and dear to his household, so that he roused everyone's most ardent affections for himself.

[209]Cf. Rom 1:18-21.

31:32 The stranger did not remain outside.

That which was recorded in the first place among the great virtues that he had recounted seemed inadequate. He heaped up more by an addition when he said, "My door was open to the traveler." That is, The gate of my hospitality received not only those whom either previous acquaintance or dignity had recommended but all whom the necessity of traveling had brought [to me].

31:33 If as a man I have hid my sin.

A sensitive brow and a foolish sense of shame did not obstruct me from making public that which I had done perversely, nor from blotting out my evil deeds by confession.

31:34 If I have been afraid at a multitude, and the contempt of kinsmen has terrified me.

The title of my office was not of such great worth to me that I was afraid to cast it down if confession of sin rendered me more vile before the people. Nor since blame stripped of honor thrust me out among neighbors, therefore I chose the concealment of silence rather than concern for publicity. "And I have not rather held my peace." Just as I repressed my voice from protecting things done wrongly, so I condemned myself by keeping the secret.

31:35 Who would grant me a hearer, that the Almighty may hear my desire?

He had been forced to admit his virtues, both by the accusations of his friends and by his pious esteem for God; that is to say, his virtues had proceeded from the fear of God. Therefore, he now desires to add the testimony of the sentence of the Judge in support of his words, so that, when God declares that he had spoken the truth, none of his opponents would be able to deny it.[210]

31:38-40 If my land cry against me, and with it the furrows thereof mourn, if I have eaten the fruits thereof without money, let thistles grow up to me instead of wheat.

He has indicated at the end of the third line what he intends to be understood by these two verses—namely, that he never oppressed his laborers by an unjust quota of work or cheated those whom he had hired out of their agreed-on wage.

[Chapter 32]

32:1 So these three men ceased to answer Job.

32:2 Because he said he was just before God.

By the recounting of his own virtues he had claimed for himself the calculation of justice, as if the portions of his life and suffering had been weighed in the balance.

32:4 So Elihu waited while Job was speaking.

Elihu does not so much rail at the virtues of saint Job as feel annoyance that he could be given preference by God when he is placed under examination.

32:6 Then Elihu the son of Barachel the Buzite answered and said, I am younger in time, and you [all] are more ancient; therefore, I was afraid to show you my opinion.

When Elihu sees that the three friends took refuge in silence from the failure of their responses, he says that he indeed held fast to the discipline of silence for the sake of the reckoning of age; but since the speech of elders yielded to Job's arguments, he is no longer able to be silent. Yet he is convicted about tracing the tracks of their thoughts through the same paths that the friends previously had worn down.

32:8 But, as I see, there is a spirit in men, and the inspiration of the Almighty gives understanding.

The gift of being wise does not pertain to the law of bodies if it is granted to each by the divine generosity.

32:9 They that are aged are not (supply in thought, "the only") wise men, neither do the elderly (supply "alone") understand judgment, lest he seem to have reputed to youths alone what he denied to the others.

32:10 Therefore I will speak: I also will show you my knowledge.

32:13 Lest you should say, We have found wisdom, God has cast him down, not man.

Since your speech ceased, you were not able to reply to those things that were said; therefore, you should believe that this summary could support you, so that you say, What we were trying to show by arguments is proven by the judgment of God—namely, that he is guilty of transgression. In fact, the divine punishment would not have had any rights against him had it not found an evil work in him.

32:14 He has spoken nothing to me, and I will [not] answer him according to your words.

I was not involved in the debate with him, as you know, nor did he provoke me to bitterness after adopting the aim of speaking against me. Therefore, the words that I bring forth are not inspired by indignation but by the mind's reason.

[210]Cf. Job 42:7-8.

32:15-17 They were afraid and answered no more. I also will answer my part.

Their silence is a taunt, because having been vanquished by the power of his statements, they would have chosen to be better if they were silent.

32:18 For I am full of matter to speak of.

That is, it is time for me to say some things, for there are many things that I could set in opposition to his statements.

32:19 And my belly is as new wine.

He shows that he endured the flood of their thoughts when they were speaking, and he had discovered many things, which, as it seemed to him, could be said wisely and suitably.

32:21 I will not accept the person of man, and I will not level God with man.

He says that he is forced into the necessity of speaking by the honor of God, lest because he is silent it should seem that Job ceased, as his friend had done, and was granted favor.

32:22 For I know not how long I shall continue, and after a while my Maker may take me away.

Therefore, it is not expedient for me to keep silent about an injury to God, lest the final end of life may find me in sin.

[Chapter 33]

33:3 My words are from my simple heart.

In confirmation of those things that he is about to say, he says that he is not impelled by the goads of anyone's sin but by the rationale of truth.

33:4-5 The spirit of God made me. If you can, answer me.

He believes that with the aid of a comparison he can do something effective against saint Job. He says, If you cannot answer me, I who am a thing created by God, know that you will be much less able to answer to God, who is the Maker of all things.

33:7 But yet let not my wonder terrify you, and let not my eloquence be burdensome to you.

The parts of the reply I seized on, after the elders were exposed, this is what ought not seem so wonderful to you that you too are *terrified. But yet let not my wonder terrify you.* The Greek has "My fear shall not disturb you, neither shall my hand be heavy on you." Here is another way. He has expressed the reason for his indignation openly, because Job wants to challenge God to judgment. And in the argument against his friends, holy Job had said, "Let him take his rod away from me, and let not his fear terrify me. I will speak, and will not fear."[211] It is as if he were fleeing for the sake of this judgment alone. For higher up nature remained against him, although he had just claims in view of the testimony of his works, which excluded every voice of opposition. Therefore, Elihu warns him and says, Behold you have what you wanted, your argument will be against an equal, whose authority does not overwhelm you, nor does terror compel you to silence.

33:8-10 Because he has found complaints against me.

As he *found complaints against me,* so "he has counted me for his enemy." Now you said in my hearing, and I have heard the voice of

[211]Job 9:34-35.

[your] words, since *he has found complaints against me*, therefore *he has counted me for his enemy*. This is what saint Job had said earlier: "And you want to consume me for the sins of my youth."[212] Therefore, [Elihu] refutes this as a curse—that is, because saint Job had not soundly believed that no faults could be found in him from his mature age, but believed that he was being punished severely in himself for the errors of his youth.

33:12 I will answer you, that God is greater than man.

If you see for yourself that this has to be admitted even by those who are ungrateful, doubtless you will agree that God is superior to all things. Therefore, since he is also the first in justice and wisdom, he should not appear to have done anything in such a way that may incur your brand mark of reproof.

33:14 God speaks once.

To ratify a verdict but not to repeat it, this pertains to God's authority, to the gravity of his constancy.

33:15-16 By a dream in a vision by night, when deep sleep falls on men, and they are sleeping in their beds, then he opens the ears of men, and by teaching them he instructs discipline.

From Elihu's words it appears that saint Job came before the time of the law. For he would never have said that God warns men by dreams and nocturnal images, or that he instructs concerning fleeing from errors or seeking virtue, if he had already conferred the teaching authority of the good life in written form.

[212]Job 13:26.

33:19 He rebukes also by sorrow in the bed.

By many and various ways[213] he shows that God displays concern for human beings, when he says he not only stands by those who are sleeping, and shows them what needs to be done, but even chastises all those who have gone astray by the scourges of illnesses and diseases. Now this statement seems to be directed properly at Job himself.

33:23-24 If there shall be an angel speaking for him, one among like ones (*similibus*),[214] he shall have mercy on him.

The affection of mercy is shown to be ready at hand in God, so that any suspicion of injustice and savageness and deformity of character is far removed from him. For he says that if in a man who is struck by adverse health, some single good is brought by his angel as by his intercessor, God is immediately ready to pardon and he takes it well when he has found something to be sparing towards.

33:27 He shall look on men, and shall say, I have sinned.

By these words it is shown what benefit comes from a chastisement and the forgiveness that follows of one already acquitted and placed at rest. For the greatness of sins becomes known at that time when the free soul sees them clearly after danger.

33:29 Behold, all these things God works three times within every one.

We should understand *three times* either as "in many ways" or, if we cling to the number recorded, we say that God's providence is present to mortals at the beginning before they sin; then, when they begin to withdraw from natural simplicity by the imitation of evils, the

[213]Cf. Heb 1:1.

[214]The online Vulgate reads *millibus* (thousands).

concern of the admonisher is present; after this, if love of transgression continues, the bitterness of scourges is applied.

33:32 But if you have anything to say, answer me, speak.

If you can defend your person against my objections or endure the weight of my statements by the strength of your reply.

[Chapter 34]

34:1-4 And Elihu continued his discourse and said this: Let us choose to us judgment.

Whether it is appropriate for us to accuse God or Job.

34:5 For Job has said, I am just.

The affirmation of his virtues and the introduction of punishments are at odds with each other. If the affirmation of his virtues is true, the introduction of the punishments is unjust. If the chastisement was just, his boasting about his virtues was false.

34:6 For in judging me there is a lie.

For I am not being examined according to the rules of fairness; I experience fruits that are in opposition to my works. "My arrow is violent without any sin." He has added something on his own that indeed seems similar to the statements of saint Job, yet it is not the same, so that the changes in the wording become the occasion for a just rebuke.

34:7 What man is there like Job, who drinks up scorning like water?

He reproves God's judgments and despises them, and he thinks that they must be considered worthless.

34:8 Who goes in company with them that work iniquity.

By thinking ill of the judgments of God, he does not differ at all from those who are proven to be impious by the injustice of their actions.

34:12 For in very deed God has not condemned without cause.

The thought of each is similar, either in view of the apportioning to men or in view of the rational reckoning of the times. For what Elihu asserts happens to many in the present, saint Job says that this is to be carried out universally in the future.

34:10-11 Therefore, ye men of understanding, hear me. Far from God be wickedness. For he will repay a man for his work.

According to the rules of the debate, both sides might quite easily be speaking falsely in their general pronouncements rather than speaking the truth. Therefore, here, since they are speaking against each other, the pronouncement of both is nonetheless proven to be true. For both what Elihu says cannot be completely proved by holy Job to be false; and what Job asserts cannot be proven to be untrue. For God is shown to *repay* according to *a man's work*, if not in everyone, yet in many; and Job is convicted by the testimony that God does not *repay*. Therefore, it is evident that what both say is partly true. According to Elihu, [God] does not repay everybody; according to Job, he has not repaid many.

34:13 What other has he appointed over the earth?

By proclaiming God's kindness, he wants to commend his justice by saying, If he is so kind to human beings that he delivered over the world and the things that are in the world to the service of man,[215] how shall he not maintain justice with respect to man himself?

34:14 If his heart speak (*dixerit*)[216] to him, he shall draw his spirit and breath unto himself.

Since his kindness shuts out any suspicion of wickedness, and his power attests that nothing obstructs what he wants to do—for if he makes known a judgment against someone to bring about his death, the destruction of the condemned man will not delay—how is it that you complain about his violence and injustice?

34:17 Can he heal one who does not love judgment?

To summon back to health by means of chastisements one who is astray, this pertains to one who does not want sins to increase by the hope of impunity. But to be unwilling to permit vices to go unpunished, this is what it means to *love judgment*. Therefore, the causes of healing have regard for the vigor of judgment. "And how do you so far condemn him that is just?" He proposes this examination of judgment, lest he believed to be unjust.

34:18 Who says to the king, Apostate, who calls rulers ungodly.

So much so does the concern for justice abide with him that he does not hesitate to brand a sinner with the mark of reproach, though he be lofty in dignity.

34:19 For all are the work of his hands.

He shows the reasons why he applies equal scales of judgments among people of disparate conditions.

[215]Cf. Gen 1:28-30.

[216]The online Vulgate has *direxerit*, "turn" or "direct."

34:20 They shall suddenly die.

Doubtless those whom the name of his power was not able to protect from harm. "And they shall pass and take away the violent without hand." That is, when egregious wickedness is consumed by its partisans. *Without hand*, without work or effort.

34:23 For it is no longer in the power of man to enter into judgment with God.

Since he has once and for all been doomed to punishment, he will not be able to appeal, as it were, for a milder verdict.

34:24 He shall break in pieces many and shall make others to stand in their stead.

The former out of severity, the latter out of goodness. For it pertains to providence to substitute others in place of those whom punishment has removed.

34:25 He shall bring night on them, and they shall be destroyed.

This is the face and appearance of severity.

34:26 He has struck them, as being wicked, in open sight.

In open sight God struck those who sinned intentionally and, as it were, with an applied zeal, so that their death would lead to the correction of the rest.

34:27-28 Who, as it were, on purpose have revolted from him, so that they caused the cry of the needy to come to him, and the voice of the poor.

Those who spurned all the ways of God, while they oppress and ravage the *needy, caused their cry* to strike the stars.

34:29 For when he granted peace, who is there that can condemn? When he hides his countenance, who is there that can behold him?

He has recorded two contrary things, that just as no one's vileness can be prejudicial to those who delight in God's appeasement, so, when he turns his countenance away and covers it, as it were, no one will have any prosperity.

34:30 Who makes a man that is a hypocrite to reign for the sins of the people.

He is replying to an implied question: If he so pleads the cause of the poor that he holds in check the acts of violence of tyrants by death, why does he allow either similar or else worse men to come to power? Therefore, they cause the faults of their subjects, so that the iniquity of those who preside seems to contradict providence and deny justice.

34:31 Since, therefore, I have spoken for God.

That is, if what I have said could vindicate the estimation of God from the injustice of evil opinion.

34:32 If I have erred, teach me.

If by asserting his justice I have wrongly inferred all these things, that he who is kind, powerful, a defender of the poor, could not fail to be just, you, by rejecting everything, are asserting that he rejoices in iniquity.

34:33 Does God require it of you, because it displeased you?

Supply in thought: justice.

34:34 Let men of understanding speak to me.

It seems that, as his friends, in view of the silence that they have exhibited in themselves, approve and ascribe to their praise the fact that they have welcomed without contradiction those statements that were made by him, so holy Job praises himself for what he has found repose in with his words and thoughts.

34:36 My father, let Job be tried even to the end.

Lest you should desire to lessen the rebuke of your severity by a milder sentence. *My father, let him be tried.* He is addressing God.

34:37 Let him be tied fast in the meantime among us, and then let him provoke God to judgment with his speeches.

Then he will rightly be able to question God if he first convinces us.

[Chapter 35]

35:1-2 Therefore, Elihu spoke again these words: Does your thought seem right to you, that you should say, I am more just than God?

The apostrophe[217] made to him intends that he examine himself, putting down his zeal a little bit, as to what he obtained by his whole disputation.

35:3 For he said, That which is right does not please you.

Elihu says that saint Job had a wrong opinion about God, and these words are gathered from his reflections, because God is rightly offended by deeds, and Job recounted the errors of others in the heap of his own honor. "What will it profit you if I sin?" This is clearer

[217]An apostrophe is a rhetorical figure, when the speaker turns from the judges or his hearers, and addresses some other person or thing. Cf. Quintilian, 9.2.38; 9.3.24.

elsewhere: "What advantage did I get from not sinning?"[218] That is, What else would I have suffered because of the iniquity of my morals if I received such misfortunes after my pursuit of virtue?

35:4 Therefore, I will answer your words, and your friends with you.

Since your friends are shown to agree with you in thinking wrongly about the judgments of God by the fact that they oppose you with no contradictions, so that by this you seem to be just, but God appears unjust, therefore I will take care to answer in order to oppose you and them.

35:5 Look up to heaven and behold the sky.

The very immensity of the infinite separation can show you that God can neither be injured by your evil deeds nor helped by your good deeds. *Look up to heaven and behold.* By the testimony of divine providence he wants to call his ventures into fault, because he had said that he wanted to come as an equal into judgment with God, whose supremacy he strives to prove from the testimony of his works and benefits.

35:6-8 If you sin, how will you hurt him? And if you act justly, what will you give him? Your wickedness will hurt a man that is like you, and your justice will help the son of man.

Even the nature of your works will not advance any further in either direction than earning the affection and offense of the judge; moreover, neither advantage nor loss will be introduced into his reality.

[218]This may be an alternative Greek version. It does not match the Brenton (Vaticanus) text.

35:9 By reason of the multitude of false accusers they shall cry out and shall wail for the violence of the arm of tyrants.

He had said that his justice could help them; now he shows that it is time to bring help. When men burst out into a voice of wailing, he says, *by reason of the multitude of false accusers. They shall cry out and shall wail.* So much so is God not in need of human offerings and gifts that when all inferiors are harassed by the violence and rapine of superiors, they ask God to avenge.

35:10 And he has not said, Where is God?

This is either the voice of one inflicting violence or the voice of one enduring violence. *And he has not said: Where is the God* "who made me?" He had spoken of the one whom they called on to avenge those whom the power of the wealthy was accustomed to join to their houses violently. Therefore, now he expresses the feeling of those very violent ones, who do not fear the judgments of God. "Who has given songs in the night?" Having made a partial beginning, he revisits the general description of providence, so that he says that God generally wants to be consulted by men, he who separates one time of night for rest, another time for work and labor. *Who has given songs in the night.* That is, He mingled the time of night with the pleasure of sleep.

35:11 Who teaches us more than the beasts.

Who gifted us beyond the other living creatures with understanding and reason, and made us capable of instruction.

35:12 There they shall cry, and he will not hear.

He recorded *there* in keeping with the custom of Scripture, as the reason, not the location. It is as if he were to say, For this reason *they shall cry. There they shall cry, and he will not hear.* For this reason, *he will not hear* the violent and the arrogant who are placed among evils, since he previously took in the cry of the afflicted with an attentive ear.

35:13-14 Therefore, the Almighty will look into the causes of every one. Yea, when you shall say, He considers not, be judged before him, and expect him.

Even if he postpones your complaints by some delay, exhibit patience and wait for his judgments.

35:15 For he does not now bring on his fury.

For now is said for "not at once."

35:16 Therefore, Job has opened his mouth in vain.

That is, He has spoken such things about God unbecomingly. "And he multiplies words without knowledge." He is saying, Failing to understand how great the difference is between God and men, he has made use of verbose and disordered speech.

[Chapter 36]

36:1-2 Elihu also proceeded, and said this: Suffer me a little.

The author of the book, while distributing the chapters of the speeches to us, connects the words that follow to the beginning. Since he had made his hearers attentive by discussing the providence of God, he also asks their patience for the things that he is about to add.

36:5 God does not cast away the mighty, though he himself also is mighty.

[By *mighty* he means] the innocent. Here is another way: he does not have reasons for jealousy that would corrupt with envy the virtue of his own judgment.

36:6 But he does not save the wicked.

This has in view the duty of justice.

36:7 He places kings on the throne forever.

First he excluded the suspicion of jealousy from him, now he excludes the vice of fickleness. For if this was his sentence when he placed a man on the highest summit of dignity, that if he did not disfigure the merit in himself, he would not change his judgment, you cannot accuse him of fickleness. *And he places kings on the throne.* He added another reason for which he claimed the side of justice—namely, that he has conferred the very kingdoms. Therefore, he is not vexed by his very own gifts, so that he judges wrongly.

36:8-10 And if they shall be in chains, and be bound with the cords of poverty, he shall show them their works; he also shall open their ear to correct them.

If those whom he set on royal thrones change their status due to merits, not even then will he cast away care for them; for he will encourage correction by means of admonition. Or else this should be understood by changing the time, that is, before they come *into the chains* and are *bound with the cords of poverty,* he pins the merits of their works on them, in order that they be corrected.

36:13 Dissemblers and crafty men provoke the wrath of God; neither shall they cry when they are bound.

Overwhelmed by a bad conscience, they will not have the confidence to cry out; or else those on the verge of crying out are denied because there will be no effect to the cry.

36:14 Their souls shall die in a storm, and their life among the effeminate.

He had said, "God does not cast away the mighty."[219] Therefore, he has said well that this one who by his own contempt kindles the avenger's anger against himself *shall die among the effeminate*; that is, he will be stripped of all strength by the misfortunes that will happen to them.

36:15 He shall deliver the poor out of his distress and shall open his ear in affliction.

Through the voices of the facts themselves he will teach them that he has not forgotten the cry of the poor.

36:16 Therefore, he shall save you at large out of the narrow mouth, which has no foundation under it.

It is as if he were to say, Out of hell, whose mouth is said to widen in order to receive people indeed by a huge gaping hole, but those who are to be sent forth are constrained by the narrowness into a tight spot. For in order to show its great void, he adds, *which has no foundation under it*—that is, because the depth of it stretched on without measure with no bottom to be reached. "But there will be rest at your table." It is logically coherent that one who is delivered from misfortunes by God's aid, with his grace generously granting this, will likewise be gifted with prosperity.

36:17 Your cause has been judged as that of the wicked; cause and judgment you shall receive.

Since the appearance of things deceive, you have endured prejudgments about merit, but whatever was thought to be lost will be restored to you completely.

[219]Job 36:5.

36:18 Therefore, let not anger overcome you to oppress anyone; neither let a multitude of gifts turn you aside.

You too then, imitate the form of your judge. When you make presumptions about things that are doubtful, let neither anger nor influence steer you away from the love of truth. Or else thus: since this hope awaits you, that you receive the cause and judgment, you ought not want to oppress the side of God, having been led into bitterness by the present circumstances; that is, you ought not think wrongly about his judgments, and you should believe that providence is present in affairs, not merely in prosperity, when you abound in his gifts.

36:19 Lay down your greatness without tribulation, and all the mighty of strength.

From the link to what is above, a twofold meaning occurs. For either since he had promised to restore his state when he said, "cause and judgment you shall receive," he is persuading him to accept without resentment the loss of his power that came to him for a time, and to teach others too to think that way who are placed in the same situation, or else let him bear it without annoyance that God has cast him down from the step of his greatness.

36:20 Do not prolong the night, that people may come up for them.

That is, do not kindle the anger of the avenger against yourself by your complaints, and though you perish, others will be substituted in your place.

36:21 Beware you turn not aside to iniquity.

That you should want to accuse the judgments of God. For unto this you have stumbled by the bitterness and offense of your mind.

36:22 Behold, God is on high, and none is like him among the lawgivers.

He calls *lawgivers* those who in different countries have established human institutions by which the assembled peoples can be ruled.

36:23 Who can search out his ways?

The very ignorance of *his ways* (that is, of his works) does not permit anyone to lay claim to confidence about his judging.

36:24 Concerning which men have sung.

Referring to all the saints who foretold things while filled with the Spirit.

36:25 Every one beholds him afar off.

Since they are unable to approach nearer leading to full knowledge.

36:26 Behold, God is great, exceeding our knowledge.

If he is great in his nature, he is also great in his wisdom and great likewise in justice. Therefore, he cannot be summoned under the censure of our judgment.

36:27-28 He lifts up the drops of rain and will pour out showers like floods that flow from the clouds.

He is inferring the providence and power of God by the things that he can point to.

36:31 For by these he judges peoples.

While he either makes lands barren with drought or fertile by the outpouring of rain.

36:32 In his hands he hides the light.

He is not saying this about the alternation of day and night but about the sign of his power, that it is just as easy for God to take away the services of all light as it is easy to cover the scantiest thing by blocking it with his hand.

36:33 He announces to his friend concerning it, that it is his possession and that he may come up to it.

Though he may somewhat be wise beyond the earth, about what could be numbered among the profits, he shows that he nevertheless does not perceive enough great things when he reckons that only the possession of light is to be given to the friends of God.

[Chapter 37]

37:1 At this my heart trembles and is moved out of its place.

So that it does not stand still in the vigor of his thoughts.

37:2 Hear ye attentively the terror of his voice, and the sound that comes out of his mouth.

Sound that comes out of his mouth refers to thunder.

37:3 His light is on the ends of the earth.

His light refers to his eyes.

37:4 And shall not be found out when his voice shall be heard.

He so wants to remove the justice of his judgments from comprehension that many of his works and dispensations escape the power of human recognition.

37:6 He commands the snow to go down on the earth.

This stands as a proof of his providence, to regulate the earth for human use by changing the weather.

37:7 He seals up the hand of all men, that every one may know his works.

By the gift of reason he has caused men to know which times correspond with his diverse works.

37:8 The beast shall go into his covert.

And this has in view the laws of his creation, that beasts know when they need to roam, when to lie concealed.

37:9 Out of the inner parts a tempest comes.

That is, from the north.[220]

37:10 When God blows, there comes frost, and again the waters are poured out abundantly.

The diversity of divine activity is summoned so that the knowledge of his justice may be removed.

37:11 The clouds spread their light.

He recorded *light* for the rains, which are desired by the farmer in the manner of light.

37:12 Which go round about, whithersoever the will of him that governs them shall lead.

This agrees with the following words of the prophet: "I rained on one city and did not send rain on another. One part was rained on, and the part on which I did not send rain withered."[221] Surely by this he shows not that they are fortuitous but that they follow the will of the one in command.

37:13 Whether in one tribe, or in his own land, he shall command them to be found.

He recorded *in one tribe* for "in one region."

37:15 Do you know when God commanded the rains, to show his light of his clouds?

He had said this obscurely earlier.[222] Here he caused it to be understood openly, that by *light of his clouds* he was referring to the rains.

37:16 Do you know the paths of the clouds?

By all these things he is trying to show the effects of providence, which undoubtedly he is commending by a lengthy speech in support of the divine justice.

37:18 You perhaps made the heavens with him, which are most strong, as if they were of molten brass?

Since he had made mention of the air, therefore he said *molten*, not that the clouds are *molten* but because it is proper to air to be dissolved and poured into another form and use.

37:20 Who shall tell him the things I speak? Even if a man shall speak, he shall be swallowed up.

As his own wish, he wants to reach the knowledge of God. It is as if he were to say, Who makes known to him the intention of my words, which I apply to unfolding his praises?

[220] *Septemtrione*, referring to the seven stars near the North Pole belonging to the Great Bear (Big Dipper).

[221] Amos 4:7.

[222] Cf. Job 37:11.

But why do I say that I praise him? Though I publish great things in his honor, they will be found to be so scanty that they could be *swallowed up* by the waves of his praises.

37:21 But now they see not the light: the air on a sudden is thickened into clouds; and the wind shall pass and drive them away.

He has made clear by the added words how it is that *they do not see light*, when he says, *The air on a sudden is thickened into clouds*. For when the clouds have condensed and the air grown dark, the brightness of the sun is shut out, which is again recalled for the use of mortals by the driving away of the clouds.

37:22 Gold comes out of the north.

The Septuagint has "From the north [come] clouds of golden color, in these is the great glory and honor of the Almighty." *Gold comes out of the north*. He said *north* for east, and *gold* for dawn, which imitates the appearance of the shining metal with its reddish color. "And to God praise with fear." For the service of praising him is not undertaken without fear because of the immensity of his public fame.

[Chapter 38]

38:1-2 Then the Lord answered Job and said, Who is this that wraps up sentences in unskillful words?

Elihu had been roused by no bitterness of mind when he approached the disputation, but was merely inflamed by the outspokenness of the complaints, and he thought of checking saint Job by the reasoning of his reply. He alleged that God—who had so much power, so much goodness, whose care for the human race he disclosed by his creation and governance of creatures—allowed for no movement leading to the injury of justice, as if he had been motivated by hatred. But he had brought forth certain things less worthily, either in respect to the honor of God or in the defense of his providence. Therefore, God reproaches him merely for *lack of skill*, not for maliciousness as well, as those three friends had been who impudently and mendaciously engaged against the past life of saint Job.

38:3 Gird up your loins like a man; I will ask you, and you answer me.

After Elihu is reproached for lack of skill,[223] not for maliciousness, because when maintaining the justice of God he had produced things inferior to what the subject demanded, the Lord's speech is directed to Job himself, and he is shown to have been given satisfaction for his request. For he had said, "Who will grant me that I might know and find him, and come even to his throne? I would set judgment before him."[224] In a logically coherent way, then, it is said to him, What you wanted is fulfilled. Behold, I am here; stand ready with your complaints with perseverance.

38:4 Where were you when I laid up the foundations of the earth?

I prepared this earth to be your possession and in service to you. *Where were you when I laid up the foundations of the earth?* The suspicion of evil intent is excluded by the proof of infinite goodness. For if God's kindness toward humanity is proven to be so great that before human beings even existed so much was prepared for their use and service, how is it all of a sudden that they are abandoned and despised? Therefore, God recounts each thing by which he shows that his care for humanity existed, even before he was formed, so that Job may understand by many proofs of facts, which

[223]Cf. Job 38:2.
[224]Job 23:3-4.

speak of God's kindness toward men, that he could not be robbed of God's providence.

38:5-6 Who laid the measures thereof? Or who stretched the line on it? On what are its bases grounded? Or who laid the cornerstone thereof?

By the terms *measure, line, base,* and *cornerstone,* he shows that he made all things with reason, so that saint Job may understand, if those things that were made for his sake have come into existence by the application of consideration, his Creator's concern for him had never completely failed.

38:7 When the morning stars praised me together, and all the sons of God made a joyful melody?

Some think that what saint Moses overlooked among the beginnings of creatures, (namely, When were the angels made?) is indicated here in the reference of his Lord, who not only says that the angels were present at the beginning of his works but even nicely testified to their good works.

38:8 Who shut up the sea with doors, when it broke forth as issuing out of the womb?

Since he says that he made new elements and things that had no previous existence, he has splendidly adopted the metaphor of birth and offspring.

38:9 When I made a cloud the garment thereof.

That is, I poured out the atmosphere over it. The following passage is similar: "And the Spirit of God was being borne over the waters."[225]

[225]Gen 1:2.

38:10 I set my bounds around it.

This too has in view that reason by which I wanted to exercise foresight for man, lest what I had made marvelously in view of its greatness should prove fatal to the farmer, if it were permitted to rush forth freely.

38:12 Did you since your birth command the morning and show the dawning of the day its place?

This too testifies to the great proofs of my kindness toward man. For I have permitted those things that I created to be administered not by his solicitude, which indeed would not have been equal to the great things, but I commanded them to obey the laws of my providence to the point that while it preserves the appointed bounds in its rising and setting, there would occur for you a pleasing alternation of labor and rest.

38:13 And did you hold the extremities of the earth, shaking them, and have you shaken the ungodly out of it?

He attests not merely that he exerted himself to bring benefits to mankind, but even ordained that he would set out to correct their customs. He is referring to the fear of future judgment in which there will be such a destruction of the *ungodly* that they are said to have been *shaken out of the earth.* This has to do with a denial of rest. Whence it is significant that he added the time when this would take place—namely, when the clay of the body dissolves in view of the condition imposed on it, and it will be restored to its original form.

38:14 The seal shall be restored as clay.

The Septuagint has "Or did you take clay of the ground and form a living creature, and set it famously on the earth?" *The seal shall be restored as clay,* "and it shall stand as a garment." It is well said that we will have a body like a garment in the resurrection,[226] since no concern for maintenance will touch us when our frailty has been laid aside.

38:16-18 Have you entered into the depths of the sea and walked in the lowest parts of the deep?

He wanted the things that he added to be relevant as an indication of the time when the ungodly are to be shaken out of the earth,[227] and he spoke briefly concerning the restoration of bodies. Therefore, he adds another indication of the last time, and he unlocks the mystery of the Lord's incarnation. For he *entered into the depths of the sea, and walked in the lowest parts of the deep.* In order to make his obscure statement a little clearer, he added, "Have the gates of death been opened to you, and have you seen the darksome doors?" The added line requires that *the deep* be understood here in view of hell's immense capaciousness.

38:18-19 Tell me where is the way where light dwells, and where is the place of darkness?

He says what he had said before but more clearly—that is, that the course of human life is regulated by the alternation of times, so that at one time people dedicate themselves to work; in another time, the body's strength is returned to them, which exhaustion had taken away.

38:21 Did you know then that you would be born?

These words are not said without purpose, but prove that God's goodness is the cause of everything. If you owe the fact that you exist to my kindness, he says, since you did not exist before, how can you think that you are estranged from this kindness, now that you live and are able to function?

38:22-23 Have you entered into the storehouses of the snow, or have you beheld the treasures of the hail, which I prepared for the time of the enemy?

He had previously mentioned things that testified to his kindness toward men. Therefore, lest he should show himself to be merely generous and not also severe, and it should thereby be believed that he could be scorned with impunity, he has of necessity added things through which he could inspire terror. For ordinarily he punishes the rebellious by these same things by which he pays back the upright.[228]

38:24-25 By what way is the light spread and heat divided on the earth? Who gave a course to the very violent showers, and a way for noisy thunder?

He says that the change of day and night, heat and cold, clear skies and rain pertain to his providence, by which he wanted to be thought of by men.

38:26 That it should rain on the earth without man in the wilderness, where no mortal dwells.

From regard not only for human beings but also for wild animals, he says that the earth is both shaken by thunder and irrigated by rains for fecundity.

38:28 Who is the father of rain, or who begot the drops of dew?

He shows that everything by which the world is made fruitful or is ruled has in view the

[226]Cf. 2 Cor 5:1-4.
[227]Cf. Job 38:13.
[228]Cf. Wisd 11:16.

principles of his good disposition. That is why he uses the term *father* improperly for his own works, since things that previously did not exist received from him the beginning of their being.

38:30 The waters are hardened like a stone.

Even things that come about as a consequence look back to the original creation.

38:31 Will you be able to join together the shining stars of the Pleiades,[229] or can you stop the turning about of Arcturus?[230]

Since in arranging the administration of the world, providence did not lack the collaboration of [divine] power, he now recounts those things that it is acknowledged properly concern the power of the Creator. Here is another interpretation. Even though the amount of space between them [i.e., the stars of Pleiades] might be small, your power (*virtus*) will never be able to promote forcing them together into a single place and location after removing whatever it is that makes them distinct. Nor will you be able to alter *the turning about of Arcturus* (that is, the seven stars of the Great Bear) and move it to a location or region different from the one that I have set.

38:33 Do you know the order of heaven?

This is effective in opposing those who promise that they have comprehended in their subtle discussions, as they think, the form of the sky and its positioning, also the courses and distances of the stars, and to transmit this to others.

[229]The Pleiades is the constellation of the Seven Stars, which according to the myth are the seven daughters of Atlas and Pleione.
[230]See the note at Job 9:9.

38:34 Will you lift up your voice to the clouds, that its force of waters may cover you?

That is, Will it hurry up and hasten to obey your command?

38:35 Can you send bolts of lightning, and will they go? And will they say to you reverently, Here we are?

It is a sign of obedience that they are said to refuse to carry out what had been commanded to them.

38:36 Who has put wisdom in the heart of man?

The Septuagint has "Who has given to woman knowledge of embroidery?" *Who has put wisdom in the heart of man,* "or who gave the cock understanding?" He had said that he established many things for mankind's benefit. Lest he should seem to have provided only for his conveniences and not for man himself, he says he has given by his own generosity that which is more excellent among his goods, and what distinguishes him from fellowship with cattle. Whence solicitously, lest he should seem to have given the same gift to the remaining animate creatures, he says that *he gave the cock* not wisdom but *understanding,* so that it could announce to the night time that the light was near at hand.

38:37 Who will declare the rational account of the heavens?

He claims that this is known to himself alone, who made these things, not to the curiosity of human beings, who have occupied their mental talents with the investigation of incomprehensible things. "And who makes the harmony of heaven to sleep?" Who could remove the voice of praise from him, since by the very beauty of his work he seems melodious in praise of his

Creator, or else, who either preserves the harmony amid the various movements of the stars or guards the imposed arrangement of knowledge?

38:38 When was the dust poured on the earth?

This pertains to the initial coming together of the elements, as if he were to say, When the addition of the tiniest parts were joined to the single mass.

38:39-41 Will you take the prey for the lioness or satisfy the appetite of her whelps? Who provides food for the raven? When do they lie down in their dens?

That he should understand all the more that God's providence does not fail human beings, he indicates by the testimonies supplied that it even reaches diverse living creatures and the very birds too. And so everything that follows has in view this meaning.

[Chapter 39]

39:5 Who has sent out the wild ass free?

Many things are compiled, not merely to indicate the riches of the divine work but also to show that the reckoning of those works for the most part is hidden, so that saint Job may understand by how much more he is not able to know the justice of his judgments.

39:10 Can you bind the rhinoceros to plow?

Both those things that I have commanded you to tame for your use, and those that I have armed with a bulk of power to defy you, will follow the laws of their creation, so that you could not lead and force them to do anything else.

39:11 Will you have confidence in his great strength and leave your labors to him?

That is, will you invite him to share in your work?

39:12 Do you trust him that he will render you the seed or gather it into your barn floor?

Will he submit his neck to your plow and gather your seed into your barn floor when the crop is multiplied?

39:13 The wing of the ostrich is like the wings of the heron.

He preserves the course taken among the foundational things, and when many witnesses have been summoned, as it were, he proves that the laws of his own creation are preserved without any alteration.

39:16-18 She is hardened against her young ones as though they were not hers; she has labored in vain, no fear constraining her. She scorns the horse and his rider.

Since love customarily does feel fear on behalf of those things to which something is expended, he has well said that fear was absent from them in whom he had shown that the feeling of passionate love was estranged.

39:19-25 Will you give strength to the horse? He breaks up the earth with his hoof; he prances boldly; he goes forward to meet armed men. He smells the battle afar off.

He made an appropriate transition from the proximity of the previously mentioned term, so that since he had said, "She scorns the horse,"[231] he showed what significance there was in the nature of the horse itself; and in order to make

[231]Cf. Job 39:18.

what he says more splendid, he proceeds to adorn in detail the inborn character of the spirited creature.

39:26 Does the hawk begin to have feathers by your wisdom?

He says that many things, which we in our leisure overlook, upon closer inspection, are greatly to be admired, while he removes these things from the orderly arrangement of human wisdom.

39:31-32 And the Lord went on, and said to Job, Is he who contends with God so easily silenced?

Who asks of him an accounting for his works and judgments? Since he began to disclose the reasons for his affairs, does he adduce in public so much approval of his deeds that the accuser of his work is dashed by the waves of his wisdom? Here is another way: he who enters into combat with one who is superior by means of challenges ought not quickly to withdraw from the heat of his argument. "Surely he that reproves God ought to answer him." He who assumes for himself the place of a superior in making accusations ought to carry out the role of debater by persistence in his replies.

39:33-34 Then Job answered the Lord, and said, What can I answer, who has spoken inconsiderately (*leviter*)? I will lay my hand on my mouth.

I will lay my hand on my mouth. Saint Job has come to understand where the whole essence of God's arguments had led—that is, that he himself had not been abandoned by that providence that had been paid out for his sake in other matters as well. And therefore he condemns himself to silence.

39:35 One thing I have spoken, which I wish I had not said, and another, to which I will add no more.

He recorded *one thing* or *another* for "a few things."

[Chapter 40]

40:1-3 And the Lord answered Job out of the whirlwind and said, Will you make void my judgment?

After he proved the care of his providence and kindness by many testimonies of creatures, it is logically coherent that he interviews saint Job about whether he abides in that opinion, whereby he believed that God had abandoned him. And he says to him, *Will you make void my judgment,* "and condemn me, that you may be justified?" That is, since there has been a concern for justice in you, do you not think that I have been concerned about your merits? Have I allowed you to be unrecompensed, since you did not experience being abandoned? *Will you make void my judgment,* whereby I neglected my concern for you, so that I could reveal your merits? And lest your virtue should have been unknown, did I want there to be doubt about my estimation of it in the meantime? *Will you make void my judgment?* The Septuagint has "Or do you think that I have dealt with you in any other way than that you might appear to be just?"[232]

40:4 And do you have an arm like God, and can you thunder with a voice like him?

He had said, "Will you make void my judgment?" that is, do you think that you could deliberate better in the ruling of things? Therefore, he describes everything that matches the power of the judge and his grace, which is compared from his character and his judicial rebuke.

[232]Job 40:8 LXX.

40:6-8 Scatter the proud in your indignation and crush the wicked in their place. Hide them in the dust of the earth.

These words are not spoken with an offended mind but with the affection of a lover, so that they may be useful in consoling and instructing him and that he may understand that to perform such a great judgment is beyond his strength.

40:9 And I will confess that your own right hand is able to save you.

If you could play the role of such a judge, as I described it in my speech, evidently you would not need any further help.

40:10 Behold, Behemoth, whom I made with you, he eats grass like an ox.

Through the creation of such a hateful and enormous beast, people are given three advantages. [First,] they can recognize that the power of the Creator not only made those beasts that served human beings, but he also fashioned those who frighten them. [Second,] they can understand the goodness of providence, because it removed from the midst [of humans] those beasts that would have been deadly, and he relegated them to live in isolated places. [Third,] they can learn how severe he is against vices. These [beasts] that are troublesome to mortals according to their size and strength are also subject to his rebuke. *Behold Behemoth whom I made with you, he eats grass like an ox.* After the intervention of a question, by which he asked whether his judgments displeased him, he set forth the kind of rebuke he himself ought to undertake. He returns again to the description of the creatures, which attested both to his power and providence, and he intentionally put off all the way to the end of the speech mention of these two beasts. This way it would be established how much more someone is to be punished for that haughtiness that arose from the vice of the will, if God did not spare that which seemed to imitate the arrogance in view of the bulk of its body and magnitude of its strength. Here is another way: they intend this to refer to a four-footed creature and an earthly animal. Here is another way: with one term among the Hebrews, all earthly animals are called *Behemoth*; similarly, everything that lives in the water is called Leviathan. For the Greek in this passage recorded as follows: "Behold, with you the wild beasts eat grass like oxen."[233]

40:12 He sets up his tail like a cedar.

Sets up: raises. For beasts, when made savage, customarily lift up their tails. "The sinews of his testicles are wrapped together." As a sign of his great strength he said that *the sinews of his testicles are wrapped together.*

40:14 He is the beginning of the ways of God, who made him.

We are constrained by the authority of the one speaking, that this one's original form proceeded into the fashioning of the diversities of the beasts. "He who made him applied his sword." Not that with which he is struck but that with which he can strike others; that is, he who made him knows at what time he ought to set him loose for the devastation and destruction of mortals. Here is another way: he is the one who, due to the bulk of his body and the magnitude of his strength, holds primacy among wild animals.

40:15-17 To him the mountains bring forth grass; there all the beasts of the field shall play. He sleeps under the shadow. The willows of the brook shall compass him about.

[233]Job 40:15 LXX.

This is said as a testimony to his size, because all kinds of beasts could dwell in the mountains, which are reputed to be his pastures with more freedom to roam.[234]

40:18 Behold, he will drink up a river, and not wonder.

He had said that he slept in the shade of willows for the sake of avoiding the heat.[235] Now he claims that he has no fear of inundations of water.

40:19 In his eyes as with a hook he shall take him.

Lest the description of his size should be believed to protect him from all destruction, he shows that he is of such little account to himself as a little fish for which a hook causes danger.

40:20 Can you draw out the Leviathan with a hook, or will you bind him with a cord?

Likewise, the making and magnitude of another brute, which is testified to be in the Indian Ocean, is described for our admiration. Holy Job himself also mentioned it at the beginning of the book.[236]

40:22 Will he make many prayers to you or speak soft words to you?

Not that a speechless animal would burst forth into a voice of supplication, but that it intends to be patient to the touch when it is treated gently.

40:24 Will you play with him?

So that laying aside his fierceness he begins to be a delight?

[234]Cf. Job 37:8.
[235]Cf. Job 40:16.
[236]Cf. Job 3:8.

40:25 Shall friends cut him in pieces, shall merchants divide him?

According to the understanding of the preceding and subsequent things, this is said not to affirm but to deny. Thus, it means, His friends will not cut him to pieces and apportion him in the fashion of meat that is for sale, will they? Here is another way: when the time of slaughter comes to him, he will be shared by the hands of many. Here is another way: the Greek has *nations* instead of *friends*.

40:26 Will you fill nets with his skin?

That is, the thing is so large that not even at that time when it is cut up and divided out would you be able to enclose its skin or head with your nets, however large those nets may be.

40:27 Lay your hand on him; remember the battle, and speak no more.

This too is said in accordance with the sense given previously. He says, If you have an arm like God, and if you thunder with a voice like his,[237] *lay your hand on him*; that is, arm yourself to destroy him and gird yourself to slaughter him. But if you distrust your strength, hold in check the outspokenness of your words too.

40:28 Behold, his hope shall fail him.

Fittingly, when the choice of combat is resolved, the greatness of the venture is revealed, and there is talk of destruction, not of one man but of many, either by the wish to attack or by the intent to catch.

[237]Cf. Job 40:4.

[Chapter 41]

41:1 I will not stir him up, like one that is cruel.

He says that he will not make him free at some point so that his violence would increase by human calamities, but in order that the power may be made known either of the one holding him or else of the one appointing him for destruction.

41:2 Who has first given to me that I should repay him? All things that are under heaven are mine.

Therefore, he shows either that its restraint or slaughter was easy for him, since the same thing by which it was made can either be held in check or killed by his power.

41:3 I will not spare him, nor his words framed to make supplication.

That power is to be feared by others, that monstrous size of body is shown to jump at words of supplication by the right of their master.

41:4 Who shall unveil the face of his garment, and who has entered the midst of his mouth?

He had revealed his submission that came from fear. Therefore, lest this should seem unique to his nature, again the cause of terror is told. *Who shall unveil the face of his garment, and who has entered the midst of his mouth?* That is, that appendage with which the voracity of its mouth is impeded.

41:5 Who can open the doors of his face?

The meaning is the same that was also found in the brief verse higher up.[238]

[238]Cf. Job 41:4.

41:6 His body is like shields.

Since an animal that is native to water is being described, it is fittingly claimed to possess rings of scales like fish.

41:9-11 His sneezing is like the shining of fire; out of his mouth go forth lamps; out of his nostrils goes smoke.

By a lengthy arrangement of a description, everything is recounted that is either truly menacing in his nature or for the sake of emphasis serves to inspire terror.

41:13 In his neck strength shall dwell, and want shall go before his face.

He will move himself in every direction. He will lay waste to all things and in order to show not only that those things that he had approached remained deserted but also he indicates that the flight of all things occurred when he moved himself along any path.

41:14 The members of his flesh even cleave one to another.

That is, they are tightly connected, bound by many bonds of sinews. "He shall send bolts of lightning against him." And because all other things were hanging from nothing, he shows only what prevailed to kill it.

41:15 His heart shall be as hard as a stone and as firm as a smith's anvil.

He will not *be made hard* by strokes of lightning, but he makes those weapons bounce off him that human strength has hurled.

41:16 When he shall raise him up, the angels shall fear, and being affrighted shall purify themselves.

By the example of punishment directed at the beast, an opportunity of fear will arise that is useful to the higher rational creation, so that it strives not to have in its character what it has seen being struck against the bodies in this way.

41:17-18 A sword shall not be able to hold up; for he shall esteem iron as straw.

He had said previously, "His heart shall be as hard as a stone and as firm as a smith's anvil."[239] Therefore, he shows that against which such callousness is prepared. Therefore, it is not the Leviathan that will be unable to hold out, but the sword that is drawn out against him.

41:21 The beams of the sun shall be under him.

It is customary in the Scriptures always to extol the descriptions of great things in an abundance of words. Therefore, in order to show him to be of immense bulk, he says that *the beams of the sun* shall rise and grow red *under him*. "He strews gold under him like mire." He does not say what he is doing, but what he is capable of doing, if his size and strength allowed no hindrances. By the term *gold* he has indicated riches that various forms of things make.

41:23 He shall esteem the deep as growing old.

Which could not oppose him, as if its strength were exhausted.

41:24 There is no power on earth that can be compared with him, who was made to fear no one.

Another way is how the Greek renders it: "There is no power on the earth of him, who was made to be sported with by the angels."

[239]Job 41:15.

41:25 He beholds every high thing; he is king over all the children of pride.

This would be the true description of the beasts according to reliability of history. Let there be no doubt about their great size in light of the power of the Creator. However, they also leave room for a deeper understanding, so that we may believe in addition to them something else is signified as well. Thus, the power of spiritual wickedness may be perceived more easily in the representation of the bodies. Just as the former beasts are deadly to bodies, so the latter are to morals, and as the sin of pride must deservedly be imputed to them, so it ought to be punished. Another way is given in the Greek: "He is king of all that are in the waters." *He beholds* is recorded for "despises."

[Chapter 42]

42:1-2 Then Job answered the Lord, and said, I know that you can do all things, and no thought is hidden from you.

For you have understood that more was involved in my feelings of bitterness than the speech of complaints had brought out. Here is another way: whoever therefore believes that what he turns over in his mind does not lie exposed to your knowledge is ignorant of reality and acts as one who is devoid of rational knowledge.

42:3 Who is this that hides counsel?

The Septuagint has "For who is he that hides counsel from you?" "Therefore I have spoken unwisely." The Greek has "What I did not know has been told to me, great and wonderful things which I understood not?" Here is another way: that I should have believed that I had been forsaken by your providence, which intervenes in all things that it has created.

42:5 With the hearing of the ear, I[240] heard, but now my eye sees you.

That which the speech of reason and teaching authority previously brought to my awareness (namely, that you care about justice) has now settled more deeply into my mind by the presence of your revelation.

42:6 Therefore, I reprehend myself and do penance in dust and ashes.

The Greek has "I esteem myself earth and ashes." Here is another way: this means either I will not take offense over the misfortunes I suffer, but will embrace them in the place of training or correction, or else I will zealously employ other things as well with my torments.

42:7 But after the Lord had spoken these words to Job, he said to Eliphaz the Themanite, My wrath is kindled against you, and against your two friends, because you have not spoken the thing that is right before me, as my servant Job has.

He deservedly incites. . . . [241]

[240]Reading *audivi* with the Vulgate rather than CCSL's *audivit*.

[241]The manuscript is defective after these words. The Latin Vulgate concludes with vv. 8-17: "Take unto you therefore seven oxen and seven rams, and go to my servant Job and offer for yourselves a holocaust. And my servant Job shall pray for you; his face I will accept that folly be not imputed to you. For you have not spoken right things before me, as my servant Job has. So Eliphaz the Themanite, Bildad the Shuhite, and Zophar the Naamathite went and did as the Lord had spoken to them. And the Lord accepted the intercession of Job. The Lord also was turned at the penance of Job, when he prayed for his friends. And the Lord gave Job twice as much as he had before. And all his brethren came to him and all his sisters and all that knew him before; and they ate bread with him in his house and bemoaned him and comforted him for all the evil that God had brought upon him. And every man gave him one ewe and one earring of gold. And the Lord blessed the latter end of Job more than his beginning. And he had fourteen thousand sheep, six thousand camels, a thousand yoke of oxen and a thousand she asses. And he had seven sons and three daughters. And he called the names of one Day, and the name of the second Cassia, and the name of the third Cornustibil. And there were not found in all the earth women so beautiful as the daughters of Job, and their father gave them inheritance among their brethren. And Job lived after these things a hundred and forty years, and he saw his children and his children's children unto the fourth generation. And he died an old man and full of days." Also noteworthy is that the LXX version of Job contains an appendix that describes him as a descendant of Esau in the fifth generation from Abraham.

TRACTATES ON THE PROPHETS HOSEA, JOEL, AND AMOS

COMMENTARY ON THE PROPHET HOSEA

[Preface]

When he recounts the marvelous wonders of the law, that most sacred lyre player, blessed David, who was distinguished both in the art of ruling and singing,[1] frequently intersperses, "Confess to the Lord, for he [is] good, since his mercy [endures] forever."[2] For whether you consider his spiritual or physical gifts, we are admonished consistently at least to give thanks to our Creator to whom we cannot compare. Yet nothing is more delightful than that diligent care, nothing more precious than that oblation; since indeed it is his very clemency that is exhausted neither by gifts nor by the ages, which makes us devout and, what is more, that we generally seem worthy of obtaining what we ask for. When, therefore, we offer to him this sacrifice of a grateful heart, let us trust that we will obtain what we pray for, since we seem already to have obtained those things that we have requested.[3] For when we were discussing the books of Solomon,[4] we described the aesthetic of his organization, to the extent that he granted the possibility, so that on no occasion did contextual coherence forsake us, in the possession of which the authority of one's explanation ought to consist.[5] But this fruit of our preceding diligence commends our zealous labor. For it is not a question of what provokes more acute investigations into novelties[6] as much as the prayed-for perception of the more excellent things. This is particularly true before so pious a Lord, who is ready to give generously those things that he commanded us to aspire for.[7] Nor should we be intimidated by the profundity of the very task. Otherwise, after the pledges of confidence have been received, our trepidation may proceed to convict us of being not merely lazy but ungrateful as well.[8] And so, let us undertake a commentary on the Twelve Prophets. They are called "Minor" not due to their worth but to the number of verses.[9] In the first place I admonish you who

[1]Cf. 1 Sam 16:16-23; 18:10.

[2]Ps 106:1; 107:1; 118:1, 29; 136:1.

[3]Cf. Mt 7:7-12; Jas 1:5-8.

[4]The Venerable Bede has preserved fragments of a commentary on the Song of Songs by Julian. This is probably the work referred to here. Cf. G. Bouwman, *Des Julian von Aeclanum Kommentar zu den Propheten Osee, Joel und Amos. Ein Beitrag zur Geschichte der Exegese* (Rome: Pontificio Istituto Biblico, 1958), 6-7; and J. Lössl, "Julian of Aeclanum's *Tractatus in Osee, Iohel, Amos*: Some Notes on the Current State of Research," *Augustiniana* 51 (2001): 18n25.

[5]I have usually rendered *consequentia* as "contextual coherence." It refers to the literal and historical meaning of Scripture, which Julian thinks can be ascertained by the close study of the context and the natural development of the narrative or argument. Julian constantly insists on following the sequence of ideas and the logical unfolding of the story.

[6]As I briefly discuss in the introduction, I believe Julian is criticizing tendencies found in Origen's and Jerome's exegesis.

[7]Cf. Mt 7:7-8.

[8]Cf. Mt 25:26.

[9]Jerome says in his *Commentary on Obadiah* 1:1b (ACT 1:278), "The prophet is 'minor' by the reckoning of the number of verses, but not in terms of its meaning. In a way that is similar to the three books of Solomon's Canticle of Canticles, the shorter it is, so much the more difficult it is."

have imposed this work on me to lend me help by your pious and concentrated prayer, that I may become worthy of understanding the truth.[10] Second, let the reader of our work recognize which version I followed and what was the main consideration I had in mind when I took up this very difficult task of writing a commentary. Especially if he belongs to those who train attention on the reading [in the liturgy],[11] let him know that it was not for no reason that I deliberately chose this most recent version known as "according to the Hebrew."[12] For in the earlier versions, faults of expression frequently corrupt the meaning of the doctrinal teaching or of the narrative, so that divination rather than work seems to be required. But this latest translation, although it has not added much rhetorical brilliance to the coherence of the original text itself, nevertheless by its integral soundness of expression it frequently avoids those previously mentioned losses of suppressed meanings. In fact, although the silence among the Latins particularly in commenting on the prophets has now been so continuous that it seems to be some sort of conspiracy, yet among the Greeks and Syrians some men have arisen who have endeavored to discuss these writings. Among them I of course happen to have read a few things written by St. John, bishop of Constantinople. He adapted nearly the whole work to his unique style, which is exhortation rather than explanation.[13] Origen, on the other hand, composes charming allegories rather than solid and tenable historical explanations as he runs along in his own uninterrupted course.[14] Furthermore, Jerome, a man of enormous intellectual capacity and persistent zeal for scholarship, wrote commentaries on the books of the prophets to be sure, but he was content to navigate between the two traditions,[15] and he was either unwilling or unable to exhibit any concern to find out about the contextual coherence [of these texts].[16] Thus, his entire speech flowed either through the allegories of Origen or through the fabulous traditions of the Jews.[17] Therefore, since it seems to me that Jerome passed over many useful things, I have decided that the work would be a religious one before God and useful to men, if in obedience to you, I should undertake to write a commentary on the prophets, as our capacity has

[10]Cf. Mt 10:11-13; Rev 5:2-4.

[11]I have followed J. Lössl, "A Shift in Patristic Exegesis: Hebrew Clarity and Historical Verity in Augustine, Jerome, and Julian of Aeclanum and Theodore of Mopsuestia," *Augustinian Studies* 32, no. 2 (2001): 167n37, in adding the bracketed words for clarification. His rendering of portions of Julian's prefaces to Hosea and Joel aided my work here.

[12]Julian is referring to Jerome's new translation of the Hebrew Old Testament. To my knowledge, apart from Jerome's disciple, Philip the Presbyter, Julian is the first Western scholar to adopt Jerome's version as the basis of his Old Testament exegesis.

[13]St. John Chrysostom (345–407) was patriarch of Constantinople. The sample of Chrysostom's exegesis of Hosea referred to here has not survived. Cf. G. Bouwman, *Des Julian von Aeclanum Kommentar*, 129. J. Lössl, "Julian of Aeclanum's 'Rationalist' Exegesis: Albert Bruckner Revisited," *Augustiniana* 53 (2003): 101, emphasizes the importance Julian attributes to patristic exegesis alongside of scriptural testimony. This is "mainly because he understands the Patristic tradition as an exegetical tradition, as Scripture mediated through tradition."

[14]Origen's commentary on Hosea is no longer extant. It is noteworthy that Julian has read it but seems to frown on it for its excessive use of allegory. In his own *Commentary on Hosea*, bk 1, preface (ACT 2:150), Jerome reports that Origen wrote a work in Greek titled "Why Is the Name of Ephraim Used in Hosea?" that Jerome claims aimed to show that whatever was spoken against Ephraim in Hosea should be referred allegorically to the persona of the heretics. Jerome adopts this application extensively in his own commentary, which contains an enormous amount of polemic against heretics, a feature largely absent from Julian's commentary. It seems noteworthy that Jerome's reception of Origen was far more positive than Julian's. In *On Famous Men* 75, Jerome reported that he possessed Origen's twenty-five-book *Commentary on the Twelve [Minor] Prophets*, transcribed by the hand of the martyr St. Pamphilus himself, "which I hug and guard with such joy, that I deem myself to have the wealth of Croesus."

[15]Julian means the Greek Christian exegetical tradition and the Jewish (Hebrew) tradition.

[16]Bouwman, *Des Julian von Aeclanum Kommentar*, 81, notes the importance of the concept of "contextual coherence" (*consequentia*) to Julian. It means the natural sequence of words and concepts. It is shown statistically by the fact that *consequentia* occurs fourteen times, and *consequenter* forty times, in his three commentaries on the prophets. It seems noteworthy that Julian thinks Jerome (and Origen) often ignored this aspect.

[17]See J. Lössl's comments on this passage. "Shift in Patristic Exegesis," 169-70, which are quoted at length in the introduction.

allowed by the help of divine grace.[18] With attentive minds then let us approach the knowledge of the work, so that we may discern how many things [these prophets] have published with broad application, how many things with acute penetration, everything with piety and logical consistency.

Book One on the Prophet Hosea

[Chapter 1]

1:1-2 The Word of the Lord that came to Hosea the son of Beeri in the days of Uzziah, Joathan, Ahaz, and Hezekiah kings of Judah, and in the days of Jeroboam the son of Joash king of Israel. The beginning of the Lord's speaking[19] in Hosea.

Indeed, from the practice of those who recount what events happened at various times, a mention also of the kings has evidently been made, so that we might learn in which ages the history was composed.[20] Yet it was far more necessary for this to be observed by the prophets. Granted they are not pursuing the work of history pure and simple (that is, recording the things that happened), but they are also declaring the future under the impulse too of those who are making predictions. Yet they affirm that these things will come to pass not by chance but by his just decision, and they discuss this before the arbitration of his prince, whose violated laws and often-defiled sacred rites they have complained about. Doubtless this is why they affix the names and generations of the kings one after another in the beginning of the work. Thus, once we know what was done during the times of those kings, with history as our teacher, we may recognize that they deserved to receive these invectives on a grand scale. And so it is contained in the annals both of Kings and of Chronicles (*Paralipomenon*) that when these men reigned, whose names have been recorded at the beginning, certainly the whole nation of the Jews was befouled with the worship of idols.[21] Yet the ten tribes that were called Israel ever since the separation that occurred under Jeroboam[22] were even crusted with extreme sacrileges and were oppressed by the disasters that threatened them. Therefore, he made mention of four kings from Judah (namely, those whose periods coincided with the times of his prophecy) and of one [king] who had reigned on the side of Israel. Now when he began the prophecy, those men whom he mentioned were in charge of their portions; but after a short time, the reign within Samaria was ended. Indeed, Zechariah, the son of Jeroboam, who obtained command by succession in the sixth month, was destroyed by civil discord, that is, when Shallum rebelled.[23] But when Shallum had reigned for one month in Samaria, "Menahem the son of Gadi went up"[24] and destroyed the previous tyrant, restoring the rebellion, and he, having obtained tumultuous power for ten years, was a slave to the king of the Assyrians, who was called Pul, under so great a burden of paying

[18]To me it seems obvious that Julian has not separated the grace of God from the endeavor of his own diligence. He explicitly acknowledges his need for divine grace here.

[19]Literally "of speaking the Lord."

[20]To refresh the reader's memory of ancient Jewish history, I use the dates given in *Eerdmans Dictionary of the Bible*, ed. D. N. Freedman, A. C. Myers, and A. B. Beck (Grand Rapids, MI: Eerdmans, 2000). Jeroboam I was the first king of the northern state of Israel (ca. 924–903). He had separated from Solomon and set up golden calves for worship in Dan and Bethel, establishing a non-Levitical priesthood. Hosea is not referring to him but to Jeroboam II, king of Israel (785–745), who was succeeded by Zechariah (746). The latter reigned only six months before he was assassinated by Shallum. Next reigned Menahem (746–737), who overthrew Shallum, taxed Israel heavily, and paid tribute to Tiglath-Pileser III of Assyria. The kings of Judah during Hosea's time were Uzziah/Azariah (790–739), Joathan/Jotham (750–730), Ahaz (742–727), and Hezekiah (715–687).

[21]Cf. 2 Kings 14:24; 15:4-35; 16:2-4; 2 Chron 26:16-20; 27:2; 28:1-4, 19, 22-25.

[22]Cf. 1 Kings 12.

[23]Cf. 2 Kings 15:8-31; 17:1-6.

[24]2 Kings 15:13-14.

tribute that extreme poverty appeared.[25] So already in that portion of the ten tribes, the whirlwinds from the awakened disasters were rushing in, and thus, while a kingdom still remained in Jerusalem, the announced captivity carried off the ten tribes.[26] Therefore, after the people of Samaria migrated to Assyrian lands, saint Hosea remained in the country of Judah and beheld the time of king Hezekiah, renowned for its miracles,[27] and under him he also exercised his gift of prophecy. Therefore, since destruction was already looming over Israel, he named only one prince on that side.[28] It was under him that he had begun to prophesy.

Now as for what he recorded, *The beginning of the Lord's speaking in Hosea,* doubtless this seems to show that he is the first to have been admitted into this kind of speech. It is not that there were no prophets previously, since even the same history of Kings mentions the deeds and words of blessed Elijah and Elisha, and of many others.[29] But of all those who were likewise commanded to write down what they foretold for eternal remembrance, Hosea was the first to take up the task.[30] Nor may we reasonably deny that blessed David and wisest Solomon consigned their words to writing. They were legitimate prophets according to the testimony of the gospel and the apostles.[31] Yet the experienced reader will notice no small difference between these latter men and the writings of those whom we are now trying to explain. For although the latter spoke some things about the captivity of the people, nevertheless, as though with quiet minds—that is, with minds undisturbed by any proximity of evil—they foretold things that they had once perceived were going to come. But the former men were placed within the very din of [God's] vengeance, with hearts wholly terrified, who would indeed even be rendered participants in the disasters. It is as though they are describing the whole thing with tearful complaints and portraying the feelings of our God, who is being compelled to take his vengeance with very great regret. They certainly implore the aid of his divine mercy now and then; moreover, they virtually describe the sequence of the calamities in the style of Greek tragedy. Therefore, let us know that the *beginning* of those prophets, who were marked out chiefly by this designation, so that they were named "prophets," was taken up by blessed Hosea. He was conspicuous for the holiness of his character and descent. He took up such work of one speaking in a public assembly, so that he bore the persona of the Redeemer and Judge. This will become clearer throughout the whole work.

1:2-5 And the Lord said to Hosea, Go, take thee a wife of fornications, and children of fornications, for the fornicating land shall fornicate from the Lord. So he went, and took Gomer the daughter of Debelaim; and she conceived and bore a son. And the Lord said to him, Call his name Jezrahel, for yet a little while, and I will visit the blood of Jezrahel on the house of Jehu, and I will cause the kingdom of the house of Israel to cease, and in that day I will break in pieces the bow of Israel in the valley of Jezrahel.

The habits, or rather, the character of holy men must be noted, that after they ascend to

[25]Cf. 2 Kings 15:19-20.
[26]Cf. 2 Kings 17:5-6.
[27]Cf. 2 Kings 18–20; 2 Chron 32. Bouwman, *Des Julian von Aeclanum Kommentar,* 129n2, 132, identifies the regular application of the prophecies of Hosea, Joel, and Amos to the events that occurred under King Hezekiah as one of the original features of Julian's interpretation.
[28]Namely, Jeroboam II, the son of Joash.
[29]Cf. 1 Kings 17–2 Kings 13.
[30]Jerome, *Commentary on Hosea* 1:1b-2a (ACT 2:152-53) says that Hosea was contemporary with Isaiah, Joel, Amos, Obadiah, Jonah, and Micah. The northern kingdom ended while he was living, and the Lord spoke first in him, then to the other prophets.
[31]David is described as a prophet in Mt 22:43; Acts 1:16; 4:25. Theodore of Mopsuestia, *Commentary on Hosea* 1 (FOTC 44) mentions Ps 14:7 as David's prediction of Israel's release from captivity.

this honor, our God uses their tongue like the pen of the scribe; not only their words but also their deeds are vested with prophetic honor.[32] And in announcing the mysteries, they diligently perform the work either by teaching or by their actions. Therefore, at the very beginning of the reprimand, he says, the sacred Creator has commanded this to blessed Hosea, that, disregarding the excellence of both his own design and blood, he should be joined through marital partnership to a most base woman, and what is more, to use the language of the street, to a whore. And he not only endured to the point of having the name of his wife of reproach, but he also threw into disorder a father's rights in respect to himself, so that he was believed to be the father of uncertain offspring, as though he had raised the children of another's lust.

Now I am fully aware of how great a contention there has been among learned men with respect to their opinion of this passage, so that whole countries disagree about his declaration. For Palestine, Egypt, and all the others, who are generally impressed by the authority of Origen, deny that this marriage was physically consummated by the prophet Hosea.[33] Instead, just as many things are told by the prophets as having been done in spirit, so they say that these nuptials with a prostitute were carried out only in words. For [they say that] the reason of that time would not have asked Hosea to be wanton, who was stepping forth to speak in a public assembly of the people, so that contrary to the instructions of the sacred law, which had proclaimed that partnership with a prostitute is wicked,[34] he who was about to bring forth his censures against sins would have himself first committed what the whole people could have subsequently accused. But how unfitting would it have been if in defense of his shameful act he would have cited the character of his commander, doubtless claiming that he certainly, as much as concerns his own character, shrank back horribly from that filthiness of marital partnership. But he had yielded to the authority of his Lord, who had appointed him to censure the people. Straightaway he would have seemed to be providing them material for mockery rather than dread, he who in his own person thought that the moral obscenities of others ought to be censured, while the preacher himself was the author of a shameful act committed by himself!

It is asked also where throughout the whole law this is supported by a similar example of either a precept or a deed—that is, if in any place our God has commanded anything to be done contrary to his precepts, the transgressors of which he surely set about to punish by the disasters announced by the prophets. If, in order to show this, the command to blessed Abraham to commit murder is brought forward, we shall be reminded by the very outcome of the action, even though this was before the time that the law was promulgated, that it was not the savageness of slaughter that was chosen, but the piety and faith of the father's mind.[35] For he who had received the promises, to whom it had been said, "For in Isaac shall seed be raised up for you,"[36] offered his only [son], showing that God could even raise from the dead.[37] However, just as a fixed, ready belief guarded him against the fear of the promise being frustrated, so God did not permit the devotion of the father to extend to the point of killing the boy, but the interjected praise of his tested virtue stayed the hand of the one who was on the verge of making the sacrifice.[38] It became clear, it says, that I

[32]Cf. Ps 45:1-2.

[33]Jerome objects to the literal reading of God's command to Hosea in bk 1, preface to *Commentary on Hosea* (ACT 2:150), and he is certainly based on Origen's antecedent views.

[34]Cf. Deut 23:17-18; 1 Kings 14:24; 1 Cor 6:16.

[35]Cf. Gen 22:1-19.

[36]Gen 21:12.

[37]Cf. Heb 11:19.

[38]Cf. Gen 22:11-12.

wanted only to make public that with you nothing is more powerful than loving and honoring me. As things now stand, spare his blood, which was neither licit for anyone to shed nor was it fitting for you to do. Yet, lest you should seem to lack a priest's gift, behold, a ram stands near at hand to you, with its horns entangled in briers. Just as its life in the present could bring aid by releasing your son, so too it shall be worthy of signifying a future mystery.[39]

But in the affairs of blessed Hosea, [sexual] mingling was not only commanded but also carried out and repeated many times. Nor does it seem possible for this to be defended by the moral uprightness of the action or by the authority of the command. At this point it is added also that the prophet's sequential ordering is not preserved in these figurations. For to signify that the tribes, which lived, so to speak, under the same tent and in the society of God, had broken out into acts of adultery (that is, sacrileges), a prostitute woman is taken in who, however, once purified by an honorable marriage, has children not from a shameful act but from an honorable husband—that is, from a prophet. And in honor of her marriage, she forgets her past vices and fully enjoys fertility rather than lust. How, therefore, shall this woman, who is shown with the matrimonial signs of honor, be approved to symbolize the persona of that nation, which just before the marriage had shuddered exceedingly at obscene vices but [now], although previously it had remained steadfast in the sacred union with its God, is described as having eagerly run after baseness? By these and many other arguments, they strive to show that the prophet was not physically united to a prostitute.

Directly opposite to this interpretation, the Syrians, and those who hold that that marriage was consummated sexually, rely principally on the testimony of the names, by which plainly both the woman and her parents as well as her country are made known.[40] And the matter of their conjugal connection is confirmed by the births that followed. But it was more out of a prophet's devotion than as a violation of the law undertaken by him. It was out of obedience that he took care to join himself to whomever needed to be called back, going against the practice of his own morals, although one could reasonably defend the virtue of that work also; that is, he had converted a woman from having the profession of a courtesan to functioning as a chaste wife for years to come.[41]

So, fighting among themselves with these sorts of arguments, they have rendered both views suspect, although really it seems more succinct and safer, and more suitable for the expression of reality, if the thing is believed to have been done in spirit.[42] Thus, just as blessed Jeremiah is said to have buried his loincloth in the land of the Parthians, but not by leaving the borders of Judaea;[43] just as holy Ezekiel, while set in the midst of the Babylonian captivity, is brought into the inner shrine of the temple of Jerusalem as an observer, assuredly by contemplating only images of the places and deeds while being situated far off in another location;[44] so also blessed Hosea, who was about to symbolize the deeds of many times by means of fitting images, saw a series of both the faults and of the punishments. Of course, by the testimony of his gift according

[39]Cf. Gen 22:13-14; Rom 8:32.

[40]Hos 1:3 describes Gomer as the daughter of Diblaim. Theodore of Mopsuestia, *Commentary on Hosea* 1 (FOTC, 42) says, "The prophet obeys this command, and marries a prostitute, whose father's name he also mentions lest what was said should seem some trifling fiction and not a true record of events."

[41]For those who object to a figural reading, Jerome also provides arguments in defense of Hosea's behavior, if his marriage to Gomer is understood as physically consummated. Cf. *Commentary on Hosea* 1:2b (ACT 2:153-54).

[42]I.e., Hosea's marriage with a prostitute.

[43]Cf. Jer 13:1-7; Jerome, *Commentary on Hosea*, bk 1, preface (ACT 2:150). In his *Commentary on Jeremiah* (ACT 2:82), Jerome says that Jeremiah's linen loincloth is "rational," and he interprets it spiritually and allegorically.

[44]Cf. Ezek 8:3-4. In his *Commentary on Ezekiel*, bk 3, on 8:3, Jerome says that Ezekiel was moved there in spirit, not in body.

to any pondered opinion, respect for the one prophesying is evident. The creator of the universe doubtless seems to clothe him with his own persona, so that the reason of the divine judgments is gathered from the deeds of a husband. And such a great bond exists between the eternal Lord and his faithful servant that it is as if the estimate of each is mingled; and if the actions of the prophet have to be washed away, an excuse may seem to be provided too in his religious duty. But if his action puts pressure on and drives out the compliance of our testimony, his majesty has transcended all things. Likewise, let him attribute it to the designs of his authority that are exceedingly pleasing to himself, so that they are shown not to require a human examination. For indeed, the reproach of the apostle Paul declares this when he says, "But to me it is a very small thing to be judged by you, or by a human law court (*die*); but neither do I judge my own self, for I am not conscious to myself of anything; but he that judges me is the Lord."[45] Therefore, both the command of the Creator and the actions of the prophet have stood firm under one and the same reverence.

But the succession and order of the statements ought to be carefully noted, which rather mocks that interpretation whereby their union was not seemingly physically consummated. It says, *Go, take thee a wife of fornications and children of fornications, for the fornicating land shall fornicate from the Lord.* Yet the commencement of the sacrilege that he accuses under the name *fornication* did not happen in that time, but it was now at its worst. For the corruption of the religion had begun chiefly in the times of Jeroboam [I],[46] and the worship of the calves that was commended to the people continued for many ages without interruption. But now, in these days in which the gift of prophecy is granted to blessed Hosea, it is not transgressions that are beginning to arise, but rather retributions. Clearly this is at odds with that interpretation that seems to show a prostitute who has been taken up in marriage in order to point to that outrage that God would endure for a long time. So now let us see what the sequence of the proclamation contains.

Go, take thee a wife of fornications, and children of fornications, for the fornicating land shall fornicate from the Lord. So he went, and took Gomer the daughter of Debelaim; and she conceived and bore a son. And the Lord said to him, Call his name Jezrahel, for yet a little while, and I will visit the blood of Jezrahel upon the house of Jehu, and I will cause the kingdom of the house of Israel to cease, and in that day I will break in pieces the bow of Israel in the valley of Jezrahel. Throughout the sacred books, this language from our God is frequently found in that he accuses sacrileges by the name *fornication*. For because the God known in Judea[47] had chosen one nation to unite with himself, and he received it like a wife, when the tablets of the law came on the scene, from whom he generated *children* by instruction, he calls those ones chaste who keep the laws of religion unviolated. But, on the other hand, he calls those ones shameful and defiled who have violated the covenants of the sacred worship by the infection of errors and by their eager pursuit of heresy. Doubtless, by this image he has expressed both the extent of his love toward the pious and the vehemence of the severity with which he hotly pursues every impious person. For he rises up not only as censor and judge but as a husband angrily demanding to lay claim to what is his own.[48] But though he makes straight toward this understanding by his own course, it must be asked, Why did he discuss this with the

[45]1 Cor 4:3-4.
[46]Cf. 1 Kings 12:25-32.
[47]Cf. Ps 76:1.
[48]Cf. Ex 34:14; Ezek 16:35; 23:2-3; Is 62:4-5.

pomp of such a great outward scheme?[49] For instead of a simple narration containing all these things, why was it necessary to command the prophet to enter into a marriage with a prostitute, whether physically or only figuratively? Of course, to those who think piously and in hidden fashion about this passage, the depth both of the divine kindness and of prophetic dignity presents itself. For our God, who interposes his providence in human affairs, has certainly taken care of humanity universally, but it is as if he values only those human beings who have attained reverence stemming from the virtues of their moral character. He shows that he is moved by their judgments, and he hastens to instruct them in particular—now by commands, now by figures. Therefore, it is either because he wanted to show what I mentioned earlier (namely, that he has a most vehement concern for holy men and women, and he does not consider their complaints unimportant) or else it is because he is accustomed to be appeased by the prayers of the saints. Thus, when it is time for him to begin to make known his vengeance, before he relates in their presence the reasons for his anger, in order to remove the impediments to his intervention by setting forth their offenses, he first establishes from his side those whom he could test as delayers of the sentence. And he exhorts them to be angry along with himself. For it is based on this, that when blessed Moses had appointed scouts of the Promised Land from each of the twelve tribes,[50] and when they returned, all the rest save for two terrified the cowardly people, and the rebellion that arose shook even blessed Moses himself. But when he had fled to the tent it says, "The glory of the Lord appeared" and showed him how great he would make him and how he would give preference to him over all those people. He says, "Permit me to wipe out that people, and I will make you a far greater and mightier nation than this one is."[51] Understanding from these words what a holy man could accomplish before God, he immediately mitigated the anger of the judge.[52] So also when the destruction of the Babylonian captivity was threatening the temple of Jerusalem, he leads the prophet Ezekiel around, at least by the contemplation of his spirit.[53] They go throughout the holiest places, which had once been venerated, so that, by his perceiving how the people were sinning, he might cease to wonder if so great a change into opposite conditions should happen. Thus, the nation, once lofty for its extraordinary reverence, might most basely perish. So then, in this way also the preparation of similar business is indicated to the blessed Hosea. Through him the impending destruction was announced to the people, (the destruction) for which clearly no merits of their ancestors would avail, no prayers of the prophets would avail, so far as he perceives and carefully considers in his own example, whether God either could or should tolerate that mass of affronts. Therefore, he says, adopt the persona of a kind-hearted husband, of a man who has for a long time put up with the courtesan behavior of his spouse. And welcome children who may either be regarded as of doubtful parentage or, more logically, who should be attributed to the unchastity of another. And try to see whether you can have constant patience or whether you think that the remedy for an ancient wound is one of a kind; or [see] if you are set free by a separation from that woman, whom you have never reformed by means of acts of kindness, however many. Or try to see if the union commanded only in the affections of the mind,

[49]J. H. Baxter, "Notes on the Latin of Julian of Eclanum," *ALMA* 21 (1951): 47, says, "*Schema* is any rhetorical device, figure of speech, trope."

[50]Cf. Num 13:3.

[51]Cf. Num 14:10-12.

[52]Cf. Num 14:13-19.

[53]Cf. Ezek 8:3-18. This is Jerome's interpretation as well in his *Commentary on Ezekiel.*

or even in an affair of a defiled body, seems to have regard for the honor of the prophet. In order to show forth faithfully the harshness of the judge, he gets a taste of the injury that God has been dealt. On the other hand, it is as though the obligation of the vengeance to be wrought against the impious is suited for this very thing, since the prophet himself endured a shameful affront in order to point out the matter. Therefore, since the reason for the parable seems to have been fitting, as we have said, let us now describe its order.

It says, *Take thee a wife of fornications and children of fornications, for the fornicating land shall fornicate from the Lord.* This repetition involves an idiom of the Hebrew language, "doing he will do," "speaking he will speak," and other things like this.[54] So then also *fornicating it will fornicate.* Now a subtle distinction could be applied to this expression, but the brevity that comes from the custom of the Scriptures should not be disregarded. Take note, of course, that he does not call the time of their entry into transgression by the name *fornication* so much as the time when they were already undergoing the captivity. And this is not illogical, for since the obscenity of profane minds has supplied the material for the condemnation, for that reason the punishment is designated by the name of its cause.[55] Thus, we may say that the people are *fornicating* when they are condemned for fornication. Indeed, in the present passage he shows that this offered a great opportunity too. For it is apparent that the punishment is not the same as the guilt. For the one is resisted by moral uprightness, the other by wantonness. And when this has been ascertained sufficiently, the definition of these realities can by no means be confused by a sharing of names, that the punishment is the same as the guilt. At any rate, it is scarcely without cause that he has pronounced the people *fornicators* at that time when they were about to approach the evils of their captivity. But because he knew that on account of the diversity of minds chastisement was going to lead to some becoming better by their suffering, others to becoming more wicked by their impudence, he says justly that they would bear punishments. This is in view of the impiety that they were perpetrating in their land. And in the very time of captivity, some people would take up the signs of correction, but others would take on an increase of crime, according to what is threatened elsewhere: "You have served gods in your own land whom your fathers did not know, [so] shall you serve strange gods in a land that is not your own."[56] Therefore, because the slave woman celebrated that profanity that the free nation had committed, it is foretold that she will *fornicate* also in the midst of her punishments.

But the first son whom the harlot gave birth to, so to speak, is given the very name of the country that the captivity threatens; for he says, *call his name Jezrahel.* By this name the valley bordering on Samaria was indicated.[57] Therefore, through the name of this place, he announces what the country is about to suffer. After all it follows, *For yet a little while, and I will visit the blood of Jezrahel upon the house of Jehu, and I will cause the kingdom of the house of Israel to cease, and in that day I will break in pieces the bow of Israel in the valley of Jezrahel.* The time to reveal vengeance is pressing on them, it says, and on account of this his anger rises against the *kingdom* of

[54]See also under Hos 10:15. Theodore of Mopsuestia mentions the scriptural custom of repeating words for emphasis in his *Commentary on the Psalms* (translated by Julian). Cf. Bouwman, *Des Julian von Aeclanum Kommentar,* 127.

[55]J. Lössl, "Pauline Exegesis in Patristic Commentaries of Old Testament Prophets: The Example of Julian of Aeclanum's *Tractatus in Amos,*" *Journal for Late Antique Religion and Culture* 4 (2010): 11, calls attention to a similar interpretation of Julian with respect to Rom 1:28 that proved offensive to Augustine. See under Hos 8:4.

[56]Jer 5:19.

[57]Cf. Jerome, *Commentary on Hosea* 1:5 (ACT 2:156).

Samaria, which, as I said, is shown by the name of *Jezrahel*, a nearby valley. Therefore, let the offspring destined for punishment be born from your spirit, so that you may know that this is to be executed against my own children, which you have seen as though arranged in your own children.

For *I shall visit the blood of Jezrahel upon the house of Jehu*. To explain this, a twofold sense would have occurred through the usage of the law, had not the natural sequence of the context confirmed one of them. For the offspring of Jeroboam ruled up to the family of Ahab, who was the husband of Jezebel.[58] But when Ahab had been befouled as much by his own crimes as by those of his wife, to whose audacious outrages he was enslaved, at the command of God the prophet Elisha raised up Jehu, the son of Nimshi, to take command.[59] Provoked by the occasions with an equal severity, he destroyed by massacre the whole family of Ahab and Jezebel, and in the same manner, all the priests and ministers of the idol of Baal.[60] For this service of retribution it was promised to him that his descendants would rule over the Israelite realm all the way up to the fourth generation.[61] But this Jehu and his children and grandchildren did not destroy the outward trappings of their own devotion for which they had hunted down the worshipers of Baal, by abandoning the sacrileges by Jeroboam [I]. That is to say, they continued to cling to the worship of the calves of Samaria[62] and were enslaved to various crimes against their morality, as their profane worship demanded.[63] For that reason, his anger could be said to rise against them too—namely, against the posterity of *Jehu*, those who had destroyed the family of Ahab—so as to avenge the *blood* of those who had been extinguished by the former ones.[64] It is not that that [initial] slaughter [by Jehu] had been unjust, but because they who had performed those deeds had forfeited the honor of being their judges, since they were emulating their crimes. And because they followed after things similar to those whom they had slaughtered, they crossed the line into the number and fellowship of the guilty. And so they whom the sword of the desecrated had annihilated seemed deserving of retribution. We could easily point out that this style is likewise used frequently in the Scriptures.

Therefore, I say the prophetic verse could be explained in two ways—namely, by the one that we have previously mentioned, and by another that shall follow, had the progression of the work not supported the latter more. For he wanted to indicate the nation itself by the name *Jezrahel*, but by the name *Jehu* the reign of that nation; that is, behold, now the time has come for the people of Israel to begin to experience the violence of the merited retribution. They must either be vanquished in the valley of *Jezrahel*, or they have a royal city situated in the same valley, so that they have the king who comes from the lineage of Jehu. After all, in confirmation of this understanding he added, *And I will cause the kingdom of the house of Israel to cease, and in that day I will break in pieces the bow of Israel in the valley of Jezrahel*. Therefore, he called the chastisement a *visitation*, but he called the end of the empire a *ceasing*. In order to indicate both of these more plainly, he says, *I will break in pieces the bow of Israel in the valley of Jezrahel.*

1:6 And she conceived again, and bore a daughter, and he said, Call her name, Without Mercy; for I will not continue to

[58]Ahab ruled Israel from 875 to 854. He was the successor of Omri (886–875 or 879–869), who had established Samaria as the capital.

[59]Cf. 2 Kings 9:1-13. Jehu ruled Israel from 843 to 816.

[60]Cf. 2 Kings 9:14–10:31.

[61]Cf. 2 Kings 10:30.

[62]Cf. 1 Kings 12:29-30.

[63]Cf. 2 Kings 10:31.

[64]Cf. Jerome, *Commentary on Hosea* 1:3-4 (ACT 2:155).

have mercy on the house of Israel, but I will forget them with forgetfulness.

Because he had determined to anticipate the outcome by means of images of the events, which would be informers of the same, a daughter is described as though born, who took up the name of the calamity inflicted by foreigners—that is, *Without mercy*. For it says, *I will not continue to have mercy on the house of Israel, but I will forget them with forgetfulness.* In these things the burden of the twofold sentence of judgment is contained. For he says, Not only shall I deny mercy at the time of woes, but neither shall I allow them to return into my memory. For there might have been consolation, albeit in the midst of extreme torment, if at some point in time he were to take up remembrance of those whom he had cast away. But now, in order that the threat brought forth might grow worse, he promises that both shall be present to himself—that is, both the memory of those to be condemned and the utter forgetting of those who have been condemned. Of course, when this is heard by a wise servant it could inflame them to resentment of the cruelty. Thus, something of the following sort might be involved, by reflection, if not by speech: And how is it that so much bitterness has flowed into that kindness of yours, which is the cause of things, that you do not forget the offenses, if you do forget the guilty, and that you are devoted to the one who transgresses, if you never remember the one cast down? I fear that the salvation even of those who repent might be a hopeless case if a forgetting of those who have fallen should steal softly on so great a ruler! Therefore, he has immediately added that he has not cast out his concern to show mercy but has applied the scales of the merited examination—that is, to forget, so to speak, only those who also gave no thought to their amendment even after their stripes.

1:6-7 For I will not continue to have mercy on the house of Israel, but I will forget them with forgetfulness. And I will have mercy on the house of Judah, and I will save them by the Lord their God; and I will not save them by bow, nor by sword, nor by battle, nor by horses, nor by horsemen.

He says, When I subject the people of Samaria, befouled by transgression, to destruction and ruin, and because of their faults permit them to be so little esteemed that it appears that I have utterly forgotten them, then not only shall I protect those who stay in the region of Judah and who place their hope and confidence of salvation in the cultivation of religion, but I shall also vindicate them in a wondrously new way. Thus it will be plain and clear that they have been defended not by their weapons but by their merits, and that they have obtained their victory not by their battle array but by their piety. Now he is announcing that time when Hezekiah ruled Jerusalem and Sennacherib, king of the Assyrians, drew near to besiege his city with a great army.[65] And there he said many things in reproach of God and the sacred religion, and he incited divine judgment against himself. And in one night all his troops fell by the smiting angel. For after losing 185,000 warriors, it is recorded that he himself fled into his own country with a few men and perished there. But let us look to the remaining things as well.

1:8-9 She weaned her who was called "Without mercy," and she conceived and bore a son. And he said, Call his name, "You[66] [are] not my people," for you[67] are not my people, and I will not be yours.

The book heading indicated that blessed Hosea continued to prophesy up to the time of

[65]Cf. 2 Kings 19:35-37; Is 37:36-38; Jerome, *Commentary on Hosea* 1:6-7 (ACT 2:157).
[66]Singular.
[67]Plural.

Hezekiah.[68] Therefore, whatever is read as having been done through the entire period of that prophecy, he puts this briefly on record in this very introduction. Thus, throughout the whole book he discloses a series and order of events already accomplished. Therefore, when the profaneness of the ungrateful nation had impelled our God to take up the work of retribution, he announced that he was going to punish the guilty and would so abandon them in their wretchedness that it would seem that he had wholly forgotten them. But lest the forgetting taken up into the sacred heart should also incite terror in the pious, immediately he indicated that he would employ this forgetting not maliciously but judiciously. For indeed, he was setting in motion a deserved separation between those who were neighbors. And having surrendered the Israelites to destruction, he would protect the people of Judah, who doubtless were still clinging to the worship of their religion. And he would do this by means of miracles rather than weapons.[69] Although this was revealed at the appropriate time, nevertheless, because also that portion of the nation of Judea had certainly not been pleasing in respect of constant devotion (but just as the other prophets reproach, he was roused to anger against their cult of idols), they too bore a similar judgment, and were transferred from their own borders when Babylon conquered them.[70] Yet a summoning back from this captivity was promised by the prediction of nearly all the prophets, and this was fulfilled under Cyrus, king of the Persians.[71]

Therefore, the words of blessed Hosea are now expressing both periods of time. Now as a signification of the Israelite captivity, a daughter has been introduced who would be called *Without Mercy*; but as a figure of Judah a boy is introduced whose name is *Not My People*. But amid the three representations of the children, it is solely of the girl alone that it is mentioned that she was *weaned*. Doubtless this is to show that the judgment against the ten tribes of the captivity that was brought in recovered its strength, so to speak. For in fact we read that the captivity of the ten tribes was far longer, and therefore the advancement of the girl's age is indicated by her weaning. But the third [child], who as the last forebodes the captivity of Judah, received the name *Not My People*. For indeed, as long as Judah remained in its own borders, it was the multitude that would be called the people of God; but after the violent storm of the captivity tore even them away, that people who of old had been separated from the confusion of the nations seemed to have perished. And therefore it says, *You [are] not my people, and I will not be yours*; that is, this mark shall be removed from you, by which you were once distinguished, lest you be called the people of God in the whole world, and lest I be called your prince or your God. For it is right that you who by your pursuit of sinning have tainted the customs of the sacred law, which distinguished you from the other nations, should also be deprived of that dignity by which you were distinguished.

But briefly announcing these things from the side of severity, he transitions to prosperous things that his admirable providence fulfilled in reality, just as he has composed in his prophetic discourse:

1:10-11 The number of the children of Israel shall be as the sand of the sea, which is without measure, and shall not be numbered. And it shall be in the place where it shall be said to them, You are not my people, it shall be said to them: [You are] the sons of the living God. And the children of Judah, and the children of Israel shall be gathered together equally, and they shall appoint themselves one head, and shall

[68]Cf. Hos 1:1.

[69]Cf. 2 Kings 19:35.

[70]Cf. 2 Kings 25:11.

[71]Cf. Jer 25:8-14; Dan 9:2; Is 44:28; 45:1; Ezra 1:1. Cyrus ruled Persia from 558 to 530.

come up out of the land, for great is the day of Jezrahel.

Now with these holy utterances he promises the return of the people from the Babylonian captivity, whose enormous procession is described in the writings of the other prophets, but principally in those of blessed Isaiah.[72] This procession, of course, avails to confirm the mercy of God and the consolation and strengthening of the faithful, who were offered the solace of hope by their endurance of the fellowship of that disaster, contrary to the worth of their merits, for the sake of communion with their own nation—namely, the solace that results from the expectation of prosperity. For indeed, those things are said to be going to be so abundant that they even require new names. For when they fell from glad times into sorrowful ones, they ceased being called the people of God, as though they had been poured back into the vileness of the rest of the nations. But when the time of liberation comes, such a change from sadness to joy is said to follow that the restoration of their prior dignity is not sufficient, but the insignia of their names are made greater. For *the number* of those returning shall surpass that of the *grains of sand*. So much reverence and grace shall shine forth in them that all are no longer called the "people" but the *sons of God*, who contains all things. If indeed they are amended by the torments of the previously mentioned slavery so that they are thus united to one another by their blood as well as by charity (and they shall especially shun that division, which was the great cause of their crimes and distinctions, and if they rejoice under one ruler), they shall go up to the temple of God with eagerness and shall set so much value in that state of happiness that they would confess that *great* was *the day of Jezrahel*. This refers either to that time in which the adversities began—about which the prophet said, "I will break in pieces the bow of Israel in the valley of Jezrahel,"[73] the liberated people shall take this up in remembrance, that their joys are enlarged by comparison—or else they shall cry out that the interpretation of the name *Jezrahel* fits them, since indeed in our language it expresses "God's seed."[74] The resultant meaning is thus: when the time of captivity expires, there shall be such a great display of exultation that a *great day* is said to have shone on the sons of God. But just like the rest of the prophets, so also blessed David describes this festivity principally in this song: "I rejoiced at the things that were said to me, 'We shall go into the house of the Lord. Our feet will stand in the courts of Jerusalem to praise your name, O Lord, because there thrones will sit in judgment, thrones on the house of David. Pray for the things that pertain to the peace of Jerusalem.'"[75]

Therefore, following the course of history that the prophetic announcement contained, it briefly pointed out everything that was going to happen: namely, the ten tribes, corrupted at the source by Jeroboam [I],[76] were borne off when Assyria captured them,[77] but Judah, who trusted in his God, was miraculously delivered under King Hezekiah.[78] But afterward that tribe, too, having followed in the footsteps of his brother's impiety, was allowed to experience Babylonian domination,[79] whose chains, however, the promised liberty loosed a second time. And the brothers no longer separated from each other but, abiding under one ruler, would celebrate the honor of God in the sacred precincts of his temple. But so great was the happiness of that time that it would even be pleasant to remember the hard

[72]Cf. Is 10:21-22; 35:10; 40:3-11; 51:11; 52:8.

[73]Hos 1:5.

[74]Cf. Jerome, *Commentary on Hosea* 1:3-4 (ACT 2:154).

[75]Ps 122:1-2, 5-6.

[76]Cf. 1 Kings 12:25-33.

[77]Cf. 2 Kings 15:29; 17:5-6.

[78]Cf. 2 Kings 19:35.

[79]Cf. 2 Kings 25:11.

times[80] and to call it the great *day of Jezrahel*—that is, that time of the captivity that was brought on them, the occasion that had created so much exultation. Therefore, *they shall appoint themselves one head, and shall come up out of the land,* at which time also blessed David says, "To you have I cried from the ends of the earth, when my heart was in anguish, you have exalted me on a rock. You have conducted me, for you have been my hope."[81]

It should also be noted that blessed Paul received the promise of that passage regarding the multitude of believers flowing in with respect to the proclamation of the gospel. That is, he claims that the announcement of the good news of piety has surpassed the narrow confines of one nation and that multitudes were coming together "not only of the Jews," who were once called the people of God, "but also of the Gentiles," who had lived in manifold errors but have taken on themselves the dignity of the divine lineage. He says, "As it says in Hosea, I will call not my people, my people; and not beloved, beloved; and it shall be in the place where it will be said, You [are] not my people, there they shall be called the sons of the living God."[82] Thus, the teacher of the nations[83] shows that in the time of the gospel, this joyous promise was fulfilled. Certainly this is not to deny what the whole context of the prophecy drives home—namely, that a release from the Babylonian captivity had also been promised. He merely wanted to show what principle we ought to observe in the interpretation of the prophetic writings; that is, when anything was revealed in a narration of Jewish matters that was vaster than the insignificance of one nation had room to contain, we need to know that it has been fulfilled partially in that people, and by [prophetic] vision (*per theoriam*[84]) it is applicable to others also—that is, to all the nations. But as the learned have agreed,[85] [prophetic] vision (*theoria*) is the perception[86] of those realities that are of greater importance, considered generally in brief images or cases.[87] Therefore, this summoning back of the Jews from Babylon was not properly spoken of according to history, but that liberation signified allegorically what has been acquired through faith in Christ—I grant that the prophetic speech has promised both without qualification.

Thus, the thing of moderate size that preceded made known the peaks that were to follow. For what had first been expressed in

[80]Cf. Virgil, *Aeneid* 1.278.

[81]Ps 61:1-3.

[82]Rom 9:24-26.

[83]Cf. 1 Tim 2:7.

[84]H. Bate, "Some Technical Terms of Greek Exegesis," *JTS* 24 (1923): 62, states that in Theodore of Mopsuestia, *theoria* is primarily used of prophetic vision. "It is that intuition of things present and future which God granted to the prophets." Bate's discussion affected my translation here.

[85]In the inaugural article of *Biblica*, the periodical issued at Rome by the Pontificium Institutum Biblicum, Fr. A. Vaccari, "La θεωρία nella scuola esegetic di Antiochia," *Biblica* 1 (1920): 3-36, understood the "learned" here to refer specifically to the Antiochene fathers; cited in Bate, "Some Technical Terms of Greek Exegesis," 62. Bate, however, suggests that it may refer rather to the teachers of rhetoric from whom the Antiochenes derived their technical equipment.

[86]*Considerata perceptio*. In the preface he uses *votiva perceptio* (prayed-for perception).

[87]"Theoria est autem (ut eruditis placuit) in brevibus plerumque aut formis aut causis, earum rerum quae potiores sunt considerata perceptio." Julian's definition of *theoria*, a word that can be translated as "vision, sight, speculation, contemplation," has given rise to abundant discussion, beginning with A. Vaccari's article cited earlier. Cf. most recently J. Lössl, *Julian von Aeclanum: Studien zu seinem Leben, seinem Werk, seiner Lehre und ihrer Überlieferung* (Leiden: Brill, 2001), 174-87. The precise meaning, nuances, and conjectured Greek Vorlage of the terms are contested. Jerome uses *theoria* in his *Commentary on Ezekiel* 12, 40, 4. It is used by Cicero (written as Greek) in *Att.* 12, 6, 1. After a lengthy analysis, Bouwman, *Des Julian von Aeclanum Kommentar,* 108, renders Julian's definition: "*Theoria ist die Erfassung einer höheren Wirklichkeit durch die Betrachtung meist unbedeutender Bilder oder Ereignisse*: '*Theoria* is the grasping of a higher reality through the consideration of generally less important images or events.'" He says that Julian's intent is not that the Old Testament's partial fulfillment in image and content is of lesser importance than the conclusive fulfillment in the New Testament but that the literary form is almost always transcended, in order that we may be made attentive to the incompleteness of the partial fulfillment.

exaggerated terms hardly equaled the magnitude of the things that were to come later.[88] So also, the announced captivity that terrified the Jewish people at that time, and the restored liberty that raised them up afterward, held aloft the signs of the captivity and liberation of others too (which were weightier by far), doubtless of that about which the apostle says, "We were by nature children of wrath, even as the rest; but God, because he is rich in mercy, for his exceeding charity with which he loved us, even when we were dead in sins, made us alive together in Christ."[89] For indeed, the stronger one who came has "bound" that enemy of the human race, who had oppressed the guilty under a long domination, "and he plundered" all "his possessions."[90] He has released the captivity of the nations, restoring their freedom, and he has ennobled with gifts of grace those who have been redeemed, so that we, who were once foreigners and guests, are suddenly his citizens and people who have obtained mercy.[91] Or rather, we are called "a chosen, priestly and royal race."[92] So in this way, what Hosea had declared about the Babylonian times, Paul transferred to the affairs of salvation. This certainly does not mean that the prophet would, so to speak, deny or reluctantly follow where he is being led [by the apostle]. Rather, it is that the prophet very much favors the apostolic understanding throughout the course of the prophecy, in which he taught that both gifts and joys were here increased nearly all the way up to the consummation, which had already begun in that age.

But up to this point the speech of the prophet proceeded along that course so that it briefly indicated whatever matters and times it was about to speak of. But now it returns to the order of the appointed censure and complaint, which he has deliberately managed with foresight, lest what had validity in respect to the pomp of the prediction should begin to be unsuitable to the salvific teaching. For he touched on those things that were going to follow a long time afterward with the vehemence of one prophesying. And the boldness of his preaching proposed faith as a substitute both in the adversities and in prosperity. Otherwise, by this very thing, I say, he might seem to have abolished fear and prayer equally, seeing that it accomplished nothing toward the adoption of a zeal of amendment. For the crisis of the pre-announced punishment was impinging once and for all. The wish for prosperous times does not seem necessary all over again, though it was to be restored in all ways on behalf of the truth of the one preaching. For that reason the speech is directed to the people, and they are called together into a mutual participation in judgment so that with attentive eyes they might proceed to examine "their mother"[93] (namely, the multitude of their ancestors whose crimes have angered God) and to remind her of divine mercy, which is accustomed indeed to remove announced torments if it sees that the guilty have taken refuge in amendment. Therefore, let them not despair of their salvation if they become better through fear, because he is in charge who blots out merited punishments, who delights far more in resplendent forgiveness than in bitter severity.

[88]H. Bate, "Some Technical Terms of Greek Exegesis," 63, summarizes an interpretation of Theodore of Mopsuestia on Zech 9:9 ("Rejoice greatly, O daughter of Sion") in words that seem to fit well with Julian's explanation here: "Here, he says, we have a passage which must not be understood to speak at one moment of Zerubbabel and at another of Christ, but one which primarily applies to Zerubbabel, yet speaks of him in language so hyperbolical that the prophecy could not be completely fulfilled in him; its final fulfillment is only to be found in Christ."

[89]Eph 2:3-5.

[90]Cf. Mt 12:29.

[91]Cf. Eph 2:19.

[92]Cf. 1 Pet 2:9.

[93]Hos 2:2.

[Chapter 2]

2:2 Judge your mother, judge [her], because she is not my wife, and I am not her husband.

Your liberation, it says, stands out as a great monument to my kindness, and for that reason the faults of your filthy mother are laid bare, for which she was driven from my society, but of such a filthy woman that it is not possible for you who are judging to be absolved. But because in the present appraisal we are examining not one person but the whole nation, we hope that there will be some whom the announced severity might move to better pursuits. Therefore, pay attention to what I am waiting for:

2:2-3 Let her put away her fornications from her face (*facie*), and her adulteries from between her breasts, lest I strip her naked, and set her as in the day that she was born.

That is, she had banished shame from her face (*vultu*), which usually prevents obscene behavior, and she had hardened her face by the profession of disgrace. So now let her eagerly take up affections opposite to these, and clothe her brow, stripped of wantonness, with modesty. And not satisfied with having done only this, on the surface, as it were, with her lips, let her cast out the poison drawn out *from between her breasts*, so that she might henceforth be made pure in her whole heart. But if she neglects to do this, I shall gird myself for the work of severity, which I employed during that time in which this woman was born into my people. Now he is showing the exodus of the synagogue from the land of Egypt, in which time obviously it had received no trappings or ornaments of legal institutions, nor was it flourishing with any signs of vestments,[94] but, as far as the value of their morals went, it remained in that same baseness of Egypt.[95] Nevertheless, it was rescued by great miracles solely on account of the honor of its ancestors.[96] Of course, this display of a manifold victory procured no prejudice, as it were, no impediment to the one judging later on—that is, that those whom so many miracles had rescued unto liberation would see their sins go unpunished in the future. After all, because they resisted the precepts of God, at one time by wantonness, at another through idleness, one reads that all of them were wiped out in the solitude of the desert. Out of six hundred thousand men of military age who marched forth, no one entered the Promised Land save for two, Joshua and Caleb.[97]

Therefore, this is what the Lord of the universe now threatens through the prophet. He is saying that if that nation does not cleanse the secret places of their heart and make progress toward the better by effecting change, the fact that they lived for so many ages as set apart from other nations, and flourished by the institutions of the law and by spiritual gifts will provide them no shelter—I mean, shelter whereby that closely pursuing judgment on their crimes would be softened. In the same way it did not profit the wretches at all in that age in which they went out from Egypt and rejoiced as it were in their recent adoption. And what is more, if they were stripped of all their privileges, they were not kept from utterly perishing. When writing to the Corinthians, the apostle Paul also carefully cultivated this sense. He says, All those freed by miracles alone made use of the same spiritual food; they drank from the same springs bursting forth from the rock. Yet, he says, all of them, or many, displeased God, but in that age of exile they bristled with various sins, and they perished by various punishments.[98] In showing

[94]Priestly vestments are described in Ex 28–29.

[95]Cf. Jerome, *Commentary on Hosea* 2:2-3a (ACT 2:160).

[96]Cf. Ex 14:26-31.

[97]Cf. Ex 12:37; Num 1:45-46; 14:23-30; 32:11-12; Deut 1:34-40.

[98]Cf. 1 Cor 10:1-11.

why he has recalled these things, he says, "They were written for our instruction."[99] This is to keep us from emulating the pursuits of those whose failure we have read about. Therefore, through this prophet our God has disclosed the affection of his design, and he warns so that that people might run to him for help by means of an immediate correction. And he warns them to expel *from between their breasts* (namely, from their heart) the impiety that he calls *fornication,* lest they should feel the trials of that severity, whose dispensing no difficulty can defer. For whether he proceeds to devour the impious in his vengeance, the multitude of those perishing shall not have the strength to resist, or whether he has consigned the children of those punished to be restored to salvation out of esteem for their innocence or due to the merits of their correction, the heaping up of the calamity previously mentioned shall not be able to make any impediment. Therefore, in order to indicate all this briefly, the prophet showed the same orderly arrangement in the example that he preserved in his prophecy. And, just as in the very title by mentioning the kings he indicated the whole age in which he had prophesied,[100] so likewise he showed some of the matters his preaching would contain—namely, the captivity, first of Israel,[101] then of Judah. Then, when in turn the captivity of the same people was released, he shows their concord and, once liberty has been restored, he shows their coming together to worship at the temple of the true God.[102] Yet the splendor of this return was described in a way that was effective to indicate a matter of greater significance; namely, it expressed the freedoms as well as the liberality of the gospel, which surpassed their hopes in respect of its gifts.[103] He called those whom he had freed from deadly servitude not only "the people of God" but also "sons of God." Therefore, having briefly covered those things, he has returned to the discourse that matched those times, and he shows the duty of a mother, as it were, rebuking and teaching her children, so that she who had taken no care to preserve her chastity should at least think about taking hold of repentance. And let her not consider herself to be protected against the repayment for her practices only by virtue of the nobility of her blood. For the adoption would not profit those whom devotion also did not fortify. For in order to infer the future from the past, he thought on the destruction of those multitudes that had been miraculously led out of Egypt. Their iniquity, as we have said, was assuredly not defended by the nobility of their ancestors, nor did their slaughter create an obstacle to the leading of their children to the happiness that was promised. Therefore, he says, this manner of judgments shall also be preserved now in your examination[104] so that those who are defiled by sacrileges might be overwhelmed by destruction and so that their posterity, who differed from the design of their progenitors by their better pursuits, might either acquire the liberty that had been despaired of or increase more abundantly by the good results of prosperity. Because these changes of times, it says (namely, of both grievous times and joyful), mark out the reckoning of divine providence and of just governance, right now let us describe what the present case demands. Therefore, declare it so that they may forestall the mass of the damnation that is threatening them, both by an earnest endeavor to make correction and by the groaning of repentance. Otherwise, when the vengeance begins to rage, this whole nation, just as it had not been marked out by any special rights, would perish by slaughter.

[99]1 Cor 10:11.
[100]Cf. Hos 1:1.
[101]Cf. Hos 1:4-5.
[102]Cf. Hos 1:11.
[103]Cf. Rom 9:25-26; 1 Pet 2:10.
[104]Baxter, "Notes," 30, suggests this meaning of *expunctio*.

2:3-5 Lest I strip her naked, and set her as on the day that she was born, and make her as a wilderness, and set her as a land that none can pass through, and kill her with thirst. And I will not have mercy on her children, for they are the children of fornications, for their mother has committed fornication; she that conceived them is covered with shame.

Because he had once introduced the reminder of and comparison to the Egyptian exodus, he ran through a description of the same passages, obviously naming the *wilderness* and the *land that none can pass through* and one that was destitute even of the consolation of springs. And again, taking up the words from the circumstances, since the wasteland of the desert had been called to mind, he added also the peril of *thirst*, saying, *I will kill her with thirst*. It is not that we read that the people who were led out from Egypt were consumed by lack of water, but because, as the apostle says, "they drank from the spiritual rock that was following";[105] that is, the power of the one guiding them, not the conditions of the region, supplied drinks for their encampments. Indeed, if this power had been absent, the people would have been destroyed first by the peril of *thirst*. For that reason he declares that the wicked may be led away into similar distresses and that mercy shall not come to meet them. For he admits that even the offspring of such people were obscene parents unto themselves by imitation of those vices. And because both the children are ashamed of their parents and the parents of the children, he promised that they were going to perish of *thirst*.

2:5-7 For she said, I will go after my lovers, who give [me] my bread and water, my wool and my flax, my oil and my drink. Wherefore, behold, I will hedge up your way with thorns, and I will stop it up with a stone wall, and she shall not find her paths. And she shall follow after her lovers and shall not overtake them, and she shall seek them and not find.

From the beginning of the book he has adapted the character of a prostitute to the profaned nation. Therefore, he executes the rest of it as well with a similar description, and he introduces an address made by the whore, which doubtless she is convicted of having blabbed, if not with her lips, yet by her works. And so, according to the custom of the Scriptures, those things are exposed that every impious person is able to say in consequence of a rather evil life, since they speak to themselves also in words. Therefore, it says, even that shameless woman alleged the pretext of service for the eager pursuit of her shameless deeds. Thus, she tells the lie that her lovers pursued her on account of her generosity rather than on account of her baseness. For she confides that those men supplied her with *wool and flax, oil and drink*—that is, food and clothing overflowing even to the point of luxury. Although plainly by these statements she is adding to the sin of sacrilege the crime also of an ungrateful mind, nevertheless she seems to introduce also what even now is constantly on the lips of the profane—namely, among diverse opinions, no testimony of sure religion is stronger than that which the voice of favorable circumstances conveys. Therefore, by announcing that she goes in eager pursuit of her lovers, she also conceals her passionate deed with silence and portrays the motives with which she is enticed as though they are quite honorable. But he calls her *lovers* either pagan noblemen, by whose eager pursuit she has been desecrated,[106] or those national gods that are more worthy of ridicule than of any

[105] 1 Cor 10:4.

[106] Cf. Ezek 16.

veneration. Obviously it was to them that this synagogue succumbed when she forgot about the law of her fathers and about the one true God. For this reason, therefore, the just judge (*arbiter*) now upbraids them and says, She remains hardened with a calloused brow of impudence. All those gifts that were created as an aid for mortal life—by which the nakedness of the human body was covered, its weakness nourished, and its meanness adorned—she dared even to direct more to the corruptions of unclean spirits than to the creation of strong ones by services. Therefore, let misfortunes succeed in the place of her hopes, and let her be entangled in unforeseen torments. In the first place, let no opportunity of entering into a covenant be at hand for her with those nations that she desires the most. In her adversities let her not enjoy the assistance of those by whose example she transgressed in good times. And in this way shall I *hedge her path with thorns*, and not only with thorn bushes but also with *stone walls*, so that from now on she cannot enter the narrow ways that she had tread earlier. All of these things surely he wove in below as a consequence while having in view the persona of the woman whom he introduced, the authoress on secret paths, as it were, of her repeated shameful deeds. Surely he does not say this because the people of Israel were intermingling with wicked nations secretly, but because the similitude given by the woman (as we have often said) demanded this arrangement of the description. Therefore, because the avenging severity will begin to come upon her, and none of her lovers will be able to produce any wealth by her torments, now she is moved no longer by reason but by anguish. She begins to recall her previous happiness:

2:7-8 And she shall say, I will go and return to my first husband, because it was well with me then, rather than now. And she did not know that I gave her corn, wine, and oil, and multiplied her gold as well, which they made into a Baal.

If she was aroused at least by the perils of the events and was considering *returning to her first husband*, how was it logical to add *And she did not know that I gave her corn and wine and oil?* Therefore, the sense is of this kind, whereby consistency is maintained in the prophetic statements. At the first appearance of punishment, this woman experiences what all [do] who pursue empty things—namely, she is utterly dismayed at the nullification of her wishes. So she tries to seek what she had repudiated not through the amendment arising from the judgment sentence but due to the lightness of the judgment. Moreover, she promises anew that she would be subject to God alone, so as to escape the losses of prosperity hanging over her, as it were. This agrees with the reproach expressed by blessed David: "When he slew them, they sought him; and they returned early in the morning, and came to him, but their heart was not right with him, nor were they counted as faithful to his covenant."[107] Therefore, while the guilt of her nation remained, she is impelled not by the teaching authority of the Word but, like a beast, under the impulse of the lash. And my anger will not be mitigated on account of this because, she has said, *I will go and return to my first husband*. Moreover, I shall lead her into long experiences of blows, she who does not take the trouble to know and judge that all these things could have been given by no one but me, the one by whom they had certainly also been created. Therefore, what he says, *And she did not know that I gave her corn and wine and oil*, has in view the hatefulness of her voluntary delay. This accords with the following words of David: "She was unwilling to understand so as to act well."[108] And so, amid

[107]Ps 78:34-37.
[108]Ps 36:3.

the perils of her hardships, she shall begin to admit what before she did not take the trouble to know—namely, that I was the one by whom her sustenance was being supplied, who also brought forth the very substance of human beings. *That I gave her corn and wine and oil and gold, which they made into a Baal.* Thus, she was not only instructed but also well supplied when she abused my gifts by committing her criminal acts. And from these riches that she had received from me, she fabricated idols to insult me. Therefore, at length even I shall take up the duty of condemnation. The highly extolling prophet wisely sang about my providential governance, "With the holy one, you will be holy, and with the innocent man you will be innocent, and with the elect you will be elect, with the perverse you will be perverted."[109] The result will be that I lead on those who had been gathered unwillingly, and their wealth would achieve some benefit of deliverance when it is withheld from being used by the profane.

2:9a I will take away my corn in its season, and my wine in its season.

He distinctly says this because there has not been a single gathering of the crop. Moreover, each is gathered in individually at different seasons of the year; and for that reason also the summer shall refuse its harvest, the fall the grape vintage, the winter shall bear off with its olive harvest, and a certain freedom, it says, shall lay hold of created things, if those who use them are not undeserving. "And I will set at liberty my wool and my flax, which covered her disgrace."[110] To be sure, this tastefully alluded to feminine adornment, since in this way she covered her whole body, in which there are some shameful things, to make that part attractive as well; but this pointedly seems to show that generally a hideousness in the guilty lurks beneath their prosperity in life. If a well-earned scarcity should again touch them, their offenses also, which had lain hidden, are exposed.

2:10a And now I will lay open her folly in the eyes of her lovers.

That is, the outcome of events shall force those who stood forth as the authors and partners in crime to admit that there is nothing more stupid than this nation. Counsel could not guide it, nor could dangers correct it. But by the sins of their ungrateful minds they have aroused the anger of that God whose power holds all things together. She has experienced this power both in her adversities and in her good fortune. Therefore, *I will lay open her folly in the eyes of her lovers,* "and no man shall deliver her out of my hand."[111] That is, not one of those noblemen whose profanity she has pursued shall be able to protect her from my wrath. It is not that anyone would dare to try this, but the speech that was adopted is composed using the similitude of a woman and her husbands. For that reason, it says, when the divine anger has struck her down, her crowd of lovers will not be able to run to her aid or offer her any consolation during the misfortunes in which she is to be overwhelmed.

2:11 And I will cause all her joy to cease: her solemnity, her new moon, her Sabbath, and all her festive times.

He has recorded here the names of the religious holidays on which she was most accustomed to rejoice, when the whole nation would become wanton with their dances, their songs, their feasts. Certainly such extravagance flourished only when the people were enjoying a deep peace. All these things will be changed into their opposites, he says. Thus, when joy

[109]Ps 18:25-26.
[110]Hos 2:9b.
[111]Hos 2:10b.

ceases, mourning shall be brought in; captivity shall replace the times of the festivals; the weariness of a wretched servitude shall fill up the leisure of the Sabbath. Not only shall freedom change into slavery but also the fertility of the ground shall change into a deadly barrenness:

2:12 I will destroy her vineyard and her fig tree, of which she said, These are my rewards, which my lovers have given me. And I will make her as a forest, and the beasts of the field shall devour her.

He has described what the damage of the portions would accomplish—that is, when constant frustration had overtaken the diligent care for cultivation. Their farms shall put aside the former delightfulness, when squalor follows after. And the whole country shall become very like unto wild areas rather than fields; that is, they will be considered more fitting for wild beasts than for human beings. Since the scarcity of cultivators would introduce that appearance, he has elegantly discerned that *the beasts of the field* would feed on its fruits. Of her own free will, it says, she has cast out the light of reason, and after her abundance and fattening, "the beloved one kicked."[112] And that most shameless nation was so much inclined toward their own error that they dared to attribute to their own corruptors the joys of peace and the abundance of things, the continuation of which I had promised to them, if they would have remained chaste and devout. For that reason, as I said, this portion shall be the first for retribution, so that they may be deprived of these joys and this abundance, which they did not use well, and may know that he who gave these things earlier out of kindness was thereafter able to take them away when angered. It says, *I will make her as a forest, and the beast of the field shall devour her.* He is saying, I shall allow her to be consumed by the enemy's assault, and just as no farmer surrounds forests and wild areas with toilsome fences, so my disposition will not protect her by any intervention.[113] And because he seemed to have carried out a severe judgment, he adds the reason for this agitation a second time so as to teach that whatever rage he has exhibited is evidence more of his justice than of his anger:

2:13 And I will visit on her the days of Baalim, to whom she burnt incense, and decked herself out with her earrings and with her necklace, and went after her lovers, and forgot me, says the Lord.

He is saying, It is hardly with just the beginning stages of sinning that she is involved. One would think that she has been suffused with it by the advancement of time. Of old our patience has contended against her depravity, but we have not succeeded in seeing her make amendment, as she has grown old in her wickedness. Therefore, let not the long period of her going unpunished stain the reputation of the judge as well. Let me not seem to be in favor of what for so long a time I permitted to flourish. Though the hour may be late, nevertheless, ultimately I shall gird myself for the work of retribution, in order to blot out those feast days also, on which she would serve *Baalim* (namely, the idol of her shamefulness) while being decked out all over with *necklaces*. But since he mentioned not only *necklaces* but also *earrings*, we can certainly say that he named a few of the many things with which women are adorned. Nevertheless, this passage allows that we might bring out something loftier; that is, obedience seems to be shown by the term *earrings*. And because at that time the Jewish people alone had received the precepts of the law that they were to obey, fittingly they

[112]Deut 32:15.

[113]Cf. Jerome, *Commentary on Hosea* 2:10-12 (ACT 2:164).

wore the ornaments of *earrings*, as it were; but when they were ensnared by deadly error, such that they were subjected to the rituals of idols, we may now consider that very object especially as a matter of reproach. It is as if he were to say, By my lavish gift the synagogue took up the gold and silver that the earth that I created had brought forth. And once it had been defiled with sin, it brought together the abundance of the remaining things for the worship and adornment of idols. And it transferred to shameful rituals that sign of obedience by which it alone flourished among the rest of the peoples. And thinking that it was remaining in that beauty in which it had once been, she followed *her lovers* with such great trust that a complete *forgetting* of our name came upon her.

2:14-17 Therefore, behold, I will allure[114] her and will lead her into the wilderness, and I will speak to her heart. And I will give her vinedressers out of the same place, and the valley of Achor for an opening of hope. And she shall sing there according to the days of her youth, and according to the days of her coming up out of the land of Egypt. And it shall be in that day, says the Lord, [that] she shall call me My husband, and she shall call me no more Baalim. And I will take away the names of Baalim out of her mouth, and she shall no more remember their name.

The arrangement of the prophet's speech should be carefully noted. Whenever he needs to announce torments and to show the extent of divine severity, immediately he adds the causes that merited this. And not content with having enumerated the sins of mortals, he describes the joys of the prosperous times that will follow. This shows that our God adopts that brief negligence of pardon in a certain manner in preparation for reconciliation; yet by this argument, as the divine mercy is praised, so human iniquity is suppressed—namely, the magnitude of it brings about that the Lord of such great benevolence is sometimes roused to anger. Therefore, after he had announced that a sorrowful cessation to all their joys had to be introduced and that no one could run to meet the wretched ones, as one who was going to bring help or comfort [to them], immediately he expounded the crimes of the people. That is, he gives the reasons for his indignation, and he calls to mind the magnitude and the period of those crimes. He shows that their punishment should not be in greater suspicion for anyone on account of its excess, since, if it was amassed by the quantity or periods of their crimes, he would regard his sparingness as excusable, his lateness as excusable. But by not commending his mercy familiar to himself and sweet in this one condition, I say, he also consigns this very same thing concerning the onset of prosperities that cleaves to the blows, and he describes these things with an extent greater by far, like one who wanted not only to compensate but also to apologize for what he destroyed. Therefore, he had said that he would place her in a forest, so that the beast of the field would devour her;[115] that is, all fortifications of the kingdom and of the cities will be cut off. She will be handed over to the power of her enemies. She will experience, as previously in Egypt, the contumely and hardship of filthy slavery, for she had forgotten her God in her eager pursuit of idols. However, because he is tenderhearted and one who pities, he announces the joys of their return after the end

[114]*Lacto* means "give milk to, give suck to." There seem to be two etymologically different Latin verbs *lacto*; the first derives from the noun for "milk," the other, from *lacio*, the verb for "to allure, entice." The Greek of Hos 2:14 uses πλανῶ, "to lead astray, deceive, seduce," which indicates that the Old Latin translators employed *lacto* in its second meaning. Cf. Jerome, *Commentary on Hosea* 2:14-15a (ACT 2:165).

[115]Cf. Hos 2:12.

of the captivity. And because he mentioned the Egyptian liberation earlier, he asserts that this would be conveyed on the Israelite peoples like that also, in fact now even more extensively. But he scans the same example briefly and says, *Behold I will allure* (lactabo) *her, and will speak to her heart, and I will give her vinedressers out of the same place, and the valley of Achor for an opening of hope.* Because he calls the time of the Egyptian liberation the "birth" of the synagogue, "suckling" (*lactatio*) also seems to point to the food of manna.[116] But the speech directed *to her heart* points to the promulgation of the law, which transformed the hearts of the hearers.[117] But take heed of what this signifies: *I will give her vinedressers out of the same place, and the valley of Achor for an opening of hope.* Before the people entered the Promised Land, the scouts sent in carried the choice fruit of the vine—that is, a grape cluster of such size that a single porter could not lift it.[118] But after they seized the exceedingly wealthy city named Jericho by a wondrous victory, a man from the tribe of Judah named Achan, the son of Charmi, secretly stole some of the plunder, which had been set apart to be burned.[119] And when the success of the conquerors was impeded by sudden adversities, the accursed thief is discovered by the casting of lots, and, when he produced everything that he had concealed, we read that he was destroyed and buried in the Valley of Achor, where the people stoned him.[120] This atonement, of course, had the power to appease God, so that thereafter they were the masters of bloodless victories. And thus that *valley opened up* new fields for those who took up the *hope* of success, *hope* that the previous guilt had closed off. Therefore, having recalled these things, which corresponded to the events of that time, he promises also that there would thus be a joyful return of the Jews from the Babylonian captivity. After all, it follows, *And she shall sing there according to the days of her youth, and according to the days of her coming up out of the land of Egypt.* For just as then, when the waves were cut through and they crossed through the open sea by a dry passage, and Miriam (*Maria*), the sister of Moses, snatched up her musical instruments and began to sing the praises of God with choirs of dancers following her,[121] in this way they will sing when they come forth from the Assyrian captivity. Certainly this will not be as those about to destroy some Jericho or about to find grapes again, but such joyful times will turn out for them that they would seem to have attained to the glory that they possessed under Moses and Joshua.

But consider carefully how the memory of this history was made, clearly both as an example of sad things and of joyful. For he had said earlier, "Lest I strip her naked, and set her as on the day that she was born, and make her as a wilderness, and set her as a land that none can pass through, and kill her with thirst."[122] Certainly this would be in imitation of those "whose corpses," as the apostle Paul says, "were scattered in the desert."[123] But now, since he promised that their servitude would be released and that joys would come, arising from their freedom, he has recalled just as many of those times—namely, those in which their glorious liberation had been praised with sacred songs. Of course, just as the sweetness of that happiness (that is, that which would be experienced after the Babylonian captivity) would be a consolation to the Jews, so its greatness would indicate that people would flock to the preaching of the gospel, who truly sing "a new song"[124] to God. For "he has made

[116]Cf. Ex 16:13-36. See note under lemma.
[117]Cf. Deut 6:5-6.
[118]Cf. Num 13:24.
[119]Cf. Josh 7.
[120]Cf. Josh 7:26.
[121]Cf. Ex 15:20-21.
[122]Hos 2:3.
[123]Heb 3:17.
[124]Ps 98:1. Cf. Jerome, *Commentary on Hosea* 2:14-15 (ACT 2:165).

known his salvation to the world and has revealed his justice in the sight of the Gentiles."[125] And by his free forgiveness and sanctification he has abolished that slavery in which we were subdued by sins and unclean spirits, so that having been freed from our iniquities, we serve justice.[126] And we have been made the "people of possession"[127] and are resplendent with the marks of a divine lineage. And we have *vinedressers* from our body, I say, from our people—namely, those who hand over the delight of the enormous grape cluster to us in the mysteries or who exhibit that very skill and diligence by which the vineyard of God is tended.[128] Hence in that time, when these desired things that we have recounted come to pass, even the amendment of their ways shall reveal how much benefit shall have come about from the promised punishment. He says, If indeed she shall cleave to me with her whole heart in such a way that she no longer worships me sporadically, but devotes constant worship to me, has constant affection for me, and shall call me alone her husband and Lord, and shall no longer ascribe my name to Baal, that is, to idols. Of course, from this term *Baal* the tradition of the Jews wanted to contrive some meaning,[129] but the following appears to be more true, through which the whole logical sequence runs—namely, that he is promising that the names of the idols would be removed from the mouth of the chastised nation and that they would invoke only the Lord God. But by saying *she shall no more remember their name*, either he indicated the correction that was complete or it looked toward that which he had recorded earlier, "She went after her lovers, and forgot me, says the Lord."[130] Therefore, shutting out this fault by her correction, she shall turn into the opposite affection, so that with complete forgetfulness she puts aside her pursuit of wickedness.

[125]Ps 98:2.
[126]Cf. Rom 6:18.
[127]1 Pet 2:9.
[128]Cf. Mt 20:1-16; 21:28-41; Mk 12:1-9; Lk 20:9-16; Jerome, *Commentary on Hosea* 2:14-15 (ACT 2:166).
[129]According to Jerome, *Commentary on Hosea* 2:16-17 (ACT 2:168), in the Hebrew and Syrian languages, Baal means "one who has [in wedlock]."

2:18-20 In that day I will strike up a covenant (*foedus*) with the beast of the field, and with the fowl of the air, and with the creeping thing of the earth; and I will destroy the bow, and the sword, and war out of the land, and I will make them sleep secure. And I will espouse you to me forever, and I will espouse you to me in justice and judgment, and in mercy and in commiserations, and I will espouse you to me in faith, and you shall know that I am the Lord.

He says, It is fitting that she who had been polluted (*foedata*) was subjected to lashes, and once corrected should obtain all good things; and therefore, just as our indignation had rendered every creature not only hostile but even dangerous, so also our reconciliation makes these same creatures friendly and agreeable. And so, *I will strike up a covenant with the beast of the field*, that the wild beast's savageness might not lay waste to the crops of the fields, and that a multitude of *fowl* might not snatch away from their grapevines or olive groves, and that serpents might not inject venom into the limbs of the exhausted. All these things are said to be going to cease when the time of liberation comes; at any rate, they are shown to have been introduced in the days of chastisement. But along with these misfortunes, *wars* too shall cease, in such a way that they would be able to *sleep* in their ancestral lands (that is, to rest confidently), for they will fear neither invasions nor ambushes. *I will espouse you to me forever*; that is, having been

[130]Hos 2:13.

instructed in these matters, you shall come to know that that separation with which you were afflicted happened not by my fault but by yours. Moreover, I was prepared to have you remain my spouse forever; that is, if you would have been the sort as the punitive judgments have now rendered you, the previous covenant with you shall be preserved forever. For thus I make a contract that you will remain in our fellowship, so that the judgments applied might bring out your justice; or if negligence sneaks up on you and wounds you, and you shall nevertheless ask for a remedy from me with a full display of weeping, nonetheless I shall espouse you to me *in mercy and in commiserations*. When, of course, you shall have felt them faithfully and persistently—for this is what he says, *I will espouse you to me in faith*—you shall announce with the ardor owed that *I am the Lord*. As we have taught,[131] all of this shall stand firm as fulfilled more clearly if we apply it to the calling of the gospel. For "[You are] beautiful in form beyond the sons of men."[132] The grace poured out from your lips gave salvation to the world.[133] The queen, whom he betrothed to himself, he received into the union of the wedding chamber for the honor of her virginity,[134] *in justice*, which he gave to justify. He received her *in judgment*, since he loved her, who was to be duly afflicted. He received her *in mercy and in commiserations*, since he forgave her past debts, and he espoused her *in faith*, whereby either "with the heart one believes unto justice, with the mouth confession is made unto salvation"[135] or, which is not to be doubted, because "to them that love God, all things proceed to the good."[136]

[131]Cf. Julian's comments under Hos 1:10-11.
[132]Ps 45:2.
[133]Cf. Ps 45:2.
[134]Cf. Ps 45:9-11.
[135]Rom 10:10.
[136]Rom 8:28.

2:21-24 And it shall come to pass in that day, I will hear, says the Lord, I will hear the heavens, and they shall hear the earth, and the earth shall hear the corn,[137] the wine, and the oil, and these shall hear Jezrahel. And I will sow her unto me in the earth, and I will have mercy on her that was Without Mercy; and I will say to Not My People, You are My People. And they shall say, You are my Lord.

He extends the series of the wished-for promise, and by means of various outward forms composes a trope familiar to the sacred volumes, so that the elements alternately desire to carry out his work in supporting human frailty, but they are unable, unless the Creator gives his assent. At that time, of course, in which he has been appeased and has driven off the adversities, he promises that he will supply all things sufficiently. Their felicity shall indeed begin to be deficient if their desired freedom should long for fullness for so many ages. But as we have said,[138] this sweetness of joys only made a prelude even in that age, when the captivity of Babylon was released. And it was rendered in a more abundant way in the time of the apostles, when the whole multitude of believers indulged in such a sober abundance of things that "they had but one heart and one soul."[139] And then at first the equality proclaimed by all the wise shone all around, so that in so great an assembly of disciples there was no one more lifted up in respect of wealth, no one pressed down in respect of poverty. Moreover, just as there was one agreement in the virtue of all, so also possessions were justly held in common. For "no one said that any of the things that he possessed was his own, but" because "all things were common unto them," they would bring even the prices of

[137]Referring, of course, to wheat.
[138]Cf. Hos 1:10-11.
[139]Acts 4:32.

their fields to the feet of the apostles, so that a distribution might be made for the needs of each.[140] And because the spiritual state of the people was contained within the history of the Jewish people, he returns to those names with which he had begun his prophecy, and he says, *The earth shall hear the corn, the wine, and the oil, and these shall hear Jezrahel*—that is, the people who are shown by the name of the valley in which they were conquered. Earlier he expressed that he was about to punish this people's sins. He receives that nation into his fellowship, I say, not the one that continues in the same character but in the same tribes, and the one that has been expiated by the scourges of their blows, for he has been appeased. And he plants the diverse seeds of his precepts *in earth* that is "good,"[141] so to speak. Thus, even that day of Jezrahel on which the disaster was brought in is judged to have been valuable and desirable, on account of the great extent of the prosperity that followed. For now *I shall have mercy on her*, at whose name shortly before I had shuddered. And I shall call *My people*, the one who had stood out as my deserter and who had defected from me by the law of those who rise up in opposition. And trust would again be conferred on them, so that they call me the one true *Lord*.

But with the proclamation of prosperity being issued up to this point, he again leads his speech back to the state of the present time. For it follows:

[Chapter 3]

3:1-5 And the Lord said to me, Go yet again, love a woman beloved of her friend, and an adulteress, as the Lord loves the children of Israel; and they look to strange gods and love the husks of the grapes. And I planted her for myself for fifteen pieces of silver, and for a core of barley, and for half a core of barley. And I said to her, You shall wait for me many days, you shall not play the harlot,[142] and you shall be no man's, and I also will wait for you. For the children of Israel shall sit many days without king, and without prince, and without sacrifice, and without altar, and without ephod, and without teraphim. And after this the children of Israel shall return and shall seek the Lord their God, and David their king, and they shall fear the Lord and his goodness on the last of the days.

Here the prophet under the persona of God had taken up the sad things of the prophecy that promised the captivity of that people with various voices, just as he had taught in the beginning. But now, by the same guidance of the Holy Spirit, he was beginning to announce the things that threatened them, as though he has composed his oracle out of opposites.[143] For indeed, though he raged on with savage things, at once he added joyful things by which he soothes the wounded. This is either in order that the people might grow accustomed to hearing sorrows or to show the same God delaying and, as we have said earlier, putting off his pursuit, since he is about to take his vengeance. By this means he simultaneously teaches that they should never despair of salvation under such a judge, who without a doubt is so ready to forgive that while narrating peaceful things in the midst of adversities, he appears zealous to excuse what he was angry about. Therefore, he directs the prophet not to put aside the love that he had devoted to the impure woman at her first offense. Instead he should contend with her shamelessness by means of a professed kindness. He should

[140]Cf. Acts 4:32, 34-35.

[141]Cf. Mt 13:8, 23. Cf. Jerome, *Commentary on Hosea* 2:21-24 (ACT 2:170).

[142]Or "fornicate."

[143]There may be textual corruption here. I have followed the printed CCSL text.

learn by the reality itself, or, what seems logically coherent, solely by his spirit revealing it,[144] that that prostitute could be hired for a meager price not only to be contented by prophetic company but to abstain equally from union with him and others. It is as though she was able to show that she prostituted herself more for the necessity of providing food than for the eager pursuit of lust.[145] After all, if even a scanty sustenance should be offered, she would easily do without the pleasure of her shameful actions. Certainly by this example the synagogue's cause is rendered more base. Clearly, though it had been invited by abundance, it did not keep this agreement that any prostitute respects, even during excessive scarcity! Therefore, he says, we grant time to those who have gone astray, so that they may either break through unto amendment by their weeping or may at last succumb to the grave vengeance. Since they now esteem vile things over things that are precious, they forget their own God and follow foreign ones. It is no different than if they had scorned grapes and were collecting the *husks of the grapes*, which are more fitting for swine than for men.[146] Therefore, the measure of a *core* is named first, which contains thirty pecks; secondly, he says *half a core of barley*, which constitutes a bargain.[147] I have matched the duty of continence from the woman to the image of that condition that the synagogue is about to suffer in the Babylonian captivity, where it will endure exile, to be sure, but with the hope of a return. And the synagogue shall be lawfully united neither to God nor to idols, but it shall live as though stripped of every consolation. For that is why it says, *You shall not play the harlot, and you shall be no man's, and I also will wait for you.* The Jews and those who follow them strive to relate this passage to the signs of the present time—namely, that those who have been driven away from Jerusalem certainly have no marks of their priestly duty, which the prophet recounts, when he promises that they would be *without king, without prince, without sacrifice, without altar, without ephod, and without teraphim.*[148] Yet [he says] that he himself held assurances of their return—that is, the voice of God, who promised that he also shall *wait* for them. But the evidence of all the nations received into the faith of Christ is convincing to show that they are deceived in this opinion or that they deceive. For when they refused to believe in the gospel of Christ, the vineyard was taken away from them and entrusted to other husbandmen "who shall return his fruit in due season."[149] Therefore, in that age in which they were enslaved to the Babylonians, rightly are the nation and God said to have mutually *waited* for each other. It is not that the whole people were free from pagan wickedness, which is imputed to them even by the other holy teachers,[150] but because in that place there was an admixture of just men and because the offspring would possess the joys of liberation better than their parents. For the sake of a portion of these, God certainly promises to *wait*; that is, he will not immediately admit any other nation into the place of the one driven out, till they *return*, just as we have said even earlier. They will be better for their chastisement and will receive the ornaments of the ancient priesthood that they had lost. In the frequent gathering of the faithful he will surround the horns of the altar, "paying their vows to God, which their lips have marked off."[151] *And they shall fear his goodness on the last day.*

[144]I believe he means that he prefers the interpretation that Hosea's relations with the fornicating woman were played out in his spirit and not in reality.

[145]Cf. Jerome, *Commentary on Hosea* 3:2-3 (ACT 2:172).

[146]Cf. Lk 15:16.

[147]Cf. Jerome, *Commentary on Hosea* 3:2-3 (ACT 2:171).

[148]Cf. Jerome, *Commentary on Hosea* 3:4-5 (ACT 2:174).

[149]Cf. Mt 21:41.

[150]Cf. Dan 13:56.

[151]Ps 66:13-14.

Accordingly, he has set forth the reason for this expulsion, obviously, so that through it the afflicted nation might become accustomed to withdrawing from wickedness, until they have been corrected by lawful scourges and have merited to be received into his companionship once more. From this union the pious and rejoicing multitude came forth.

[Chapter 4]

4:1-2 Hear the word of the Lord, ye children of Israel, for the Lord shall enter into judgment with the inhabitants of the land. For there is no truth, and there is no mercy, and there is no knowledge of God in the land. Cursing, and lying, and killing, and theft, and adultery have overflowed, and blood has covered[152] blood.

Again and again I have called to mind what the rationale was that in the very onset of the threat, he spoke also about those prosperities that would come after a long period of time—that is, so that the nation on the verge of exultation might have comfort or so that the mercy might be plain of the Creator who was drawing near to punish, but as one who was, so to speak, unwilling. So, having spoken also about the future with this purpose, he returns to the present era, as he had done earlier.[153] And he examines the faults of the people who have to be punished, so that he might solve that question that the dispatching of divine duty had caused.[154] For it was appropriate that a reflection of the following sort would arise: if the judgment remained fixed, so that the captivity brought in is released and the glorious return comes to pass, why is there not uninterrupted liberty? Or how many faults could there be that would inflame the spirit of our ruler unto so great a severity? Therefore, a recounting of their crimes is added by necessity, so that the gravity of the one avenging may be made clear. He says, *Hear therefore the word of the Lord, ye children of Israel.* For he does not refuse to enter into the conflict with you and to cite the reason for his judgments and of your offenses. He is the one to whom blessed David says, "That you may be justified in your words and may overcome when you are judged."[155] *Hear,* I say, *the word of the Lord, ye children of Israel.*[156] Judge for yourselves entirely on your own about what is going on and about which pursuits of the people we complain when we see them. If any sense remains to you, flee together to confession and repentance. *For there is no truth, and there is no mercy, and there is no knowledge of God in the land.* They transgress, he says, with scarcely any intermission, as it were, so that there seemed to be a certain intermingling of vices and virtues, but in such a way that the praiseworthy things yielded to the worst, so that no trace of goodness appears anywhere. There remained, I say, no reliability in the giving of testimony, no justice in court cases, no piety in religious rituals. What should I say about the fact that their hearts are devoid of the fear of God, since forgetfulness even of his name has seized hold of everyone? Cruelty and lust fight it out between themselves mutually. Shameful acts also rush in; crimes overflow. They are restrained neither by the peril of shame nor of *blood*, but, joining *cursing* to their lies, *killing* to *thefts*, *adultery* to sacrilege, they have filled every locale of the once-holy country with bloodshed, so that through the multitude of the slain, *blood* is mingled with *blood.* History reveals that this has been said not as an exaggeration, but reliably. For indeed, there are those times in which even blessed Elijah was asked by God what he was doing in the

[152]*Tegit*. Jerome reads *tetigit* (touched).
[153]Cf. Hos 3:1-5.
[154]Cf. Jerome, *Commentary on Hosea* 4:1-2 (ACT 2:175).
[155]Ps 51:4; Rom 3:4.
[156]Cf. Jerome, *Commentary on Hosea* 4:1-2 (ACT 2:175).

wilderness, and he responded with sorrow: "Lord, they have killed your prophets, they have demolished your altars, and I alone am left, and they seek my life."[157] So the people had been corrupted by such great wickedness that they sought to destroy every pious person (that is, the worshipers of God) with the utmost slaughter. Indeed, this unspeakable corruption of religion was not worth the pleasure for which it was sought, but it promised impunity for deeds that were both disgraceful and savage. For this reason the worshipers of Baal and of the calves became subject to the madness of Jezebel by shedding the blood of the pious.[158]

4:3 On account of this the land shall mourn, and everyone who dwells in it shall languish with the beast of the field and with the fowl of the sky, but also the fishes of the sea shall be gathered together.

Once the causes of his indignation were set forth, consequently he cries out that that *land* must be covered with mourning, as it had been covered with crimes. If these crimes, which were both many and enormous, had gone unpunished, his providence would also have been denied. Therefore, *every* worshiper of the country *shall languish with the beast of the field and with the fowl of the sky*. He is accustomed to call the cattle and the flocks *beasts of the field*.[159] Therefore, he says, when want of fruits and crops shall have occurred, a failure and lack of cattle shall also follow. And clearly this is not the end of their torment, *but even the fishes shall be gathered together*; that is, they will fail in the sense that they are gone, so that food cannot be found in the waters.

4:4-5a But yet let not any man judge, and let not a man be rebuked. For your people are as those who contradict the priest. And you shall fall, and the prophet also shall fall with you.

He says, If while the commonwealth was standing, some wrongdoers perished by the sentence of the judges, doubtless one would have been *rebuked*, another would have *rebuked*. For indeed the censure would have exercised its proper duty, by which at the same time it is shown that the corruption of their crimes, like sickness or pestilence, had not had mastery over all the people at once but, just as some pursued shameful deeds, so the majority pursued honorable deeds. But when iniquity, as though sworn together in a conspiracy, shall have taken over almost every assembly, which the prophet Hosea laments had happened in his times, deservedly also both teaching and judgment shall cease, so that the punishment poured out may rage against the impious. Therefore, the force of the evidence has been expressed in the form of a command: *But yet let not any man judge, and let not a man be rebuked*; that is, no one shall judge, nor shall anyone be rebuked. For you must be laid waste by the enemy's fury, not assessed by the sentences of judges. *For your people are as those who contradict the priest; and you shall fall, the prophet also shall fall with you.* The prophet added this *as* (*sicut*) as evidence, not in order to make a comparison. Therefore, you shall observe nothing new in the vengeance, but what you have practiced in your faults, you shall recognize in your punishments. For *your people* resisted *the priest*; that is, by eagerly pursuing idols you have withdrawn from the true priesthood. Therefore, *you have contradicted the priest*, he says, when you rejected the sacred rites, when you spat out salutary warnings and the precepts that informed you about morality; and, as you entrusted yourself to impious leaders, so also to wicked prophets. Deservedly, therefore, the sentence let in shall now surround both groups, so that you also

[157] 1 Kings 19:10; cf. Rom 11:2-3.
[158] Cf. 1 Kings 19:2-3.
[159] Cf. Hos 2:18.

may fall with your *prophets*—that is, with your soothsayers.

4:5b-6 In the night I have made your mother to be silent. My people have been silent, because they had no knowledge. Because you have rejected knowledge, I will reject you, that you shall not do the office of priesthood to me. And you have forgotten the law of your God; I also will forget your children.

As I have frequently called to mind, this is an idiom of the Scriptures, that because the speech is directed to the nation, at one time it seems to match its proper name, at another the name of the parent whose daughter it was.[160] And for that reason, when he had said, "You shall fall today, and the prophet also shall fall with you"[161] (that is, the time of your desolation approaches, and now also shall you cease from a wicked voice, you who have long ago left off from learning and speaking justice), he added, *In the night I have made your mother to be silent.* But this should not be understood as though he permitted her to speak during the day, and only at night made her keep silent, but he wanted to express the mass of unspoken silence. And for that reason, so as to show that, once destruction rushes in, she would become dumb, he made mention of *night,* as if he were to say, I shall clothe her with sorrow poured out like the night that is accustomed to envelop the lands, so that, just as the conditions of a dark time introduce a general and universal silence, so that crowd of old persons, which I have called *your mother,* who a little while ago was screaming garrulous profanity, may fall silent during the night of a hostile time. After this, according to the order established, when he has made terror resound, he adds the reason for the commotion: *My people have been silent, because they had no knowledge.* For, he says, it was just that the lips of my people should be closed in mournful silence, which were unwilling to learn how to speak well. Accordingly, since he said that his people lacked knowledge, lest you should attribute this to any necessity, immediately he shows why he had made this accusation: *Because you have rejected knowledge, I will reject you, that you shall not do the office of priesthood to me; and you have forgotten the law of your God, I also will forget your children.* "You refused to understand that you should do well," it says, but "you devised iniquity in your bed."[162] By your own choice you have dared to destroy sections of my law among you, so that, with the part about justice neglected, you retained the instructions about sacrifices.[163] For that reason a fitting frustration shall rise to meet your perversity, so that for the one who did not care to pursue the virtues there may not be freedom to offer sacrifices. A harsh silence shall hang over you, who drove out the salutary warnings from your ears. *You have forgotten me, I also will forget your children,* so that you who have suffered a freely chosen blindness in your duties may experience the bitterest bereavement of children. This, of course, should not be understood in such a way that we suppose that that people who had given themselves up to idols were serving the true God even by their offering of sacrifices. For the chief reason they consecrated the bull calves in their land was to keep from having the opportunity to go to the temple to offer their sacrifices.[164] Therefore, a twofold sense should be adopted. Either this was recorded conditionally, as if we were to say, Although

[160]Cf. Hos 2:2; Jerome, *Commentary on Hosea* 4:5b-6 (ACT 2:176).
[161]Hos 4:5a. The lemma at 4:4-5a lacked "today."
[162]Ps 36:3-4.
[163]Cf. Mt 23:23.
[164]Cf. 1 Kings 12:26-31.

you carried out parts of the priesthood diligently, in fact this was ineffectual for your defense, whom a hideousness of morals condemned, but consequently you lost even that confined space of your superstition and those solaces that deserved ridicule, you who lost the aids of your merits. Or else it means that since both prophets and lawful priests were living here and there among those tribes, some had even become accustomed to offer small gifts from the same people. And by this means they believed that they had obtained impunity for their crimes. Under the persona of the people he threatens such persons as these also, that, when captivity has rushed in openly, they would be deprived of the supports of that fancy by which they considered themselves to have been generous in respect of God even intermittently.

4:7 According to the multitude of them, so have they sinned against me; I will change their glory into shame.

The people resolved to fight against my kindnesses with concentrated effort, so to speak, and with ample zeal, so that the more profusely I gave to them bountifully, so much the more insanely did they openly abuse this. After all, when I had brought them forth by a succession of assurances, such that the worshipers advanced and filled up the extent of the exceedingly widespread lands, they compensated for their growth by crimes that kept spreading out to insult me. The result was that they actually seemed to be afraid that there would be more members of the people than crimes to commit. Therefore, because they placed *their glory* in the *multitude* both of their wicked deeds and soldiers, when disgrace arrives, *I shall change* it—namely, so that when hardships devour them, they would be brought to the utmost scarcity.

4:8(-9) They shall eat the sins of my people and shall lift up their souls to their iniquity.[165]

This whole thing needs to be read as a reproach of the priests; or of those who were the attendants of the idols, and through this who claimed that they were sacrificing to God; or of the leaders who were with the people who had surrounded themselves with the pursuit of their deadly error. Among the other things that they were doing worthy of punishment, they began to adopt also the terms that stemmed from the tradition of the law. For, just as the Samaritan tribes were preserving "circumcision" and the "Sabbaths," although they served idols, so also one must believe that those prophets (*hariolos*) usurped some of the institutions of the law. Through the institution of blessed Moses, therefore, there were various kinds of offerings, among which were also those that were offered for sin. Yet from that offering, once the fat and certain parts were consumed by fire, they granted the remaining portions to become the food of the priests.[166] And because these rites appeased God, the priests were said to *eat*—that is, to consume *the sins of the people* for whom they were praying. According to this manner of the prophet (*harioli*), in order to promise impunity of various offenses through their gainful profits, they claimed that they consumed *the sins of the people*. For this reason, therefore, through the prophet God now criticizes them, with the voice and countenance of one who is indignant. It is as if he were to say, Behold these marvels, things that aim at fame but never based on any noble deeds but on shameful acts alone! They have disgraced the institutions of the venerable law by usurping its words—namely, in order to promise the people going about that if they offered

[165]The remainder of v. 9 reads in Jerome's version, "And it shall be like people, like priest."

[166]Cf. Lev 7:16; 8:31; 10:13.

sacrifices through their hands, they would immediately be made innocent, and they would consequently obtain forgiveness of sins. And thus *they lifted up the souls* of the guilty; that is, they comforted them and made them haughty, in whom no trace of remorse was accustomed to dwell. Therefore, since the teacher was not accustomed to speak, nor was the disciple accustomed to hear that which pertains to salvation, but the guilt that defiled them made both equal, deservedly too shall the judgment that followed after place them together, so that they receive the fruit of their works without deceit, and the priest and people suffer one destruction.

But in this passage we can produce an easier understanding if we introduce also the character of Judah, whom he names a little later.[167] Thus, since he chastises that tribe as well with a grave warning, although they were less guilty up to this point yet were not pure in every respect, he may seem to have introduced this already, that the priests are devouring the sacrifices offered for sins. A meaning of the following kind would result: But what wonder is it that the tribes that have withdrawn from worship and fear of God and who have been delivered up to the worship of idols are soiled by various sins, since even that portion of the people that up to now seems to preserve the mystical ceremonies is deranged by a similar error? Corrupted priests flatter sinners—namely, by saying that impunity falls to their lot through the offering of the sacrifices that they consume. Therefore, with these consolations *they lifted up their souls*, which were weighed down by the awareness of their crimes. And the people listened most willingly to what the priests were most shamelessly promising. For that reason, even in the time of disaster there shall be no distinction between the people and the priests, but those who have lived promiscuously shall also perish vilely.

[167]Cf. Hos 4:15.

4:9(-12) I will visit their ways on them, and I will repay them their thoughts. They shall eat, and shall not be satisfied; they have committed fornication, and have not ceased.[168]

Because, he says, the punishment of his vengeance has begun to reveal itself, these measures of sorrows that they themselves created by their sins shall be filled up. Thus, they will experience in their punishments what they perpetrated in their desires. For *they have committed fornication* by following either obscenities or wickedness, nor were they ashamed of the horridness they employed, so that those who had fallen down from their first position might at least consider the second set of remedies and cease even to frequent what it was not fitting to have touched. And thus the cessation conducted might resemble a refraining from error. On the contrary, when *they committed fornication, they did not cease*. Therefore, what they have wrought in vices, they will experience in their punishments, so that *they shall eat, and shall not be satisfied*; that is to say, they are filled with torments, but they do not cease to drain them, so that they seem to be enduring some kind of insatiable hunger. For when you hear of *fornication*, do you not think of the temperate use of that bodily pleasure? But it says those who violate the terms of the holy covenant have *forsaken* the all-powerful *Lord*,[169] into whose fellowship they had been adopted. And for that reason they were deprived of the light of understanding. They did not reflect after these marks of religion devolved into such defilements of religious rituals. Truly what foolishness of opinions failed to creep

[168]The remainder of the lemma in Jerome's version reads, "Because they have forsaken the Lord in not observing [his law]. Fornication and wine and drunkenness take away the heart. My people have consulted their wood, and their staff has declared unto them. For the spirit of fornication deceives them, and they have committed fornication against their God."

[169]Cf. Hos 4:12.

into their spirits that was not produced by *drunkenness* and intoxication? And for that reason, though they claimed to be wise, they became so foolish,[170] so that from dry *wood* they sought the service of prophets, and the *staff* indicated what each one's future would be.[171] The Greeks call this kind of profanity "rhabdomantias."[172] Therefore, the *spirit* of profanity, which they call *fornication, ensnared them,* so that they departed from the true *God* and were intermixed with many and various demons, naturally with the manner and look of adulterers.[173]

4:13 They offered sacrifice on the tops of the mountains, and burnt incense (*thymiama*) on the hills, under the oak, and the poplar, and the terebinth tree, because the shadow thereof was good.

He says those who despised the divine ordinances were not content to have erred in only one way, but they eagerly pursued old wives' tales,[174] so that not only are they moved unto any deception with smoothed staffs,[175] but now they do so on hills that rise up a little bit or in the slightly darker shadows of the trees. And they believed that the greatest divination existed where they had seen something delightful. Therefore *they offered sacrifice on the tops of mountains,* an accusation that history frequently makes, since it says about the kings, He did this or that, "yet he did not remove the high places, but the people still sacrificed in the high places."[176] But here he adds that they would even burn incense (*incensum*)[177] *under the oak and the poplar.* And he records the reason for their wonder when he added *because the shadow thereof was good.* Having rejected the author of light and life, like true children of darkness, they were caught in the shady places of the grove. Therefore, let us hear what punishments that madness merits.

4:13-14a Therefore shall your daughters commit fornication, and your spouses shall be adulteresses. I will not visit on your daughters when they shall commit fornication, and on your spouses when they shall commit adultery.

He says, You have engaged in foul things and did not leave off from the deed. Thus, if you did not have those feelings that are harmless, you should at least have felt those feelings that the guilty are accustomed to have (that is, those which make the violators of moral integrity ashamed of the things they have done). Instead you have established your audacity in harmful works, to the point of pursuing what was shameful. Thus, you esteemed the shadows of tree trunks and rocks above the Creator of all the elements. Therefore, may the bringing in of the final calamity compensate for this impiety in such a way that in a marvelous manner the punishment of the vengeance may be conformed to resemble their guilt. And thus it would be harsher because the judgment will not have been tried. For indeed *your spouses and daughters* shall be subjected to the lust of the conquerors, and neither husbands nor fathers shall expose that disgrace before any judges, but the whole shameful act shall be employed unto dishonor, so that none of it remains to the one charged. Thus, as though sharply, with the reproof of the offense denied, he concludes that there is nothing more bitter than to have remained

[170]Cf. Rom 1:22.
[171]Cf. Hos 4:12.
[172]ῥαβδομαντεία, divination by a wand. Cf. Jerome, *Commentary on Hosea* 4:10-12 (ACT 2:178).
[173]Cf. Hos 4:12.
[174]Cf. 1 Tim 4:7.
[175]Cf. Hos 4:12.
[176]Cf. 1 Kings 22:44; 2 Kings 12:3; 14:4; 15:35; Jerome, *Commentary on Hosea* 4:13a (ACT 2:179).

[177]He alters the word used in the lemma.

fixed under the state of servitude of such a kind, in which you continue to see the utter outrages committed against relations, and you do not dare to reproach them. Therefore, since he had considered this to be the ultimate misfortune, which indeed only captivity could inflict, he immediately added the reason for so great a commotion by the repetition of the things previously stated. "Because they themselves conversed with harlots and offered sacrifice with the effeminate, and the people who do not understand shall be beaten."[178] He is saying, They do not know how much I suffer from the perversity of the one who of late conducted herself in my fellowship of people. For that reason, in the disgraceful treatment of their relations they shall recognize the magnitude of their own crimes, so that those who have pursued the *effeminate* and the prostitutes, from whom they took up the worship of demons, are torn to pieces by obscene enemies who will abuse them. They will experience the fruits of their voluntary foolishness in the indignities that the tyrannical victors inflict.[179]

Book Two[180] on the Prophet Hosea

[Chapter 4 (continued)]

4:15-16 If you play the harlot,[181] O Israel, at least let not Judah offend. Go ye not into Galgal, and come not up into Bethaven. For Israel has gone astray like a wanton heifer; now will the Lord feed them, as a lamb in a spacious place.

Although the judgment of this prophecy shows that all the tribes were defiled by the worship of idols, nevertheless he announces an even worse arrangement for Israel and for the one who seems to have more room for condemnation than for correction. For they did not confine the impudence of their profaneness only to within their own borders and customs, but they sought the corruption also of their brother as though that would be some sort of gain. For indeed the prophet rebukes this pursuit of rousing [others] to sins, when he announces to *Israel* that *at least let not Judah offend*. For concern for his brother's way of life had not been imposed on Israel, who is reminded to be diligent, but through this kind of command he criticizes that sin of his that preferred to make Judah resemble himself all the more than that he should give any thought to his amendment. And the sense becomes something like this: O Israel, you who followed the prince of error (namely, Jeroboam), you have withdrawn from the companionship of your own brother (namely, Judah) for no other reason than that there should be no opportunity for you to recover and turn back to better things through the honor of the temple and the celebration of the sacred feasts days.[182] If you do not maintain the truce of your nation, or of your sin, and you who did not want to preserve the laudable harmony, keep to the division once begun. Do not insinuate the profession of the brotherhood that has been repudiated by the cunning of a corrupter. Instead, at least be content with your own ruin and suffer the innocence of your brother to remain. And cease to invite him into this condition, which you shall mourn having gone into. For now your lack of prudence proceeds to a greater kind, if out of love of sacrilege you enter into fellowship with these same ones, separation from whom you have chosen out of fear of the remedy. At least preserve that feeling in yourself, which was accustomed to arise in sinners—namely, that you be ashamed of becoming guilty of moral deformity. Why do you shut out a doubtless tenuous comfort from yourself so that you

[178]Hos 4:14b.

[179]Cf. Jerome, *Commentary on Hosea* 4:13b-14 (ACT 2:181).

[180]Jerome begins his second book on Hosea at Hos 5:8-9.

[181]Or "fornicate."

[182]Cf. 1 Kings 12:25-33.

might seem to have been beguiled? For the approbation[183] will not escape the guilty; but he points out that there is a distinction between the thoughtless and the insolent, doubtless so that audacity may render some odious, while fear may render others pitiable. But you, since you allow no immunity from your filthy disgrace, what else is there but that you acknowledge that you are completely guilty, not by wandering away but by a freely chosen detestable judgment? *If you play the harlot, O Israel, at least let not Judah offend.* Why, I say, do you join that error to your previous ones, so that you think that you will perish with less sorrow if you perish with more than if with few? Why do you waste your own goods[184] and defile the rights of your brother as well? Why do you want the whole race (*genus*) rolled into one grave? Permit some portion of your race[185] to survive, by whose support you may be aided, by whose example you may be reformed.

If you play the harlot, O Israel, at least let not Judah offend. Go ye not into Galgal, and come not up into Bethaven, and do not swear: The Lord lives. By the things added below he has disclosed how he had commanded Israel *not to let Judah offend* by keeping them from *coming up into Galgal and Bethaven,* places that were near the tribe of Judah, with the aim of getting mixed up in their religion, and from *swearing, The Lord lives.* This should be understood as follows, that, because they had consecrated the calves in these very places, just as in Samaria, they ascribed to these also the name of the true God, and swore by the name and divinity of those same things. For that reason he now warns that, because the people of Judah as well were flocking in from that vicinity (namely, to *Bethaven* and *Galgal*), they are eager to *come up* and to *swear, The Lord lives.* That is, in those places consecrated by the consent of the people, let not Judah be deceived by these familiar words and at first fail to shrink back from the calves, and then begin even to swear by them. However, he seems also to show the following, that the impiety of the people was confused—namely, so that those who served the calves also swore by the true God, whom Judah worshiped, in whatever affairs they had. And they would bind their solemn invocations by his name, as though by swearing on the best. They revered both religions with equal honor, so that they persuaded even those who had remained in the faith to worship this and to take up the worship of the calves, I say, while reverence of the former religion remained. Thus, it was not so much a change of religious devotion as a certain addition to it that seems to have occurred. However, this was undertaken contrary to the precepts of the law,[186] and doubtless it defiled those wretched people with an abundance of wickedness. Therefore, do not frequent those places with this pursuit, places that you have made very renowned by your sacrilegious rites, so that even the heart of Judah was poisoned by your sin. For let Judah take care, if up to now he has not completely withered, a condition that has laid hold of Israel. Then let him recognize what else is threatening him if he does not take heed.

4:16 For Israel has gone astray like a wanton heifer. Now will the Lord feed them, as a lamb in a spacious place.

Aptly he takes up the analogy from a heifer again, so that the outward form of that sin and the protuberance of those sinning and the lowing of those perishing may be indicated. When the yoke of my law was cast off, he says, the audacity of Israel has offended in the worship of bull calves, and they have *gone*

[183]*Assensio.* A variant reading is *ascensio,* which is discussed by Baxter, "Notes," 20.

[184]Cf. Lk 15:13.

[185]*Sanguinis.* Literally, "blood."

[186]Cf. Ex 20:4-5; Deut 6:13; 12:2-7.

astray from the paths of virtue, believing that they would enjoy abundant goods without interruption. But so great a disappointment of wishes has overtaken the impious that they have declined from their bullish bulk, as it were, into the littleness of a *lamb*. Thus, the whole nation, which placed its trust in their strength, saw their glory changed by the ignominy that followed.[187] And they were placed under a shepherd's staff with as much ease as a *lamb* is customarily restrained. Yet not only this, but, just like the lamb that has been guided into desert places (that is, one that is weak and alone) is stripped of the comfort both of its mother and of the flock, and it fears whatever it sees and whatever sound it hears, so also when the nation is subjected to the savagery of its enemies, it will be forced to wander through a wilderness. Yet divine providence did not completely abandon them (on account of which he said, *Now will the Lord feed them*). But this happened so that by the authoritative instruction of the imposed disaster, they might understand and confess that the precepts of the sacred law were not to be despised, nor did their sins go unpunished, nor were their desires fruitful.

4:17-19 Ephraim is a partaker with idols; let him alone. Their banquet is separated; they have fornicated with fornication, they who should have protected them have loved to bring shame [on them]. The spirit has bound them up on its wings, and they shall be confounded because of their sacrifices.

After the prophetic discourse addressed Israel about their vexation and announced their end, for they had not listened to his word, as a consequence he turns his admonitions to Judah. For lest the censure aimed at Israel should seem to have exempted Judah from guilt, who would certainly never be ruined except by voluntary assent, for that reason he appeals to them too with a similar vigor. He says, You have seen that he has decreed *Ephraim* to be a *partaker with idols* for his leading ungrateful and unfortunate necks out from under the yoke of my law. Therefore, be not joined to that one by any treaty, but *let him alone*, and thus be separated from the whole end of his pursuits, just as from the border of his places. Moreover, if any association has bound you to him, doubtless an equal calamity shall seize you as well. Do you wish to escape the contagion of his wickedness? Surround yourself with a palisade of constant separation; never enter into either public alliances or private *banquets* with his sacrileges. For "what fellowship has light with darkness? What agreement has the temple of God with idols?"[188] *They have fornicated with fornication*; and lest you should think that this simply befell those who had been deceived by error, *they who should have protected them have loved to bring shame [on them]*. With dedicated zeal and inflamed love, they pursue wickedness, nor do they offend only in the portion of the common people, but from their leaders unto the uttermost dregs they have been thoroughly pervaded with deadly obscenity.[189] Therefore, if the mysteries of pure faith please you, never mingle with their mind and assembly. Indeed, the hastened condemnation of such ones has been foreseen, O tribe of Judah, with the intention of aiding your judgment. Otherwise, upon seeing that the outcome for the guilty has been delayed, you may also become uncertain about your merits. While you are still unscathed, a sudden action like the wind shall snatch Samaria away, *and they shall be confounded because of their sacrifices*; that is, they shall be ashamed and shall acknowledge the vanity of their hope who were promising freedom and security to themselves in these

[187]Cf. Hos 4:6-7.

[188]2 Cor 6:14, 16.

[189]Cf. Jerome, *Commentary on Hosea* 4:17-19 (ACT 2:183).

sacrifices, which they were offering to idols. Now he recorded *wings* (alas) *of the spirit* with which the *bound* nation departed, according to the general belief, which was wont to furnish representations of the wind with wings (*pennis*). Therefore, he is saying the following: those who have pursued sacrileges shall be destroyed and shall be conveyed unto various exiles by the tornado of captivity, so that they seem to have been caught up in the *wings* of the wind. But when we read such things, we ought to think how lightly the insane people valued the words of the prophets. For when the priests, kings, and common multitude conspired together in open error, a certain opportunity of rebuking and of addressing the public in assembly was offered to a few spiritual poor people. But, just as Scripture testifies elsewhere, they were called "raving mad,"[190] and they were derided in public as portents, as it were. But those who were equally lacking both works and honors merited to enter into conversation with God and, as if from the throne of heaven, to proclaim his sentence against souls that were scattered on and cleaving to the ground.

[Chapter 5]

5:1(-2) Hear ye this, O priests, and hearken, O ye house of Israel, and give ear, O house of the king, because there is a judgment for you.[191]

Certainly all of you are advancing toward sacrileges, nor have you offered any discrimination in sinning of the kind that you were accustomed to have in your ranks. So now, all of you exalted with priestly or kingly dignity, and you whole crowd of Israel, because destruction is now hanging over you, it is fitting that you understand that you are perishing not on account of your strength but on account of the just decision of the judge. Indeed, you have perpetrated two things that seem to be opposed—namely, that you became "a snare and a net,"[192] but so spread out on the top of a mountain that it was as if it was in the location of a projecting watchtower. But the sacrifices, which it would have been fitting to offer to the one who presides in heaven, and to be carried on high like rising smoke, these you have plunged into the depths, having utterly changed their arrangement. But it is this which I call to account in the priests and kings. For they were allotted this place in the nation in order to act no less with moral integrity and religious duty than with power and dignity of worshiping. And in addition to what was right, they should have inspired those who were placed under them both by word and by example. Instead, they offered either reconciliation for crimes directly or the outward ritual. They retained only this from their previous eminence, in order that what they had done might seem far removed from them: they stretched out their *snares* and *nets* by which the unfortunate crowd was ensnared. And with this same perversity, he says, you have "turned your sacrifices into the depth"[193]—that is, toward hell, as it were. Why not? For you sacrificed these things either to demons or to the spirits of the dead. Therefore, because by your love of sinning you have mixed up the order of doing things, so that being ignorant of discernment a certain ostentation appeared in you, heed what follows.

5:2b-4 I shall be the instructor of you all, [so that with retribution as your teacher you may learn what you did not know when you spurned instruction]. I know Ephraim, and Israel is not hid from me, for now Ephraim

[190]Cf. Jer 29:26.

[191]The remainder of the lemma reads in Jerome, "Because you have become a snare to them whom you should have watched over, and a net spread on Thabor. And you have turned aside victims into the depth."

[192]Hos 5:1b.

[193]Hos 5:2a.

has committed fornication, Israel is defiled. They will not set their thoughts to return to the Lord their God, for the spirit of fornication is in the midst of them, and they have not known the Lord.

No one knows better than I, he says, with how much stubbornness Israel has offended, I who perceive the inner depths of their sins. After all, there is no part of their inmost being that can escape my gaze. Therefore, by carefully examining all of them, I know that he has now fornicated completely and has become completely defiled. Lest you should think that this was said as an excuse for their past sins, with the speech added beneath he immediately revealed what he wanted to indicate with such an affirmation. For he says, *They will not set their thoughts to return to the Lord their God, for the spirit of fornication is in the midst of them. And they have not known God.* Therefore, after their acceptance of sin, a feigned remorse, and not merely the adoption of the sin that was received into their hearts but even forgetfulness of amendment, are so preferred to the former errors that this iniquity alone is assessed as the foremost or the greatest. He says, *They will not set their thoughts to return to the Lord their God, for the spirit of fornication is in the midst of them.* He showed that this was the reason why they did not think about amendment, that an unclean *spirit*, the very demon, or love of sacrilege, was dwelling *in their midst*. For if they were transgressing intermittently, an unclean spirit would be believed to have drawn near to them. But now, because they are devoting the whole time of their life to sins, the author of the sacrileges is rightly said not to be near them, but *in their midst*. Therefore, since that one resides in their hearts, they give no thought to amendment, and for that reason they are subjected to destruction.

5:5 The arrogance of Israel shall answer in his face, and Israel and Ephraim shall fall in their iniquity; Judah also shall fall with them.

According to the metaphor of the labors of the peasant, to which (labors) fruitfulness often *answers*, he says that these also will receive the reward of their pursuits immediately. Fittingly, he says, shall their diligence *answer*—that is, so that they who were *arrogating* so much to themselves from their crimes might be ashamed during the disasters.

5:6-7 With their flocks and with their herds, they shall go to seek the Lord and shall not find [him]: he is taken away from them. They have transgressed against the Lord, for they have begotten children that are strangers; now shall a month devour them with their offspring.[194]

When he had said earlier that it was consistent with the justice of the judge that those who had handed themselves over to sins should also take home a fitting wage, he associated Judah as well with Israel, whom he knew would enter into similar guilt, though somewhat late.[195] But after he pointed out the justice of the examination, he returns to distinguishing the times and proceeds against the deeds of Israel, whom he knew was about to perish immediately. And indeed at first, when he had said that Judah had to be involved in the calamity with Israel, he added that he had more care for Judah, which was keeping the temple consecrated to God. For although it was being defiled with idols, nevertheless they were also offering sacrifices to God. And though they did not take enough pains to correct their morals, they believed that they would obtain help from constant sacrifice. Therefore, he says, *With their flocks and with their herds they*

[194]*Partubus*. Jerome reads *portions* (*partibus*).
[195]Cf. Hos 5:5.

shall go to seek the Lord, and shall not find [him]: he is taken away from them. Now he has recorded *they shall go* (*vadent*) for "they were going" (*ibant*).[196] For indeed the whole reproach is described by changing it from the past tense. Therefore, walking on the narrow path of superstition rather than religion (for this is how the offering of sacrifices is assessed, if concern for virtues is missing from it), they were not able to find this God, to whom no one is led except by the narrow path of complete devotion. *He is taken away from them.* It is not that God can be carried off, but it should be understood to mean that nowhere do they encounter his help. It is as if seemingly he had been entirely *taken away* from them. But afterward casting back his words to Ephraim (that is, to the Samaritans), he criticizes another kind of transgression, which, however, shows the long duration of the impiety they have committed; namely, they have so despised the statutes of the law that they were intermingled through marriages even with the unholy nations.[197] They actually pursued these and endeavored to lay aside the name of their race and to be called anything but the people of God. *They have transgressed against the Lord, for they have begotten children that are strangers.* They have conceived such a great hatred of my name, he says, that they believed that they were freed from threats, or that they would be delivered from troubles, if they had passed over into the number and offspring of those foreign nations.[198] For this reason he says, *now shall a month devour them with their offspring.* By the term *month* he shows that the disaster is near and impending, in which he promises that both the sprouts and the fruits are to be cut down by a single sword.

[196]These are two different verbs in Latin meaning "go," but Julian's point seems to be the tense used. The former verb is future tense, the latter imperfect.

[197]Cf. Lev 18:24; Ps 106:35; Ezra 10; Neh 13.

[198]Cf. Jerome, *Commentary on Hosea* 5:6-7 (ACT 2:186).

5:8-9 Blow ye the cornet in Gabaa, the trumpet in Rama, howl ye in Bethaven, behind Tergum of Benjamin.[199] Ephraim shall be in desolation.

He had declared that in a short time they would be devoured, and he knew the gravity of the sentence that was advancing into fulfillment without any delay. Therefore, as though the events were already fulfilled, he ordered it to be indicated with blowing trumpets and resounding lamentations throughout these cities that were most populous that a desolation would take possession of all Ephraim. But we gather that all the places of which he has spoken—that is, *Tergum of Benjamin,* a tribe that bordered on the country of Judah, as well as *Gabaa, Rama,* and *Bethaven*—were near the borders of Judah.[200] Therefore, although the calamity of these cities that preceded ought to have made them anxious, doubtless by that example of fear, not only were they not at all moved to amendment, but they even showed an increase in transgression. And so he upbraids them strongly and says that they were shown to be made worse by the very thing that ought to have made them better in view of its being an act of kindness.

5:10 The princes of Judah have become as those who take up the boundary; I will pour out my wrath on them like water.

That is, he is referring to the time of the Assyrian captivity, which drove the ten tribes from their borders. *The princes of Judah* should have been moved to mourning by this disaster that had come upon their brother. They should have carefully considered the dignity of their character—namely, lest they also should fall into similar tribulations. Not only did they

[199]Julian seems to understand *Tergum* as a place name, whereas Jerome had read it as the word *back*.

[200]Cf. Jerome, *Commentary on Hosea* 5:8-9 (ACT 2:188).

feel no fear or remorse, but they revealed a murderous spirit—namely, by rejoicing at the extent of the lands annexed to themselves, when their brother was driven out.[201] Therefore, *in the day of desolation* (that is, in the time when the Israelite tribes departed from their borders), supply in thought, "I have shown faithfulness," O Judah, whose latent desire the opportunity has uncovered. And thus he regarded the critical moment of their brothers as a matter of insignificance, so that he said that these things were fitting for them also. This, of course, is a sin so great that it compelled the anger of the avenger to increase. For it follows, *I will pour out my wrath upon them like water*—that is, after he had said *I shall pour out*, he aptly added *like water*. Judah showed itself worse, he says, by their crime of exultation, and for that reason it shall be buried in the flood of punishments. For when, among other acts of kindness our mercy presented this to them as well, that destruction was being threatened to Ephraim for his fear and amendment, he abused this by increasing his insolence. He did not believe the example of his brother that had been provided to him but rather believed in collecting the spoils.

5:11-15 Ephraim, suffering a false charge, has been broken by judgment because he began to go after filthiness. And I [will be] like a moth to Ephraim and like rottenness to the house of Judah. And Ephraim saw his sickness, and Judah his chain. And Ephraim went to the Assyrian, and sent to the avenging king; and he shall not be able to heal you, neither shall he be able to loose the chain from you. For I will be like a lioness to Ephraim, and like a lion's whelp to the house of Judah. I, I will catch, and go and take away, and there is none who can rescue. Going I will return to my place, until you faint and seek my face.

God earnestly points out that he has been offended, because they felt no remorse about the condemnation of their brother, but Judah remained insulting toward the one exiled. They rejoiced that their borders had been extended by any circumstance whatsoever. Therefore, God rated this sin so serious that he promised not [merely] to summon his anger but to completely pour it out like water. And because through increases in punishments he had made Judah seem more wicked, which was certainly about to be laid waste by overflowing chastisement, he proceeded to develop the condition taken up, and says that the guilt of Judah was so much worse that, compared to it, Israel seems to have borne a *false charge*. And the sense becomes like this: if the reckoning of their offenses demanded the evil of the captivity, why has Judah, befouled by the customs of the nations and infected with hatred of their brother, postponed the violence of the retribution? But if indeed after so many sins they still did not merit to be driven out, is not that one who was taken captive shown to have been overwhelmed more through a *false charge* than through justice? *Ephraim, suffering a false charge, has been broken by judgment*. He has taken care to show what was the *suffering a false charge*—that is, to be overwhelmed not by the fairness of the judge but by his power. But it looks back on the same sense, which says, *He began to go after filthiness*. For in earlier passages he had upbraided Israel for the multitude and the ancient duration of their sins. But when he reproved the crime of

[201]Julian supports the interpretation of Jerome, *Commentary on Hosea* 5:10 (ACT 2:189), whereas Theodore of Mopsuestia seems to understand the line as referring figuratively to the adoption of idols, *Commentary on Hosea* (FOTC 62). D. A. Hubbard, *Hosea: An Introduction and Commentary*, Tyndale Old Testament Commentaries (Downers Grove, IL: IVP Academic, 1989), 132, appears to agree with Jerome and Julian: "Judah's crime seems to have been the land-grab implied in the battle language of verse 8. With a zeal born of frustration and opportunism, they marched north to snatch back their own territory and, apparently, much more. Moving boundary markers to expand, by force or deceit, one's own allotted holdings, was an intolerable offence in ancient Israel (Deut 27:17)."

Judah—namely, of his seeking to gain from his brother's captivity and feeling joy over it[202]—he appraised this as of greater importance than the other crimes. And he added the rest as well in the same uninterrupted course, in order to say that even Ephraim was afflicted in the judgment, and it was they who had begun the error. It is as if he were to say, You, O Judah, have revealed such great cruelty in your heart that in the crimes for which Israel has been condemned, you seem more dreadful and of longer standing. Whence even the movement of my judgment shall be sharpened on account of the differences in merits. Thus, I will spoil Ephraim *like a moth*, but you I shall consume like a clinging *rottenness*. Now it is well known how much less those things are consumed and destroyed that a moth eats than those things that a rottenness pervades. *And Ephraim saw his sickness, and Judah his chain*: that is, you both shall perceive and shall endure the retribution, which is destined for your pursuits. It will not benefit you to beseech aid from various kings,[203] but you shall confess in reality that they have supplied you only with examples of corruption, and not with aid to your salvation. *And Ephraim went to the Assyrian, and sent to the avenging king; and he shall not be able to heal you, neither shall he be able to loose the chain from you. For I will be like a lioness to Ephraim, and like a lion's whelp to the house of Judah.* He promised that he would encounter both peoples under the appearance of a *lion*, but the vehemence that he had not made in the outward form, he preserved in the sex, so that he said he would appear to the one as a *lioness* but to the other as a *lion*. But he ended the simile taken up by saying, *I, I will catch, and go; I will take away, and there is none who can rescue. Going I will return to my place, until you faint and seek my face.* There is no shepherd, he says, who dared to rescue the prey taken away by me; but contemptuous of the crowd of peasants, I shall put forth my strength until the hunger of my indignation shall be satisfied. But he recorded *I will return to my place* for "lair," where the unfrightened lion was accustomed to betake himself. But this is what shall be, he says, *until you seek my face*, exhausted by tribulations and sorrows. Clearly this is based on the truth of the matter and goes beyond the example taken under the image of the lion. Moreover, as far as concerns the comparison, what weary person would have desired to look on that face, which not even the strong could have stood up to? Accordingly, when he had expressed the indignation felt through the hunger of the lion, now he added regarding the majesty of his person that he will not come to set them free unless the people advance from their worn-down condition, long to see his face, and begin to request a remedy from him alone, by whom they had perceived that their punishment had been brought in.

[Chapter 6]

6:1-3 In their affliction they will rise early to me. Come, and let us return to the Lord, for he has taken us and he will heal us; he will strike, and he will cure us. He will revive us after two days; on the third day he will raise us up, and we shall live in his sight. We shall know, and let us follow on, that we may know the Lord. His going forth is prepared as the morning light, and he will come to us as the early and the latter rain to the earth.

He had said that he was raging against the wicked people like a lion that had come forth to hunt[204]—namely, by carrying on the work of retribution, which once it was set in motion began to crush the impious. He would not cease inflicting punishments before they had

[202]Cf. Hos 5:10.

[203]The critical edition does not specify the instances, but cf. 2 Kings 15:14; 16:1-20; 17:4; Is 7:1-2.

[204]Cf. Hos 5:14.

in turn gathered themselves to seek God by a total display of prayers.[205] But because there is a great distinction in that expression of supplication, and those who have been struck by fear alone offer one thing, but those who at that time have been reverentially and rationally amended offer something else, he took care to express what might occur in either circumstance. Thus, although one face appeared for both, yet we should understand that they were supported by different roots—namely, the former only by confusion, the latter by the amendment of virtue as well. Therefore, because he had said that he would certainly not go forth to aid them unless they yielded to the correction of seeking his face,[206] if that nation turns itself around, he will necessarily proceed to show what sort of supplication he was expecting. And he first runs through their words with derision, a prayer that he shows must be shunned on account of its inconstancy—that is, which flatters with words alone but pleads in a way that is destitute of the gravity of these matters. The holy song as well accuses this demeanor and kind [of supplication] when it says, "When he slew them, they sought him, and they returned and came to him early in the morning; but their heart was not right."[207] *In their affliction they will rise early to me. Come, and let us return to the Lord, for he has taken us and he will heal us, he will strike, and he will cure us, he will revive us after two days, on the third day he will raise us up, and we shall live in his sight, we shall know, and we shall follow on,*[208] *that we may know the Lord. His going forth is prepared as the morning light, he will come to us as the early and the latter rain to the earth.* He says, When you begin to "seek my face,"[209] I shall not be pleased by that prayer that you bear on your lips (nor if you should praise my power and my mercy both, saying that I am so prepared to forgive, that I will anticipate your prayers with rewards, nor will I permit the destruction that I have brought in to remain for the space of two days, but on the third day I will arrive to bring you back to life). As you have taught, this will take place: *in his sight.* We who have obtained the happiness of the life that he had given should know him and search for him carefully. He drives away the nights of our torments and sorrows *as the morning light.* And by bestowing abundance, he flowed down like *the early and latter rain.* I say, I shall despise those things that characteristically you are accustomed to sing about without amending your ways. But observe what I am referring to.

6:4 What shall I do to you, O Ephraim? What shall I do to you, O Judah? Your mercy. . .

Namely, the mercy from me that in your previously mentioned old songs you claimed would be present to you (if I may borrow from your imagery)—vanished like "the morning cloud," and like the moisture of the evening is dried up when the sun comes out. This has the following meaning: my custom of sparing you is being taken away by the exhalation of our indignation, so that the source from which you obtained relief from your evils is failing. The reason this is happening is not because my judgment has changed, but because yours did not. For I preserve equally the principles of justice and of mercy. I did not want to punish those whom I have frightened; but you were unmoved by the threat of blows and have forced these terrors to go into effect.

6:5(-6) For this reason have I hewed [them] by the prophets; I have slain them by the words of my mouth. Your judgments shall go forth as the light.

That is, I applied the axes of the prophetic threats, and with such great increases I have

[205]Cf. Hos 5:15.
[206]Cf. Hos 5:15.
[207]Ps 78:34-37.
[208]The lemma had used the subjunctive.
[209]Hos 5:15.

described the evils that are to be brought in, that everyone may be easily dismayed by hearing about that matter.[210] But because the display of terror that was particularly detailed could not restrain your impudence, it is necessary to inflict what it was not profitable to intimate. For that reason *your judgments shall go forth as the light,* so that no one may now fail to know what you deserve, nor may your deformity conceal itself under any outward appearance of religion, which you possessed in the offering of sacrifices. Moreover, it would wholly light up when the outcome of events is displayed that I sought good affections rather than opulent sacrificial victims, and that person was acceptable to me who had stood forth as one who was diligent in helping his neighbor through mercy rather than by staining an altar through sacrifice,[211] and who preferred the "knowledge of God"[212] and his commands to all sacrifices. You, therefore, who scorn to have learned these things and have pondered nothing of morals, nothing of virtues, but you thought that with gifts of praise and sacrificial victims you could placate me whom you were exasperating by your daily actions, at least understand how serious I am about the dangers of these matters. The *mercy* that you were unfittingly praising has passed away *like a morning cloud;* but the *judgments* to which you will be handed over as one found guilty shall shine like the day at its height.

6:7 But they, like Adam, have transgressed the pact: there have they dealt treacherously against me.

He proceeds with the established order of the discourse so that, after he had threatened them with punishments, he adds their material cause—namely, the sins by which they roused him to be offended. Whence even here, after he promised that there would be open retribution, he added the guilty charge for which they were held liable. In order to show its gravity, he called to mind an ancient example. Here, of course, the prophet's mode of expression should be noted, because in many passages of such a kind it bears the light of explanation. For he says, *Like Adam, they have transgressed the pact, there have they dealt treacherously against me.* Certainly he does not mean that they apparently committed transgression in Paradise, but, because he had said that they, *like Adam,* have trespassed against a precept, he added that they sinned *there,* doubtless by offending in the same likeness; but this requires a shrewd understanding. For although *Adam* was a violator of a precept,[213] nevertheless one does not read that he knelt down before any idols, nor that he committed any of those sins of which Israel is accused. Why then does he compare the people who were practicing the worst crimes to that first man? Scarcely for any other reason indeed than that, although they are not equally sacrilegious, yet they are shown to be equally ungrateful. For they are like Adam, who had been led into Paradise in order to enjoy its abundance acquired without labor, with no occasion of affliction, with no complaint having arisen. He preferred to fulfill the command of the tempter over that of his Creator.[214] And with him an alluring promise springing from a lie carried more weight than the decree of the Creator that was filled with so many gifts, with so many miracles—namely, a decree that had granted the use of all things with the exception of one fruit.[215] And the violator of the precept immediately experienced banishment,[216] and traded the highest

[210] Cf. Jerome, *Commentary on Hosea* 6:4-5 (ACT 2:194).
[211] Cf. Hos 6:6a.
[212] Hos 6:6.

[213] Cf. Gen 2:17; 3:6.
[214] Cf. Gen 3:4-5.
[215] Cf. Gen 2:16-17.
[216] Cf. Gen 3:24.

happiness for almost the worst misfortune, in such a way that thereafter the fields punished his sin by denying their fertility.[217] In this way, the people of Ephraim, who were enjoying the abundance of the land like the delights of Paradise, finding no occasion for offense (that is, nothing that they might complain about concerning the kindness and generosity of God), preferred errors to the truth, as though they were afflicted solely by a hatred of virtues. They spurned the religion that was salvific, and they defected to the worship of idols. Therefore, they are said to have fallen into the same fault of the one whose situation they seem to have imitated, and they are struck down with the great hatred of the ungrateful nations. They preferred the author of no service, and one skilled only in subversion, to their Maker, the One who abundantly bestows every good thing.[218]

6:8-9 Galaad [is] a city of workers of idols, supplanted with blood, and like the jaws of highway robbers, participants with the priests who murder in the way those that pass out of Sichem. For they have wrought wickedness in the house of Israel.

As we have often said, he did not prove any one person guilty, but rather the people. Sometimes with a general speech he runs through what they did. Sometimes he recounts the things in which individual cities practiced wrongdoing, as it were, more than the rest. Therefore, although that whole country bristled with the worship of idols, nevertheless, without a doubt certain places had accrued more sacrileges there, where they would have had a greater number, whether from the opportunities arising from commerce or from the number of inhabitants. From among these, therefore, he introduces *Galaad* and *Sichem*, cities renowned for their wickedness. *Galaad*, he says, the foremost city of those who fashion idols, boasts hardly less in its pursuit of cruelty than of wickedness. For *like the jaws of highway robbers*, thus do its citizens open their mouths wide to the blood of the innocent. For while being enslaved to the persuasions of their *priests* (that is, of their soothsayers), if anyone had wanted to go up to the temple of God, they would have attacked him on the way, turning him away from the temple of God and dragging him into the fellowship of their own error.[219] And what is more, as if they were not accomplishing enough by leading him astray, they would even carry out the matter by *murder*. This is why he says, *Participants with the priests who murder in the way those that pass out of Sichem, for they have wrought wickedness*. That is to say, at first they do this by sinking themselves into sacrileges, then because they were not content with their own fall but would lead others also into a similar ruin either by persuasion or compulsion. Deservedly this is declared to be *wickedness*—namely, to have had such great zeal for impiety that they strove to impart it even to the unwilling and to those resisting.

6:10 I have seen a horrible thing in the house of Israel, the fornications of Ephraim there; Israel is defiled.

In order to show that the whole country was polluted, he also calls to mind the various

[217]Cf. Gen 3:16-18.

[218]For Julian, Hosea's point is that Israel fell by imitating Adam's transgression. Because he says nothing about Israel's inheriting Adam's guilt, G. Morin, "Un ouvrage restitué à Julien d'Eclanum: Le commentaire du Pseudo-Rufin sur les prophètes Osée, Joel et Amos," *Revue Bénédictine* 30 (1913): 20, claims that Julian shows himself to be a disciple of Pelagius in his exegesis of these verses. On the other hand, Bouwman, *Des Julian von Aeclanum Kommentar*, 79, contests Morin's claim, arguing that the passage is completely orthodox and that Pelagian expressions are not found in Julian's *Commentaries on the Prophets*. As Bouwman notes, Jerome's exegesis of the passage is substantially the same as Julian's: "But they imitated Adam, so that what he did in paradise, they did on earth, disregarding my pact and law." *Commentary on Hosea* 6:6-7 (ACT 2:195).

[219]Cf. Jerome, *Commentary on Hosea* 6:9b (ACT 2:196-97).

places. And, just as he says previously that the residents of Galaad, like highway robbers, sprang upon the travelers in order to lead them from the right path,[220] so now he announces that he saw a matter that was *a horrible thing in the house of Israel* (either in Samaria or in the whole region). He means that without exception, the whole people of Ephraim was stained with sacrileges. Because he had already said repeatedly that punishments were threatening these sins, now content with the enumeration of their offenses alone, he goes over to Judah and reminds them that they should know that the severity of the judge cannot be misled. On the contrary, they too are going to receive the wages of similar disasters if they do not hasten to amend themselves.

6:11 And you also, O Judah, set thee a harvest, when I shall bring back the captivity of my people.

Therefore, do not reckon, O tribe of Judah, that you shall be immune from condemnation because you remain within your borders, while the people of Israel goes into captivity.[221] They had indeed surpassed you in their iniquities, and it was fitting that they should anticipate you in their misfortunes. But you will follow up also in disasters the one whom you accompanied in shameful deeds. Yet one must rate this as worse: that their previous condemnation did not profit you. Therefore *set thee a harvest, when I shall bring back the captivity of my people*. Behold, he says, have no doubt about it. When the time of the owed retribution comes, the captivity, which *my people* (that is, your brothers) have now endured as justice that was announced ahead of time, is *brought back* to you, so that you also might similarly *reap a harvest*. For just as "those sowing in tears" of repentance carry back their "bundles" of joys,[222] so also those who chase after polluted pleasures shall gather a harvest of sorrows and lamentations.

[Chapter 7]

7:1 When I would have healed Israel, the iniquity of Ephraim was revealed, and the wickedness of Samaria, who have wrought falsehood. And the thief came in to steal; the robber is out in the open.

He undertakes carefully to show how ready he is to pardon, and since he, so to speak, unwillingly adopts the persona of one who is avenging, how much more and with what great delight will he indulge his lenient side, if only justice would allow it. When, therefore, he says, I had conceived an impulse, as it were, to be indulgent, and was considering rising up to run to the aid of a wretched people, I turned my eyes a little to see those whom I was about to set free. And behold, a column of iniquities rushed into my face, which Ephraim had committed, of men shouting, as it were, that no such men should be spared without committing a disastrous injury to justice. For they were so drenched with hatred of the truth that they were constantly heaping up deadly *falsehoods* with great zeal. He says, *When I would have healed Israel, the iniquity of Ephraim was revealed, and the wickedness of Samaria, who have wrought falsehood*. But in addition to their different vices of character, here he criticizes by name the sacrilege of *falsehood*, just as earlier he had criticized obscenity.[223] For they fabricated the gods whom they worshiped, they who had ceased worshiping the true God, and thus they are exposed as having *wrought falsehood*, who ascribed the divine name to images.[224] Whence even the

[220]Cf. Hos 6:8-9.

[221]Cf. Jerome, *Commentary on Hosea* 6:10-11 (ACT 2:197).

[222]Cf. Ps 126:5-6. Cf. Jerome, *Commentary on Hosea* 6:10-11 (ACT 2:198).

[223]Cf. Hos 4:9-14, 17-19; 6:10-11.

[224]Cf. Ex 32:4; 1 Kings 12:25-33.

teacher of the nations[225] says, "God handed them over to the desires of their heart to uncleanness, to the dishonoring of their bodies among themselves, who exchanged the truth of God for falsehood, and worshiped and served the creature rather than the Creator, who is blessed forever. Amen."[226]

Therefore, they have discharged me of my consideration whereby I was thinking of sparing them. The magnitude of the crimes committed by them does not allow to escape those who have fashioned falsehoods even as an affront to sacred truth. Thence the swiftly moving plunderer invaded every inner chamber of the guilty ones, entering safely like a victor and with the diligence of a thief—namely, so that he should neither leave anything behind through negligence of those things that had to be plundered, nor feel disgust due to the abundance. Therefore, he employed both the comparison to and the name of thief to one who was laying waste to things both inside and *out in the open*, so that you would understand that the enemy compared with him was not hesitant but swift.

7:2a And lest perhaps they may say in their hearts that I remember all their wickedness.

This verse was inserted for the sake of commending modesty; but the things said first hold good for the context that follows; that is, "the thief came in to steal; the robber is out in the open."[227] "Now their own devices have beset them about; they have been done before my face."[228] *And lest perhaps they may say in their hearts, that I remember all their wickedness*, or I will set forth a certain part of the profaneness that has been committed so that they may understand that the punishments are less by far than what is deserved. And so, enemies *have beset them about* and become masters over them by the rights of victory. They searched through all things so carefully that it was as if thieves had rushed into the interior rooms of houses, or as if robbers were out in the open fields. *Their own devices have beset them about, which have been done before my face*. This is similar to what he had said earlier: "When I would have healed Israel, the iniquity of Ephraim was revealed, and the wickedness of Samaria."[229] This agrees with what blessed David confesses under the persona of the same people: "You have set our iniquities before your sight, our age in the light of your countenance; and all our days have failed, and we have failed in your wrath."[230] Therefore, you are entangled in your crimes, you bear the weight of your *devices*, you have fabricated the falsehoods of gods (*deorum*), but in truth of griefs (*dolorum*). But let us hear what things he says have been revealed.

7:3-7 They make the king glad with their wickedness, and the princes with their lies. They are all adulterers, like an oven kindled by the baker. The city rested a little from the mingling of the leaven, till the whole was leavened. The day of our king. The princes began to be mad with wine. He stretched out his hand with the scorners; for they have applied their heart like an oven, when he laid snares for them. He slept all night baking them; in the morning he himself was kindled as a flame of fire. They were all heated like an oven and have devoured their judges.

He has called to mind that festivity and time the sequence of which is contained in the history of Kings. For when through Rehoboam's foolishness a separation of the people

[225]Cf. 1 Tim 2:7.
[226]Rom 1:24-25.
[227]Hos 7:1.
[228]Hos 7:2b.
[229]Hos 7:1.
[230]Ps 90:8-9.

had been carried out,[231] and Jeroboam had begun to take charge of the ten tribes, it says, "He said in his heart, Now shall the kingdom return to the house of David, if this people goes up to offer sacrifices in the house of the Lord at Jerusalem. So when a plan had been thought up, he made two golden calves, and he said to them, Behold your gods, O Israel, who brought you up out of the land of Egypt. And he set one in Bethel and the other in Dan. And this thing became a sin, for the people went as far as Dan to worship the calf. He also made shrines on high places and appointed priests from among all the people, who were not of the sons of Levi. And he appointed a feast day on the fifteenth day of the month in the eighth month, like the feast that is celebrated in Judah. And he went up and likewise made an altar in Bethel to sacrifice to the calves that he had made. And in Bethel he appointed priests of the high places that he had made. And he went up to the altar that he had made in Bethel on the fifteenth day in the eighth month, in the month that he had devised of his own heart; and he ordained a feast for the sons of Israel."[232]

Therefore, he reports that King Jeroboam, who was only looking after his own power, for a capricious fabrication expelled the worship of the true God, which was commended to the people by so many miracles and through so many ages. And the entire nation yielded to the royal profanities. In order to point out with greater contempt that they had no truth in their observance, he describes that there was a kind of contest between the impiety of the flatterers and the rulers—namely, as to who should precede whom in their crimes. Therefore, if the people should go up to the temple to worship, the tribes *made the king glad* since he was diffident, as it were, in his own affairs.[233] By their scorn for religion they removed the scruple of religious dread from his spirit. *Their princes with their lies* too. That is, they caused either the royal attendants or the neighbors to rejoice in their lies. They applied such great fervor to their deadly schemes that they seemed to be burning like an oven to which a flame is applied. Or else, just as leaven is accustomed to be hidden in a lump that is leavened, and the whole thing becomes sour in a short amount of time, so the iniquity of one man who summoned them to depravity permeated and infected all the tribes. And thus being unworthy of their profession of virtue, as terrible men characterized by impiety, they began to call that time *the days of their king* (that is to say, days to be celebrated with games and banquets)—a time, I say, at which either the life of their king or carefree security had come to pass for them. As a consequence, drunkenness lays hold of that sort of festivity, so that not merely all the common people but even the nobles, whom you could call the princes of the nation, began *to be mad with wine*. But the king himself, a fellow profaner of that office of his and the inventor of the sacrilegious error, *stretched out his hand with the scorners*, who were flattering him with their professed adulation. Thus, because they had *prepared their hearts like an oven*, which was kindled by the object of impiety, *he slept all the night baking them*. That is, he did not remove the fire that was kindled, but, as if with a furnace crammed with wood, he allowed himself a deep and carefree sleep, knowing that through the whole night their drunkenness and profaneness would bake them. Nor did belief deceive the craftsman, for when all light of reason is extinguished, everyone was discovered at dawn to be so seething in their crimes. Thus, without ambiguity they overcame their own judges—namely, those whom they had as teachers of impiety.

[231]Cf. 1 Kings 12:6-11.

[232]1 Kings 12:26-33.

[233]Cf. Jerome, *Commentary on Hosea* 7:4 (ACT 2:199-200); 7:5-7 (ACT 2:200-201).

[7:7b.] All their kings have fallen; there is none from among them who cries to me.

Why then are you amazed if all are compelled to endure torments, since they all carried out such crimes that no one (I do not say of the common people, but even of the nobles) was found who escaped from the fall of the public impiety?

7:8 Ephraim himself was mixed among the nations.

Earlier he had shown the transgressing nation by the portions that had run their course (namely, by marking out the people who had followed the kings), and then he showed that the princes likewise had fallen with the common people. Thus, there was no one to take up the duty of intervening. By this line that comes next, he has abundantly and concisely indicated the same thing. He says, *Ephraim himself was mixed among the nations*; that is, not this person or that, few or several, coming from all the stock of Israel were engrafting themselves into the errors of the nations, but the whole of Ephraim, as great as it could be, *was mixed* with the profane nations and was campaigning for this very thing. From this it was clear that they destroyed their name and were assessed instead with the name of the Gentiles. Though of course this desire was always breaking out for him in adverse circumstances, it was never corrected even by affliction. And therefore, that he might mark him out as imprudent amid the extreme miseries, he produced a fitting image of this.

7:8-9 Ephraim has become as bread baked under the ashes that is not turned. Strangers have consumed his strength (*robur*), and he knew it not.

He says, As a little bread that is not made by the art of the baker, but is made up, as it were, impulsively by a hungry man (which is not turned while it lies under the ashes, but it happens to be baked on one side only, clearly while the other side remains unbaked), thus, he says, when repeated affliction has consumed Ephraim's strength, notwithstanding he continued in his zealous pursuit of impiety. Thus, he may be called at the same time unbaked, in the sense of untamed, and burned, in that he groaned over his being afflicted by decay. But he has preserved the metaphor so that, because he had accommodated the foolish and worn down people to bread baked under ashes, but that was not turned over, he likewise called their destroyers devourers. For he says, *Strangers have consumed his strength, and he knew it not*. That is, he did not have the discernment of good and evil, which comes from the meditation on virtue, nor did he receive it from the lashes that were inflicted. But *he knew it not* at all, who was using up *his strength*, and he chose his own destruction with wondrous stupidity. Not, of course, that this was the final form of education or that he came to his senses after the trials. Instead the foolishness that he had embraced in his youth persisted until his "gray hairs"[234]—that is, continuously till the time of old age. He points out that the grayness did not shine in abundance but that it was faded and "spread about,"[235] to show that it had not drawn near but had, as it were, fulfilled the years of old age. And yet in infants one is hardly to excuse ignorance of wrong and right until they have attained extreme old age. But earlier we noted that he calls the infancy and adolescence of the people that time when they came forth out of Egypt and occupied the Promised Land.[236] Their youth is the middle period when they reigned in their own country, but he calls old age the years of captivity, the end of which the prophet names the renewal, in which doubtless

[234]Hos 7:9b.
[235]Cf. Hos 7:9b.
[236]Cf. Hos 2:14-17.

they seem to be flying like eagles with their youthfulness restored to them.[237]

7:10-11 And the pride of Israel shall be humbled before his face, and they have not returned to the Lord their God, nor have they sought him in all these. And Ephraim has become as a dove that is decoyed, not having a heart.

The prophets indeed freely change and alter the times. Yet a consideration of the statements should be able to find logical coherence in them. Hence here too he recorded, *the pride of Israel shall be humbled before his face,* for "it was humbled"; that is, even to themselves it appeared how hideous they were. He beheld that they had lost the beauty of their long-lasting security; they were covered with sores from their wretched slavery, and not even then did they seek after God, whom they knew they had offended. *And Ephraim has become as a dove that is decoyed, not having a heart.* What he called the foolishness that had progressed all the way till old age,[238] now he names this simplicity, doubtless of one who lies exposed to the tricks of deceivers. But we ought to remember that every similitude that the divine Word is accustomed to adopt from the created world can stand both for something blameworthy and for something praiseworthy. Thus, here the prophet has compared blameworthy foolishness to doves, whereas in the gospel the Lord named them for their praiseworthy innocence when he said, "Be wise as serpents and innocent as doves."[239]

7:12 Ephraim has become as a dove that is decoyed, not having a heart. They called on Egypt, they went to the Assyrians. And when they set out, I will spread my net on them; I will bring them down like fowl of the sky; I will strike them as their congregation has heard.

When they were stripped of the help of God, whom they had forsaken, and were being struck by now regular invasions, as the history of Kings relates, they requested aid from the Egyptians to protect them from the Assyrians.[240] But though they sensed that the cost would be nothing more than a few coins, they were captured by those to whom the divine judgment had subjected them.[241] This then is what he is saying: that when *they called upon the Egyptians, they went off to the Assyrians;* for when the Egyptians were not able to assist, the Assyrians transported them to the country of Media.[242] And because he had called Ephraim a *dove,* which he also calls *a fowl of the sky,* he preserves the metaphor and announces that he will drag it down and cover it with his *net;* that is, you indeed have forsaken my authority by having transgressed, yet you will not subsist outside of my choice, even in captivity, but it will hang over you, even as you move on to others' fields. The dominion of my power is fixed; therefore, lest you think that you are discharged by this migration, behold, I say beforehand that even there you will experience the net of my punishment, and you will not be able to escape my indignation unless you should correct those pursuits by which it was stirred up.

7:13-16 Woe to them, for they have departed from me; they will be destroyed, for they have transgressed against me. And I redeemed them, and they have uttered lies against me. They have not cried out in their

[237]Cf. Ps 103:5; Is 40:31.
[238]Cf. Hos 7:9.
[239]Mt 10:16; Jerome, *Commentary on Hosea* 7:11-12 (ACT 2:203).

[240]Cf. 2 Kings 7:6; 17:4; 18:21; Is 36:9. Hubbard, *Hosea,* 127, speculates that the background may be the Syro-Ephraimite war sketched in 2 Kings 16:1-9 (2 Chron 28:5-7) and alluded to in Is 7:1-8:22 and, perhaps, Mic 7:7-20.
[241]Cf. 2 Kings 15:29; 17:5-6.
[242]Cf. 2 Kings 17:6.

heart, but they howled in their beds. They were ruminating for wheat and wine; they have departed from me. And I have instructed and strengthened their arms, and they have devised evil against me. They returned that they might be without the yoke; they became like a deceitful bow. Their princes shall fall by the sword because of the rage of their tongue. This shall be their derision in the land of Egypt.

It is necessary, he says, that they be harassed by the calamity that presses down on them since *they have departed from me* and have transgressed the statutes of my law. And they were not content with having done this once; they resisted all the remedies of my judgments that I have employed to heal them. And they have, so to speak, paid back gifts and kindnesses by taking offense. They fought, as it were, against my benevolence by the wickedness of an ungrateful mind. For just as formerly thence out of Egypt, thus often they even made loud noises with their voices at other things too, and when they should have been freed from anguishes, they paid back true remedies by false services. For this is what he says: *They have uttered lies against me*; that is, they were offered to me not from their heart but from the surface of their lips. In order to indicate this more plainly, he objected, *They have not cried to me with their heart, but they howled upon their beds.* For where a disposition of a sincere mind is lacking, a supplication poured out by drunkards is rightly named by *howling.* After all, he added the consequence: *They were ruminating on wheat and wine; they have departed from me.* This means, Since I had given them the fertility of all those crops, so that they passed from feasts to renewed feasts, like cattle, for whom ruminating is instinctual, they were reconsidering the food that they devoured, either by praising it or by renewing it, as if they knew of nothing better, and they were continually departing from me, who was the giver of the abundance itself. *And I have instructed and strengthened their arms, and they have devised evil against me.* He is saying, But when it was time for them to proceed to war, I fulfilled the office of a vigorous leader so that their upper arms were made strong for combat and tasted the sweet glory of victory. But they abused my kindness and used it against me. They immediately revealed the strength of the hearts, which they had gathered, in contempt of the law, and, because they had averted the hostile yoke, they also refused to be made subject to me, saying the following by a voice of deeds: "Our lips are our own; who is our master?"[243] *They became like a deceitful bow*; that is, they had such great perversity that they seemed like a treacherous bow—namely, one that by a monstrous deceit shot arrows at the very person by whose hands it was extended.[244] Thus, he says, they turned the audacity that they had conceived by my good will against their own enemies into contempt and mistreatment of us. *Their princes shall fall by the sword for the rage of their tongue. This shall be their derision in the land of Egypt.* This can be understood in two ways—namely, he is proclaiming it to be absolutely right that, when their crimes are tallied up from various times, the *princes* should have perished along with the people, and they would know by a fitting end what was their *derision in the land of Egypt* (that is, by which they despised the threats of the prophets, while they were expecting help from the Egyptians). And therefore it seems to have been reported, as it were, insultingly and convincingly after a reckoning of plagues brought in, *This is their derision in the land of Egypt*—that is, the downfall of princes and of the people also. Or else, since he had said, *They returned that they might be without yoke* (that is, they had removed their necks from the

[243]Ps 12:4.
[244]Cf. Jerome, *Commentary on Hosea* 7:14b-16 (ACT 2:205).

law of God, and they desired to be free from its dominion), now is not the first time that they began to want this, he says, but when they were in Egypt, before they were delivered from the power of Pharaoh, they resounded both to Moses and Aaron with a similar impiety.[245] Therefore *their princes will fall by the sword,* who so dishonored the law of God by their atrocious blaspheming that they seemed not so much to be going astray as to be *raging.*

[Chapter 8]

8:1-3 Let there be a trumpet in your throat like an eagle on the house of the Lord, because they have transgressed my covenant and have violated my law. They called on me, My God, we, Israel, know you. Israel has cast off the good; the enemy shall pursue him.

In the earlier section I have warned that the manner of prophetic speech must be noted. Whenever it sounds out with a serious threat, either by supplying reasons then and there for the indignation, or by producing similar examples, it defends its judgments even from the report of iniquity and proves that they correspond with justice in all things. So then even now he has laid out the faults and calamities of the Israelite people. He showed that they dreaded not only its severity but also its long duration. Lest it seem that they indeed had been convicted of wickedness (but nevertheless were reckoned to be more worthless than the tribe of Judah, which even if they were defiled by errors, granted not as great but similar), therefore suddenly he has called to mind the captivity too, which was certain to be fulfilled after many long years. And he says, *Let there be a trumpet in your throat;* that is, let your mouths shout out like a trumpet, because a fierce predator is coming like an *eagle on the house* of God—namely, on the temple situated in Jerusalem.[246] It is not that the religion of the place and the power of the deity that was accustomed to appear there was unable to fight back, but because even the natives of that city have *transgressed the covenant* that had been made between God and men. That is, they violated the religious agreements by serving the images of the Gentiles. And the sense becomes of this nature: Understand how great the severity of judgment is. I did not put off striking down that tribe, I say, when its morals fell into ruin. It had kept the ceremonies of the law for some time while you were transgressing. It was vindicated at the time of Sennacherib by a very great miracle.[247] It carries on conspicuously in the sight of the altar and temple and is revered for its aid. For indeed it has grown cold and has no defense, its sole boast being its name, which proclaims the impudence rather than religion of "one who confesses."[248] That is, those who have become stained by profane pursuits nevertheless dare to say, *My God,* deliver us, we who alone in the whole world *know you,* and we boast in the name *Israel* given by you.[249] For in the presence of the good judge, the weight of works counts more than that of words. And therefore the Israelite people, who have *cast off* their own good (namely, the worship of the sacred religion) will lie exposed to the pursuing enemies.

8:4 They have reigned, but not by me; princes have arisen, and I knew not. Of their silver and gold they made idols for themselves, that they might perish.

He says, This madness toward me of the defiant people is an old one; long ago they hurried to cast aside my control. As if it were a

[245]Cf. Ex 5:19-23; 6:9.

[246]Cf. Jerome, *Commentary on Hosea* 8:1-4 (ACT 2:207).

[247]Cf. 2 Kings 19:35-37; Is 37:36-38.

[248]The name Judah derives from *confess.*

[249]Cf. Gen 32:28.

small thing that they decided to obey kings rather than priests, like the remaining nations round about! Thus, in a short time they abandoned even such reverence by which they had demanded a king from me.[250] And desiring to exist wholly outside our dominion, they appointed princes for themselves. Neither the choice of the priests ennobled them nor did the blessing of the prophets consecrate them. But they took up palace laws, as if I were in ignorance of it. And thus they obtained a context for their crimes. Elections went to those who were the most undeserving, and so they spent their wealth on images. *Of silver and gold they made idols for themselves, that they might perish.* He had already said about them, "I . . . multiplied her gold as well, which they made into a Baal."[251] Therefore, when they had been enriched by my liberality, they squandered the favors sacrilegiously, devising mockeries of shrines from the decorations of their houses: Therefore, *of their silver and gold they made idols for themselves, that they might perish.* One should take note of the manner of speaking that the authority of sacred Scripture frequently uses. That which follows principally is recorded in a result clause—namely, *they made idols for themselves, that they might perish,* though they did not make the images with the purpose of perishing, but they deserve to perish because they made them.

8:5-6 Your calf, O Samaria, is cast off. My wrath is enraged against them. How long will they be incapable of being cleansed? For itself also is [the invention] of Israel; an artisan made it, and it is no god.

In every verse the complaint is full of indignation: that you have fallen into iniquity of your own free will, he says, O nation that is ungrateful for the benefits of your founder, it is proven above all by the evidence of adversity. For so be it, that your material prosperity and carefree security has dulled the edge of your discretion, and you supposed that the divinity existed in the images of cows. For you saw that that is what the neighboring nations also imagined. At least you exchanged joyful things for sorrows, and the victorious enemy, in whom you had placed confidence, ravaged those shrines, and at the choice of him who was nevertheless a servant of my indignation, whom you had forsaken, the bull calves that you had consecrated were either cast down or melted. You should have trembled at the guilt of your belief, so as to perceive that no power can be given to you from the images of speechless cattle, which not even they had claimed for themselves, either by mockery or by destruction. And that we may go over what things were done, I say, O people, you were aware yourself that you had donated the material for those images. You produced the effigy, and through this you understood that you were impiously addressing them as gods. They stood forth for your benefit, things obviously to which you had not been able to give life but only form. Nevertheless, although that whole time has flown by during which as you indulged [yourself] in leisure you were occupied by these drunken ceremonies too, at the least after the troubles that followed exposed the vanity of such worship, you should have immediately shown concern for correction. And from the besetting trials you should have stoked the fire of reason that had been covered with mud, and stripped off your filth with which you had been clothed. Since you did not do this, the prophet justly exclaims, *How long will they be incapable of being cleansed? For itself also is [the invention] of Israel, an artisan made it, and it is no god.*

8:6-7 For the calf of Samaria was turned into spider's webs. For they shall sow the wind and reap the whirlwind; there is no

[250]Cf. 1 Sam 8:4-9.
[251]Hos 2:8.

standing stalk among them, the bud shall yield no flour, and if it should yield, strangers shall eat it.

He says, If imitation had not confounded your counsels, you would have judged that they were not gods, those things that you knew had been constructed by the hand of an artisan. Then there followed the enemy's invasion, and your defenses perished along with their worshipers. These things were no more able to be delayed in their devastation than *spiders' webs*. Yet with stubbornness and imprudence you even resisted these perils of events, and you did not take care to cast off the filth of such profaneness. Therefore, justly will such a tearful disappointment follow both your prayers and works that you will seem to have *sown* not grain but *the wind*, to have *reaped* not stalks but *the whirlwind*. This means that no fertility and stability will remain among you, as is customary with straw, whose height, when it is damaged by the wind, does not produce the fullness of the grain. In this way then, I say, neither will you obtain any advantage from your labors. No amount of industrious cultivation will give a return, but even if some of the former fertility begins to manifest itself from the remains, the whole thing shall come under the power of the enemy.

8:8-10 Israel has been swallowed up; now he has become among the nations like an unclean vessel. For they went up to Assyria, Ephraim a wild donkey alone by himself. They gave gifts to their lovers, but even though they shall have hired the nations with a wage, now will I gather them together. And they shall rest a while from the burden of the king and the princes.

By constant repetition he exasperates the things that he threatens, in order that a drawn-out description of the adversities may provoke a feeling of fear. His hope is that somehow the guilty might be stricken with terror and correct themselves before they are punished. So then, now he introduces the very state of the captive people and logically calls them *swallowed up*, who were placed under the choice of those who devoured them and for whom there is no further room to slaughter, except as much as the complete ferocity of the conquerors has granted for their advances. He says, *Israel has been swallowed up; now he has become among the nations like an unclean vessel.* Indeed, the obvious sense[252] of the judgments resounds; but as far as the sense is concerned, the things said first are explained by the things added below. For he is showing why he called them *swallowed up*; that is, all their strength has been exhausted, and they could easily be consumed by slaughter, if the anger of the masters demanded this too. Further, the fact that they have ravaged them in a lesser degree compensates for the added indignities, and the reason they do not destroy everyone is so that they may have some who always stand in dread of them and who would seem to envy more the consolation of death than that they be granted the benefit of life. For they did not save these miserable people to enjoy the light, but to bear contempt. And therefore he says, *Israel has become among the nations like an unclean vessel.* Some translators have rendered this "chamber pot."[253] He says, Israel has not been singled out for honorable service, so that, after his bearing the signs of liberty and dominion, at least he might be graciously judged to be among the servants. On the contrary, he is as a vessel prepared to meet the requirements of nature; thus he was filled with the filth of indignities.

[252]For this meaning of *superficies*, see Baxter, "Notes," 51.

[253]Jerome, *Commentary on Hosea* 8:8 (ACT 2:210) renders the word "unclean vessel" in the lemma and reports that the Septuagint rendered it "empty vessel." In his discussion Jerome indicates that the Hebrews call an empty or unclean vessel *matula*, which we use to collect feces. Bouwman, *Des Julian von Aeclanum Kommentar*, 124, concludes that Julian has not understood Jerome correctly.

And by mentioning the *nations*, he augmented the condition well by speaking of the injury. *Now Israel has become among the nations like an unclean vessel.* It is as if he were to say, Alas, alas! How lamentable he was and how great was the change as that people, who alone had learned by the authority of the sacred law to distinguish between clean and the unclean things,[254] who had lived set apart from all the nations in order that they not be defiled by them by any contact, now he is proven to be unclean by the judgment of those nations too, which, from infancy to old age were soiled by the filth of all shameful deeds. And so, *He has become among the nations like an unclean vessel, for they went up to Assyria, a wild donkey alone by himself.* This refers to what we said they will suffer when the Assyrian afflicts them. They will see clearly that such great eminence in strength has been given to him, that those who reach him are said to have *gone up*. But the words *a wild donkey alone by himself* need to be referred to Ephraim. That is, *Ephraim, a wild donkey alone by himself has given gifts to his lovers.* He is saying, the Jewish people, who allowed no commands from outsiders, but like a *wild donkey* that did not know the yoke and burdens, about whom blessed David had sung in praise of God, "He who makes those who are strong of one custom live in the house"[255]—that is, by a singular foundation he has made them dwell in the Promised Land. This one, therefore, I say, he who was free from human domination, who was placed solely under divine authority, now is so prostrate and crushed that he considers himself blessed if even an honest slavery happens to him. *They gave gifts to their lovers, but even though they shall have hired the nations with a wage, now will I gather them together.* Since the throng of the ten tribes deserved to be punished on account of their profanities, the domination of the Assyrians was promised them by the announcements of the prophets. But the Jews exhibited exactly that spirit toward the threats that the tribes likewise had. They stood out as defiant in all things and preferred even to hire the Egyptians at a wage than to be subjugated to the Assyrians to whom the divine sentence subjected them. This, then, is what he is saying, that with a resolve to fornicate, they wished to try out the Egyptians as their lovers, so to speak. And by their own free will they sent bribes to them, and they promised to bring them yearly payments, if they would help to drive off the Assyrians, and the threat of the prophets would be overcome.[256] Next he says, since they *hired the nations with a wage* (that is, the Egyptians), *now will I gather them together.* This means, I will drag them into captivity, and I will doom them to the decreed tyranny of the Assyrian nation. For *I will gather them together,* he says, lest anyone seem to have escaped, *and they shall rest awhile from the burden of the king and the princes.* This seems to have been introduced with derision—that is to say, that he should speak of the captivity that had been brought in as *rest*. The meaning is that they will recognize the extent to which they incited it by their own counsels and pursuits when they have been *gathered together,* when they have migrated as exiles into foreign lands. If indeed they either cease with the commands to the Assyrians or offer voluntary tribute to the Egyptians, they will be carrying out the commands of masters with all their strength. Thus, they would admit that what they ceased to bring as tribute resulted in an increase of evils for themselves.

8:11-14 Because Ephraim has made many altars to sin, altars have become to him unto transgression. I shall write to him my manifold laws, which have been reckoned as foreign. Offer victims, offer; and they shall

[254]Cf. Lev 10–18.
[255]Ps 68:6 LXX.
[256]Cf. 2 Kings 7:6; 17:4; 18:21-24; Ezek 16:33.

sacrifice flesh and shall eat it; the Lord will not receive them. Now he will remember their iniquity and will visit their sins; they shall return to Egypt. And Israel has forgotten his Maker, and has built temples; and Judah has multiplied fortified cities. I will send a fire on his cities, and it shall devour his houses.

He is showing that he had summoned help from the Egyptians as a consequence of transgressing—that is, by resounding with holy counselors through everything, so that, as he had scorned the teaching prophets, so he also scorned those who were threatening, and he not only scorned them but even fought against them. And as far as it lay within him, he accused them of falsity—doubtless he means that those prophets would have been proven false if Ephraim would have repelled the Assyrians by hiring the Egyptians.[257] Rightly then blessed Hosea now recounts the evils of the coming captivity. He runs through the punishments, then the transgressions, and he laments the many altars Ephraim had made to idols. Moreover, he complains that he had converted these altars to criminal use. It is as if he were to say, Naturally the reason the treatment of the divine affair was established was in order that the altars might expiate those whom shameful acts had defiled. But now calamitous things so envelop miserable persons that nowhere will they happen to be expiated with greater difficulty than at the altars. *I shall write to them my manifold laws, which have been reckoned as foreign.* He is saying, By fleeing to the nations and by going around and mingling with their rites, an ungrateful nation has judged itself to be absolved from the difficulties of our law. But because he is ready to wear down the profane faces of the obstinate with the bridle and muzzle of my rebuke, the outcome itself reveals that the one who was unbridled with respect to the precepts was not treated with contempt for these. For *I shall write to them my manifold laws, which have been reckoned as foreign.* But he has expressed the thing that he was about to do with the circumlocution of a judge, who customarily reads aloud the written verdict from a little book: my laws, therefore, which were promulgated long ago and are contained chiefly in the book of Deuteronomy, *I will write* in them in manifold ways; that is, I will describe them and augment them. But they are the ones that were proclaimed by an enumeration of all the commandments between the mountains of Gerizim and Ebal (Hebae), when the tribes were divided up equally. In that place, therefore, to recall a few things of the many, the sermon concludes in this way: "But if you will not hear the voice of the Lord God, to keep and to do all his commandments and ceremonies, which I command you this day, all these curses shall come on you and overtake you. Cursed shall you be in the city, cursed in the field. Cursed shall be your barn, and cursed your stores. Cursed shall be the fruit of your womb, and the fruit of your land, the herds of your oxen, and the flocks of your sheep. Cursed shall you be coming in, and cursed going out."[258] And so he threatens that he will multiply these laws for the defiled people. *They will offer victims; and they will sacrifice flesh and eat it; the Lord will not receive them. Now he will remember their iniquity.* Certainly the people of Samaria (that is, the ten tribes) had scorned his judgments and precepts no less than the sacrifices that had to be offered to the true God; but the tribe of Judah, though growing dirty through the imitation of his sister, nevertheless had not yet abandoned paying attention to the sacrificial victims. Therefore, in the prophecy he proceeds to join them together in the nature of their character, and he makes a transition to Judah while

[257]Cf. 2 Kings 7:6; 17:4; 18:21-24; Ezek 16:33.

[258]Deut 28:15-19.

accusing Israel, so that, as he has already done,[259] he might make a reproach. For by giving no thought to the justice of their morals, they are establishing the hope of salvation solely in the offering of sacrifices. And he introduces the voice of those mutually exhorting themselves, as it were (that is, *Offer, offer victims*); and he immediately responds, *The Lord will not receive them. Now he will remember their iniquity.* Without doubt, the gravity of the judgment must be considered. For he says that he was brought at that time especially to the remembrance of their iniquity, when they thought that they ought to be protected by offering victims, fully conscious that they had neglected and despised justice. For surely gifts would be pleasing at that time when they were offered not in the person of enemies but by beloved persons. Moreover, it is closer to being an outrage if you give soothing gifts to him whom you had exasperated by your crimes, not with the ostentation of one who is making supplication but giving. Therefore, that verdict befits you that the murderer Cain sensed,[260] that you will offer flesh, and when the Lord does not receive it, you yourselves will devour it. Why not? Since he wants obedience rather than sacrifice, and concern for justice more than burnt offering.[261] Now, therefore, especially he is accelerating the punishment, he says, because you place the confidence of your liberation in the shedding of the blood of animals. Now *he will visit the sins* of all who *return to Egypt*—namely, in spirit and in esteem. For all of Israel together (that is, both Judah and Ephraim) have so *forgotten their own Maker* that, when they had rendered him most hostile to themselves, they did not show concern for improvement, but partly for restoring the fortifications, partly for hiring out nations. They used up their wealth and works, as if they did not know that it had been declared by a sacred song that "Unless the Lord builds the house, those who build it labor in vain. Unless the Lord guards the city, those who guard it stay awake in vain."[262] Therefore, their impiety increased so much that though they had provoked the almighty Judge to wrath, they thought that they would no less be blessed through their own effort—namely, if they should construct a large number of fortifications against the enemies' sorties. And thus they would remain happy, not merely apart from God's help but even with God fighting against them. Therefore, he says, a well-deserved disappointment will strike them down, so that they would seem confined to their own fortifications rather than defended by them, and a raging flame would consume all the *houses* of the same.

Since these things are so—that is, since no difficulty hinders the justice of God—nor does any deceit delude it.

[Chapter 9]

9:1a Be not joyful, O Israel! Exult not.

For you withdrew from the covenant of the law by your sacrilegious defilement; that is, do not think you will remain unpunished for having mixed yourself with the remaining nations. For such a desire for vain flight does not appropriate for you the freedom that you had desired. It only subjects you to severe retribution.

9:1b-3 You have loved a reward on all the corn floors. The floor and winepress shall not feed them, and the wine shall deceive them. They shall not dwell in the Lord's land.

Be not impudently *joyful*, I say, O nation of ours, but know that you will change all your vows into their opposites; for you have shown

[259]See Job 6:10, 11.

[260]Cf. Gen 4:1-16.

[261]Cf. Hos 6:6; 1 Sam 15:22; Eccles 5:1 (4:17 in the Hebrew); Mt 9:13; 12:7.

[262]Ps 127:1.

yourself to be worthless and licentious not only in your religious duties but also in every action. Truly, *you have loved a reward on all the corn floors*; that is, you have judged nothing better, nothing dearer than the fertility of your lands and the money laid out for your belly. Therefore, the entire abundance of your crops and fruits will be carried off, and in order that your vows may torture you all the more, the vintage that has been evident for a long time will be wiped out by sudden storms, so that it would seem not only to have been injured unto your sorrow but even *deceived*. But why do I recall lesser losses? For exiles will follow your scarcity, nor will any ability of cultivating the soil of your homeland be granted to you. Nevertheless, you will not be able to wonder at the magnitude of his calamity, as if complaining about it. For you will be guilty of having been a voluntary deserter of that land as far as one looks back at your pursuits. For at one time you desired the crimes of the Assyrians and the Egyptians, at another you desired their aid. By what shamelessness then do you seize the fertility of that country whose defining marks you rejected both in respect to religious rituals and morals? Rather, having been struck by it, you will depart to that one where you had been previously corrupted, and you will be brought forcibly both to Egypt, by your wishes, and to the *Assyrians*, by captivity. And you will endure that poverty so that you feed with sorrow on the *polluted* foods that are at hand.

9:4 They shall not pour libations of wine to the Lord; and they shall not please him. Their sacrifices [will be] as the bread of mourners. All who eat of it shall be defiled, for their bread shall be for their soul; it shall not enter into the house of the Lord.

Now he is describing the evils of captivity, and he says that when material wealth has been exchanged for extreme poverty, neither any happiness nor consolation occurs, and they spend all their time in lamentations. For they are neither allowed to offer sacrifice to God nor to expect anything from the expiation of faults—namely, through those duties by which they thought they would be pleasing to God. Therefore, every oblation of theirs is more suitable not for holy days (*feriis*) but as offerings for the dead (*inferiis*).[263] It will defile rather than cleanse those who draw near. *For their bread shall be for their soul; it shall not enter into the house of the Lord.* It is the same attentive thought, which was found earlier, when the sacrifices of those who offer are said to be rejected by God.[264] And now, therefore, he says, I have rejected their offerings, which on account of excess guilt I have been aroused to drive out from the soil of the homeland. That bread shall turn out to be their deadly nourishment. They do not deserve to bring it into *the house of the Lord*.

9:5-6 What will you do on the day of appointed festival and on the day of the feast of the Lord? For behold, they have set out because of destruction; Egypt has gathered them, Memphis will bury them. Nettles will inherit their beloved silver; thorns will be in their tents.

Although the larger intention for blessed Hosea is to review the deeds of the ten tribes, and to devote attention either to criticizing their crimes or unfolding their calamities, nevertheless, because of the authority of his prophecy, he touches on things that have happened to the tribe of Judah as well. And since he knew that the residents of Jerusalem, though a little later, will compare with the Samaritans because of the equality of the merits, he remembered the temple and their sacrifices as well, as if ascribing to the whole nation what agrees particularly with two

[263]Notice the play on words.
[264]Cf. Hos 8:13.

tribes. Hence when he said that they lost the solace of their offerings, by means of which they thought they would be purified, he refined the coinciding conditions. And because the commanded cessation of the same offices becomes rough especially on those days on which an *appointed festival* was being carried out, therefore he says, *What will you do on the day of the appointed festival of the Lord?* Namely, what darkness, what bitterness, what anxiety of spirit will fill you, when you, as exiles, silent, in chains and in barbarous servitude, spend that *day of the feast of the Lord*, which the coming together and singing of the people rendered it as distinguished and sweet to you? And because, as we have said, on the occasion of Ephraim he signified also things that would come to Judea, it follows, *For behold, they have set out because of destruction; Egypt will gather them together,*[265] *Memphis will bury them.* He is saying, When a hostile dominion will have ravaged their country, it will come to pass on all the tribes, as the punishment follows, what they perpetrated before in their sinful desire. Thus, just as a portion was led to the Assyrians, so Egypt too will gather a portion, and the land of Memphis will consume those taken in. Now both the blessed Jeremiah and the history of Kings recount that this happened after the victory of Nebuchadnezzar, who destroyed Jerusalem, to those Jews whom the Babylonians had left behind as cultivators of fields.[266] But as for what he adds, *Nettles will inherit their beloved silver,* this happened during the experience of the captivity. Would that the reading alone, and not also experience, had taught us this! For it is a well-known fact that when the inhabitants are gone, houses built at great expense get covered over with forests; frequently even buried treasures of gold and silver perish in everlasting oblivion when those who had concealed these things are wiped out.[267]

9:7 The days of visitation have come; the days of retribution have come. Know, O Israel, that the prophet was foolish, the spiritual man was mad (*insanum*). Because of the multitude of your iniquity, [there is] also a multitude of madness (*amentiae*).[268]

It would have been fitting, certainly, he says, that reason rather than calamity should teach you to be discerning. But since you have forced the use of whips and goads, as if you were utterly devoid of reason, or already now, since the time of *visitation* has arrived (that is, of your condemnation), wake up and understand what you deserve. Admit that such harsh wages are owed to your pursuits, which certainly you reckon you have amassed by despising spiritual teachers. Indeed, you had burst forth to the point of madness (*furoris*) when they announced the prophets, who spoke according to the choice of the Holy Spirit and who endured you with the devotion of parents, in the hope that perchance the previously expressed fear would act its part, to prevent vengeance from finding someone to punish. You said not only that they had foreseen nothing beyond the rest but even that they were deprived of human reason and that they were moved by madness (*vesania*) rather than by revelation. But the history of the kings also expands on how it was thus customary at that time to address prophets using an abundance of profanity. For when a certain prophet on a mission from the blessed Elisha had come to Ramoth Galaad to anoint Jehu as king, the nobles sitting around say to Jehu, "What does

[265]The lemma said, "has gathered."

[266]Cf. 2 Kings 25:26; Jer 41:17; 43:7; Jerome, *Commentary on Hosea* 9:5-6 (ACT 2:215).

[267]According to Gennadius, Julian had distinguished himself by almsgiving during a period of famine and want that apparently came in the wake of the barbarian invasions. Thus, these are autobiographical reflections. Cf. on Amos 2:13-16; 8:10.

[268]It is interesting to note the variety of Latin words for "madness" in this section.

that raving madman (*fanaticus*) want with you?"[269] So then, the authority of the divine Word had so deteriorated among them that they assessed the precepts of the virtues to be no longer medicinal, but maddening (*furiosa*). The one addressing the public dreaded the magnitude of this crime and exclaims in judgment, *Because of the multitude of your iniquity, [there is] also a multitude of madness* (amentiae). It is as if he were to say, This is not some simple error, but a madness (*dementia*) that has multiplied—namely, to despise as foolish madmen (*vesanos*) the spiritual teachers and those capable of prophetic splendor, especially at that time when they themselves were enduring such a great lack of prudence that they esteemed as gods things that they had melted down.

9:8 The watchman of Ephraim [was] with my God. The prophet has become a snare of ruin on all his ways; madness (*insania*) is in the house of his God.

Some have thought that here Jeroboam has been signified by the name *Ephraim*.[270] He is known to have come from the tribe of Ephraim and to have been zealous at cultivating the temple, and on account of this he offended Solomon.[271] But after he secured command over the ten tribes, he proved to be the author of profaneness as well when he converted the hearts of his subjects to the worship of the calves.[272] Therefore, they think that Jeroboam is being addressed by the name of *Ephraim*, who was called a watchman with God, because at first he had concern for religion and carefully considered those things that were right. But once he was a prophet, I say, he fell so suddenly into depravity that he became a ruin and a snare to his followers. Why not? When *in the house of his god*, whom he had chosen, how great is the greatest madness he got involved in! But this passage can be explained more briefly in the following manner. Let us say, because he added in uninterrupted succession the complaint taken up concerning the mistreatment of the prophets, it is as if he were to say, O you people, subject to profane religious rituals, to the heap of your iniquity you have added insults of your spiritual teachers, so that you have called the prophets of God madmen (*insanos*) and spiritual teachers fools. What madness (*amentia*) has broken out from the multitude of iniquity. For you dared sometimes to engage in combat, so to speak, with their promises, and to say, Behold let us both equally be allotted the service of watch duty, and let us see whether all these things come to pass, which they announce to us as about to come. And you added that the prophets ought to be thought of as nothing more than an enemy's snare, fashioned for the ruin of wretched citizens. And so having united blasphemy to insults, you said that the madness (*insaniam*) of the prophets was in the house of God. The invective that is added clearly accuses this opinion of being the greatest sacrilege. For he exclaims,

9:9 They have sinned deeply, as in the days of Gabaa [RSV: Gibeah]; he will remember their iniquities and will visit their sins.

He says, It is not the kind of crime that the rebuke of the judge would prevail to forget it. And because he had made mention of the ancient history, he says, *He will remember their iniquities*. He is saying he will punish the present mistreatment of the prophets no differently than if he were bringing up for examination that crime that they committed

[269]Cf. 2 Kings 9:11; Jerome, *Commentary on Hosea* 9:7 (ACT 2:216). Hubbard, *Hosea*, 169, also identifies this passage as well as Jer 29:26 as the background to Hosea's remark.
[270]Cf. Jerome, *Commentary on Hosea* 9:8-9 (ACT 2:216).
[271]Cf. 1 Kings 11:26-40.
[272]Cf. 1 Kings 12:29-33.

before the age of the kings,[273] when judges ruled the nation of Judea. Indeed, at that time there was a certain Levite who returned to the place of his own residence in a city of the tribe of Benjamin named *Gabaa*.[274] As the day was already advancing toward evening, he turned aside, and when he had found no host in that place, he stayed in a public inn with his wife.[275] But the degenerate youth of the city were not satisfied with having sinned by denying him lodging. They abducted the priest's wife for obscene use and carried out such a great act of the most insolent shame that the degraded woman was deprived even of her life, just as she had been robbed of her chastity.[276] But on the following day the Levite got up and placed the body of his dead wife on his own beast. He cut it into pieces and sent it throughout all the tribes of that nation, so that they might take joint vengeance once knowledge of this savage spectacle had become known.[277] And thus publicly declaring war against the Gabaonites, they were handed over even if they were not guilty.[278] In the third conflict they wiped out those who had scarcely been overcome, so that from the entire tribe of Benjamin no more than five hundred men are reported to have survived.[279] The prophet has compared the present sin to that crime, then—namely, which they were committing by calling spiritual men foolish and mad. But by equating the faults he is commending reverence for the prophets. He is showing that proper respect for them has been outraged to such a degree by their reckless speech that it is counted as being no less a crime than the earlier public obscenity provoked, and that bloodshed and pollution.

[273]Cf. Judg 19:1; Jerome, *Commentary on Hosea* 9:8-9 (ACT 2:217).
[274]Cf. Judg 19:1-15. The more familiar spelling is Gibeah.
[275]Cf. Judg 19:15.
[276]Cf. Judg 19:16-26.
[277]Cf. Judg 19:27–20:11.
[278]Cf. Judg 20:12-26.
[279]Cf. Judg 20:27-48.

9:10 I found Israel like grapes in the desert, like the firstfruits of the fig tree in the top thereof I saw their fathers; but they went in to Baalpegor and were estranged to shame, and they became abominable, as those things were, which they loved (*dilexerunt*).

As we have said, he compiles things that were done at different times in order to equate the guilt of the outraged religion and of the abusive treatment of the prophets. But he made a digression in order to praise the ancestors, through which praise ill will for the degenerate sons increases, and it is made apparent from what peak of sanctity they have descended into such depths of crimes. He says, When mortal natures become filthy and covered over by dense thorn bushes of impiety, Abraham, Isaac, and Jacob furnish evidence of excellence.[280] Thus, they produce the attractiveness of the confession owed to God, as if they bear grapes and figs. I have not despised their faith and virtue due to their small number; but to the extent that I judged them to be of greater honor and grace, so much the more did they show contempt for the several examples of the profane nations. Therefore, just as the vine sprouting forth in a desolate waste, as ripened figs, for which both their ripeness and sweetness have wakened a longing after, so have I gathered them into my lap with the obligatory sedulity, lest any of their fruit or praise should be lost. But although I had chosen to be called their God, I who was the Lord of all things, I had also proceeded to multiply their progeny. But the degenerate people, equally forgetful of both their own ancestors and of the Creator, entered into the worship of their idols, things that obscenity alone had consecrated. That is to say, they went to Beelphegor, which they say contains a

[280]Cf. Jerome, *Commentary on Hosea* 9:10 (ACT 2:217).

statue of Priapus.[281] Now the history of the book of Numbers points this out—namely, that according to the counsel of Balaam, Midianite women were instructed to come forth to meet the Israelite army, fitted out in the dress and bearing of courtesans. Their aim was to inflame them with lustful desires, that they should occasion the means of sexual immorality, but not before they had defiled themselves before the idol of Beelphegor with their own sacrifice.[282] Ultimately such a plague arose among the people that twenty-three thousand perished together in a single day.[283] Therefore *shame* seized these obscene men, so that they became no less *abominable* to God than the idols themselves, by whose eager pursuit they had transgressed (*deliquerant*). Therefore, it is hardly the people of that age whom the prophet Hosea rebukes, who are said to have sinned in *Beelphegor*; but because he has introduced a remembrance of antiquity, and has praised the excellence of the holy fathers, he sets forth what things their descendants did in different ages, in order that it may be evident to whom they compare who are convicted in the present time. It is as if it were being said to them, Behold those shameful deeds that emanate from the illustrious race! Behold the extent of forgetfulness of ancestral dignity there has been in them. Though their ancestors merited to be chosen for salvation, when the world was perishing, those thereafter worshiped the Priapi and the calves, when folly and obscenity went to war against them!

[281]Priapus was the god of procreation—hence, of gardens and vineyards, where his statues were placed. For reproductions of photos of some of his quite obscene statues in antiquity, see Kristi Upson-Saia, "Gregory of Nyssa on Virginity, Gardens, and the Enclosure of the Παράδεισμος," *Journal of Early Christian Studies* 27, no. 1 (2019): 125.

[282]Cf. Num 25:1-9; 31:16. Jerome, *Commentary on Hosea* 9:10 (ACT 2:218), does not make explicit the link to Num 25, but Theodore of Mopsuestia, *Commentary on Hosea* (FOTC 79) alludes to it.

[283]Cf. 1 Cor 10:8.

9:11-12 As for Ephraim, their glory has flown away like a bird from the birth, and from the womb, and from the conception. Because even if they should bring up their children, I will make them without children among men. Yea, and woe to them when I shall depart from them.

Ephraim, he says, *has flown away like a bird*. And he had already said, "Ephraim has become as a dove that is decoyed, not having a heart. They called on Egypt, they went off to the Assyrians."[284] Therefore, that people, who were unwilling to distinguish between pious and impious things, but was made abominable even as the images themselves, they will be transferred justly into captivity with such great speed that they would seem not so much to have walked there but to have flown. Nevertheless, they will experience not only the scourge of exile, but the preceding calamity of want and sickness will devour throngs of their *children*, so that bereavement would punish their hearts, which fertility previously brought forth. He says, *Their glory from the birth and from the womb and from the conception; because even if they should bring up their children, I will make them without children among men*. That is, although they had provoked the eternal judge by their sins, showing no concern to appease him, they were eager to have large families, thinking that this was their own happiness and glory, if it would be permitted at one time to unite in marriage, then to look after those who were pregnant, then to listen to the childbirths. In that place, therefore, I will strike them, where they were especially rejoicing. Either it will not be permitted for them to raise the children they have conceived or, if one happens to raise them, they would perish, until they at last be conducted to the filth of solitude by the passing away of the

[284]Hos 7:11; cf. Jerome, *Commentary on Hosea* 9:11-13 (ACT 2:218-19).

desired offspring. And in this way they would perceive that though it cannot be well for those whom I abandon, it would be much worse for those against whom I fight.

9:13-14 Ephraim, as he saw, was a Tyre founded in beauty, and Ephraim brings out his children to the murderer. Give them, O Lord; what will you give, Lord? Give them a womb without children, and dry breasts.

Even among the other prophets we read a description of the loveliness and great population of the city of Tyre. Thus, blessed Ezekiel named it a harlot's song,[285] obviously on account of the multitude of songs with which the whole city made extravagant noise throughout the whole night. Therefore, because here he had threatened a change for the people of Samaria, in order to increase the sense of sorrow, he marvels at its beauty, which was in prosperity. It is as if he were saying, No one well understands the magnitude of this calamity, whereby the Jews have migrated from their own territories, with their offspring destroyed, unless he considers the former things. For then he will notice how great a change for the worse has occurred when he considers with what a great flower of gladness they blossomed before. He says, *Ephraim, as he saw, was a Tyre*, seething with people, overflowing with wealth, resounding with sumptuousness, and resonating in songs. Its location was so favorable both to those who left from its shores and who came from the mainland[286] that it could be said its very foundations were established in a certain *beauty*.[287] But, I say, he has commanded this city, which indeed overflowed with delights yet had prepared no protection for itself concerning justice and religion, to lead forth its own children to the slaughter and to experience the choices of savage enemies, a city that had trampled on the precepts of our law. But when the times were changed into a period of decline, he recalls actions that are still to come under Nebuchadnezzar, as if in another time.[288] *Ephraim*, therefore (that is, Samaria and the multitude of the remaining tribes), is oppressed by such great terror of the punisher that he nearly hastened to offer his own offspring to the killers. Surely, he is said to have carried this out not in action but in what they deserve. But it occurs in scriptural usage as a figure of speech of one questioning, and, as a request of the one announcing what may come, *Give them, O Lord—what will you give?* He says, *a womb without children and dry breasts*. He says, Let him condemn these wounds, and let them know that they are to be destroyed by a slaughter. For he had said that, if they had raised sons, they should immediately endure the loss of them.[289] But now he has added that their women must endure *dry breasts* and an ominous sterility. Thus, among the people whom captivity has consumed, there is not even hope of restoration.

9:15-17 All their wickedness is in Galgal, for there I hated them for the wickedness of their inventions. I will cast them forth out of my house. I will love them no more, all their princes are withdrawing. Ephraim is struck, their root is dried up; they will yield no fruit. And if they should have issue, I will slay the best beloved fruit of their womb. My God will cast them away because they hearkened not to him; and they will be wanderers among the nations.

They are reported to have worshiped idols chiefly in *Galgal*, to be sure, and therefore he

[285]Cf. Is 23:15. Notice the misattribution. Ezek 27:2 speaks of a lament for Tyre.

[286]Tyre, the famous maritime and commercial city of the Phoenicians, was an island in ancient times.

[287]Cf. Ezek 27:3; 28:12.

[288]Cf. Ezek 26:7.

[289]Cf. Hos 9:11-12.

declares that *all their wickedness* has been collected there, on account of which he testifies that he hates them. Now some have thought that the prophet remembered this passage too because of Saul;[290] for in Galgal he took over the leadership of the nation. The city had transgressed at Jeroboam's instigation—namely, by consecrating the calves.[291] Therefore, on the occasion of the present guilt he also accuses that original error, when it scorned the guidance of the priests and desired to be under kings in imitation of the neighboring nations.[292] So then, he says, *All their wickedness is in Galgal.* It is as if he were to say, That impiety that now devoured them, which caused it, from there it received its beginning, when they transferred the republic from the priestly rule to kingship. But this meaning would seem to be rather subtle. Now the following would be clearer and more applicable, which without interruption of the discourse convicts the worship of idols both in Gilgal and in other places. For the sake of inspiring dread, the just judge threatens to *cast them forth from his house.* And he adds to that sentence something else, which burns all the more (that is, *I will love them no more*), because even in the beginning he showed that that daughter would be without mercy.[293] He is announcing that the tribes are to be *cast forth from their own house* (that is, from the Promised Land) because, as far as concerns the temple, long ago they had withdrawn from it through the destructive fabrications of King Jeroboam.[294] Therefore, he promises that his severity, by which the profane are cast forth from their own territory, will remain so fixed that it would seem to be tempered by no succession of mercy. Because he was showing only the heavy weight of punishment, immediately he added the cause of it, which was great: for *all their princes are withdrawing,* he says. Surely, he recorded this not in order to signify that only the nobles had fallen into sins but in order that no doubt would remain concerning the iniquities of the common crowd. For no prince had arisen who had not withdrawn from the worship of God. The remaining verses, of course, repeat the sentence stated a little bit earlier—that is, by which he had threatened them with both bereavement and barrenness at the same time. *Ephraim is struck, their root is dried up; they will yield no fruit. And if they should have issue, I will slay the best beloved fruit of their womb. My God has cast them away,*[295] *because they hearkened not to him; they will be wanderers among the nations.* Captivity will swallow them up, he says, but numerous and diverse calamities will consume their offspring, than whom nothing is sweeter to the parents.

[Chapter 10]

10:1-3 Israel a vine full of branches, the fruit is agreeable to it; according to the multitude of his fruit he has multiplied altars, according to the plenty of his land he has abounded with images. Their heart is divided; now they shall die. He shall break down their images; he shall destroy their altars, for now they will say: We have no king; for we fear not the Lord, and what shall a king do to us?

It is one and the same subject by which the prophet's speech runs on—that is, to scold the crimes of that people, to announce punishments. And therefore, generally he treats again similar and identical arrangements. Yet to the extent that he is able, he mixes in something by which they may be renewed. Therefore, by

[290]Cf. Jerome, *Commentary on Hosea* 9:15a (ACT 2:220).
[291]Cf. 1 Kings 12:28-31.
[292]Cf. 1 Sam 10:1-9; Jerome, *Commentary on Hosea* 9:15a (ACT 2:220).
[293]Cf. Hos 2:21-24.
[294]Cf. 1 Kings 12:25-33; Jerome, *Commentary on Hosea* 9:15b (ACT 2:221).

[295]The lemma said, "will cast them away."

naming *Israel* a *vine full of branches*, he proclaims that its *fruit* is *agreeable to it*. But this *vine*, when it was transferred from Egypt, filled the Promised Land.[296] It established glad things by spreading out its branches, he says, and it produced such great *plenty* of fruits (namely, children and grandchildren) that the narrowness of the lands that it had received were rendered spacious. But what good was it to have attained an increase in offspring? Their pursuits so much broke out into the opposite direction that for the sake of the number of the multitude they armed themselves against my reproaches, I who had been the author of such a great gift. And it was as if they were striving to match their wealth to their wickedness. In public and in private they fabricated gods for themselves to worship. And so that *vine* that had been planted from the stock of the chosen fathers was converted into a cluster of bitter grapes and a vine of Sodom.[297] Thus, both the common people and the princes, all of them, not only neglected justice but even rejoiced in having fought against it. Therefore, *their heart is divided; now they will die*; that is, they have been separated from me with their whole intent, and they have departed from the worship of the law by a definitive judgment. What remains except for them to perish by a definitive disaster? And let them understand the vanity of their own opinion by which they had been accustomed to console themselves so that they were saying that their situation, even in captivity, ought to be rated as better than when they were governed by holy men or by priests or kings. Therefore, he says, they will converse shamelessly among themselves; at that time they would obtain a certain amount of liberty since they are compelled to obey neither law nor king. For an enemy will have led away their prince, and they will have driven off the yoke of religion by their impiety of long duration. Exulting in these crimes, therefore, he says, they think it happiness that they are not summoned to daily duties of their kings, but living far away they pay annual tribute to the victors. For they are like those of whom the apostle says, "Who without hope have given themselves up to lasciviousness by the working of all uncleanness and covetousness,"[298] or those whom the prophet brands because they said, "We will magnify our tongue; our lips are our own; who is our Lord?"[299] This is how they are whom the blessed Hosea proclaims that they have burst forth so far into profanity that they seem capable either of having said or of saying, *There is no king; for we fear not the Lord, and what shall a king do to us?* That is, we are released from the troubles of a divine fear, and we do not have a king, who could punish this license in our statements. Because he is stirring up a serious sense of dread in the one who considers this well, he exclaims in reproach,

10:4 You speak words of an unprofitable vision, and you will make a covenant, and judgment will spring up as bitterness on the furrows of the field.

That is to say, in the soil of the heart, if you sense in such madness that you have entered into a covenant with extreme disasters. And your country will be so filled with different disasters that in these lands dangers would seem to be sprouting rather than seeds. Suitably, however, because he had indicated that they had sinned not by negligence but with zeal and dedicated effort, he called them *furrows* cut by the plow, in which the *bitterness* of *judgment* arose (that is, severe vengeance), and they would know that they will reap what they had sown.

[296]Cf. Ps 80:8-9.

[297]Cf. Deut 32:32; Jerome, *Commentary on Hosea* 10:1 (ACT 2:222-23).

[298]Eph 4:19.

[299]Ps 12:4.

Book Three[300] on Hosea the Prophet

[Chapter 10 (continued)]

10:5-6 The inhabitants of Samaria have worshiped the cows of Bethaven. For the people thereof have mourned over it. And its wardens exulted over it in its glory. Because it is departed from it. For itself also is carried into Assyria, a present to the avenging king; shame shall capture Ephraim, and Israel shall be confounded in his own will.

Jewish tradition was accustomed to explaining this passage in the following way.[301] In those times when the Israelites were still settled in their own country and had not yet been transferred to the lands of the Medes, they paid tribute to the Assyrians.[302] When their treasury was emptied out, they directed that the calves that they were worshiping be sent as a substitute for the taxes owed to Assyria. However, since Jeroboam [I] had made them out of gold, the *wardens* who had been delegated to guard them turned them into bronze. When, therefore, the necessity arose for the calves also to be sent as a supplement to the tribute, certainly the people *mourned*, who thought that they had lost their deities. But the guards who were aware of the deception *exulted* because, since the images had been transferred elsewhere, they ceased to fear any longer an investigation into the theft. However, although the reading may seem to present an occasion for this interpretation, nevertheless it can also be clear by holding fast to the continuous course of explanation established at the beginning.[303] Thus, after his threatening authority had announced that a bitter vengeance against the wretched people would sprout forth throughout the furrows of the land, immediately he added the cause of indignation, in keeping with his own custom. He says, *The inhabitants of Samaria have worshiped the cows of Bethaven*—that is, the inhabitants of the royal city, who should have called back the others from their error (namely, those who were resorting frequently to the poor towns to worship the images of the calves). After this the order of the following verse is changed through a hyperbaton.[304] Thus, a distinction is made so that the people of Samaria *will be confounded* when adversities will have revealed the worthlessness and uselessness of the gods *thereof*. For when need compels, they too will be added to supply the taxes—namely, since they have no more importance than the transaction of the metal demands. And therefore with tears the unhappy people will follow after those objects that a little while before they had hallowed with the greatest honor and by the rejoicing of their soothsayers. *Shame shall capture Ephraim; and Israel shall be confounded in his own will.* Doubtless he will recognize the deformity of that will as being very great, and its wage very bitter.

10:7-8 Samaria has made her king to pass as foam on the surface of the water. The high places of the idol, the sin of Israel will be destroyed. The bur and the thistle will grow up over their altars. And they will say to the mountains, Cover us; and to the hills, Fall on us.

As far as concerns devotion to the divine and his mercy, he says, I would have wished that their possession of their own land might have been long and secure. But their grave sacrileges put up resistance, and they had forced their king (that is, their own kingdom) to be

[300]Jerome also begins his third book on Hosea at Hos 10:5-6.

[301]Cf. Jerome, *Commentary on Hosea* 10:5-6 (ACT 2:226).

[302]Cf. 2 Kings 15:19-20.

[303]It seems noteworthy that Julian often is skeptical of interpretations Jerome transmits seemingly sympathetically that stem from Jewish tradition.

[304]A transposition of words from their natural order.

destroyed by a swift end. Thus, both the profaneness and the dignity of the nation faded away like *foam* floating on the waves of the *water*. Therefore, when all the shrines have been devoured by the enemy's fire, the frequenting of which used to provoke me, thorn bushes will cover their altars, so that the one who is left, from an impulse of either shame or fear, would desire to lie hidden, if possible, even under the ruins of some mountains. Now it should be noted that in the Gospel as well the Lord cited this verse to signify the desires of those who are afraid, and yields according to the custom of the Scriptures that the judgments brought forth in a certain case are applied fittingly to similar distresses.[305]

10:9(-10) From the days of Gabaa, Israel has sinned; there they stood. The battle in Gabaa against the children of iniquity does not overtake them.

He had already mentioned this time, when he says that those who had scorned the statements of the prophets sinned just as those youth of the Gabaonites did who violated the wife of the Levite even to the point of death.[306] But in order to avoid a paltry repetition, here he prefers those whom he had compared there. He says that the crime, to be sure, seems similar, of those who [in Judges] had sinned by an unclean obscenity, and of those [here] who had rated spiritual men as madmen and fools.[307] Therefore, captivity will wreak havoc in a manner that resembles that disaster, which had almost completely blotted out the Benjamites by slaughter.[308] Now, therefore, as if hanging the critical moments of the crimes and punishments in the balance, in order to examine them, he declares that the one that occurred later is a heavier vengeance, surely not for no reason, but because in the former the conflict wavered for a long time between the battle lines of the ten tribes against the one. And granted that the Gabaonites were fewer in number, nevertheless they were overcome only by a very great effort. But here disasters and the sudden attacks consumed all the wealth of the Samaritans that preceded the final overthrow, so that there was no one who had the confidence to put up resistance. He declares, therefore, that *Israel had sinned from the days of Gabaa*. But at that time it had stood firm for a long time and had issued proof of their strength by very fierce conflicts. For at last, in the third battle all the Israelites accomplished victory by beseeching God's help with tears.[309] But now, not only has no one advanced into the battle line against the Assyrians, but they could not even protect their own walls. This is why the prophet says that the amount of sin ought to be understood from the heap of miseries. For at that time, he says, the Benjamites fought back so courageously that they seemed for a long time not to be *overtaken* in *battle*. But here, these people of the ten tribes, together with their kings and princes, did not stand firm, because they had offended me.

Therefore, because I must promulgate the sentence against the guilty without any *battle*, "According to my desire I will chastise them."[310] This seems to have been brought forth altogether according to our usage, we who when we are roused by any anger say that we *desire* vengeance and that we feel pleasure from the affliction of the guilty. And so, now he promises to *chastise* them *according to his desire*; for it follows, "The peoples will be

[305]Cf. Lk 23:30; Rev 6:16. Whereas Jerome, *Commentary on Hosea* 10:7-8 (ACT 2:227) cites the Lord's citation of Hos 10:8, Theodore of Mopsuestia, *Commentary on Hosea* 10:8 (FOTC 83) ignores it.

[306]Cf. Judg 19:22-30. See Hos 9:9.

[307]Cf. Hos 9:7-8.

[308]Cf. Judg 21.

[309]Cf. Judg 20:26-28.

[310]Hos 10:10a.

gathered together against them."[311] That is to say, they are like a band of plunderers coming together for the booty that has been prepared. Thus, they receive punishment for a twofold iniquity. For he says the following: "They will be chastised concerning their two iniquities."[312] Yet when he indicated their number, he did not record their forms. We could consequently say that he has indicated those iniquities that another prophet distinguished—namely, that they abandoned God, the fount of living water, and they have constructed for themselves broken cisterns (namely, idols), from which they would not be able to experience any refreshment.[313] But because the rule of explanation is best that is taken from the context of the reading,[314] doubtless we believe that in the present passage he named them *two iniquities*, which he reproaches because the people were not only drenching the true prophets with insults and scourges but also, from the opposite direction, they were honoring the false ones with services and gifts and, what is more, were serving demons. Through this surely they were shown to have fallen not by mistake but on purpose. They did both of these things with equal persistence, both by honoring pernicious teachers and by cursing the beneficial ones. For everyone who is holy is portrayed as traveling down the opposite road: "O Lord, who shall dwell in your tabernacle, or who shall rest on your holy mountain? He that walks without blemish and works justice; he that speaks truth in his heart, who has not used deceit in his tongue and has not done evil to his neighbor, nor taken up a reproach against his neighbor. In his sight the evil man is brought to nothing, but he glorifies them that fear the Lord."[315] Therefore, on account of these *two iniquities*, I will devour these impious men by means of that affliction that is exceedingly delightful to me.

10:11-12 Ephraim is a heifer taught to love to tread out corn, and I passed over on the beauty of her neck; I will ride on Ephraim, Judah shall plough, Jacob breaks the furrows for himself. Sow for yourselves in justice, and reap in the mouth of mercy. Break up your fallow ground. But the time to seek the Lord is when he shall come who shall teach you justice.

He has made public his disposition of anger by his mocking words. Thus, he named the nation that was liable to receive punishments a *heifer* that is suitable and fit for threshing the crops. Obviously, he has thus signified their weakness, both in terms of sex and age, which he laid completely by the wayside in the comparison to the Gabaonites made earlier.[316] Therefore, with mockery he names her both a *heifer* and *beautiful*, one who *loves* those afflictions, which she has earned by her evil pursuits. It is not, of course, that one who is afflicted can love the troubles but that she is bound to them thus through the judgment, just as hearts inflamed with love are accustomed to be joined to each other. Therefore, the neck worthy to be exposed to torments is promised to be going to bear heat and wind.[317] And so that the one who is threatening might mock her with scorn, he declares that she is both desirous of and skilled in those evils of which she is most deserving. He says, *Ephraim is a heifer taught to love to tread out corn, and I passed over on the beauty of her neck; I will ride on Ephraim, Judah shall plough, Jacob will break*[318] *the*

[311]Hos 10:10b.

[312]Hos 10:10c.

[313]Cf. Jer 2:13; Jerome, *Commentary on Hosea* 10:9-10 (ACT 2:229).

[314]This is a very important principle of Julian's literal Antiochene exegesis. Cf. Marialuisa Annecchino, "I Temi Dottrinali-Esegetici nell'Expositio in Iob di Giuliano D'Eclano," in *Munera parva: studi in onore di Boris Ulianich*, ed. Gennaro Luongo (Naples: Fridericiana Editrice Universitaria, 1999), 290.

[315]Ps 15:1-4.

[316]Cf. Hos 10:9.

[317]Cf. Jerome, *Commentary on Hosea* 10:11 (ACT 2:229).

[318]The lemma has "breaks."

furrows for himself. He says, I will break the haughty necks of Ephraim as far as this, so that the one whom he treated with scorn when he was a kind and forgiving teacher, he will at last experience as a punisher. It is not, of course, that the benefit desired will leave my rebuke high and dry. For although he subjects some to destruction, he will heal others by their example. For since Ephraim was unwilling to be grain, and was not filled up with the marrow of piety, but the whole of it disappeared in the chaff due to the levity of his mind, he will endure the distress of the threshing floor in which he burns himself up. But Judah will succeed the yoke of fear by a happier condition. For he will distinguish between good and evil, with the plowshare of the precepts having been driven in deep. And he will subdue the soil of his heart by religious pursuits and plant the seed of knowledge by works of justice and mercy. And he will entrust it to renewed fallow land (namely, that from which he gets rid of the woody brushwood) so that a matching abundance can answer to such a great work. This seems to have been fulfilled at that time, when help sent from above delivered Hezekiah and the whole city from the hands of Sennacherib.[319] After all, it follows, *But the time to seek the Lord is when he shall come who shall teach you justice.* For the sacred annals say that blessed Hezekiah had a zeal to commend the religion, so that he carried out the office of prince and teacher. And not content with having summoned the inhabitants of his tribe back to the worship of God, he sent out messengers and edicts even through the neighboring regions, in which some had remained from the captive and exiled Israel. He told them to repudiate the errors of the idols and to turn back to the worship of the true God.[320] This, then, is what he is saying, that the residents of Jerusalem will reap mercy when the devotion of the one who is teaching them justice has roused them to seek the God of the prince also. Although of course this work and service seems to have been effective briefly during the time of Hezekiah, nevertheless it is shown to have been effected more fully by our Lord, who is the King of kings and Lord of lords.[321] Through him the light of piety is shown and the instruction in the virtues is delivered, not to a single tribe or region but to all lands and nations. And this is why the apostle says, "Behold, now is the acceptable time, behold now is the day of salvation. Give no offense to any man, that our ministry be not blamed."[322] Accordingly, the opportune time for seeking the Lord appeared at that time when "the Word became flesh and dwelt among us; and we have seen his glory, glory as of the only-begotten from the Father, full of grace and truth."[323] But let us also consider the rest.

10:13-15 You have ploughed wickedness, you have reaped iniquity, you have eaten the fruit of a lie, because you have trusted in your ways, in the multitude of your strong ones. A tumult is arising among your people, and all your fortresses will be destroyed, as Zalmunna was destroyed by the house of him who judged Baal in the day of battle, the mother being dashed in pieces on her children, so has Bethel done to you, because of the evil of your iniquities.

On the occasion of Ephraim, whose sins he criticizes nearly throughout the whole book, a mention of Judah had been introduced. In this it became evident what his faith and devotion had merited during dangerous times. Therefore, content to have noted this digression of remembrance briefly, he returns to the order of

[319]Cf. 2 Kings 19:32-37; Is 37:21-36.
[320]Cf. 2 Chron 30:1-11, 18; 31:1.
[321]Cf. 1 Tim 6:15; Rev 19:16.
[322]2 Cor 6:2-3.
[323]Jn 1:14.

the drama he has undertaken, and he continues to accuse the wickedness of Israel. He says, But you people of Samaria, exactly like Judah and often Benjamin, when you had come into extreme peril, *you trusted* not in God but in your own plans and in the power of your own armies. Therefore, you will receive the appropriate reward so that the *tumult* of the enemy kills and destroys your *people* and *fortresses*, and you will be devoured like the very wicked leader whose name was *Zalmunna*. In the book of Judges we read that Gideon was victorious over him and blotted him out.[324] And he destroyed him together with either his relatives, which he showed by the name of his wretched mother, or with the city itself, in which he had ruled, which can seem to have been named *mother*. Therefore, he says, just as Gideon himself, who had torn down the idol *Baal*, destroyed *Zalmunna* completely in a massacre, so too *has Bethel done to you*—that is, the city in which you set up idols[325] that you worshiped, being a deserter of your God. Now it is customary in the Scriptures to express the heap of the profaneness by repeating the same words. Thus he says, *so has Bethel done to you, because of* [a facie = *in the face of*] *the evil of your iniquities*. Therefore, he is eager to show that the *face of evil* is composed of manifold *iniquity* and is nothing more than the fitting wage that they have received for their morals—namely, captivity.

[Chapter 11]

11:1(-2) As the morning passes, so has the king of Israel passed away. Because Israel was a child, and I loved him, and out of Egypt I called my son.

He had already said, "Samaria has made her king *to pass* as foam on the surface of the water."[326] And now, therefore, he has taken care to repeat the same thing, by saying, *As the morning passes, so has the king of Israel passed away*. The meaning is, the kingship of your nation, which you desired by sinning,[327] you have also destroyed by sinning. And all the pomp of your arrogance has faded away, because the royal power, which you lusted after in imitation of the neighboring nations,[328] did not make you ready for anything without the help of my protection. On account of this the prophet also warned you and said, "Do not trust in princes nor in the sons of men, in whom there is no safety. Their spirit has departed, and it will return to its earth; on that day all their plans will perish."[329] Therefore, just as nothing of theirs is a mark of distinction for you, so your applause was not beneficial to them. For indeed the whole of what seemed capable even of life has been consumed speedily, so that it was seen no longer than the morning twilight, which of course is constricted by the departure of the night and by the appearance of the day. This agrees with what we read in a similar case in the writings of blessed David, who says, "Though sinners have arisen like grass, and all who work iniquity have appeared, [it is] that they may perish in the age of the age and beyond."[330] So then, even the principate of Israel has fallen, since vengeance adheres closely to its crimes, so that he appears not so much to have flourished as to have suddenly appeared. *Because Israel was a child, and I loved him, and out of Egypt I called my son*. Blessed Matthew, the writer of the Gospel, cited the last part of this verse with reference to the person of our Lord Jesus Christ. He affirmed that it was accomplished in the [divine]

[324]Cf. Judg 8:5-21; Jerome, *Commentary on Hosea* 10:14-15 (ACT 2:232-33).

[325]Cf. 1 Kings 12:30.

[326]Hos 10:7; cf. Jerome, *Commentary on Hosea* 11:1-2 (ACT 2:233).

[327]Cf. 1 Sam 8:19.

[328]Cf. 1 Sam 8:5.

[329]Ps 146:3-4.

[330]Ps 92:7.

dispensation, with the result that Joseph and Mary proceeded to Egypt to avoid the rage of Herod, who persecuted the infancy of our Redeemer. For indeed, "It was necessary that what the prophet had announced be fulfilled: 'Out of Egypt I called my Son.'"[331] Well then, seeing that the text of the prophecy shows that this was said concerning the people, apostolic authority wanted to point out that this can also be transferred to the person of the Lord Jesus Christ. He is the one—namely, through whom those things that had been given to the Jews as insignia of the divine religion were conferred even more abundantly and more graciously on us. But the context of the explanation [in Hosea] shows the force of one who is rebuking. He mentions their past nobility for the purpose of branding them more seriously, those whom he complains have degenerated. Therefore, after recounting their crimes and announcing their punishments, he suddenly recalled their past dignity. It is as if he were to say, Come sorrow! Come tears! And what race of human beings is this that is appraised with such worthlessness? After these things, as if he has received a reply, he proclaims, *Because Israel was a child, and I loved him, and out of Egypt I called my son.* This is he, he says, for whom I cried bitterly that he reaped sorrows after sowing seeds of impiety. I announce that he would be ravaged like Zalmunna, which was destroyed by Gideon.[332] This is he, I say, who has caused his own kingdom to be obliterated, so that it passes away as swiftly as the time of the morning light can exist. He is the one, I say, who descends from holy stock, and whom I had consecrated to myself from the very beginning. And among so many nations that were scattered throughout the whole world, he was chosen as the one who would be called the one people of Israel, whose merits I anticipate by my affection. I have called you my child, I say, my son, and I have put so much glory on him, when he was still being led out from Egypt, that he was spread out in a certain measure by both words and affairs, because with me such a great distinction existed between that people and the common people of Egypt as was accustomed to exist between the best of sons and the worst of slaves. Already at that time, therefore, beyond all the miracles of liberation and the sweetness of that freedom, he had taken this distinguishing mark from me, to be called my son.[333] But now he has degenerated to such low depths of profaneness that he has equally forgotten me and himself. He has hearkened only to the worshipers of demons, who to prove how no religion and no reason resided in the mind of that people, seduced them to themselves, to promote fabrications that were not elaborately wrought, but were like cattle prepared for death. Thus, *they called them*, and with an easy expression of approval they dragged them where they wanted. *They offered victims to Baalim, and sacrificed to images*—that is, to the worship of various idols, which they were going to serve by diverse rites. They *called* them and followed them so easily that they were found guilty of having had the desire for the same opportunity.

11:3(-4) And I was like a nurse to Ephraim, I carried them in my arms, and they knew not that I cured them.

These two verses are inserted and interrupt the context of the simple narrative.[334] Thus, they offered an interpretive difficulty. Moreover, his words, *Like a nurse to Ephraim, I carried them in my arms*, answer that statement that came before; that is, "Israel was a child, and I loved him, and out of Egypt I called my

[331] Mt 2:15.
[332] Cf. Hos 10:14.
[333] Cf. Ex 4:22.
[334] Verse 4 says in Jerome's version, "I will draw them with the cords of Adam, with the bands of love. And I will be to them as one that takes off the yoke on their jaws and I came down to him that he might eat."

son."[335] But after this he inserts the crimes they had perpetrated and returns to the sequence of remembering his leniency. This certainly seems effective as a witness to the flood of indignation. It is not, of course, that a speech once begun should run on with one uninterrupted course, but that the force of the present complaint bursts forth also at the time when he remembers the things that were done long ago. It is as if the speech is impatient even of a brief dissimulation. Therefore, when he had established that the ancient marks of distinction had occurred, doubtless in order to lay stress on the guilt of the degenerate people, and because he loved them with his own free devotion, and because he honored them with the name of son, suddenly he exclaimed that they had surrendered their ears to the deranged ministers of demons, and they had followed them so swiftly that it required no effort for them to give their assent. This is inserted impulsively, as we have said, as a complaint. If you separate it off a little bit, the things that follow will have a clear context that coheres with the things earlier—that is, "Because Israel was a child, I loved him, and out of Egypt I called my son,"[336] *and I was like a nurse to Ephraim and carried them in my arms, and they did not know that I cured them.* It is as if he were to say, The profaneness of this people is not new, for at the very beginning they showed me signs of having an ungrateful mind. For when I had called them a son, I added enticements to my kindnesses as well, and I exercised care as a very indulgent *nurse* for a small child. Why not? This happened when I did not allow them to feel the hardships of the desert waste, nor to be vexed by the weariness of the new and long journey. Instead, as his "cord" (that is, "Adam's" allotment)[337]—namely, that of the first man, when he had fallen from happiness, who had been made the cultivator and inhabitant of paradise),[338] he fed on the abundance that was acquired without labor. In the same way, he took the food and drink unknown to the multitudes and prepared by miracles alone. And thus I have bound them only by the "bands of love" and by the reins of the precepts. The only reason was this, that they might advance safely, [having] mouths I have provided for, showing that the reason I turned aside to guide them was so that they might enjoy adequate rest and delight. For those who do not perceive power as oppressive, but necessary for the one traveling through the desert regions, had an "exalted yoke"—that is, free and clear, just as we see is done with chariots in which the yokes are raised up when they are released. That people, however, does not consider either my providence or my forgiveness by which it was to be both fashioned and healed. They always showed me the spirit of one leaping backward, until with obstinate shamelessness they reached that state in which they are now.

11:5-7 He shall not return into the land of Egypt, but the Assyrian [shall be] his king, because they were unwilling to be converted. The sword has begun in his city, and it shall consume his chosen men and shall devour their desires.[339] And my people shall long for my return. But a yoke shall be put on them together, which shall not be taken off.

Earlier he had said, "They called them, so they went away from before their face."[340] But now he says, *They were unwilling to be converted;* that is, those who lent willing obedience to those who dissuaded them from religious duty now have been compelled by various afflictions

[335]Hos 11:1.
[336]Hos 11:1.
[337]Hos 11:4.
[338]Cf. Gen 2:15.
[339]*Cupita.* Jerome had read *capita* (heads).
[340]Hos 11:2.

to return from perverse things to better things. For when they lost their wealth and endeavored to change their condition of servitude, so that they would be placed under the power of the Egyptians rather than of the Assyrians, they did not even deserve to obtain that. For the sentence proceeding from our mouth is unalterable—namely, that they will hardly be slaves in the meantime to any others but to Assyrian masters. Whence the beginnings of revenge will advance in its own work, so that the *sword* (*gladius*) tears through cities, and sword (*ferrum*) and flame ravage all nobility equally, and the enemies would plunder everything that usually is valued by the wealthy. Thus, this *people of mine* of long ago will be stripped of all its strength and of all consolations as well and *shall long for my return* with a delayed hope—namely, by demanding with prayers that are too late and with groans that do not please me, that I should deign to become his helper. *But a yoke shall be put on them together, which shall not be taken off.* Namely, he will prove that their tears have been ineffective in reality, because I will not undo this public announcement, which I have commanded at last to go into effect, compelled by their many wicked deeds. And because he had said that his decree remains, and they will submit to the yoke of captivity to Assyria immediately, he also assumes the attitude of one who is deliberating—namely, over what kind of punishment he will use to consume the guilty. And he proposes examples of cities, which fire brought down from heaven had destroyed.

11:8-9 How shall I give you up, O Ephraim? How shall I subdue you, O Israel? How shall I make you as Adama? Shall I set you as Seboim? My heart is turned within me, my repentance is stirred up as well. I will not act according to the fierceness of my wrath, I will not return to destroy Ephraim, because I am God and not man, the holy one in the midst of you, and I will not enter into the city.

By recalling those things that had been done long ago, he shows that the Israelites, no less than the Sodomites, could have been or deserved to be consumed.[341] Nevertheless mindful of the benefits that he had given in honor of the holy ancestors, even on their undeserving children, he is unwilling to rescind them so as to destroy them absolutely by an unrestrained slaughter. And therefore he announces that he has been roused and struck, as it were, with the affection of a father and has adopted a kind of *repentance*.[342] For he will threaten Israel with the destruction of the Sodomites even under the appearance of one who is deliberating; and he immediately adds, *I will not act according to the fierceness of my wrath, and I will not return to destroy Ephraim.* This means, I will not continually change my mercy to indignation, so as to allow no Israelite to survive, *because I am God and not man*—namely, one whose benevolence flows forth by flooding veins and for whom an offense would not be capable of exhausting, or whose disposition takes delight in a once and for all dedicated firmness and does not change due to the fault of the ungrateful. Even the teacher of the nations[343] pointed this out briefly when he said, "For God's gifts and calling are irrevocable."[344] "For I say," he says, "did God reject his people whom he foreknew previously?"[345] That is to say, he will never allow that people to be destroyed in the manner of the godless nations. And now, therefore, when he had announced the

[341]Cf. Gen 14:8; 19:24-29. Adama and Seboim are listed as allied with Sodom and Gomorrah in the former text. They are not explicitly mentioned in the account of the destruction of Sodom and Gomorrah recorded in Gen 19, but their destruction is assumed in Deut 29:23 and Hos 11:8.

[342]Cf. Jerome, *Commentary on Hosea* 11:8-9 (ACT 2:238).

[343]Cf. 1 Tim 2:7.

[344]Rom 11:29.

[345]Rom 11:1-2.

punishments that were owed to the defiled multitudes, he shows that he nevertheless has kept an account of those whom he will spare. He says, *the holy one in the midst of you, and I will not enter into the city*. When Jerome wished to explain this verse, he proceeded to list those who are read as having founded cities.[346] And he says that Cain first constructed the protection of a city for himself.[347] Later on, too, several founders of cities were distinguished for their crimes. And he said that the reason that God commended reverence for his sanctity is because he avoids entering the city. And in this manner Jerome proceeded to assert that holy men too and those who surrender their lives to philosophy stay away from the feasting of the cities and choose the hidden places of the mountains. But who can consider the character of such an explanation without mockery? For when our God here says that he will not enter a city, he has not proclaimed that he shrinks back from cities generally.[348] For we read it said of him, "The Lord loves the gates of Zion more than all the tents of Jacob"[349] and "God is within her; she will not be moved. God will help her with his countenance."[350] But he had brought in the remembrance of Sodom and of the neighboring cities because, as we read in the book of Genesis, he entered them in order to destroy them. And he had said, *How shall I give you up, O Ephraim? How shall I subdue you, O Israel? How shall I give you up as Adama, shall I set you as Seboim?* And he had mentioned immediately, *I will not act according to the fierceness of my wrath, and I will not return to destroy Ephraim*; consequently he added, *Because I am God and not man; the holy one in the midst of you, and I will not enter into the city*. The meaning is, From all peoples I have chosen you, whom I guard by my own divine will, and that is in honor of your ancestors, who had lived most acceptably to me. I have decreed and promised that even if you have earned my being offended at your defilement of the sacred law, I would visit your iniquities, but I would not remove my mercy entirely, doubtless so that I would have allowed you to be consumed and the memory of your name to be altogether abolished. And *because I am God, and not man* (namely, one whose ordinance no change shatters), therefore I dwell *in the midst of you* as one who certainly is conspicuous for everlasting holiness. This is why I also arise as the chastiser of your sins, and I do not violate the covenants that have been established with your fathers, yet I shall never enter your cities in such a way as I entered the gates of Sodom, when it had to be destroyed. And because he had introduced a speech from the side of the prosperous, he was not content with having said that the Israelites would never perish like the other nations, but the merciful one ran through something else as well concerning those things he has ordained. And he mentioned that time when they would be led back to the soil of their fathers, when the captivity has been released.

11:10-11 They shall walk after the Lord; he shall roar like a lion, because he shall roar; and the children of the sea shall fear. And they shall fly away like a bird out of Egypt, and like a dove out of the land of the Assyrians; and I will place them in their own houses, says the Lord.

How is it surprising indeed, he says, if our religious duty should be regulated by a seething punishment, especially when at that time I am already sketching the joys of bestowing freedom? Nor would I wish it to be hidden

[346]Cf. Jerome, *Commentary on Hosea* 11:5-9 (ACT 2:237-39).
[347]Cf. Gen 4:17.
[348]Julian normally ignores or dismisses Jerome's allegorical interpretations, deriving from Origen, in this case that God does not enter the cities of the heretics. Bouwman, *Des Julian von Aeclanum Kommentar*, 130, thinks he has not done justice to Jerome's interpretation.
[349]Ps 87:2.
[350]Ps 46:5 LXX.

with what great majesty I am arranging both their liberation from barbarous servitude and their summons back to the home country? The time shall come, I say, that when I lay hold of my task of punishment, *the children of the sea* (namely, the multitude of hostile nations) would be terrified and would feel hardly more easily than the raging whirlpools of the Red Sea were torn apart when Israel passed through, and they flowed back by the same power of command, leading to the destruction of the Egyptians.[351] A little while before, the safety of the pious had depended on this power. Therefore, as flocks of *doves* returning to their former nests, they will fill up their ancestral regions with a stable habitation, both *out of Egypt,* to which the Israelites had fled after the Babylonian triumph, and *out of the* country *of the Assyrians,* to which Sennacherib had led them away.

11:12 Ephraim has compassed me about with business,[352] and the house of Israel with deceit; but Judah went down as a witness with God and is faithful with the saints.

[Chapter 12]

12:1 Ephraim feeds on the wind and follows the burning heat. All the day long he multiplies lies and desolation, and he has entered into a pact with the Assyrians and carried oil into Egypt.

In the midst of the roaring of the threats that the reckoning of that time demanded, he touched on the joys of freedom in a brief digression. Then he returned to the succession of the drama undertaken and describes the pursuits of Ephraim, either as one grieving or as one who is indignant. As I have frequently observed, he is very careful to interweave with the announced punishments the outward forms and the magnitude of the offenses, which they do not forsake, due to the agitation of their malicious spite, and they show that those punishments have been brought forth not viciously but by his just judgment. If, therefore, you separate the things that were inserted as a digression, you shall make the context of the present verse [consonant] with the things earlier. That is, "A yoke shall be put on them together, which shall not be taken off."[353] But why? "Ephraim has compassed me about with business, and the house of Israel with deceit."[354] That is, like some bad businessman, the people rejoiced in the deceit that they had brought to me, and they thought they had fooled me when they prayed, and they did not confess their error at the time of the punishments, knowing that my mercy helps those who are troubled. But they also did not promise correction faithfully, because their heart was not right with me. They were like that Pharaoh, who as soon as he had received respite from the calamities, returned to his shameful acts.[355] Or else, as the prophet has remonstrated within the very pages of his book, they transferred to the worship of idols gold and silver and other things related either to living or to worship, things that they had received from God. Likewise, now too he wanted this to be understood when he complains about the business of Ephraim to its own shame—namely, when they lied that they had obtained from the idols everything that they had received from God. But when during the time of those kings who are displayed in the title[356] the ten tribes defiled themselves by those iniquities that we spoke

[351]Cf. Ex 14:21-31.

[352]*Negotiatio.* Jerome had read "denial" (*negatione*).

[353]Hos 11:7.

[354]Hos 11:12.

[355]Cf. Ex 7:23; 8:15, 32; 9:34.

[356]Cf. Hos 1:1.

about, Judah, still a little different from his brother, *went down as a witness with God and is faithful with the saints*; that is, he followed the pious ruler Hezekiah and was zealous to show the majesty of divine protection and the reliability of the promise. And he placed the confidence of his salvation in his strength, even amid extreme miseries, and thus he deserved to be delivered by a miraculous defense.[357] He shows that their ancestors were not deceived when they worshiped this one Lord with all their mind, and that those who rejoiced in the true defender could not be overwhelmed by the flood of captivity. Therefore, each people reached their corresponding territories, so that Judah, by following the true God, escaped as a witness of both the holy fathers and of miracles, but the Samaritans, just as they worshiped the false gods after abandoning the truth, are thus *fed on the winds*, having *followed the burning heat*; that is, they are exposed to vanities and destruction. For when they forsook the defense of God, which needed to be obtained by merits, not by a price paid, then they bought help at one time from the Assyrians,[358] at another from the Egyptians[359] —namely, by arranging for gifts from their fertile soil money to the Assyrians and oil to the Egyptians.[360] For by the one outward form, he indicated many things. Let us then hear what has followed.

12:2 Therefore, there is a judgment of God with Judah, and a visitation for Jacob. He will render to him according to his ways and according to his devices.

By the name Jacob he has indicated the people of the ten tribes. The difference of their pursuits, he says, has required a difference too in their settlement, so that the Lord's judgment continued on behalf of the salvation of Judah, but a severe visitation struck down the Samaritans.

12:3-6 In the womb he supplanted his brother, and by his strength he had success with an angel. And he prevailed over the angel and was strengthened; he wept and begged him; he found him in Bethel, and there he spoke with us. And you will turn toward your Lord, keep mercy and judgment, and hope in your God always.[361]

As he began to do earlier,[362] he recalls their ancient nobility and shows that any honors or virtue the chosen race deserved leads to the exposure of the worthlessness of the descendants. It is as if he were to say, Behold from what an ancestor they were begotten and have reached the point of this mockery! How far have they degenerated from the virtues of the ancients! Indeed, Jacob was so eager for glory that before he came forth into this light from his mother's womb he engaged in a prophetic struggle with his brother—and what nature itself scarcely permits one to believe, he seized hold of the sole of his brother's foot,[363] whose rights of the first born he was ready to snatch away, not by deceit but by merits.[364] If that is the case, then he adopted the token of light with the testimony of dignity. Clearly this shows that he was strong by a nobility that was pleasing to God, to whom he happened to promise the fruit of the virtue that will follow even before he experienced the times. And thus next in succession, when he had come to the age of youth and, already stood out, having secured the blessing of the firstborn,[365] he was

[357]Cf. 2 Kings 19:32-37; Is 37:1-38.
[358]Cf. 2 Kings 15:19.
[359]Cf. 2 Kings 17:4.
[360]Cf. Jerome, *Commentary on Hosea* 12:1 (ACT 2:241).

[361]He omitted v. 5, which reads in Jerome, "Even the Lord the God of hosts, the Lord is his memorial."
[362]Cf. Hos 11:3-4.
[363]Cf. Gen 25:24-26.
[364]Cf. Gen 25:29-34.
[365]Cf. Gen 25:33.

attacked by a savage plot of his brother and headed eagerly into a long exile, following the plans of his holy mother.[366] And he trusted in no human resources but in God alone, to whom he had dedicated a tithe when God appeared to him at Bethel.[367] And he was made prosperous by his help, and he acknowledged the greatness of his power and strength, which he did not know before the experience.[368] For when after a long interval of time he returned as a wealthy man to his ancestral habitation, and suddenly had become terrified by an encounter with his brother, an angel met him in the form of a man, and he condescended to wrestle with the fearful man—in such a way, of course, that he would not overwhelm him by a full display of his grandeur, but he wrestled as would an equal or an inferior with a rival.[369] When blessed Jacob saw this, he was happy in his strength and was thus also furnished with eyes of wisdom. He realized that his own Lord submitted himself with a great sense of religious devotion in order to point out the things that he had arranged concerning the deliverance of his servant. Jacob realized that he would be delivered by that protector, in comparison with whom he had stood out as nearly superior to as a wrestler. And when he became capable of understanding that no mortal could harm his protector, since his superior nature could not see such thing brought into effect, then the patriarch perceived also that profound plan and immediately he assumed a spirit of humility, not of elation. And with supplicating tears he requested earnestly to be blessed by the one over whom he had seemed to prevail.[370] He was not deceived by the pretense of his fellow wrestler so as to think of himself as the stronger. On the contrary, just as he had been great-hearted in the endurance of adversities, so he was solicitous in discerning secret things. And he understood that he was the one who had deigned to adopt comprehensible images, the one whom he had seen at Bethel leaning on the tips of a ladder that reached from the earth into the sky.[371] In that place, therefore, he merited to learn from a brief confrontation both how great was the divinity of the one who appeared to him and what the duty of a faithful servant was, without which he could not please God at all. That is, he learned that he should believe in his almighty power, confess his authority, and trust in him with his whole mind throughout the entire period of his life. *Lord God of hosts, the Lord is his memorial.*[372] This means you ought to be so mindful of your God that you always acknowledge him as your defender and Lord. He will regard this as a tenet; but from the aspect of morals, hold fast to the pursuit of justice and mercy, and *hope in your God always*. Thus, you will remain with him continually in virtue, or, if your devotion is interrupted, you should run to him and receive correction. By holding to these rules of virtue by a sure course to the apex of beatitude, he also exercised them successfully and left them behind to be preserved by his descendants. And this is why from an insignificant location he raises up a dignity so great that the Promised Land was handed over to his descendants.

12:7-8 Canaan, with a deceitful balance in his hand, has loved calumny. And Ephraim said, But yet I have become rich, I have found an idol for myself, all my labors shall not find me the iniquity that I have sinned.

When he was describing the noble deeds of blessed Jacob, from whom he complains that his descendants had degenerated, he suddenly

366Cf. Gen 27:41-45.
367Cf. Gen 28:22.
368Cf. Gen 28:16-21.
369Cf. Gen 32:22-32.
370Cf. Gen 32:26; 33:4.
371Cf. Gen 28:12-17.
372Hos 12:5, which was omitted from the lemma.

mentioned *Canaan*. It is not that the discourse was moving on to another nation but that in the manner of the prophets, in excessive indignation, he has called Israel's own descendants *Canaan*, to whom doubtless they had shown themselves to be very similar in character. Now we find this form of invective both in others, to be sure, but especially in the writings of blessed Isaiah, Ezekiel, and Daniel, when he was convicting the old adulterers.[373] Therefore, in the course of this rebuke in the present passage too, a mention of *Canaan* is brought in (that is, of a profane nation) so that the meaning would be of this sort: But why do I unfold the various indications of ancestral nobility, from which that crowd, whom I am bewailing, is found guilty of having fallen so far into ruin for such a length of time that it is named not without cause the offspring of *Canaan*? *In his hand* therefore, of one who *loves calumny*, there stands a *balance*, but an extremely *deceitful* one. For it is good for this, that I may show that he has transgressed not by an error but rather on purpose and by his judgment. For when such an affection of the spirit is involved, that he engages in impious deeds not impulsively or out of negligence, but with deliberation, he is said to have sinned under a pair of scales, as if with weights suspended on each side. We read about this meaning also in the writings of blessed David in the following passage: "But the sons of men are liars in the balances, that by vanity they may together deceive."[374] Since, therefore, this is the chief gift of the human spirit, that it weighs by the plumb line of reason and by critical reflection and comparison what it should obey, what it should avoid, the profane people, by suppressing the truth in their lying, has indeed applied a *scale* to their business, but a *deceitful* one. That is, it is one that prefers worse things to what is better. It comes to rest in harmful things rather than in what is profitable. But as for what he says, he *loved calumny*, this can be referred to the accusation he raised earlier—namely, that the thankless common people had covered themselves with such great shamelessness, like a polluted wife, that everything that the sole Creator of the universe had given them either for worship or for livelihood, they lied about, to the effect that they had obtained it from their lovers. On this account the Lord was angry and has promised to remove both the wool and the linen, which covered over their disgrace, that the accompanying hideousness and nakedness might expose the wicked deeds of the hateful people. *Calumnies* of this [sort] are branded with reproach in the writings of blessed Jeremiah also; for when Jerusalem had perished after its calamities had been announced by many prophets and when the whole Jewish nation had been transferred to Babylon, a few were left behind to tend to the fields. They revealed such great obstinacy of mind in their transgressing that they were not afraid to say that from the time when they had ceased to worship the queen of heaven and the remaining idols of the neighboring nations, from that time also all adversities followed them.[375] Therefore, by thoughts like this they incited *calumny*, as it were, against the true and most merciful God, by declaring most falsely that the days had been blessed for them after they had departed from him, and wretched since they had returned to him. Hence the false pair of scales caused them to be called descendants more of the mind of *Canaan* than of Israel. As we have said, they were sinning not as a momentary outburst but by searching for impious actions. And therefore, since they do not have the weights of true judgment, they have placed the confidence of their safety and prosperity in things that are very fleeting and that slip away like shadows. He says, *All my labors shall not find me the iniquity that I have*

[373]Cf. Is 1:10; Ezek 16:3, 29; 17:4; Dan 13:56; Zech 14:21; Jerome, *Commentary on Hosea* 12:7-8 (2:244).
[374]Ps 62:9.
[375]Cf. Jer 44:18.

sinned. This means, though they were beset by the wicked crimes they had perpetrated, nevertheless they claimed that they would be safe in their elaborate wealth, saying that they had amassed such great opulence that hardships would not be able to reach them. Hence, they were deluded by these frauds of their own balance. For when the most high God revealed the work of judgment, they thought that the various house furnishings or money that was shut away would protect the guilty.

12:9 And I the Lord your God from the land of Egypt will yet cause you to sit in tabernacles, as in the days of the feast.

With the outcome of events as witness, therefore, you will recognize the deceits of that scale (that is, of your deliberation), that you may confess from anguish what you refused on the basis of reason, that I am *your* one *Lord God*, who deigned to adopt you as my special people from the time of the liberation of Egypt. For that matter, you will not be able to remove my censure by any protections or by wealth, so that not only is it necessary for you to submit to the yoke of the servitude that has been announced, but you will have to remain under it for the established time. When you are finally extricated from them, you will taste the joys of freedom afterward. Therefore, by this meaning, amid the roaring of the threat, something seems to have been brought in concerning the prosperous times, as an effective confirmation of the captivity that will precede those times. That way no one would doubt that the miseries that he had learned were to be inflicted would be ended by the succession of prosperity. Now we could offer the following as well. Doubtless, it would come from the usage of the Scriptures that a declaration of sorrows and joys is mixed together so that minds not be softened by uninterrupted joys, nor weakened by continual sorrows. But the context of the passage seems to support the former sense. After all, it proceeds, as it had begun, with severe speech.

12:10 I have spoken through the prophets, and I have multiplied visions, and I have used similitudes by the hand of the prophets.

This means, I have never laid aside the concern to heal, but *through* my *prophets* I have stood firm both by speaking and by enduring, that they should understand my providence and confess. It was I who counseled them with such great indulgence; I assumed outward appearances that were not sufficiently worthy of my majesty in which I could relate more intimately with them. Therefore *by the hand* (that is, the works) *of the prophets* I did not scorn to use similitudes in those forms or personas, which, although they corresponded well to my mercy, nevertheless in a certain measure they were not fitting as an expression of our power. It is like what I said a little earlier, that I drove out fear from the heart of Israel by adopting the persona of a powerless wrestler.[376] I elected to be transfigured into fire at the time of blessed Moses, when the bush was not consumed,[377] or when I fortified the thresholds of the Israelites with the blood of the lamb.[378] And there were many other things that we read were done in this manner at different times—namely, so that our God appeared in these images, which his providence demanded and assumed, things that did not correspond to his majesty. But let us consider what remains.

12:11a If Galgal [be] an idol, then will they be in vain in Galgal sacrificing with bullocks?

After the mention of those things that he had conducted mercifully, he was led back to the

[376]Cf. Gen 32:24-28. See Hos 12:3-4.
[377]Cf. Ex 3:12.
[378]Cf. Ex 12–13.

source from which the complaint had begun with a meaning of this nature: Behold, what wicked deeds of a thankless people I experience after so many of my benefits, after so many gifts, and so many miracles! They run after open errors as an affront to me, and not deceived by some subtlety of arguments, they are subjugated to a professed insanity! *If Galgal [be] an idol, then will they be in vain in Galgal sacrificing with bullocks?* Earlier as well he said of this place, "All their wickedness is in Galgal."[379] With a logical connecter, therefore (that is, *if*), he has introduced the verdict of one who is accusing—that is, since there is no doubt that the sole images of brute beasts were set up in those places, in which they certainly set them up even though they were cattle, they could not help the supplicants.[380] But now, when images more worthless than worthlessness itself and things without feeling are visited there, they will give no benefit either to themselves or to others. *Then will they be in vain in Galgal sacrificing with bullocks?* It is as if he were saying, Would they have believed that this could be done before it happened, that people once famous for their virtues should follow open foolishness and profanity? These things contain nothing in itself beyond ultimate guilt. After reverencing those rites of evident majesty, should they stoop to the worthless institutions of fanatics? Should they believe idols, which are subject to the derision of those who possess even a modicum of wisdom?[381] This is *in vain*—that is, without any usefulness even of fleeting profit. But though the madness is clearer than daylight, if people should think that supplications ought to be made to cattle, then will there be crowds that think that happiness can be given them from images of bullocks? "For their altars also shall be like heaps [of stone] on the furrows of the field."[382] Consequently, however, the very worthlessness of the observances also exposes the profane rites, so that without any distinction of places they build altars and adore the shameful gods with raised altars. Therefore, as if with groaning and wonder, which we discussed,[383] a voice is produced: *If Galgal [be] an idol, then will they be in vain sacrificing with bullocks? For their altars also are like [stone] heaps on the furrows of the field.* But let us hear what is added.

12:12-13 Jacob fled into the country of Syria, and Israel served for a wife and was a keeper for a wife. But the Lord by a prophet led Israel out of Egypt, and he was preserved by a prophet.

He has mentioned the ancestors not from the course of the historical narrative, but impulsively and painfully he has recalled the deeds of the forebears to expose the degeneracy of their posterity. Therefore, the sermon proceeds like waves, as it were, so that reproach and praise succeed each other in turn. By proclaiming their ancient nobility he is adding weight to the rebuke. Hence, as he had established, he recounts the labors and successes of blessed Jacob, who was also called Israel.[384] By his name, of course, the whole nation is signified; this is why he made mention especially of him. And as we had begun to say, Jacob, from whose stock they descend, obeyed the counsels of his holy mother and placed the hope and trust for future prosperity in his God alone. He left his home country and entered the land of Mesopotamia alone and as an exile.[385] He had no assistance to commend him except his noble character. With that connection of his, his maternal uncle Laban immediately desired his company, and, lest the work of

[379]Hos 9:15.
[380]Cf. Jerome, *Commentary on Hosea* 12:11 (ACT 2:246-47).
[381]Cf. Is 46:1-7.
[382]Hos 12:11.
[383]Cf. Hos 11:5-7.
[384]Cf. Gen 32:28.
[385]Cf. Gen 29:15-30.

the noble young man be gratuitous, he promised him marriage to his beloved virgin daughter for the endurance of seven years of service.[386] In time, when his great faithfulness and diligence had become known, the terms of his service and marriage were repeated.[387] For this is what he says, *He served for a wife*—that is, he carried out the duty of a shepherd in order to obtain marriage, as the story says. But as for the words, *And was keeper for a wife*, this means, when the recompense of marriage was offered, he kept the flock of his father-in-law. When *the Lord led Israel out of Egypt*, he was led out *by a prophet*, and *by a prophet he was preserved*. Truly he was from small beginnings, so small in fact that he was nourished by hired work, until he attained to that great abundance of people and of riches, so that in a way all of Egypt could not now contain him. And, as at first he [the nation of Israel] had envied his [Moses'] happiness, so thereafter his freedom, when Pharaoh perished together with his whole army.[388] And he [Israel] recognized that he obtained that glory of diminished Egypt scarcely by human strength, but both by declaring the merits of the fathers and by establishing the sacred rites. But *he was preserved* not by some warlike leader, but *by a prophet* (namely, by blessed Moses), who vindicated him by those famous miracles that we have read about.[389] What complaint will be sufficient, then, since the nation that was so famous for its illustrious stock is now marked out by its foolishness? It acts as one that is famous for its crimes alone.

12:14 Ephraim provoked me to wrath with his bitterness, and his blood shall come on him, and his Lord will render his reproach unto him.

The mention of the fathers renders the crime of the sons more terrible, and the exclamation added by the one who is rebuking indicates the same. He testifies that he has been driven to *bitterness* and indignation, which will avenge the impious. And therefore, although he rises up with the vigor of one declaring, nevertheless he rejects the hatred from himself of such vengeance and announces that Ephraim, who deserted the salvific instruction and completely corrupted himself and degenerated from his source, has perished by the punishments that have been worked out.

[Chapter 13]

13:1-2 When Ephraim spoke, a horror seized Israel, and he sinned in Baal and died. And now they have added to the sinning, and they have made to themselves a molten thing of their silver as the likeness of idols; the whole is the work of craftsmen; to these they say, Immolate, men, you who adore calves.[390]

He has brought in a mention of those things that they had engaged in from the time of the division of the tribes, but he does so in a sequence that his indignation more than the narrative demanded. For indeed, in the present passage he calls Jeroboam, the leader of the division, *Ephraim*. He is the one who decreed that the people should worship the images of cows.[391] But later on Ahab, together with Jezebel, adopted the worship of the idol Baal.[392] We read that Jehu punished this profanity with a corresponding severity.[393] Consequently,

[386]Cf. Gen 29:19-20.

[387]Cf. Gen 29:27.

[388]Cf. Ex 14:30-31.

[389]Cf. Deut 18:15, 18; 34:10; Jerome, *Commentary on Hosea* 12:12-13 (ACT 2:247).

[390]Julian appears to punctuate this last command differently than Jerome and Theodore of Mopsuestia. He adds a comma after "Immolate," so that the thought of sacrificing human beings is not explicit in the lemma.

[391]Cf. 1 Kings 12:28-30; Jerome, *Commentary on Hosea* 13:1-2 (ACT 2:248).

[392]Cf. 1 Kings 16:31.

[393]Cf. 2 Kings 10:28.

that eager pursuit of idols first began among the people and ceased in the last time. Although this is the sequence of history, which we mentioned, the invective has now changed part of it. For *when Ephraim spoke*—that is, when Jeroboam was summoning people to the worship of demons—*a horror seized Israel*; for either he immediately adopted the fear of the superstition and dreaded it, as if it were the true divine will, or else he undertook the emotional disposition of one who was worshiping it, through which he deserved to dread the eternal judge. Not content with having done this, he submitted their necks to other sacrileges also and embraced the customs of Baal.[394] He also felt deeply the trials of the calamities and did not adopt any zeal for correction from the collapse of those who had overthrown various things by the attack of the enemies. On the other hand, when by Jehu's vengeance the idol itself was completely destroyed together with its worshipers,[395] yet no disposition of correction, he says, could be stirred up by such things. He says, But *now they have added to the sinning, and they have made to themselves a molten thing of their silver as the likeness of idols*. Surely, he says this not because they began to adore the images of the calves after the time of Ahab but because those things that they did not abandon after the verbal chastisement are said to have been *added*. For such profanity is only increased by the zeal to rebel, nor could it be continuous. He says, *The whole is the work of craftsmen; to these they say, Immolate, men, you who adore calves*. He has repeated this not without reason. He has already waved it back and forth throughout the entire book. But in order that the sense should be the same, the fickleness of affairs makes the rebuke worthless, when a delay actually counterbalances, even if an unexpected novelty unites. Nor is continuous veneration exhibited, except with respect to those things that stood out with certain fixed markings. But in this situation, since both reason and the long period of time has revealed the worthlessness and vanity of a work (that is, that in the deities of the nations, to say nothing of their possessing no power, there is not even any beautiful form in them, apart from that which the skillful hand of the workmen has bestowed on them in the fashioning of them), nevertheless the profane people gladly heed the voices of the soothsayers, doubtless as they command men to pray to the calves that lack reason and sense, and to attend to them by the offering of prayers and sacrificial victims.

13:3 Therefore, they shall be as a morning cloud and as the early dew that passes away, as the dust that is driven with a whirlwind out of the threshing floor, as the smoke out of the chimney.

Above he had said that his blood was on that one's head, and his reproach was rendered to him.[396] And now he has repeated the same thing, indeed piled it on by curses. He says that because they surrendered themselves to extreme folly (namely, by transferring the honor due to God to the images of cattle), they have also utterly perished in base fashion, the way smoke, dust, dew, and a morning cloud are consumed by the rays of the sun.

13:4 But I am the Lord your God from the land of Egypt; and you shall know no God but me, and there is no savior beside me.

The context of these lines is woven into the things above, so that the sense becomes the same: Though I cast off the yoke of the Egyptian master from your necks, and I made known my grandeur, and when you were

394Cf. 1 Kings 14:9.
395Cf. 2 Kings 10:25-28.
396Cf. Hos 12:14.

happily delivered by those illustrious miracles,[397] I established this also with unconditional words, that the nation should always strive after the worship of me, and never submit to another as god, because you would find no other who would offer salvation to you.[398] For at that time you seemed to have been united with those enslaved to the elements.

13:5 I knew you in the desert, in the land of solitude.

But why am I now incited, as it were, by your new sacrileges, he says, when I have always known by experience at the very time of your deliverance that you are ungrateful and full of insults of the sort that you have now revealed yourself to be? But as for what he has taken care to add, *in the land of solitude*, surely he wanted the following to be understood, that it was not always examples that corrupted them, since they transgressed even in locations in which they had no one to imitate.

13:6 According to their pastures they were filled and satiated; and they lifted up their heart and have forgotten me.

He says, the whole nation was competing with my acts of kindness, not with devotion but from wickedness. In order to make this quite clear, he links the former with these times also, and in the course of the invective he returns to the present age from which he had begun. But with a brief, hasty treatment of that sermon he makes mention of the judgment also that was published in the song of Deuteronomy when blessed Moses declared, "The beloved was satiated and grew fat, and kicked, so that he made new gods for himself, as barley bread, whom their fathers knew not."[399] For he says, *according to their pastures they were filled and satiated; and they lifted up their heart and have forgotten me*. The reason he mentioned the series of sins earlier was to show that the revenge that would be brought in was not provoked by passion, but fortified with justice and reason. For it follows,

13:7-8 And I will be to them as a lioness, as a leopard in the way of the Assyrians. I will meet them as a bear that is robbed of her whelps, and I will rend the inner parts of their liver. And I will devour them there as a lion; the beast of the field shall tear them.

He is showing that these calamities, which the barbarity of the enemy will introduce, happen at his command. He does not refuse to unfold his own admonition with images taken from wild beasts. Although he knows that these do not correspond to his nature, yet they do fit his verdict—that is, concerning the misery of the condemned. But this is elegant, when he recorded a bear, too, amid the gaping mouths of lions. He has sharpened its savagery with incitements to bereavement. And lest the comparison introduced should lose any of its vigor, he says, *as a bear that is robbed of her whelps, and I will rend the inner parts of their liver.* Namely, the liver of those who have afflicted me with similar losses. For though I formed this people into my children with much devotion, and I subdued their hearts as though licking them into shape,[400] they have robbed me of offspring that were not merely desired but labored over—namely, by committing those crimes that demanded the destruction of the entire nation.

[397]Cf. Ex 14:26-31.

[398]Cf. Deut 5:6-8.

[399]Cf. Deut 32:15-17; Jerome, *Commentary on Hosea* 13:5-6 (ACT 2:251).

[400]Suetonius reports that Virgil dictated a few lines of the *Aeneid* each day, then spent the rest of the day refining them, "licking them into shape as a she-bear licks her cubs." Donatus described the composition of Virgil's *Georgics* similarly; he molds his poems the way a she-bear licks her cubs into shape.

13:9(-13) Destruction [is] your own, O Israel; your help is only in me. Where is your king? Let now your own especially save you in all your cities. And your judges? Of whom you said, "Give me a king and princes." I will give you a king in my wrath, and will take [him] away in my indignation.

Let the sentence of judgment answer these questions, and why not if the pattern of piety does not. For it is said under the persona of God, *Destruction [is] your own, O Israel; your help is only in me.* And yet there is a definitive defense of the faithful at that time when confidence of liberation is placed in God.[401] And this is what the blessed prophet reprimands throughout the whole book against the profane morals of the people, that they were trusting not in the defense of God but in that of the shrines! How is it, therefore, that now, as if by changing the order, he announces that manifest ruin is threatening Israel, because their salvation remained in the power of God alone? Therefore, that distinction should be observed, which clarifies what was thought to be ambiguous. For here he is not mocking the faith of the people who repose the hope of their joy in the sole power of God (for assuredly their failure to do so would have offended him), but he has pronounced that such great misfortunes are threatening that nothing but divine power could bring help. Therefore, he says, *Your destruction* impends, *O Israel; your help is only in me.* But if you should consider this carefully, you will see that it has been brought in not merely not absurdly, but even characteristically and from the usage of human speech. For this is why, if ever we see someone either with a serious sickness or overwhelmed by a desperate calamity, we say that his hope is in God. Surely this does not indicate the function of his mind, but the weight of the disaster that oppresses him. Therefore, a certain *destruction* will overtake [you], he says, and one from which no one except the Almighty can rescue. For you have rendered him hostile to yourself by your sins.[402] It remains for you to be snatched from the gaping destruction. He added this thought to make it clearer: *Where is your king? Let him now especially save you in all your cities. And your judges? Of whom you said, "Give me a king and princes."* According to the prophetic custom, he reproaches that error also of the people, which they had in their quest for a king, thus withdrawing from the priest-governed republic.[403] For indeed they had derived this desire out of envy of the neighboring nations, when things were going badly.[404] Their preceding counsels also are blamed. It is as if he were to say, This insanity of yours is of long duration—namely, that you think that you can take better counsel from yourself than from me. From the commencement of this opinion, you demanded that princes be given to you in imitation of the other nations. Now, therefore, the fruit of your counsel is evident, and let the effort of the kings protect you against my indignation! Doubtless they will be obligated to show what profit those powers bring that were demanded by your ambitions. But let us move on to the rest.

13:12 I will give you a king in my wrath, and I will take [him] away in my indignation.

Some[405] have understood the *king given in wrath* as Jeroboam, who was the author of the division of the tribes.[406] But they understand the one *taken away in indignation* as Hoshea, under whom Israel was taken captive.[407] Although this could be granted, to be sure, yet

[401]Cf. 2 Kings 19:1-7, 14-37.

[402]Cf. Jerome, *Commentary on Hosea* 13:9-11 (ACT 2:252).

[403]Cf. 1 Sam 8:4-9.

[404]Cf. 1 Sam 8:19-22.

[405]Jerome reports this as the view of some in *Commentary on Hosea* 13:9-11 (ACT 2:252).

[406]Cf. 1 Kings 12:25-33.

[407]Cf. 2 Kings 17:1-7.

because he signaled both with a pronouncement about a future time—that is, *I will give you a king* and *I will take [him] away*—the sentence can be understood by the fitting summary that the Israelite prince without doubt is the one who is to be *taken away*, but the Assyrian is being proclaimed as the one who is to be *given*.

Finally, from the custom of the prophet, after the burden of condemnation, he added what had been the cause of this: "The iniquity of Ephraim is bound up, his sin is hidden."[408] That is, this has been carried out as a remuneration for those wicked deeds, I say, which he perpetrated at many times, so that they were not interrupted by any virtuous acts. Instead the crimes were heaped up by a deadly progression, as if they stood guarded under some protective seal in the memory of the judge. Thus, when the marks of freedom were lost, they were submitted to a most savage servitude, and they felt those pains and anguishes that women are accustomed to experience in childbirth.[409]

13:13 He is a senseless son; for now he will not stand in the contrition of the children.

He has already discussed this previously in the same style,[410] that he should show the open folly of Israel with a testimony of adversities. And the deformity of their offenses, which had lain hidden for a long time underneath their prosperity, was at last exposed by the troubles that proved them guilty. Therefore, with a weighty testimony he confirms that you are a *son*, and *senseless*, since at that time when the enemy invaded, you did not deserve to *stand*. And he branded their profaneness with the name of folly, to which the ten tribes surrendered themselves with all their zeal, as he has accused since the beginning of the book; and on account of this same foolishness the storm of captivity snatched them away. Thus, he fittingly moves on to Judah and exposes him not only by name but by the proof of the things they have carried out as well. This was in order to show simultaneously what conclusion would detain the wise sons, even as he had exposed to the public those who had remained foolish. Therefore, the prophetic speech moves on to prosperous things, which were granted by the great miracles that occurred under the king Hezekiah.[411] And he says,

13:14-15 I will deliver them out of the hand of death. I will redeem them from death. O Death, I will be your death. O hell, I will be your bite. Comfort is hidden from my eyes, because it itself divides brothers among themselves. The Lord will bring in a burning wind that shall rise from the desert, and it shall dry up his springs and shall make his fountains desolate, and he shall carry off the treasure of every desirable vessel.

First, as is customary, he announces the joys of freedom by promising prosperity; but afterward he heaps up the same things with a pleasure for revenge. Therefore *I will deliver them out of the hand of death*. This means, when they come into such great hardship of affairs that death seems to have seized hold of them with its hand thrown in, then I will arrive as deliverer. Now it was especially the prayer of the blessed Hezekiah that expressed this when he said, "Days of distress and reproach have come; since indeed children have come to the point of birth, but there is no strength to deliver them."[412] When, therefore, they were beset by the power of the Assyrians, and the enemy had shut the city with a siege, destruction was so imminent that at any time now it seemed that it would devour the

[408]Hos 13:12.
[409]Cf. Hos 13:13.
[410]Cf. Hos 7:11.
[411]Cf. 2 Kings 19:35-37; Is 37:36-38.
[412]Cf. 2 Kings 19:3; Is 37:3.

wretched people. But because they obtained divine help by just prayers,[413] he brought forth that powerful miracle, and an angel struck down and destroyed one hundred and eighty-five thousand Assyrian soldiers, and the prayed-for liberation shone brightly on the pious. This agrees with what the holy songs had predicted: "This poor man called out, and the Lord heard him; and he saved him from all his troubles. The Lord will send his angels around those who fear him, and he will rescue them."[414] Accordingly, here the Assyrian king and his whole army are named *death* and *hell*, whom the divine judgment promises to destroy. And having first mentioned the din of vengeance, according to his custom he gives the reason that is inciting his indignation: *Comfort is hidden from my eyes. Because it itself divides brothers among themselves.* He adopted the demeanor and the words of one in mourning in order to increase the Assyrian's guilt. And as if under the persona of Judah, as one who was anxious more over the calamity of his brother (that is, of the Israelites whom Sennacherib had led into captivity) than over his own calamity, he says that his eyes had become so wet with tears that they could not recover *comfort*. For the arrogant and fierce king effected a grievous separation *among the brothers*—namely, by transferring the ten tribes into captivity to the country of Media.[415] Of course, here the diligent reader is able to ask why is this affection that mourns over the withdrawal of the brother ascribed to the tribe of Judah, seeing that earlier the prophet speaks about this same matter and reproaches the impiety of Judah's rejoicing over this? For, when he had said, "Ephraim shall be in desolation," he says, "In the day of desolation I have shown faithfulness among the tribes of Israel. The princes of Judah have become as those who take up the boundary; I will pour out my wrath on them like water."[416] Though there they are said to have rejoiced over the expulsion of their brothers, through which fact they thought that the boundaries of their fields would be expanded, how is it that now they are induced to mourning over the expulsion of their brother without any consolation?[417] This problem can be solved by two explanations. For since the discussion concerns not individual persons, as I have repeatedly said,[418] but whole multitudes, therefore we understand that there were diverse morals in that multitude as well. Thus, some things are brought forth from the characters of the pious, other things from the characters of the impious. Consequently, then, we infer that there were some there who were saddened by the expulsion of their brothers, but the majority were delighted over the extension of their boundaries. But let us now consider another way of explaining this, which doubtless shall be effectively introduced in such a way that it would seem to apply to the causes more than to the characters. This may indeed be the voice of a relation, which the prophet set near the end of his book—that is, that they are grieved over the disaster to their exiled brother and they plead with the enemies for the change that is owed. But the fact that it even brought pleasure to certain ones, this has in view the crime of murder. Thus, there results a sense of this sort: there were some in whom wickedness not only confounded the laws but even the rights of nature, as they preferred to boast over the captivity of brothers, when they should have shown compassion. *The Lord will bring in a burning wind that shall rise from the desert, and it shall dry up his springs and shall make his fountains desolate, and he shall carry off the treasures of every desirable vessel.* He is calling

[413]Cf. 2 Kings 19:20; Is 37:21.
[414]Ps 34:6-7.
[415]Cf. 2 Kings 17:6; 18:11.

[416]Hos 5:9-10.
[417]Jerome had emphasized Judah's joy over Israel's demise and the hope of acquisition of more land; *Commentary on Hosea* 5:10 (ACT 2:189).
[418]Cf. under Hos 6:8-9.

the angel who destroyed the Assyrian army in one night a *burning wind* that came *from the desert.*[419] It is not that we believe that angels live in the desert, whom gospel authority points out daily look on the face of the Father.[420] But on account of the swiftness of vengeance—one hundred eighty-five thousand are reported slaughtered in one night—he took up the comparison to fire. The reason he mentioned the desert is this, so that the whole multitude might seem to have been wasted by the wind rather than by some kind of operation. For thus even blessed David had said, "He makes his angels spirits, and his servants burning fire."[421] Therefore, he now showed that this burning is summoned from places that are uninhabitable due to the heat of the sun. This burning destroyed the Assyrian *springs* and *fountains*—that is, the king with his army and race. *And he shall carry off the treasure of the desirable vessel.* If you look at the usage of the prophets, who do not observe changes of the times with sufficiently meticulous care and attention, he seems to have intended the riches of the king Sennacherib compiled from his triumphs.[422] That is to say, the reason he was devoured by the previously mentioned burning was because he carried out many things cruelly, and his plunder did not sate his avarice. And now he is being compelled to vomit forth whatever he had devoured previously through iniquity.

[Chapter 14]

14:1 Let Samaria perish, because she has stirred up her Lord to bitterness; let her perish by the sword, let their little ones be dashed, and let their fetuses be ripped up.

A little earlier he had said, "Comfort is hidden from my eyes, because it itself divides brothers among themselves,"[423] and he had shown that affection with which he pities Israel. But now he describes the slaughter of the Assyrian and has grown hot against Samaria again. Surely he did not do this for the sake of variety, but due to the gravity of the judgment. For he had showed both the due regard and power of the true God, who had destroyed the arrogant king as if it were no trouble. He had showed that he was so prepared to defend the pious that for their joy he threatened vengeance on all the great nations, deservedly on Samaria, so that it would utterly perish, as if it desired to be set on fire. This, of course, was something it had brought about by its crimes. Thus, here the Lord stood out as so good, not as their champion but as their opponent. It is as if he were to say, When I consider the kindnesses of our leader, who is eternal, more and more do I dread Israel's sin—namely, those who labored to lose such protection.

14:2 Return, O Israel, to the Lord your God, for you have fallen down by your iniquity.

The oration proceeds with wonderful coherence. For he had exclaimed that the sin of Samaria was strong enough to become oppressive; but because he had done this very thing more in order to show pity than to curse them, he brings in at least secondary remedies, which will heal the wound. And because they were unwilling to embrace the protection of continuous devotion, they receive the help of a corrective repentance. If, therefore, even dangers make you better, O Israel, *return to the Lord your God,* from whom you should never have turned away. And since I have cursed the very fact that *you had fallen down by your iniquity,* take up the duties of confession. For this is what he says:

[419]Cf. 2 Kings 19:35; Is 37:36.
[420]Cf. Mt 18:10.
[421]Ps 104:4.
[422]Cf. 2 Kings 18:15-16.
[423]Hos 13:15.

14:3a Take with you words and return to the Lord, and say to him, Take away all iniquity, and receive the good.

For you alone are able to remove the guilt by which we are oppressed. Now the following verse shows what the *good* is, which he was begging to receive, "And we will render the calves of our lips."[424] For this is what holy songs also have taught, that we should sacrifice to God "the sacrifice of praise."[425] For grateful praise from a pure heart is offered to him "rather than a new calf bearing hooves and horns."[426] "Speak forth, therefore, against yourself," O Israel, "your iniquities to the Lord," whose remission you desire to earn.[427] But let us hear what he adds to this.

14:4 Assyria shall not save us, we will not ride on a horse; neither will we say any more, the works of our hands are our gods; for you will have mercy on the people (*populi*)[428] of the one who is in you.

What he says, *Assyria shall not save us,* seems to have been taken up from the example of Judah. For the history of Kings narrates that when the Assyrian leader by the name of Rabsaces arrived, who had been sent by King Sennacherib to challenge and terrify those who were enclosed within Jerusalem, among the other things that he proclaimed pompously and arrogantly concerning the Assyrians, he added that Sennacherib was prepared to bring out two thousand horses. The whole army of Judah was not able to offer riders for them.[429] Then by what madness were they rousing the forces of such a great prince against themselves! If they took counsel for their own safety henceforth, they should surrender to the command of him who would show himself no less generous to his subjects than severe toward the defiant. But the inhabitants of Jerusalem placed confidence of their liberation in the power of God alone. They silently scorned the boast of the threatening enemy. Therefore, the sermon of the one now giving warning is instructing Israel as well by the example of Judah's trust—namely, that when he too has been corrected by a long servitude, he should begin to imitate the devotion of his brother, which he showed at the time of the Assyrian siege. He says, *Neither will we say any more, the works of our hands are our gods;* that is, we shall leave off worshiping those images that are made by the hand of craftsmen. This will happen after we have learned even from the witness of our brother that you are a good judge and you do not cease *having mercy on the people* who abide in your worship. But hear what is related by our God to this offering of your confession.

14:5-8 I will heal their distresses; I will love them freely; for my wrath is turned away from them. I will be as the dew to Israel; he shall spring forth as the lily, and his root shall shoot forth as that of Libanus. They shall be converted who sit in his shade, they shall live on wheat, and they shall blossom as a vine; his memorial [shall be] like the wine of Lebanon.

With diverse similes he describes the sweetness of deliverance, the marks of freedom, and the delightfulness of the cultivated fields. Doubtless just as at the time when the enemy prances about, they are covered with so much filth, so, when the security of peacetime trains the effort of the cultivators, both fruitfulness and delightful conditions are seen everywhere. So then, O Israel, when the prosperity that was promised shall drive off your captivity, the beauty of freedom and the sweetness of

[424]Hos 14:3b.
[425]Cf. Ps 50:14.
[426]Cf. Ps 69:31.
[427]Cf. Ps 32:5.
[428]Jerome reads "orphan" (*pupilli*).
[429]Cf. 2 Kings 18:17-36.

rejoicing will so fill you and cover you that meadows will appear glistening, not with any worthless plants but with lilies and roses. For my mercy and my grace will flow into you like the *dew*, so that, when every filth has been laid aside, you may perceive the ornaments of renewal. Lest in view of its greatness you be in doubt that this can happen to you, he has anticipated it in the brother—that is, in the liberation of Judah from the hands of the Assyrians. The deliverance, desired, to be sure, but hardly expected, will bring the kind of glory that will likewise remain with you, if only you show yourself worthy of the one by whom it is being granted. You *will live on wheat* and *will blossom as a vine*, which when transferred from Egypt filled the spacious lands of Palestine.[430] And your *memorial* will be *as the wine of Libanus*; that is, the fragrance of your glory will be as great as the best wine produced on the mountain of Libanus.[431]

14:9 Ephraim [shall say], What have I to do any more with idols? I will hear and make him straight like a green fir tree, from me is your fruit found.

Since these things are so, he says, as our discussion has taught thoroughly (that is, that this is the one way of salvation, which the worship and religion of our name has revealed), at least set a limit to your profanity. You should never have allowed a beginning of this profaneness to become perceptible. Cleave to the one Lord, who is true, with complete faith and devotion. Do not think that his truth is to be held onto with falsehood so as to ascribe to idols the incommunicable name. But know what you have learned not only by precepts but by the very voice of troubles, that I am one whose worshipers may obtain eternal blessedness, just as those who desert me are plunged into eternal miseries. For it is I who *hear* those who offer supplications, who am able and accustomed to save the contrite, to *make straight* the twisted, to make fertile the barren, to find the perishing, to raise the dying, and to lift on high those whom I have invigorated, so that from the shrubs or bramble bushes they may seem to have grown into *fir trees* and cypresses.

14:10 Who is wise, and he shall understand these things? Prudent, and he shall know these things? For the ways of the Lord are right, and the just shall walk in them; but transgressors shall fall in them.

Fittingly he has concluded his book with an expression of wonder, the usefulness of which he had showed both by precepts and examples. At the same time, in order to show that the cause of all the sins and miseries had occurred from foolishness, he praised the one who is *wise*, who by weighing carefully everything that had been discussed, recognized the usefulness and end of the sacred ways—namely, that by them the *just* may walk with security. But all *transgressors will fall*—namely, by committing sacrilege and by enduring destruction.

One should note, of course, that these passages, which I have explained to the best of my ability in accordance with the history predicted by the prophet, are likewise capable of signifying even greater things. For that which was said about Sennacherib, "O Death, I will be your death; O hell, I will be your bite,"[432] can likewise be understood of grander matters. This is what the teacher of the nations[433] showed. For when he was speaking to the Corinthians about the manifestation of the resurrection, he said, "Where, O death, is your sting? Where is your victory? But thanks be to God who gave us victory through our

[430]Cf. Ps 80:8-9.

[431]Cf. Jerome, *Commentary on Hosea* 14:5-9 (ACT 2:259-60).

[432]Hos 13:14.

[433]Cf. 1 Tim 2:7.

Lord Jesus Christ."[434] For he is cited here as a "burning wind"; indeed, he who came to cast fire on the earth[435] rose up "from the desert,"[436] because he sprouted forth from the womb of a virgin to whom no man had submitted as cultivator in accordance with the laws of nature.[437] And he caused the fountain of death and its spring to run dry,[438] so that it did not have the right to attack them a second time, those whom the Redeemer had once raised up in everlasting joy. For indeed, by the mystery of the incarnation itself, the dew of grace came down on the fields of the churches,[439] so that far and wide a fruitful vine and lilies came up with diverse virtues.[440] And the blessedness of the multiplication of the faithful would become as great as the fields that were filled with crops, with fruit, with glorious blossoms.[441] And thus "they shall be converted who sit in his shade."[442] This means diverse nations will long to rest under the protection of the church, so that in the wine and the wheat[443] they would attain the nourishment of both bodily and spiritual vigor. Therefore, that liberation that was accomplished under Hezekiah is unfolded more abundantly and graciously by the freedom that Christ bestowed. *Who is wise, and he shall understand these things? [Who] understands, and he shall know them?* Namely, that the Lord was "appointed for the fall and resurrection of many."[444] Let them not advance confidently on the rough paths in which pursuers of crimes *will fall*. But those who confess with their whole heart that Christ is the power of God and the wisdom of God[445] strive to become one spirit with him[446] by their prayers and pursuits.

[434]1 Cor 15:55, 57. Jerome, *Commentary on Hosea* 13:14-15a (ACT 2:254-55) says that no one can dare to interpret the Hosea text otherwise than as the apostle understands it. Robert C. Hill notices that Theodore of Mopsuestia, *Commentary on Hosea*, ignores the New Testament citation (1 Cor 15:55) of Hos 13:14 (FOTC 98, n. 109).

[435]Cf. Lk 12:49.

[436]Cf. Hos 13:15.

[437]Cf. Jerome, *Commentary on Hosea* [13:15a] (ACT 2:255).

[438]Cf. Hos 13:15.

[439]Cf. Hos 14:5.

[440]Cf. Hos 14:5-6.

[441]Cf. Jn 4:35-38.

[442]Hos 14:7.

[443]Cf. Hos 14:7.

[444]Lk 2:34; cf. Jerome, *Commentary on Hosea* 14:10 (ACT 2:261).

[445]Cf. 1 Cor 1:24.

[446]Cf. 1 Cor 6:17.

COMMENTARY ON THE PROPHET JOEL

[Preface]

I approached these prophecies, or hidden matters, or perhaps better called, remote things, boldly, to be sure, but as an investigator who relies on the aids of religion rather than temerity. I was hoping it would be permissible to employ meanings not transparent to the common light, but ones that are in awe of that concealed brilliance. Therefore, I took note [at the beginning of the *Commentary on Hosea*] of the version that I had chosen to adopt (for there are several versions out there). Namely, I selected the most recent one, which is called "according to the Hebrew."[1] For in it there is a greater completeness of the expressions, which [better] communicates the emotional state of the one who is teaching, or threatening. Therefore, from the information found in [Jerome's] translation, we have learned that the order of the twelve prophets among the Hebrews is different from that which the more common edition had.[2] And because superscriptions are not recorded in all the prophets as indications of the times, uncertainty about the epoch in which each of them was prophesying scarcely occurs, because the tradition that was passed down from hand to hand pointed out that the teaching of those prophets who are read without superscriptions flourished under those kings under whom the prophets before them prophesied, who were equipped with superscriptions.[3] So then, let it be tested whether you, blessed Joel, seem to be of the same epoch and among the contemporaries of saint Hosea, whom we read before him. That is to say, Joel is one who experienced the same cruelty and abuses of the kings. He accused the same sacrileges of the raving people. He predicted the same impending torments against those who slandered him.

But he begins more with the feeling of one who is expressing wonder and, so to speak, commiserating.

[Chapter 1]

1:1 The word of the Lord that came to Joel the son of Phatuel.

He says, The eternal teacher has imposed on his own servant this task of teaching, or rather, of reproaching. For by the term *word* he has indicated at the same time the entire teaching that he will use. Also, it is not for nothing that the prophet's father is mentioned, but this is because whenever not only the virtues of those who possess holiness are named, but also their ancestors, the result is an equality of dignity

[1]Julian is referring to St. Jerome's new translation of the Old Testament that was made directly from the Hebrew, as opposed to the Old Latin version, which was translated from the Greek Septuagint (LXX).

[2]*Vulgatior editio.* The more common version would be the Old Latin translation of the LXX. Jerome discusses the differing order of the Twelve Prophets in the preface to his *Commentary on Joel* (ACT 2:262). The Hebrew ordering is Hosea, Joel, Amos, Obadiah, Jonah, Micah, Nahum, Habakkuk, Zephaniah, Haggai, Zechariah, Malachi. The LXX ordering is Hosea, Amos, Micah, Joel, Obadiah, Jonah, Nahum, Habakkuk, Zephaniah, Haggai, Zechariah, Malachi.

[3]Julian intends here to agree with Jerome's preface to the *Commentary on Joel*, that the prophet Joel, whose book lacks a superscription indicating the times, prophesied under the same kings that are mentioned in Hosea 1:1. Theodore of Mopsuestia, *Commentary on Joel* (FOTC 104), agrees that Joel lived at the same time as Hosea.

with their parents. And thus those men as well are pointed out, whether they be just ones, prophets, or priests.[4] Therefore, this cause of praising the root in the offspring is shown to be both noble and grave. Now some commentators have likewise pursued the etymologies of the names, obviously in order to gather the seeds of praises from them.[5] Thus, Joel is ἀρχόμενος, which we can translate as "a beginner." And Phatuel means "the breadth of God," and the rest in this way. These are childish and unsuitable things, and seem to offer more trouble than profit.

1:2 Hear this, you old men, and perceive with your ears, all you inhabitants of the earth. Has this ever happened in your days, or in the days of your fathers?

He proceeds in the manner of one who is speaking in a public assembly of the people, who is about to relate the greatness of the disaster that has befallen the Israelites. He says, Behold, I anticipate the sound of your weeping, and I announce first what your complaining was going to move to ill will—namely, that you all were subject not to one or another set of floggings; you always drove away the preceding afflictions with new ones, disasters that were stirred up like frothing waves.[6] Therefore, all of you inhabitants, come together to *hear*: whether those of you who have gathered up many perils in the old age of this life, or you who, although you are a little younger in years, nevertheless, with a vigorous memory you are able to comprehend if you received something similar from your parents of such a nature that it has flowed into your present age. Nay, what will I say? Let us consider only the annals, as if looking for comfort from the examples, since I judge that the afflictions of our nation have gone up into that heap, so that no such thing could even arise among future [generations]. And therefore the *old men and the inhabitants of the land* are commanded either to *perceive with their ears* or to *hear*. [The use of two phrases] does not indicate different merits or pursuits, but the command is given in an absolute way, that they should *hear*. This is similar to what is said in the psalm: "Hear these things, all you nations, perceive with your ears, you who inhabit the world. All you that are earthborn, and you sons of men, both rich and poor together."[7] Certainly, by this proclamation it is none other than humanity that he summons in many ways. The reason I have briefly noted this is because certain people thought that there was a big difference in these terms, and thus they wasted lots of the unprofitable words.[8] But let us listen to what the prophet brings forth with this show of such great astonishment.

1:4 That which the palmerworm has left, the locust has eaten, and that which the locust has left, the young locust[9] has eaten, and that which the young locust has left, the mildew has destroyed.

He comprehends different forms of disasters, which he laments have been inflicted on the Jewish people. When each of these happen, they consume the year's crop and hope in such a way that hardship and dread equally crush the hearts of the farmers. We gather, of course, either from the very prophet whom we are discussing, or from the threats of Deuteronomy, that these inconveniences happened to them not once but at many times.[10] Whence also we oppose the opinion of those who think

[4]Cf. Jer 1:1; Ezek 1:3.
[5]Cf. Jerome, *Commentary on Joel* preface (ACT 2:262-63).
[6]This simile is used in Julian's *Commentary on Hosea* 12:12-13; *Commentary on Job* 31:23; 37:20; 39:31-32.

[7]Ps 49:1-2.
[8]Jerome, *Commentary on Joel* 1:2-3 (ACT 2:264), would be one who (presumably following Origen) reads in different audiences for these distinctive phrases and distinguishes hearing from perceiving.
[9]*Bruchus* refers to a wingless locust.
[10]Cf. 1 Kings 17; 2 Kings 7:4; 8:1; Deut 28:38-39, 42.

that all these things have been said about [Israel's] enemies. For they thought that *palmerworm, locust, young locust,* and *mildew* were being used to signify the Assyrian, Chaldean, Macedonian, and Roman people, by whose resources the commonwealth of the Jews doubtless was wasted away. That is, they believe that under the representation of the locusts the alternation of the enemies has been made public.[11] Assuredly, they would have seemed to surmise this with some measure of logical coherence if the Jews had endured no disasters except those brought about by enemies. But since they are shown to have endured both the most severe famine, and a prodigious drought, such as the one that occurred at the time of blessed Elijah,[12] and sudden death and different forms of ruination, why was it necessary, whenever he mentions locusts and young locusts, to link this destitution too to the invasions of nations?[13] Therefore, understanding the prophetic words in a literal fashion, rather than transferring these same things into another form that pleases, we should understand *locusts* and *palmerworms* not as horsemen clad in mail, or foot soldiers bearing shields, but as long-legged grubs[14] or small, winged creatures. They will have advanced themselves in such a way at that time as a means of tormenting the profane nation that they took turns in their persistence in wreaking harm, and, if anything was leftover [from] the preceding ones, those that followed consumed the remainder. Saint Joel, of course, looks on this impending destruction with a prophetic look more than on that one already inflicted. And for that reason, to those concerning whom he is pleading, who are sluggish in respect to their own wretched security, as a kindly prophet and one who is perplexed by such a spectacle, he exclaims,

1:5 Wake up, you drunkards, and weep, wail, all you who drink wine unto sweetness, for it is cut off from your mouth.

Characteristically the complaint that has just begun first addresses those in the general disaster, who are shown that they will bear the same things more heavily than the rest. For scarcity hurts more bitterly those who are accustomed to pleasures; and to those addicted to luxury, not only is want a torment but so is frugality itself. Therefore, since he was about to relate the troubles of the destitution, he began with ordinary things, and he only touches on the loss of pleasures, which are not common to all but can only be feared by the wastrels. And he rates them so poorly that he proclaims that they wished to live for pleasure alone, [and to show] that the state of such persons is merited, he adds that they should stay alert and *wake up,* at the least since the expense is under threat of those things after which they strove as their partner in falling asleep. He says, Up to now no concern for these pursuits has distracted you, and the awareness of such great faults has not goaded you to remorse, but you have been enslaved to all desires; you have acted as if you were free from justice. The patience of the eternal judge has been conquered by the shamelessness and

[11]Jerome, *Commentary on Joel* 1:4 (ACT 2:265), reports as the view of the Hebrews, which he says is also supported by Josephus, that the species of locusts and the mildew refer to the Assyrians, Chaldeans, Medes and Persians, Macedonians, and Romans, respectively. Theodore of Mopsuestia, *Commentary on Joel* (FOTC 105), says that the locusts and blight figuratively convey the troubles inflicted on Israel by the Assyrian kings Tiglath-pileser, Shalmaneser, Sennacherib, and the Babylonians. It is interesting that Jerome further reports under 1:6-7 (ACT 2:268) that the Jews think a literal plague of locusts occurred in the days of Joel. And under Joel 2:1-11 (ACT 2:277) Jerome says that he himself recently saw a real locust plague in Palestine. Strikingly, under Joel 2:4-11, Julian supports an allegorical interpretation of the locusts, derived almost verbatim from Jerome, as representing the emotions of the soul.

[12]Cf. 1 Kings 17:1.

[13]J. Lössl, "Julian of Aeclanum's Tractatus in Osee, Iohel, Amos: Some Notes on the Current State of Research," *Augustiniana* 51 (2001): 35n68, defends the integrity of Julian's interpretation here against the charge of banality and inconsistency made by De Plinval.

[14]*Raripedes.* Literally, "with feet wide apart."

obstinacy of sinners. He has decreed to subject you to the flogging that you deserve, and to remove those chief instruments of your delights, which you were abusing. Of course, although the progression of this destitution reaches even to the ordinary people and those without wealth, yet even the very commencement of it will torment you. You, then, whom instruction in justice has taught nothing, begin at least to experience the goads of fear, and shed some tears for your vices, which you did not give to your duties. All of you who never felt pain over your wounded innocence, *weep* at last for your destitute drunkenness. *Wake up, you drunkards and weep, wail all you who drink wine unto sweetness, for it is cut off from your mouth.* He is saying, You have supplied the causes of this most severe offense by your pursuit of extravagance; and you were not content with sumptuous seasonal banquets or simple intoxication. You corrupted the wine with sweets mixed in and you craftily provided a provocation to banquets, so that the whole scope of your life was ruined amid wantonness and drunkenness. Behold, now the time of the same sort of revenge has arrived, a revenge that removes chiefly the instruments of your pleasures by means of the devastation of the crops of the lands. Therefore, I say, this tribulation will torment you first, because the diminution of abundance becomes a punishing experience for those who are not acquainted with frugality. And since you have forgotten reason and have made yourselves like the beasts, at least *wail* on the very couches and beds on which you lie. *Wake up, you drunkards and weep, wail all you who drink wine unto sweetness, for it is cut off from your mouth.* Since the skillful reproach of a censor is mixed in with the prophetic announcement, he shows that "man who is established in honor did not understand, and therefore he is compared to the brute beasts,"[15] to which he has rendered himself similar. For as we have said, he does this when he considers loss an injury to his life so that he is vigilant from a diseased extravagance during the very din of the punishment that has been set in motion. Thus, since he does not know how to weep, he indeed howls in the manner of the psalm: "They shall suffer hunger like dogs, and shall go round about the city."[16] Therefore, it would have been suitable that reason aroused you by the spurs of remorse rather than that tribulation do so by the biting of pain. But since you have *cut off* counsel by excessive gormandizing, with the result that now you are no longer able to show foresight, but only to feel, *wail* when you are struck, you who did not fear when you were warned. And what is the cause of such tears?

1:6-8 For a nation has come up on my land, strong and without number; its teeth are like the teeth of lions, its molars like those of a lion's whelp. It has laid waste my vineyard and has pulled off the bark from my fig tree; stripping it bare, it has uncovered it and has cast it away; its branches have been made white. Lament like a virgin girded with sackcloth for the husband of your youth.

Indeed, during these times that are contained in the superscription of blessed Hosea,[17] the repeated invasions of the Assyrians are related.[18] But because the Creator of the universe was not afflicting the violators of his law in just one race, therefore we conclude that these plagues that the prophet threatens also occurred among the enemy populations. Clearly he eagerly expends much effort in describing these things, doubtless with the intention and skill of a medical doctor. His aim is to excite in the hearts of those listening

[15]Cf. Ps 49:12.

[16]Ps 59:15.

[17]Cf. Hos 1:1.

[18]Cf. 1 Kings 15:18; 20:1; 2 Kings 7:6; 8:20; 10:32; 13:7, 20-22; 15:19, 29; 17:4.

that wholesome fear, which would compel them to shrink back from the enticements, and not to pass by the goads of the menacing terror due to the brevity of the disclosure. Instead he wants to teach the listener to linger in the consideration of facts, for whose correction this entire campaign of punishments was being prepared. Not content simply with having described this, he proceeds also to increase the weight of his words by telling them what was going to happen. Finally, he attributed the name of *nation* to the battle line of the locusts, as if it were moving by throngs and companies, and whose novelty was no less than the greatness of the dread. For if you consider its efficiency rather than its members, you will see that it has been given *teeth like the whelps of lions*, or rather, like those very lions that are already skilled in plundering. For [these locusts] lay waste to plants with less difficulty than those lions devastate herds of cattle. And to the extent that it is clear that flocks are less suitable than crops for mortals to live on, so much the more is the plunderer and throats gaping with the blood of wild beasts unsuitable for crops rather than flocks. But the raging locust devours the very milk of the fruits and the grass, and therefore it even kills the cattle, which it does not eat. For it robs all the forests of their greenness, and by the force of the disaster it imitates the state of nature itself, as it were. Thus, just as it is customary in the decline of winter for the moisture of trees to be driven toward the insides, and thus, with the glory of their foliage having been cast off, the hardwood stands bare, which if someone who is inexperienced with living in the country saw them, he would doubt that they could become green again, so that battle line, which I lament is coming, will devour not merely the soft grass but also the ripe vineyards. And once the grape harvest has been removed, it will not restrain itself with respect to the fruits, for it will destroy the sweet *figs* with a bitter tooth. And thus, with dedicated effort, it will pursue the entire *bark*, through which doubtless the life-giving sap could flow, so that one beholds a *white* forest instead of a green one. Therefore, since the land will neither yield the fruit entrusted to itself, nor will the fruit voluntarily bend down the bough, nor will the year supply the consolations of fruits to the suffering tillers of land, what remains, O people of ours, save that you let tears follow in the train of your disaster? But let them be well watered and abundant, as women are accustomed to shed whom the sorrow of widowhood crushes, and who are deprived of the companionship of their husbands, to whom they had been united from the time of their virginity.

1:8-9 Lament like a virgin girded with sackcloth for the husband of your youth. Sacrifice and libation is cut off from the house of the Lord.

Fittingly the discourse turned to religious duty. For because he had said that the sorrow of widowhood was to be regarded as equivalent to the lamentations of the entire nation, by mentioning religious duty he solved the question of why he had brought forth this comparison. For just as often elsewhere, so also in the writings of the blessed Hosea, our God declares that he has received the synagogue as his wife, as it were, but that she violated the terms of the union in the fashion of adulteresses, and, what is more, she subjected herself to the worship of different gods.[19] Therefore, here too he proceeded from the beginning of the threatening disaster into a boundless extent by a narration, and, after the initial costs, as it were, of drunkenness, which signaled the sufferings of the luxuriant, a tribulation of very abundant poverty has been brought in. It has laid waste the cultivated fields and the brothels equally, and on account

[19]Cf. Hos 1–3; Jer 2:32; 3:1.

of this there remained not merely no nourishment for the community but not even that which was due to be offered according to religious duty. Therefore, it corresponds with the comparison of the widowed woman, for through this seeming torment over her husband's departure, she has lost the means of offering and of performing the sacred rites, by which through the daily sacrifices she believed she appeased God and cleaved to him.

1:9-12 The priests, the Lord's ministers, have mourned. The country is destroyed, the ground has mourned, for the [wheat] corn is wasted, the wine is confounded, the oil has languished. The farmers are ashamed, the vinedressers have howled for the wheat, and for the barley, because the harvest of the field has perished. The vineyard is confounded, and the fig tree has languished; the pomegranate tree, and the palm tree, and the apple tree, and all the trees of the field have withered, because joy is confounded from the children of men.

By the destruction inflicted by the locust, young locust, and mildew, common scarcity has reached the point that a deprivation of animal sacrifices also followed, and the loaves of proposition were not placed on the altar.[20] Consequently the first *priests* and the Levites *mourned*. But let the rest of the people groan after the manner of widows (as we have said),[21] as if rejected by the eternal spouse, because even the very land has been covered over with the squalor of one who is in mourning. All its green adornment and fertility have been lost. For the reaper did not pull up the grain for this sad devastation, the grapevine did not bring its own fertility with which it was loaded to the point of sweet grape juice, but it deceived the tillers with such great frustration that his own lie would seem to turn red with embarrassment. A similar envy struck the olives, the *pomegranates* languished with the figs, and no kind of fruit was able to subsist in a better condition, but with the joys and hopes of mortals both the sprouts (*germina*) and the grass (*gramina*) perished. It is not the time for hiding sorrow. Everyone, take up the attitude and mindset of mourners, for the most hideous kind of destruction threatens, by which both the hope of the year and the thing itself are to be bewailed.

1:13-14 Gird yourselves, and lament, O priests; howl, you ministers of the altar; go in, lie down in sackcloth, ministers of my God, for sacrifice and libation is cut off from the house of your God. Sanctify a fast, call an assembly, gather together the old men, all, all the inhabitants of the land into the house of your God, and cry out to the Lord.

The greatness of the disaster has been set forth. Indeed, he had related the weeping that threatened all the peoples, but it is the duty of one who is showing pity rather than teaching to be roused solely by the sight of the tears. Yet the prophet is arrayed with the spirt of a parent and does not conciliate except for the sake of serving a useful purpose. Now too in an orderly manner it is conducive to laments not to waste time with empty weeping, doubtless attending their own afflictions with mournful voices. This would undoubtedly have been unbecoming to religious and strong minds. But they arrange the very gifts of tears according to the rules of the sacred law. They prepare a harvest of joys, and they indulge in the hardships of the mind to the extent that suffices, to grieve their offense rather than their loss of things, before the anger of the judge. Therefore, he says, You *priests*, exchange your soft clothing for rough, adopt the attitude and heart of mourners, but also recount what especially belongs to your care—namely, that

[20]Cf. Ex 25:23-30; Lev 24:5-9.
[21]Cf. Joel 1:6-8.

you failed at the source from which you serve the divine worship. But that which concerns the people, *sanctify a fast*—that is, proclaim with an announcement, that if someone perchance disregards it, he should be charged as if he did violence to the holy things. That is what he says: *Sanctify a fast*. But at the same time he says, *all, all*—that is, not only those vigorous in their age but also those he regards as weak, whether infants or the elderly, in view of the greatness of the danger, *call* them together for common duty. For it is consistent that the affliction of everyone should drive away this catastrophe, which was about to rage on everyone in common. A favorable time of a keen understanding ought not slip away from us. If only the *fast* is commanded universally for everyone. He says, *Call the old men, all, all the inhabitants of the land into the house of your God*. But if that want, which was described earlier, seized the region to all the boundaries, so that a solemn sacrifice could not be offered, how is the fast commanded again to the same people by the ostentation of a great sanctification? For surely for those set amid such great destitution it would be more difficult in fact to provide food than to continue to fast. Therefore, we ought to call attention to the fact that it is one thing to be hungry, something else to fast. The latter concerns training in virtue, but the former concerns a mortal hardship. Therefore, the affliction of guilty ones does not appease God, but the correction of those who are penitent; neither is it necessary to be cured by wasting away but by remorse. For common hardship by no means drives away the filth of extravagance from the good and the bad, but only friendly instruction drives it out of honorable minds. And therefore I seek fasting, he says, because it comes from duty. I do not seek hunger, which generally happens as a punishment. Or, I say to those who are hungry, bring about a fast so that piety may render very fruitful what lack had made troublesome. But we have said these things in order to build up those who are listening; for the rest the contextual coherence can be vindicated for the prophetic statements by a larger abridgement: for the soothsayer is proclaiming a threatening disaster more than one that has already rushed in. He justly admonishes the priests to summon the people to fasting and to let them meet these catastrophes, which they hear are threatening, with lawful supplications. After all it follows,

1:15-18 Ah, ah, ah, for the day, because the day of the Lord is at hand, and it shall come like destruction from the mighty. Is not [your] food cut off before your eyes, gladness and exultation from the house of our God? The beasts of burden have rotted in their dung; the barns are destroyed; the storehouses are broken down, because the corn is confounded. Why did the beast groan, why did the herds of cattle bellow? Because there is no pasture for them, but even the flocks of sheep have perished.

After the prophet arranged the appearance of the mourners—namely, that they should come together covered in sackcloth (that is, wrapped in goat's hair)—he now adds also what speech they ought to carry out. And he repeats twice and three times the exclamation of the one in sorrow, as if he is expressing the force of the blows with which the plagues are striking. He does this for hardly any other reason certainly than that the display of the foretold disaster might incite terror and remorse in the hearts of the listeners. It is as if he were to say, Trust my eyes; trust the senses that see with a prophetic keenness of vision not only what has been brought in but also the things to come. Doubtless he means his sharp-sightedness, which cannot be allowed to endure the weight of the calamity, and we are collapsing as if wrenched in our vital organs before each of these blows. For thus will the palmerworm, the locust, the young locust, and the mildew succeed one another,[22] so that the cessation of the preceding disaster, which seemed to promise some relief, brings more burdensome anguishes for the wretched people. And that *day of the Lord* (namely, on which he has appointed vengeance on the guilty) is not dreadful as if by a trifling annoyance, but it brings that devastation, which every most powerful avenger would have brought in—namely, by whose strength neither the bravery of those who resist was able to withstand, nor would the cunning of those who hide be able to rescue anyone. Therefore, as for what he says, *Destruction shall come from the mighty*, understand this as recorded either as a comparison, so that we know that the chastisement will be no less efficacious than if a victory of some very powerful king were about to rage—the following passage in the psalm speaks in these tones: "And the Lord was awaked as one out of sleep, and like a *mighty* man that had been made drunk with wine; and he struck his enemies on the hinder parts, he put them to an everlasting reproach"[23]—or else we should understand the mention that was made of *the mighty* not as an example but in view of its uniqueness. He accomplishes without difficulty not one or two things, but everything that he wants, and thus *the mighty* seems to have represented the Almighty. *Because the day of the Lord is at hand, and destruction shall come from the mighty. Is not [your] food cut off before your eyes?* He says, It is not the time for you to be afraid of an ordinary setback, and of a disaster that is inflicted only in the gathering of the produce that has hardly even been gathered in. But rather, this will occur under your very eyes, so that you all are assured that the food is being stored up already. I cry out that scarcity threatens not only your private homes but also the treasury of the temple, in such a way that *gladness*—nay, rather, universal comfort—will go to ruin; and of course, the *beasts of burden* will not provide the nourishment when the crops have been taken away, because to these very ones both the mountains that have been grazed down and the consumption of the green plants will announce the calamity. Certainly the prophet shows that he himself is struck by these evils that are approaching. For either it has an effect as an indication of spiritual meanings that extend themselves far beyond the bodily ones, or as a solemn procession, as we said, that provokes the emotion of fear in the hearts of the people. Therefore, it is as if he took up the appearance of an inquirer when he said, *Why did the beast groan, why did the herds of cattle bellow?* so that on the part of the one replying it might be suggested, *Because there is no pasture for them, but even the flocks of sheep have perished.*

[22]Cf. Joel 1:4.

[23]Ps 78:65-66.

1:19-20[24]

Accordingly, since insufferable affliction encompasses me on every side, I lift up my hands, my voice, and my prayers to you, the one Lord. Prostrate in soul and body, I entreat you to look on the disasters of the land, you who are sometimes propitious, sometimes mild. For behold, the flames have destroyed *the beautiful places of the desert*. Of course, in this passage the attentive hearer may ask, what beauty of fields will be proclaimed with respect to deserts, which this recent and invidious conflagration has destroyed, especially since nowhere has any complaint about fire preceded? Accordingly, the coherence of the reading shows that here he calls the forests putting forth leaves and the glad pastures *the*

[24]Julian provides no lemma. To facilitate comprehension of his commentary, I will supply Jerome's lemma for Joel 1:19-20: "To you, O Lord, I will cry out, because fire has devoured the beautiful places of the desert, and the flame has set every tree of the region on fire. But even the beasts of the field, like ground thirsting for rain, have looked to you, for the springs of water have dried up, and fire has devoured the beautiful places of the desert."

beauty of the fields. But the reason he has praised the pleasant rural places, not of the tilled fields but of the desert, is because he had mentioned the flocks and the herds. Since those are gladdened by the groves and the pastures, surely when these have been marred by some calamity, those also are subjected to destruction. But he recorded *fire* in view of the devastation that the locust and the young locust inflicted, just as we also read in the psalm: "He gave them hail for rain, a burning fire in their land. And he struck their vineyards and their fig trees, and he broke in pieces all the trees of their country."[25] Accordingly, the locust and the young locust so devoured the greenness of all the forests and the grass that they do not seem to have been eaten but burned up. Consequently, even the wild beasts have fallen into the perils of famine. And things that have been taught by natural governance look up to you alone, that you may be appeased and may bring a remedy to the peril. Indeed, the sacred songs bear witness with truth and sweetness: "All things wait for you to give them food in season. What you give to them they shall gather up; when you open your hand, they shall all be filled with delight. But if you turn away your face, they shall be troubled. You shall take away their breath, and they shall fail, and shall return to their dust."[26] Thus, accordingly, the herds of wild beasts also request from you a remedy, even if they lack clear voices. Yet they do so with different sounds from their throats, just as the level areas of the lands that are fit for the seeds they have received wait for either dew or rain, by which sprouts are produced. But if you examine this closely, dear listener of ours, you will see that importance inheres in this example. For he has compared the thirst of living creatures with the natural longing of the elements, which is by all means stronger by far. But let us consider the rest as well.

[25]Ps 105:32-33.

[26]Ps 104:27-29.

[Chapter 2]

2:1-2 Sound the trumpet in Zion, howl on my holy mountain, let all the inhabitants of the land tremble, because the day of the Lord will come, because it is near: a day of darkness and gloom, a day of cloud and whirlwind, as the morning spread on the mountains.

Since the time of the great devastation draws near, he says, let the inhabitants of the city and the fields assemble, and with prayers and weeping let them anticipate the time of the announced calamity. If I were able to explain their bitterness by speaking before the very experiences of the events, it seems to me that the *darkness* of the torments will be of such nature that it is as if it came to pass that the blackness were doubled, as when the *gloom* and mists make the night more intense. Or rather, imagine you were to combine this darkness with dense *clouds* and *whirlwinds*, so that, when the comfort of the stars has been completely excluded, terror gleams forth through the blind air of the thunderbolts. Yet these representations are concerned to point out solely the quality of the evil, whose quantity the bitterness increases in a greater measure. For the violence of the evil of which we are speaking will fill up all the spaces of our country, as if the boundary limits were taken down and a bright *morning* (that is, a red dawn) will spread out at once on all the *mountains* and hills. Therefore, he compared the single event both to the night and to the light, not to bring in some opposite thing but to express both its enlargement and bitterness with a diversity of metaphors. "A numerous and strong people; the like to it has not been from the beginning, nor shall be after it even to the years of generation and generation."[27] He shows by the progression of the speech that

[27]Joel 2:2 (left out of the lemma).

the narrative that has been undertaken concerns locusts rather than enemies. For the very swarm of locusts and young locusts whose invasion is represented as having brought with it a manifold destruction, now he has compared to a roaring army that is well armed.[28] Surely he would not have been able to introduce this as a comparison if the description that had been undertaken concerned soldiers. Therefore, he proceeds to display the effects of the evil, I say, through its different aspects, and he speaks of the kind of "face of the lands" he found when it came, what sort it left behind when it departed.[29] The times of our ancestors saw nothing like this, he says; none of our posterity will see the like.

2:3 Before the face thereof a devouring fire, and behind it a burning flame; the land is like a garden of pleasure before it, and behind it a desolate wilderness; neither is there any one who can escape it.

When he said, *Before the face* (faciem) *thereof,* he wished to point out the very assault of the locusts. Surely he did not mean that some sort of fiery conflagration preceded the appearance (*faciem*) of the locusts, and then afterward they destroyed the burned-out countryside. But he says, the assault devastated their entire country in such a way that it was as if nothing less than fire had consumed it. Now the reason he proclaims that the fire is vigorous both before and after is because the efficacy of the blaze is unproven. Yet fire is accustomed to devour quickly and wholly everything that is light, like foliage, straw, chaff, with its crackling and flying flames, but the lingering of the fire overcomes all the more the things that have more firmness of substance. But by skillfully preserving the orderly intensification, after he compared the locust to fire, he says that the country that was destroyed could be compared to pleasant and well-watered lands: *the land is like a garden of pleasure before it, and behind it a desolate wilderness, neither is there any one that can escape it.* Thus, at that time surely the violence of the assaulting evil becomes clear, since it consumed those things that had been exceedingly pleasant.

2:4-11 The appearance of them is as the appearance of horses, and they shall run like horsemen. They shall leap like the noise of chariots on the tops of mountains, like the noise of a flame of fire devouring the stubble, as a strong people prepared to battle. At their presence the people shall be in grievous pains; all faces shall be made like a kettle. They shall run like valiant men, like men of war they shall scale the wall; a man shall march on his ways, and they shall not turn aside from their paths. No one shall press on his brother; they shall walk everyone in his footpath. But they shall even fall through the windows and shall take no harm. They shall enter into the city, they shall run on the wall, they shall climb up the houses, they shall come in at the windows as a thief. At their presence the earth has trembled, the heavens are moved, the sun and moon are darkened, and the stars have withdrawn their shining. And the Lord has uttered his voice before the face of his army, for his camps are exceedingly great, for they are strong and execute his words. For the day of the Lord is great and very terrible, and who shall withstand it?

A little earlier I called to mind that with the progression of the speech he was unfolding the established narrative more and more, not concerning armed battle lines (as some have conjectured), but literally concerning young

[28]Cf. Joel 2:4-9; Jerome, *Commentary on Joel* 2:1-11 (ACT 2:276).
[29]Cf. Joel 2:3.

locusts and locusts.[30] And so he has assembled similes of armed soldiers and horsemen so that their power and effect might be expressed. He has followed not merely the outward display of narrating this but also the erudition of making comparisons, as he splendidly and also elegantly unfolded what he had perceived. He does this obviously by comparing the very course of the invading locusts to the going about of four-legged animals and by comparing the *noise* to that crackling that *fire* is accustomed to make among *stubble*. Since he has seen these images fittingly adopted, he has very deliberately lingered on them. And he not only compared the harsh noise and the raids with fires and cavalry, but he intentionally made the following point as well, that they came with a battle line that was orderly and in lockstep, not one that was scattered. He indicated clearly that certain armies went under banners and commanders, because the narrative required this for the sake of terror. He says, *As a people prepared to battle, at their presence the people shall be in grievous pains, all faces shall be* rendered *like a kettle*. He says, Even the military training arranges the power of the forces so that they do not resemble marauders and highway robbers. Rather, they are organized into squadrons and battle lines. They advance to war with constant hearts and ranks. Before the occurrence of the conflict, enemies are easily shaken by fear, so that their *faces* generally grow completely pale due to their approaching death. If this is so, he says, the armies of our nation will not be strong enough to endure the very *appearance* of the disaster that is breaking in. But just like the *kettle*, which smoke has stained, they not only will grow pale but also will turn completely black. For neither the aid of physical strength in the field nor of walls in their cities will secure help for them. If indeed armies of the locusts will hasten forth, which I declare are about to come, complying with their duty of laying things waste, like the most warlike of men, whithersoever indignation or passion will have summoned, they not only will lay waste the fields but also will enter within the houses of the cities. There will be no multitude of resisters who create a hindrance, no obstacle to delay the attackers; the conquering swarm will advance along the *footpaths* unobstructed. For this is what he says: *No one shall press on his brother, they shall walk everyone in his footpath. But they shall even fall through the windows, and shall take no harm*. He says, Not only will they attack the temples of the cities, as if content with causing public fear, but they will enter into the interiors of private homes, like robbers. And thus deadly anxiety will seize[31] all the inhabitants of that region, so that to them the *heavens* will appear to be *moved* and the *earth* to quake, the stars to remove their own *shining*, and the *sun and moon* to be covered with a tangible *darkness*. Now we should not be in doubt that all these things will come with so great a mass of evils, since the very one who is the all-powerful leader will announce these columns, and he is making use of such an army for the destruction of the guilty. And he raises aloft the sign of the command by which they are roused, and he furnishes strength to them, with which they execute the judgment. *For the day of the Lord is great*, and it is to be feared by the very management and display of vengeance. Its first appearance shows that its overwhelming ruin cannot be endured.

Now although by the very din of their severity they are effective for edification, we can nevertheless transfer these complaints of blessed Joel, who is speaking in a public assembly of the people, by means of a loftier understanding, and make them figurations of souls. Thus, through the portrayal of the catastrophes that he announces are threatening

[30]See Joel 1:4.

[31]Reading *occupabit* for CCSL's *accupabit*.

all the regions for the sake of punishing sinners, one may believe that he has signified the filthiness of criminal minds. For the critical discernment of a wise person does not assess those whom he sees subjugated to tribulations as more wretched than those subjugated to vices. Based on this principle, at one time out of pity, at another time indignant, he accused the state of a most profane nation that abstained from absolutely no forms of wickedness. At first he declares that he neither remembers what has been done nor confides in what will be done, since he sees that these are things that have happened in his own times. That is, by the mass of paltry little grubs, and things that hardly seem capable of being named living creatures, so much violence has been brought in like waves (which follow one another uninterruptedly) that they have destroyed everything prepared in the region and the look of it. For "that which the palmerworm has left, the locust has eaten, and that which the locust has left, the young locust has eaten, and that which the young locust has left, the mildew has destroyed."[32] If, therefore, you examine human souls judiciously and inspect vices that have not yet been chastised, you will assuredly discover such a state in them as the pitiful plague had brought to these regions. There were indeed four forms of corruption that he inflicted—namely, the palmerworm, the locust, the young locust, and the mildew. They bring injuries that are linked to each other by a certain affinity. We can suitably apply these to those four emotions of the soul—namely, to hope, joy, fear, and grief.[33] For all evils and diverse injuries are produced from these four overflowing affections, but from one source—namely, of the motion by which we are influenced. But we should designate these things with such an agreement that we ascribe to hope and joy the palmerworm, which pursues only the green leaves of the trees, and the locust, which advances more with leaps than steps, doubtless with some sort of faulty dancing from below. But on the other hand, we distinguish as fear and sorrow the young locust and the mildew, which devours by settling on and cleaving, without any energetic effort. Therefore, when we see anyone sinning through those things that are called joyful things, as one estranged from modesty and shame, after he has ruined the adornments of moral integrity, and even yielding his inheritance and livelihood to shameful acts, it will be permissible for us to exclaim, "That which the palmerworm has left, the locust has eaten."[34] But suppose, on the other hand, [we see] someone else so enslaved to sloth that he reckons the glory of freedom as nothing. Instead he exults without a mantle of serious honor, if the depravity of some superior even detects him desiring to lie concealed. He even demands a helper or attendant to his crimes, or else he may threaten to say no to the one who is attempting something evil or some harmful thing, and immediately you see that he will be enslaved to even greater crimes than you had thought. If that happens, say with the prophet, "That which the locust has left, the young locust has eaten, and that which the young locust has left, the mildew has destroyed."[35] And so if we keenly focus our vision according to this principle, we take offense at the entire life of mortals, in various matters, to be sure, but in nearly all their pursuits and times, when we fittingly use these exclamations of the prophet. If indeed it is accomplished by such a multiplication of vices, that not only meadows and sprouts, as if the excellence of nature perished, but even the very fruit trees and hardwoods were ruined, even of the vines and olive trees and fig trees, which of

[32]Joel 1:4.
[33]Cf. Jerome, *Commentary on Joel* 1:4 (ACT 2:265-66); *Commentary on Zechariah* 1:18-21 (ACT 2:12); Virgil, *Aeneid* 6.733.
[34]Joel 1:4.
[35]Joel 1:4.

course had been established for the services of the country. I say, therefore, when you see even those who have been constituted with the Christian name and who rejoice in the reception of the mysteries—yet who have no concern for the virtues, or rather, who are attendants of the altar itself by outward display only and are enslaved to luxury—you should cry out pitifully and indignantly, "It has laid waste my vineyard and has pulled off the bark from my fig tree; stripping it bare, it has uncovered it and has cast it away; its branches have been made white."[36] "The wine is confounded, the oil has languished. The farmers are ashamed . . . because the harvest of the field has perished."[37] But this situation of the churches, the kind we see especially in this storm, kindles that anger of God at which the prophet trembled—that is, "The day of the Lord is great and very terrible, and who shall withstand it?"[38] But let us hear by what counsel he is betrayed, who cannot endure it.

2:12-14 Now, therefore, says the Lord, Turn to me with all your heart, in fasting, and in weeping, and in mourning. And rend your hearts, and not your garments, and turn to the Lord your God, for he is gracious and merciful, patient and rich in mercy. Who knows if he will turn and forgive, and leave a blessing behind him and a sacrifice and libation to the Lord our God?

You then who behold the display of severity with which the eternal Lord is accompanied as he comes forth for vengeance, keep your spirits from desperation, come to have a better hope, know that he has not terrified out of the desire to rage but to spare. For he has sounded forth with such a multifaceted din of the punishment that has been set in motion, not as one who is forgetful of his special *graciousness,* but in order to stir up the disposition of fear in you. After all, he addresses you with the very voice of reality so that you may at least bring your sick hearts to him, bandage your internal wounds with his medicine—that you may carry out not merely the outward appearance of mourners but their entire disposition, and may rend your *hearts* rather than your *garments.* He has given this warning both abundantly and even elegantly. Thus, since it is the custom of mourners to tear their garments from their chests, he warned them too, as if they should apply their hands and press them deeper into their chests, to rend not only their clothing but their very hearts, if possible. He found a word most suitable for the thing he was discussing: *Rend your hearts, and not your garments.* Surely this rending seems to point beyond the striving of the mourner to the discrimination of good and evil too, or a separation from shameful acts by which they had defiled themselves by mingling in them. Therefore, change your purpose for the better, and weep over those things that you previously did evilly, that there might be a reason for the *gracious and merciful Lord,* who is "eminent over evil,"[39] to freely grant abatement from this disaster, which he calls *evil,* if he sees that those whom he had terrified by his threat have repented. But by scriptural custom he has adopted the outward appearance of one who is in doubt, as it were, when he says, *Who knows if he will turn and forgive, and leave a blessing behind him?* Surely this is inserted out of respect for the judge. He wants them to be so terrified of him that they fear even the things that are safe. The reason he says *and leave a blessing behind him* is because he had said earlier that the violence of the want that was to be inflicted by the ravaging locusts was so great that after their passage the land would

[36]Joel 1:7; cf. Joel 1:10, 11.
[37]Joel 1:10-11.
[38]Joel 2:11.

[39]The phrase was not recorded in Julian's lemma for Joel 2:13 but is found in Jerome's.

remain like desolate wilderness.[40] Therefore, he says now, offer tears, offer groans; the violence of the punishment that has been announced will perhaps be moderated by such sacrifices, so that if he has diminished your abundance, he might not take away also the sustenance. The words *And leave a blessing behind him, a sacrifice and libation to the Lord our God* correspond in an ordered fashion to the things said previously. For earlier he had said that the greatness of the want will reach so far that sacrifice and libation would perish from the house of the Lord.[41] And so, here, when he laid claim to the hope of consolation to those who had been corrected and were repenting, he added that he would leave behind a blessing, which would serve the libations of the altar.

2:15-17 Blow the trumpet in Zion, sanctify a fast, call an assembly. Gather together the people, sanctify the church, unite the old men, gather together the little ones and them that suck at the breasts. Let the bridegroom go forth from his bed, and the bride out of her chamber. Between the vestibule and the altar, the priests, God's ministers, shall weep and shall say, Spare your people, O Lord, and do not give your inheritance to reproach, that the nations should rule over them. Why do they say among the peoples, Where is their God?

It is customary in the prophets that in short digressions they do not solicitously preserve the tenses or kinds of words that are said, but they are content with having satisfied the meaning and make use of common expressions. Thus, even now when he said in the imperative mood, *Let the bridegroom go forth from his bed, the bride out of her chamber,* he added, *Between the vestibule and the altar the priests shall weep,* instead of saying, "Let the priests weep." For he was content with the duty of a censor; he was not careful about moods. Or else, in order to reveal that his exhortation was effective, he said that they *shall* take care of the matter, because he had commanded them to do it. And so he says, *Between the vestibule and the altar,* sound forth the assemblies of the lamenters; and especially you *priests,* to whom the overseeing of the sacred rites has been assigned, wet your faces with weeping and shout out: *Spare your people, O Lord,* and do not allow those whom you have decreed to possess by hereditary right now to become hated and scorned by the nations by whom we are surrounded. And, if nothing else, at least let that cast a favorable vote for us in the presence of your clemency, for we cannot perish without having affronted you. Therefore, with respect to us whom you willed to be believed to be and to be called your servants and sons, not only by creation but also by adoption, do not allow the nations to say, *Where is their God?*—that is, Where is their defender, in whom they were accustomed to rejoice? After he explained this in his office as teacher, with the confidence of one prophesying uninterruptedly, he promises that the prayers of the people were effectual and that the Lord of the universe was aroused by jealousy (*zelo*), as it were, to take up a defense of the faithful.

2:18 The Lord has been zealous (*zelatus*) for his land; he has spared his people.

He says, Looking on it, he has kept it from taking part in despair over its proper worth, lest the nation that was reckoned specially with his name should perish, as though lacking a defender, and he has filled it with hope of joy. From his response, then, it is added,

2:19-20 Behold, I will send you corn, wine, and oil, and you shall be filled with them. And I will no more make you a reproach

[40] Cf. Joel 2:3.
[41] Cf. Joel 1:13.

among the nations. And I will remove far off from you the one from the north. And I will drive him into an unpassable and deserted land; with his face toward the eastern sea, his back toward the last sea; and his stench shall ascend, and his rottenness shall go up.

To be sure, blessed Jeremiah and the other prophets say that the Assyrians and Chaldeans will come from the north.[42] Here too then, the Assyrian could be understood, except that as I have noted earlier,[43] in accordance with what he had enacted in Deuteronomy, he fixed other plagues as well to be inflicted on the profaned people.[44] Consequently, according to the established order, we should understand the locusts and young locusts. The Lord promises to remove them once he has been placated. He added this, of course, for the favor and sweetness of freedom, because he commanded those armies to die in the desert, lest the great *stench* caused by the corpses beget disease for the inhabitants. Therefore, the *stench* and *rottenness* will rise up from there "because he acted arrogantly."[45] Now when he declares that he *acted arrogantly*, he has not expressed the vice of the mind but the extent of the calamity.

2:21-23 Fear not, O land; exult, be glad, for the Lord has done great things. Fear not, ye animals of the country, for the beautiful places of the desert have sprouted, for the tree has brought forth its fruit, the fig tree and the vine have yielded their virtue. And you, O sons of Zion, exult and be glad in the Lord your God, because he has given you a teacher of justice.[46]

It is contextually coherent that the words are directed to the entire *country*, as it were, so that the return of fertility may be promised to the one to whom devastation had been announced. And the speech runs through these same outward forms[47] by which it had also passed under the adversity. And so he says that the mountains will be clothed with pastures, a leafy appearance will return to the forests, figs and vines will offer the gifts of their fruitfulness. For this is what he has called their *virtue*. Since all these things are delivered up for the enjoyment of human beings, he has fittingly added, *And you, O sons of Zion, exult and be glad in the Lord your God, because he has given you a teacher of justice*. He has entirely crowned the preceding warnings with a full pronouncement of instruction. He has signified the joys that the people ought to experience after the expulsion of the afflictions and the very much desired successes of prosperity.[48] But from which respect in particular? Surely it is not because they sought the things that were to be enjoyed, but because they had found the *teacher of justice*. He says, *And you, O sons of Zion, exult and be glad in the Lord your God, because he has given you a teacher of justice*. He is indeed merciful, he says. He is indeed one who drives out sadness and brings in favorable things with the singular virtue of bringing help. But you, O my people, ought to rejoice especially in him by whom you surpass the other nations—namely, because you have received the teachers of a just way of life, by whose instruction you have lived modestly and blessedly. This sort of thing is said in another prophet: "We are blessed Israel, because the things that are pleasing to God, are made known to us."[49]

---

[42]Cf. Is 14:13, 31; 41:25; 43:6; 49:12; Jer 1:14-15; 4:6; 6:1; 10:22; Jerome, *Commentary on Joel* 2:18-20 (ACT 2:283).

[43]See under Joel 1:4.

[44]Cf. Deut 28:38-39, 42.

[45]Joel 2:20.

[46]Jerome's version, "he has given you a teacher of justice," does not agree with the LXX, which reads "food of justice." The RSV renders "he has given the early rain for your vindication."

[47]*Species*. J. H. Baxter, "Notes on the Latin of Julian of Eclanum," *ALMA* 21 (1951): 49, says that Julian uses this word in the unusual rhetorical sense of "images, illustrations, pictures."

[48]Cf. Jerome, *Commentary on Joel* 2:21-27 (ACT 2:285).

[49]Bar 4:4.

2:24-25 And I will make the early (*matutinum*) and the latter rain to come down to you in the beginning. And the floors shall be filled with wheat, and the presses shall overflow with wine and oil. I will restore to you the years, which the locust, the young locust, the mildew, and the palmerworm have eaten. My great strength that I sent on you.

By diverse images he describes what he began, and he portrays the coming change from sadness into joy. Therefore, when he is about to promise fruitfulness, he announces the falling of the early and late rain, saying, *He will make the early and the latter rain to come down to you in the beginning.* The Septuagint did not translate this *in the beginning*, but "as from the beginning." Thus, they made the sense to be that when the offenses are removed, due to which the occasion of the yearly rains was upset, so to speak, the year would return to its own custom, so that due to the diversity of seeds, the fields would be watered either by *early* or *late* rain showers. These, of course, will generate such great fruitfulness that both your *floors* and your jars would be overwhelmed. Therefore, his words *the early and the latter rain to come down to you in the beginning* can be understood in such a way that he appears to have indicated the order of favorable conditions. And let there not be any opposition in the ideas, as if somehow even the rain that is called *late* is said to be *in the beginning.* But [this is] in order to say that the rains will precede the fruitfulness of the crops. And the sense is, I will send the first rain, and later the joy of the crops will follow When this fills their farmers with joys and strength, it will infuse forgetfulness of the previous want and will proceed to blot out the traces of the affliction. Thus, not only would the trouble of scarcity be laid to rest, but even the losses that had preceded would be made good. For this is what he has said: *I will restore to you the years, which the locust has eaten.* Surely he does not mean that the moments of time would be restored, but the fruitfulness of the fields. One should also take note that God has called the palmerworm and the locust his own *great strength.*[50] Surely this is not because worms are related in any fashion to the eternal power of God, but because by their service and devastation in the affliction of things it carried out the work of revenge. Therefore, the very littleness of the palmerworms and locusts points to the power of the Creator and avenger. When he has decreed to wipe out the peoples, he uses neither the teeth nor venom of any wild beasts, but he devours what were wealthy kingdoms a little while before by means of the young locust and mildew. And the reason it is called the *power of God* is because it carries out his sentence, like an eager lictor.[51]

2:26-27 And you shall eat and shall be filled, and you shall praise the name of the Lord your God, who has done marvelous things with you, and my people shall not be confounded forever. And you shall know that in the midst of Israel I am the Lord your God, and there is none besides, and my people shall not be confounded forever.

He says this when the longed-for fertility erases the losses of those times. It indeed comes from the prophetic fashion that as often as he promises things that are joyful, so too he announces that they will remain forever. We should understand this either as conditional up to a point, which is frequent in the

[50]Cf. Jerome, *Commentary on Joel* 2:21-27 (ACT 2:285).

[51]According to Lewis & Short's *A Latin Dictionary* (http://logeion.uchicago.edu/lexidium), lictors were attendants granted to magistrates as a sign of official dignity, who bore a bundle of rods, from which an axe projected. Their duty was to walk before the magistrate in a line, one after the other, to call out to the people to make way and to remind them of paying their respects to him. They had also to execute sentences of judgment, to bind criminals to a stake, to scourge them, and to behead them. Cf. Livy, 1.26; 8.7; 38; 26.16.

Scriptures—that is, *if* they persevere in pursuing moral goodness, *then* too the prosperous conditions will continue—or else he says this because it is always part of the prophet's function to add something from the aspect of what he is wishing for. But a third meaning can also be brought in to which, of course, the progression of the speech itself alludes. For he had already said, "O sons of Zion, exult and be glad in the Lord your God, because he has given you a teacher of justice."[52] Although this could be understood in a variety of ways, yet as far as the reckoning of the times is concerned, he seems to be pointing to Hezekiah in particular. He is the one whom the credibility of the yearly chronicles reveals was seething with great zeal for the worship of God.[53] And as the prophet Isaiah in particular shows, the persona of this king seems to have been chosen to signify greater matters.[54] Therefore, we should apply the things that were done by Hezekiah to the affairs of our Redeemer. Thus, though they were indeed fulfilled somewhat in that time, yet under the gospel they seem to have acquired vast surpluses. For he is the true "teacher of justice,"[55] "in whom all the treasures of wisdom and knowledge are hidden."[56] He was "handed over for our transgressions and was raised for our justification,"[57] so that "having been justified freely through his grace, through the redemption which is in Christ Jesus,"[58] we were also set free[59] from ancient errors and were put under the sun of justice.[60] And with respect to matters of salvation, he drove away all the past scarcity by a renewed fertility and filled us with teaching in abundance, as the gospel promises: "Seek first the kingdom of God and his justice, and all these things shall be assigned and added unto you."[61] And so the *people* of his possession[62] *will not be confounded forever,* who rely on the pronouncement of the Redeemer: "Behold I am with you all the days until the consummation of the age."[63] Well then, with that commander living in their midst, the armies of the faithful always remain secure and courageous, and whatever adversities they endure in combat, they perceive these things as rendered obsolete by the good fortunes that have succeeded, so that they seem to result merely in the commendation of the joyful things.

2:28-31[64] And it shall come to pass after this, [that] I will pour out my spirit on all flesh, and your sons and your daughters shall prophesy, your old men shall dream dreams, and your young men shall see visions. Moreover, on [my] servants and handmaids in those days I will pour forth my spirit.

Blessed Peter recalled this passage in the Acts of the Apostles, saying that this prophecy was fulfilled at that time, when the Holy Spirit came down into the apostles.[65] Hence, one should observe that from the context of the prophet's speech the apostle adopted this alone that corresponded to his own time—namely, *I will pour out my spirit on all flesh, and your sons and your daughters shall prophesy.* For since the apostles had miraculously attained the knowledge of tongues,[66] the teacher of the church showed that this *outpouring* of the *Spirit* was

[52]Joel 2:23 Vulgate.
[53]Cf. 2 Kings 18:3-7.
[54]Cf. Is 1:27-28; 4:2-6; 7:14-25; 9:6-7; 10:12; 11:1-6, 10-16; 28:5-6; 31:4-5; 32:1-3; 33:1-6; 37–38.
[55]Joel 2:23 Vulgate.
[56]Col 2:3.
[57]Rom 4:25.
[58]Rom 3:24.
[59]Cf. Rom 6:18.
[60]Cf. Mal 4:2.
[61]Mt 6:33.
[62]Cf. 1 Pet 2:9.
[63]Mt 28:20.
[64]In the Hebrew these verses are now numbered 3:1-4.
[65]Cf. Acts 2:17-21; Jerome, *Commentary on Joel* 2:28-32 (ACT 2:287).
[66]Cf. Acts 2:4-8.

foretold, and he called the knowledge of tongues *prophecy*. Although he [Peter] discussed these things not concerning future mysteries but about the recent ones of the Lord's incarnation, yet it happened none other than by the power of the Holy Spirit. But he was not content with having merely mentioned the gifts; he adds too those things that concerned the fearful display—that is, "And I will show wonders in heaven and in earth, blood and fire, and smoky vapor. The sun shall be turned into darkness, and the moon into blood, before the great and dreadful day of the Lord comes. And everyone that shall call on the name of the Lord shall be saved."[67] And so he hastens to persuade by this whole continuation that, when *the day of the Lord comes* (that is, the time of final judgment), since it will come with such great power and uproar that the framework itself will dissolve as if burned,[68] when the stars shake and are struck down,[69] it would be faith alone that protects the throngs of the pious when the world collapses. They need to believe in the gospel if they desire to attain salvation.[70] Since, therefore, blessed Peter had not taken up the concern to expound the prophet but to preach the gospel, he seized hold only of those statements as far as it suited him. Surely he did not thereby repeal that explanation of the prophet's work that the context creates. The reason we offer this brief admonition is so that the audacity of those may be renounced who recklessly and ignorantly contend that the prophet had indicated solely that time about which the apostle Peter preached. For, I say, the entire context of the work is shown to embrace, first of all, the times of the Jewish people, but secondly, ours, as a finishing touch, as it were. Therefore, just as it does not interfere with the prophet's meaning to apply what the whole book describes as Jewish history to the situation of the gospel, so also, or rather, far more, at least with the well-educated reader, it is never allowed to deny the credibility that is suitable to the context, if some prophecy can be applied to the situation of believers from the nations too.

Therefore, let us see how the uninterrupted course, as it were, of the historical explanation proceeds. We gather, of course, that saint Joel prophesied under blessed Hezekiah.[71] Grave battles and enormous miracles attended the lifespan of this king.[72] But among the other disasters by which we read that the ten tribes were also afflicted up to their removal, several cities from the allotments of Judah and Benjamin also fell.[73] We understand that the Jews were also harassed by disease and scarcity. After all, when Rabshakeh addressed the besieged people and threatened destruction unless they immediately surrendered to the Assyrian king, he promises that they must put up with the evils of hunger and thirst.[74] And for this reason, then, the merciful Lord promises them that when the grievous things are changed into joys, the losses of scarcity too would be made good. But let us hear how he made the succession of events and times: *I will pour out my spirit on all flesh, and your sons and your daughters shall prophesy, your old men shall dream dreams, and your young men shall see visions. Moreover, upon [my] servants and handmaids in those days I will pour forth my spirit, and I will show wonders in heaven above.* The promise is furnished, of course, from the prophet's mouth: for after he ran through the advantages of the present life, he added spiritual markers in which assuredly the people of God especially boasted. And so, it is contextually coherent that he promises them physical goods beyond these things, as we have said, also that they would grasp hold of the

[67]Joel 2:30-32.
[68]Cf. 2 Pet 3:10-12.
[69]Cf. Mt 24:29.
[70]Cf. Mt 24:14.
[71]Cf. Hos 1:1; preface to Joel.
[72]Cf. 2 Kings 18:2; 2 Chron 32:1.
[73]Cf. 2 Kings 18:13.
[74]Cf. 2 Kings 18:27; 2 Chron 32:11.

trappings of revelations and would obtain an abundance of spiritual gifts. Therefore, his words *I will pour out my spirit on all flesh* signified both sexes and various time periods. After all, it follows, *Your sons and your daughters shall prophesy, your old men shall dream dreams, and your young men shall see visions*—namely, by various forms of revelation, they will see the things that are coming. *Moreover, upon [my] servants and handmaids I will pour forth my spirit*—that is, from these tokens of holiness, just as no age is excluded, neither is any condition that is thought worthless, but this holy outpouring will visit even the slaves, if they are found capable of such gifts. All these things are said to be fulfilled in the times of blessed Hezekiah, at least as a first stage, as it were.[75] For because he was compelled by assailing dangers into grave straits, and against the expectation of the neighboring nations he was defended by religion alone, therefore the prophet describes that very time as if with great ostentation and with a matching style, doubtless in order to express the power of God, by whose aid the city could have come forth from such a great deluge. No doubt it was in accordance with this meaning that the orderly speech of our prophet ran on. For in addition to the consolation of the returning abundance, he promised also the gifts of the Spirit (that is, the tokens of revelation) by which that people were uniquely shown to belong to God; and for that reason they ought to trust amid adversities, seeing that one who is dear to God and therefore also stands forth as precious could not perish as something worthless. But since the prophet himself testifies to what we speak of, we conclude that something had been shown even in dreams, as it were, in lesser and private oracles, which was effective in bringing comfort. Of course, on the occasion of this passage it seems that what we read in Deuteronomy needs to be set apart—that is, that we are not supposed to believe in dreams.[76] For how is it that dreams are now referred to as gifts of the Holy Spirit, if in that passage trust in them is believed to have been completely renounced? Whence it appears that a rational distinction needs to be employed, since both [scriptural] pronouncements are of equal authority and, if the subject matter of the person dreaming coincides, so that, just as the one case is to be respected on account of merits, so the other should be esteemed on account of its own importance, we should understand that some support was attained through the dreams. But if there is no testimony present that either the time or the person merits, then the apparitions of the dreamers are to be rejected by the authority of the law.

But let us hear those things that we already said were added by him proudly. He says, *I will show wonders in heaven and in earth, blood, and fire, and vapor of smoke. The sun shall be turned into darkness, and the moon into blood, before the great and dreadful day of the Lord comes. And it shall come to pass [that] everyone who shall call upon the name of the Lord shall be saved.* It is prophetic custom that as often as God is proclaimed as rising up either to fight or to avenge with indignation, the appearance of the heavens (*polorum*) is described as changed, and the very elements are portrayed as trembling. This is the sort of thing that is found in the writings of blessed David, who portrayed the encounter and appearance of the heavenly (*aetherii*) defender by saying, "There went up a smoke in his wrath, and a fire flamed from his face, coals were kindled by it. He bowed the heavens (*caelos*) and came down,"[77] and the rest. In this fashion, then, as we said, which comes from the custom of the law, even now the prophet, [who is set] under

[75]Cf. Is 37:30-32.

[76]Cf. Deut 13:1-5; 18:10.

[77]Ps 18:8-9.

the time of punishment about to be inflicted from heaven, speaks first of the elements being penetrated with fires, of stars being covered either with smoke or with the character of blood. He says this not because these things would be brought about just as they are said, but either because a display of this kind would be fitting for the director of the heavens, or because his judgment is brought into effect so easily that it is as if the cover of the universe and the movement of the elements were guiding it. For such great anxiety would at last seize the souls of the guilty ones, it would be as if the framework of the heavens were dissolving, and the moon turning to blood, the earth turning to ash, the stars turning black.[78] Therefore, what was taking place in the souls of the fearful is thus described as if it were happening to the very elements. For indeed that one final convulsion is believed to be inflicted either on the lands or on the stars—namely, at the very end of the world. But in that bit of the prophet that we are discussing, one must believe that such a disturbance occurred at the time, not to the sky and lands (as I said earlier), but only in the minds of the guilty ones. For let us trace out the succession of the story as well whose outward form and manner we have perceived.

Therefore, he proclaims that all those things which are read were fulfilled in the times of blessed Hezekiah. For when the ten tribes were already transferred to the fields of the Medes,[79] the Assyrian army rushed into the boundaries of Judah, and, while Sennacherib was besieging other cities, he directed a certain Rabshakeh to Jerusalem with a great portion of his troops.[80] As we began to say earlier,[81] using the Hebrew language in which he was skilled, he enticed the people to surrender. Those who were in charge of the walls began to request with money that he should speak in the Syrian language and not in Hebrew. Then Rabshakeh added the weight of the greatest dread, claiming that he had brought calamities and final destruction not to a few noblemen but to an entire nation, since it did not accept the empire of the Assyrians. So, crushed by these threats, both blessed Hezekiah and the rest of the very people turned to Isaiah the prophet with a full display of tears, and said, "The children have come to the birth, and there is no strength to bring forth."[82] This means they reached the point of having spiritual contractions, which women feel at the time of birth, because of the labor of bringing forth the child, when there is no strength left in the one giving birth. Therefore, Hezekiah and the Jews were placed in the fires of the threatening danger, and doubtless it seemed that *the sun and the moon were turned into darkness and blood, before the great and dreadful day of the Lord*—namely, the day that removed that mass of dreadful destruction from the Jewish people and by an unexpected miracle turned it against the Assyrians.[83] Hence he called the day of the Lord *great* and *dreadful*, not because it was sad to the faithful ones but because it was to be revered for the majesty of the work.

2:32 And it shall come to pass, that everyone who shall call on the name of the Lord shall be saved: for in mount Zion and in Jerusalem there shall be salvation.

In that mountain, I say, in which a little while before the wearing away of strength promised that there would be the least defense—in that city, I say, which, just as a weak mother had conceived her own people for liberty, as

[78]This line reads well rhetorically in the Latin: "ac si polorum machina solveretur atque luna sanguesceret, terra cineresceret, astra nigrescerent."

[79]Cf. 2 Kings 18:11-12.

[80]Cf. 2 Kings 18:13–19:37; Is 36–37.

[81]See under Joel 2:28-31.

[82]Is 37:3.

[83]Cf. 2 Kings 19:35; Is 37:36.

children brought forth for this world, or rather as a mother who lacks the strength to give birth and threatened certain destruction to her offspring—suddenly such a glorious defense has appeared that apart from it there was no certain deliverance.[84] *And it shall come to pass, [that] everyone who shall call upon the name of the Lord shall be saved: for in mount Zion and in Jerusalem there will be salvation, and in the remnant whom the Lord shall call.* But all these things, which were completed *summa cum laude* (with highest distinction) by God our defender, are shown to have been fulfilled more abundantly at the time of our Lord's incarnation in the spiritual gifts, so that these very miracles that came in advance in the days of the fathers seem not only to have had a historical meaning but also a prophetic force. For they were rendered effective for the signification of those things that happened a long time afterward in the ages to come. For thus at the time of the Lord's passion, when the author of life[85] entered upon the bitterest death, an unforeseen night took away the middle of the day. For it says, "from the sixth hour there was darkness until the ninth hour."[86] Thus, because with a black countenance the heavens laid aside the glory of unbegotten brilliance, it seemed to be showing regard for the duty of one either weeping or showing fear, because it did not wish to look on the outrage done to the Creator, or on the deed of the Jews, before *the great and dreadful day of the Lord comes*—namely, before the glory of the resurrection showed forth. Or else it refers to that day that our Lord interpreted in the Gospel, as it were, with a narration that is twofold.[87] For when he was fully communicating the signs of the end times, he first described the destruction of Jerusalem and the calamities with which the country of the Jews would be filled. Therefore, just as there he adjoined the end of the world to the destruction of Jerusalem, so also in the prophet that entire shaking of the elements and of the stars will be fully carried out at the end of the world. As blessed Peter says, this is when "the heavens shall pass away in flames with great violence, and the elements shall be melted with the heat of fire."[88] For at that time faith alone will shelter its own, *and everyone who shall call upon the name of the Lord shall be saved: for in mount Zion, and in Jerusalem there shall be salvation, as the Lord said, and in the remnants whom the Lord shall call.* He is speaking of heavenly Jerusalem, which is the mother of the devout. Everyone who will move to eternal joys will be reckoned among her citizenry; yet they are all called *the remnants* because "many are called, but few are chosen."[89] But let us also consider the rest.

[Chapter 3]

3:1-3[90] For behold, in those days, and in that time when I shall convert the captivity of Judah and Jerusalem, I will gather together all nations and will bring them down to the valley of Josaphat, and I will plead with them there for my people and for my inheritance Israel, whom they have scattered among the nations and have divided my land. And they have cast lots over my people; and the boy they have put in the brothel, and the girl they have sold for wine, that they might drink.

He has finished that digression of meaning, which had gone on at length, and returns to the times about which his prophecy had begun. And he tarries on those things that he perceives are to be fulfilled very soon, so that either by their testimony he confirms also the

[84] Cf. Is 37:32.
[85] Cf. Acts 3:15.
[86] Mt 27:45; cf. Mk 15:33.
[87] Cf. Mt 24–25; Mk 13; Lk 21.
[88] 2 Pet 3:10-12.
[89] Mt 20:16; 22:14.
[90] Verse 1 appears as 4:1 in the Hebrew.

credibility of those things, which he promised would come after a long time, or it is to show that he had not set aside the pursuit of providing counsel through that impulse that he had assumed of one who was prophesying. It is as if he were to say, Those things that one day are to come will rest on reasons of their own time, but now let us describe what impends and threatens. Certainly the ten tribes already departed, when the Assyrian transported them,[91] and the hostile army lays waste to the allotment of Judah as well. And no hope of strength remained, by which we could resist. Therefore, I declare that now the defender especially appears, and he drives away the captivity of his people (namely, of Judah), which now was seeming to have gaped, and what is more, after despairing of his salvation, he imparts the glory of revenge that is celebrated throughout the whole world. For when the Assyrian throng came together for the siege of Jerusalem, let us so make them subject to vengeance, he says, that they would seem not so much roused up for battle as brought before the judgment seat. Therefore, when I will have begun to set in motion the *pleading, in the valley of Josaphat* I will pay back to the Assyrians and to the different enemies what they deserve, so that the destruction introduced both ruins the princes and the people left behind are subjected to the evils of captivity, and they themselves would suffer the whims of those who traffic the children of my people, those who even sold them into slavery or disgrace. And they would sense what kinds they are before the fruits of stirred-up boldness, who on account of this suffer the most bitter dividers of their fields, because they recently spread through my fields.

3:4-8 But what have you to do with me, O Tyre, and Sidon, and all the coast of the Philistines (*Palaestinorum*)? Do you pay back vengeance on me and avenge yourselves on me? Very soon and speedily I will pay you back a recompense on your own head. For you have taken away my silver and gold, and my desirable and most beautiful things you have carried into your temples. And the children of Judah, and the children of Jerusalem you have sold to the children of the Greeks, that you might remove them far off from their own country. Behold, I will raise them up out of the place wherein you have sold them, and I will return your recompense on your own head. And I will sell your sons and your daughters by the hands of the children of Judah, and they shall sell them to the Sabeans, a nation far off, for the Lord has spoken it.

It was often indeed a trivial occasion that exposed the wickedness and hatred of the neighboring peoples who surrounded the Jews. For since they were not able to storm the Jews with their own strength, they joined themselves to the battle lines of more powerful enemies. A poem accuses this deed of theirs, saying, "The tent of the Idumeans, and the Ishmaelites, Moab, and the Aggarens, Gebal, and Ammon and Amalek, and the Philistines (*alienigenae*) with the inhabitants of Tyre. Yea, and the Assyrian also came with them; they have come to the aid of the sons of Lot."[92] Therefore, following this custom, the neighboring peoples had joined forces with the Assyrians to overthrow Zion. The rigid judgment of the divine speech was fit for them, and it is as if he is demanding from them the reason for such harm. But thereafter he responded on behalf of the conquered ones and the silent ones, lest perhaps they took up the remembrance of the past pain—namely, when they came forth from Egypt and entered the Promised Land under the leadership of Joshua son of Nun, and they occupied the land that

[91]Cf. 2 Kings 17:5-6; 18:9-12.

[92]Ps 83:6-8.

was handed over to them with certain dimensions. Therefore, he says, are you not preparing with a rebellious spirit that time of vengeance, and are you not striving, as it were, by the occasion that has been found to retake the occupied boundaries? But if a consideration of this kind roused you all, the invading vengeance will conquer your feebleness and profaneness. For not only will you not be able to change concerning the old decrees, but you will stay under the power of those whom you reckoned will be overpowered by your plots. But through different outward forms he recounts the evils of captivity, which are introduced doubtlessly on behalf of the whims of the attackers. And therefore when he said that they had taken away gold and silver by the covetousness of those plundering, he added, *And my desirable and most beautiful things you have carried into your temples,* so that he indicated either the rest of the furniture, obviously, or the different necklaces. You have even sold the children of the wretched people along with these decorations of their houses. In the bringing in of *recompense* you will feel what sort of sorrow this begets in bereaved parents. For when he punishes, whose judgments you incite to destruction, the time will come that not only do the Jews obtain the joys of the freedom but also they would feed on the pleasure of vengeance and sell your children not to the neighboring nations, from whom they may hope for a return, but to the peoples of *Saba,* whom pagan literature called Meroen.[93] All of this seems reasonably to have been fulfilled either immediately after the destruction of the Assyrians or after the return from the Babylonian captivity in the times of the Maccabees.[94] But one should note that not everything that was done in those times is plausibly applied to the spiritual understanding (that is, to the significance found under the gift of the gospel) as are those other things that we said a little earlier about the convulsion of the stars, about the greatness of the wonders, and about the outpouring of gifts—namely, that these things both happened in Joel's times and they are also believed to have been fulfilled more abundantly at the time of the Lord's passion, and they will be fulfilled at the final judgment. I say, therefore, Not everything that the prophet weaves into these things in this way is connected to a spiritual understanding. For beyond the literal meaning, what Tyrians or Sidonians, or what remaining *coasts of the Philistines* will we conjecture to be walking about who we imagine have sold the children of the faithful? Yet if they are said to have handed them over even for sale, whom they enticed to commit vices, how will we threaten them with the same *recompense*—namely, that we wholly deliver over their children once more to Sabean merchants? Therefore, that rule of understanding needs to be retained, that when an established speech runs on in its simple, uninterrupted course, those things that agree with the prophecy that are also able to fit with future mysteries sometimes sound forth in the midst by means of digressions. But on the other hand, when this function is accomplished, the subject is led to the main point of its own time, and it proceeds with contextual coherence, either by threats or exhortations. Whence blessed Joel also, after he pointed out the things to come even in the last ages by the impulse of his prophesying (but briefly), he returns to the reckoning of his own time. He threatened destruction for the neighboring enemies and proceeds to unfold those joys, which he already perceived to be drawing near. Thus, they should place their trust in the things to come after a long time, which he announces as being exhibited very soon, and he inspires those for whom he is preparing consolation to grasp hold of the delight

[93]I have not been able to determine what Meroen refers to. Based on PL 21, the CCSL cites Josephus, *Ant.* II, 249 = II, 9, 2.

[94]Cf. Julian, *Commentary on Amos* 1:11-12. This goes against Jerome's interpretation, *Commentary on Joel* 3:1-3 (ACT 2:291).

beforehand. But he substitutes a solemn procession, as he had taught, by the things that are to be announced.

3:9-12 Shout this among the nations, sanctify war, rouse up the strong. Let all the men of war come up. Cut your ploughshares into swords, and your spades into spears. Let the weak say, I am strong. Break forth and come, all ye nations, from around, and gather yourselves together; there will he cause all your strong ones to fall down. Let them arise, and let the nations come up into the valley of Josaphat.

By the image of this exhortation he has expressed the violence of the successive disclosure, with what great desire for war they were coming up to destroy Judah. Every tiller of fields, he says, has taken hold of weapons. They have turned sickles into *swords,* and plowshares into javelins. Some likewise, though declining the business of war, whether on account of weakness of the body or the disadvantage of old age, nevertheless they spontaneously ran to the battles—that is, in advance of the throngs of military forces, whom both the Assyrian prince of war and the rest of the neighboring little enemies were enticing. They supposed that they would obtain an indubitable victory. In the end, of course, you will learn the profound plan of our defender! For he says while all your throng is coming together to the *valley of Josaphat* (that is, to the siege of Jerusalem) with a haughty and savage spirit, at that time a just destruction will exact a payback on you. And since you have thus directed insults against me, just as you were accustomed to cast spears at those in the way, thence "you all will tremble"[95]—that is, you will experience destruction from a source that you were by no means able to detect. That is, no battles lines will labor to bring in their banners against you, and no shouting of fighters will sound forth, but you will all collapse in a single night, when the angel strikes.[96] And as if incapable of a great battle, with a certain scorn and derision, the formerly pleasant nocturnal rest will hand over the ones who are caught to a never-ending slumber.

3:14-16 Peoples, peoples in the valley of destruction, for the day of the Lord is near in the valley of destruction. The sun and the moon are darkened, and the stars have withdrawn their shining. And the Lord shall roar out of Zion, and utter his voice from Jerusalem; and the heavens and the earth shall be moved, and the Lord [shall be] the hope of his people, and the strength of the children of Israel.

Fitly, he says, the valley of Josaphat[97] is called the place of *destruction,* for the enemies imagined that the destruction of the Jews would take place there; but because profane hope forsook them, and the judgment of revenge was directed against themselves, this valley will indeed be called that of *destruction,* but of the Assyrian destruction. When the enemy forces had first assembled at this valley, such great anxiety and fearfulness spread through those confined in Jerusalem that no great *stars* shined on them at all. But when the all-powerful defender took up the work of vengeance, that darkness that the vexation of the soul was begetting fell on the souls and eyes of the barbarians. Our God sprang forth for vengeance with such great majesty that he seemed to have brought forth not only a shout like that of leaders making war but also certain roars and growls, the strength and greatness of which could not be endured not merely by the hearts of men but not even by the very elements. Indeed, he says, *The Lord shall roar out of Zion,*

[95]Ps 14:5; 53:5.

[96]Cf. 2 Kings 19:35.

[97]Cf. Joel 3:12.

and utter his voice from Jerusalem; and the heavens and the earth shall be moved, and the Lord [shall be] the hope of his people, and the strength of the children of Israel. Therefore, that conversion will take place, as we said, so that the darkness, which the Jewish people at first perceived had struck not the stars but the breasts of the ones in fear, thereafter the throng of the enemy would experience, so that both the stars would seem to them to have become black and the elements to shake. But *strength* will come *to the children of Israel,* and by the dangers of the events the learned will know that their God is the *Lord* of the whole earth, who nevertheless condescends to dwell on mount *Zion* on account of his exceeding mercy.[98]

3:17b-18 And Jerusalem shall be holy, and strangers shall not pass through it any more. And it shall come to pass in that day, the mountains shall drop down sweetness, and the hills shall flow with milk, and waters shall go through all the rivers of Judah.[99]

The appearance of the whole country will be changed, he says, from sad things into happy things. And since it is the singular mark of our nation that it should be called *holy,* the wonder of the fortunate ones will cause not only the temple but also all the walls of the city to be so revered that no one unholy will be believed to be able to enter into it. Moreover, such great richness will follow sweet freedom, that not only from the beehives or the trees but also from the very *mountains* honey will seem to flow down, and so each of the *torrents* would seem to be changed into the charm of *rivers* flowing from *springs*—that is, so that they never set aside the abundance of the flow. But they will attain this new blessedness of water courses from that fount, which breaks forth from the inmost recesses of the house of God. All these things certainly are said either with exaggeration or because the peoples were rejoicing over their regained salvation and experienced emotions of this kind. Thus, just as earlier the stars seemed to be rendered invisible by the sadness that was appointed in the final critical moment,[100] and the elements seemed to tremble, so on the other hand by the outpouring of drunken joy, milk seems to trickle from the rocks, honey from the mountains, torrents are overflowing from the springs, and not merely the meadows but even the rocks are blooming with various flowers. Moreover, a fountain will go forth from the house of God, which waters the *torrent of thorns;* that is, it makes the places that had been occupied by thorn bushes suitable for cultivation, through that which supplies in abundance the relief of uninterrupted irrigation. Now this context in which the blessedness of Jerusalem is foretold embraces the mysteries of the church, which endured both the assault of hostile power and that of the Jews together with that of the pagans. But while all of these were flowing away into nothingness like water, in a wonderful fashion the church grew strong and advanced as a vine that stretched out to the boundaries of the world.[101] And she grew strong by putting down the profanity of idols, and she established herself with majestic authority in a certain seat of perceived supremacy. And as far as the rules of her constitution are concerned, she was so fortified by the holiness of her precepts that no *stranger* (that is, an unholy and criminal person) would be able *to pass through her.* Why not? Because "Christ delivered himself up for her, that he might present to himself a church, not having spot or wrinkle," but she stood forth "holy, and without blemish."[102] Therefore, this virgin of the eternal King was

[98]Cf. Joel 3:17a.

[99]Joel 3:18b reads in Jerome, "And a fountain shall go forth from the house of the Lord and will water the torrent of thorns."

[100]Cf. Joel 2:31.

[101]Cf. Ps 80:8-11.

[102]Eph 5:25-27.

consecrated as his partner. Just as she is separated from each bad thing in the present arrangement of virtues, so also in the age to come she is separated also by the blessedness of the rewards. Thus, no one finds rest "in your tabernacles" unless it is "he that walks without blemish and works justice."[103] Therefore, to the one to whom the eternal blessedness of that citizenship comes, as "he will be made drunk with the abundance of the house of God," so he "drinks from a certain river of holy delight."[104] And he senses that pain and sadness have equally fled. Just as this happiness will be given in full at the time of the resurrection, so also in this life the apostles and their disciples appropriated its greatest part to themselves; for indeed, when they were flogged by persecutors, they began to rejoice, "that they had merited to suffer mistreatment for the sake of Christ's name."[105] Therefore, we see that the honey of saving doctrines has flowed down from these lofty mountains; for the prophet is witness, "How sweet are your words to the palate" of the devout, "beyond the sweetness of honey and the honeycomb."[106] From the hearts of the apostles, I say, trickled a flow that gave life to the world. And from the thorn bushes on which they had fallen, fields were made, painted with flowers, weighed down with fruits. Why not? For they perceived the abundance of that fountain from which the one who had drunk would thirst no more, but "rivers of living water were flowing from his belly."[107] Therefore, by means of these increases of gifts he promises to those who stand out the sweetness of vengeance leading to the increase of blessedness.

3:19 Egypt shall be a desolation, Idumea a desert of perdition, because they have acted unjustly against the children of Judah and have shed innocent blood in their land.

The prophet concluded his speech as a prediction for his own time, and just as previously he announced the recompense of disaster to the Tyrians and the Sidonians,[108] so now he threatens the *Egyptians* and the *Idumeans* because of the same wicked deeds. Indeed, we can apply this to the business of the church by that reckoning, if we call hardhearted and dark souls *Idumeans* and *Egyptians*.

3:20-21 And Judea shall be inhabited forever, and Jerusalem to generation and generation. And I will cleanse their blood, which they[109] had not cleansed; and the Lord will dwell in Zion.

Once the Assyrians have been obliterated by a wonderful vengeance, he says, and the other peoples who joined them in battle, the inhabitants of *Zion* will be increased in all their hopes and actions, and they will take up a concern for religion, and they will be made clean by the sacred rites, by the neglect of which they had been defiled before. And they will become conspicuous to me, their protector. Just as we read that this was done in part under Hezekiah, so also we proclaim it was fulfilled more abundantly under the "mediator of God and men."[110] He indeed died "for our transgressions, and rose again for our justification," so that "having been justified by faith, let us have peace with God,"[111] who promised that he would *dwell* in the midst of the city of *Zion* when he said, "Behold I am with you all the days, even to the consummation of the world."[112]

[103]Ps 15:1-2.
[104]Ps 36:8.
[105]Cf. Acts 5:41.
[106]Ps 119:103; cf. Jerome, *Commentary on Joel* 3:18a (ACT 2:298).
[107]Cf. Jn 4:13-14.
[108]Cf. Joel 3:4-8.
[109]Jerome reads "I."
[110]1 Tim 2:5.
[111]Rom 4:25–5:1. Notice the subjunctive reading of Rom 5:1.
[112]Mt 28:20.

COMMENTARY ON THE PROPHET AMOS

Book One on the Prophet Amos

[Preface]

We have completed a commentary on saint Joel and carried it through to the best of our ability and with God's help. We are now summoned to the third prophet in that series of duty, whose name is Amos.[1] This man is glorious no less for the humility of his descent than for the eminence of his virtue. For unsupported by any distinguishing marks of his parentage, he obtained a place in the number of the prophets solely by his merits—of the prophets, I say, who provided not only the teaching authority of the synagogue but also the foundation of the church, as the teacher of the nations testifies,[2] who points out that the church is built on the teaching of the apostles and of the prophets.[3] Therefore, he was promoted to that assembly that shines with a heavenly light even without the assistance of more distinguished origins, but by the sanctity of his moral character, as we have said, and also of his entire life. Even if he had taught without speech, he will prove abundantly by his own example that the piety and devotion of his mind sufficed for laying hold of the true glory of blessedness, since neither his poverty nor his obscurity could provide an impediment to him.[4] And since we have made known how much he merited, let us hear what he taught.

[Chapter 1]

1:1(-2a) The words of Amos, who was among the shepherding regions of Tekoa, which he saw concerning Israel in the days of Uzziah, king of Judah, and in the days of Jeroboam, son of Joash, two years before the earthquake, and he said.[5]

One should first notice that his times are the same as those of the preceding prophets—namely, of Hosea and Joel.[6] For indeed, at that time impiety was especially seething among the ten tribes, which are called Israel, and the light of discernment was altogether buried, so to speak. The people so loved the darkness with which they had clothed themselves that neither by salutary warnings nor by

[1]Jerome discusses the ordering of the Twelve Prophets in his preface to Joel (ACT 2:262). In the Hebrew Bible, Amos is third after Hosea and Joel. In the LXX, he is second after Hosea and followed by Micah.

[2]Cf. 1 Tim 2:7.

[3]Cf. Eph 2:20-21; 1 Cor 14:3, 4. J. Lössl, "Pauline Exegesis in Patristic Commentaries of Old Testament Prophets: The Example of Julian of Aeclanum's *Tractatus in Amos*," *Journal for Late Antique Religion and Culture* 4 (2010): 17, comments on this text: "Thus for Julian the message of Amos and Paul is essentially the same. *Prophetia* is *doctrina*. Paul is *doctor* and *magister gentium* in the same way as Amos is prophet. God's *gratia* is man's *virtus*, *humilitas* is *modestia*, low birth is spiritual aristocracy, achieved by merit alone, *solis meritis*. This is not mere moralism, as can be found in Jerome, this is some kind of synergism, similar perhaps to that of John Chrysostom." Lössl (19) adds that Julian's link from Amos to Paul distinguishes him from Jerome: "Therefore, far from being an obscure commentary of a remote and minor Old Testament prophet, *tr. Amos* [Julian's Tractate (or Commentary) on Amos] is an important document for understanding Pauline exegesis in the fifth century in general and in the second Pelagian controversy in particular."

[4]Cf. Amos 7:14-15. The language is reminiscent of Julian's description of Job in the Preface to Job.

[5]In Jerome's version, Amos 1:2a reads, "And he said: the Lord will roar from Zion."

[6]See Julian's preface to Joel for an explanation of this. For the dates of these kings, see note under Hos 1:1-2.

severe scourges would anyone repent at all. Instead they joined shamelessness with impiety, such that they seemed to embrace their faults and miseries equally. Therefore, our God girded himself with the duty of vengeance and foretold this very thing in various ways. For the intention that motivated him was that of correcting rather than of punishing. He foretells what he knows he is about to bring forth. It says, *Two years before* the *earth* was shaken by an ominous *quake*. Although the history of Kings does not reveal that this happened, we are nevertheless satisfied with the prophet himself as the source, and do not doubt that an earthquake preceded as a sign of the disaster that was coming.[7] Therefore, the people are admonished throughout the intervening intervals of this time period, which postponed the vengeance too late for them to think of amendment. And a display of terror occurs to keep them from beginning to experience the very bulk of the revenge. Of course, when this superintendence accomplishes nothing with them, they are deprived not only of safety but of excuse. But take note of the insignificance of this preacher addressing a public assembly, one who is lifted up by the greatness of the revelations.[8] For he attained that dignity by which he became resplendent by the approbation of character alone, not also of origins, like others (namely, those whose ancestors are recorded in the titles[9]). And yet he did not conceal the lightly esteemed activity in which he was trained, but he indicated that he had always been placed among the cattle feeders of *Tekoa*. Now *Tekoa* is said to be a small village in which there are a great number of shepherds. It is separated from the city of Bethlehem by about seven miles, beyond which an empty wilderness extends all the way to the ocean.[10] Therefore, he was among the herdsmen in Tekoa who sought out places that were uncultivated but favorable for the flock. The reason he points out that he was led forth was to prevent his seeming puffed up on the occasion of a new duty and thinking a bit too highly of himself. He has explained this theme of his earnest thriftiness in the progression of the work as well when he says, "I am not a prophet, nor am I the son of a prophet, but I am a herdsman plucking sycamore figs. And the Lord took me when I followed the flock, and he said to me, Go, prophesy to my people Israel."[11] Now this is the virtue of modesty, which also the teacher of the nations[12] displays when he says, "And lest I be puffed up by the greatness of the revelations, there was given me a goad of my flesh, an angel of Satan, to buffet me. For which thing thrice I besought the Lord that it might depart from me, and he said to me, My grace is sufficient for you; for virtue is made perfect in weakness."[13] Therefore, it was made evident to the sight of the prophet that that earthquake was effective in signifying the violent wrenching of the authority to command. And this is what he calls the roaring of the angry Lord.[14]

1:2b(-c) And he will utter his voice from Jerusalem.[15]

Doubtless this voice would correspond with his anger, not his nature. Therefore, the

[7]Cf. Zech 14:5 where there is reference to an earthquake in the days of Uzziah king of Judah.

[8]Cf. 2 Cor 12:7-9.

[9]Cf. Is 1:1; Jer 1:1; Ezek 1:2; Hos 1:1; Joel 1:1; Zeph 1:1; Zech 1:1.

[10]Jerome, *Commentary on Amos*, bk 1, preface (ACT 2:301), alluding to Sallust, *Bellum jugurthinum* 48.3, says that Tekoa is six miles from Bethlehem and that beyond it the desert stretches as far as the Red Sea and to the borders of the Persians, Ethiopians, and Indians.

[11]Amos 7:14-15.

[12]Cf. 1 Tim 2:7.

[13]2 Cor 12:7-9.

[14]Cf. Amos 1:2a.

[15]The second part of Amos 1:2 reads in Jerome, "And the beautiful places of the shepherds have mourned, and the top of Carmel has withered."

shaking of the world expresses in words that the eternal judge has roared. Its force was such that immediately the greenness of the pastures disappeared, and the nourishment was removed not only from men but also from the flocks. For he has named the glad pastures "beautiful places of the shepherds,"[16] and he intended the same meaning to apply to "the top of Mount Carmel has withered."[17] For herdsmen customarily look for summer pastures especially on hilltops. When he declares that all these things are to be *withered* by that earthquake, it seems that something also happened[18] by natural estimation. For the majority of those who have shown themselves inquisitive in matters of that sort are of the opinion that earthquakes are caused by drought. They endeavor to prove this by examples and to persuade by arguments.[19] At this time, however, it is not necessary for us to go over this, but I briefly have taken note of the following, that the initial quake brings in the double misfortune.[20] Now if a large concussion creates the drought by disturbing, as it were, the veins of the springs, this looks back to the power of the Creator, at whose nod the elements carry out their service; or if a preceding lack of moisture first caused the ground to dry up, and afterward to shake as well, and thus to have laid open the misfortunes of the drought to the perishing pastures, this no less shows the same power of him who judges. Just as he sustains with his devoted care that which he has created, so, when it is necessary, he disturbs these same things with his indignation. Now we could think by tropology that the great men and the kings of diverse nations are indicated under the name of *shepherds*, and that the *top of Carmel* indicates that power that they held when they had lived happily, especially because the words of this prophet are directed toward different nations. But the first explanation is both simpler and more suited to the history if various forms of grievous sufferings are said to have beset the impious. But now let us see what the roaring avenger exclaims.

1:3-5 For three crimes of Damascus, and for four, will I not convert it, because they have threshed Gilead with iron carts? And I will send a fire into the house of Hazael (*Azahel*), and it will devour the houses of Ben-Hadad. And I will break the bar of Damascus, and I will destroy the inhabitant from the plains of the idol, and him who holds the scepter from the house of pleasure, and the people of Syria will be deported to Kir (*Cyrenem*), says the Lord.

The apostle says, "We know that everything that the law speaks, it says to those who are in the law."[21] Since, therefore, it was the intention of the prophets to convict the crimes of the people who were living under the law, and since the blessed Amos took his stand chiefly against the ten tribes that are called Israel, nevertheless, out of his providential care and by reason of his manifold counsel, our God mentioned other nations as well. He examines them by reason of his equitable judgment, just as he also examines the Jewish people. The latter claimed for themselves on the basis of this that they lived separate from the rest, but this for the most part contradicted the deserts of their lives. For when they hear that the neighboring nations are also called to the examination no less zealously than their own

[16]Amos 1:2c.

[17]Amos 1:2c.

[18]Presumably CCSL's *cintigisse* is a mistake for *contigisse*.

[19]Democritus of Abdera and Anaximenes made such speculations. Cf. P. A. Cartledge and J. R. Sallares, "Earthquakes," in *The Oxford Classical Dictionary*, 3rd ed. (Oxford: Oxford University Press, 1996), 501.

[20]Lössl, "Pauline Exegesis," 18n70, aids us in grasping Julian's meaning here: "The 'twin plague' ['double misfortune'] consists in the scorching of the pastures and the singeing of Mount Carmel" (Amos 1:2; this verse is not cited in the lemma).

[21]Rom 3:19.

tribes, they really understand that God is the one founder of all the nations, and that all exist under the providence and governance of one! For in the very fact that the grief of the Israelites over the neighboring nations is punished, their pride is put down at the same time, so that they at last perceive that he is not only the God of Jews but also of the Gentiles.[22] For indeed no people's pursuits are deprived either of consolation or of punishment in the recompense owed. Finally he shows how he who rises up in anger with such great difficulty is more disposed to spare. Thus, no single fault incites him, or two, but only when some *three* or *four* come together. Yet this number was adopted to show an endless amount; it is not that he was really expressing *four* crimes, but many. But the same one attests that he himself is also zealous to forgive even the other nations round about, when he excuses his own commotion by the multitude of foreign iniquity. He says, *For three crimes of Damascus, and for four, will I not convert it, because they have threshed Gilead with iron carts?* He says, the coeternal justice has pleaded before my throne that at length I should take on the duty of a judge and should teach clearly that I shrink back from manifold and shameless cruelty equally, when the state of the guilty ones has been *converted* to sadness. For the people of Damascus ravaged the cultivated lands of Israel not once or twice, but numerous times.[23] Moreover, it so crushed *Gilead* likewise *with iron carts* and caltrops,[24] that it thought it a pleasing sight if the limbs of the inhabitants were threshed randomly in the *plains* like ears of corn and stalks. Therefore, because I could not bear this unpunished savagery for long, nor should I have, *I will send a fire into the house of Hazael* (he is the king of Damascus[25]), *and it shall devour the houses of Ben-Hadad* (he is the one who succeeded his father Hazael in command[26]). *And I will break the bar of Damascus, and I will destroy the inhabitant from the plains of the idol, and him that holds the scepter from the house of pleasure.* This means, I will overwhelm with the evils of captivity the impious inhabitants of [those] places, either all the high-ranking men or the nobles, who spent all their time on *pleasures.* And what is more, lest they fail to recognize the burden of the captivity, or employ a hope of return, they themselves will be led to the fields of *Kir* when they see that their houses have collapsed in ashes. Now we read again in the book of Kings of those kings whom the prophet mentioned—that is, Hazael and Ben-Hadad. They harassed the ten tribes by frequent attacks and they led them into extreme miseries.[27] Therefore, lest that victory appear to have come to pass fortunately for the Syrians, it is described as the cause of their calamity and punishments. But now let us proceed to the rest.

1:6-8 Thus says the Lord: For three crimes of Gaza and for four will I not convert it, because it has carried away a perfect captivity to shut them up in Idumea? And I will send a fire on the wall of Gaza, and it will devour the houses thereof. And I will destroy the inhabitant from Azotus, and him who holds the scepter from Ascalon, and I will turn my hand against Ekron, and the rest of the Philistines shall perish, says the Lord.

In the same order of the narration, which he had also maintained earlier against Damascus,[28] he recounts the crimes and

[22]Or "nations." Cf. Rom 3:29.

[23]Cf. 1 Kings 20:1; 2 Kings 7:6; 10:32; 13:7, 22; 2 Chron 24:23; 28:5; Is 20:1-2.

[24]A device with four metal points so arranged that when any three are on the ground the fourth projects upward as a hazard to the hoofs of horses.

[25]Cf. 2 Kings 8:28.

[26]Cf. 2 Kings 13:24.

[27]Cf. 2 Kings 8:25-29; 13:1-9, 22-23.

[28]Cf. Amos 1:3, 5.

punishments of the city of *Gaza* too. And it is as if he takes on the appearance of a questioner. Is he obligated to maintain such continuous patience for men who were so attached to their wicked deeds that they thought that they had not done anything with cruelty unless they had repeated it three and four times? And they had maintained an astonishing ostentation in sinning. And, what is more, they were nurtured not only by their own crimes but also those of foreigners. For it [Gaza] took pains that the Idumeans administered punishments on the nation of the Jews. The Idumeans were the descendants of Esau, whom history reveals to have been the brother of the blessed Jacob.[29] Therefore, the prophet says, he who was separated from us by his murderous hatred, although he was joined by blood, employed the help of the people of Gaza. Nor did the cruel nation give my blood to the enmities of foreigners for its own gain. It raged as much against me as the murderers were satisfied to command. He shows how he will blot out this declaration of malice: *And I will send a fire on the wall of Gaza, it will devour the houses thereof. And I will destroy the inhabitant from Azotus and him who holds the scepter from Ascalon, and I will turn my hand against Ekron, and the rest of the Philistines shall perish, says the Lord.* On the occasion of one city he has also run through the names of other towns. We frequently read about them in the history of Kings, that they were engaged in nearly continuous conflicts with the Jewish nation. But these are the ones who slaughtered the Jewish army and transferred the ark of the covenant like a captive to the temple of the idol whose name was Dagon.[30] However, afterward its power was revealed by the crumbling of his statue followed by the calamity that afflicted the people, when they sent it back for its needed functions.[31] Admittedly they did not adopt the worship of God in the face of such miracles, but they persisted in their native rites and customs. These ones, therefore, who were raging with constant hatred toward the people of God, since they had not been able to inflict war in their own name, have joined forces and arms with stronger enemies. As they did this especially at that time, when the Assyrians invaded the borders of the Jews, the prophet whom we are discussing is complaining about what they repeatedly had done. And he shows that all the nations that surrounded the Jews have labored toward their destruction, as though they were in competition with each other in their pursuits. Therefore, because you also have added heaps of evils in their time of adversity, and their misery did not stir up in you a more neighborly disposition (that is, one of mercy) but instead one of cruelty, you will know the greatness of your crime, which you did not want [to know] by reason, at least by an extension of vengeance. For the fire of the siege that has been sent in will devour not only the roofs but even the walls—that is, it will consume both the decorations and fortifications equally. And in this way it will blot out your inhabitants by a slaughter such that no exception would be found, not even among the leaders who wield *scepters,* who were really those who had been reliant either on authority or conspicuous for the delights and pleasure of that life, to such a degree that they can even be called *kings.* But I will stretch out the hand of our opposition in such a way against everyone that even *the rest of the Philistines* would be consumed, and from top to bottom a single desolation will rage. Now this is what the preceding prophet also expressed—namely, when he accused Tyre and Sidon and all the borders of the Palestinians of carrying off silver and gold and everything that was

[29]Cf. Gen 25:25-26.
[30]Cf. 1 Sam 5:1-5.
[31]Cf. 1 Sam 5:6-12.

valuable from the territory of Israel.[32] They had also sold the children of the people, who had been born in freedom, to Greek and Barbarian merchants, so that they were carried off far from their fatherland and endured exile as well as servitude.

1:9-10 Thus says the Lord: For three crimes of Tyre and for four will I not convert it, because they have shut up a perfect captivity in Idumea, and have not remembered the pact of their brothers? And I will send a fire on the wall of Tyre, and it shall devour its houses.

He accuses Tyre of this crime, that it had recently shut off even Gaza—that is, it had hastened to *shut up* not some small portion but *a perfect captivity in Idumea,* so that it filled the Idumean nation with the perils of the Jews (namely, with hatred of his antagonistic brother). Hence, vengeance will come that conforms to and surpasses the form of your crime: for you have incited by your aids the still smoldering ill will that desires the destruction *of brothers,* and you *have not remembered* that *pact*—that is, you were completely unwilling to think about that fact that between brothers nature itself has established that for them to love each other is not so much a source of praise as it would be a crime for them to hate each other. But you have even provoked not merely to wrangling but even to war those who are most foreign, as it were, and who were known to each other neither by their common language nor by reputation. And so the consequence will be that a burning vengeance will seize you and will turn the enormous pleasures with which you had carried on infamous things to a horrible squalor. And it will dole out so much devastation that both the foundations and the tops of your lofty tower and wall will be reduced to ashes.

[32]Cf. Joel 3:4-6.

1:11-12 Thus says the Lord: For three crimes of Edom and for four will I not convert him, because he pursued his brother with the sword, and violated his mercy, and held on to his fury, and kept his wrath to the end? I will send a fire into Theman, and it shall devour the temples of Bosra.

He follows the order of the established sermon and addresses the different nations with a rebuke; at any rate the nations that he knew were cleaving both to the crimes and the borders of the Jews. But he has recorded the Idumeans in order after Tyre, since they seethed with a murderous impiety against the Jews. Therefore, what he had announced was to be punished among the Tyrians—namely, that they had aided the raging Idumeans with either troops or counsels, so that they could more easily feast on their brother's miseries, in a contextually coherent way he now addresses them too on account of the same crimes of Esau. And he destines them for punishment, lest the one who had announced to their allies that a price for these offenses had to be paid should seem to have spared those who were the authors of the crime. Therefore, he says that that people offended by their murderous spirit, not once but often. Doubtless, the result was that, if a fault deserved to be pardoned, their deadly persistence demanded vengeance. For *he pursued his brother* not with reproaches but *with a sword.* He forgot about the *mercy* and love that brotherhood demanded. And not content with having boiled over with some outburst of *wrath,* it says that he threatened criminal action for a long period of time. He added a lot of weight to the accusation when he said, *And he held on to his fury, and kept his wrath to the end.* For he not only departed from the customary behavior of brothers by pursuing his brother in battle, but he did not preserve the custom of those whom [anger] incites to bloody conflicts with the flames of *wrath.* For he raged like one who will not quickly leave off;

thus, he persevered in his hatred as one aroused by justice more than fury. Justly, then, he will allow the burning to be delayed until the consummation, so that just as the cities and the strongholds were made dirty by single crimes, so they may be destroyed by these same calamities. Now he is indicating one people (namely, Esau) by many names—that is, *Edom, Theman,* and *Bosra,* whose capital city went by the name of Bosra.[33] He says, therefore, that they are to be conquered in both war and siege, they will suffer terrible things at the whim of their conquerors, and they will perish by slaughter and fire. All these things are shown to have been inflicted partly by the Chaldeans and partly by the Maccabees.[34]

1:13-15 Thus says the Lord: For three crimes of the children of Ammon and for four will I not convert him, because he has ripped open the pregnant women of Galaad to enlarge his border? And I will kindle a fire in the wall of Rabba, and it shall devour the houses thereof with shouting and in the day of war, and with a whirlwind and in the day of trouble. And Melchom shall go into captivity, both he and his princes together, says the Lord.

These peoples too (namely, Ammon and Moab, which stem from Lot[35]) are not free from murderous envy. For they are indeed revealed as neighbors of the Israelites, yet they bear none of their original glory and did not bypass the opportunity to harm Galaad. After all, the Ammonites hastened to invade the country that shared a border with them, which as Scripture says the two and a half tribes had received.[36] Moreover, they did not abstain from slaughtering *pregnant women,* desiring namely to kill the offspring of the Jews, so that when the inhabitants were destroyed, the whole country of the Galaadites could be joined to their lands. Therefore, he says, I will pay back to this people as well what it deserves, and I will cause its buildings to begin to burn with the enemy's *fire* of *Rabba,* which was its capital city. Obviously this will result in their being so consternated by the *whirlwind* of *war* that they seem even to die prematurely. But not only its *princes* but also *Melchom* (that is, the image whose divinity they believed they had to protect) will be transferred into the laughing-stock of *captivity.*

[Chapter 2]

2:1-3 Thus says the Lord: For three crimes of Moab and for four will I not convert him, because he has burnt the bones of the king of Idumea even to ashes? And I will send a fire into Moab, and it shall devour the houses of Carioth, and Moab shall die with a noise and with the sound of the trumpet. And I will cut off the judge from the midst thereof and will kill all his princes with him, says the Lord.

One should notice that when he imputed to all the nations that he listed the abuses and dangers that they had heaped on Israel, he now objects that the people of the Moabites stood out in their violence against the Idumean king. And he pleads that they raged so insanely that they were not content with waging war against a living man but displayed their hatred even around his grave. Surely by this also the arrogance of the Jews is suppressed, who thought that they alone mattered to God, and either the comfort of hope or the light of understanding is set out as a defense of the nations, so that they would perceive that they are under the same providential governance of their Creator—namely, he who will avenge not only the injustices inflicted on the Jews but also those of foreign nations.

[33]Cf. Is 34:6; 63:1; Jer 49:13. What Julian says does not agree with Jerome, *Commentary on Amos* 1:11-12 (ACT 2:311).
[34]Cf. 1 Macc 4:29, 61; 5:3; 6:31; 2 Macc 10:16.
[35]Cf. Gen 19:30-38.
[36]Cf. Josh 13:8-32.

2:4-5 Thus says the Lord: for three crimes of Judah and for four will I not convert him, because they have cast away the law of the Lord and have not kept his commands? For their idols have deceived them, after which their fathers have gone. And I will send fire into Judah, and it will devour the houses of Jerusalem.

When he had objected to the crimes of violence among various nations, he came to Judah and imputed to him the crime of feigned religion. He is declaring with the same form of deliberation with which he had begun that those who had pursued with obstinacy everything base and profane will undergo a needed conversion—namely, from joyful things to sad things. But we should not think that he assessed those peoples whose crimes he reviewed a little bit before as worthy of approval in respect to their religion, that concerning that matter he thought that nothing deserved reproach among them. On the contrary, there was professed profaneness among them. They had always sold themselves out to the worship of idols and were unwilling to have a suitable judgment concerning the duty of religious rites. Therefore, he does not charge them in particular with the crime of feigned religion, but with those wounds of moral behavior that they were capable of knowing clearly and avoiding even while set outside the true religion. But to Judah he objected this at the beginning, that he was quite uncouth with other shameful acts, and other crimes as well had sprouted forth deservedly from his stock. For they had *cast away the law of the Lord,* he says, by which they alone in the whole world were distinguished, and not content with having *cast it away,* they too went over to the worship of idols. Therefore, they will receive the wages they deserve—namely, that the enemy's fire would consume Judah and Jerusalem. This was fulfilled when Babylon conquered them.[37]

[37]Cf. 2 Kings 25:8-9.

2:6(-7) Thus says the Lord: For three crimes of Israel and for four will I not convert him, because he has sold the just man for silver and the poor man for a pair of shoes?[38]

He accuses the ten tribes, which he names *Israel,* not as [he accused] Judah but as the rest of the nations for moral crimes. Doubtless this is to show the degree to which they cleaved to profaneness, insofar as they were neither ashamed nor afraid of being exposed in this respect. Therefore, he accuses the wounds of morality, not because these things were more serious than the religious rites but either because these fruits of a defiled religion were clearly visible or because also in their sharing of actions they were shown to be worse than the other nations. Therefore, our rebuke will scarcely put up with this any longer, he says, so that the impudent one abides in that state in which he does not sigh for better things. On the contrary, a change will come on them from prosperity to adversity, so that what they were unwilling to learn when warned, they would begin to know when condemned—namely, that I am pleading for the "poor,"[39] and that those who lack the wealth of this age are not deprived of the protection of my providence. Only let concern for uprightness flourish among them, and that inferior state in which they had lived more humbly than the rest will render them acceptable and dear to me. But I have said this because the people of Israel neglected to notice the just man and the poor man striving, as it were, before me with a double approval, but the one who was always hostile to my judgments was trampling on the poor, and

[38]Amos 2:7, which is also discussed under this lemma, reads in Jerome's version, "They bruise the heads of the poor on the dust of the earth and turn aside the way of the humble; and the son and his father have gone to the [same] young woman, to profane my holy name."

[39]Cf. Amos 2:7.

with the shoes of his feet he was quite vilely esteeming the adornments of the world—that is, those sinning either in duties or in business with such great foulness that not only allured by short-lived profits for the most part but often even fed on the gratuitous outrages of the just, thinking it some form of pleasure if they trampled on the very heads mixed with dust of men lowly in respect of power (that is, men who avoided the evil of arrogance by the holiness of innocence). But his words, "They turn aside the way of the humble,"[40] can be understood in two ways. Either they turn away from it and follow a far different road of life, or else in their courts they ruin the just cause of the poor through fraud, the kind of thing that is spoken of in the psalm: "When you see a thief, you go with him, and with adulterers you have common cause. You sat and spoke against your brother, and callously laid a scandal against your mother's son."[41] The guilt of the transgressors is enhanced by that understanding, because by pursuing with dedication works that were deadly, they were exposed as not merely neglecting but as actively hating justice. But the prophet goes on to recall various crimes; for after injustice and pride he touches on the sins of lust. He says, "The son and his father have gone to one young woman, to profane my holy name."[42] He shows in what large numbers of transgressors custom proceeds: First, he says, you deny citizens justice in the law courts; you deny compassion in adversity. It directly follows that among you the laws of nature itself do not apply, but by going from shameful acts to incestuous ones, sons rushed with their fathers to prostitutes, exhibiting no respect, first to other citizens, and eventually not even to their own parents. Surely, by this wicked deed of yours "my holy name was profaned"—namely, as the Gentiles discuss among themselves, "What sort of God is this, whose people, said to be his very own,[43] appear so terrible?"[44]

2:8 And they have lain down on the garments taken in pledge by every altar, and they drank the wine of the condemned in the house of their God.

It was indeed consistent that the worshipers of idols should have persisted under multiple forms of depravity. Here, however, the prophet is careful in all that he has accused to express that they, so to speak, fought back against works that were dedicated to the divine injunctions, and by all these outward forms they tore up the precepts. Therefore, while recounting all that is prohibited in the law, he even declares that they had reclined on clothes *taken in pledge*,[45] but he carefully added *by every altar* since their impiety had multiplied their altars. And therefore *they drank the wine of the condemned*—that is, they feasted in the temples using that money that they had received from the payments of the innocent, doubtless from whom he said a little earlier that "they sold the just man for silver and the poor man for a pair of shoes."[46]

2:9(-12) Yet I have cast out the Amorite before their face, whose height was like the height of cedars, and who was strong as an oak; I destroyed his fruit from above and his root beneath. It is I who brought you up out of the land of Egypt, and I led you forty

[40]Amos 2:7.
[41]Ps 50:18, 20.
[42]Amos 2:7.

[43]Cf. Ex 19:5.
[44]Lössl discusses this passage and links it to *Turb. Frg.* 321. "Pauline Exegesis," 14-15. He concludes, "After looking at this passage the references to hyperbole and exaggeration in *Turb.* may read slightly differently from the way Augustine would have liked them to be read" (14).
[45]Cf. Ex 22:26; Deut 24:12-13.
[46]Amos 2:6.

years through the desert, that you might possess the land of the Amorite.[47]

He keeps to his custom of calling to mind previously dispatched acts of kindness in order to exasperate the wickedness of the hateful. And that is why after he had run through their twisted and profane pursuits to which they had dedicated themselves, he tossed in mention of good things too, the forgetting of which had misled them. It is as if he were to say, He has been quite deceived, the one who drove out the nations of old, who were stronger in strength and power, in order to prepare a habitation for them, since they reckon this combat to be glorious, if they emulate and surpass their crimes. He says, *I have cast out the Amorite, whose height was like that of cedar, and who was strong as an oak; I destroyed his fruit from above and his roots beneath.* He is saying, Like a careful measurer[48] of encampments I have cut down the forest of nations that was for a long time now very strong, even threatening the lofty treetops and relying on deep roots, so that at least they would not perceive that the baggage and equipment of their habitation was light. Whatever strength they had, therefore, I have cut it off root and branch so that the native forests that our judgment sentence removed would never sprout again, but abundant security would follow the joys of the victory given. Why not? I conferred kindnesses on them even in former times; for when they were oppressed by Egyptian servitude, I raised them up to the heights of liberty, and through impassible wilderness I led them about for forty years, providing food and drink along with miracles, so that the inheritance of blessed lands that was decreed might taste more sweet in that it was attained quite late. And at the same time they would know that human life does not consist in fertility of fields but in the providential governance of God. And yet not content with having given merely the tools for the present life, I rendered you conspicuous through spiritual adornments as well. He says, "I raised up [some] of your sons for prophets and [some] of your young men for Nazarites."[49] This means he raised up men and women who were effective both with a unique form of devotion and also with a holy illumination. Some of them possessed sure knowledge of the future;[50] others had a glorious contempt for licit things.[51] You have not only regarded all these things as worthless but have even very much repudiated them, daring to decree to the prophets not to prophesy and to the Nazirites to ingest wine in order to become intoxicated.

2:13-16 Behold, I will screak under you as a wagon screaks that is laden with hay. And flight shall perish from the swift, and the strong (*fortis*) shall not possess his power; neither shall the strong (*robustus*) save his life. And he who holds the bow shall not stand, and the swift of foot shall not be saved, neither shall the rider of the horse save his life. And the stout of heart among the valiant shall flee away naked in that day, says the Lord.

It is common in the sacred Scriptures to use images taken perhaps even from everyday things, to express what they desire, but this is done in such a way that an inner core of mystical meaning exists in these things. Whence even now, since the just judge endured the people who had been sinning for a long

[47]The commentary under this lemma also covers Amos 2:11-12, which reads in Jerome's version, "And I raised up [some] of your sons for prophets and [some] of your young men for Nazarites. Is it not so, O children of Israel? says the Lord. And you will present wine to the Nazarites and command the prophets, saying: Do not prophesy."

[48]*Metator* occurs in Tertullian, *Adv. Marc.* 1.8.

[49]Amos 2:11.

[50]Cf. Num 12:6; Deut 13:1; 18:22; 1 Sam 1:11; 3:20-21.

[51]Cf. Num 6:1-21.

time, he has claimed that they are *laden* like a *wagon* but for whom the load turned out to consist in worthless material. Therefore, as for what he says, *I will screak under you as a wagon that is laden with hay,* he did not want this to be understood in such a way that a wagon full of hay appears to screak in one way, one full of silver in another way. On the contrary, since he was adapting the metaphor of the screaking wagon to his own purposes, he skillfully combined the meanings, as if he were to say, If a wagon that is laden had some sort of ability to distinguish, doubtless it would screak more indignantly if it were carrying worthless things rather than precious. So then, since as the apostle teaches, on the foundation of religion, in view of the diversity of merits, some are heaped up as gold, silver and precious stones, but others as hay, wood, or stubble,[52] our God justly declares that he experiences greater sorrow by putting up with their sins in whom he could find nothing precious in their pursuits but who have all approached him as being worthless hay, and that which would easily be consumed by fire.[53] But when I *screak* (that is, rage), either your arrogance or self-reliance will perish on the spot. For no one's speed will keep him from destruction, nor will courage protect the one ready to fight, nor will a battle line of foot soldiers nor companies of horsemen ultimately put off the divine sentence of judgment, but those who were famous for the art of waging war will throw away their armor and long to lie hidden, so that even the naked would make use of hiding places to save their lives. We acknowledge that all these evils happened during the enemy's victory in yearly disasters more than in literary chronicles. In this passage the Jews, of course, follow some view that says that the persons of different leaders have been signified by the various preparations.[54] We do not think this holds much importance, and so let us move on to other things.

[Chapter 3]

3:1-2 Hear the word that the Lord has spoken concerning you, children of Israel, concerning your whole family that I brought up out of the land of Egypt, saying, You only have I known of all the families of the earth; therefore, will I visit on you all your iniquities.

He says, You rejoice especially, of course, in this mark of distinction, that I who am the Creator of the world was made known to no nation in the whole world except to you alone. And, though I formed all the nations by the same devotion with which I formed you, nevertheless I chose to be and to be called your God alone, and I forestalled all the duties of your devotion by gifts and miracles. I destroyed unto your honor the powerful kingdoms, first of the Egyptians, then of the Palestinians—namely, so that a glorious exodus and a rich inheritance would be offered to you. And not content only with having given you joy by driving off your condition of slavery, I added the light of spiritual doctrine as well. At any rate, I showed by all these things that I had chosen you from all the nations, you whom I likewise educated by sacred information, so that those who had received many things without merits would understand how they would likewise be deserving. But that generosity did not render the judge more neglectful of your way of life, but I reprove your evil deeds all the more by the very fact that I preferred you over all nations. For it was consistent that things that are reckoned to be

[52]Cf. 1 Cor 3:12.

[53]Cf. Jerome, *Commentary on Amos* 2:13-16 (ACT 2:320).

[54]Cf. Jerome, *Commentary on Amos* 2:13-16 (ACT 2:320-21), who says that the Jews refer the various descriptions of the passage to Jeroboam, Bashan, Omri, Jehu, Manahem, Pekah, and Hoshea.

more precious be more carefully examined. Therefore, the grace provided to your nation either by my forgiveness or by the virtues of your ancestors permits that no fault remain unchastised. For a nobility that has been granted becomes worthless if it is not taken away from those who are unworthy. And so, the nobility acquired scarcely commends impunity for crimes committed, but it affirms the keeping of the commandments. But let us consider the rest.

3:3-8 Shall two walk together except they be agreed? Will a lion roar in the thicket, if he have no prey? Will the lion's whelp utter his voice out of his den, if he have taken nothing? Will the bird fall into the snare on the earth, if there be no fowler? Shall the snare be taken up from the earth, before it has taken anything? Shall the trumpet sound in a city and the people not be afraid? Shall there be evil in a city that the Lord has not done? For the Lord God will do nothing without revealing his secret to his servants the prophets. The lion shall roar, who will not fear? The Lord God has spoken, who shall not prophesy?

There have been various opinions of certain people on this passage, but they do not harmonize well enough with the sense of the examples.[55] We will now render the meaning by making a needed distinction. For the established speech touches on various sentences of judgment. And indeed, the first verse shows that the rejection of the thankless nation was necessary—that is, it was just, namely, a nation that he declared earlier as the single one that had been adopted from all nations.[56] Therefore, since it had inflamed the anger of the judge when they changed their pursuits to perverse things, and they were repudiated and subjected to destruction, he explains why discord within the same nation had occurred. He says, *Shall two walk together except they be agreed?* That is, why are you surprised that you have been stripped of the protection of our accompanying presence, when the just association of travelers cannot abide for long unless they are in agreement? You then, who chose to have desires that were contrary to my laws, acknowledge that it was logically consistent for you to be stripped naked of the help of my companionship, since you began to travel on roads that were not mine, as one set apart. I, I will not be content with having abandoned you, nor will our indignation be enclosed within this limit, but I will convert from being your protector into a raging *lion*, which doubtless traverses over desolate haunts. It is hardly levity but *prey* seen from afar that provokes it to roar. When, of course, he vanquishes what he wished for and brings back the destined game to his *lair*, the cave itself will force it to belt out a growl, and he never growls in this way without reason, but always when in possession of *prey*. In these two verses he has expressed the campaign of one taking vengeance. But it follows, *Will the bird fall into the snare upon the earth, if there be no fowler? Shall the snare be taken up from the earth, before it has taken anything?* When the aspects of the avenger are acquitted, he appeals to those against whom vengeance is being carried out, whom he declares are to be crushed with such great ease that they seem like a bird that has entered a snare. He says, *Will the bird fall into the snare upon the earth, if there be no fowler?* It is as if he were to say, Even if all the prophets were equally silent, the very voice of the events could instruct you sufficiently that these calamities by which you are being worn out could have corresponded to your destruction, not of their own accord or by some chance but only if the hand of the *fowler* (that is, of the judge) brought them in. And so, by the

[55]Cf. Jerome, *Commentary on Amos* 3:3-8 (ACT 2:324).
[56]Cf. Amos 3:1-2.

prophet's announcement, miseries are shown to be exposed like a *snare*, so that all who forsake the footpath of justice fall into them. Accordingly, let no intervening postponement generally console you. For the *snare* is set—that is, the judgments published by the mouths of the prophets will not be removed until they fulfill the function of their capturing. *Shall the trumpet sound in a city, and the people not be afraid? Shall there be evil* (malum) *in a city that the Lord has not done? For the Lord God will do nothing without revealing his secret to his servants the prophets.* He has publicized that our explanation harmonizes with itself through the things supplied (namely, *snare, trumpet,* and evil [*malitiam*])—that is, the affliction by which the cities of the sacrilegious would perish would not have been set in motion apart from divine indignation. But [it was set in motion] when he confirms equally the purpose of his own pious duty whereby he was determined to be lenient, if they allowed this, and he points out his respect for the sacred judgment, which he showed could not be despised with impunity. Now as often elsewhere he names as "evil" (*malitiam*) not sins but the punishments—namely, those by which the guilty are tormented, the innocent are not stained. *For the Lord will do nothing without revealing his secret to his servants the prophets.* The dignity of the saints is commended absolutely fittingly, after contempt for the guilty had been made public. For because they seemed to have been reckoned as worthless (for they were to be overwhelmed by so many punishments), lest this very thing have in view the state of nature rather than the odium of a depraved way of life, it was set in place as a means of providential governance and for the purpose of bringing benefit. For it was effectual for the honor of human beings—that is, of the *prophets,* who of course exist in that same nature that all others have, yet they differed completely in the worth of their moral character. Thus, God could say of them, "I will not take their names on my lips."[57] But he said this because he did not do anything about these things without first informing those prophets. Therefore, he says, just as no calamity will arise in those cities unless it be one that the divine sentence of judgment has roused, so no reproach shall be brought forth against you unless it be one that was previously carried through to the awareness of the saints. But he condensed what he had pleaded with a larger abridgment when he said, *The lion shall roar, who will not fear? The Lord God has spoken, who shall not prophesy?* Therefore, since earlier he had expressed his indignation using the image of a lion,[58] thereafter he finishes with what he meant, so as to say, *The lion shall roar*—that is, when God threatens and makes public a rebuke that is imminent, what mortal is there who would not be undone by dread? But let us now see what is the outward form and display of the threats.

3:9-10 Make it heard in the houses of Azotus, and in the houses of the land of Egypt, and say, Assemble yourselves on the mountains of Samaria, and behold the many follies in the midst thereof, and them that endure false accusation in the inner rooms thereof. And they have not known how to do the right thing, says the Lord, storing up iniquity and robberies in their houses.

The divine Word keeps to its custom of attributing the extent of the difficulty he has in being moved to punish. Therefore, now too after he unfolded the form of the terror, he repeats and reconsiders the complaints, and he instructs the neighboring peoples to assemble together to see by what defilements and crimes of the people of God they are coated and raving mad. He says, Announce to the

[57]Ps 16:4. The context of the psalm indicates that he is speaking of the names of other gods.
[58]Cf. Amos 3:3-8.

Philistines and Egyptians to *gather themselves together,* as it were, to a spectacle on the *mountains of Samaria*—that is, from their height let them look down on the cities and valleys and consider that there is neither a shameful act nor any crime that I do not say approaches their pursuits but exists, as it were, with its seat having been established *in the midst thereof.* For if you turn your eyes to them, who are burdened with *false accusation,* you would discover that the gates of the cities, where court cases customarily took place, as well as the *inner rooms* are crowded, so that no other voice seems to be heard except that of those who are afflicted with sufferings. For all who had undertaken the duty of judging have fallen into such great forgetfulness of the *right thing,* whether through avarice or through arrogance, that they seem not only not to love but not even to know any longer what is *right.* Therefore, let no one begrudge my severity, I who have offered so much extended patience to wayward servants that even the censure of them was forgotten. I say, You nations that I crushed leading to their liberation and glory, you, I say, come together once again, so that the greatness of my pardon and the impiety of Ephraim may be revealed with you yourselves being the witnesses.

3:11 Therefore, thus says the Lord God: The land shall be in tribulation, and will be surrounded, and your strength shall be taken away from you, and your houses shall be plundered.

As we have said, he has often complained about their crimes and shameful acts so that he could at least make public his judgment, and in the explanation he responded to that meaning that he had made in the opening—that is, "For three crimes of Israel and for four will I not convert him?"[59] Therefore, when justice demands it, a conversion is decreed for Israel and for Judah—namely, so that they do not perish by extermination when they fell from joyful things into grievous things. Now hear in what manner the ravager is about to wreak his havoc.

3:12 As if a shepherd would rescue two legs out of the lion's mouth, or the tip of the ear, so shall the children of Israel be rescued that dwell in Samaria, on the bedspread of a bed, and on the couch of Damascus.

He means that our God chastised the Israelites with the intent of correcting them. He indicated this very thing both by the prophets pointing it out as well as by the voice of his acts of providential governance. For though their cherished profaneness always made them detestable, the Almighty nevertheless changed their condition—namely, at one time by afflicting them with griefs, at another time by nurturing them with prosperity. Therefore, as the history of Kings reveals, the Syrian who was the nearer neighbor (that is, "the inhabitant of Damascus"[60]) harassed the ten tribes by repeated invasions.[61] The result of this was that at one time the Samaritans reached the point of such scarcity after a long siege that their women fed on the flesh of their children.[62] Moreover, in the whole army scarcely ten horses could be found.[63] But when blessed Elisha commanded king Joram that on the next day the greatest abundance of the year's crop would be seen in the gates of Samaria,[64] such a great change took place all of a sudden that when the Syrians who had attacked fled, not only did the Israelites invade them but they even captured rich spoils as if of a

[59]Amos 2:6.

[60]Cf. Amos 1:3-5.

[61]Cf. 2 Kings 6:24-27; 16; Is 20:1-2.

[62]Cf. 2 Kings 6:24-31.

[63]Cf. 2 Kings 13:7.

[64]Cf. 2 Kings 7:1-2.

triumph.[65] We read that they frequently experienced salvation and joys in this manner. And so, our God, hesitant to punish and rich in showing mercy, announces that although he has assumed the office of judge, he is nevertheless not forsaking his duty of being a shepherd. On the contrary, he would deign to *rescue* the remnants of them from *the couch of Damascus,* by whose fevers they were being held as if by ropes as they endured the lengthiest disease throughout the vicinity. And he would extricate the limbs of the people, who had been torn to pieces, as if from the jaws of lions—that is, of the kings.

3:13-14 Hear ye, and testify in the house of Jacob, says the Lord of hosts, for in the day when I shall begin to visit the transgressions of Israel, I will visit on him, and on the altars of Bethel; and the horns of the altars shall be cut off and shall fall to the ground.

As far as the context of the reading is concerned, he is indeed promising devastation by the enemy, and he says that *the horns of the altar* that Jeroboam set up in Bethel are to be destroyed. Indeed, one reads that he placed one of the two calves in Dan, the other in Bethel.[66] Therefore, the sense is the same in the present passage, that although I will not allow you to be blotted out by extermination, I am prepared to extricate a remnant of your nation from captivity. Otherwise, the neighboring enemy (namely, the ruler of Damascus) would destroy you. Nevertheless, I will not allow what you are doing to take place with impunity. Now it could be said that by the name of *Jacob,* he wanted Judah to be understood, if the progression of the speech was not instead distinctly expressing Israel—that is, the ten tribes. Now we read about this destruction of the altar also in the books of Kings, that a prophet had already come to Jeroboam who had constructed the calves, and with a threat he promised this very thing to the one who made sacrifice.[67] When Jeroboam commanded him with outstretched hand to be chastised, he felt deeply the power of the prophet when his right hand immediately withered.[68] And immediately the altar was broken, and when prayers were said he recovered the use of his hand.[69] But he heard that Josiah would arise to avenge that sacrilege.[70] Therefore, since either the chastisement of the people or the final captivity comprised long periods of time, the things that were to be brought in at various times are equally indicated in the present prophecy.

3:15 And I will strike the winter house with the summer house, and the houses of ivory shall perish, and many houses shall be destroyed, says the Lord.

He does not just criticize one single vice among the profane nation. He touches on the sins of avarice and affluence too, and that is why he complains about the different dwellings they had constructed, which match their pleasures for different seasons of the year—instruments of their luxury, as it were. And though they were involved in multiple faults, they gave absolutely no thought to regret or amendment, but were careful only about pursuing their delights, to have made some houses for the summertime, others for cold seasons. And these are equally to be removed at the time of punishment, and the various building are to be burned down by the enemy's fire.

[Chapter 4]

4:1-3 Hear this word, you fat cows that are on the mountain of Samaria, you who make

[65]Cf. 2 Kings 7:3-8.
[66]Cf. 1 Kings 12:29.

[67]Cf. 1 Kings 13:1-6; Jerome, *Commentary on Amos* 3:13-15 (ACT 2:330).
[68]Cf. 1 Kings 13:4.
[69]Cf. 1 Kings 13:5-6.
[70]Cf. 1 Kings 13:2.

a false accusation against the needy and crush the poor, who say to your masters, Bring, and we will drink. The Lord God has sworn by his holy one that, behold, the days will come on you, and they will lift you up on pikes, and your remains in boiling pots. And you will go out through the openings, one after another, and you will be cast forth into Armon, says the Lord.

Although the profaneness of the whole nation had to be rebuked, nevertheless he was directing his reproof especially against the rich and the wealthy, who did not make use of just one house, but they used various dining rooms to suit the occasion, and they adorned them with resplendent ivory.[71] Justly then he ascribes to them the name *fat cows.* For their speech was earmarked by lowings, and "their belly was god, and their glory was in their shame."[72] The following can be appropriately added as well, that they are said to have been named not merely from the vices of their character but from the brand of their very impiety. Thus, those who had accepted the worship of bull calves[73] should be marked with the name of *cows.* But they are denoted as *fat* in accordance with what blessed David finds fault with: "Their iniquity has come forth, as it were, from fatness; they have passed into the affection of the heart. They have thought and have spoken wickedness, they have spoken iniquity on high."[74] Therefore, you who sit *on the mountain of Samaria* (that is, in the royal city), and you who are swollen with royal acquaintances, you have worn down *the poor* so as to provide instruments for your own luxury by despoiling them. But as for what he says, *You who say to your masters: Bring, and we will drink,* this should be understood as follows. Either they have called their very idols their *masters* (namely, those from whom they were earnestly begging for an abundance of things, for they had placed all their happiness in timely and elegant feasts) or at least [they have called] their inferiors "masters," all who by farming out works even to the leaders of their crimes sought this reward from them, at whose profit they often sinned, so as not to lack a drink. But what will they attain in exchange for this impudence? *The Lord God has sworn by his holy one*—that is, he has decreed, he has established that they be maltreated by the unknown holiness of his own judgment. For it is coming, or rather, the time is already approaching, when your flesh *will be lifted up on pikes and [your] remains in boiling pots.* However, he has changed the comparison from cows, which are served to those feasting, either to barbarians or soldiers; and since he had branded them as profane by the way he designated them, he announces a second time that they will be subjected to the destruction of themselves. Therefore, here he has recorded *pikes* for spits—that is, for the awls with which cow meat is pierced and roasted over the smoke of burning coals. But we should understand the *remains* either as the guts or as those portions that, being rather crumbly, are boiled in pots rather than roasted on awls. And since he had said that they had completely forgotten their honest character and fear, they measured even the rewards of their crimes by their gluttonous stomachs, he justly added, because I invaded with the very fire of captivity; they are exposed to those who are reveling and to enemies about to swallow them down, as it were. *And you will go out through the openings, one after another, and you will be cast forth into Armon, says the Lord.* With the lines above he had concluded the metaphor derived from cows and feasting, but at the end he returns to a simple piece of information and says that they are to be dragged forth from their broken-down walls. This indicates the overthrow of the city. Now according to Hebrew idiom, *one after another*

[71]Cf. Amos 3:15.
[72]Phil 3:19.
[73]Cf. 1 Kings 12:25-33.
[74]Ps 73:7-9.

shows that the captives meet each other in turn or mutually accompany each other.[75] They will be removed to the mountains of Armenia in the Assyrian conquest.[76] But let us consider the remaining things as well.

4:4-6 Come to Bethel and act wickedly, to Gilgal and multiply transgression. And bring your victims in the morning, your tithes in three days. And offer a sacrifice of praise with leaven, and call free-will offerings, and proclaim it. For so you have wanted it, O children of Israel, says the Lord God. Therefore, I also have given you dullness of teeth in all your cities and want of bread in all your places. And you have not returned to me, says the Lord.

The whole text of the reproof itself shows that this was the chief or, rather, the sole motive of the prophets in announcing the disasters that were looming over those who were in sin, that dread would give rise to correction in them. For since due to shamelessness in the one transgressing they resisted this counsel of the judge who was quite ready to forgive, a sort of struggle seemed to arise between God and human beings. But since it was not an equal contest—namely, since it was God who decrees, but humans are the ones subject to things that were bitter—for that reason sometimes he addresses them with derision and reproaches the very struggle that they had chosen for themselves.[77] He says, *Come to Bethel and act wickedly*. In the imperative mood, but using irony and scoffing, he announces those things in which he is offended. This figure of speech [irony] is praised in noble literature.[78] Therefore, he insolently upbraids desecrated Israel, in order to threaten them for the pursuits that they had chosen. And he tells them not to cease visiting *Bethel* and *Gilgal*. These are cities that the earlier prophets showed to be teeming with idols.[79] But let them accumulate an increase in their transgressions and offer *victims in the morning*; let them serve zealously by the offering of *tithes*; let them place *leavened* bread on the altar, which were called "praise," so to speak, or *free-will offerings*. All of this should be understood as follows. They had transferred to idols the orders and rites of the religious ceremonies, which they had received from the holy law. For those things they had decreed were to be venerated for God's sake. But just as they had impiously transferred these same observances to the idols, so also they impudently altered the greater part of them as well. Hence he reproves both equally—that is, since they had either transferred the legal institutions to the idols to which they had defected or they had arbitrarily deformed these things, both of which succeeded in achieving the same impiety, doubtless they should either transfer these observances, which God has commanded are to be rendered unto himself, to godless shrines or else, as if he is speaking with scorn and with the spirit of one who is correcting, they should change something from these that had been established. Finally, satirizing that criminal fault of their arrogant mind, he says, *For so you have wanted it, O children of Israel, says the Lord God*. Therefore, he says, Keep after the pursuits that you have chosen, so that the appropriate rewards may accompany you, a taste of which you already took from the greatest part. For *I have given you dullness of teeth in all your cities, and want of bread in all your places. And you have not returned to me, says the Lord*. By *dullness of teeth* he meant to be understood not that which comes from illness but from scarcity. However, the reason he placed *want of bread* after *dullness of teeth* is so that the sense would be the same, because

[75]Cf. Jerome, *Commentary on Amos* 4:1-3 (ACT 2:332).
[76]Cf. 2 Kings 19:37 Vulgate.
[77]Cf. Jerome, *Commentary on Amos* 4:4-6 (ACT 2:334).
[78]Quintilian speaks of irony in *Inst Orat* 9.2.
[79]Cf. Julian's *Commentary on Hosea* 4:15-16; 7:3-7; 9:15-17; 10:13-15; 12:3-6, 11a.

their teeth seemed to be pressed together by their forgetting how to work, and they had grown disaccustomed to cutting into or grinding foods, and after a long period of time they experienced a kind of numbness. But although the chastisement had struck you so bitterly, *you have not returned to me, says the Lord.* Clearly by this line he has indicated two things at once—namely, their stubbornness in transgression and his kindness in counsel, he who had certainly inflicted these scourges not in order to punish but in order to correct. But they resisted this counsel to their own misfortune, and they entered into a kind of struggle (as we said earlier[80]). And therefore let us listen to what he goes on to say.

4:7-8 I also withheld from you rain, when there were still three months until the harvest. And I rained on one city and did not send rain on another. One part was rained on, and the part on which I did not send rain withered. And two and three cities went to another city to drink water and were not filled. And you have not returned to me, says the Lord.

Above he showed that the abundance of crops had been destroyed by a sudden plague.[81] Since no amendment followed, he provided even clearer evidence of his indignation and shows that, by withholding the rains, he also choked the first sprouts that were growing from the roots. Consequently he added that he has not removed the comforting rains from all people in common, lest they attribute what had happened to their fortune rather than to his anger.[82] But in order that you may perceive that the drought came about by my judgment, he says, *I rained upon one city, and did not send rain on another city.* Thus, at the same time as comfort is denied to you, O people, you might be tormented by the example of your neighbor. The scarcity of rain was so great also that it did not satisfy the thirst of those places that it seemed to have sprinkled. Nevertheless, you who ran like cattle to the rumor of rain refused to return to me by the amendment of your will; and this was done to such an extent that both your constant misfortunes and my ministrations were rendered completely unfruitful.

4:9 I struck you with a burning wind and with mildew. The caterpillar has eaten up your many gardens, and your vineyards, your olive groves, and fig groves. And you have not returned to me, says the Lord.

That pile of your iniquities will be duly reckoned, because although I have so often taken up a work of severity, nevertheless I have accomplished nothing in the way of your correction. Therefore, instead of acts of kindness I will recount whatever troubles you have heaped up. And I admit that it is as if I had forgotten my kindness, even while I exert myself to overcome your pernicious obstinacy in wrongdoing. Therefore, I did not delay to double your misfortunes, or rather, even to multiply them. And when the people were deprived of the aid of crops, I removed also the comforts of fruits and of gardens so that, just as the long drought devoured the hope of the harvest, so also either the pestilential air or the swarming caterpillar destroyed the good things of autumn and winter; *and you have not returned to me, says the Lord.*

4:10 I sent death to you in the way of Egypt. I struck down your young men with the sword, even to the captivity of your horses. And I made the stench of your camp to come up into your nostrils; and you have not returned to me, says the Lord.

The mention of Egypt can be understood in two ways. That entire people, which is said to

[80]See under Amos 4:4-6.

[81]Cf. Amos 4:6.

[82]Cf. Jerome, *Commentary on Amos* 4:7-8 (ACT 2:336-37).

have numbered six hundred thousand from twenty years and above,[83] is shown to have died out in the desert, apart from Joshua and Caleb.[84] Rightly, therefore, God says here that those whom he declares must be destroyed by slaughter lay dead in the manner of the Egyptian departure. Or else, as blessed Hosea teaches, when the Assyrians threatened, the Israelites requested help from the Egyptians, yet they obtained no remedy.[85] Consequently, the prophetic speech announces that the *death in the way of Egypt* has been sent against them. Doubtless it was not allied armies but rather a very furious enemy that fell on them along that way. The things that follow agree more with this sense—that is, it indicates that both young men and horses in the camp were destroyed in the siege or crushed by captivity. But he says, although the *stench of your camp* tormented you in your confinement, and though you saw that the evils of captivity were to be inflicted on you immediately, not even then did you *return to me, says the Lord.*

4:11 I overthrew you as God overthrew Sodom and Gomorrah, and you became as a firebrand plucked out of the burning; and you have not returned to me, says the Lord.

How, therefore, can you believe that I will allow so much fruit of my chastisements to perish on account of you? I say, *I overthrew you as God overthrew Sodom and Gomorrah, and you became as a firebrand plucked out of the burning; and you have not returned to me, says the Lord.* "Who is wise, and knows these things? Then he will understand the mercies of the Lord,"[86] which of course he does not cease to offer in all his ministrations. Therefore, even in the present passages, though the speech certainly proceeds with a great show of severity, nevertheless he demonstrates that these mercies overflow and superabound. Thus, he teaches that the blows he has inflicted seem heavier by far to himself than to those who suffer them. He says, *I overthrew you as God overthrew Sodom and Gomorrah.* Surely the hope of the promised deliverance likewise confirms that this did not happen to the Israelite people. Accordingly the same meaning is found, since the disasters that I inflicted raged against your blood to such a degree that the Sodomites themselves do not seem to me to have endured greater things. For according to the measure of necessity by which I had claimed you for myself, that accumulation of calamities must be equated to those fires by which that filthy multitude went up in flames with their houses and lands.[87] For although I granted you the hope of recovering your liberty, nevertheless you seem to me to be like some half-burned *firebrand* that is removed from the flames rather than one that continues with vigorous strength.

4:12-13 Therefore, I will do these things to you, O Israel. And after I have done this to you, prepare to meet your God, O Israel. For behold, he who forms the mountains and creates the wind, and proclaims his word to man, he who makes the morning mist and walks on the high places of the earth, the Lord the God of hosts [is] his name.

And because you have decided to contend with my kindness with shameless obstinacy, and you are forcing me to reveal my severity, *I will do to you* that which the order of chastisements itself demands. For it is not proper that your shamelessness should seem to have possessed more strength than our rebuke and that the latter, as if exhausted, should stop before either your iniquity or your life is

[83]Cf. Ex 12:37; Num 26:51.
[84]Cf. Num 14:29-30.
[85]Cf. Hos 7:11; 12:1; Jerome, *Commentary on Amos* 4:10 (ACT 2:339).
[86]Ps 107:43.
[87]Cf. Gen 19:24-25.

ended. Therefore, as far as I am concerned, I will prolong my resolve to heal; but it will stand to your account whether that manifold chastisement should lead to your correction or instead to punishment. Therefore, I recently enumerated those misfortunes—that is, the scarcity of crops and rain, but an abundance of locusts and caterpillars, the consumption of any surviving greenness, the pestilence ravaging the sprouts and the stems of the season, and finally the evils of the enemy's siege turning the whole camp into a ruin. Moreover, the sword raged at home and abroad. Certainly, he says, I compared all this to that destruction by which through my compassionate mercy Sodom had perished. Thus, the captivity that is about to return your survivors seems like scorched firebrands. I say that all those things have been ineffective of your betterment. But I will do this to you who are clearly under the uninterrupted course of the same purpose—namely, so that when the ruinous impiety has been driven off, you might adopt a disposition of amendment. And for that reason, after you see that what I announce to you is being carried out, gird yourselves to meet your Lord, having come to a better hope, that having been struck down by the aspect of judgment, you might not either despair of salvation or dread to appear before the eyes of the judge. For your reckoning is with him who does not desire the death of the one dying[88] but who runs to the aid even of persons who have been doomed, if he sees that they have repented of their crimes.[89] Some people[90] have thought that this passage—that is, where he says, *Therefore, I will do these things to you*—is to be understood in the following way. The outward form of the threat has been concealed intentionally, so that to whatever extent the listener could imagine anything that was the most horrible, that too is what he would believe had been promised. But it may be observed that the matter was not allowed to match the suspicions of those who were frightened, but after a little while he made public what he said would happen. For as if by way of repetition he appended to the things that came in between, which came into effect at the power of the Creator, "Hear this word, which I speak concerning you as a lamentation. The house of Israel has fallen, has fallen, and it shall rise no more. The virgin of Israel has been cast forth on her land; there is no one to raise her up."[91] And the arrangement of meanings is woven together in such a way that our God in his customary manner has carefully declared the reasons for the inflicted captivity, which doubtless seems to have been carried out, as it were, against his will. But let us return to the arrangement of the reading. Therefore, after he said, *I will do this to you, O Israel. And after I have done this to you, prepare to meet your God, O Israel—For behold,* he says, *he who forms the mountains and creates the wind, and declares his word to man, he who makes the morning mist, and walks upon the high places of the earth, the Lord of hosts is his name.* For the sake of inspiring reverence for the judge in the hearts of the guilty ones, he interposes the works of the Creator, so that either the prudent hearer may understand the censurer's affection for himself or so that the one who sees that the universe subsists by the power of the One who is threatening him may not be in doubt about the execution of punishment. That is, You, *O Israel*, consider who is the assessor[92] of your offenses; surely it is the One through whom all things were made, and without whom nothing is made;[93] he who fashioned and separated the elements by his

[88]Cf. Ezek 18:23, 32.

[89]Cf. Jon 3:5-10; Jer 18:7-8.

[90]Cf. Jerome, *Commentary on Amos* 4:12-13 (ACT 2:341).

[91]Amos 5:1-2.

[92]Baxter, "Notes," 31, suggests this meaning of *expunctor*.

[93]Cf. Jn 1:3.

command;[94] he who caused the stars to shine, the valleys to sink down, the fields to lie flat, the mountains to rise up; he who instructed the breathable air with which is filled the middle empty space from the sky to the earth, at one time to condense into a *mist,* at another to be moved in the *wind.* The daily works of his providence are revealed by the various functions of the elements. Though he is so great in the preeminence of his power, yet he deems it worthy to communicate to mankind *his word*—that is, his law. And among the wonders of his rule, by which he causes the *mists* to issue forth from the earth, when the morning sun has breathed on them, until they are either amassed together by the lingering of the same vapor or they are wholly dried up, or rather, when suitable, they are led to higher regions mingled in the clouds, and the higher ones return from every mountain and pour out the waters of the gathered rains on what lies below. And thus the imprinted traces of his own rule attest to him, him, I say, the Creator of the elements, whose name is *Lord of Hosts*—that is, whose power is such that the throngs of angels serve his will, and they acknowledge him as their king and creator—he who, I say, strives with you by means of that benevolence. Insofar as he declares that torments have to be inflicted on you, if in some way, when the feelings of the penitent one have been awakened in your hearts, assuredly the late amendment may remove the accused from the punishment. Since obviously you are ruining this relief by your stubborn depravity, "Hear this word, which I speak concerning you as a lamentation,"[95] whose warnings you have always rejected: "these words," I say, by which we are pursuing what is best for you.

[94]Cf. Gen 1:1-31.

[95]Amos 5:1a.

[Chapter 5]

5:1b-2 It is fallen, it is fallen and it shall rise no more. The virgin of Israel has been cast forth on her land; there is no one to raise her up.

That is, that nation that descends from the renowned root of Israel, and that either previously merited or was accustomed to be called a *virgin* (for no profaneness had violated her chastity by which she had been associated in fellowship with her own leader, or no captivity had contaminated her thriving happiness of its constant integrity). Having now been exposed to being trampled on by the conqueror, she bears abuses and torments simultaneously. And she does not enjoy any comfort from the disasters being removed. Moreover, she lies out of bed *on her land* like a woman subjected to defilements, and has come even to the graves by the oppressing misfortunes. And *no one* is able to help and to *raise up* the downcast whom the censure of the Almighty has crushed. Therefore, from that line in which it says, "he who forms the mountains and creates the wind,"[96] up to the present passage, the statement can be understood as spoken from the persona of the prophet—namely, from the power of the discoursing God. However, as for what he says, that *Israel has fallen on her land* in such a way that she will absolutely *rise* no more, notice that both the preceding and the following sentences promise relief by the removal of the misfortunes at some time. Moreover, they threaten the diminution of the people at the time of the attentive punishment itself rather than their annihilation. Therefore, we should understand that either he has reckoned the dangers brought in with the affection of one who is mourning too copiously, and thus has called them utterly destroyed whom he saw were in large part crushed; or else under the

[96]Amos 4:13.

personae of those whom captivity was consuming he has said that they are sunk, and he did not indicate that the nation of Israel could be raised up by anyone.

5:3 For thus says the Lord: The city from which came forth a thousand, there shall be left in it a hundred; and from which there came a hundred, there shall be left in it ten, in the house of Israel.

The history of Kings makes clear that the misfortunes of captivity did not rush in all at once, but the people were chastised at many times while their amendment was awaited.[97] And for that reason also our God addresses them through the prophets by a voice that changes its tone. At one time he says that their ruin is definite since ruin had to be declared. At another time he promises them prosperity if they amend. Therefore, do not surmise that there is any discrepancy in the statements, as though he were restricting them to one time; rather, he distributes the judgments that have been set forth over long periods of time, and they are appropriate for the circumstances. Then you will find that coherence is maintained in everything, and truly the reign of the profane people was diminished bit by bit by increasing adversities, until it reached the destruction of the final captivity. Accordingly we should understand that the decimation of the nation was carried out in those cities and regions that were laid waste while the capital city of Samaria was still standing.[98] Thus, while nine parts had perished, the one that was the last portion remained. For this decimation was carried out for this purpose, so that, just as he gave some over to just destruction, so he corrected others by the example of those who perished. The exhortation of the judge himself has sounded forth immediately.

5:4-6 For thus says the Lord to the house of Israel: Seek me, and you will live. Do not seek Bethel, and do not enter Gilgal, nor pass over to Beersheba. For Gilgal will be led away as a captive, and Bethel will be useless. Seek the Lord and live, lest the house of Joseph be burned with fire, and it will devour, and there will not be one to quench Bethel.

He says, This is what you should have learned from the law and from piety, O Israel—namely, to cleave to the one God, your creator, by the duty of continuous devotion. He is the one who paid you back quite graciously when you were blessed, and when he became angry he paid you back as one who was very wretched. At last fierce trials have taught you this. Even now, if you want to live, take up the pursuits of one who is repenting, and reflect on the amendment of your actions. Therefore, seek me, the one whom you abandoned in your devoted service to profaneness. Seek me, I say. I am ready to be found, and I will meet you as soon as you begin to seek. For "everyone that asks will receive, and he who seeks will find, and to him who knocks, it shall be opened."[99] Do not add to your sacrileges by hesitating to seek me. Otherwise, by neglecting the remedies that have been offered, you may be betraying yourself as being more terrible than you would be by defiling precepts that had been promulgated. *Seek me, and you will live. Do seek Bethel and Gilgal and Beersheba.* Now as the account of Kings relates, these were the cities that had transferred their devotion to the calves that Jeroboam had made and to the rest of the idols.[100] Therefore, the Lord has regard for them and announces that they should cease frequenting those [idols] that profaneness has rendered hateful. Otherwise,

[97]Cf. 1 Kings 15:18; 17; 20:1; 2 Kings 6:25, 28; 7:4; 8:1; 10:32; 13:7, 20, 22; 15:19, 29; 17:3-6.
[98]Cf. 2 Kings 15:29.

[99]Mt 7:8; Lk 11:10.
[100]Cf. 1 Kings 12:28-29; Jerome, *Commentary on Amos* 5:4-5 (ACT 2:347).

they might perish along with them, having indeed been equally appointed for destruction. *Seek the Lord*, therefore, for he does not desire the death of the one who dies.[101] Seek him and return to him, *and live*, lest you begin to be consumed by the fire that is cast down on the roofs of the temples. But let us consider the things that remain as well.

5:7-8 You who turn judgment into wormwood and forsake justice in the land, [seek] him who makes Arcturus and Orion,[102] who turns darkness into morning, and who changes day into night, he who calls the waters of the sea and pours them out on the face of the whole earth. The Lord is his name.

By the same arrangement that he used earlier, in order to unfold the judge's power, he has warned that he is the same Creator; and he shows the purpose of him, who wanted to give counsel to everyone, as far as it lay within him. For his goodness alone had provided the reason for their existence. He says that they had rendered his *judgment*, which would have been sweet to the innocent, as very bitter to themselves, like *wormwood*. Therefore, we ought to understand his words, *You who turn judgment into wormwood*, as follows. Either he is complaining that they have turned the divine judgment into bitterness, judgment that due to their merits they have compelled to be deadly to themselves, or else he may be saying that the very consideration of human reason was corrupted into bitterness—namely, by their preferring the worship of idols to the sacred rites that they had received through Moses. But as for what follows, *and you forsake justice in the land*, we can apply this to the fault of the choice itself, which had abandoned the standard of judging as something to be trodden underfoot, unless he was pointing to that which he had called *justice* in the lines added below this. For it says, *him who makes Arcturus and Orion, and who turns darkness into morning*. Therefore, he has called our very God *justice*, who is rightly named both "power" and "wisdom."[103] And complaining that he has been forsaken by the wicked (that is, spurned), he recounts his works by which he governs the world, doubtless in order to amass the criminal charges against those who were not afraid to exasperate a God of such great majesty. Now he has introduced those names of the stars (*astrorum*) that seem to have been imposed by pagans, although other translators have only said "constellations" (*sidera*).[104] We could coherently understand that the prophet has made use of the familiar names in order to distinguish the stars, not to provide verification of fables. This agrees with the fact that the apostle did not scorn to adopt statements of the poets.[105] Now the following should also be noted. When he wanted to treat a description of the arrangement of the heavens, he described the four zones, which are also called directions, by the names of the stars; that is, he establishes the north as *Arcturus*, the south as *Orion*, which is in that direction. But he marks out the rising and setting of the sun by the interchange of day and night. At this point having excellently admired the power of the Creator, he says that he *turns the* very *darkness into morning*. For in this way the sphere of the sun, when it has unfurled its rings, suddenly pours forth its splendor on the lands, so that it seems not to have driven off the *darkness* it has found but to have changed it into light. *Who calls the waters of the sea, and pours them out*

[101]Cf. Ezek 18:23, 32.

[102]For Arcturus and Orion, see the note at Job 9:9.

[103]1 Cor 1:24.

[104]Cf. Jerome, *Commentary on Amos* 5:7-9 (ACT 2:348-49). G. Bouwman, *Des Julian von Aeclanum Kommentar zu den Propheten Osee, Joel und Amos. Ein Beitrag zur Geschichte der Exegese* (Rome: Pontificio Istituto Biblico, 1958), 125-26, emphasizes that Julian's knowledge of Hebrew is derived from Jerome's commentaries and from Theodore of Mopsuestia's *Commentary on the Psalms*.

[105]Cf. Acts 17:28; 1 Cor 15:33; Titus 1:12.

upon the face of the earth. The Lord is his name. While speaking very elegantly and knowledgeably of the functions of the elements pertaining to the disposition and governance of the Creator, he said indeed that God made all things. By his power doubtless he both formed and watches over these same arrangements. Yet he showed especially that he made use of the service of his star for creating the crops. Doubtless he means the sun that prepares the night for us by its departure, the day by its return. Therefore, since his discourse had touched on a depiction of natural things, he added likewise the fact that either liquid evaporated from the lands or rivers drawn from the marine depths were seized on high in the same way by evaporation and suspended from above from the clouds, which, now no longer able to rise to the heights of the sky with that very weight, deposited the bitter saltiness in a downpour. And in this way at last they were returned to the parched lands, and thus by the intermingling of opposites (namely, of liquid and of evaporation), remarkable fruitfulness occurred in the nourishing of the crops. For it would not have been possible in any case to explain an enterprise of such magnitude apart from him who alone is shown to be the Lord of the whole world by right of creation. But let us consider the things that remain as well.

5:9 He who smiles at the destruction on the strong, and brings plundering on the mighty.

He has disclosed the consequence of the business that the previously spoken description of his power prepared—that is, in order to awaken fear in the hearts of those listening, and they might understand how great a mass of disasters was hanging over them, with whom the judge of such great authority was incensed. He says, He who is the Creator of the universe continues to blot out merits as well; and although no one is able to oppose his strength, nevertheless *he smiles* at the torments of the guilty, who seemed to themselves to be mighty, namely those whom he will crush with such ease, that he makes his disdain known with a smile rather than an outcry. Why not? Since all things are subject to his will, and in view of the diversity of merits both adversities and prosperity ensue on the audience from his statement. Therefore, *he smiles at the destruction on* those who seemed to themselves to be powerful and who were accustomed to say, "We will magnify our tongue; our lips are our own; who is our Lord?"[106] I say, while they most impiously arrogate to themselves misfortune of this kind stemming from their own strength, he says, the eternal avenger himself *smiles* at the torments of affliction, and he indicates his indignation by the employment of the same gaping mouth, which is at odds with his warmth. Accordingly, he calls the Israelites *strong* and *mighty*, either on account of envy of pride or on account of the memory of their ancient good fortune. He has already forewarned them, that for the most part they have been destroyed and are to be transferred by the impending captivity.

5:10-11 They have hated him that rebukes in the gate and have abhorred him that speaks perfectly. Therefore, because you robbed the poor and took the choice prey from him, you built houses with square stone, and will not dwell in them; you will plant most delightful vineyards and will not drink their wine.

The arrangement of the prophet's discourse is preserved—namely, that after the punishments were foretold, immediately the reason for that same harshness is added, clearly so that the Lord of such great devotion may not seem to have done anything out of indignation rather

[106]Ps 12:4.

than out of sound reason, and likewise in order to show that he takes care of the poor with so much kindness since he links their humiliations and the plundering to the violation of religion. By this he demonstrates that it is consistent, since no concern for civil justice is present in profane minds, no feeling of humanity, but rather they spring up with their companions as though attacked by a gadfly of frenzy, and they tear apart all the poor with acknowledged savagery; whence even these ones, who had fallen away to the worship of idols by a sacrilegious mind, inwardly do not hold back from any acts of wickedness, but they are as pernicious to their companions and to their fellow citizens as they are to the Lord himself, whom they hatefully opposed. Now as for what he says, that they pursued with *hatred* those who *rebuke in the gate,* he is showing the custom of the Jewish institutions, which had been arranged in such a way that the witnesses of the affairs resided in the gates of every city, lest the one who had need of their consideration should grow weary from some legal question, but rather in the very entrance could meet with those with whom he was going to court. Now we may suppose that this custom, which had been established through blessed Moses for the priestly nation,[107] did not remain among the Israelites, especially when they lived under the authority of the kings and of the wicked. Rather, he is showing that these ones violated even the civil laws with religious observances, and with the proclaimers of these rites they assumed a hatred of the virtues; and, if someone had wanted to exhort [them] to amendment and holiness, they immediately destroyed him by their conspiracy of hatred. But he shows why they opposed the warnings of the censors when he says, *You robbed the poor and took the choice prey from him.* Therefore, in order that you might go on without any hindrance—namely, of either shame or fear, through the injuries and humiliations of the poor—you hated the temperate people issuing the warnings. But one should take note of what he says, that they took the *choice prey* from the poor, though assuredly it would be considered more logical to say that they took one of the two things [they possessed], so that either those whom he acknowledges were *poor* did not have great things that they lost or that they should rightly be called "wealthy" if the robber took every precious thing from them. Therefore, one should understand either that he has called them *poor* whom the wealthy had rendered poor by their pillaging; or else he was considering the feelings of those who own the things rather than the instances of the losses. Although their property was scanty, yet due to that very scarcity it was precious to the poor people, and it was removed by an atrocious act of greed. As a testimony about this matter, let us indeed call to mind at least one example. The very stupid king Ahab coveted the vineyard of Naboth, a holy man, which was indeed small in size but most pleasing to its owner and precious on account of its very delightfulness.[108] And when the king had ordered the owner to sell it, Naboth answered that he could not despise his paternal inheritance, nor if possible did he want to be deprived of it. Then the king, spurred on by the urgings of his utterly profane wife, added the crime of cruelty to his avarice. After killing Naboth, he seized the vineyard that he had coveted. So then, by their cruel ventures they *took the choice prey*—namely, that than which the owners valued nothing to be more precious. Let us hear what is declared to them for these deeds.

5:11-12 [Therefore, because you robbed the poor,] you built houses with square stone

[107]Cf. Deut 17:5; 21:19; 22:15, 24; 25:7.

[108]Cf. 1 Kings 21:1-16.

and will not dwell in them; you will plant most delightful vineyards and will not drink their wine. Because I know your many crimes and your great sins.

Up to this point the audacity of your plundering was, of course, aimed to make available equipment for your luxury, and you were adorning your dwellings very expensively, as if they were going to be both for protection and for pleasure. But two things are going to happen to you simultaneously, that you build them indeed, but you will not be able to live in them; and so you would be tormented as much by the construction of your work as by the loss of it. And, what is more, in this you would feel your sorrow piling up, since you would be deprived not of makeshift but of elegant dwelling places; nor, of course, would you be able to complain about this misfortune or, in the midst of your groans, to hope for divine relief. The mass of blameworthy faults stands opposed to their prayers. Why is that? Because they see at once that they themselves committed crueler deeds against both citizens and neighbors. Now those ten tribes of Samaria endured all these things, as the history has revealed, often from their neighboring enemies, to be sure,[109] but especially from the Assyrians.[110] In fact, Judah shared in the same destruction when Babylon was on the rampage.[111] Since, therefore, you have been deprived of your homes that were very spacious and beautifully adorned, and of fruitful vineyards planted by your own labor (which is even more), when the captivity comes on you as well, attribute this to the sins you have committed, which were very great.

[109]Cf. 2 Kings 13:1-9, 22-23 (Hazael); 2 Kings 13:20 (Moabites).
[110]Cf. 2 Kings 15:19, 29; 17:3.
[111]Cf. 2 Kings 24:1.

5:12 Enemies of the just,[112] taking a gift, and oppressing the poor at the gate. Therefore, the prudent will keep silent at that time, for it is an evil time.

He disturbs the condition of the corrupted city by means of various notions, and just as he said that they had spurned or, rather, had even struck down those exhorting [them] to justice,[113] so logically he calls these same people *enemies of the just*. This may be reasonably understood in two ways. If *just* is taken to be a genitive singular, then they are being proclaimed to be *enemies* of justice; that is, I am accusing you of being not merely heedless of justice but haters of it. From this passion flows the deadly perversity of your pursuits, when, uniting shamelessness to iniquity, you do not even wish to conceal what you are doing; but *at the gate* of the city (namely, in the locations of the judicial investigations, with the people watching) you assess lawsuits but not according to their merits, but for a price. You even support the injustice of the wealthy out of the resources of the poor. Or else they may be thought to have been called *just enemies*, with *just* being a nominative plural. In that case, when their many great crimes have been listed, he added that they were *just enemies*; that is, they exhibited themselves to be, as it were, legitimate adversaries to religion and to God. Now the mode of expression is familiar to those who possess eloquence—namely, those who are in the habit of calling large armies and large provinces "just armies" and "just provinces."[114] But let us consider the things that remain as well.

[112]*Iusti* here can be genitive singular (of the just one) or nominative plural (just enemies). Jerome seems to have understood it as a genitive singular.
[113]Cf. Amos 5:10.
[114]*Iustus* in the sense of full, complete, in full number; cf. Livy 9.43. Bouwman, *Des Julian von Aeclanum Kommentar*, 124, claims that Julian's discussion here proves that textual criticism was foreign to him..

5:13 Therefore, the prudent will keep silence at that time, for it is an evil time.

The time has changed in its declension; for in recounting either the past or present acts of the people, it would have been more logical to say, "The prudent *kept* silence." Instead he says, *will keep silence*. Since, therefore, he had announced that they had undertaken a "just" (that is, a lawful) war against virtue and religion, fittingly, he says, they have silenced the mouths of those who called them back to justice. And any prudent person has ceased speaking with a groan and anguish, doubtless since he was contemplating that no place remained for the salvific teaching, and for that reason they ought to take counsel by keeping silence, since arguing does no more good. However, those ones are *prudent* who were compelled to silence by a common dread. Above he had said about them, "They have hated him that rebukes in the gate and have abhorred him that speaks perfectly."[115] Since, therefore, the audacity of the profaned people has conspired in this way, so that it pursues truth and piety of the teaching as though a state of war had been declared, any *prudent* teacher will weep, to be sure, but *will keep silent* when he sees that they have stopped their ears like deaf vipers,[116] lest anything be able to penetrate them from the salutary prophecies. This same thing, of course, seems to be conveying a question, which needs to be cleared up by a brief explanation. For indeed the guarded prudence of a teacher is praised who interiorly subdues himself with silence if adversity blows back from the side of his audience; and the teacher of the nations[117] "warns, reproaches, implores in season, out of season."[118] And nearly all sacred Scripture commends this perseverance. There is, therefore, a distinction that must be admitted, which is able to vindicate the harmony in the commands. As long as the people remain under the registry of being learners, even though they may be perpetrating many things through negligence, the lawful teacher certainly ought not to fear [rebuking] anyone's hidden offenses, but to take thought for all who gather to listen, with perseverance in teaching. For he hears that the money given to himself must be entrusted to the money changers, but another will come to demand back both the deposit and the interest.[119] But if there be such a great change for the worse, that they submit their necks in discipleship to the impiety of the common people and put up with the itch of the ears and assent only to silly stories,[120] then silence is obviously necessary, as the teachers say together with the prophet, "I was dumb, and was humiliated, and kept silence from good things, and my sorrow was renewed."[121]

5:14-15 Seek good, and not evil, that you may live. And the Lord the God of hosts will be with you, as he has said: Hate evil, and love good, and establish judgment at the gate; it may be that the Lord the God of hosts may have mercy on the remnants of Joseph.

These lines seem to have been inserted in the name of the merciful prophet—namely, as a reminder to the Israelites that they likewise have already been placed under that ruin, so that they might agree in their prayers and pursuits for their own amendment, lest perchance the God of hosts, whose mercy is as great as his power, may be appeased by amendments of this sort and might at least refrain from destroying the remnants of the worn-down nation. But he adds the ordered scheme that he has to the things above.

[115]Amos 5:10.
[116]Cf. Ps 58:4.
[117]Cf. 1 Tim 2:7.
[118]Cf. 2 Tim 4:2.
[119]Cf. Mt 25:14-30.
[120]Cf. 2 Tim 4:3.
[121]Ps 39:2-3.

5:16-17 Therefore, thus says the Lord the God of hosts, the sovereign Lord: In all the streets there shall be wailing. And in all places that are outside, it will be said, Alas, alas! And they will call the farmer to mourning, and those who know how to mourn to lamentation. And in all vineyards there shall be lamentation, because I will pass through in your midst, says the Lord.

When those lines are removed, which we have said were brought in under the persona of the prophet showing mercy,[122] the order of the invective flows on. Thus, after his words, "Enemies of the just, taking gifts, and oppressing the poor at the gate. Therefore the prudent will keep silence at that time, for it is an evil time,"[123] he seems to have connected what was brought in: *Therefore thus says the Lord God,* and the rest that follows—namely, the lamentations that are to be heard *in all the streets. And in all places,* he says, *that are outside it will be said: Alas, alas!* Since he had said that there would be wailing in the streets, he added also those that are outside by an intermingling of similar lamentation. Thus, he certainly does not seem to be threatening merely the cities. And so, *alas, alas, will be said* throughout the whole region, and the vineyards, fields, and mountains will resound with wretched lamentations. *Because I will pass through in your midst, says the Lord.* For a long time, he says, you have in no wise tested me, as though I were absent and simply did not see what you were doing. For you gave no thought to amendment during so many long periods of respite. At this very moment I, your very censor, am advancing on your nation, which has been polluted with sacrileges. I am he whom you will no longer be able to mock. But he says that he is *passing through,* in order to call to mind a memory of that time when one reads that he entered either Egypt or Sodom, destroying the firstborn of the Egyptians and the houses of Sodom.[124] Therefore, he says, *I will pass through* in this manner, in order to bring about the retribution that their offenses demand.[125] And this is why in the blessed Hosea, when he was discussing the alleviation of the judgment, he says, "For I am God and not man, the holy one in the midst of you, and I will not enter into the city."[126] Therefore, what there he had mercifully promised not to carry out, now in his anger he promises will happen—that is, he will pass through the midst of the people in the spirit of a punisher. But when the mass of these calamities has rushed in, *farmers* will assemble not to cultivate but *to mourn.* They will summon to themselves *those who know how to mourn.* This was introduced according to the custom of that region, which also flourished among other nations; for there were funeral songs, which the crowd sang to a rhythm, with the others singing chants. Therefore, in order to express a lawful funeral of the people, as it were, he announces that those who *know how to mourn* will be summoned.

5:18-20 Woe to those who desire the day of the Lord. So that it will be what for you? That day of the Lord [is] darkness and not light. As if a man should flee from the face of a lion, and a bear should meet him. Or enter into the house and lean with his hand on the wall, and a serpent should bite him. Shall not the day of the Lord be darkness and not light? And gloom, and no brightness in it?

The teacher of the nations[127] shows the plan and purpose of divine religion when he says,

[122]Julian thinks that Amos 5:14-15 interrupt the prophet's invective.
[123]Amos 5:12-13.

[124]Cf. Ex 12:29; Gen 19:24-25.
[125]Cf. Jerome, *Commentary on Amos* 5:16-17 (ACT 2:355).
[126]Hos 11:9.
[127]Cf. 1 Tim 2:7.

"The goodness of God leads you to repentance, but according to your hardness and impenitent heart, you treasure up for yourself wrath in the day of wrath."[128] Thus, by the very postponement [of punishment] you receive your amassed vengeance. Therefore, with this having been proposed for deliberation, the prophetic threat resounded throughout the generations of many kings.[129] And the display of terror, which rekindled a feeling of dread and amendment in the hearts of those listening, preceded the description of the calamities. But those who had grown accustomed to misusing the remedies prolonged the delay of punishments and deaths to support the lie—namely, by saying that the deceptive prophets were provoking terrors by mentioning *the day of the Lord*. Therefore, among the other things that they were speaking licentiously and wickedly, they said the following things too with derision—namely, that they *desired the day of the Lord* and wished that it might be revealed at last. It is not that they asked for it with true desires but because the falsity of the prophets' threats was proven, so long as the day of the Lord did not come. Hence the censor, conscious of his rectitude, announces to the impious that the suffering of the looked-for day follows that declaration, but the affliction will be multifaceted. Thus, that time does not correspond to the evidence of their good, but to harsh wages. Such storms of calamities would arise that a more violent crisis would always appear wherever those wretched ones thought to take refuge. *That day*, he says, will lie so neglected in the *darkness* of the torments that it leaves no light to reflect, but the most wretched ones would run to and fro from destruction to destruction, with terror driving them on, as though someone flees a pursuing *lion* only to run into a raging *bear*. And having suddenly experienced increased fear, he rushes into another *house* to hide, and when he puts his *hand* on the *wall* in order to rest a little after such great trouble, he incurs the bite of a serpent lurking in a crack, and so he perishes from the venom coursing through his veins. *Shall not the day of the Lord be darkness, and not light; and gloom, and no brightness in it?* I declare that that night is not only dark but also gloomy, on which obviously both the light of safety will be driven out, and the consoling stars will not even faintly gleam.

5:21-24 I hate, and have cast out your festivals, and I will not receive the odor of your assemblies. But if you offer me whole burnt offerings, and your gifts, I will not accept them, nor will I regard the vows of your fat beasts. Take away from me the tumult of your songs, and I will not hear the canticles of your harp. But judgment will be revealed as water, and justice as a mighty torrent.

Although in the greater part of his speech he set out to accuse Israel (that is, the ten tribes), nevertheless he touched on the transgressions of Judah as well. Indeed, even at the beginning of the work, when he mentioned the various nations, when he reached Judah he said, "For three crimes of Judah and for four will I not convert him, because they have cast away the law of the Lord and has not kept his commands? For their idols have deceived them, after which their fathers have gone. And I will send fire into Judah, and it will devour the houses of Jerusalem."[130] Therefore, although he started out against Israel quite vehemently, nevertheless, after the speech reached the depiction of the day of the Lord (that is, the time of punishment) and strove to explain his severity with various images—assuredly this terrible display of vengeance threatened the people of Judah no less than those of

[128] Rom 2:4-5.
[129] Cf. Amos 1:1; Hos 1:1.

[130] Amos 2:4-5.

Samaria—Judah still seemed to be celebrating the comforts of the religious ceremonies also, which he showed were completely weakened and cast down, while Israel had been desecrated.[131] That is to say, he showed that he himself would be the just judge of both [sets of] tribes at the fitting time of the censure that was to be displayed. At that time, when they were beset by the loss of their customs, this sort of means of assuaging would be inefficacious. Therefore, with the postponement of the sentence, he announces both to Judah and to Israel that he loathes their assemblies and sacrifices, and he despises their vows in which they are accustomed to offer fat sacrificial victims, and he is so displeased by their songs, in which they sing the praises of God, that he proclaims that he senses *tumults* more than songs. For indeed all these services of religion are shown to be pleasing to God at that time, at that acceptable time, when they are presented with good morals. But if they practice those things while serving sacrileges and wickedness, then they achieve nothing in procuring salvation, so that their prayer "is turned to sin."[132] So, when all these comforts have been rebuked and driven out, *the judgment of God will be revealed as water.* To keep this from being obscure, he added, *and justice as a mighty torrent.* Doubtless the inundation of the calamity sent against you will carry you away and will destroy you like a flood. For he eagerly desires to express his power and the acquaintance of his punishment with various images. Just as it can be mitigated by weeping before it strikes, so also, when it happens, it cannot be eluded.

5:25-27 Surely you did not offer sacrificial animals and sacrifice to me in the desert for forty years, O house of Israel, did you? And you carried the tent for your Moloch, and the image of your idols, the star of your god, which you made. And I will cause you to move beyond Damascus, said the Lord, the God of hosts [is] his name.

The blessed Stephen recalled this passage as well at the time of his glorious suffering. For when he was surrounded by multitudes of raging Jews, he explained the divine mystery foretold by the holy prophets of our Redeemer and said, "God turned and gave them up to serve the host of heaven, as it is written in the book of the prophets: Did you not offer victims and sacrificial animals to me for forty years, O house of Israel? And you took up the tent of Moloch, and the star of your god Rephan (*Rempha*), figures that you made to adore them; and I will carry you away beyond Babylon."[133] Now although this very passage seems to have its motive laid bare (that is, it is a censure reproving iniquitous peoples), nevertheless it has so intermixed the judgment sentences that pertain to various times that no little obscurity emerges from it. After all, Jerome adopted such an unfortunate opinion on this passage that he said that during the forty years that they are reported to have spent in the desert, they seem to have served not God but rather idols.[134] Yet surely the historical account does not attest to any such thing, but only that they forged a calf's head when blessed Moses was delaying. Yet they immediately ground it to pieces at Moses' command.[135] Therefore, it was not to the stars

[131]Cf. Jerome, *Commentary on Amos* 5:18-20 (ACT 2:356-57).
[132]Ps 109:7.

[133]Acts 7:42-43. In his citation of Amos, Stephen follows the LXX but substitutes Babylon for Damascus.
[134]Cf. Jerome, *Commentary on Amos* 5:25-27 (ACT, vol. 2, 360-61). Bouwman, *Des Julian von Aeclanum Kommentar,* 130, thinks Julian has misrepresented Jerome here. But also in his *Commentary on Isaiah* 1.15 (on Isa 1:11), Jerome says that God never willed the sacrifices of the Jews. At 1.16 (on Is 1:12) he qualifies this slightly and says, "Sacrifices, therefore, and the immolation of victims have not been requested by God as a matter of principle, but in order that they not be made to idols, and in order for us to make a transition from fleshly victims to spiritual sacrifices."
[135]Cf. Ex 32:1-20.

or to angels that they were offering lawful ceremonies. Our Creator composed the manner and arrangements of those things with his own mouth, and he commanded that all things must be offered to himself alone. In accordance with the custom of the Scriptures, therefore, a discourse of one who is reproaching has indeed joined together varying times, but times that are in other respects similar. This was done to show that in their present sacrileges they were imitating their impious ancestors, who wickedly asked that gods be made for them, and who perished in the desert waste. What wonder then, he says, if even these are driven out of their own borders beyond Damascus—namely, to perish in Babylon and beyond? But as for what he recorded, *the star of your god*, it is said that in Hebrew this is the name of a star—that is, the morning star (*luciferi*), whom the Saracens are reported to worship up to today.[136] Yet Scripture recounts no such thing about this—namely, that they decided to serve the stars too at that time when they made the head of an idol, doubtless in imitation of the Egyptian bull, whom they call Apis.[137] But we gather that for their imitation of the Egyptian superstition they are being compared also with the other Gentile nations, as if there would be no profaneness, since their reputation is not based on their venerating and worshiping through the taking up of one idol. A connection is made in the meanings, however, if those things that had been inserted are set aside. If what he had said, "Woe to those who desire the day of the Lord,"[138] has in view that which he says, *Surely you did not offer sacrificial animals and sacrifice to me in the desert, did you?* the meaning would be, this is how your profanity takes advantage of my patience and kindness, which postpones my vengeance for a long time. From this you conclude that that destruction is never going to come, since it has not come yet, although it has often been promised. You act as though examples are not at hand by which you may recognize my custom, that to those who are doubtless destined for destruction, he exercises forbearance for a long time to cause them to repent. But to pass over the rest, at least consider this, that when the people had come to Mount Sinai after being led out of Egypt, and when they halted in the midst of the miracles that were worthy of my powers, yet they reverted to the worship of idols, a worship that they had forsaken. And they merited to be appointed for destruction. Nevertheless, I for my part was not appeased by any sacrifices or gifts of theirs, but I granted them a period of forty years; nor did I permit my wrath to vent itself against the guilty, but I destroyed their multitudes already doomed to judgment. And thus the length of the time granted did not nullify the judgment that was announced, nor did my revulsion of the crime hasten the enkindled revenge. Why, therefore, do you doubt that what you see has already been done will take place? This means the reason the disasters that must come are being announced to you, and these same ones are not being inflicted, is so that a time of amendment may be offered. It is not that the retribution disappears, which no amount of time will be able to prevent. But since you are shamelessly taking advantage of the goodness of God, the end that came to your ancestors, whom you have imitated in your sacrileges, will attend you. Thus, just as their corpses fell in the desolate wilderness,[139] so also you too will die in a foreign land, having been driven from the borders of your fatherland.

[136]Cf. Jerome, *Commentary on Amos* 5:25-27 (ACT 2:360).
[137]Apis is a bull worshiped in Egypt; cf. Herodotus 2.153.
[138]Amos 5:18.
[139]Cf. Heb 3:17; 1 Cor 10:5.

Book Two on the Prophet Amos[140]

[Chapter 6]

6:1 Woe to you who are wealthy in Zion, and who trust in the mountain of Samaria, you nobles, heads of the peoples who enter the house of Israel with a great pomp.

Certainly the Scripture often points out that pride has always been hateful to God. Indeed, it was the beginning of sin, such that it changed angels into demons.[141] And this is why blessed David anxiously prays that he not be subjected to being trampled on by the proud. For he says, "There have all the workers of iniquity fallen."[142] Yet here he preserves the prophetic order while rebuking, in order to show that pride is more or less the fruit of impiety. By this course, the apostle's discourse also appears to have proceeded, when he said that they abandoned the Creator and served creatures.[143] He then added a list of crimes and shameful acts, and proclaimed that on account of those things they abounded in abominable deeds, since they had violated the laws of piety toward God.[144] Therefore, he says, *Woe to you who are wealthy in Zion, and who trust in the mountain of Samaria.* It is not that we esteem the crimes of the poor as less serious, but a greater hatred of your crimes strikes you, whom greater wealth has magnified. For what is the point of your being more illustrious in respect to public honor and wealth? It behooved you to have a greater zeal for religion. But now you strive to be rich no less in impiety than in money. Therefore, the lamentations will lay hold of you, but serious ones. For with respect to the divine judgment, some mercy may be applied to them that are of little account, "but the mighty shall be mightily tormented."[145] Therefore, among such great misfortunes of the lands, which experience such things either on account of lost strength or on account of the calamities that are already invading, *you trust* in the defenses and fortification of your locations (namely, in *Zion* and *Samaria*) thinking that you will be guarded against the wrath of the judge. *Woe to you who are wealthy in Zion, and who trust in the mountain of Samaria, you nobles, heads of the people who enter the house of Israel with a great pomp.* For you have never prostituted yourself more than in the time of adversities, so great was the greed for excess that filled you. When the power of your nation was already for the most part destroyed, nevertheless you swell with opulence and are abandoned to luxury within your besieged cities.

6:2 Pass over to Calneh, and see from thence into Emath the great, and go down into Gath of the Philistines (*Palaestinorum*), and to all the best kingdoms of these, [to see] if their border be larger than your border.

Suitably he has mentioned foreign nations, and through the circumstance of another discourse he showed that the Creator of the universe had assigned to others the lands that they were inhabiting and the kingdoms in which they were flourishing; [and] in fact those peoples were not desiring more things, but these ones are shown to be both ungrateful and profane. They had been so pestilential to their cities that those whom they had destroyed before as examples, these same ones afterward they tread underfoot with a deeply spiteful arrogance. Indeed, the form of the divine judgment must be noted. In its presence the merits of

[140]Julian divides his commentary into two books, Jerome into three. Jerome's second book covers Amos 4:1–6:1 and his third book covers Amos 6:2–9:15.

[141]Cf. Sir 10:13; Ezek 28:15-17.

[142]Ps 36:12.

[143]Cf. Rom 1:18-32.

[144]J. Lössl treats this passage as demonstrating Julian's pattern of linking Amos with Paul. "Pauline Exegesis," 15-16.

[145]Wis 6:6; cf. Jerome, *Commentary on Amos* 6:7-11 (ACT 2:367).

those doing the afflicting are also taken into consideration, not in place of the qualities of the afflicted. Thus, if they who are brought to ruin are not innocent, the injury of the oppressors would also seem pardonable, but if the latter treat saints with violence, they would thus be blamed as guilty. For they are leaping in not with a hatred of the foreigner's malice but by the violent impulses of their own iniquity, displaying the spirit of robbers, not of judges. A certain modesty and uprightness of the profane and of the border nations is placed before them in order to express their iniquity. It says, *Pass over to Calneh, and into Emath the great, and Gath of the Philistines,* and carefully see if they have received wider lands than yours to cultivate. They are so satisfied with their allotment that they seem to seek after nothing else. Clearly he longs to explain this reproach in what follows, in order to accuse them of acquisitiveness; for it seems incoherent that, after he has upbraided them for the crime of wealth and luxury, he would bring them into approval, those who seemed to inhabit smaller lands. For it could have been said in reply that the reason they had more ostentation was because they had gathered to themselves greater wealth by taxation of the annihilated lands. The comparison that was referred to possessed no strength for reproaching, since the reason it was happening was because logical consistency demanded it. What then is the meaning here, which the words are leaving behind? Doubtless that meaning that demonstrated clearly that there were murderous souls among the sacrilegious people, whom another prophet (that is, the blessed Hosea) plainly noted when he said, "In the days of desolation I have shown faithfulness. The princes of Judah have become as those who take up the boundary."[146] That is, when the ten tribes were conquered by Assyria and transferred, the people of Judah, estranged from mercy and remorse, were glad to have acquired for themselves an extension of their borders. Therefore, based on this consideration, the prophet is now showing also that the impious leaders ran riot not only in Judah but even in Israel itself, which was previously subjected to captivity. For when the citizens and inhabitants of the region were wiped out by various disasters, a more extensive inheritance would have come to those who, being within the walls of their cities, as it were, were going to be freed. Yet he upbraids this crime of the tribe of Judah more, for he speaks its name in what follows. Therefore, he justly condemned both their animal sacrifices and their gifts and praised the moderation of the neighboring nations. But let us consider the things that remain as well.

6:3-6 You have been set apart for an evil day. And you are drawing near to the throne of iniquity, you who sleep on beds of ivory, and frolic on your couches, who eat a lamb from the flock, and the calves out of the midst of the herd, you who sing to the sound of the psaltery. Like David they thought they had instruments of music. They drink wine in bowls, and anoint themselves with the best ointment, and they have not suffered for the affliction of Joseph.

Consequently he looked over the feasts and pleasures of those whom he had called "nobles who enter the house with a great pomp," who glory in their riches and feasts and crush the *heads* of the lowly,[147] who even rejoice in their brother's captivity. He says, Woe to you *who have been set apart for an evil day*—that is to say, for whom the time of vengeance is imminent, for which you have been consecrated in such a way that you seem to have been chosen precisely for this. But as for what he says, *and you draw near to the throne of iniquity,* either

[146] Hos 5:9-10.

[147] Cf. Amos 6:1.

we ought to understand it thus, that a single linking conjunction that has been placed first (that is, *and you draw near*) possesses the force of a causal conjunction meaning "because," making the sense, They are *set apart for an evil day* because they *draw near to the throne of iniquity*—that is to say, the reason they must be punished is because they have administered unjust judgments unto others—or else he is calling it *the throne of iniquity*, from which the examined injustice will be condemned. It is similar to the way we speak of a "judgment (*iudicium*) of money and murder," not in order that embezzlement and homicide may be perpetrated, but punished when subjected to examination. However, while living with such enormous crimes, thus far you are giving no thought to pursuing repentance, so that you are chasing after every instrument and every kind of luxury. Not content with having devoted all your days to sport, you lie on ivory beds and soft-cushioned couches so that your bodies may be warmed by silk fabrics and may carry out obscene activities. However, you even season your feasts with the delight of the ears. For when you consume *lambs* chosen from your *flocks* and the *calves* from your *herds*, and you pour out *wines* up to the point of intoxication, you make the *psaltery* and the cithara resound. And to these shameful acts you have even joined the affronts of antiquity—namely, when you say that you have the musical instruments that were available to the most blessed *David*. And you do not perceive, you wretches, how different your pursuits and merits are from his! For in his holy songs David resounded with praises of the Creator, of virtuous laws, and of remedies for troubles. But you, on the contrary, make noise intended to inspire luxurious indulgence, insulting your Creator and spurning his law. David delighted in sober banquets with prophets present, and he was fortified by ointments; but you are languid with intoxication and overindulgence, and you are drenched with vulgar olive oil, which has also been artfully spoiled. Finally, he was filled with feelings of mercy; with weeping and prayers he attended to the calamities that were coming to his nation after many ages.[148] But you look on these same calamities that have already been brought in and the rioting that is already here with eyes so dry that you are murderously glad that they have come. In what he says therefore, *they have not suffered for the affliction of Joseph*, he has referred them back to the compassion that he knew customarily arises in the hearts of those who love or who show mercy. The following song even reproaches this hardness under the persona of the just man: "I looked for one who would grieve together with me, but there was none, and for those who would comfort me, and I found none."[149] Therefore, when the captivity seized *Joseph* (that is, the ten tribes), Judah felt no feelings of pity, no compassion. Why was that? Because it was thinking instead of the opportunity that was being offered to increase its own wealth, to see whether it could join its kinsmen's fields to its own borders.[150] But let us hear what such a choice and such a resolution receives in turn.

6:7 Therefore, now they will go away at the head of those who are transmigrating, and the faction of the luxurious ones will be taken away.

That is, forthwith they will acknowledge the inanity of their hopes, when the captivity that had been delayed a little lays hold of them also. For they will be driven out from their borders *at the head of those who are transmigrating*—that is, those who had believed they would be safe will be the first to be exiled there, and thus will the multitudes of those living in luxury perish.

[148]Cf. 2 Sam 15:30; 19:1; Ps 6:6, 8.

[149]Ps 69:20.

[150]Julian discusses this theme, in dependence on Jerome, at Hos 5:10; 13:14-15.

6:8(-10) The Lord God has sworn by his own soul. The Lord of hosts says, I detest the pride of Jacob, and I hate his houses, and I will deliver up the city along with its inhabitants. But if ten men are left in one house, they also will die.[151]

He took an oath in the words of the vengeance to be carried out, in order to show that their disregard for their brother's captivity was grievously shocking to him. But as for what the prophet says, that God has sworn *by his own soul*, understand that this has been said in our own fashion, as of those to whom he was speaking.[152] Thus, since we value nothing more preciously or sweetly than our souls, he too, not like a brute beast that is composed of soul and members, but like one who has expressed his majesty and life by the term *soul*, has sworn that he *detests the pride and the houses of Jacob*, and that he will subdue them with such great disasters that the populous families will be consumed by so many unremitting deaths, that no one would remain among them who would be able to bury the dead. Now with the name of *Jacob* he has indicated both Judah and Israel equally. For a little earlier he had already mingled them together in the calamity.[153] Hence, when many houses come to this desolation, so that they do not find anyone to bury them, those who live nearby will come and tend the tombs of their neighbors; and they will not settle them in honored graves as is traditional but will cremate them in a communal fire. And lest anyone lie concealed or remain in secret places, those who come, whom we have called their neighbors, will search carefully, and by turns will converse with one another, saying that this desolation has happened to those families, so that no one at all remains alive.

6:11-12 And he will say to him, Be silent, and do not remember the name of the Lord. For behold, the Lord has commanded, and he will strike the greater house with breaches, and the lesser house with clefts.

What is this which he says, *Be silent, and do not remember the name of the Lord?* For assuredly the greatness of their wretchedness could have turned their stubborn hearts back to the remembrance of their judge and creator. And therefore it would have been more logical to say, Let us remember *the name of the Lord*, whose anger has laid us waste with such manifold destruction. Therefore, from the things said previous to this, we may infer a hidden sense in this passage. He says, "Woe to those who desire the day of the Lord. So that it will be for what for you? The day of the Lord is darkness and not light."[154] It is not that they can demand the time of their condemnation but that, as we have shown, those abusing the delay of retribution were bringing the prophets themselves into ill repute from their falsehoods, as if the prophets were threatening those evils, none of which were going to come in their age. For that reason he now says, when the promised captivity will have taken hold of the multitude of miscreants, and that "day" (that is, time) arrives, which they in mockery had boasted that they desired, so great a terror of the divine name will fill them that they may converse in turns, lest anyone dares to remember the name of the Lord, whose severity in this offense appears so great that the commotion is thought to be stirred up even by [the wrath] of the one named. *For behold the Lord has commanded, and he will strike the greater*

---

[151]Amos 6:10 is also discussed under this lemma. Jerome renders it, "And a man's kinsman will take him and burn him in order to carry the bones from the house, and he will say to the one in the inner rooms of the house: there is not any still with you, is there? And he will answer: There is an end."

[152]Cf. Jerome, *Commentary on Amos* 6:7-11 (ACT 2:367).

[153]Cf. Amos 6:1-6.

[154]Amos 5:18.

house with breaches, and the lesser house with clefts. We have said that a little before both Judah and Israel were pointed out by the name of *Jacob*—that is, all the tribes together that had been distributed among themselves.[155] And so the present verse completes this, which announces that both the *greater and lesser house* are being struck with *clefts* and *breaches*. Now he seems to be showing one thing by different words, that is, the overthrow of the *houses*. For indeed *clefts* in the walls customarily precede their *breach*, and he has indicated the breach of both by their collapse and *cleft*. Now he has called Israel the *greater house* on account of the number of its tribes, but Judah is called the *lesser*,[156] and he proclaims that both of them will perish by a similar destruction, just as they have both been defiled with a similar wickedness.

6:13 Can horses run on the rocks, or can anyone plough with buffalo? For you have turned judgment into bitterness and the fruit of justice into wormwood.

The meaning is most pleasing, and it is one that may have been concealed by the manner of expression. For with allegorical words he upbraids the vices of the people with which they were filthy. For he has not literally indicated four-footed beasts here, either horses or buffalo, but he is censuring the pride of the unholy nation. For already they had turned the sweetness of the judgments to bitterness by trampling on innocent people, and they were claiming for themselves so much strength that they thought they could not be harmed by any troubles. For they had acquired so much wealth for themselves, that like buffalo that never submit their necks to the plow, they enjoyed constant freedom, and they ran not on paths made difficult because of the rocks, as a horse free from the bridle, but through fields and meadows. Therefore, he says, it is certain that the *buffalo* does not carry a yoke, nor does the *horse* travel over rocks of its own accord; but you who rejoice at having shattered your yokes and broken free of your bridles, you seemed to be like *horses* in your excess, like *buffalo* in your power and freedom. Prove by the facts what you have derived from your hopes—that is, that you are not subject to any commands. At any rate, since things are falling out to the contrary, and you are coming into the judgment of the enemy and by the roughest paths, and you are enduring heavy labors with a broken neck, you must acknowledge that your resources or your minds have provided neither horses nor buffalo, no protection and no strength.

6:14-15 You who rejoice in what is nothing, you who say, Have we not taken horns for ourselves by our own strength? For behold, I will raise up a nation against you, O house of Israel, says the Lord of hosts; and I will destroy you from the entrance of Emath even to the torrent of the desert.

These words have offered complete support to the explanation that was set out before—namely, that they had believed themselves to be free and strong like buffalo and horses, hardly from an awareness of their strength, but rather this came from their own fancy and vain hope. He says, For you have rejoiced *in what is nothing*. You say to yourselves, *Have we not taken horns for ourselves by our own strength?* Doubtless he means the horns that seemed to show the form of buffalo. Therefore, you have arrogated to yourselves so much strength for yourselves that you thought you could safely scorn his precepts. A mighty army will come *against you* and will lay you waste first, *O Israel*, and by the efficacy of those who

[155]See under Amos 6:8-10.
[156]Cf. Jerome, *Commentary on Amos* 6:12-15 (ACT 2:369).

conquer: *from the entrance of Emath* (that is, from Antioch[157]) *even to the torrent of the desert* (the direction that touches the desert); that is to say, it will ravage all your borders with the cruelty of an enemy. And you, O Judah, while you wait under a brief delay, nevertheless it will blast you from the vicinity and will level with fire.

[Chapter 7]

7:1-3 These things the Lord God showed to me, and behold, the creator of the locust in the beginning of the shooting up of the latter rain, and behold, [it was] the late one after the shearer of the herd. And it came to pass that when it had made an end of eating the grass of the land, I said, O Lord God, be merciful, I beg you. Who shall raise up Jacob, for he is very little? The Lord had pity on this. It will not be, said the Lord.

He is composing his speech in the prophetic fashion; or rather, he is showing whatever revelations were customarily perceived in the spirit of the prophet (whence they were also called "seers"[158]). That is, those brief images of future events indeed appeared to them under diverse forms, but they understood the meaning[159] of them through their intelligence, and in this way they were moved by various emotional responses, tending doubtless either toward censure or to mercy.[160] Hence, after he announced that a nation will be roused up, which would bring destruction to them, lest that brief warning sign fail to move the hearer enough, he lingers in the unfolding of the images that he had seen. And on the occasion of those images, he shows how diligently he prayed for them, to keep anyone from thinking that he was announcing those calamities either with a spirit of a reviler or of one who had no grief. Therefore, listen to the sights and images to which our God has introduced me. A certain person was standing there who, like the creator of locusts, fashioned (that is formed) swarms and dispatched multitudes to those who were dying from this trouble, so that they fed on every root of the fields and every seed as though by tireless chewing. But as for what it says, *in the beginning of the shooting up of the latter rain,* he is showing that he has power to increase the disaster: that is, a severe drought may appear to take up the time of the seasonal rains, and the farmers, who are exhausted and distressed by the long wait for the rains, may even begin to have the relief of the latter rain and thus may hastily employ the despaired-of sowings. But when those seeds begin to sprout, although they were sown exceedingly late, before they rise into stalks and ears, they are destroyed by the feeding locusts. Nevertheless, lest any even scanty hope should mitigate that evil, another *late one* came after the locust, for it says, *behold, the late one after the shearer of the herd*—that is, the one that followed consumed all the way down to the roots those sprouts that the locusts had "shorn." Seeing that he has not named it here, we may infer from the preceding what the prophet means. For blessed Joel says, "That which the palmer-worm has left, the locust has eaten, and that which the locust has left, the young locust (*bruchus*) has eaten, and that which the young

[157]Bouwman, *Des Julian von Aeclanum Kommentar,* 131, described Julian's identification of Emath with Antioch as a "practically comical" (*fast komisch*) misreading of Jerome, *Commentary on Amos* 6:2-6 (ACT 2:364); 6:12-15 (ACT 2:370). In the latter passage Jerome indeed says that Emath is called Epiphania from Antiochus (Epiphanes). Bouwman thinks that Julian read Jerome's reference to the person of Antiochus Epiphanes as the name of the city. However, in the earlier passage (not cited by Bouwman), Jerome says that there are two Emaths, a greater and a lesser, and the greater one is now called Antioch, whereas the lesser one is Epiphania. Thus, according to Jerome, there was an Emath called Antioch.

[158]Cf. 1 Sam 9:9.

[159]Or "force" (*vim*).

[160]Cf. Jerome, *Commentary on Amos* 7:10-13 (ACT 2:378).

locust has left, the mildew has destroyed."[161] Therefore, the prophet Amos also indicated the "late one" as the young locust (*bruchus*) that proceeds to the remnants of the *shearer*. However, because he sees the *creator of the locust*, since he could have been shown as a summoner of a creature that has already come into existence, it is doubtless valid that to reveal the countless multitude of those living beings (namely, of which no swarming multitude as great could be found being gathered on the earth), yet they are fashioned anew through the power of the judge, who is also the Creator of the universe. Accordingly, when the full devastation had revealed the cause of this design, and the destruction had revealed the abundance of the decaying food provisions, I cried out, he says, *O Lord God, be merciful, I beg you. Who will raise up Jacob, for he is very little?* That is, if through your indignation our nation comes to so great a scarcity as those figurative visions promise, who will be able to raise it up later on, a nation that you will have brought to such great ruin? *The Lord had pity upon this. It will not be, said the Lord.* That is, the subsequent change of the judgment sentence taught me that my prayerful appeal was effective. For God is inclined to show mercy, and he withdrew that plague when he saw that its magnitude had terrified me. And he responded that that will not come to pass, since I had implored that it not come to pass, but he sent in something else, which he judged to be milder.

7:4-6 [For] the Lord God showed to me this: behold, he was calling for judgment unto fire, and it will devour the great deep, and it ate up a part at the same time.

Unless we grasp what has been said with prudence and care, no little incongruity will be exposed in the meaning. After these injuries, which the destroying locust and the subsequent young locust (*bruchus*) had inflicted, fire is introduced as being a milder plague. For there is absolutely no doubt that the calamity of the shearing of the sprouts that he was bringing to all is greater by far than would have been achieved by the conflagration that was sent. Why then does the prophet say that the merciful God and the one who has been turned, as it were, by the tears of an intercessor, *called for judgment unto fire*—that is, regarded them liable to fire, those from whom he had removed the danger of scarcity? Wherefore one should take notice that here with the name *fire* he wanted to indicate the darting of a flame, which, although its intensity may burn around what it has touched, nevertheless, as long as it does not linger on the things it is blown on, it neither reaches those things that are down deep nor does it consume the tough core that it seemed to have laid hold of. Therefore, with the images of locusts and young locusts settling down for the work they had undertaken, he wanted to show the slaughter of the doomed nation.[162] When the prophet had seen this in his spirit, he was alarmed and he objected, both out of affection for his people and out of the reverence owed to the judge. And he succeeded in changing the harshness of the judgment sentence. But since the age-old perversity of the people did not permit a full pardon to be granted, such a punishment takes its place, which although sent to consume the greater part, nevertheless allows a remnant to survive. For thus it says, *And behold the Lord God*[163] *called for judgment unto fire, and it devoured*[164] *the great deep, and will eat up*[165] *a part at the same time*. But the prophet may have been inspired by the effect

[161]Joel 1:4.

[162]Cf. Jerome, *Commentary on Amos* 7:1-3 (ACT 2:372-73); 7:4-6 (ACT 2:374).

[163]The lemma lacked "Lord God."

[164]The lemma had "will devour."

[165]The lemma had "ate up."

of the first prayer and dares to stand in the way of this pronouncement too. He calls Israel a *little one*—namely, in respect to its reduced resources, which are going to be erased by utter destruction if the one who judges should inflame the anger of the enemy, like one who is not acting as a corrector. Now some interpreters have thought that the Assyrians were being signified by the image of the locust, and the Babylonians by the image of fire.[166] They fail to see that this is inconsistent with history. For the prophet says that the plagues of both locust and fire were warded off by his prayers, and that the Lord answered him when the prophet implored him about both, and the Lord said, "This will not be"[167]—that is, that devastation will surely not rush in. But the Assyrian and Babylonian enemies were victorious and with a terrible slaughter laid waste to both Israel and Judah. Therefore, our God is showing the following to us through the prophet, who had become a beholder of the images, that the Jewish people deserved a ruin greater by far than what they endured, that the heavenly arbiter could have wiped them out by a slaughter had he wanted to multiply the number of enemies or to inflame his indignation, and that he was, as it were, enduring the necessity of afflicting his people, whom he did not want to perish entirely.

7:7-9 The Lord showed me this. And behold, the Lord was standing on a coated wall, and in his hand a mason's trowel.[168] And the Lord said to me, What do you see, Amos? And I said, A mason's trowel. And the Lord said to me, Behold, I will lay down the trowel in the midst of my people Israel. I will plaster them over no more. And the high places of the idol will be thrown down, and the sanctuaries of Israel will be laid waste, and I will rise up against the house of Jeroboam with the sword.

He says this when he had warded off those two kinds of impending crises. The vision of the prophet about whom we are speaking showed the people a large part of the arrangements of God by which the life of mortals runs its course. For when the preceding judgment sentences showed a judge who was either menacing or growling like a lion and gaping over the deaths of the guilty—surely these passions and feelings are shown to be estranged from the nature of God, who rejoices in constant tranquility, according to reasonable doctrine—the occasion of the present passage has chiefly disclosed the manner by which our God rises up to punish (namely, by abandoning rather than by growling). For seeing that a heap of calamities would have set in immediately if he had ceased pleading, he says that they fell down when he struck. And on account of the remorse awakened in the hearts of the guilty, he writes that God was inclined and moved with respect to himself, whom when he was raging he had regarded as an enemy, while he permitted this. Therefore, because his intervening prayer had done away with God's twofold judgment, which he had resolved to do on account of the merits of the Jews, he brought in a third judgment, which assuredly the prophet dared not oppose, since it was exceedingly mild, but which contained the fullest accomplishment of punishment. For it says *upon a coated wall* (that is, one constructed with architectural skill) *the Lord* of the universe seemed to me to be *standing*, holding *a mason's trowel in his hand*. By this he was clearly indicating the duty that he had been accustomed to perform—that is, that he was accustomed to guard them with a constant defense, and he applied that frequent remedy by which they were healed and restored; but if that [remedy] should remove his directing providence from the wretched ones, none of

[166]Cf. Jerome, *Commentary on Amos* 7:4-6 (ACT 2:374).

[167]Amos 7:6 (not included in the lemma).

[168]A trowel is a tool having a flat blade with a handle, used for depositing and working mortar, plaster, etc.

them would be able to stick together or to exist. Therefore, he says, *I will lay down* this *trowel* (that is, my care) by which those things that were corroded were *coated* and those things that were battered were fortified, and I will also declare a certain leisure for kindness, since Israel compels in this way, nor will I endure the work any longer, doubtless with the shameless profanity of striving earnestly after an ineffective piety. And thus at length they will come to know what they have done, since they are perishing though I am not the one smiting them, but I am merely not protecting them. *And the high places of the idol shall be thrown down, and the sanctuaries of Israel shall be laid waste, and I will rise up against the house of Jeroboam with the sword.* For the enemies will come, and they will rave furiously, conducting a full triumph with fire and the sword, burning down the temples and the profane places together with whole cities, and they will lay waste the house of Jeroboam with the avenging sword.

7:(10-)11[169]

But when the speech of the prophet, who is addressing a public assembly, proceeded up to this point, a certain man by the name of Amaziah, a priest of the idols, sent to Jeroboam [II], who held command over the ten tribes at that same time. He announces to him that Amos was declaring destruction with a spirit of rebellion rather than an impulse of prophecy, and that in particular the destruction was aimed at him (that is, the king) and that he was terrifying all the people with his variously compounded threats in such a way that it even became a matter of doubtful judgment concerning which king the waverer should follow. Comprising briefly the purpose of the whole prophetic book, he says, **"For thus says Amos: Jeroboam shall die by the sword, and Israel shall depart as captives out of their own land."** From these words we coherently observe (which we also experience in affairs in our own time) that since the humbler portion of the people (that is, every countryman) did not have any of the pride of the nobility, they were likewise more easily swayed by the words of the prophets; but since the priests and aristocrats strive to support even their own vices, they rejected his statements, nay rather, they incriminated them, and, if it would have been allowed, they would have destroyed the salutary teachers.[170] But let us keep following the order of the reading.

7:12-13 [Therefore, when he had sent orders to king Jeroboam, by which he could kindle a flame against the prophet of God, as though not content to wait for the end of the contest that had been stirred up, but greatly desiring that the holy man might be put to flight in some manner or other, the counsellor came up to him,] And Amaziah said to Amos, You who see, go, flee away into the land of Judah, eat bread there, and you shall prophesy there. And you shall not prophesy any more in Bethel, because it is the king's sanctuary, and the house of the kingdom.

I believe he was afraid that the anger of even the king might be bridled by respect for the prophet. So he tried to drive him out on his own.[171] He greets him with honor and says, *You who see*, go away, and flee to the neighboring region of Judah for refuge, where you may be able to live and teach safely. But do not continue to sound out in such a manner in this place (that is, Bethel), in which you look on a

[169]Julian's lemma omits v. 10, which reads in Jerome's version, "And Amaziah, the priest of Bethel, sent to Jeroboam, king of Israel, saying: Amos has rebelled against you in the midst of the house of Israel. The land will not be able to bear all his words." Julian includes this verse in his discussion below.

[170]This strikes me as an important autobiographical reflection of Julian that is worth noting.

[171]Cf. Jerome, *Commentary on Amos* 7:10-13 (ACT 2:379).

constructed palace and on the *king's sanctuary*—namely, the image to whose worship we have devoted ourselves, along with our prince himself. You will come to understand that these utterances of yours will not go unpunished.

7:14-16 Amos answered and said to Amaziah, I am not a prophet, nor am I the son of a prophet, but I am a herdsman plucking sycamore figs. And the Lord took me when I followed the flock, and he said to me, Go, prophesy to my people Israel.

Frequently even things that are left unspoken concerning the occasions of the responses occur to the mind as necessary to understand, just as now, when the diviner had told him to flee, the prophet responds that he neither descends from a line of prophets nor did he receive this gift from the beginning. Yet he should not on that account be an object of scorn to his listeners, as though he is one who is prophesying false things. Instead, he likewise admits with joy what they were accustomed to say as a reproach to him—namely, that he was from neither the chorus nor the lineage of the prophets, but he was merely dedicated to the duty of being a shepherd and led livestock through the woodlands and gathered food from the trees in a very common fashion. He was chosen by God, who sees into the heart,[172] and was appointed to this duty of prophesying.[173] The apostle likewise boasts in this fashion when he says that "when it pleased God to reveal his Son through me, immediately I did not find rest in flesh and blood, nor did I go to Jerusalem, to the apostles who were my predecessors, but I went off into Arabia, and from there I returned to Damascus."[174] That is, I did not rest in any authority or special prerogative, but immediately I obeyed our Redeemer who was calling me, so promptly and readily that I tackled the task of preaching. Therefore, the blessed Amos also admits that he is a shepherd of flocks, with no ambition for this work, but that he came to it solely by the choice of the One who called him, who *said to me*, he says, *Go, prophesy to my people Israel.* Therefore, you, O Amaziah, as well as all your fellows, ought to receive these things that I have presented earlier as threats—not as my own words but as the statements of God speaking through me. Do not doubt that what I was proclaiming are things that I had known were coming by the will of God. To keep you from not knowing this, receive proof of him who is speaking in me, Christ.

7:17 Your wife will be a prostitute in the city, your sons and your daughters will fall by the sword, and your soil will be measured by a line. And you will die in a polluted land, and Israel will go into captivity out of their land.

So what use is it for you to be unwilling to hear what you need to endure, when it is not the proclaimer's words that torment you but the wounds of the one pursuing you? So then, that you may perceive that the impending judgment sentence is not to be withdrawn in any way, I proclaim that you are going to feel the torments of all your affections—that is, the affections that the husband experiences, the father, the well-known citizen. For your wife will be defiled with a disgrace that is not secret, but she will lie subject to the lust of the conquerors in the middle of the city, and a sword will destroy your children as you look on. You will not be allowed to mourn for them, and having been cast down in shame and bereavement *you will die in a polluted land*—that is, either in the country of the Jews, which of course the sacrileges of the citizens first defiled, but then the crimes of their enemies,

[172]Cf. 1 Sam 16:7; Prov 24:12.
[173]Cf. Jerome, *Commentary on Amos* 7:14-17 (ACT 2:380).
[174]Gal 1:15-17.

or else in foreign lands, which you always regarded as polluted, and Israel will be driven out into exile by the tornado of captivity.[175] But let us look to the remaining things as well.

[Chapter 8]

8:1-3 These things the Lord God showed to me. Behold, a hook for the fruit. And he said, What do you see, Amos? And I said, A hook for the fruit. And the Lord said to me, The end has come on my people, I will not again pass by them anymore. The hinges of the temple will creak in that day, says the Lord. Many will die; silence will be cast in every place.

Up to the present passage he had announced both that the disasters that were owed for their crimes were going to come and that they were being kept within limits by a fixed judgment of the eternal judge, so that those unholy ones would certainly not escape unpunished. But since the extended strength of the discourse had spoken this, just now it shows that the time is near for the punishments that have to be inflicted, and following the custom of the prophets, he has introduced an image that portrayed this very thing. For just as the trowel of the mason revealed the concern of providence,[176] which the judge, laying down from his own hand in the time of (his) indignation, taught that he had stopped protecting them, so now he shows the nearness of condemnation and takes up a *hook for the fruit*—that is, one that they were accustomed to have who climb up into trees to pluck the fruit. And on account of the thinness of the branches they are not able to reach the ends of the branches. They stand on solid ground, bend the tips of the branches toward themselves, and collect the fruits that they see are ripe.[177] Therefore, when the eternal judge was already deciding that the appropriate punishment had so to speak ripened for the taking of it, he made the people understand. And he announces that he has undertaken the duty of punishment. Israel can remain unpunished no longer: *I will not again pass by them anymore*—that is to say, just as the gatherers of fruits, which they see are now becoming bitter, pluck the ones that are truly suitable for eating. Therefore, now the image of a hook showed the time of the judgment about to be executed—namely, a hook that drags to the punishments that are owed those who seemed to be flourishing in their riches and abounding with their children. *The hinges of the temple shall creak in that day, says the Lord. Many will die; silence will be cast in every place.* Lest you think, O you people, that what this image of a hook announces is doubtful, *The hinges of the temple will creak*—that is, all the shrines in which you trust will be demolished with the cities.[178] For their gates will not be opened softly for the functions of the worshipers, but they will burst apart by the violence of those storming them, and the unholy mob *will die* by a disorderly slaughter, and thus the crossroads that were accustomed to resound with a multitude of citizens will be filled with mournful silence. However, by the name of *temple,* whose hinges are said to creak, it would seem to be announcing also the disaster of Judah and the destruction of the temple that was located in Jerusalem, except that the whole context itself is more consistent with the ten tribes. Therefore, he is saying that the hinges will be wrenched away of that temple of which he also says earlier, "And the high places of the idol will be thrown down, and the sanctuaries of Israel will be laid waste,"[179] and after a few things he says

[175]Cf. Jerome, *Commentary on Amos* 7:14-17 (ACT 2:381).
[176]Cf. Amos 7:7-8.
[177]Cf. Jerome, *Commentary on Amos* 8:1-3 (ACT 2:381).
[178]Cf. Jerome, *Commentary on Amos* 8:1-3 (ACT 2:381).
[179]Amos 7:9.

more openly, "They swear by the transgression of Samaria, and say, Your Lord God, O Dan, lives, and the way of Beersheba lives. And they will fall and will rise no more."[180]

8:4-6 Hear this, you who crush the poor and make the needy of the land to be in want, saying, When will the month be over, and we will sell our wares, and the sabbath, and we will open the grain, that we may lessen the measure, and increase the shekel, and convey in deceitful balances, so that we may possess the needy by money (*argento*) and the poor for a pair of shoes, and may sell the refuse of the grain?

The prophetic speech is composed by the same rules by which it was established. Thus, although he accuses their worship of idols above all their crimes, whereby obviously those who abandoned God were rendered most profane, nevertheless he is not silent about the other aspects of life as well—that is, the remaining transgressions against morality. And so either he shows that they have despised the authority of the sacred law by their love of vices, or the impiety produces such fruits of character, which (impiety) although it may diffuse itself through nearly every kind of depravity, nevertheless it is devoted to greed before all others. Even in the apostle it is called "service to idols."[181] Therefore, when this divine speech too had convicted these wicked persons and threatened them with an already approaching destruction, it suddenly called out, like one who wanted to shatter the deafness of their profanities. Thus, if they did not trouble themselves to pass judgment on the merits of their pursuits but rather gave preference to what was ugly over against what was beautiful and beneficial, at the least when things were now reduced to a state of distress, and with the resounding din of the punishment that had been aroused near at hand, they might perceive to what use they might collect their money or with what facial expression they should strive to fill their purses, which were sure to come at once under the power of their enemies. He says, *Hear this, you who crush the poor, and make the needy of the land to be in want.* "O ye sons of men, how long will you be dull of heart, why do you love vanity"[182] and shamelessly regard *deceitful* riches with longing? You shall experience no help from these, or rather, no consolation. They produce the cause both of your guilt and of your punishments. With what credible hope did you corrupt the gifts of those judging, such that you have seized the bloodstained spoils from the poor who were oppressed and put to death? And you had no harmless kind of activity. For you have not merely transgressed by corruption in the decisions of judgments, but also, when you were continuing to collect money from the fruits of the fields, you defiled even those trades that could have been conducted honorably, and you mingled crimes with the lawful activity of vows. For you said, *When will the month be over, and we will sell our wares, and the sabbath, and we will open the grain, that we may lessen the measure, and increase the shekel, and convey in deceitful balances?* Therefore, sinning no less in greed than in injustice, you waited for public income and you wished for scarcity, and, although exceedingly immoderate, and on account of this exceedingly indolent, nevertheless you loathed the Sabbaths' days of rest because, with its appointed leisure, on at least one day you were restrained from deceits. Therefore, it says, you inveighed against the slowness of the passing of the time of leisure, doubtless since you were in a hurry to get to the times for business, in which not only you would sell grain to the hungry people at high prices but also the *refuse*, which normally you were

[180]Amos 8:14.
[181]Col 3:5.

[182]Ps 4:2.

accustomed to throw away. You practiced such things in your houses and were silent about the injustice of it: *That we may possess the needy by money, and the poor for a pair of shoes.* Therefore, since you have conducted yourselves in this way as the enemies of humanity, so that, because you were wealthier than others, by this the crowd of citizens began to perceive you as rather cruel, and an abundance of things in and of itself did not invite you to give generously, surely you ought to obtain no mercy from the eternal judge. You denied such mercy to your neighbors with such stubbornness and such shamelessness.

8:7 The Lord has sworn against the pride of Jacob, Surely I will never forget all their works.

The indignation of your Creator, O Israel, has revealed the magnitude of your iniquity. He has also girded himself with a solemn witness that he will not forget any of these evils, which are so many. On the contrary, he will direct the force of his severity until he has finished you off with final destruction. At the same time also he exposed the latent affections of the guilty, who, though they seemed to have transgressed on account of greed alone by cheating in the measurements and weights, he threatens to rise up *against their pride.* Assuredly this shows that they would never have permitted so many crimes if it were not on account of their contempt of the law and also that they valued money excessively, just as they also reckoned the precepts of God as worthless. He says, It is not that you limit their arrogance by the scorn of the poor. The unbridled audacity of impious persons proceeds further by far, I say; they have drained our contempt. On account of this, I who am the examiner of souls justly detest their pride, and "I swore in my wrath that they shall not enter into my rest."[183] For what mercy can restrain my judgment when they proceed to act with such hatefulness, that the whole of their country deserves to tremble since it longs to be freed from the burden of those immoral ones whom it is feeding?

8:8(-9) Will not the land tremble for this, and every one mourn who dwells there, and rise up altogether as a river, and be cast out, and run down as the river of Egypt?[184]

He has made clear in the added speech what it means for the *land to tremble,* which assuredly he had declared on account of the attitude of terror. He says, *and every one mourn who dwells there.* He is saying the captivity that was promised long ago and has been postponed up to now will come; for already that one whom I said earlier was the "hook" of our judgment has dragged in the business of punishment, and all will be fulfilled that he who was both despised and bound by an oath produced, and all the people of Israel will flow out with no greater difficulty than the *river of Egypt* (namely, the Nile), and they will be forced to cross into Assyria. The appearance of this time will truly be so sad and bitter that in the middle of the day the sun may seem to have failed and the night may seem to have rushed in.[185] For thus there will be no distinction of order, no light of counsel will remain, as if tangible darkness had removed the earth and the sky equally from the eyes of those wretched ones.

8:10 And I will turn your feasts into mourning, and all your songs into lamentation; and I will place sackcloth on every back of yours, and baldness on every head; and I will make it as the mourning of

[183]Ps 95:11.

[184]Amos 8:9 is also discussed in this section, which reads in Jerome's version, "And it will come to pass in that day, says the Lord, that the sun will set at midday, and I will make the earth dark in the day of light."

[185]Cf. Amos 8:9.

an only begotten and the latter end thereof as a bitter day.

Because the established speech points out not one person but all the people simultaneously, for that reason the change of number and of gender came to pass, so that at one point it addresses them in the plural, then in the singular. It says, *I will turn your feasts into mourning, and your songs into lamentation*—that is, all things that rival the joyful things will succeed, and the incited captivity will subject to mourning the things that you free persons have prepared for your enjoyment; and sackcloth and rags will clothe the bodies of the high-born, which a little earlier were covered with precious jewels. If only we knew from the indications of the reading what all occurred at the time of captivity! But so often in our times such is the situation produced, that we marvel at the audacity of those who hope for anything better.[186] He says, *I will place sackcloth upon every back of yours, and baldness on every head,* and you will lose the ornaments of your bodies and the supports of your strength, so that your grey hair will begin to fall out, either by mocking humiliation or by consuming disease. *And I will make it as the mourning of an only begotten, and the latter end thereof as a bitter day.* That is, the condition of the Israelite nation will descend from the height of their ancient happiness to the depths of wretched slavery, since they are worthy of an affliction as bitter as that bereavement that was accustomed to happen over only begotten [sons], when not only lost security but also extinct posterity are mourned. But let us look to the remaining things as well.

8:11-12 Behold, the days are coming, says the Lord, and I will send a famine in the land, not a famine of bread, nor a thirst for water, but of hearing the word of the Lord. And they will be troubled from sea to sea, and from the north to the east; they shall go about seeking the word of the Lord and shall not find it.

He showed that a lack of salvific teachers would be reckoned among the final disasters of his people, [teachers] who had flourished under the condition of the law. Why not? Since this is the arrangement, as if you do not hear the things that you must learn, may you toss and turn in the night of ignorance under and through this lack of experience, and may you also encounter manifold miseries, as though captured by lights. For as another prophet announces, one who will not learn justice shall not effect truth on the earth.[187] And thus "those speaking lies shall perish."[188] On account of this the prophet Hosea had reproached the people as well, that they "had rejected knowledge."[189] And on account of this they merited to be rejected by the all-powerful God. Likewise, in the present passage under the announcement of the punishment, the same crime is presented, so that those who had hated the teachers of piety in their pursuit of profanity might recognize the extent to which they had labored for their own destruction. Namely, those who by this sinning have wrought that the judge threatens them among other things, or rather, more than other punishments (that is, in the midst of the hardships of captivity), they must be struck by want of instruction, so that they might be

[186]J. Lössl, "Julian of Aeclanum's Tractatus in Osee, Iohel, Amos: Some Notes on the Current State of Research," *Augustiniana* 51 (2001): 23, comments on this passage: "Yet despite his rather dim view concerning the general prospects of his day and age Julian seems far from succumbing in principle to the gloom surrounding him. This impression of a Julian who remains optimistic and confident, always ready to act and respond to oncoming challenges is confirmed by Gennadius, who reports that 'in a time of famine and anxiety Julian managed to procure alms for those in need.'"

[187]Cf. Hos 4:6.

[188]Prov 19:9.

[189]Hos 4:6.

forsaken by that mark by which they had conspicuously ruled among the other nations and so that no one might instruct those ignorant of the prophets nor comfort the afflicted. Constant dangers have shown us that all of this takes place under hostile rule.[190] However, the blessed Isaiah also exposed these kinds of threats—namely, by foretelling that the prince must be removed from Judea, and the senior counselor and the teacher, and that boy-kings and effeminate princes are to be substituted in their place.[191] But as for what he says, that he must inflict on those peoples *not a famine of bread, nor a thirst for water, but of hearing the word of the Lord,* as far as pertains to the continuous course of the reading, it seems to be introduced in this sense, that he says that this want will be not only a famine of bread, nor just a thirst for water, but also of hearing the word of the Lord, so that in no place would they be able to find a teacher, even if they sought for one most earnestly. For he would not have terrified them by decreeing the removal of the only teachers, as if they were desirous of spiritual teaching and on account of this reckoned the cost of this heavily. For surely in the whole book he had threatened lack, sickness, sufferings, swords, and fires to those who were guilty of both cruelties and of acts of moral disgrace! Therefore, following the familiar speeches in the Scriptures, he has certainly not denied that they must be vexed by hunger and thirst, but he has left this to be supplied in thought. Thus, they are to be subjected not only to those things, which on account of the condition of mortal life, with its goods and evils, occasionally come to pass commonly, as it were, but by another greater calamity, and one that looks to the soul and is not able to come about without harm, that they are about to be punished in such a way that the divine doctrine would not instruct them but rather would leave their ears unvisited, even if they swear that they want to learn. The following words that we read in another prophet would nearly agree with this: "But to the sinner God said, Why do you declare my justices, and take my covenant in your mouth."[192] The meaning is fashioned from everything he has said. On account of their religious and moral crimes, the formerly chosen nation of the Jews is being subjected to a foreign captivity. Indeed they have fallen so far from their ancient height of glory that they recognized their willful crimes in the retributions. Moreover, they have endured the commands of savage masters. Nowhere do they hear the teaching of the sacred law resounding. Doubtless while the nation was established within the borders of their fathers, until now it had despised its precepts that gave them light.

But as the context of the reading itself demanded the continuance of this understanding, so also we ought to notice that the same things are also valid for signifying future things—namely, those times in which the Jews sinned most criminally and fell most gravely. For after that "vine," which "was transferred from Egypt,"[193] was planted in fertile lands and received a "wine-press" of the sacred high altar in the temple that had been built, "it was expected to bring forth grapes, but it brought forth thorns," and not "justice" but "a cry."[194] So then, its cultivators turned wild against the very son of the father of the household and believed that since they had prevailed with the annihilation of the lawful heir, they would try for the rest without trouble.[195] Therefore, "the Lord God has sworn against the pride of Jacob, Surely I will never forget all their works."[196] This atrocity emerged as so great that their very land trembled, and a mournful darkness

[190]Note this autobiographical comment.
[191]Cf. Is 3:1-4.

[192]Ps 50:16.
[193]Ps 80:8.
[194]Cf. Is 5:2, 7.
[195]Cf. Mt 21:33-46; Mk 12:1-12; Lk 20:9-19.
[196]Amos 8:7.

removed midday.[197] For indeed "from the sixth hour there was darkness until the ninth hour, and the earth quaked, and the rocks were rent."[198] And thus did their festivals turn to mourning, and their songs to lamentation, and the backs of the impious were covered with sackcloth, and their heads felt their baldness.[199] And when the nations came as a retribution of the sin offering, Jerusalem was surrounded by a siege and was dashed to the ground so that it would certainly not be able to rise up any longer.[200] Hence [Jerusalem] felt the mourning as of an only begotten, and that nation has been enclosed by a bitter end. They treated the only begotten of God with violence by their insults and blows. And a time truly followed in which we see that they who had been stiff-necked with respect to the word of the Lord are devoured by a famine for spiritual goods, and they experience not a hunger for bread nor a thirst for water but for hearing the word of the Lord. Or is this very disaster of theirs not wholly illuminated by the very attestation of the facts? For since the commencement of spiritual philosophy departed from them (namely, pious devotion toward the Lord, kindness toward neighbors, and the worth of a teacher), they sank down into such a great a lack of studies and of teaching that they were scattered from the rising of the sun to its setting—that is, into the whole world.[201] And they never hear the word of God by which they might be enlivened. Nor are they touched by the lightning flash of the gospel.[202] But like infants, they are puffed up with the shameful parts and with games, in place of virtues of character and life-giving mysteries—that is to say, they boast in mutilating the flesh and in Sabbath feasts. Consequently, therefore, no learned teacher, nor prince, nor priest by which they might be reformed has arisen among them. For when Moses speaks, their eyes are covered by a veil, which is not removed otherwise, than when it is dispelled in Christ, who has redeemed us.[203] He says, *They shall go about seeking the word of the Lord and shall not find it,* because they have denied him who is "the Word made flesh,"[204] and so "the light shines in the darkness, and the darkness did not comprehend it."[205]

8:13-14 In that day beautiful virgins and young men will faint because of thirst. For they swear by the transgression of Samaria, and say, Your Lord God, O Dan, lives, and the way of Beersheba lives. And they will fall and will rise no more.

Although the prophetic discourse may accuse the character of its own time, nevertheless through the accumulation of the censure, as we have shown as being consistent with this,[206] the things to come are also pointed out. Also on that account, although the continuing speech turned its attention to the matters that seemed to be urgent, nonetheless it is also possible to agree with that situation that now detains the Jews. For it is not nonsensical if the tribes themselves are called "beautiful virgins" from past merit, who, just as one reads that they were doomed back then to destruction by following idols, so now, since they have denied their Redeemer, they are said to have committed the same thing, that [which they did] when they worshiped the calves set up in Dan and Beersheba. Thus, the sense is that in vain the Jews think that they are free from impiety when they do not believe in Christ the Lord—namely, on the grounds that they worship no idols. For they have not retained any of the

[197]Cf. Jerome, *Commentary on Amos* 8:9-10 (ACT 2:385).
[198]Cf. Mt 27:45, 51.
[199]Cf. Amos 8:10.
[200]Cf. Lk 19:43-44.
[201]Cf. Jerome, *Commentary on Amos* 8:11-14 (ACT 2:386).
[202]Cf. Mt 24:27; Lk 17:24.
[203]Cf. 2 Cor 3:14-16; Gal 4:5.
[204]Jn 1:14.
[205]Jn 1:5; cf. Jerome, *Commentary on Amos* 8:11-14 (ACT 2:386).
[206]Cf. Amos 8:11-12.

ancient devotion of the patriarchs. Thus, they are exposed as sharers and comrades with the worshipers of idols by their dishonoring of the name of Christ by their stubborn faithlessness. On account of this also the examiner of souls pronounces in the gospel, "He that hates me, hates my Father also."[207] Hence, their accumulated condemnation dooms them, who by denying the Son, are also proclaimed enemies of the Father. But as for what it says, *Your Lord God, O Dan, lives, and the way of Beersheba lives,* he has indicated the custom of the common people, who obviously falling into superstition also mostly swear by the journeys on which they go to the temples. He says, *They will fall and will rise no more*; that is, they will no longer be allowed to lean on consolations of hope, so that they should think that threats of such a kind resound all the way to the point of terror, and then suddenly they would encounter the joys of liberation, as one reads they frequently experienced. On the contrary, because the "hook"[208] that was seized at last has drawn in the time of revenge, they perceive by suffering what thus far they had learned by hearing, and thus *they will fall* so that they are ground down by these things oppressing them.

[Chapter 9]

9:1a-c I saw the Lord standing on the altar, and he said, Strike the hinge, and let the lintels be shaken. For there is covetousness in the head of them all, and I will slay the last of them with the sword.

Some have believed that this is the lawful altar, on which the avenger stood—namely, the one that was placed in the temple of Jerusalem.[209] According to what another prophet says, "Begin with my sanctuary,"[210] it would seem that the destruction of the temple itself is also being threatened. But the context of the passage refutes such an understanding. For no mention of Judah had preceded, but he was expressly threatening the ten tribes. After all, after he said, "They swear by the transgression of Samaria, and say, Your Lord God, O Dan, lives, and the way of Beersheba lives," he says, "they will fall and will rise no more." And then he added, *I saw the Lord standing on the altar.* Since, therefore, he has most notably struck at the ten tribes and Samaria, we ought to understand that the altar and the temple also, which he warns would be overturned, is that one about which he said a little before this, "And the end has come upon my people Israel, I will not again pass by them anymore. And the hinges of the temple will creak in that day, says the Lord."[211] And a little bit earlier it says, "Amos said to Amaziah, Now hear the word of the Lord: You say, you will not prophesy against Israel, and you will not drop [your word] against the house of the idol. Therefore, thus says the Lord: Your wife will be a prostitute in the city, and your sons and your daughters will fall by the sword, and your soil will be measured by a line, and you will die in a polluted land, and Israel will go into captivity out of their land."[212] Therefore, since he had said that those swearing by the transgression of Samaria would be subjected to a deserved destruction, there follows the effectual achievement of the threat itself. And he says that he *saw the Lord* standing ready to demolish the altars of the profane people. And although he may appear under varying images, now of one running, now of one standing, nevertheless, because he completes everything with a command, it says, *And he said* to his attendants (doubtless either to angels or to the

[207]Jn 15:23.

[208]Cf. Amos 8:1.

[209]Cf. Jerome, *Commentary on Amos* 9:1 (ACT 2:388). Theodore of Mopsuestia, *Commentary on Amos* 9 (FOTC 167), agrees that Amos has in view the Jerusalem temple.

[210]Ezek 9:6.

[211]Amos 8:2.

[212]Amos 7:16-17.

nations who came by his will), to *strike* the double-doors and burst asunder the *shaken lintels,* and thus the total collapse of the buildings would follow. And it immediately shows the causes of the shaking when it says, *For there is covetousness in the head of them all, and I will slay the last of them with the sword.* There seems to be something left out in this speech, but, if you examine it carefully, it was done by design rather than by chance. For since he had distributed their crimes throughout the whole book and the punishments owed to them, justly now he has chosen to abbreviate the sermon so as to point out the wounds of their morals by the disclosure of a single vice, and doubtless so as to touch on the weight of condemnation with a concise discourse. For by striking the *hinges* and shaking the *lintels,* he is announcing the ruin of the temples; but by the term *covetousness* lingering *in the head of them all,* he proclaims that everyone, from the first to the last, bristles with stinginess and sacrilege; indeed, because he has indicated that the *last of them* are to be killed by the enemy's blade, he shows also that there would be no sparing of the poor, but nobles and common people would perish in a confused slaughter. It says, "There will be no flight for them. One will flee, and no one will be delivered from those who flee."[213] He had called it a "flight" instead of an "escape" because, as it has explained, after he said "there will be no flight for them," it immediately added, "One will flee, and no one will be delivered from those who flee." Therefore, fleeing did not profit the captives, and he does not announce that they are going to be arrested in their flight. Lest there be any uncertainty about this, he added what availed for the explanation. He says, "One will flee, and no one will be delivered from those who flee." The following words of the psalm are based on this meaning also: "Let their way become dark and slippery, and let the angel of the Lord pursue them."[214] Lest this very thing briefly mentioned should escape the sense of the listeners, he proceeds to expand the sentence by means of ideas that would provoke a feeling of fear by the length of the description. And at the same time he points out that, when he who is the examiner of the whole world becomes angry, there is no land, no creature that would be effective in offering any help or consolation to the condemned. That is why he said afterward, "There will be no flight for them. One will flee, and no one will be delivered from those who flee."

9:2-4a If they go down as far as hell, my hand will bring them out from there. And if they go up to heaven, I will drag them down from there. And if they are hidden on the top of Carmel, I will search and take them away from there. And if they conceal themselves from my eyes in the depth of the sea, there will I command the serpent and he will bite them. And if they go into captivity before their enemies, there will I command the sword, and it will kill them.

He produced examples from things impossible, not because captive Israel either was able or wanted to go to any of those places that he recounted but so that the greatness of the eternal judge might proclaim itself. That is, If, while I was pursuing them, they were able either to fly up to the heights of heaven or to be swallowed up by gaping clefts in the ground in order to hide; or, just as the folly of the fearful generally is, if they sought out the *top of Carmel,* as though that were a safe hiding place; or if they were plunged into the depths of the oceanic whirlpools, yet nowhere would they be able to escape the power of our vengeance. Of course, lest by chance this very

[213]Amos 9:1d.

[214]Ps 35:6.

situation delude them, by which they are being punished, and they should think that they are going to die thus during the captivity that has to be endured, so that I would have no remaining rights over them whom I will have delivered up to savage rule, I announce that they may not be able to be defended from the fate of the captives—namely, those whom his harshness, when it either grows weary or is satiated, is accustomed to spare. But there also javelins will pierce their throats at my command: for no one will be allowed to have mercy on them, against whom I too will have been compelled to act harshly. However, the writer of the sacred songs in praise of God refined this condition, saying, "Whither shall I go from your spirit? Or whither shall I flee from your face? If I ascend into heaven, you are there; if I descend into hell, you are present. If I take my wings early in the morning, and dwell in the uttermost parts of the sea, there also your hand will lead me, and your right hand shall hold me."[215] Even if I should say, Darkness will cover me, and night will be my consolation, I reflect again and I understand that "the darkness and the light thereof are alike to you"; that is, the darkness of night, however thick, is as pervious to the eyes of God as is also the light of day. Therefore, as blessed David reckoned all these things in his wonder at the divine strength, so also now through Amos our Lord has set forth his powers both for the disclosure of his strength and for the increase of fear. And he showed that they would not be able to find any consolation, when he says, "And I will set my eyes on them for evil, and not for good."[216] That is, I, who am about to punish them, will look on them so that they may sense in the midst of their griefs the Lord whose power the wretches have despised for a long period of time.

[215]Ps 139:7-10; cf. Jerome, *Commentary on Amos* 9:2-5 (ACT 2:390).
[216]Amos 9:4b.

9:5 And the Lord [is] the God of hosts who touches the earth, and it melts; and all who dwell on it will mourn.

As a sign of his power he certainly seems to have mentioned the whole world under the term *earth*. For obviously the world would melt away without any difficulty if God commanded it, according to what the apostle Peter says: "What manner of people ought we to be in holy conversation, looking for the coming of the Lord, by which the heavens shall pass away with a huge, violent motion, and the elements shall melt with the burning heat."[217] And the sense would be the same: O you people of the Jews, give up your profaneness, lest you thus receive this which I have said, that you be unable to avoid the force of my revenge by any flight, as though I have weighed out all that I am capable of in the vastness of your misfortune. For you may understand how paltry this execution of my strength is from this: that if when angered I will have looked on the whole mass of the earth, it is hardly more difficult for it to be dissolved than for wax to be melted by the smoke of a fire. For I [am] the *Lord* "Sabaoth," that is, *of hosts*, for whom truly innumerable multitudes of angels fight as soldiers.[218] Although it is too late in respect to you, yet I am indeed girded as the punisher. Therefore, may you suffer the vastness of your misfortune, everything he can whose anger now pursues you. But he looks back more at the contextual coherence of the reading if he seems to have said this also about the country of Judea, against which threats resounded from the beginning of the book.[219] For since he had said, "I will set my eyes on them for evil, and not for good,"[220] and since none of the elements either dared or were able to conceal them, in a contextually consistent way he

[217]2 Pet 3:11-12.
[218]Cf. Mt 26:53.
[219]Cf. Jerome, *Commentary on Amos* 9:2-5 (ACT 2:390).
[220]Amos 9:4b.

added that the king of powers was also the Lord of lords, who covered the defiled country in that squalor. "And it will rise up as every river, and will run down as the river of Egypt";[221] that is, the whole nation will depart into captivity. And as another prophet says, "They shall come to nothing, like water running down."[222] For he calls the Nile the "river of Egypt," which when it covers the Egyptian fields with its annual flood brings its streams back again into their riverbed in such a way that almost no traces of its waters remain in the fields. So also the people of Samaria, who once had filled the land of Palestine as those about to overflow, will enter the gates of a foreign domain, with their honor and liberty taken away from them, and will retain no signs of their former glory.

9:6 He who builds his ascension into heaven and has founded his bundle on the earth.

The proclamation that is now imparted proceeds, being composed out of the praises of God. For to that which he had said, "The Lord the God of hosts who touches the earth, and it melts; and all who dwell on it will mourn,"[223] there is united this: *He who builds his ascension into heaven and has founded his bundle on the earth.* This means you cannot escape his sight if you ascend to heaven or if you sink into the depths of the sea. He is the Lord of angels, who also contains the world that he created. *He who builds his ascension into heaven and has founded his bundle on the earth.* Now the sense is that though he sits on his heavenly throne in view of his own majesty, nevertheless he has deigned to have his own *bundle,* as it were, on earth—namely, the descendants of Abraham, Isaac, and Jacob, whose God he chose especially to be called,[224] though he is the Lord of the universe. Therefore, he called it a *bundle,* as though it were his possession. This agrees with the following passage from Deuteronomy: "When the Most High divided the nations, he appointed their bounds according to the number of the angels of God, and Jacob became his portion, and Israel his inheritance."[225] Surely by introducing this word briefly he has shown how great is the kindness he has borne toward the Jews and how great are their crimes by which they have spurned him. Therefore, he *who builds*—that is, who has built and has ordered it with sacred laws from the beginning of creation, so that its very master might ascend into heaven, just as into the high places of the world, and might sit there in his eternal reign. But he has assigned the earth to be the dwelling place of his servants, according to what blessed David also expresses: "The heaven of heaven is the Lord's, but the earth he has given to the children of men."[226] Therefore, although he is lofty with his throne and scepter, and not only the stars but even the heavens of heavens look on him with trembling, nevertheless he turns the eyes of his dutiful responsibility to the lowest depths and "looks down on the lowly things"[227] in such a way that he allows no creature to be destitute of the guidance of his providence. For although in honor of Abraham, Isaac, and Jacob he deigned to regard the *bundle* (that is, as we have said, the nation) as worthy of instruction in the sacred rites, nevertheless, according to what the holy song states, "The Lord is good to all, and his tender mercies are over all his works."[228] "He makes his sun to rise on the good and bad, and rains on the just and the unjust."[229] He gives nourishment in abundance not only to men but also to birds

[221]Amos 9:5b.
[222]Ps 58:7.
[223]Amos 9:5.
[224]Cf. Heb 11:16.
[225]Deut 32:8-9 LXX. The Vulgate reads "sons of God" instead of "angels."
[226]Ps 115:16.
[227]Cf. Ps 113:6; 138:6.
[228]Ps 145:9.
[229]Mt 5:45.

and to cattle. This agrees with David's words: "All expect you to give them food in season; what you give to them they shall gather up; when you open your hand, they shall all be filled with good; but if you turn away your face, they shall be troubled."[230] And elsewhere it says, "He who gives food to the cattle, and grass for the service of men, that he may make the face cheerful with oil, and strengthen men's hearts with bread."[231] So then, in order that the produce and fruits of the earth may provide for the sustenance of men, they are made fruitful by the rain fallen from the clouds.[232] Its mildness has been created so that they may be filled up like sponges cast on the waves and may bedew the thirsting fields as these same waters are cleansed from their natural saltiness by this very transfusion and pass into drinkable sweetness. And they multiply the variety of seeds with an extraordinary fruitfulness, confessing that the Lord is one, who has obviously ordered these things by a fixed law. But let us see how the previously stated description of divine power proceeds.

9:7a Are not you as the children of the Ethiopians to me, O children of Israel, says the Lord?

"Or is he the God of the Jews only? Is he not also of the Gentiles? Yes, of the Gentiles also. For God is one, who will justify the circumcision by faith, the uncircumcision through faith."[233] Therefore, although by the testimony of my providence, which takes thought for all mortals in common, you could have and ought to have recognized that I chose your race especially in honor of your holy ancestors, nevertheless I did not reject other nations from my care and concern. At least you should come to understand from these things that have happened that I am the Lord of all, not merely of you. Though you have sunk into crimes, you plead for vindication, so that you may esteem yourselves alone to be preferred to others on account of the fact that you were miraculously led forth from Egyptian slavery, and you possess a fertile country, with its inhabitants having been cast out, which is an even greater thing. For I have not carried out the office of such a management with respect to you alone, but just as I have sent in Israel from the land of Egypt, so also the Palestinians were received from Cappadocia, and the Syrians from Cyrene,[234] into the locations of those who had merited to be driven out. Therefore, do not think that your virtues have merited that which I have always paid out in view of my justice—namely, that I blot out kingdoms that have been defiled by sacrileges.[235] I attest that this is the chief concern of the lawful Lord, to leave no one unpunished, whom he has observed takes no thought for his own amendment.

9:8 Behold, the eyes of the Lord God are on the sinful kingdom, and I will destroy it from the face of the earth.

Learn then at least from the dangers of the events, that no mortal is protected by wealth nor by strength, who has not been surrounded by innocence and moral uprightness. Therefore, my justice has always demanded from me that not only one or two people but also the whole kingdom go to ruin if it has been subjected to sins. However, the sanctity of your ancestors obtained from me that I not allow you to be destroyed by slaughter, but, even if in consideration of the changes of merits with regard to your crimes, I will have awakened my revenge; no forgetfulness of showing mercy as well would ever steal in on

[230]Ps 104:27-29.
[231]Ps 104:14-15.
[232]Cf. Jerome, *Commentary on Amos* 9:6 (ACT 2:391-92).
[233]Rom 3:29-30.
[234]Cf. Amos 9:7b.
[235]Cf. Deut 9:4-5.

me. But, although I may crush the guilty, I shall not even yet allow the name of the Israelites to perish. Therefore, there will be a distinction between you and between the rest. For you will be taught by having been chastised, but they will be taught by having been annihilated. And because even in this very attack of indignation God has nevertheless revealed to the rest that they shall be spared, he follows up with things that are joyful.

9:9-10 For behold, I will command, and I will shake the house of Israel among all nations, as [corn] is shaken in a sieve, and a little stone will not fall to the ground. All the sinners of my people will die by the sword, those who say, Evil will not come near and will not come on us.

Therefore is it hither that my anger has resounded in the whole volume; it will not proceed with poured out swiftness, but as though with a cautious hand and attentive consideration it shall *shake* you—namely like a *sieve*, by which the corn is purified, the narrow openings of which allow neither grains nor *little stones* to fall through, but separate out only dust and darnel and the rest, things that are useless. But when he says that *little stones* remain among the corn, he seems to be recalling the custom of things that are purified. Generally they throw little stones into a sieve so that those struck from the sides might add strength to the shaking and none of the refuse might be allowed to remain. But according to the subtler sense touching more closely this reality for which it had been taken up, by the name of *little stones* he indicates the strength of those who are not easily corrupted by bad examples, as we read that in those times there were both prophets and other just men who, when the rest of the common people perished like wood and stubble, remained like firm and therefore precious stones, on which the church, which no storm can collapse, was rightly founded.[236] Therefore, he says, even if the captivity that has been sent in snatches all away equally, nevertheless I will certainly not value you cheaply—namely, that you should perish in a disorderly slaughter. But the scales of justice will be employed so that the sword befalls no one who is innocent and passes by no one who is guilty. *All the sinners of my people will die by the sword, who say, Evil will not come near, and will not come on us.* This refers to those who have resisted the sacred prophets, and as though managing to overcome them, they claimed that none of the disasters that they were announcing will come, and they will not arrive at any of the evil trials. He says, A raging vengeance will hunt them down, but our hand will defend all those who are conspicuous either for their innocence or tested virtue. Thus, they would indeed be taught by having been trained, but they will not be annihilated. But let us consider the things that remain as well.

9:11-12 In that day I will raise up the tabernacle of David that has fallen, and I will rebuild the breaches of its walls and repair what had fallen, and I will rebuild it as in the ancient days so that they may possess the remnant of Idumea, and all nations, because my name is invoked on them, says the Lord who does these things.

He had promised that he also would have consideration for mercy regarding the nation of the Israelites in the time of the kindled anger, in such a way that he would not allow them to be destroyed to the last man. But in the very whirlwind of captivity, when the savage barbarity already had mastery over them, nevertheless those endowed with innocence and justice shall be defended with miraculous aid, so that death might not have power against them. Certainly because this

[236]Cf. Mt 7:24-25; 16:18; Lk 6:47-48; 1 Cor 3:12.

seemed to be difficult, he has suitably and necessarily added words about the prosperity that would come in the future. Obviously he does this in order to heap up even more clear proofs of his mercy, the signs of which he had spoken of in advance, and to show that he cares for them, he who was accustomed to judge them in view of their offenses. And thus they would understand that he will permit no one to perish without judgment, since indeed this distinction stood out prominently, not only in respect of persons but also among nations. For when the ten tribes were already in the grip of Assyrian rule, he defended Judah and Benjamin from the siege of Sennacherib, who of course are designated only together by the mention of Judah.[237] Therefore, in prophetic fashion he calls the time a *day* and says, *In that day I will raise up the tabernacle of David that has fallen, and I will rebuild the breaches of its walls, and repair what had fallen, and I will rebuild it as in the ancient days.* Surely with these words he indicates that age in which even the tribe of Judah with the rest was liberated from the Babylonian captivity. For just as nearly all the prophets harmoniously had predicted these things, so also the outcome of events has proven it. So here, when he had told every sad thing under the persona of the ten tribes, when he came to the preaching of joyful things, he ran through their lineage on the occasion of Judah, simultaneously indicating that the residents of Jerusalem were to come under adversities, from which doubtless he is foretelling that they would be led forth. Of course, the signs of this freedom preceded under Hezekiah—namely, when in Jerusalem with his marvelous protection God defended the oppressed from the bands of the besiegers and from grave destitution.[238] Therefore, whatever adversities there were when all those besiegers were driven off, I shall take up again that trowel of the mason worker, which I had put aside in my indignation, so that I may build up the shattered parts of the walls, which had been shaken by the assault of the enemies.[239] And I shall raise all of the buildings that had grown old and lead it back to the vigor of their ancient blessedness. I shall allot not only the delights of victory but also of punishment—that is, so that they might possess the remnants of the Idumean nation, obviously from the race of Esau who is coming, by whose murderous hatred they had suffered perpetually.[240] And they shall so establish every nation under their own dominion that it is evident how much fruit of piety they have obtained, they who have obtained abundant and numerous victories by *calling on my name.* It must be noted, however, that blessed James called this passage to mind in the Acts of the Apostles. He prophesied the mystery of our Redeemer by using a loftier understanding—namely, by calling the body of Christ the *tabernacle of David.*[241] When it had fallen into death on account of this same condition of nature, it was raised up by the power and mystery of the resurrection, and truly *the faithful* (that is eternal) *holiness of David* shone forth when God did not suffer his "holy one to see corruption"[242] but made him resplendent "before the face of all peoples, to the glory of thy people Israel."[243] Therefore, by following the teaching of the apostles, we have come to know that the books of the prophets must be understood in such a way that the events of their own times are embraced according to the context. And through the sudden digressions or accumulations of senses, they also have

[237]Cf. 2 Kings 18–19.

[238]Cf. 2 Kings 19.

[239]Cf. Amos 7:7-9.

[240]Cf. Num 20:14-21; 2 Kings 8:20-22; Ps 137:7; Lam 4:21-22; Amos 1:11-12; Is 11:14; 21:11-12; 34:5-17; Jer 49:7-22.

[241]Cf. Acts 15:15-17; Jerome, *Commentary on Amos* 9:11-12 (ACT 2:394-95).

[242]Cf. Acts 13:34-35; Ps 16:10.

[243]Cf. Lk 2:31-32.

indicated future events and have taught that their greatness is seen in the narration of epitomes. For thus has the form of the present passage established, that, as far as the history is concerned, both the rule of the Babylonians has been dissolved and the captivity that the Jews suffered has been abolished, and the long-awaited freedom that was often promised has shone forth on the troubled. Nevertheless, if you examine this freedom against the measuring rod of virtue, you will say indeed that an excessively small amount happened to mortals and to those who endured the bitter things of this life. But this liberation, which the mysteries of Christ have brought to the faithful, when it finally came, was limitlessly longer, incomparably higher. The walls of strength and sweetness are compared to it in such a way that the riches laid up within them can fear neither a siege nor deceit. But one must believe that that liberation will possess the *remnant of Idumea*, when this body, which appears to be shown by the red complexion of the Edomites,[244] "shall rise in glory," just as it had been "sown in dishonor."[245] Nor shall it produce out of weakness any troubles either for the understanding or for the senses, but "God shall be all in all."[246] But since these things have been explained briefly, let us turn back to the order of the reading.

9:13 Behold, the days are coming, says the Lord, and the ploughman shall overtake the reaper, and the treader of grapes the one that sows seed. And the mountains shall drop sweetness, and every hill will be tilled.

Not content, it says, only to have restored your freedom, I shall also make you rejoice in the abundance of your crops in such a way that the fruits to be gathered may give abundantly throughout the whole year, and a rich and abundant harvest would proceed at the appointed time of the grape harvest, and the sowers would receive the grapes. This agrees with what is sung in the writings of the blessed David: "Blessing the crown of the year of your goodness, and your fields will be filled with plenty; the borders of the wilderness shall grow fat, and the hills will be girded about with joy."[247] Therefore, in this way here too after the things stated first he added, *The mountains shall drop sweetness, and every hill shall be tilled*. For if indeed in the time of adversities there was a great scarcity of husbandmen, now on the other hand, when tranquility has been restored, he shall multiply the cultivators, and the cultivation of the *mountains* shall bear witness to the good of the public peace in such a way that they *shall drop sweetness*—that is, wine would seem to flow out from the cliffs, honey from the mountains.

9:14 And I will convert the captivity of my people Israel, and they will build the abandoned cities and inhabit them; and they will plant vineyards and drink the wine from them, and shall make gardens and eat the fruits from them.

Because he had spoken with an exaggeration—that is, he wrote in a subordinate narrative that it would be as if far and wide nectar would burst forth from the mountains[248]—he was obviously saying that by using the goods of freedom, they would build the walls of the city and repair the buildings, plant vineyards, and not fear the plunderer, but they would be filled with the richest fruits of these, and not only the wealthy but also the humble would diligently cultivate gardens and would freely feed on the abundance obtained.

[244]Cf. Gen 25:25.
[245]1 Cor 15:43.
[246]1 Cor 15:28.
[247]Ps 65:11-12.
[248]Cf. Amos 9:13.

9:15 And I will plant them on their own soil, and I will no more pluck them out of their land that I have given them, says the Lord your God.

This means, When I shall have led the people, whom the scourges of captivity have set right, back to the possession of their own lands, I shall make them rejoice with constant security in such a way that they no longer experience the commands of arrogant masters, nor taste again bitter exile, but would remain fast in their own country with an eternal possession. In saying this he has assuredly not promised that they are never to be changed into a malformed will, since it is an established fact that later on they both denied the Redeemer of the human race and outraged him by their persecution until they were driven out from those lands, which they had received, so that they are continually kept from cultivating them.[249] But the Lord of the universe has made known his own design—namely, that he shall reestablish them in their paternal lands in such a way that he would never want them to be expelled if their life should allow it. And thus it would be open to be understood that every adverse thing that followed one after another must be imputed to their habits. But in the body of Christ (that is, the members of the church), all these things appear faithfully and abundantly fulfilled (namely, in those to whom this happiness of hope has been brought) so that, when the time of the resurrection comes and they attain the happiness that is true, thus would they confess their own goods, both with sweetness and with a precious eternity.[250]

[249]Under the Roman emperor Hadrian (117–138) the Bar Kokhba Rebellion (132–136) was suppressed, resulting in the destruction of the city of Jerusalem. Jews were then permanently expelled from Palestine.

[250]Bouwman, *Des Julian von Aeclanum Kommentar*, 8, thinks it probable that in spite of Julian's announced plan to interpret all twelve Minor Prophets (*Commentary on Hosea*, preface), his work actually came to an end here, since no break is indicated, even if he does not offer concluding words.

BIBLIOGRAPHY

Annecchino, Marialuisa. "I Temi Dottrinali-Esegetici nell'Expositio in Iob di Giuliano D'Eclano." In *Munera parva: studi in onore di Boris Ulianich*, edited by Gennaro Luongo, 287-309. Naples: Fridericiana Editrice Universitaria, 1999.

Bagby, S. *Sin in Origen's Commentary on Romans*. New York: Fortress Academic, 2018.

Bate, H. N. "Some Technical Terms of Greek Exegesis." *JTS* 24 (1923): 59-66.

Baxter, J. H. "Notes on the Latin of Julian of Eclanum." *ALMA* 21 (1951): 5-54.

Beatrice, Pier Franco. "Chromatius and Jovinus at the Synod of Diospolis: A Prosopographical Inquiry." *JECS* 22, no. 3 (Fall 2014): 437-64.

———. *The Transmission of Sin: Augustine and the Pre-Augustinian Sources*. Translated by Adam Kamesar. Oxford: Oxford University Press, 2013.

Bede, The Venerable. *On the Song of Songs and Selected Writings*. Edited by Arthur Holder. Mahwah, NJ: Paulist Press, 2011.

Behr, J. *Formation of Christian Theology*. Vol. 2, *The Nicene Faith*. Crestwood, NY: St. Vladimir's Seminary Press, 2004.

Bonner, Ali. *The Myth of Pelagianism*. Oxford: Oxford University Press, 2018.

Bonner, G. "Augustine and Pelagianism." *Augustinian Studies* 24 (1993): 27-47.

Bouwman, Gisbert. *Des Julian von Aeclanum Kommentar zu den Propheten Osee, Joel und Amos. Ein Beitrag zur Geschichte der Exegese*. Rome: Pontificio Istituto Biblico, 1958.

———. "Zum Wortschatz des Julian von Aeclanum." *ALMA* (1957): 141-64.

Brenton, Sir Lancelot C. L. *The Septuagint with Apocrypha: Greek and English*. Peabody, MA: Hendrickson, 1987. First published 1851. Based on Codex Vaticanus.

Brown, P. *Augustine of Hippo: A Biography*. Berkeley: University of California Press, 1967.

———. "The Patrons of Pelagius: The Roman Aristocracy Between East and West." *Journal of Theological Studies*, N.S., 21, no. 1 (1970): 56-72.

Brückner, A. *Julian von Eclanum: Sein Leben und seine Lehre. Ein Beitrag zur Geschichte des Pelaginismus*. TU 15/3. Leipzig: Hinrichs, 1897.

Burnett, Carole C. "Dysfunction at Diospolis: A Comparative Study of Augustine's *De Gestis Pelagii* and Jerome's *Dialogus Adversus Pelagianos*." *Augustinian Studies* 34, no. 2 (2003): 153-73.

Burns, J. Patout. "Augustine's Role in the Imperial Action Against Pelagius." *JTS* 30, no. 1 (1979): 67-82.

———. "The Interpretation of Romans in the Pelagian Controversy." *Augustinian Studies* 10 (1979): 43-54.

Cartledge, P. A., and J. R. Sallares. "Earthquakes." In *The Oxford Classical Dictionary*. 3rd ed. Oxford: Oxford University Press, 1996.

Clark, E. *The Origenist Controversy: The Cultural Construction of an Early Christian Debate*. Princeton, NJ: Princeton University Press, 1992.

De Bruyn, Theodore S. "Pelagius's Interpretation of Rom. 5:12-21: Exegesis Within the Limits of Polemic." *Toronto Journal of Theology* 4 (1988): 30-43.

De Plinval, G. "Julien d'Éclane devant la Bible." *RSR* 47 (1959): 345-66.

———. *Pélage: Ses écrits, sa vie et sa réforme*. Lausanne, 1943.

Duhm, Bernhard. *The Twelve Prophets: A Version in the Various Poetical Measures of the Original Writings*. Translated by Archibald Duff. London: Adam and Charles Black, 1912.

Dupont, A. "The Christology of Pre-Controversial Pelagius." *Augustiniana* 58 (2008): 235-57.

———. "Die Christusfigur des Pelagius. Rekonstruction der Christologie im Kommentar von Pelagius zum Römerbrief des Paulus." *Augustiniana* 56, nos. 3–4 (2006): 321-72.

Dupont, A., and G. Malavasi. "The Question of the Impact of Divine Grace in the Pelagian Controversy." *Revue d'Histoire Ecclesiastique* 112 (2017): 539-68.

Duval, Yves-M. "Iulianus Aeclanensis restitutus. La première edition—incomplète—de l'oeuvre de Julien d'Éclane." *Revue des Études Augustiniennes* 25 (1979): 162-72.

Evans, Gillian R. "Neither a Pelagian nor a Manichee." *Vigiliae Christianae* 35, no. 3 (1981): 232-44.

Evans, Robert F. *Four Letters of Pelagius*. New York: Seabury Press, 1968.

———. *Pelagius: Inquiries and Reappraisals*. New York: Seabury Press, 1968.

Ferguson, John. *Pelagius*. Cambridge: W. Heffer & Sons, 1956.

Freedman, D. N., A. C. Myers, and A. B. Beck, eds. *Eerdmans Dictionary of the Bible*. Grand Rapids, MI: Eerdmans, 2000.

Garcia-Sanchez, C. *Pelagius and Christian Initiation: A Study in Historical Theology*. Washington, DC: Catholic University of America Press, 1978.

Harkins, Angela Kim. "Job in the Ancient Versions and Pseudepigrapha." In Harkins and Canty, *Companion to Job in the Middle Ages*, 13-33.

Harkins, Franklin T., and Aaron Canty, eds. *A Companion to Job in the Middle Ages*. Leiden: Brill, 2016.

Heine, R. *The Commentaries of Origen and Jerome on St Paul's Epistle to the Ephesians*. Oxford: Oxford University Press, 2002.

Holder, Arthur. "The Anti-Pelagian Character of Bede's Commentary on the Song of Songs." In *Biblical Studies in the Early Middle Ages*, edited by Claudio Leonardi and Giovanni Orlandi, 91-103. Florence: SISMEL, Edizioni de Galluzzo, 2005.

———. "The Patristic Sources of Bede's Commentary on the Song of Songs." In *Studia Patristica* 34. Louvain: Peeters, 2001.

Hubbard, David Allan. *Hosea: An Introduction and Commentary*. Tyndale Old Testament Commentaries. Downers Grove, IL: IVP Academic, 1989.

———. *Joel and Amos: An Introduction and Commentary*. Tyndale Old Testament Commentaries. Downers Grove, IL: IVP Academic, 1989.

Hwang, A. Y. "Augustine's Interpretations of 1 Tim 2:4 in the Context of His Developing Views of Grace." In *Studia Patristica* 43. Louvain: Peeters, 2006.

Hwang, Alexander Y., Brian J. Matz, and Augustine Casiday, eds. *Grace for Grace: The Debates After Augustine and Pelagius*. Washington, DC: Catholic University of America Press, 2014.

Jerome. *Commentary on Ezekiel*. Ancient Christian Writers 71. Translated by Thomas P. Scheck. New York: Newman Press, 2017.

———. *Commentary on Isaiah*; Origen: *Homilies 1-9 on Isaiah*. Ancient Christian Writers 68. Translated by Thomas P. Scheck. New York: Newman Press, 2015.

———. *Commentaries on the Twelve Prophets*. Vol. 1. Ancient Christian Texts. Edited by Thomas P. Scheck. Downers Grove, IL: InterVarsity Press, 2016.

———. *Commentaries on the Twelve Prophets*. Vol. 2. Ancient Christian Texts. Edited by Thomas P. Scheck. Downers Grove, IL: InterVarsity Press, 2017.

Julian of Eclanum. *Iuliani Aeclanensis expositio libri Iob, tractatus prophetarum Osee, Iohel et Amos, accedunt operum deperditorum fragmenta post Albertum Bruckner denuo collecta aucta ordinata*. CCL 88. Edited by L. De Coninck and M. J. D'Hont. Turnhout, Belgium: Brepols, 1977.

Kelly, J. N. D. *Jerome: His Life, Writings, and Controversies*. New York: Harper & Row, 1975.

Lamberigts, Mathjis. "Augustine and Julian of Aeclanum on Zosimus." *Augustiniana* 42 (1992): 311-30.

———. "Augustine, Julian of Aeclanum and E. Pagels' *Adam, Eve, and the Serpent*." *Augustiniana* 39 (1989): 393-435.

———. "Competing Christologies: Julian and Augustine on Jesus Christ." *Augustinian Studies* 36, no. 1 (2005): 159-94.

———. "A Critical Evaluation of Critiques of Augustine's View of Sexuality." In *Augustine and His Critics: Essays in Honour of Gerald Bonner*, edited by R. Dodaro and G. Lawless, 176-97. London: Routledge, 2000.

———. "The Italian Julian of Aeclanum About the African Augustine of Hippo." In *Augustinus Afer. Saint Augustin: africanité et universalité. Actes du colloque international Alger-Annaba, 1–7 avril 2001, Paradosis, 45,1*, edited by P.-Y. Fux, J.-M. Roessli, and O. Wermelinger, 83-93. Fribourg, Switzerland: Éditions Universitaires, 2003.

———. "Julian of Aeclanum: A Plea for a Good Creator." *Augustiniana* 38 (1988): 5-24.

———. "Julian of Aeclanum on Natural Virtues and Rom 2:14." *Augustiniana* 58 (2008): 127-40.

———. "The Philosophical and Theological Background of Julian of Aeclanum's Concept of Concupiscence." In *Die christlich-philosophischen Diskurse der Spätantike: Texte, Personen, Institutionen: Acten der Tagung vom 22.-25. Februar 2006 am Zentrum für Antike und Moderne der Albert-Ludwigs-Universität Freiburg*, edited by Therese Fuhrer, 1-18. Stuttgart: Franz Steiner Verlag, 2008.

———. "Recent Research into Pelagianism with Particular Emphasis on the Role of Julian of Aeclanum." *Augustiniana* 52 (2002): 175-98.

———. "Was Augustine a Manichaean? The Assessment of Julian of Aeclanum." In *Augustine and Manichaeism in the Latin West*, edited by J. van Oort et al., 113-36. Nag Hammadi and Manichaean Studies 49. Leiden: Brill, 2001.

Lössl, Josef. "Augustine, 'Pelagianism,' Julian of Aeclanum and Modern Scholarship." *Journal of Ancient Christianity* 11 (2007): 129-50.

———. "Julian of Aeclanum's 'Rationalist' Exegesis: Albert Bruckner Revisited." *Augustiniana* 53 (2003): 77-106.

———. "Julian of Aeclanum's *Tractatus in Osee, Iohel, Amos*: Some Notes on the Current State of Research." *Augustiniana* 51 (2001): 11-37.

———. *Julian von Aeclanum: Studien zu seinem Leben, seinem Werk, seiner Lehre und ihrer Überlieferung*. Leiden: Brill, 2001.

———. "Pauline Exegesis in Patristic Commentaries of Old Testament Prophets: The Example of Julian of Aeclanum's *Tractatus in Amos*." *Journal for Late Antique Religion and Culture* 4 (2010): 1-27.

———. "Sallust in Julian of Aeclanum." *Vigiliae Christianae* 56 (2004): 179-202.

———. "A Shift in Patristic Exegesis: Hebrew Clarity and Historical Verity in Augustine, Jerome, and Julian of Aeclanum and Theodore of Mopsuestia." *Augustinian Studies* 32, no. 2 (2001): 157-75.

———. "Who Attacked the Monasteries of Jerome and Paula in 416 A.D.?" *Augustinianum* 44 (2004): 91-112.

Malavasi, Giulio. "The Involvement of Theodore of Mopsuestia in the Pelagian Controversy: A Study of Theodore's Treatise *Against Those Who Say That Men Sin by Nature and Not by Will*." *Augustiniana* 64 (2014): 227-60.

———. "John of Jerusalem's Profession of Faith (CPG 3621) and the Pelagian Controversy." In *Studia Patristica* 98. Louvain: Peeters, 2017.

Malavasi, Giulio, and A. Dupont. "The Question of the Impact of Divine Grace in the Pelagian Controversy." *Revue d'Histoire Ecclesiastique* 112 (2017): 539-68.

Markus, R. A. "The Legacy of Pelagius: Orthodoxy, Heresy, and Conciliation." In *The Making of Orthodoxy: Essays in Honor of Henry Chadwick*, edited by R. Williams, 214-34. Cambridge: Cambridge University Press, 1989.

McGuckin, John A. *The Path of Christianity: The First Thousand Years*. Downers Grove, IL: IVP Academic, 2017.

Moreschini, C., and E. Norelli. *Early Christian Greek and Latin Literature: A Literary History*. 2 vols. Translated by Matthew J. O'Connell. Peabody, MA: Hendrickson, 2005.

Morin, Germain. "Un ouvrage restitué à Julien d'Eclanum: Le commentaire du Pseudo-Rufin sur les prophètes Osée, Joel et Amos." *Revue Bénédictine* 30 (1913): 1-24.

Murphy, Roland E. *The Book of Job: A Short Reading*. Mahwah, NJ: Paulist Press, 1999.

Nazzaro, A. V. *Giuliano D'Eclano et L'Hirpinia Christiana*. Naples: Arte Tipografica Editrice, 2004.

Ogliari, Donato. *Gratia et Certamen: The Relationship Between Grace and Free Will in the Discussion of Augustine with the So-Called Semipelagians*. Bibliotheca Ephemeridum Theologicarum Lovaniensium 169. Louvain: Peeters, 2003.

Outrata, Filip. "Differing Defenders of Free Will: Possible Origenian Influences in Julian of Aeclanum." In *Origeniana undecima: Origen and Origenism in the History of Western Thought*, edited by M. Schatkin and F. Outrata, 489-500. Louvain: Peeters, 2016.

Paciorek, P. M. "The Controversy Between Augustine and Julian of Eclanum: On Law and Grace." In *Studia Patristica* 98. Louvain: Peeters, 2017.

Papageorgiou, P. "Chrysostom and Augustine on the Sin of Adam and Its Consequences." *St. Vladimir's Theological Quarterly* 39, no. 4 (1995): 361-78.

Paucker, C. *Vorarbeiten zur lat. Sprachgeschichte*. Edited by H. Rönsch. Berlin, 1884.

Pelagius. *Pelagius's Commentary on St. Paul's Epistle to the Romans*. Translated by Theodore T. De Bruyn. Oxford: Oxford University Press, 1993.

———. *Pelagius's Commentaries on Thirteen Epistles of St. Paul*. Ancient Christian Writers. Translated by Thomas P. Scheck. New York: Newman Press, forthcoming.

———. *Pelagius's Expositions of Thirteen Epistles of St. Paul*. Texts and Studies 9. 3 volumes. Edited by A. Souter. Cambridge: Cambridge University Press, 1922–1931.

Plumer, E., trans., *Augustine's Commentary on Galatians*. Oxford: OUP, 2003.

Quasten, Johannes. *Patrology*. 4 vols. Allen, TX: Christian Classics, 1975.

Rackett, Michael R. "What's Wrong with Pelagianism? Augustine and Jerome on the Dangers of Pelagius and His Followers." *Augustinian Studies* 33, no. 2 (2002): 223-37.

Rees, B. R. *Pelagius: A Reluctant Heretic*. Wolfeboro, NH: Boydell Press, 1988.

Refoulé, F. "Julien d'Éclane, théologien et philosophe." *Recherches de science religieuse* 52 (1964): 42-84.

Rist, John M. *Augustine: Ancient Thought Baptized*. Cambridge: Cambridge University Press, 1994.

———. "Augustine on Free Will and Predestination." *JTS* 20, no. 2 (1969): 420-47.

———. *What Is Truth? From the Academy to the Vatican*. Cambridge: Cambridge University Press, 2008.

Rotelle, John E., OSA, ed. *The Works of Saint Augustine: A Translation for the 21st Century, Answer to the Pelagians*. Vol. 1.23. Translated by Roland J. Teske, SJ. New York: New City Press, 1997.

Scheck, Thomas P. *Origen and the History of Justification: The Legacy of Origen's Commentary on Romans*. Notre Dame, IN: University of Notre Dame Press, 2008.

———. "Pelagius's Interpretation of Romans." In *A Companion to St. Paul in the Middle Ages*, edited by Steven R. Cartwright, 79-113. Leiden: Brill, 2013.

Souter, A. *The Earliest Latin Commentaries on the Epistles of St. Paul*. Oxford: Oxford University Press, 1927.

Squires, Stuart. *The Pelagian Controversy: An Introduction to the Enemies of Grace and the Conspiracy of Lost Souls*. Eugene, OR: Wipf & Stock, 2019.

Steinhauser, Kenneth B., ed. *Anonymi in Iob Commentarius*. CSEL XCVI. Vienna: Verlag der Oesterreichischen Akademie der Wissenschaften, 2006.

———. "Job Exegesis: The Pelagian Controversy." In *Augustine: Biblical Exegete*, edited by Frederick Van Fleteren and Joseph C. Schnaubelt, 299-311. New York: Peter Lang, 2001.

———. "Job in Patristic Commentaries and Theological Works." In Harkins and Canty, *Companion to Job in the Middle Ages*, 34-70.

Stiglmayr, J. "Der Jobkommentar von Monte Cassino." *ZKT* 43 (1919): 269-88.

———. "Zum Jobkommentar von Monte Cassino." ZKT 45 (1921): 495-96.

TeSelle, E. "The Background: Augustine and the Pelagian Controversy." In *Grace for Grace: The Debates After Augustine and Pelagius*, edited by Alexander Y. Hwang, Brian J. Matz, and Augustine Casiday, 1-13. Washington, DC: Catholic University of America Press, 2014.

Teske, R., SJ. "1 Timothy 2:4 and the Beginnings of the Massalian Controversy." In Hwang, Matz, and Casiday, *Grace for Grace*, 14-34.

Theodore of Mopsuestia. *Commentary on Psalms 1-81*. Translated by Robert C. Hill. Atlanta: Society of Biblical Literature, 2006.

———. *Commentary on the Twelve Prophets*. Translated by Robert C. Hill. Washington, DC: Catholic University of America Press, 2004. Abbreviated in notes as FOTC (Fathers of the Church, series).

Upson-Saia, Kristi. "Gregory of Nyssa on Virginity, Gardens, and the Enclosure of the Παράδεισος." *Journal of Early Christian Studies* 27, no. 1 (2019): 99-131.

Vaccari, A. "La θεωρία nella scuola esegetic di Antiochia." *Biblica* 1 (1920): 3-36.

———. *Un Commento a Giobbe di Giuliano di Eclano*. Scripta Pontificii Instituti Biblici 27. Rome, 1915.

Vessey, Mark. "*Opus Imperfectum*: Augustine and His Readers, 426–435 A.D." *Vigiliae Christianae* 52 (1998): 264-85.

Vinzent, Markus, ed. *Studia Patristica*, Vol. XCVIII. *Papers Presented at the Seventeenth International Conference on Patristic Studies Held in Oxford 2015*. Vol. 24, *Augustine and His Opponents*. Louvain: Peeters, 2017.

Walsh, P. G., trans. *The Poems of St. Paulinus of Nola*. ACW 40. New York: Newman Press, 1975.

Wermelinger, Otto. *Rom und Pelagius: Die theologische Position der romischen Bischöfen im pelagianischen Streit in den Jahren 411–432*. Stuttgart: Anton Hiersemann, 1975.

Weyman, C. "Der Hiobkommentar des Julianus von Aeclanum." *Theologische Revue* 11/12 (1916): 241-48.

White, C. *The Correspondence (394–419) Between Jerome and Augustine of Hippo*. Lewiston, NY: Edwin Mellen, 1990.

Williams, N. P. *The Ideas of the Fall and of Original Sin*. London: Longmans, Green, 1927.

General Index

Abbreviations: Jb = *Commentary on Job*; Hos = *Commentary on Hosea*; Jl = *Commentary on Joel*; Am = *Commentary on Amos*

Scripture Index (RSVCE)

Locations are given according to the chapter/verse lemma of the individual commentaries contained in this volume

Abbreviations: Jb = *Commentary on Job*; Hos = *Commentary on Hosea*; Jl = *Commentary on Joel*; Am = *Commentary on Amos*; Pref = Preface

ANCIENT CHRISTIAN TEXTS

SERIES EDITORS

Gerald L. Bray

Michael Glerup

Thomas C. Oden†

Ancient Christian Texts is a series of new translations, most of which are presented here in English for the first time. The series provides contemporary readers with the resources they need to study the key writings of the early church for themselves. The texts represented in the series are full-length commentaries or sermon series based on biblical books or extended scriptural passages.

This series extends the ecumenical project begun with the Ancient Christian Commentary on Scripture, promoting a vital link of communication between today's varied Christian traditions and their common ancient ancestors in the faith. On this shared ground, we gather to listen to the pastoral and theological insights of the church's leading theologians during its earliest centuries.

Many readers of the Ancient Christian Commentary on Scripture have wished to read the full-length works from which excerpts were selected. Several of those texts have not been available in English before or have existed only in cumbersome English in isolated libraries. The work begun by Thomas C. Oden and the Institute for Classical Christian Studies to make more of these texts available to the general reading public continues today.

The volumes, though not critical editions, provide notes where needed to acquaint general readers with the necessary background to understand what the ancient authors are saying. Preachers, pastors, students and teachers of Scripture will be refreshed and enriched here by the ancient wisdom of the church.

www.ivpress.com/act/